EGON R
Ford Gu

...and Baby Comes Too

900 family-friendly hotels and eating places in Great Britain

mothercare

Egon Ronay's Guides
73 Uverdale Road
London SW10 0SW

Consultant **Egon Ronay**
Editorial Director **Bernard Branco**
Managing Editor **Andrew Eliel**
Publishing Director **Angela Nicholson**

First published 1994 by Pan Macmillan
Publishers Ltd, Cavaye Place,
London SW10 9PG

987654321

Cover Design © **Elizabeth Ayer**

Cover Concept and Illustration
© **Chris Ackerman-Eveleigh**

ISBN 0 333-61001-6

Typeset in Great Britain by Spottiswoode Ballantyne,
Colchester, Essex.
Printed and bound in Great Britain by BPCC Hazell Books Ltd

**All restaurant and hotel inspections are
anonymous and carried out by Egon Ronay's
Guides' team of professional inspectors.
Inspectors may reveal their identities in order
to check all the rooms and other facilities.
The Guide is independent in its editorial selection
and does not accept advertising, payment or
hospitality from listed establishments.**

Contents

How to Use This Guide

Order of Entries

London appears first and is in alphabetical order by **establishment name**.
Listings outside London are in alphabetical order by **location** within divisions
of England, Scotland, Wales, Channel Islands and the Isle of Man. See
contents page for specific page numbers and the index for individual entries.

Types of Establishments

Categories such as **Hotel, Restaurant, Pub, Tea Room** are printed within
the header for each establishment. If a hotel features in our *Hotels and
Restaurants Cellnet Guide 1994* then it is given the % grading from that
Guide; several private house hotels, more modest London hotels and country
inns (many of which include 'hotel' in their title) also feature in both Guides
but are not given a grading as their range of public rooms is limited;
nevertheless, good facilities for families are offered in all establishments.

Hotels

Prices given are high season rates and are accurate at the time of research
but may well have changed by the middle of 1994. We urge readers to ask
about weekend break prices as many hotels that fill up with business people
during the week offer reduced prices at weekends; family facilities may also
be extended at weekends and during school holidays. The price quoted in
the header for each establishment entry is for a double room (occupied by
two adults) with private en-suite facilities and a cooked breakfast; children's
beds and cots may well attract an extra charge. The percentage shown is an
individual rating arrived at after careful testing, inspection and calculation
according to Egon Ronay's Guides' unique grading system. **The size of a
hotel and the prices charged are not considered in the grading.**

Please note: *only* in those hotels that feature a separate entry for their
restaurant do we specifically recommend the food for adults; children's
meals are considered separately and, where information has been provided,
details are given. Where a hotel's brochure says 'Egon Ronay listed' this
does *not* automatically include the restaurant; there are many hotels in the
UK where the food continues to disappoint but where the overnight
accommodation is perfectly acceptable. Children may be easily satisfied with
homely offerings such as fish fingers and baked beans but once they are
safely tucked up in bed their parents have a right to expect higher
standards.

The majority of chain hotel groups are listed only under the separate section
at the rear of the Guide; they are not plotted on the maps but are listed in
county order.

Pubs

We include establishments where our team of professional inspectors found
good-quality **bar food**. Reference may also be made to the pub's restaurant,

but our chief concern has been with bar food and facilities for families, both inside and outside. Typical dishes are usually listed, with prices valid at the time of our visit. Prices may, however, have risen a little since then. We indicate when bar food is served and also any times when food is not available. Times of restaurant meals may differ and are then listed separately.

Where a pub offers accommodation suitable for families we give the relevant statistics at the end of that establishment's story. The price quoted is for a double room with en-suite facilities and a cooked breakfast. If residents cannot check in at any time during the day then we print the appropriate check-in times; if it's advisable to arrange a check-in time (say, out of pub hours) when booking, we print *by arrangement*.

Pubs recommended as pleasant or interesting places for a drink rather than for their bar food or accommodation have very short entries and no statistics for bar food times or accommodation. Invariably these offer outdoor areas where children can let off steam and are thus a useful family 'pit-stop'.

Restaurants

Wherever possible we have given an indication of a restaurant's attitude towards children; some obviously attract families like bees to a honey pot, others may have a menu, room layout and staff attitude that offer more subtle attractions. Prices given in the header are for two people and include a *three-course meal for two including one of the least expensive bottles of wine, coffee, service and VAT.* Set-price menu prices quoted often do not include service, usually exclude wine and may not necessarily comprise three courses. Many restaurants and hotel dining rooms now offer *only* a set-price menu, although this will usually include a choice. Vegetarians should inform the establishment of their requirements when booking. Facilities such as the provision of high-chairs and children's cutlery have been listed where known. We urge readers to confirm facilities that they require for their children when booking.

Map references

Entries contain references to the map section at the rear of the Guide (before the index). **Map 8 C2**, for example, refers to map square C2 on page 8 of the maps. Use this section to help select establishments in areas you wish to visit.

Credit Cards

We list credit cards currently accepted by each establishment. If it is vital to your visit that an establishment takes a particular credit card then we suggest that you always confirm this information at the time of booking; credit card facilities sometimes change after we have gone to press.

Symbol

   Henry the Duck award for outstanding family facilities.

Introduction

Children may be noisy, messy, picky, disobedient and upset other people in public, but they *are* good business. Parenthood may mean financial cutbacks and a change in life's priorities but it doesn't have to mean purgatory. Dining out *en famille* should be a joy and one of life's pleasures, but all too often it's a disappointing and (most importantly) a difficult affair. Similarly, staying in a hotel should not break the bank and involve transporting the contents of house and home just to take the family away for a night or two.

High-chairs, changing facilities, cots and extra beds, high teas – these are the basic requirements that we look for when comparing hotel and restaurant facilities for . . . *and Baby Comes Too*. Many establishments that we recommend go further and provide much more – from bibs to bottle-warming, baby baths to baby-sitting and fun packs to fridges. Nevertheless, the starting point will always be the *attitude* of restaurateurs and hoteliers; without the right attitude they're a non-starter. Our Henry the Duck symbol is awarded sparingly to those establishments that we consider cater exceptionally for families.

Entries for this Guide are collated from research conducted by our team of professional hotel and restaurant inspectors for *Egon Ronay's Cellnet Guide 1994 Hotels & Restaurants*, *Egon Ronay's Heineken Guide 1994 Pubs & Inns* and *Egon Ronay's Britvic Guide 1994 Just a Bite*. Over 150 entries are new to the Guide this year; some entries feature only in . . . *and Baby Comes Too*. It has been impossible to visit with children every establishment listed, since not all our inspectors are parents, but they have kept a watchful eye on how both staff and proprietors have reacted to families during their visits; however, it's not easy for a gentleman inspector to inspect changing facilities in the Ladies (or vice versa)! In addition, we have requested details from all establishments with regard to the provision of facilities for toddlers and their parents.

We commend restaurateurs who carefully set out their stall before selling you their goods. 'Families welcome' all too often has a hollow ring to it. One restaurant boldly states on its menu that "manners are more important than age", another (*Hobbs Pavilion* in Cambridge) states that ". . . all children have 'bad days', but it is unreasonable to expect other customers to have to share the consequences of them. It is also unreasonable to wait for us to tell you when the child in your care is dominating the restaurant's atmosphere and then take offence at that request." Sound advice, clearly stated. Hoteliers are also getting wiser: the *Evesham Hotel* says "well-behaved youngsters are as welcome as well-behaved grown-ups" – a chicken and egg syndrome? Two new hotel entries this year (the *Trevelgue Hotel* in Porth, winner of our Family Hotel of the Year award and *Wringford Down* in Cawsand) even actively dissuade adults without children from staying (unless, like grandparents, they are part of a family group). We've even come across a couple of restaurants (*Grapevine* in Carlisle and *Glaister's* in London) who are happy to remove children altogether (to a supervised crèche next door) while parents enjoy their meal in peace.

The magnificent *Bath Spa Hotel*, a jewel in Forte's crown, opened its own commercial crèche last year; this not only satisfies the demand from the hotel's own staff but also offers a convenient facility for guests at weekends and bank holidays. For older children, hotels like the *Norwich Sport Hotel*, *Crieff Hydro* and *Palace Hotel* in Torquay are recommended as all-singing, all-dancing destinations with extensive sports facilities for active teenagers.

The unique 'group hotels' section (listed in county order) at the rear of the Guide helps you find a hotel in a particular area, perhaps when location is the most important criterion – for example, when touring or when attending a wedding. These hotels are not plotted on the map unless they also feature in the main gazetteer section.

Many smart restaurants in hotels are recommended not because they are child-friendly but because they are havens of peace for parents once the little ones are safely in the Land of Nod. We have to emphasise, year after year, that the food is *not* positively recommended in a hotel when that hotel's entry doesn't feature a separate restaurant entry. Alternative, informal eating arrangements within hotels are often noted.

Always ring before visiting – a wedding party or private function can seriously affect the character of a hotel at weekends, likewise, a conference mid-week; special offers are also almost always offered at weekends. And always state your requirements regarding early supper, bedding for a cot, baby-listening, baby-sitting and so on **before** arriving. Although even the most clued-up hoteliers know the problems that youngsters can create for themselves, parents should still be aware that hazards – lamp and kettle flexes, cups and saucers with tea-making facilities, telephones, exposed electrical sockets, sharp corners, glass-topped tables – exist at every turn.

Readers should note that in the course of our research many establishments have stated a wish *not* to be included in the Guide; thus, while many readers may think they have found a delightful family retreat and written to tell us about it, it may not be listed in this year's Guide because of the proprietor's wishes. *Egon Ronay's Cellnet Guide 1994 Hotels & Restaurants* lists hundreds more hotels, many of which cater for the odd family very well and many that specifically do not want children under certain ages. We hope that readers who are looking for something a little different from undistinguished motorway service stations, catering-pack pubs, sanitised chain restaurants and tired holiday hotels will find this 5th edition of . . . *and Baby Comes Too* an invaluable Guide.

One final moan – why do so many restaurants continue to fail to supply even the most basic facilities to change a baby? Just a table and chair would do, but so many restaurateurs continue to see their loos as a liability rather than providing a service for their customers, both young and old. Not surprisingly, our Restaurants and Hotel of the Year supply superb, separate baby-changing facilities. Changing baby on a stone-cold floor in a tiny pub loo while at the same time extending a leg in order to prevent anyone else from coming in through the door is not an ideal service. At least this is one area where the family-themed chain pubs excel: Whitbread's *Brewers Fayre* pubs all have a pull-down changing shelf in a separate disabled loo; similarly, *Harry Ramsden's* chain of fish'n'chip restaurants recognise that Dad takes his turn nowadays, providing separate facilities. Changing baby is part of everyday life for a young family and yet it remains the most common obstacle confronting parents who want to eat out with babies and toddlers. No changing facilities, no high-chair – no chance!

Finally, a word on our Family Hotel of the Year (see page 9), about which many readers have written in praise; one couple described their stay at the Trevelgue as "the perfect holiday", another parent said "my children thought they were at a party for seven days". 'Parents' Haven' and 'Children's Paradise' are the hotel's self-styled epithets, and – on this occasion – we wholeheartedly concur.

FOREWORD

The Ford Motor Company Limited and the establishments in the fifth edition of *Egon Ronay's Guide...and Baby Comes Too* share common objectives. They both seek to provide a comfortable, safe environment in which the family can enjoy itself.

When it comes to car safety features, Ford is the front runner in Britain. The first volume manufacturer to offer a complete safety package including driver's side airbag as standard and optional passenger airbag across the whole range, with the exception of Maverick which has different requirements because of its off-road capabilities. The package also includes a safety cell, with side impact bars, to protect passengers by absorbing energy generated in an accident. All internal fittings are designed to minimise the risk of injury and most models are available with anti-lock brakes. Integral security systems, RAC breakdown cover, a range of baby and child seats and even Ford mobile phones can all play their part in keeping you and your family safe and sound.

You choose a hotel or restaurant because it's going to look after you well. Choose your car for the same reasons - Ford.

1994 Duck Awards

London

Benihana **NW3**
Chicago Pizza Pie Factory **W1** - *NEW*
Glaister's Garden Bistro **SW10** - *NEW*
Newtons **SW4**
PJ's Grill **WC2** - *NEW*
Planet Hollywood **W1** - *NEW*
Rock Island Diner **W1**
Smollensky's Balloon Bar & Restaurant **W1**
Smollensky's on the Strand **WC2**
Spices **N16**

England

Avon, Bath **Bath Spa Hotel** - *NEW*
Avon, Bristol **Browns**
Avon, Bristol **Café Première**
Cambs, Cambridge **Browns**
Cambs, Cambridge **Hobbs Pavilion Restaurant** - *NEW*
Cheshire, Chester **Francs**
Cornwall, Camelford **Lanteglos Country House Hotel**
Cornwall, Carlyon Bay **Carlyon Bay Hotel**
Cornwall, Cawsand **Wringford Down** - *NEW*
Cornwall, Mullion **Polurrian Hotel** - *NEW*
Cornwall, Porth **Trevelgue Hotel** - *NEW*
Isles of Scilly, St Martin's **St Martin's Hotel**
Cumbria, Borrowdale **Stakis Lodore Swiss Hotel**
Cumbria, Carlisle **Grapevine** - *NEW*
Cumbria, Carlisle **Hudson's Coffee Shop**
Cumbria, Ullswater **Old Church Hotel** - *NEW*
Devon, Saunton **Saunton Sands Hotel**
Devon, Thurlestone **Thurlestone Hotel**
Devon, Torquay **Palace Hotel** - *NEW*
Devon, Weston **Otter Inn** - *NEW*
Devon, Woolacombe **Woolacombe Bay**
Dorset, Bournemouth **Chine Hotel** - *NEW*
Dorset, Bournemouth **Royal Bath**
Dorset, Bournemouth **Swallow Highcliff**
Dorset, Branscombe **Bulstone Hotel**
Dorset, Poole **Sandbanks Hotel** - *NEW*
Dorset, Studland Bay **Knoll House Hotel**
Glos, Kingscote **Hunters Hall Inn**
Glos, Stow-on-the-Wold **Fosse Manor**
Hants, Odiham **Blubeckers**
Hereford & Worcester, Evesham **Evesham Hotel** - *NEW*
Hereford & Worcester, Kington **Penrhos Court**
Humberside, Willerby **Grange Park Hotel**
Isle of Wight, Chale **Clarendon Hotel & Wight Mouse**
Isle of Wight, Shanklin **Hambledon Hotel**
Kent, Hythe **Hythe Imperial**
Kent, Rochester **The Knowle**
Lancashire, Blackpool **Pembroke Hotel**
Lancashire, Lytham St Annes **Dalmeny Hotel**
Leicestershire, Stretton **Ram Jam Inn**
Lincolnshire, Louth **Mr Chips** - *NEW*
Gtr Manchester, Manchester **Harry Ramsden's** - *NEW*
Middlesex, Shepperton **Blubeckers**
Norfolk, Great Bircham **Windmill Tea Rooms** - *NEW*
Norfolk, Norwich **Norwich Sport Village Hotel** - *NEW*
Oxon, Oxford **Browns**
Oxon, Wantage **Vale & Downland Museum Centre**
Shropshire, Norton **Hundred House Hotel** - *NEW*
Somerset, Batcombe **The Batcombe Inn** - *NEW*
Staffs, Stafford **Soup Kitchen**
Suffolk, Lavenham **Great House** - *NEW*
Surrey, Richmond **Refectory**
Surrey, South Holmwood **Gourmet Pizza Company** - *NEW*
E Sussex, Alfriston **Toucans Restaurant**
E Sussex, Brightling **Jack Fuller's**
E Sussex, Brighton **Dig In The Ribs**
E Sussex, Brighton **Dove Hotel**
E Sussex, Eastbourne **Grand Hotel**
Wilts, Bradford-on-Avon **Woolley Grange**
Wilts, Marlborough **Polly Tea Rooms**
Wilts, Swindon **Blunsdon House**
N Yorks, Harome **Star Inn**
N Yorks, Harrogate **Bettys**
N Yorks, Northallerton **Bettys**
N Yorks, Skipton **Randell's Hotel**
N Yorks, Whitby **Magpie Cafe**
N Yorks, York **Four Seasons** - *NEW*
N Yorks, York **Taylor's Tea Rooms**
W Yorks, Ilkley **Bettys**
W Yorks, Leeds **Salvo's**

Scotland

Borders, Peebles **Peebles Hotel Hydro**
Borders, Selkirk **Philipburn House**
Dumfries & Galloway, New Abbey **Criffel Inn**
Grampian, Banchory **Raemoir House**
Lothian, Ratho **Bridge Inn** - *NEW*
Strathclyde, Largs **Nardini's**
Tayside, Crieff **Crieff Hydro**

Wales

Clwyd, Bodfari **Dinorben Arms** - *NEW*
Clwyd, Llanarmon Dyffryn Ceiriog **West Arms Hotel**
Gwynedd, Abersoch **Porth Tocyn Hotel**
Powys, Machynlleth **Centre for Alternative Technology** - *NEW*

Channel Islands

Jersey, St Brelade's Bay **St Brelade's Bay Hotel**
Jersey, St Peter's Village **Star & Tipsy Toad Brewery** - *NEW*

. . . and Baby Comes Too
Family Hotel of the Year

Trevelgue Hotel
Porth, nr Newquay, Cornwall

The Trevelgue gets off to a head start with its superb cliff-top position and views out to sea from 42 large family suites; most unusually, these suites can each accommodate up to two adults and four children. Self-styled as a "parents' haven" and "children's paradise", for once the brochure-speak and epithets have real substance. Owner Nicholas Malcolm realises that children can be good business and, by creating an environment that is genuinely a family home-from-home, he manages to give their parents a happy holiday destination as well. Parents and children (together with their grandparents) *are* the Trevelgue's business and so the hotel's resources are directed into providing facilities that manage to keep even the most active families busy.

A team of childcare staff look after, amuse, entertain and teach the children of all ages that come to stay; there's a Hobby Club room, indoor adventure play room, children's café and even a closely supervised Teddy Bear evening calm-down 'club' for toddlers and youngsters, while teenagers can try their hand in the air-rifle range, play pool or work up an appetite on the assault course. Additional activities range from a comprehensive playground complete with a pirate ship and Wendy houses, large outdoor swimming pool, bouncy castle and organised family cycle trails to a golf driving net and 3-hole practice course, squash, tennis and health and beauty treatments for mum and dad. Eating arrangements are cleverly versatile (and comprehensive) for the children and the wine list is exceptionally keenly priced! It's all run with commendable enthusiasm by well-motivated staff, and parents' everyday needs are all provided: a daily pint of milk, jars of baby food, changing room, hiring a baby-carrier, walker, baby bath, double buggy – you name it and they've thought of it!

Previous Winners

1993	**Crieff Hydro** Crieff, Scotland	**1991**	**Saunton Sands** Saunton, nr Braunton, Devon
1992	**Woolley Grange** Bradford-on-Avon, Wiltshire	**1990**	**Knoll House** Studland Bay, Dorset

...and Baby Comes Too
Family Restaurants of the Year

Browns
Oxford & Cambridge

Browns is a conspicuously well-run small chain of brasseries offering a winning combination of varied menu, reasonable prices, children's facilities and cheery staff. There is no earth-shattering, keep-the-kids-occupied-for-hours entertainment, simply good food that children seem to lap up in droves – the Oxford branch serves over 1000 meals a day, from breakfast at 11am (from noon on Sundays & Bank Holidays), through lunch and afternoon tea (3-5.30pm with cucumber or egg and cress sandwiches plus freshly baked scones or toasted muffins) to late-night evening meals. The long, all-day opening hours make feeding children's odd-hours hunger pangs easy and the children's menu offers enough favourites to satisfy even the most picky of junior diners: hamburger, barbecue ribs, fillet of fish, spaghetti, club sandwich with crisps, or cheese and fruit salad (all main courses are around £3). If you have a budding gourmet in the family then he or she can tuck into a Caesar salad, toasted tuna sandwich, venison steak with pepper sauce or profiteroles with chocolate sauce, all from the long main menu. Other nice touches include numerous high-chairs, plastic bibs, daily blackboard special dishes that include good vegetarian options, interesting cocktails, and an assurance that the 10% service charge (for parties of 5 or more only) "goes directly to your waitress". Nursing mums or dads can use the conveniently separate mother and baby facilities in the disabled loo, but they will have to nurse their credit cards as they are not accepted (neither are table reservations). The original branch of Browns is in Brighton and the latest outlet is in Bristol (see entries). Our award goes to the two busy branches in the famous university towns.

Previous Winners

1993 **Smollensky's on the Strand & Smollensky's Balloon**
London

1992 **Blubeckers**
Odiham, Hampshire

1991 **Toucans**
Alfriston, East Sussex

1990 **Bettys**
Harrogate, North Yorkshire

Until now, one of the major causes of crash injuries has been the driver's head hitting the steering wheel.

Mondeo from Ford has changed all that. Every single Mondeo has a steering wheel airbag.

But this technology is not new to Ford. Worldwide over 3.2 million airbags, more than any other manufacturer, have been fitted by Ford.

The system detects an impact, senses how hard the car has been hit, and if necessary inflates the airbag to cushion your head.

All this takes place in less time than it takes to blink; under a tenth of a second.

At the same time, seatbelt pre-tensioners and grabbers hold you firmly against the seat.

Specially designed seats prevent you from sliding forward under the seatbelt. Side impact bars and crumple zones absorb crash impact.

Before.

The fuel is cut off. We call these safety features
Dynamic Safety Engineering.

Before an accident you wouldn't have been
aware of them. But you'd certainly appreciate
them after one.

For further information on
airbags and the new Mondeo,
call free on **0800 111 222.**

Everything we do is driven by you.

Telephone in

Ford Cellular Systems has a wide choice
of reliable, value for money phones. If you
want a phone permanently fixed in your car,
have a look at the Ford phone Mobile or the
Integral. If you want a phone to take away,
we've a range of portable, pocket and palm
phones. And if you want the best of both
worlds we've car kits available to turn most

or take away

portables into hands-free car phones at the click of a switch.

We have all the airtime tariffs from both Cellnet and Vodafone available plus a special Ford Personal Safety tariff for people who just want a phone for emergencies. Want to use your phone abroad? Then we have GSM phones and airtime too.

For further information and prices, see your local Ford dealer. Or phone us free on **0800 52 66 57.**

CELLULAR SYSTEMS

You Can Bank on us.

Ford Credit Europe plc, The Drive, Brentwood, Essex CM13 3AR
Telephone (0277) 224400

The only thing that responds quicker

is us

Since 1963, Ford Credit has been growing. Growing by responding to the needs of our customers.

- When Ford wanted a specialised contract hire company, Ford Credit launched Ford Contract Motoring. We are now the largest Ford contract hire fleet in the UK.

- When your vehicle needs servicing, we have the largest Dealer network in the UK to respond to your needs.

- And, when you need a quotation, over 90% are given inside one hour.

Ford Contract Motoring

Leading the Market by Example

For all your Contract Hire needs call 0277 692543

The Family phone

Whether Dad's away on business, Mum's running her parents home to the country or daughter Zoe's going to the disco, wouldn't you feel happier if they had a mobile phone with them? Just in case.

We have a choice of reliable, value for money phones, including the highly recommended Ford phone Compact. And a choice of airtime tariffs too.

For further information and prices, see your local Ford dealer. Or phone us free on **0800 52 66 57**. And keep it in the family!

"The Compact is undoubtedly a remarkable phone offering peak reception and transmission. Don't shop around any more. This is definitely a hit."

October 1993

WHAT **MOBILE**
and cellular magazine
Recommended

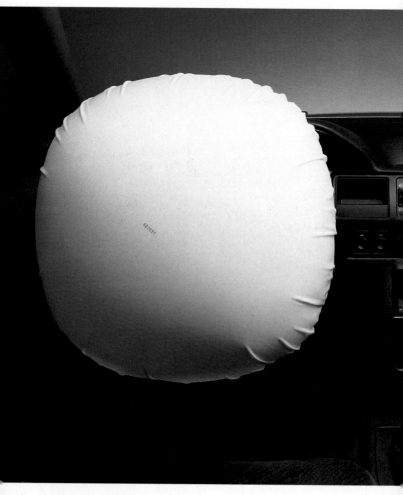

As you're driving along, have you ever wondered what might happen to your other half in the event of an accident?

Or, for that matter, what would happen to you?

For instance, would your car give you the extra protection of a driver or passenger airbag?

If you're fortunate enough to be driving a Ford, yo would automatically be cushioned by an airbag, sinc most of our new models currently have one fitted a standard equipment. By the beginning of 1994,* ever single car we make will include a driver's airbag.

For a longer lasting relationship, you can provid your partner with an optional passenger airbag fo less than the price of an eternity ring.

*Fiesta, Fiesta Van and Courier standard driver's airbag and optional passenger airbag available from January 19

See how the other half live.

But airbags aren't the only important safety features you'll fall in love with.

Our Dynamic Safety Engineering system (or D.S.E.† for short) is designed to make sure that in the event of an accident, you won't crumple like our crumple zones, absorb an impact like our door beams, or collapse like our steering columns.

In fact, both of you have an extremely strong chance of keeping your romance alive forever.

So next time you're proposing to buy a new car, test drive a Ford and gain an insight into how the other half live. You never know, it could be the start of a very long lasting affair.

For more information on D.S.E., call **0800 111 222**.

Everything we do is driven by you.

THE BIGGER, NEW BOTTLE

NOW LASTS THE ROUND

With the new,
bigger Britvic bottles, you
now get better value with nearly
60% more juice. And it's even tastier.
So fill your glasses and sink a
few more ice cubes.
Cheers!

Our brewers never do things by halves.

You would think, in times like these, what with costs soaring and the recession lingering, that the chaps in our brewery would act a little less extravagantly for once and employ a few prudent... how shall we put it... *economies.*

Couldn't they, for example, drive a harder bargain on a bushel of barley?

Perhaps select some other hops rather than those notoriously exorbitant females? (There must be varieties just as fragrant closer to home than Czechoslovakia.)

And, really, if other lagers can ferment inside a month, don't they think that six weeks is labouring the point?

No, comes the answer. No, no and no again.

They will not budge. They refuse to budget. You may as well try and argue with that brick wall over there.

Their attitude, frankly, can be a bit much. But then you already know this.   **Stella Artois. Reassuringly expensive.**

Britvic
5̌

SPARKLING
ORANGE JUICE DRINK

Pop
a bottle of juice.

Britvic 55

is the champagne

of juices.

It's more than just a juice.

More than just a fizzy drink.

Why

settle for less?

Choose Cellnet...

Thanks to Cellnet's initiative in opening up the market, the mobile phone is now available to simply anyone who needs to keep in touch – and mobile communications have really come of age.

With this maturity come new benefits for our customers – the most important being ever increasing choice...

Call the BIG network for small phones on
0800 21 4000

Cellnet – making more of the mobile phone.

Since the launch of cellular communications in the UK in 1985, Cellnet, with the support of its parent companies BT and Securicor, has invested more than £700 million in the continuous development of its network and customer services.

More support for handportable phones.

If you've bought, or are considering a handportable phone you'll need to be connected to Cellnet – the mobile communication network that offers in-depth coverage, locally and nationwide.

We are investing over £30million on 230 new local network base stations, which will bring the total number of Cellnet cellular stations to over 1,000 and help to ensure Cellnet continues to offer handportable users the best possible service nationwide.

More coverage nationwide.

Embracing over 98% of the UK population and stretching the length and breadth of the nation (including exclusive coverage of the Channel Islands and the Isle of Man), you can make calls on Cellnet, nationally and internationally, from almost anywhere in the UK.

And the widest choice of tariffs to suit your lifestyle.

Recognising that different users have very different needs, Cellnet offers a choice of tariff packages designed to offer high volume and less frequent users – not only in London, but throughout the country – more flexibility and greater value for money.

More services. More support.

Cellnet offers a comprehensive range of sophisticated services, too. Supporting both business and personal needs, including International Calls, Information Lines (such as AA Roadwatch, Cellnet Weathercall and Talking Pages), and intelligent messaging.

With Cellnet, personal communications can mean so much more than personal efficiency and peace of mind. With Cellnet, your mobile phone will not only make life easier – it will help to make life more enjoyable, too. Keeping you in touch, wherever life takes you.

THE CREAM OF MANCHESTER.

Boddingtons Draught Bitter. Brewed at the Strangeways Brewery since 1778.

London

N1   Anna's Place   £44

Tel 071-249 9379	Restaurant

90 Mildmay Park Newington Green N1 4PR   **Map 16 D2**

Anna Hegarty's eponymous restaurant continues to draw in the
crowds so booking is essential. Decorated with Swedish posters and
colourful vinyl tablecloths, it has a friendly, informal atmosphere.
The food is also uncomplicated and approachable, featuring a good
smattering of Swedish specialities. Marinated herrings, gravad lax
(delicious with a glass of ice-cold schnapps), and roast turbot with
grated fresh horseradish are typical fishy choices, while hearty meat
hot pots are a popular winter order. Among the desserts the Swedish
waffles with blueberry compote and cream should not be missed.
Outdoor eating in a partly covered garden area in summer. Children's
portions of most dishes are available and puddings are especially child-
friendly. There is one booster seat and storage for push-chairs. The
atmosphere is rather grown-up in the evening although children are
welcome at any time. No specific baby-changing area. Wheelchair
access over one small step, but no disabled toilet access. *Seats 45.*
Parties 30. L 12.15-2.15 D 7.15-10.45. Closed Sun, Mon, 2 weeks
Christmas, 2 weeks Easter, Aug. No credit cards.

W1   Arisugawa   £60

Tel 071-636 8913	Restaurant

27 Percy Street off Tottenham Court Road W1P 9FF   **Map 18 D2**

A smart, modern restaurant in a basement with a menu of more than
usual interest. Teppanyaki cuisine (griddle cooking done in front of the
diner) is offered in the ground-floor room, traditional Japanese in the
basement. While there are no specific facilities for children the staff are
patient and friendly and will gladly help with choosing dishes, clearly
describing each one (children should try the tempura); the food
is delicate, fresh and beautifully presented. The decor is sophisticated
and it's certainly not a place for anything less than best behaviour from
baby-san. Pictorial menu at lunch, when it is considerably cheaper
to dine here. Sometimes the private room is shared by families who
wish to eat in a traditional style. *Seats 100. Private Room 20.*
L 12.30-2.30 D 6-10. Closed L Sat, all Sun, Bank Holidays,
Christmas/New Year. Set L from £7 Set D from £20. Access, Amex,
Diners, Visa.

W1   Aroma

Tel 071-495 4911	Café

273 Regent Street W1   **Map 18 D3**

Recently opened at the corner of Regent Street and Great Castle Street
(north of Oxford Circus), the shop is bright in colours with Mexican
background music. In line with the decor, colourful crockery
is offered for customers who eat in. Every detail has been carefully
considered except for air conditioning and the shop can get hot
on summer days. A limited selection of sandwiches and salads, all
neatly wrapped up, is stocked on the self-serve cold counter. Excellent
bought-in pastries. Coffee is their speciality and there are dozens
of ways of enjoying it. No particular family facilities, but a good place
for a snack stop. *Seats 45. Open 7.30am-8.30pm (Sat from 9-7.30pm,*
Sun & Bank Holidays 11am-6.30pm). Closed 25 & 26 Dec. Access,
Amex, Visa.

Also at:
1b Dean Street off Oxford Street W1 Tel 071-287 1633   **Map 18 D2**
36a St Martin's Lane WC2 Tel 071-836 5110   **Map 21 B3**

EC2   Barbican Centre, Waterside Restaurant

Tel 071-638 4141	Restaurant
Barbican Centre EC2	Map 20 B1

The Waterside Restaurant, operated by De Blank Restaurants, has been
fully refurbished; there is now plentiful seating outside, although
youngsters will need to be secured in one of the four high-chairs
or closely supervised to prevent accidents in the ornamental lake.
Inside, the new decor is a fashionable mix of wood, glass and metal.
Counters are attractively displayed, food is served by helpful staff.
Dishes follow a Mediterranean theme, offering such dishes as stuffed
aubergines (£5.35) or boeuf en daube (£5.95) with tempting salads
as an alternative. The focal point is the dessert counter, strategically
placed in the centre, offering the likes of tiramisu, pavlova and
summer pudding (from £1.75 to £2.95). The dining room extends
into an agreeable terrace in the summer. A new addition is the
Cappuccino bar located at the back of the food counters (open from
10am to 8pm) serving ciabatta sandwiches, pastries, muffins and
scones. No smoking. One floor up is the Balcony Bar where the prices
are lower but the food is not so good. *Seats 180. **Open** noon-8pm.
Closed 24 & 25 Dec. Access, Visa.*

SE3   Bardon Lodge   56%   £84

Tel 081-853 4051 Fax 081-858 7387	Hotel
15 Stratheden Road Blackheath SE3 7TH	Map 17 D5

Close to Blackheath and Greenwich, Bardon Lodge comprises two
Victorian houses. Most bedrooms are fairly modest in size, with
modern furniture and compact carpeted bathrooms. The hotel
is in new hands. Within walking distance of the maritime attractions
of Greenwich. *Rooms 37. Garden. Access, Amex, Visa.*

SW3   Basil Street Hotel   71%   £178

Tel 071-581 3311 Fax 071-581 3693	Hotel
Basil Street SW3 1AH	Map 19 C4

An Edwardian English atmosphere pervades a privately-owned hotel
just 191 steps (according to their publicity) from Harrods. Public areas
have a country house feel, from the antique-lined corridor leading
to the dining room to the spacious lounge in sunny yellow with rug-
covered polished parquet floor. Well-kept bedrooms are of a good size,
usually with a sitting area, traditionally furnished and decorated with
understated good taste. Most have equally roomy private bathrooms.
Old-fashioned standards of courteous and obliging service include shoe
cleaning, servicing of rooms in the evenings and 24hr room service.
Children under 16 stay free in parents' room. *Rooms 92. Access, Amex,
Diners, Visa.*

NW3   Benihana   £75

Tel 071-586 9508	Restaurant
100 Avenue Road Swiss Cottage NW3 3HF	Map 16 B3

American-style Japanese teppanyaki griddle cooking in large and often
lively basement surroundings lavishly furnished with chrome, marble
and mirrors. Surf 'n' turf is served with showbiz flair by knife-flailing

chefs at hibachi tables. Great value week-day lunches and children's menu (5 dishes, including ice cream or sorbet, for £4.75-£5.50; chips, frankfurters and tempura sold as side orders £1.50-£2.85). Entertainment is provided on Sundays, for which time we award the Duck symbol; nevertheless, the cooking show is always a spectacle and the infectious atmopshere (particular at weekends) should be enough to interest any children in the food presented in front of them. Alcohol-free cocktails are always a big hit with children; try a Shirley Temple or a Strawberry Pussy (£1.75-£2.50). Specialities include vegetable ginza (stuffed green pepper with textured soy, asparagus, baby corn, spinach, shiitake mushrooms, carrots, lotus roots and potato). The entrance, which isn't immediately obvious, is next to the Hampstead Theatre. Branches around the world, from Beverly Hills to Bangkok; the newest branch was set to open in Kings Road, Chelsea as we went to press. *Seats 120. L 12.30-3 D 6.30-12. Closed L Mon, 25 Dec. Set L from £8.45. Access, Amex, Diners, Visa.*

W1   Bentinck House Hotel   £76

Tel 071-935 9141 Fax 071-224 5903	Hotel
20 Bentinck Street W1M 5RL	**Map 18 C2**

Large comfortable bedrooms (three family rooms at a small extra charge, 9 rooms not en suite) in a small hotel behind Oxford Street. *Rooms 20. Access, Amex, Diners, Visa.*

SW3   Big Easy

Tel 071-352 4071	Restaurant
332/334 Kings Road Chelsea SW3 5UR	**Map 19 B6**

Describing itself as the first authentic American Bar BQ and crabshack in Europe, Big Easy is relaxed, cheerful and often very busy. Specialist dishes are Bar BQ, shrimp and crab and 18oz Scotch steaks, supported by a large selection of burgers and salads. Prices are very reasonable, with the best value provided by Early Bird special dinners (£4.95 – soup or salad, a main course such as garlic roasted chicken or minute steak, plus tea, coffee or a soft drink). The Sunday Bar BQ is similarly priced. Children's meals £2.95. Live music seven nights a week. *Seats 130. Open 12-12 (till 12.30 Fri & Sat). Closed 25 & 26 Dec, 1 Jan. Access, Visa.*

SW3   Blair House Hotel   £85

Tel 071-581 2323	Hotel
34 Draycott Place SW3 2SA	**Map 19 C5**

Well-equipped bed and breakfast hotel conveniently located near Sloane Square with quiet bedrooms at the back. Extra bed supplied (£15). *Rooms 17. Access, Amex, Diners, Visa.*

E1   Bloom's

Tel 071-247 6001	Restaurant
90 Whitechapel High Street Aldgate E1	**Map 20 D1**

For over 70 years the Bloom family have dispensed authentic Beth-Din supervised cooking at this large Kosher East End institution. Chopped liver (£2.90), gefilte fish (£2.90), tzimmas (£1.50) and gedempte meat-balls (£6.90) are familiar favourites, but the salt beef (£8.90) is still the one to go for. Service from suitably sardonic staff is so slick you can order course by course if you wish. Great fun.

Childrens' portions and take-away service available. **Seats** *130.*
Open *10-9.30 (Fri to 3, 2 in Winter).* **Closed** *D Fri, all Sat, 25 Dec,
Jewish Holidays. Access, Amex, Diners, Visa.*
Also at:
130 Golders Green Road NW11 Tel 081-455 3033   **Map 16 B1**
Open Sat eve till very late.

WC1 **Bonnington Hotel** **61%**	**£108**
Tel 071-242 2828 Fax 071-831 9170	**Hotel**
92 Southampton Row WC1B 4BH	**Map 16 C3**

In the same family ownership for 80 years, the Bonnington is just
south of Russell Square – close to the British Museum and within easy
walking distance of the Oxford Street shops. Extensive public areas
include a lounge bar, breakfast room and many meeting/function
rooms for up to 250 delegates. Bedrooms with all the usual accessories
include 56 (and increasing) designated non-smoking. Rooms
on Southampton Row are double-glazed. **Rooms** *215. Amex,
Diners, Visa.*

SW18 **Brady's**	
Tel 081-877 9599	**Fish'n'Chips**
513 Old York Road Wandsworth SW18	**Map 17 B5**

Fresh fish from Grimsby or Cornwall is prepared without fuss or frills
in Luke Brady's simple, uncluttered restaurant. With grilled
or battered fish (main courses around £5) come good chips and
various flavoured mayonnaises. Starters could include smoked salmon
(£3.50) or half-a-pint of prawns (£2.50), and there are regularly-
changing specials among the main course. Treacle tart is a popular
pud. **Seats** *38.* **Open** *7-10.45 (Fri to 11.15).* **Closed** *Sun, 10 days
Christmas/New Year. No credit cards.*

W10 **Brasserie du Marché aux Puces**	
Tel 081-968 5828	**Brasserie**
349 Portobello Road W10 5SA	**Map 16 B3**

Open from 10am, serving coffee, tea, bagels and croissants, with the
kitchen starting operations at noon. This is a bright, informal brasserie
with plain wooden tables, a long mahogany bar and plenty of light
from the many windows. Six tables set out front provide alfresco
snacking in summer. Many dishes on the menu (served throughout
the day) have a modern Mediterranean ring, others the similar echo
of California: grilled radicchio and fennel with extra virgin olive oil
(£3.55), roast goose breast with green tomato and walnuts (£9.55),
grilled squid with mango and coriander salsa (£4.25), chicken Kiev
with wild garlic and roast oatflakes. One or two others have a more
distant provenance, like savarin of Indonesian rice. Seared tuna with
pumpkin won tons is a new speciality. Sunday brunch (11-4) has its
own similar menu, which changes every week. No particular family
facilities, but the long opening hours, unusual menu (perhaps only
for the adventurous child – ask for a child's portion) and its situation
on Portobello Road (for the hectic Saturday market) make it a useful
place to know about. **Seats** *35.* **Open** *10am-11pm (4-11pm Sun).*
Closed *D Sun, Bank Holidays. No credit cards.*

WC1   British Museum, Milburns Restaurant

Tel 071-636 1555	Café/Restaurant

British Museum Great Russell Street Bloomsbury WC1   **Map 18 D2**

Milburns has recently taken over the café and restaurant at the British
Museum. Both are self-service and offer drinks, cakes and pastries all
day (10am to 4.30pm). Between 11.45am and 2.45pm, the restaurant
offers a comprehensive lunch menu. Assorted salads (£2.50), ham
in Cumberland sauce (£4.85) and chicken curry (£5.80) are examples
of the pleasant, daily-changing dishes. Light cakes like carrot and
hazelnut (£1.10), fruit muffins and scones (80p), freshly baked on the
premises, are perfect for morning coffee or afternoon tea. Four high-
chairs were "on order" as we went to press, but there are no baby-
changing facilities, not even in the museum. *Seats Restaurant 50,
Café 270. Open Restaurant and Café 10-4.30 (Sun 2.30-6.30).
Closed 25 & 26 Dec, 1 Jan. Access, Visa.*

W1   Brown's Hotel

Tel 071-493 6020	Afternoon Tea

Albermarle Street Mayfair W1   **Map 18 D3**

A Forte flagship, where afternoon tea in the panelled lounge is a long-
established tradition. Every day between 3 and 6 the order is the same:
tea sandwiches, brown bread and butter with preserves, hot toasted
scones with clotted cream, home-made cakes and pastries, and a choice
of eight teas. This treat will set you back £13.95, while £15.50 gets
you high tea in the restaurant between 4.15 and 5.45. Here the bill
of fare is salmon fish cakes or high tea griddle or ham with hash
potatoes and cabbage, then sultana scones, tea pastries, Scottish
shortbread or mixed fruit loaf. Gentlemen are required to wear jackets
and ties for both these occasions; children are not! A high-chair can
be provided and the Ladies is "extremely spacious". For the well-heeled
junior gourmet afternoon or high tea at Brown's sounds idyllic – now
all one has to do is pick a day without moods, tantrums and turns
from junior! *Seats 60 (restaurant) 80 (lounge). Open 3-6 (Tea)
4.15-5.45 (High Tea). Access, Amex, Diners, Visa.*

W1   Bryanston Court   61%   £102

Tel 071-262 3141 Fax 071-262 7248	Hotel

56 Great Cumberland Place W1H 7FD   **Map 18 C2**

One minute away from Marble Arch and Oxford Street, the family-
run Bryanston Court is well situated for shopping and sightseeing.
Day rooms and bedrooms offer home-from-home comfort.
Improvements have recently been made in the bathrooms, most
of which have shower/WC only. No charge for cots provided; extra
bed £15. *Rooms 54. Access, Amex, Diners, Visa.*

SW1   Café de Blank

Tel 071-730 6400	Café

General Trading Company 144 Sloane Street SW1   **Map 19 C5**

Convenient for the Sloane Square shopping area, Justin de Blank's café
at the 'GTC' is popular for breakfast, lunch, tea, and early evening
snacks. Reached through the shop during the day or down the
basement steps in the evening, the café serves breakfast (£3.95) from
9 till noon with a choice of croissants, brioches or breads, freshly
squeezed orange juice and unlimited cafetière coffee, or there's toast

with scrambled eggs and flat-capped mushrooms (£3.50) or sausages
and bacon (£3.50). Home-made cakes and pastries are available
throughout the day, and a number of savoury dishes are served outside
the main eating times. Lunchtime is à la carte, with dishes such
as spinach roulade with salad (£6.75), smoked salmon rillettes (£5.75)
and gratin of endives and Parma ham (£7.20). From 6pm 2- or 3-
course set menus (£12.25/£14.95) operate. For weary shoppers,
a cream tea is available in the afternoons (£2.75); for weary mums,
a garden table is a peaceful haven in summer; ask a member of staff
to help you carry a push-chair down the steps (there's no lift).
Babies eat free and under-12s for half price (booster seats supplied).
No smoking inside. **Seats** 72. **Open** 9am-9pm. **Closed** D Sat, all Sun,
Bank Holidays, 1 week over Christmas.

SW14   Café Coco
Tel 081-878 4800	Café
361 Upper Richmond Road West Sheen SW14	**Map 17 A5**

A clean-lined neighbourhood café at the rear of a take-away
bakery/patisserie with grey marble tables, tiled floor and prints on the
walls. Enjoy a good, strong espresso or freshly-squeezed orange juice
with a selection of croissants, pastries and panettone. Sandwiches
on baguette, ciabatta or granary bread and main course salads (around
£3.50) are joined by hot pasta dishes – lasagne, tagliatelle, tortelloni
(some vegetarian) – and a daily special, perhaps lamb and apple curry
(£4.95). Ices, frozen yoghurts and various pastries and gateaux
to finish. Filled jumbo Yorkshire puddings (£4.25) make a novel
Sunday lunch. Two high-chairs and booster seats. **Seats** 47. **Open** 9-6.
Closed 25 & 26 Dec, 1 Jan. No credit cards.

WC2   Café in the Crypt
Tel 071-839 4342	Café
The Crypt of St Martin-in-the-Fields Duncannon St off Trafalgar St WC2	**Map 21 B3**

As its name suggests the café is found underneath beautiful vaulted
arches and has original gravestones on the floor. Open for morning
coffee with croissants and Danish pastries. The lunchtime buffet
include soup, perhaps mulligatawny (£1.50) and a couple of hot
dishes: coq au vin (£5.90), mushroom and pepper stroganoff (£5.50)
and more extensive cold buffet, plus hot and cold desserts. Dinner
is served from 5-7.30, and soup and desserts are available from noon.
Minimum food charge of £5. Children's portions and two high-chairs
provided. **Seats** 80. **Open** 12-7.30pm (Sun to 3.15pm). **Closed** D Sun,
25 & 26 Dec, 1 Jan. Access, Visa.

NW3   Café Flo
Tel 071-435 6744	Restaurant
205-7 Haverstock Hill NW3	**Map 16 B2**

Opposite the Screen on the Hill cinema, one of a very successful small
chain of five bistro-cum-cafés, each chock-full of Gallic style and spirit.
French plates decorate the walls while seating is on cane chairs around
neat, if small, tables. Lighting is soft and low. A feature is the range
of cheap set menus which start with a basic but good L'idée Flo
at £6.95 for two courses plus coffee. The regular à la carte features
French standards such as soupe de poissons (£3.95) with rouille,
croutons and Gruyère, fricassée de volaille à l'estragon (£7.95) or steak
sandwich and frites (£5.95). Seasonal specialities can include pan-fried

medallion of pork with an apple and calvados sauce (£7.50)
or smoked salmon and crab with a lobster sauce (£7.95). Opening
times vary from 8.30am onwards when a range of breakfasts
is available. All Café Flos have high-chairs and a special children's
menu offering goujons de poulet, steak grillé, saucisse and frites
or gateau de poisson (!) followed by glace au choix or mousse
au chocolat, all for £3.95. Wonderful value, long opening hours and
(usually) very busy at peak times. **Seats** 70. **Open** *10am-11pm (Sun
to 10.30)*. **Closed** *3 days Christmas. Access, Amex, Visa.*
Also at:

51 St Martin's Lane WC2 Tel 071-836 8289   **Map 21 B3**
9am-11.45pm (Sun 10am-11pm). Convenient for theatre land.

334 Upper Islington Street N1 Tel 071-226 7916   **Map 16 D3**
Open 9am-11pm (Sat 8.30-11.30, Sun 8.30-10.30).

127/129 Kensington Church Street W8 Tel 071-727 8142   **Map 18 A3**
Open 9am-11.30pm (Sun to 10.30). Converted pub at the Notting Hill
Gate end of Church Street.

676 Fulham Road SW6 Tel 071-371 9673   **Map 17 B5**
Open 9am-11.30pm (Sun to 10.30).

W1   Café Royal

Tel 071-437 9090	Brasserie

68 Regent Street W1	**Map 18 D3**

The arrival of chef Herbert Berger has produced many changes at the
Café Royal. The Grill Room decor has been dusted and the menu
given a light Mediterranean boost. Things have also improved in
The Brasserie. Caryatids highlighted by direct spotlights, dark wood,
polished brass rails and immaculate white tablecloths give a smartly
traditional ambience. Open all day for a simple snack menu of potato
skins and salsa (£2.50), bangers and mash (£7.50) or scrambled eggs
with smoked salmon and toasts (£5.65), they also offer traditional
afternoon tea (served 3-5 Mon-Sat, 2-6 Sun, £11) gently accompanied
by a harpist. Things get more elaborate for lunch and dinner when the
Brasserie's balcony offers a well-priced high-standard menu
of carpaccio of Provençal vegetables with rocket and balsamic vinegar
(£5.75), braised knuckle of lamb with roasted garlic and root
vegetables (£8.20), or salmon confit with flageolet and bacon stew
(£12). For one single dish or a three-course meal, the service will
be professional and courteous. Six high-chairs are provided; a special
offer at Christmas allows one child to eat at half price and another free
of charge. Also within the Café Royal is *Café Nichols*, a sandwich and
cappuccino shop with a street frontage, the famous *Grill Room* which
offers classical French cuisine in splendid Baroque surroundings and
Daniels Piano Bar. **Seats** *90*. **Open** *12-11 (Sun and Bank Holidays 12-6).
Access, Amex, Diners, Visa.*

SW18   Calico

Tel 081-947 9616	Restaurant

573 Garratt Lane Wandsworth SW18	**Map 17 B6**

White paper squares over red check cloths and a bare-board floor set
the tone at this informal café/restaurant in the same stable as *Gavin's*
in Putney, the *Depot* at Barnes and *Ciao* in Fulham. Crudités and dips
(£3.10), smoked trout and pink peppercorn paté, chicken and ham
bouchée (£6.95), pan-fried lamb's liver and prawn stir-fry (£6.60)
show the range. A midweek lunchtime special offers pasta, side salad,
garlic bread and a glass of house wine for £4.99. There's a short

children's menu and a courtyard with tables for summer eating.
Seats 70. **Open** *12-3 & 6-11 (Sun to 10.30).* **Closed** *25 & 26 Dec.*
Access, Amex, Diners, Visa.

NW3	**Charles Bernard Hotel**	**60%**	**£65**
Tel 071-794 0101 Fax 071-794 0100			Hotel
5 Frognal Hampstead NW3 6AL			Map 16 B2

Just off Finchley Road and well connected by public transport to the
West End, this is a 70s' hotel with open-plan day rooms and practical
overnight accommodation. Children up to 12 stay free in parents'
room. Cot (£6.50) and extra bed provided. No dogs. **Rooms** 57.
Access, Amex, Diners, Visa.

E2	**Cherry Orchard**	
Tel 081-980 6678		Vegetarian
241 Globe Road Bethnal Green E2		Map 16 D3

A brightly decorated vegetarian café run by a team of Buddhist
women affiliated to the London Buddhist Centre. Cakes (sugar-free
and dairy-free available) are priced between 75p and £1 and
accompany an excellent range of teas. Baked potatoes come with
cheese/cottage cheese (£2), houmus or sour cream and hot specials
(£3.35/£3.65) on offer at lunchtime could include mushroom
moussaka with green salad (£3.65). On the cold front there are salads
(houmus salad plate £1.75). Children's portions; two high-chairs.
Unlicensed (£1 corkage when you bring your own wine).
No smoking inside but allowed at the seven garden tables. **Seats** 55.
Open *11-4 (Tues, Wed 11-7).* **Closed** *Sat, Sun, 1 week Christmas/New
Year. Access, Visa.*

W1	**Chicago Pizza Pie Factory**	
Tel 071-629 2669		Restaurant
17 Hanover Square off Oxford Street W1		Map 18 C2

Tucked away in the north-western corner of Hanover Square
with a glossy red facade is one of London's original American deep-
base pizza restaurants. Opened in 1977, it still attracts the crowds and
nightly buzzes with noise and activity. Sited in a large basement lined
with wall-to-wall posters on a Chicago theme. Thin-crust pizzas
are a recent introduction but it's the deep-pan pizzas that are the
mainstay of what's on offer: they come as regular (from £6.45 for
two people) or large (from £12 for 3 to 4). A good choice
is 'everything and the pan' (£11) which has peperoni, sausage,
mushrooms, onion, green peppers, tomato, oregano and cheese.
Hamburgers, chili and lasagne are also on offer, with carrot cake and
home-made cheesecake to finish. Our Henry the Duck symbol
is awarded for 'Sunday Funday' when an entertainment programme
is offered for 3- to 10-year-olds and accompanying parents. Face-
painting, party games, disco dancing, storytelling, theatre workshop
and 'absolutely no computer games' is the order of the day in The
Boardroom from noon to 5pm, while a children's menu (£6) offers
pizza with mushrooms or ham or 'London's best' cheeseburger and
fries with bottomless Coke (or Diet Coke) and 'build your own
dessert' from the ice cream trolley; set-price, three-course adult menu
£10 includes coffee. Watch out for the Wicked Witch of Chicago and
the Pointed Pizza Bird who make regular appearances in the
restaurant; children's entertainer Smarty Arty appears at 1pm,

2pm and 3pm. Children are given a Pizza Bird mask, button badge
and balloon with which to go home. High-chairs, booster seats and
nappy-changing facilities are all provided, as are crayons and paper for
drawings to be entered into the CPPF Annual Art Show. Due to the
success of Sunday Funday there may be two sittings (at noon and
at 2pm), so don't expect to stay for the afternoon – business is business!
The staff are as gregarious as ever. *Seats 250. Open 11.45am-11.30pm
(12-10.30 Sun). Access, Amex, Visa.*

SW7   The Chicago Rib Shack

Tel 071-581 5595	Restaurant
1 Raphael Street Knightsbridge Green SW7	**Map 19 C4**

Loud and busy, the restaurant doesn't suffer from being slightly tucked
away. A 15-minute wait in the separate bar area is fairly average for
a weeknight. The menu is simple, mainly based on ribs (£9.60 full
rack), chicken (£7.25) and barbecue sauce, served with coleslaw, corn
on the cob and oven-roasted potatoes. Other alternatives include
an excellent chili (con carne £6.45, vegetarian £5.95), giant spinach
salad (£5.95) or spicy grilled halibut (£9.95). Even if the mud pie
(£4.75) is not completely authentic, the delicious chocolate sauce will
make up for it. Very much a family restaurant, with bibs (even for
adults), ten high-chairs, six booster seats, colouring menu, crayons and
balloons provided; the background music is usually loud enough
to cover any kid's scream of delight as they tuck into a messy rack
of ribs. A children's menu offers child-size rack, burger, barbecue
chicken or nuggets, plus soft drink and mud pie or ice cream for
£5.95. Happy hour 5.30-7.30 (Mon-Sat). Valet parking. *Seats 220.
Open 11.45am-11.45pm (midday-11pm Sun). Access, Amex, Visa.*

W1   Chuen Cheng Ku

Tel 071-437 1398	Restaurant
17 Wardour Street W1	**Map 21 A2**

One of the fixtures of the Chinatown eating scene, Chuen Cheng
Ku is a vast place stretching through the block to Rupert Street and
up a couple of floors. In an atmosphere that's often reminiscent
of a bustling bazaar local Chinese and Westerners make their choice
from a very long Cantonese menu. Best value for snackers is provided
by the daytime dim sum (£1.65-£3.30), which are served from little
metal wagons steered along the tables by reserved but not unfriendly
waitresses. One prepares and dispenses noodle soup, another carries
a payload of fried items, others deal in bamboo steamers filled with
pork, beef and prawn dumplings. A fun Chinese food factory.
*Seats 400. Open 11.30am-11.45pm. Closed 24 & 25 Dec. Access, Amex,
Diners, Visa.*

NW3   Clive Hotel   64%   £64

Tel 071-586 2233 Fax 071-586 1659	Hotel
Primrose Hill Road NW3 3NA	**Map 16 C3**

Modern Hilton-owned hotel on the fringes of Hampstead, between
Swiss Cottage and Chalk Farm. Children up to 12 free in parents'
room; no charge for cot provided. Extra bed £25. Free car park.
Rooms 96. Access, Amex, Diners, Visa.

SW1   Collin House   £54

Tel 071-730 8031	Hotel
104 Ebury Street SW1W 9QD	Map 19 C5

Privately-owned bed and breakfast hotel in a mid-Victorian town house just minutes from Victoria railway and coach stations. Most rooms have their own shower and WC. Good cooked breakfasts. No charge for cot provided; triple-bedded rooms offer extremely good value. No dogs. **Rooms** 13. *Closed 2 weeks Christmas. No credit cards.*

W9   Colonnade Hotel   60%   £80

Tel 071-286 1052 Fax 071-286 1057	Hotel
2 Warrington Crescent W9 1ER	Map 18 A2

Close to Warwick Avenue underground station in residential Little Venice, the Victorian grade-two listed building offers a friendly welcome and comfortable accommodation. Best of the bedrooms are the suites and four-poster rooms, all recently refurbished; some bathrooms have been done in marble, some have spa baths. Unrenovated rooms need attention too, though they are quite big and comfortable. Family owned and run; guests are well taken care of and the management is happy to deal with children. At mealtimes there are high-chairs, children's portions, baby food and baby bottles; all this and a garden too. **Rooms** 49. *Access, Amex, Visa.*

W2   Columbia Hotel   £55

Tel 071-402 0021 Fax 071-706 4691	Hotel
95 Lancaster Gate W2 3NS	Map 18 B3

Returning guests provide much of the business at a privately-owned hotel facing Hyde Park 400 yards west of Lancaster Gate underground station. Reasonably priced bedrooms (many with park views), roomy lounge and cocktail bar. £8 charge for cot provided; triple-bedded rooms available. **Rooms** 102. *Access, Amex, Visa.*

SW5   Concord Hotel   £60

Tel 071-370 4151	Hotel
155 Cromwell Road SW5 0TQ	Map 19 A5

Bed and breakfast hotel with some family-size bedrooms. Situated on the main road west to the airport, handy for Earl's Court, Olympia and the South Kensington museums. No cots; extra bed no charge (breakfast charged as taken). Unlicensed. **Rooms** 40. *Access, Amex, Visa.*

W1   Concorde Hotel   £84

Tel 071-402 6169 Fax 071-724 1184	Hotel
50 Great Cumberland Place W1H 7FD	Map 18 C2

Next door to the *Bryanston Court Hotel* and under the same ownership, it offers cheaper accommodation with colour TV tea/coffee facilities, hair dryer, brand new bathrooms and a friendly welcome. No charge for cot provided; £10 for extra bed in room. **Rooms** 27. *Closed 1 week Christmas. Access, Amex, Diners, Visa.*

W8   Costa's Fish Restaurant

Tel 071-727 4310	Fish'n'Chips
18 Hillgate Street Notting Hill Gate W8 7SR	**Map 18 A3**

Behind the takeaway fish and chip shop there's a licensed restaurant
serving cod, plaice, haddock, rock, skate and lemon sole in normal
or large portions (cod £4.30/£7.60, lemon sole £5.40/£9.60). Also
cod roe, taramasalata, simple salads and sweets. One minute from the
Notting Hill Gate cinemas. *Seats 40. Open 12-2.30 & 5.30-10.30.
Closed Sun, Mon, Bank Holidays & 10 days Christmas. No credit cards.*

W8   Costa's Grill

Tel 071-229 3794	Restaurant
14 Hillgate Street Notting Hill Gate W8	**Map 18 A3**

This two-roomed restaurant has long been popular for its friendly
service and reliable cooking of Greek dishes at very low cost. A short
wait in line is sometimes necessary but always worth it. In summer,
the garden offers a pleasant option for al fresco eating. Classic dishes
include kleftiko (£4.50) and charcoaled spicy chicken (£4.50).
Among the chargrilled choices are fish specials (£6-8). *Seats 70 (plus
30 in garden). Open 12-2.30 & 5-10.30 (Sat 12 to 10.30). Closed Sun &
Bank Holidays. No credit cards.*

W1   Cranks

Tel 071-437 9431	Vegetarian
8 Marshall Street W1	**Map 18 D3**

Under new management, Cranks has been through a few changes.
Dishes are of Mediterranean-Oriental inspiration but though healthy
and worthy tend to lack excitement in their preparation: spinach and
coconut soup (£1.80), cheesy lasagne, Bombay swede or sweet and
sour vegetables (from £6.50); popular salads (from £2.35) might
include macrobiotic rice, carrot, watercress and peanuts plus Cranks'
wide range of cakes, biscuits and dry fruit slices (from 55p). Best value
for money is provided by the salad platter (£3.45) or savoury platter
(£3.95), combining a couple of favourite dishes. As we went to press
there were plans for evening opening Friday and Saturday at Marshall
Street. Four high-chairs are provided. *Seats 140. Open 8am-8pm
(Wed/Thur to 9pm, Sat from 9am). Closed Sun, Bank Holidays.
Access, Visa.*
Also at:

9 Tottenham Street W1 Tel 071-631 3912	**Map 18 D2**
23 Barrett Street by St Christopher's Place W1 Tel 071-495 1340	**Map 18 C2**
Unit 11 No. 8 Adelaide Street WC2 Tel 071-836 0660	**Map 21 B3**
17 Great Newport Street WC2 Tel 071-836 5226	**Map 21 B2**
11 The Market Covent Garden WC2 Tel 071-379 6508	**Map 21 B2**

Phone for individual opening hours.

W2   Craven Gardens Hotel   £66

Tel 071-262 3167 Fax 071-262 2083	Hotel
16 Leinster Terrace W2 3ES	**Map 18 B3**

Comfortable, well-kept bed and breakfast hotel just off Bayswater
Road, handy for Hyde Park, British Rail Paddington, London
Underground stations and the cosmopolitan appeal of Queensway.
Basic facilities. Triple-bedded rooms attract a small supplement.
No dogs. *Rooms 43. Access, Amex, Diners, Visa.*

W1   Deals West

Tel 071-287 1001	Restaurant
14 Fouberts Place off Regent Street W1V 1PB	**Map 18 D2**

Styled as an American dealing room with cream-painted wood, mock gaslights, TV and a bar running the length of the room. There should be something on the long menu to suit most people, be it a steak (from £9.75), fish and chips (£5.50), bangers and mash (£4.95), salads or undistinguished burgers (from £5.25 with fries or baked potato) – don't expect gastronomic miracles, but it's a lively place that will probably be enjoyed by the over-5s. An Eastern influence is evident on the menu (Thai soup and curries and Gado Gado Indonesian salad) and the wide choice is supplemented by a daily-changing blackboard Dealer's Choice. Desserts include the likes of chocolate mud (£2.95), New England apple pie (£2.75) or home-made waffle (£2.95) with extra topping at 50p. Live music from 9.30pm on Friday and a DJ on Saturday. Tea and coffee aslo served in the afternoons. No-smoking area. Tables on the pavement in summer. *Seats 160.* ***Open*** *11-11 (Sun to 5). Access, Amex, Visa.*
Also at:
Deals Chelsea Harbour SW10 OXD. Tel 071-376 3232.   **Map 19 B6**
Packed at weekends with families. Easy parking. New changing facilities in the Ladies. Nursing mothers should ask for a booth seat (which afford a little privacy).

EC1   Diana's Dining Room

Tel 071-831 7261	Restaurant
30 St Cross Street Clerkenwell EC1	**Map 20 A1**

A small family-run deli restaurant just off Leather Lane market, specialising in Middle Eastern and vegetarian cooking. Diana runs the front of house, while her husband Bernard cooks up generous portions. Regular dishes are hot salt beef with latkes (£6.50), stir-fried chicken with ginger (£6.75), chicken or lamb kebabs, and a daily vegetarian special. A wide range of sandwiches and filled pittas are also available to eat in or take away. Desserts include apple strudel, pecan pie, toffee apple crumble (£2.50) or frozen yoghurt. Breakfast special (£3.50) served until 11.30. Minimum charge of £3.50 between noon and 2pm. *Seats 40.* ***Open*** *8am-late (evening booking available) (Mon/Tue to 3.30pm).* ***Closed*** *Sat, Sun, 1 week Christmas, Yom Kippur. Access, Visa.*

W1   The Dorchester, The Promenade

Tel 071-629 8888	Tea
53 Park Lane W1A 2HJ	**Map 18 C3**

The first tea arrived in Britain from China in the 17th century, but it was only in the 1840s that afternoon tea became a fashionable event and thence a British institution. The tradition is continued in notable style in the opulent surroundings of the Dorchester's Promenade. £13.20 (with champagne £19.50) brings you the most dainty and delicious finger sandwiches, scones with Devonshire clotted cream and a selection of mouthwatering pastries, plus a choice of tea that includes jasmine, Earl Grey, Darjeeling and the Dorchester blend of broken orange pekoe. Continental breakfast is served until noon with a selection of light snacks and meals at other times. High-chairs provided. *Seats 100.* ***Open*** *3-7pm. Access, Amex, Diners, Visa.*

EC1   East West Restaurant

Tel 071-608 0300	Vegetarian
188 Old Street EC1	**Map 16 D3**

An exclusively vegan, macrobiotic restaurant geared towards
maintaining a healthy body through strict dietary principles. Hence
a rota of around 30 well-balanced set meals forms the mainstay
utilising a strong Japanese influence. No smoking. *Seats 46.*
Open *11-8.30 (Sat/Sun to 3.30).* **Closed** *10 days Christmas. Access,
Amex, Diners, Visa.*

SW3   Ed's Easy Diner

Tel 071-352 1956	Restaurant
362 Kings Road Chelsea SW3	**Map 19 B6**

As is common to the majority of Ed's Easy Diners, this is a small,
buzzy restaurant with tall bar stools round a curved counter.
American diner-style record selectors appear at regular intervals along
the counter. Service is always with a smile and usually with a good
line in backchat. Jaw-stretching 5oz hamburgers are the main
attraction, served in a bag on a paper plate (£3.95). Fries are big and
sloppy, particularly when drenched in school gravy (wet fries £2.45),
while the malts and milk shakes (£2.10) are suitably generous and
made with real ice cream. Hot dogs (from £3.50), tuna melt (£4.25),
and veggie burgers (£3.65) are other choices. The Choco Lat with
KitKat dessert (£2.50) may be naughty but it's also extremely nice.
Brunch menu from 9am-noon Sat & 9am-3pm Sun. Happy, busy
places – not for the faint-hearted or old-at-heart. *Seats 34.*
Open *11am-midnight (Fri/Sat to 1am), Sat & Sun from 9am.*
No credit cards.
Also at:

16 Hampstead High Street NW3 Tel 071-431 1958	**Map 16 B2**
335 Fulham Road SW10 Tel 071-352 1952	**Map 19 B5**
12 Moor Street Soho W1 Tel 071-439 1955	**Map 21 A2**

See also entry under **Brighton**

SW1   Elizabeth Hotel   £70

Tel 071-828 6812	Hotel
37 Eccleston Square SW1V 1PB	**Map 19 D5**

Friendly privately-owned bed and breakfast hotel in a garden square
near Victoria station. Bedrooms range from singles to family-size; en-
suite facilities are being extended to more rooms. No dogs. *Rooms 40.*
No credit cards.

SW15   Enoteca

Tel 081-785 4449	Restaurant
28 Putney High Street SW15	**Map 17 B5**

Just south of Putney Bridge and occupying a large-windowed corner
sight overlooking it (and the cinema), Enoteca offers an opportunity
to sample a wide range of first-class modern Italian food at fashionably
reasonable prices. While the dinner menu features some slightly more
elaborately prepared dishes, lighter dishes for lunch are nevertheless
full of interest. Tender mussels and creamy cannellini beans make
a deliciously warming winter dish (£3.90), as do grilled peppers,
courgettes and aubergines served with broad bean purée (£3.90) and
Tuscan sausages on a bed of rocket (£3.90). Pasta dishes can be both

traditional or modern. Service and atmosphere are both friendly and relaxed. Adventurous young palates can get into gear here. *Seats 45.* *Open* *12.30-3 & 7-11.30.* *Closed* *L Sat & Bank Holidays, all Sun, 24-30 Dec, 1 Jan. Access, Amex, Diners, Visa.*

NW1   Fanari

Tel 071-586 1969	Restaurant
40 Chalcot Road Primrose Hill NW1	Map 16 B3

A cheerful and well-patronised Greek restaurant with a family feel. Neither the decor nor the food is sophisticated but the prices are certainly kind – two adults and a child will eat very well for around £35. Portions are notably generous, and the meal ends with a complimentary plate of cool fresh fruit. *Seats 95.* *Open* *D only 6-12.* *Closed* *Sun, 25 & 26 Dec, 1 Jan. Access, Visa.*

WC2   Fatboy's Diner

Tel 071-240 1902	Restaurant
21 Maiden Lane Covent Garden London WC2	Map 21 B2

A classic 40s' diner imported from the States after being restored to its gleaming original state. The friendly banter of the staff is as much part of the character as the colourful decor, burnished stainless steel, the background music and the vinyl-upholstered bar stools and banquettes. Food here is mostly a choice of burgers (from £3.95) or hot dogs (£3.25) but be prepared to be cajoled into trying a host of extras – all worthwhile – like the fat fries (£1.30) or crisp onion rings (£1.50). Unlicensed but the soda fountain milk shakes (all £2.45) are good and thick. A most unsual setting for a bite – teenagers with a taste for Americana should enjoy a visit. *Seats 42* (*plus 40 outside*). *Open* *11am-midnight (Sun to 10.30)* *Closed* *25 & 26 Dec. No credit cards.* Also at:

296 Bishopsgate (by Liverpool St BR Station) EC2 Tel 071-375 2763	Map 16 D3

E8   Faulkners

Tel 071-254 6152	Fish'n'Chips
424/426 Kingsland Road Hackney E8 4AA	Map 16 D3

Take-away is big at this fish and chip restaurant in a parade of shops, but the eating-in area has been considerably extended of late. Groundnut oil is used to fry generous portions of fresh fish, from traditional favourites like cod (£6.70, half portions available), haddock and rock salmon (£5.50), ranging up to halibut and Dover sole at £9.50. Jellied eels, rollmops and cod roe among the starters; children's menus at £2.95. One high-chair. *Seats 60.* *Open* *12-2 & 5-10 (Fri from 4.15) Sat 11.30-10, Sun 12-9.* *Closed* *Bank Holidays, 10 days Christmas. No credit cards.*

WC2   Food for Thought

Tel 071-836 0239	Vegetarian
31 Neal Street Covent Garden WC2H 9PA	Map 21 B2

The food at this friendly self-service restaurant is healthy, varied and vegetarian. You can sit either downstairs (where the back alcove is most suitable for families) or upstairs, watching the salads and hot dishes being prepared. In summer, some tables are set outside. Typical dishes: spinach and coconut soup (£1.90), rigatoni al vino bianco (£2.50), three-cheese casserole, almond and apple scones, Oriental

plum and ginger hot pot. No bookings. Unlicensed (BYO –
no corkage). *Seats 50.* **Open** *9.30-8 (Sun 10.30-4.30).*
Closed *Christmas/New Year. No credit cards.*

NW3   Forte Posthouse   65%   £68

Tel 071-794 8121 Fax 071-435 5586	Hotel
215 Haverstock Hill NW3 4RB	**Map 16 B2**

Close to Belsize Park underground station and a short walk from
Hampstead. Top-floor bedrooms offer splendid views; 30 recently
converted Executive rooms are equipped with various extras,
including mini-bars and stereo in the bathrooms. Ample free parking.
Brasserie with outdoor seating. Special weekend price of £41.50 per
room (breakfast extra) as we went to press, with no extra charge for
a cot or extra bed in the room. This is probably the best value
weekend accommodation for families in London, the only drawback
being its less than central location (although it's only a short drive
away). **Rooms** *140. Access, Amex, Diners, Visa.*

W1   Fortnum & Mason, The Patio

Tel 071-734 8040	Restaurant
181 Piccadilly W1	**Map 18 D3**

Something of an institution in the world-famous comestibles store, the
Patio tries to be all things to all people serving a huge variety of food
and drink, from lobster bisque (£2.75), salads and "Fortnum & Mason
famous pies" – chicken with apricots, venison (£7.25) to shepherd's
pie, grills, roast beef and vegetarian dishes. Ice cream sundaes (£3.95),
lattice Bramley apple pie, waffles (£3.50), sodas and shakes and
afternoon tea sandwiches, scones(£3.20) and speciality teas. Lunch
(11.45-2.30) carries a minimum charge of £4.50, a full à la carte
breakfast is available in the Fountain restaurant, and high tea in the
St James's restaurant also has a minimum charge of £4.50 between
3 and 5.30pm. Six high-chairs are provided; a mother's changing area
was promised to open within the store by the end of 1993.
Seats *160 (Patio).* **Open** *9.30-5.30 (Fountain Restaurant 7.30am-11pm).*
Closed *Sun, Bank Holidays. Access, Amex, Diners, Visa.*

W1   Four Seasons Hotel, The Lounge

Tel 071-499 0888	Hotel Lounge
Hamilton Place Park Lane Mayfair W1	**Map 18 C3**

Each hotel lounge has its own character. This one has an elegant
relaxing feel, with comfortable sofas, panelled walls, leafy plants,
a view over the rear gardens and soft piano music. Light breakfast
with assorted pastries, muffins and croissants (£6.50) is served till
noon. Elaborate sandwiches (from £6.45) are available all day while
the hot selection like galette of prawns and vegetable with plum
ginger sauce (£8.50) is only served during meal hours (12 to 3pm,
6 to midnight). Traditional afternoon tea (served 3-6pm £11.50)
is the climax with impeccable service, 60 different teas from which
to choose, plus hot crumpets, scones and teacakes, assorted sandwiches
and, for a perfect ending, delicate French pastries and optional
'afternoon desserts' (for really indulgent lounge lizards) – one of the
best afternoon teas in London, but at a luxury treat price! Children are
offered colouring books and milk shakes (fresh seasonal berries with
vanilla ice cream £4.50) and generally taken good care of; nursing
mums can use the excellent Ladies room. Snacks are served way past

the witching hour (until 1am), by which time the little ones should
be well in the Land of Nod. The hotel was previously known as the
Inn on the Park. *Seats 60. Open 9am-1am. Access, Amex, Diners, Visa.*

N16   The Fox Reformed

Tel 071-254 5975	Restaurant

176 Stoke Newington Church Street N16 0JL   Map 16 D2

Re-formed (from *La Fin de la Chasse*) into a much simpler brasserie
and now without tablecloths and with only the most basic
appointments, the restaurant features a short blackboard of daily
specials and an equally short printed menu of snacky as well as main
dishes. Prices have tumbled and wines represent excellent value.
Typical fare is a ceviche of plaice (£3.25), pea and ham soup (£2.75),
baked Spanish cod (£7.25) and steak haché (£6.95). Open all day,
though only light dishes are available between 2 and 6pm.
The garden at the rear is excellent for alfresco dining. *Seats 40.*
Open noon-10.30pm. Closed 25 & 26 Dec. Access, Visa.

SW15   Gavin's

Tel 081-785 9151	Restaurant

5 Lacy Road Putney SW15   Map 17 B5

Part of the consistently impressive group that embraces *Ciao* (Fulham),
The Depot (Barnes) and *Calico* (Garratt Lane), with a winning formula
of good-value brasserie-style food, bustling surroundings and strong
management. Fresh pasta can be had as either starter or main course
(£2.55-£5.50) with other starters ranging from oven-baked garlic
mushrooms (£3.20) to goat's cheese and tomato tartlet (£3.25). Main-
course salads are joined by prawn stir-fry (£6.65), lamb's liver pan-
fried with bacon and onion with a port and orange sauce (£5.95)
and chargrilled breast of chicken (£7.50). A lunchtime special of pasta,
side salad and garlic bread offers good value at £4.99 from midday
to 3.30. Candle-light in the evening. A friendly place, appreciative
of the fact that parents with youngsters are a good source of business –
besides, most children seem to like pasta. No-smoking area. *Seats 80.*
Open 12-3.30 & 6-11. Closed Bank Holidays, 24, 25, 26 Dec. Access,
Amex, Diners.

W8   Geales

Tel 071-727 7969	Fish'n'Chips

2 Farmer Street Notting Hill Gate W8   Map 18 A3

For longer than most of the locals can remember Geales has been *the*
place for fish and chips. Fresh fish is delivered daily, and the choice
is listed on a big board – haddock (from about £4.50), cod, plaice,
sole, rock salmon and fish cakes with white fish and salmon (£2.40)
are occasionally joined by more exotic offerings such as Thai king
prawn rolls, deep-fried clams and shark. The batter's crisp, cooking
(in beef dripping for the fish, vegetable fat for the chips) spot on, and
two will dine in style for around £12. Drinks are paid for separately.
No bookings, so the occasional wait is necessary. You can leave the
buggy at the entrance as there are three high-chairs and two booster
seats. Upstairs you will find a room that doubles as an unofficial
playroom on Saturdays and can be used for nursing. *Seats 100.*
Open 12-3 & 6-11. Closed Sun, Mon, Bank Holidays (and Tuesday
after), last 2 weeks Aug, 2 weeks Christmas. Access, Visa.

WC1   George Hotel   £50

Tel 071-387 8777   Fax 071-383 5044   Hotel

58 Cartwright Gardens WC1H 9EL   Map 18 D1

In a crescent near the British Museum, the George and its neighbour
the Euro (recently refurbished and now attracting slightly higher
prices) offer very reasonably priced accommodation, with children
up to 13 staying free in parents' room at weekends and at reduced rates
at other times. No charge for cot provided; excellent value triple-
bedded rooms. Unlicensed. No dogs. *Rooms 75. Access, Visa.*

SW10   Glaister's Garden Bistro   £45

Tel 071-352 0352   Restaurant

4 Hollywood Road SW10 9HW   Map 19 B6

Restaurant, café/bar and garden in a road opposite the new Chelsea &
Westminster Hospital. The bistro-style menu offers dishes like sausages
and mash with onion marmalade, grilled vegetable bruschetta with
melted mozzarella, Caesar salad, eggs Benedict, salmon fish cakes,
spaghetti with pesto and steak, Guinness and mushroom pie with
prunes; ask for half portions at half prices for youngsters. Traditional
roast sirloin of beef (or occasionally lamb, £7.95) with Yorkshire
pudding is served on Sundays, when younger children can be looked
after in *Nipper Snippers*, a registered crèche next door; it operates from
12.30-4.30 on Sunday only (except during a summer holiday period)
and costs £2.50. Older children can play with toys, play with
Nintendo, paint or watch videos, while being offered peanut butter
and jelly sandwiches, chips, biscuits and fruit juice. Our Henry the
Duck symbol is awarded for the unusual Sunday arrangements – the
management's aim is to give younger children a good time, but
to keep them separate from their parents so that *they* can have a good
time – which is fair enough. No high-chairs or changing facilities.
*Seats 80. L 12.30-3 (Sun to 4) D 7-11.30 (Sun to 10.30). Closed Bank
Holidays, 2 weeks Christmas. Access, Amex, Diners, Visa.*

SW1   The Goring   79%   £192

Tel 071-396 9000   Fax 071-834 4393   Hotel/Afternoon Tea

17 Beeston Place Grosvenor Gardens SW1W 0JW   Map 19 D4

Close to Victoria Station and directly behind Buckingham Palace,
a very English hotel in the old style, "loved and nurtured" by the
Goring family since it was built in 1910. George Goring, the owner
for more than 30 years, believes the place has a soul, and he could just
be right! Behind the splendid Edwardian facade is a high level
of service and elegant, busy day rooms that make a good first
impression with polished marble, paintings and leather sofas.
Bedrooms are individually decorated, but with the unanimously
traditional feel of solid furnishings using various woods and
comfortable settees. Brass bedsteads often feature and bathrooms are
particularly good, mostly fitted out in marble; 24hr room and
evening maid turn-down services are offered. Many rooms are air-
conditioned and the best have balconies that overlook the manicured
Goring garden (which, sadly, has no access for guests); similarly, the
Garden lounge and Garden bar have delightful outlooks. Children
up to 14 stay free in parents' room. Afternoon teas are served in the
Garden Lounge from 3.30-5pm, around an open fire in cooler
weather; Chesterfield sofas and armchairs are set round low tables laid
with white tablecloths for this most enjoyable ceremony. From

morning till midnight a lounge menu of sandwiches and snacks is also
available. A high-chair is provided and if baby needs changing the
hotel reception will happily arrange for private facilities. Weekends
are always popular with families. *Rooms 82. Valeting. Access, Amex,
Diners, Visa.*

Restaurant   £90

A traditionally elegant dining room (with service to match), where
chef John Elliott prepares a good choice of dishes on both the table
d'hote and à la carte menus, ranging from the classics – lobster bisque,
eggs Benedict, lamb cutlets, liver and bacon – to those representing the
more modern school, such as warm goat's cheese with sun-dried
tomatoes, or brochette of monkfish with Parma ham. A splendid
carefully-chosen wine list offers many bottles at quite reasonable prices.
Note the mature classics and succinct comments from the pen
of George Goring himself! *Seats 75. Parties 20. Private Room 55.
L 12.30-2.30 D 6-10. Closed L Sat. Set L £16.50/£19.50 Set D £26.*

SE1   Gourmet Pizza Company

Tel 071-928 3188	Pizzeria

Gabriels Wharf 56 Upper Ground London SE1   Map 20 A3

Deservedly busy and popular pizzeria right on the banks of the
Thames in a colourful development that includes arts and crafts shops.
An open-plan kitchen allows diners to watch the preparation of what
are some of the best pizzas in town. Everything is prepared freshly
every day and the choice of toppings is highly imaginative and well
thought-out. The range extends from the plain and simple (£4.25)
with mozzarella, beef tomatoes, basil and olive oil to the more
adventurous such as BLT (£4.95) with bacon, tomatoes, mozzarella
topped with shredded lettuce and served with mayonnaise; Cajun
prawn and chicken (£7.95) with spinach, roasted yellow peppers,
roasted garlic, ginger, mozzarella and sweet pickle to a vegetarian
pizza and calzone (folded pizza) filled with either Camembert, spinach,
tomato, aubergine and coriander or oriental-style smoked loin of pork,
spring onions, Chinese mushrooms, water chestnuts, bean sprouts,
ginger, mozzarella and Hoi Sin and plum sauce (£6.95). No starters
as such but salads are super, particularly the likes of ripe avocado with
toasted pine kernels, mixed leaves, Parmesan shavings with a balsamic
vinegar and grain mustard dressing (£3 and £6). There are a few
pasta dishes too and desserts to finish include an excellent pecan pie
served with scoops of quality vanilla ice cream. Staff, even the chefs,
are chatty and amiable as well as efficient. *Seats 82. Open 12-10.45
(Sun till 10.30). Closed 5 days Christmas. Access, Amex, Visa.*
Also at:
18-20 McKenzie Walk Canary Wharf E14 Tel 071-712 9192   Map 17 D4
The 1929 Building Merton Abbey Mills Watermills Way SW19
Tel 081-545 0310   Map 17 B6
42 New Oxford Street WC1 Tel 071-580 9521   Map 21 B1
Branches also in South Holmwood (near Dorking, Surrey) & Oxford (see entries).

W1   Govindas

Tel 071-437 3662	Vegetarian

9/10 Soho Street Soho W1V 5DA   Map 21 A1

The International Krishna Organisation owns this counter-service
restaurant just south of Oxford Street off Soho Square. As much
organic produce as possible is used in their enjoyable vegetarian dishes,
which include quiche (£2.40) or lasagne (£4.50) with salad and

mixed vegetables with rice (£2.50). Some vegan dishes, no eggs, no animal products, no garlic, onions or mushrooms in any dishes; no smoking either! Perhaps one for the serious vegetarian shopper only... *Seats 64. **Open** 12-7. **Closed** all Sun, Bank Holidays, 25 Dec & 1 Jan. No credit cards.*

W1   The Granary

Tel 071-493 2978	Restaurant
39 Albermarle Street off Piccadilly W1	**Map 18 D3**

Impervious to fashion and the passing years, the Granary still operates as a self-service restaurant with courteous waiters carrying the trays to the tables. Baked avocados with prawn, spinach and cheese (£6.95), seafood pie (£6.95), pan-fried fresh cod with new potatoes and salad (£7.50), lamb casserole with mint (£6.95), vegetarian spinach roulade (£6.95), vegetarian stuffed mushrooms (£6.80) are examples of the varied choice of dishes prepared with the same care every day. The display also includes about eight salads and many cakes, all delicious and freshly made. Gigantic portions and above-average quality, it is a useful spot for mums with babes in arms who want to shop in the smart part of town. Sundays usually feature a roast. Half portions for children. Pavement tables for fine weather eating. *Seats 120. **Open** 11.30-8 (Mon/Tue to 7.30, Sun to 5.30). **Closed** D Sun, 24, 25 & 26 Dec. No credit cards.*

N1   Great Northern Hotel   60%   £83

Tel 071-837 5454 Fax 071-278 5270	Hotel
King's Cross N1 9AN	**Map 16 C3**

The Great Northern Hotel, opened in 1854 as London's first purpose-built hotel, is a convenient pausing point for travellers and meeting point for businessmen; it's right next door to St Pancras British Rail Station, one minute from King's Cross and five from Euston. Accommodation is comfortable rather than stylish and includes family rooms, all but ten with en-suite facilities. No charge for cot provided; extra bed £10. No dogs. *Rooms 89. Closed 25-27 Dec. Access, Amex, Diners, Visa.*

NW8   Greek Valley

Tel 071-624 3217	Restaurant
130 Boundary Road St John's Wood NW8	**Map 16 B3**

Prices are still as reasonable as ever at this immensely popular Greek-Cypriot restaurant next to the Saatchi gallery. Succulent meat dishes start at £5.50 (souvlaki, shish kofte) and go up to £6.95 for stifado. Vegetarians get an equally good deal with plenty of choice from briani (casseroles) and dolmades to a vegetarian moussaka and there are always the same fish dishes (grilled trout £5.95, calamari £7.50, baked king prawns £8.50). Start with spicy sausages, cheese pastries or stuffed vine leaves, and finish with some glyko – intriguing candied fruit or vegetables. Pavement tables in summer. Particularly good value three-course set meals (limited choice) at lunch and either side of main evening hours. Children seem to particularly love tarasamalata, shish kofte (minced lamb sausages), fried kalamari and chicken kebab. A more informal coffee shop opened just along the road in September 1993. *Seats 65. **Open** 12-2.30 & 6-12. **Closed** L Sat, all Sun. Access, Visa.*

W11   Gumbo Ya-Ya

Tel 071-221 2649	Restaurant
184a Kensington Park Road W11	Map 16 B3

A newcomer in 1993 (previously the *Gate Diner*), now with
an original Cajun theme menu. The decor is simple: terracotta-
coloured walls on which a few Mardi Gras masks hang. Tables are
covered with thick craft paper printed with the cocktail menu. Iron
chairs are fashionably uncomfortable. Appetisers are a success: fiery hot
seafood gumbo (£2.65), freshly fried veggie fritters (£2.35) with
a sour cream spiced dip and corn bread which shouldn't be missed.
Compared to these, snapper pecan (£8.95), pasta Mardi Gras (£5.50)
and jerk chicken (£6.95) lack excitement. Good home-made desserts.
Good bargain 2-course lunch menu on weekdays (£4.95). Six high-
chairs and booster seats; "kiddies menu" (£4.95). Sunday brunch
served 11.30-4pm. **Seats** *110.* **Open** *11.30am-11.30pm.* **Closed** *25 Dec.*
Access, Visa.

WC2   Häagen-Dazs

Tel 071-287 9577	Café
14 Leicester Square WC2H 7N	Map 21 A2

Don't be discouraged by the long queue in front of the shop; it might
be for the take-away counter. For those wanting to eat from the
à la carte menu, tables are available in the attractive caramel-coloured
restaurant. The menu is extensive and not just ice cream. Pecan pie
(£1.50), New York cheesecake (£1.50), chocolate brownies (£1.20)
are just like American grandmas are supposed to make. For ice cream
lovers, the list is long and covers just about everything possible:
chocoholic sundaes (£3.95), praline basket (£4.25), chunky peanut
crunch (two scoops £2.65), various sauces, toppings and liqueur
toppings and even breakfast (£2.95) with croissant, cappuccino and
a scoop of ice cream. The restaurant is licensed and has champagne
on its list. No smoking. Four high-chairs; pull-out plastic changing
shelf in the Ladies. **Seats** *65.* **Open** *10am-midnight (Fri & Sat to 1am).*
Closed *25 & 26 Dec, 1 Jan. No credit cards.*
Also at:

138a Kings Road SW3 Tel 071-823 9326	Map 19 C5

Last orders 11pm. Outside tables. One high-chair.
Further outlets at **Hampstead** (75 High Street), **Covent Garden** (Unit 6,
The Piazza), **London Airport Heathrow** (Terminal 1), **Brighton** (4/5 Prince
Albert Street, The Lanes), **Oxford** (56 Cornmarket Street), **Bath** (11 Old
Bond Street), **Windsor** (22 Thames Street). Some outlets have no seats.

SW1   Harrods

Tel 071-730 1234	
87-135 Brompton Road Knightsbridge SW1X 7XL	Map 19 C4

Shoppers at this world-famous store have a wide choice of places
in which to take a break and enjoy a snack. The *Café Espresso*★ is found
in the fruit and vegetable hall, the *Bar Fromage*★ next to the long
cheese counter and the two new bars *Oyster and Champagne*★ (serving
seafood) and the *Salt Beef*★ (cooked to Harrods famous recipe) are both
situated within the fish and meat hall. *The Dress Circle*★, on the first-
floor, is a self-service restaurant offering a variety of cold dishes, while
up on the fourth floor there's the self-service **Upper Circle** (high-chairs
provided), the conservatory *Terrace Bar, Way In Restaurant*★ (a menu
of light, imaginative dishes) and the more formal **Georgian**

Restaurant serving lunch (12-2.45) and afternoon tea (3.45-5.15 £8.95). In the Georgian restaurant reservations are only taken for lunch (from £12 minimum: carvery, cold buffet or à la carte) and there are high-chairs provided; children under 12 eat for half adult price. The Mother & Baby room is also on the fourth floor. Finally, on the lower ground floor, are the oak-panelled *Green Man* pub (pies and ploughman's) and the *Health Juice Bar.* ★No smoking. *Store open 10-6 (Mon/Tue/Sat), 10-7 (Wed/Thur/Fri). Access, Amex, Diners, Visa.*

SW1   Harvey Nichols

Tel 071-235 5250	Restaurant
Knightsbridge SW1	**Map 19 C4**

In the basement, *Joe's Restaurant & Bar* (071-245 9573 Open 10-6.30, Sat to 6, closed all Sun) is on the same lines of Joseph Ettedgui's other fashionable cafés, with black and white 80s' decor, low lights and fashion photographs on the walls of its 150-seater basement setting. The menu offers light dishes of stuffed aubergine with marinated salmon (£5.75), raw spinach, pancetta and avocado salad (£8.50), focaccia filled with ham, cheese and salad (£6.50), ravioli with wild mushroom cream sauce (£8.50). A short menu of daily specials always includes salmon fishcakes (£8.95). Cooking is unpretentious, above average and well complemented by excellent coffee. There is a minimum lunch charge of £5.50 and between 12 and 4pm the cover charge is £1. Things have changed again on the fifth floor, where the *Fifth Floor Café* has been extended to create more covers and the bar is reserved for coffee and pastries. Bright, airy and lively, it is one of the most fashionable department store cafés. Pastries and kedgeree from 10am-11.30 and afternoon tea (up to £7.50) from 3.30-6. At other times, wonton-wrapped prawns with chili sauce (£4.25), tagliolini with sundried tomatoes, ricotta and basil (£7), lightly grilled tuna with green beans, sesame and soy dressing (£8.75) are examples from the menu. Portions have improved in size to the detriment of seasoning and overall quality, but the café's popularity is not in doubt. No-smoking area. Good-value prix-fixe menu (£12.50), interesting vegetarian menu and a long list of desserts. Small terrace overlooking Knightsbridge. As we went to press there was live jazz in the Café every Thursday evening. It's all rather adult (there are no high-chairs), but at least there's a Mother & Baby room on the fifth floor (by the express lift, ready for emergencies...). *Seats 140. Open 10am-10.30pm (Sundays brunch only, 11-4.30) Closed D Sun, 25 & 26 Dec. Access, Amex, Diners, Visa.*

W13   Haweli

Tel 081-567 6211	Restaurant
127-129 Uxbridge Road West Ealing W13 9AU	**Map 17 A4**

Just past the fire station between Ealing Broadway and West Ealing, an unusually bright, white Indian restaurant offering a varied menu ranging from spinach pakora (£2.35) and prawn puri (£2.05) to tandoori trout (£4.45) and lamb kata masala (£5.95). Good breads and kind prices, especially the nine-course Sunday buffet (£6.50, children half that price) from 12-12. Two high-chairs. *Seats 70. Open noon-3 & 6-12 (Sun 12-12). Access, Amex, Diners, Visa.*

W1   Heals, The Café at Heals

Tel 071-636 1666	Café
The Heals Building 196 Tottenham Court Road W1	Map 18 D2

At the back of the second floor of Heals department store, the café is a quiet, relaxing spot for croissants and baguettes in the morning and lunchtime dishes such as spinach, bacon and goat's cheese salad (£6.50), or monkfish, pepper and saffron stew with Basmati rice (£7.50). Sweet items like treacle tart or chocolate fudge cake (£2.95) are available throughout the day along with good espresso and cafetière coffee. No-smoking area. *Seats 56.* **Open** *10-5.30 (Thu to 6.30).* **Closed** *Sun, Bank Holiday Mondays. Access, Amex, Visa.*

SW6   Henry J Bean's Bar & Grill

Tel 071-381 5005	Restaurant
490 Fulham Road SW6	Map 19 A6

This is one of a chain of themed American bars created from former pubs with a Mexican-influenced menu. A monitor displays 'chow-time' when food orders are ready for collection. 'Loaded potato skins' (£2.10), nachos (£2.75), chili flautas (flour tortillas) (£2.75) are starter choices, followed by fajitas (£7.95), spinach salad (£5.10), barbecued ribs (£6.25 half rack) and variations on hamburgers (from £5.25) served with relishes and chunky, crisp fries. Finally, try their mud pie (£3.25), ice cream (£1.50) or dessert of the day, if you've got any room left. Happy Hour is from 5.30-7.30 on weekdays when cocktails and spirits are half price. Cooked English breakfast plate (£4.75) on Sundays only between 11.30 and 4. The atmosphere is young and buzzy. Children's-size burgers (£3.25) also available. *Seats 85.* **Open** *11.45-11 (Sun 11.30-10.30).* **Closed** *25 Dec. Access, Amex, Visa.*
Also at:
54 Abingdon Road off Kensington High Street W8 Tel 071-937 3339   **Map 19 A5**
Open 11.45-11 (Sun 12-10.30). High stool, pub-style seating only.
195 Kings Road Chelsea SW3 Tel 071-352 9255   **Map 19 C5**
Open 11.45-11 (Sun 12-10.30). Large, attractive open-air garden area to the rear.
See also entries under **Aberdeen** (Scotland) and **Manchester**.

SW5   Hogarth Hotel   62%

	£85
Tel 071-370 6831 Fax 071-373 6179	Hotel
Hogarth Road SW5 0QQ	Map 19 A5

Modern hotel located in the quiet part of Hogarth Road (off Earl's Court Road) and convenient for Earl's Court exhibitions. Recently renovated bedrooms have an attractive emerald green decor. Amenities include satellite TV, trouser press, hairdryer, tea and coffee facilities and a small safe. Most bathrooms still need renovation. Children under 12 stay free in their parents' room; make clear your requirements for children when booking. Secure underground parking (£10 per night). Marston Hotels. Limited 24hr room service is available. *Rooms 85. Access, Amex, Diners, Visa.*

WC1   Holiday Inn Kings Cross/Bloomsbury   69%

	£135
Tel 071-833 3900 Fax 071-917 6163	Hotel
1 Kings Cross Road WC1X 9HX	Map 16 C3

Opened two years ago, the capital's newest Holiday Inn is just a few minutes from Kings Cross station. A large floral display takes pride

of place in the cool, marble-floored lobby and the lounge, decorated
in autumnal shades, is roomy and restful. Bedrooms have all the
Holiday Inn hallmarks: large beds (even single rooms get double
beds), open clothes-hanging space and powerful showers over short
tubs in the bathrooms. Extensive room service can run to a choice
of hot dishes around the clock. Conference-room facilities for
up to 250. Children under 19 stay free in parents' room. The whole
hotel is air-conditioned. Very limited parking. Highlighted here for its
convenient location and competitive pricing policy. *Rooms 405. Indoor
swimming pool, gymnasium, squash, sauna, spa bath, steam room, solarium,
beauty & hair salon. Access, Amex, Diners, Visa.*

SE1   Horniman's

Tel 071-407 3611	Pub

Hay's Galleria Tooley Street London Bridge SE1 2HD   Map 20 C3

Right at the entrance of the newly developed Hay's Galleria on the
south bank overlooking the Thames by London Bridge, Horniman's
is a modern interpretation of Victorian style in the premises of the
family's tea-packing company. The tribute to Frederick John
Horniman's travels is discreetly paid through a painted mural on top
of the bar. It's part pub, part café and the tables on the gallerias have
views of the river and the City in the background. The Pantry (within
the bar area) offers good hot and cold dishes (turkey pie, liver and
bacon, lamb chasseur casserole, broccoli and leek pie – all served with
chips and vegetables £4.95) throughout the day; there's also a hot salt
beef bar (platter with salad £4.75) area within the bar. Upstairs is the
Carvery Restaurant (£10.50, "ask for children's portions"). Horniman's
is a popular pub with both businessmen during the week and tourists
(it's also close to Tower Bridge). Families are welcome in a special area
in the Pantry and children should ask for special portions (and special
prices). *Open 10-11 Mon-Fri, 10-4 Sat, 11-3 Sun. Bar Food 12-3 (hot)
to 7 (cold), 11-4 Sat, 12-3 Sun. Carvery Restaurant Meals 12-2.30
(closed Sat L, open Sun L), evening group bookings by prior arrangement
only. Children's portions. Beer Burton, Nicholson's Best, 6X. Pub closed
weekend evenings. Access, Visa.*

SW5   Hotel 167   £77

Tel 071-373 0672 Fax 071-373 3360	Hotel

167 Old Brompton Road SW5 0AN   Map 19 B5

Frank Cheevers has transformed a Victorian private house into
a most delightful little hotel. Each room has its own character, with
inspiration ranging from pine to art deco. Central heating and double-
glazing keep things warm and peaceful. Cot or extra bed provided
£10. Breakfast is served in the bedrooms or in a pleasant reception
room. Light evening meals also available. Unlicensed. No dogs.
The hotel is located on the corner of Cresswell Gardens. *Rooms 19.
Access, Amex, Diners, Visa.*

W1   Inter-Continental Hotel, Coffee House

Tel 071-409 3131	Coffee Shop

1 Hamilton Place Park Lane W1   Map 19 C4

The coffee house menu at this luxurious Park Lane hotel offers,
along with more expensive dishes, sandwiches (chicken, Cheddar and
bacon melt, burgers all £7.50), salads (from £6.50) and egg and pasta
dishes (eggs Benedict, penne rigate, wholemeal spaghetti).

Afternoon tea in the lounge, served with musical accompaniment between 3 and 6, is either à la carte (two French pastries £2, finger sandwiches £3.90, choice of teas or coffees £2.60) or a fixed-price menu at £9.50; £4.50 minimum charge for non-residents at weekends. The breakfast buffet is served from 7am (Continental £9.50, full £13). **Open** 7am-11pm (Sat to 11.30). Access, Amex, Diners, Visa.

SW6   Joe's Brasserie

Tel 071-731 7835	Brasserie
130 Wandsworth Bridge Road SW6	Map 17 B5

Most popular in the evenings with both diners and drinkers who can imbibe either at the bar or outside at pavement tables. The interior is quite rustic and includes a conservatory area that is somewhat quieter than the main brasserie, so a good spot for a light lunch. A blackboard list of daily dishes supplements the straightforward brasserie menu. Limited menu between 3 and 7pm. **Seats** 60. **Open** 12-10.45. **Closed** 4 days Christmas. Access, Amex, Diners, Visa.

W1   John Lewis, The Place to Eat

Tel 071-629 7711	Restaurant
Oxford Street W1	Map 18 C2

A spacious third-floor restaurant with seven separate food counters. The choice is breakfast all day (full £5.95, Continental £2.95), creperie (crepes from £2.45), crockpot (lasagne £5.25), cold table (fresh salmon salad £7.95), seafood (from £6.65), ice cream soda fountain (£1.70-£3.55) and a patisserie counter. The breakfast of scrambled eggs with smoked salmon and a glass of Buck's Fizz is as popular as the fresh fish from the seafood counter. Pancakes and ice creams are generously laced with liquor. Set children's menu; six high-chairs available. No smoking. The Mother & Baby room is on the fourth floor. **Seats** 299. **Open** 9-5 (Thur 9.30-8). **Closed** Sun, Bank Holidays. No credit cards.

SW10   Johnny Rockets

Tel 071-370 2794	Restaurant
140 Fulham Road SW10	Map 19 B5

US diner-style restaurant conveniently located by the MGM cinema. Sit at well-padded, shiny red bar stools around the long bar or at the high counter tables beside the picture windows. The staple diet is two hamburgers: the original (£3.65) and No. 12 (£3.95) embellished with cheese and the house "red, red sauce". Alternatives are sandwiches (tuna salad £3.40, grilled breast of chicken £4.05, peanut butter and jelly £1.75), with good American-style fries and straw-clogging floats and milkshakes (£2.25). Mini juke boxes on the counters play 50s' and 60s' music. No smoking. The singing and dancing staff should brighten up any child's mealtime. **Seats** 41. **Open** 11.30am-midnight. **Closed** 25 Dec. No credit cards.

WC2   Joy King Lau

Tel 071-437 1132	Restaurant
Leicester Street WC2	Map 21 A2

Just north of Leicester Square, a busy Chinese restaurant set on four floors where snackers can enjoy a particularly good selection of daytime dim sum (served to 5pm). Steamed examples (from £1.40) include stuffed chicken, spare ribs in black bean sauce and ginger beef ball dumplings; cheung fun buns have char-siu, beef, prawn, fish or pastry fillings; deep-fried offerings run from yam or mixed meat croquette through spring rolls to turnip paste and wafer-wrapped king prawns. Less familiar varieties, too, like squid with satay sauce or tripe with chili and black beans. The main menu is extensive. Should the children get a snack attack before the flicks then this is the place to bring them – they may enjoy the challenge of conversing with waiters about the dim sum! *Seats 200. Open 11.30am-11.30pm (dim sum to 5pm). Closed 24 & 25 Dec. Access, Amex, Diners, Visa.*

SW17   Kastoori

Tel 081-767 7029	Vegetarian
188 Upper Tooting Road Tooting SW17 7EJ	Map 17 C6

The Thanki family have introduced a small selection of African dishes to this very traditional Indian vegetarian menu: so now a green banana curry (£3.75) and kasodi (£3.25), a Swahili dish of sweetcorn in coconut milk with a peanut sauce, feature alongside chapatis (from 50p) and curries (from £2.75). On Sundays there are extra dishes available, some of which are included in a thali set meal (£6). Pleasant, pretty decor and willing, friendly staff. No high-chairs but a "traditional Indian welcome to children". Spacious Ladies for changing. *Seats 82. Open 12.30-2.30 (Wed-Sun), 6pm-10.30 (all week). Closed L Tues, all Mon, 2 Jan. Access, Visa.*

SW10   Ken Lo's Memories of China

Tel 071-352 4953	Restaurant
Harbour Yard Chelsea Harbour SW10	Map 19 B6

Best value at Ken Lo's airy restaurant overlooking the Marina is provided by the bar snack menu. A plate of crispy fried dim sum is a good way to start, followed by a large bowl of shredded chicken noodle soup (£2.95) and one of the main dishes – beef chow mein, chicken with cashew nuts, prawns in hot black bean sauce, all priced under £3. A quarter of crispy duck with pancake, plum sauce, spring onion and cucumber is very reasonable at £4. There are several other menus available here, but they're considerably more expensive. Parking is easy within the Chelsea Harbour complex and a lift takes you direct to the restaurant floor from the underground car park. Disabled loo. *Seats 40. Open 12-2.30 Mon-Fri, other menus available lunch and dinner all week. Closed 25 & 26 Dec. Access, Amex, Diners, Visa.*

NW3   Kenny's

Tel 071-435 6972	Restaurant
70 Heath Street Hampstead NW3	Map 16 B2

Gospel singers perform during Sunday brunch at this buzzing and popular bar-cum-restaurant serving South Louisiana food. Starters include Louisiana crab cakes with creole sauce (£4.95), black bean soup (£2.95), turtle black beans with ham hocks topped with jalapeno sour cream, or baby taters (£3.50 – cheese, potato, onion and peppers French fried and served with garlic mayonnaise). Grilled chicken and jalapeno cornmeal pancakes (£6.95), shrimp creole (£6.50), jambalaya (£6.95) or chicken étouffée (£6.50) are typical main dishes while pecan pie makes a delicious dessert. Boisterous staff and a fun place

when it gets busy. *Seats 70*. *Open 11.45am-11.45pm*. *Closed 25 &
26 Dec. Access, Amex, Visa.*
Also at:
2a Pond Place SW3 Tel 071-225 2916   **Map 19 B5**
Airy, basement premises where Sydney Place meets Fulham Road (by the
top of Sydney Street). Steep steps down from street level.

SW5   Kensington Court Hotel   £59
Tel 071-370 5151 Fax 071-370 3499	Hotel

33 Nevern Place SW5 9NP   **Map 19 A5**

Six-storey modern block in a Victorian terrace. Decent-size bedrooms,
bar, basement restaurant. No cots; all rooms have at least three beds.
Car parking facility for 10 cars. *Rooms 35. Access, Amex, Diners, Visa.*

W1   Kettners
Tel 071-734 6112	Pizzeria

29 Romilly Street Soho W1V 6HP   **Map 21 A2**

Just north of Shaftesbury Avenue (south of Old Compton Street),
a veritable London institution, founded in 1867 by Auguste Kettner,
chef des cuisines to Napoleon III. It's part of the Pizza Express group,
and, along with *Pizza on the Park* (see entry), the top of the range.
The pizza oven provides the bulk of the menu (napoletana £6, potato-
based King Edward £5.75) but there are also charcoal grills (burgers
from £4.75, lamb chops £9.55), BLTs, salads, chili, ham and eggs
(£5.20) and plenty of desserts. Morning coffee and afternoon tea.
Live piano music nightly and lunchtime Thur-Sun in one of the three
spacious dining areas. Separate champagne bar. Two high-chairs and
four booster seats provided. *Seats 200*. *Open 11am-midnight. Access,
Amex, Diners, Visa.*

W11   Kleftiko
Tel 071-603 0807	Restaurant

186 Holland Park Avenue Kensington W11   **Map 17 B4**

Straightforward Greek dishes are served among kitsch Greek-Cypriot
trappings in this two-floor restaurant (the oldest and smallest
of a group) at Shepherds Bush roundabout, opposite the Hilton
International Kensington. Taramasalata is light and lemony and other
well-known Greek dishes (stifado, tava, sheftalia and souvla) are all
well prepared. The charcoal grill is used for most main courses
(mainly £5-£9) which always include market fresh fish – perhaps sea
bass (from £9) or halibut. Meze (fish £15, meat £12.50) are
specialities. Good-value, three-course set dinner menus (£10.95 inc
coffee) and special offers at lunchtime. No special children's facilities,
but it's a group of friendly restaurants. *Seats 44*. *Open 12-3 &
5.30-11.30. Closed L Sat & L Sun, 25 & 26 Dec. Access, Amex,
Diners, Visa.*
Also at:
163 Chiswick High Road Chiswick W4 Tel 081-994 0305   **Map 17 B4**
Open all the week (7am-midnight Mon-Sat, 9am-10.30 Sun).
English breakfasts. Live bouzouki music Fri & Sat evenings.
7a The Green High Street Ealing W5 Tel 081-840 3297   **Map 17 A4**
Smaller, more intimate mews setting close to the Broadway Centre.
Open all the week.
The Kings Arms Kew Bridge Rd Kew Surrey Tel 081-940 3182 **Map 17 A5**
Open all the week. A converted pub with a large garden. Two minutes'
walk from Kew Gardens.

E1   Kosher Luncheon Club

Tel 071-247 0039	Restaurant
13 Greatorex Street E1	Map 16 D3

Located in the Morris Kasler Hall, this is the last survivor of the East
End tradition of the Kosher Lunch Clubs. A warm welcome awaits
families in the large white and blue refectory dining room. Everything
is prepared and cooked on the premises. The speciality here is fresh
fish, properly fried in matzo meal, steamed or grilled. Traditional hors
d'oeuvre include bean and barley soup (£1.80) and gefilte fish
(£1.50). Portions are extremely generous but if you're still hungry,
try the lockshen pudding (£1.50). *Seats 140. Open 12-3. Closed Sat,
Bank Holidays, major Jewish Holidays. No credit Cards.*

NW1   Lemonia

Tel 071-586 7454	Restaurant
89 Regent's Park Road Primrose Hill NW1 8UY	Map 16 C3

One of the best (and most popular) of all London's Greek restaurants,
with peak-time booking an essential. It's a large, lively and sunny place,
with lost of plants and an airy conservatory section. The regular menu
sticks largely to the more familiar dishes, with meze (£8.25 per
person) providing a filling feast – it's also an inexpensive way
to introduce youngsters to new tastes. Kleftiko, chicken shashlik and
moussaka (all around £6) are favourite main courses, and there are
always some interesting specials, notably seafood (octopus, mussels, sea
bass, red mullet). If your children have enjoyed a Mediterranean
holiday then they'll probably enjoy themselves here... *Seats 140.
Open 12-3 & 6-11. Closed L Sat, D Sun. Access, Visa.*

W8   Hotel Lexham   £63

Tel 071-373 6471 Fax 071-244 7827	Hotel
32 Lexham Gardens W8 5JU	Map 19 A4

In a surprisingly peaceful garden square within walking distance
of Kensington's shops and museums, the Lexham has been in the same
family ownership since 1956 and provides good-value bed and
breakfast accommodation. Cheapest rooms (from £45 twins) are
without private facilities. Cots and extra beds provided at a charge.
No dogs. *Rooms 66. Garden. Access, Amex, Visa.*

W1   Lok Ho Fook   £35

Tel 071-437 2001	Restaurant
4-5 Gerrard Street W1V 7LP	Map 21 A2

On two floors at the east end of Chinatown's main street, Lok
Ho Fook does a 12-hour trade in the cuisine of Canton. After the
starters and soups (crabmeat in sweetcorn £1.40, fried prawn cake
with sesame seeds £3) comes a vast selection of 'Popular Chinese
Dishes' both familiar and less so (chicken blood with ginger and spring
onion £4.50), plus a long vegetarian list and 'Popular Provincial
Dishes': sea-spice braised aubergine (34.30), crispy duck (quarter £5),
quick-fried scallops with hot spicy sauce (£6.80) and a hot pot of belly
pork and yam (£5.10). Five high-chairs. *Seats 100. Open 12-12.
Closed 25 & 26 Dec. Access, Amex, Diners, Visa.*

NW3   Louis Patisserie

Tel 071-722 8100	Café
12 Harben Parade Finchley Road NW3	Map 16 B2

Customers for twenty years, Hungarian brothers Amyr and Emil Gat liked Louis Patisserie so much that they bought it five years ago. Its namesake in Hampstead still supplies the fine cakes (£1.60-£1.75) – cream horns, chocolate éclairs, millefeuilles, strawberry cups, cheesecake slices, chocolate mousse gateau triangles covered in crisp chocolate, and Danish pastries (£1.15) among others. The menu includes goulash soup (£3.25), toasted sandwiches (£2.45) and quiches (£2.50 with salad). A pianist plays every afternoon. Continental breakfast £3.20. No-smoking area. More sticky treats, and there are two high-chairs for even younger sweet-toothed tots! *Seats 50.* *Open* 8.30-7. *Closed 25 Dec. No credit cards.*

NW3   Louis Patisserie

Tel 071-435 9908	Café
Heath Street Hampstead NW3	Map 16 B2

The Louis Patisserie is a Hampstead institution. A bakery is at the rear and the cakes, pastries and breads are sold either at the front of the shop or in the tea room. The clientele is distinctly cosmopolitan and due to its popularity a short queue is a common sight at weekends. Sausage rolls (£1.20) and croissants are the only savoury items – so forget your waistline and indulge in a chocolate truffle, coffee cake, florentine, fruit gateau or cheesecake (all £1.70). Unlicensed. No-smoking area. No high-chairs, but youngsters will enjoy the sticky treats on offer. *Seats 50.* *Open* 9.30-6. *Closed 1 week at Christmas. No credit cards.*

W4   Mackintosh's

Tel 081-994 2628	Brasserie
142 Chiswick High Road W4	Map 17 A4

A newly-opened brasserie which singles itself out from the profusion of restaurants on Chiswick High Road, although it was still getting itself into gear as we went to press. The green-and-eggshell airy dining room is enlivened by a colourful hand-painted mural. Tables are attractively set with corn stems in terracotta pots and tartan ribbons wrapped around green paper napkins. Mainly Italo-American, the multifaceted menu offers interesting toasted sandwiches (from £3.50, 8am-5pm only) or *caffè latte completo* (£2.75) for breakfast (8am-11.30am only) and extends from fritto misto (£4.95) and Caesar salad (£4.25) to Cajun chicken (£8.50), Jackson Hole Wyoming burger and excellent thin-crust pizzas. To complete the menu, afternoon teas are served from 4-5.30pm and brunch from 12-3 on weekends. Sunday is family pasta night with spaghetti pomodoro, house salad, soft drinks and crayons on the tables (£20 for a family of four). *Seats 55.* *Open* 8am-midnight. *Closed 25 Dec. Access, Visa.*

W2   Maison Péchon Patisserie Française

Tel 071-229 0746	Café
127 Queensway W2	Map 18 A3

The highlight here is the mouthwatering display counter with 100 different cakes and dozens of breads. Savoury items for lunchtime snacking run from ham and cheese croissants (95p) and vol-au-vents

to spinach quiche (£1.15) and Cornish pasties. Cake prices range from
40p (cinnamon buns) to 95p (meringues with fresh cream). Breakfast
till 3pm. Pavement tables. Close to Whiteleys shopping centre.
No high-chairs. *Seats 35. Open 8-8 (Mon-Wed to 6). Closed 25 Dec.
No credit cards.*

W8	Malabar	£40
Tel 071-727 8800		Restaurant
27 Uxbridge Street Notting Hill W8 7TQ		Map 18 A3

Indian restaurant behind the Coronet cinema, with a look and style all
its own. The look is Mediterranean (an Italian restaurant was on the
site previously) but the home-style cooking features unusual dishes like
charcoal-grilled chicken livers, chili bhutta (sweetcorn, chili, green
peppers), chicken cooked with cloves and ginger, and skewered king
prawns in lemon sauce. Accompaniments include preparations
of banana and pumpkin. More everyday items, too, plus a vegetarian
thali, a set menu for two and a good-value Sunday buffet lunch.
A high-chair is provided and don't be afraid to ask for half portions.
*Seats 56. Parties 15. Private Room 20. L 12-3 (Sun from 12.30)
D 6-11.15. Closed 4 days Xmas, last week Aug. Set meals from £11.75.
Access, Visa.*

NW3	Manna	
Tel 071-722 8028		Vegetarian
4 Erskine Road Primrose Hill NW3		Map 16 B3

"Probably the oldest vegetarian restaurant in Europe" – indeed little
has changed here since its inception in the late '60s. Varnished pine
trestle tables (non-smoking area at rear) and a very laid-back
atmosphere with enjoyable and filling vegetarian food – three courses
are almost impossible to complete. Blackboards list the daily changing
chef's hot specials and there's also a menu of mostly cold dishes, salads
and drinks. Typical offerings are crispy falafels (£2.30), corn chowder
(£1.90) or feta and cashew paté (£2.30) to begin with, followed
perhaps by mixed vegetable masala in pesto sauce (£5.50)
or mushroom lasagne (£5.50). There's a daily choice of two flans such
as sweetcorn and mushroom or parsnip and carrot. Hefty, enjoyable
sweets to finish including the perennial favourite, apple crumble
(£2.50). *Seats 60. Open Daily 6.30-11. Closed 3 days Christmas.
No credit cards.*

SW1	Manners	
Tel 071-828 2471		Restaurant
1 Denbigh Street Victoria SW1		Map 19 D5

One of the better of many cheapish eateries south of Victoria Station.
The owner's smokery supplies the smoked salmon, Dorset pheasant,
trout and chicken for the various dishes. Alternatives may
be watercress and nettle soup, salmon mousse, seafood provençale,
lamb's liver and bacon, chicken chasseur, saddle of lamb. Very good
value set-price menus (2-course lunch £5.95, 3-course dinner £7.95).
No smoking on most of the first floor; the ground floor was due to be
refurbished as we went to press. Children under 12 half price. High-
chairs available. *Seats 55-80. Open 11.45-2.30 & 5.30-11. Closed L Sat,
all Sun, Bank Holidays. Access, Amex, Diners, Visa.*

W11   Manzara

Tel 071-727 3062	Restaurant
24 Pembridge Road Notting Hill W11 3HG	Map 18 A3

Bright, well-lit frontage featuring an enormous selection of delectable-looking cakes and pastries all baked freshly on the premises. Many are French and there's also a good selection of Turkish patisserie – these tend to be much sweeter in character. To the rear is a small and neat, modern restaurant where regional Turkish specialities appear on a six-week rota. Try some genuine, imported Turkish delight with a cup of really fine Turkish coffee (95p). Two high-chairs. *Seats 40.*
Open 8am-midnight (Sun 11-5, 6-11.30). Access, Amex, Diners, Visa.

W1   Marché Mövenpick

Tel 071-734 1291	Restaurant
Swiss Centre Leicester Square W1	Map 21 A3

The setting is the basement of the Swiss Centre, the layout a large circle and colourful food stands in the centre surrounded by dining areas of French, German and Italian influence. Browsing through the different stands is like being at a food fair, and queueing while watching the cook prepare your dish is entertaining. Each counter has its own speciality: salads, salami and Swiss cheeses sliced to order; bloomer, cheese, walnut and onion breads are kneaded and baked on the spot. Rösti is prepared to order and served with the roast of the day (£3.50). Pasta, freshly out of the pasta machine, is cooked on demand and tossed in frying pans with fresh ingredients of the day. Fondue (£7.90) and raclette are available in the evening from 6pm and all day Sunday. There is, of course, Mövenpick ice cream by the scoop and a special pastries counter with freshly-baked strudel, fruit squares or chocolate marbled cake (£1.20). Beer, wine, cocktails and Mövenpick's own brand of coffee served as espresso, cappuccino or the Swiss way with whipped cream and chocolate flakes. Children's portions, five high-chairs and baby-changing facilities in the Ladies. *Seats 400. Open 8am-11pm (bistro 11am-midnight). Closed 25 Dec. Access, Diners, Visa.*

NW3   Marine Ices

Tel 071-485 3132	Restaurant
8 Haverstock Hill Chalk Farm NW3	Map 16 C2

One part of the smooth-running operation is an ice-cream parlour, the other a good, conventional Italian restaurant with a minimum food charge of £5.50 excluding drinks and ice cream. There's a wide choice of pasta (fusilli, linguini, ravioli, panzerotti, etc), pizzas (from £4.25), veal, chicken and calf's liver, and specialities include ricotta and asparagus crespoline (£5.45), gnocchi (£5.10) and mushroom risotto. Superb ice creams and sorbets: try three scoops of ice cream topped with cassis, zabaglione or delicious espresso coffee for a real treat. Marine ices is located more or less opposite the Roundhouse, opposite Chalk Farm underground station. No high-chairs, but children are welcomed, with children's portions offered. *Seats 108.*
Open 12-2.45 & 6-10.15, Sat 12-10.15. Closed Sun, Bank Holidays. No credit cards.

SW11   Mariners

Tel 071-223 2354	Fish'n'Chips
30 Northcote Road Battersea SW11	Map 17 B5

Pristine premises decorated with brick-red laminate, wood-strip and mirror panelling together with red gingham tablecloths. Its selection of fried fish is a familiar one ranging from standard and large neatly filleted portions of cod (£3.55/£4.25) to plaice and haddock as well as huss and scampi. Everything comes with a lemon wedge, a garnish of sliced tomato and lettuce as well as piping hot, crunchy *real* chips, rolls or French bread and butter, tartare sauce and the choice of pickled onions and gherkins – both sliced. Tea arrives by the pot and as well as flavoured ice creams they do a good home-made apple pie with custard. To accompany the meal there's a short, basic wine list as well as minerals. Half non-smoking. *Seats 36.* **Open** *12-3 & 5-10.* **Closed** *Sun, Mon, 24 Dec-2 Jan. No credit cards.*

W1   Le Meridien, Terrace Garden

Tel 071-734 8000	Restaurant
Le Meridien Hotel 21 Piccadilly W1	Map 18 D3

A second-floor restaurant in a very smart West End hotel with half the room in conservatory-style overlooking Piccadilly. If you steer clear of the *'les grillades, les grands plats* and *menu du jour'* two courses and a glass of good wine from the Cruvinet machine will keep you around the £15 mark, and for that price and in these surroundings you're getting real quality. Potted chicken liver parfait served with a port jelly and toasted brioche is £5.50 and a risotto with wild mushrooms and grated cheese £7.95. Salads and sandwiches are other choices. Desserts are £3.85 – summer pudding, bread-and-butter pudding in autumn and winter, crème brulée or iced lemon parfait. Traditional set afternoon tea, served from 3 to 5 here or in the lounge, will set you back £11. Also late breakfasts and day-long snacks. *Seats 130.* **Open** *7am-11.30pm.* **Closed** *Bank Holidays. Access, Amex, Diners, Visa.*

W1   Merryfield House   £48

Tel 071-935 8326	Hotel
42 York Street W1H 1FN	Map 18 C2

Run by the same family since 1958 and ideally located for the West End, just off Gloucester Place and five minutes walk from Baker Street underground station. Full English breakfast is served in the small but comfortable and clean bedrooms, all of which have smart bathrooms en suite. No cots; small charge for extra bed in room. Unlicensed. *Rooms 8. No credit cards.*

W1   Minara

Tel 071-636 5262	Vegetarian
1 Hanway Street off Tottenham Court Road W1	Map 21 A1

Recently taken over by the co-owner of *Mamta* (at 692 Fulham Road), it offers a similar exclusively vegetarian menu in smaller, less spartan surroundings. A long list of starters includes well prepared patra (Indian leaves layered with chick peas £2.50), dahi vada (savoury doughnuts with yoghurt and chutney £2.95) and masala dosa (lentil and ground rice pancake served with coconut chutney and sambar £3.50), but the most interesting dishes are the chef's specialities

of stuffed baigan (aubergine with ground almond, pistachio, peanuts
and spices £4.95), bombay alu (rich curry with potatoes, cashew nuts,
cumin, chili paste and garlic £4.50) or one of the daily specials
prepared with vegetables and herbs directly imported from India.
Thali, including Vegan (£7.95) and Jaini (no onion or garlic £9.75),
are generous and the lunchtime buffet is a bargain (£2.50 for 2 items,
£3.95 for 4). **Seats** 44. **Open** 12-3.30 & 5-11. **Closed** Sun, 25 &
26 Dec. Access, Amex, Visa.

W5   Momo

Tel 081-997 0206	Restaurant
14 Queens Parade North Ealing W5 3HU	Map 17 A4

Behind a smoked glass frontage, just off Hanger Lane (by North
Ealing tube), a cosy Japanese restaurant serving budget one-dish
lunches and a choice of ten set lunches based around either sashimi,
tonkatsu, tempura or other main dishes with the addition of boiled
rice, miso soup, pickles and a piece of fresh fruit for dessert. Lunch
prices start at £6.50, while evenings are considerably more expensive.
Attentive service and hot hand towels are indicative of a well-run
venture in an unexpected setting. Two high-chairs. **Seats** 28.
Open 12-2.30 & 6-10. **Closed** Mon, 7 days August and 10 days
Christmas. Access, Amex, Diners, Visa.

W8   Muffin Man

Tel 071-937 6652	Café
12 Wrights Lane off Kensington High Street W8	Map 19 A4

A few yards from Kensington High Street, Muffin Man provides
a quiet, gentle refuge for mothers with babes in arms or pushchairs,
although it's a bit of a squeeze and the toilets (inadequate for nappy-
changing) are down treacherously steep stairs. Nevertheless, traditional
tea shops like this one, where waitresses' dresses match the flowery
tablecloths, are not often found in London and Granny might like it!
Afternoon tea (£4.70) includes a pot of tea, cucumber and tomato
sandwiches and a choice of cake. Alternatives to set teas are sandwiches
prepared to order (from £1.90); light lunches – home-made soups
(£2), muffin rarebit (£2.80) and salads (from £3.95). Breakfast
is served all day. **Seats** 72. **Open** 8-5.30pm. **Closed** 3 days Christmas.
No credit cards.

W11   Nachos

Tel 071-792 0954	Restaurant
174 Notting Hill Gate W11	Map 18 A3

Mexico meets Notting Hill in a lively 200-seat restaurant that's
banked its name on its nachos. These are warm, crispy tortilla chips
topped with cheese and onion (£2.25) spicy chicken or spicy beef
(£2.65) or served with dips. Other staples on the menu are quesadillas
(grilled tortillas), Mexican pizza, taquitos, tacos, burritos, fajitas and
chimichangas. **Seats** 200. **Open** noon-midnight. **Closed** 25 Dec.
Access, Visa.
Also at:
212 Fulham Road SW6 Clip-on and booster seats; no changing facilities.
Tel 071-351 7531.   Map 19 B5
36 High Street Wimbledon Village Surrey Clip-on and booster seats;
no changing facilities. Tel 081-944 8875.   Map 17 B6
8 Battersea Square off Church Road SW11 Tel 071-924 6450.   Map 17 B2
79-81 Heath Street Hampstead NW3 Tel 071-431 8362.   Map 16 B2

NW6   Nautilus

Tel 071-435 2532	Fish'n'Chips
27 Fortune Green Road West Hampstead NW6	Map 16 B2

Fine, fresh fish is served in this simple restaurant. Matzo meal flour
is used as standard (with an egg and matzo option) and only ground
nut oil used for frying. 18 different types of fish are offered, including
cod or rock salmon (£6.50), plaice on the bone (£8) and grilled
Dover sole (£12). Simple starters include minestrone or tomato soup
(not home-made) (£1), prawn cocktail (£3), fresh melon (£2) and
cod's roe. Portions are enormous and the chips generously sized.
Gherkins, peas, pickled onions and roll and butter charged extra (70p).
Busy fish'n'chip take-away next door. *Seats 48. Open 11.30-2.15 &
5-10.15. Closed Sun, 3 days at Christmas. No credit cards.*

WC2   Neal's Yard Bakery

Tel 071-836 5199	Café
First Floor 6 Neal's Yard WC2H 9DP	Map 21 B2

Well known for its bread, the Bakery also offers savouries and pastries
to be eaten in the upstairs dining area (no smoking). On our latest visit
the pizza and groundnut burgers were not so good as the cakes (95p),
typically including among a daily selection pear and ginger cake,
upside-down fruit cake, cheesecake, even a vegan cake. A useful
shopping stop, but the long, steep stairs make it unsuitable for push-
chairs; if you make it to the top there's a high-chair provided!
*Seats 22. Open 10.30am-4.30pm. Closed Sun, Bank Holidays, Christmas.
No credit cards.*

WC2   New Shu Shan

Tel 071-836 7501	Restaurant
36 Cranbourne Street WC2 7AD	Map 21 B2

The location is between St Martin's Lane and Charing Cross Road – an
area just outside Chinatown, but only just. This may account for the
lack of Chinese patrons and for the unusually friendly and helpful staff.
A family-run place with decor that is unfussily basic but comfortable –
paper napkins and well-used plastic chopsticks – such minor quibbles
are compensated for by some well-prepared familiar Chinese dishes
taken from the extensive Cantonese and Szechuan repertoire. There's
plenty to please both adults and their offspring with hot and spicy
dishes alongside milder offerings, all mostly in convenient bite-sized
pieces. No special family facilities for the very young; it's just a useful
place to know about – handy for Leicester Square cinemas, half way
between Piccadilly Circus and Covent Garden. *Seats 70.
Open 12 noon-11.30. Closed 25 & 26 Dec. Access, Amex, Diners, Visa.*

W1   New World

Tel 071-434 2508	Restaurant
1 Gerrard Place W1V 7LL	Map 21 A2

Join several hundred others and enjoy a meal in one of Soho's most
typical and traditional Chinese restaurants. Think of a Chinese dish
and you'll probably find it on the vast menu, which is almost the same
but marginally more expensive than at its neighbour *Lok Ho Fook* (in
the same ownership – see entry). Pushing the boat out is a bargain here
with the special offer of a whole lobster with chili and black bean

or ginger and spring onion sauce for £9.50. Ten high-chairs.
*Seats 700. **Open** 11am-midnight. **Closed** 25 & 26 Dec. Access, Amex,
Diners, Visa.*

SW4   Newtons

Tel 081-673 0977	Restaurant
33 Abbeville Road South Side Clapham Common SW4	**Map 17 C6**

Two-course, weekday lunch menu at £6.95, the Saturday Club Menu
and the Sunday Brunch are the best value at a brasserie-style restaurant
on a corner of Abbeville Road that caters for the Clapham crowd.
As eclectic as its clientele, the set lunch menu may offer carrot and
pumpkin soup or spicy Thai beef salad followed by seafood creole
with steamed rice or lamb cutlets chargrilled with tarragon and
mustard sauce and sauté potatoes. The long Sunday brunch menu runs
the gamut from spicy garlic mushrooms (£3), eggs Benedict
(£3.85/£6.05), smoked haddock kedgeree (£3.85/£6.05) and roast
beef and Yorkshire pudding (£6.50) to smoked salmon and sour
cream pizza (£4.50/£7.50). Several tables are outside on an attractive
terrace, by the roadside but protected by a small fence. No-smoking
area. Weekends are popular with kids when a special children's menu
(£2.50: chips with sausage, burger or bacon nuggets; Smartie ice
cream 95p) applies; a clown provides the entertainment on Saturdays
(for when the Duck symbol applies). *Seats 85 (plus 30 on the terrace).*
***Open** 12.30-2.30 & 7-11.30 (12.30-11.30 Sat & Sun). Access,
Amex, Visa.*

W6   Novotel   65%   £97

Tel 081-741 1555 Fax 081-741 2120	Hotel
1 Shortlands W6 8DR	**Map 17 B4**

Very large modern hotel alongside (but not accessible from)
Hammersmith flyover. It's popular for banquets and conferences
(up to 900 delegates). No charge for cot provided; double rooms
have a sofa/single bed. Much-reduced weekend rates. The restaurant
is open from 6am to midnight. *Rooms 640. Access, Amex, Diners, Visa.*

W11   Osteria Basilico

Tel 071-727 9372	Restaurant
29 Kensington Park Road W11	**Map 16 B3**

Two floors of attractive peasanty decor where delicious modern Italian
food with a good degree of authenticity is served in ample portions.
A table laden with various cold hors d'oeuvre leads one into
temptation on the ground floor, though the menu has its charms too.
Traditional pizzas and pasta dishes should please the youngsters, while
more modern meat dishes maintain the interest for their parents.
Friendly, attentive service and good espresso to finish. *Seats 70.*
***Open** 12.30-3 (Sat to 4.30) & 6.30-11 (Sun 6-10.30). **Closed** some Bank
Holidays. No credit cards.*

W1   The Park Lane Hotel   77%   £195

Tel 071-499 6321 Fax 071-499 1965	Hotel
Piccadilly W1Y 8EB	**Map 18 C3**

Built in 1927, the hotel retains some of its distinctive art deco features,
although the feel throughout the public rooms and bedrooms is very

traditional. The Palm Court lounge, where afternoon teas are served,
is brightened by a magnificent vaulted ceiling with arched art deco
stained glass. Standard bedrooms are well sized but tend to look out
on the dark inside courtyard. All rooms have double-glazing, multi-
channel TV, mini-bars and bathrobes. The best rooms are the suites,
more than 30 in number: all air-conditioned, they look out on to the
central court or Green Park and benefit from private sitting rooms
and more luxurious bathrooms. Private parking for 180 cars
is provided in a covered garage opposite the main entrance.
*Rooms 320. Keep-fit equipment, solarium, beauty & hair salons, brasserie
noon-11.30pm, business centre, garage. Access, Amex, Diners, Visa.*

Bracewells   £70

The restaurant atmosphere is traditional. The decor is of dark carved
wood, light flowery panels, mirrors and silver trolleys; jacket and tie
are a must. Jon Tindall plays comfortably with English and French
classics adding his own individual touches: salmon and sole sausage
topped with fresh crab meat on an avocado sauce, spinach and walnut
soufflé, classic sole meunière, plain grills, pot-roasted chicken served
on a potato cake with braised vegetables. Pancakes Belmonte, flamed
at the table, are the speciality dessert. The wine list is well constructed
and the three-course luncheon menu offers good value. Also good
budget eating in the Brasserie on the Park. The Palm Court Lounge
is open 24hrs a day; full afternoon tea is £9.50. *Seats 90. Parties 20.
Private Room 20. L 12.30-2.30 D 7-10.30 Set L £17 Set D £24.*

W2   Parkwood Hotel   £65
Tel 071-402 2241 Fax 071-402 1574	Hotel
4 Stanhope Place W2 2HB	Map 18 C3

Bed and breakfast town house hotel close to Marble Arch and Oxford
Street shops. Special rates for children under 13. Unlicensed. No dogs.
Rooms 18. Access, Visa.

SW10   Parsons
Tel 071-352 0651	Restaurant
311 Fulham Road SW10 9QH	Map 19 B5

Well over 20 years of success have attended this Fulham favourite,
whose best-known dishes are burgers, steaks and pies. All use high-class
beef produced by Lower Hurst Farm in the Peak District. Burgers
come in 4, 8 and 12oz sizes and prices range from £4.15 for a small
regular to £7.65 for a giant cheese and bacon burger. Chargrilled
steaks from £6.75, chili con carne (£5.10), steak and mushroom pie
(£6.10), spaghetti with a choice of sauces (from £3.95). Also salads,
cakes, ices and children's dishes (spaghetti, fish fingers or hamburgers
with chips, ice cream and drink £2.95). Four booster seats; changing
shelf in the Ladies. Directly opposite the MGM cinema. *Seats 80.
Open noon-12.30. Closed 25 & 26 Dec. Access, Amex, Diners, Visa.*

SW7   The Periquito Queen's Gate   £81
Tel 071-370 6111 Fax 071-370 0932	Hotel
68-69 Queen's Gate SW7 5JT	Map 19 B5

New owners plan major changes at the former *Eden Plaza*, with full
refurbishment due to have been completed by the time we went
to press. The hotel is very close to the South Kensington museums.
Rooms 63. Access, Amex, Diners, Visa.

SW1   Peter Jones

| Tel 071-730 3434 | Coffee Shop & Restaurant |

Sloane Square SW1W 8EL   **Map 19 C5**

The *Coffee Shop* on the fifth floor has views over the rooftops and
is self-service, offering a cold buffet (seafood platter £4.25 or open
sandwiches £3.45) and hot dishes such as lasagne al forno £3.95,
vegetarian pizzas £3.75 and baked potatoes with different fillings
from £2.95 to £3.75. Wide range of pastries, tea breads and cream
cakes from £1.75. Good coffee. Open until 6.30pm on Wednesday.
In the fourth-floor *Restaurant* the service is extremely efficient, but
queueing at lunch time has to be expected for a seat in the popular
open-plan dining room. The decor is simple: light green carpet and
curtains, flowery plastic tablecloths, and ceiling fans. The all-day menu
offers light, healthy selections like salmon fishcakes on a bed of spinach
with watercress sauce (£6.25), coq au vin on a bed of noodles (£7.95)
and cold tarragon and thyme chicken (£6.50), and from noon
to 2.30pm lunchtime daily specials (loin of lamb £8.95, Lincolnshire
sausages £6.95); children's portions £3.25. The luncheon buffet
at £10.75 (£4.75 for uner-11s), served from 11.45am to 2.30pm,
offers cold meats, prawns, rollmops, quiches and salads, pizzas
(asparagus and broccoli), plus a selection of desserts, including fresh
fruit salad and individual summer puddings, or hot cinnamon and
apple pie. Full English breakfast (£5.75) is served from 9.30am
to 11.30am. Afternoon tea between 3 and 5 includes a selection
of sandwiches, cake or pastry and a pot of tea or coffee (£4.75), or two
scones, clotted cream and strawberry preserve with a pot of tea
(£3.95). Fun food for little ones includes banana or peanut butter
sandwiches with crisps (£2.25), or Junior's grill (fish fingers, chicken
pieces or beefburger and egg) with baked beans and chips (£3.25).
The Mother & Baby room is on the third floor and there's plenty
of room in the restaurant for push-chairs; four high-chairs are
provided, as are children's portions. *Seats 150. Open 9.30-5.*
Closed Sun & Bank Holidays. No credit cards.

SW1   Pizza on the Park

| Tel 071-235 3850 | Pizzeria |

Hyde Park Corner 11 Knightsbridge SW1   **Map 19 C4**

One of the Pizza Express group, but offering a great deal more than
the standard product. The familiar range of pizzas (£5.20-£6.65)
is the mainstay, but there are also salads, sandwiches, baked potatoes
and chili (with or without carne). Breakfast (English £4.95,
Continental £3.95) is served from 8.15 (9.30 Sat & Sun) and
afternoon tea from 3.15 in the west wing – à la carte or set at £6.75.
There's jazz music nightly in the Music Room downstairs (reservations
071-235 5273 entrance fee payable). It's a cavernous place and children
are unlikley to feel constrained either gastronomically or vocally!
Within easy walking distance of the Knightsbridge shops. *Seats 260.*
Open 8am-midnight. Access, Amex, Diners, Visa.

SE1   Pizzeria Castello

| Tel 071-703 2556 | Pizzeria |

20 Walworth Road Elephant & Castle SE1 6SP   **Map 17 D4**

The most popular restaurant in an area short of good eating places –
hence the almost constant queues for both take-aways and tables.
Booking is very advisable, particularly at peak meal times. The front

of the restaurant is dominated by the huge stainless-steel pizza oven which produces good doughy-based pizzas with a familiar selection of toppings like margherita (£3.40) or mushrooms (£4.20). Starters include a good minestrone (£1.80) packed with fresh vegetables and there's a choice of about eight pasta dishes (from £2.95). Creamy tiramisu makes a good dessert and their espresso is particularly potent. Two high-chairs. *Seats 140. Open noon-11pm (Sat till 5pm). Closed Sun, Bank Holidays. Access, Amex, Visa.*

WC2   PJ's Grill

Tel 071-240 7529	Restaurant
30 Wellington Street Covent Garden WC2	**Map 21 B2**

Uncle PJ's Fun Club comes into action at weekends (from 11-4) at this American-style brasserie. It's a narrow restaurant that stretches from its entrance on Wellington Street through to Catherine Street, opposite the Theatre Royal. The rear exit is blocked at weekends (plus Bank Holidays) and a clown sets up shop with balloon bending, face-painting (£1.50 extra), indoor play equipment (bikes, slides), a box of Duplo and padded baby playrings. Food is hardly the main attraction with a pretty standard menu of grills and popular dishes like potato skins and pasta, but the staff are generally on the ball and understand the needs of little ones. Uncle PJ's Kiddies Menu (£3.95) even offers a Kiddies Combo with peanut butter sandwichman, carrot and cucumber sticks, sour cream dip, Sun Maid raisins, shredded chargrilled chicken bits and a muesli bar, all served on a plastic plate! Drinks come in a Mickey Mouse cup with a bendy straw – guaranteed to please! High-chairs, crayons, colouring menu (complete with jokes – Q. What's French, very tall and wobbles? A. The Trifle Tower) and balloons are all provided. 2-course Sunday lunch is £9.95 including a pot of coffee (tinie's roast also offered). Wobbly fruit jelly, funny face ice cream cones, fruit plate with yoghurt and hot fudge sundae complete the picture. The duck is awarded for Uncle PJ's Fun Club at weekends and Bank Holidays only. *Seats 120. Open 12-12 Mon & Tue, 12-1am Wed-Sat, 12-5 Sun. Closed 25 & 26 Dec. Access, Amex, Diners, Visa.*

W1   Planet Hollywood

Tel 071-287 1000	Restaurant
Unit 75 Trocadero Centre Coventry Street W1V 7SE	**Map 21 A3**

On the corner of Rupert and Coventry Streets (by Piccadilly Circus) and boasting a fantastic collection of original movie memorabilia, Planet Hollywood is jointly owned by three of Hollywood's biggest box office stars, Arnold Schwarzenegger, Sylvester Stallone and Bruce Willis. A no-bookings policy operates and queues of sometimes up to 40 minutes (with a further wait in the first-floor bar) are a possible deterrent. Once inside, the loud music, flamboyant decor and film artefacts do much to compensate. From Stallone's motorcycle in Rocky to innumerable other items, most displayed in perspex cases, the collection is totally fascinating. The fin from *Jaws* sits behind a large bubbling glass porthole in a room entered through the giant barrel of James Bond's Walther PPX, with 007 artefacts decorating the walls. There's also a sci-fi room, and, in the basement, an alien grotto, together with a 75-seater preview theatre. The main dining room has a midnight-blue ceiling studded with sparkling star-like spots, palm trees and a magnificent 'Hollywood Hills' set. The food plays a secondary role to all this decor, and comprises a familiar mix of pizzas, pasta (from £7.25), burgers (from £6.75) and some Tex-Mex fare. Texas nachos (£4.95) are a generous crunchy plateful with oodles of melted cheese and sour cream and chives. Sweets are mostly ice creams and whipped cream with chocolate making several come-backs. 20 high-chairs and baby-changing facilities in the disabled loo. **Seats 400. Open** *11am-1am.* **Closed** *25 Dec. Access, Amex, Diners, Visa.*

WC2   Poons

Tel 071-437 1528	Restaurant
4 Leicester Street WC2	Map 21 A2

Excellent Cantonese dishes are served in this ground-floor and basement restaurant by the side of the Swiss Centre building, just off Leicester Square. Their specialities are wind-dried foods (£4 per portion) and unusual 'original' dishes such as stewed eel with crispy pork and garlic hot pot (£5). Everything here from dumpling soup to deep-fried lamb with lettuce leaves and fillet steak with salted black beans and green pepper (£4.90) is beautifully executed and staff, though usually exceptionally busy, cope admirably. Best to book at weekends. Take only hungry kids and hide the push-chair; three high-chairs are provided. **Seats 80. Open** *12-11.30.* **Closed** *4 days Christmas. No credit cards.*

WC2   Porters

Tel 071-836 6466	Restaurant
17 Henrietta Street Covent Garden London WC2E 8QH	Map 21 B2

Though owned by Richard 7th Earl of Bradford, there's nothing lordly about this English restaurant named after the porters who plied their trade in Covent Garden market when it was London's 'fruit and veg' distribution centre. The restaurant's on two floors (ground and basement) and specialises in 'world famous' pies – their words not ours! However, you'll get good grub here, and at sensible prices, with children's portions around the £4.50 mark. No starters as such, just main courses (all pies £7.25 with either vegetables or salad, sausage and mash £6.75, salmon fish cakes £6.75) and hot and cold puddings (£2.75). To finish, try the orange tart or bread and butter pudding, served with whipped cream or custard. The fixed-price menu (min 2 people) is a very fair £15 per head, and includes any pie, a pudding, half a bottle of house wine per person, tea or coffee, VAT & service. There are baby-changing facilities in the Ladies, high-chairs and the restaurant has a stock of baby food. Minimum charge £6 per person. **Seats 210. Open** *12-11.30 (Sun to 10.30).* **Closed** *Christmas Day. Access, Amex, Diners, Visa.*

W1   The Portman Corner

Tel 071-486 5844	Hotel Coffee Shop
22 Portman Square W1H 9FL	Map 18 C2

The entrance is through the lobby of the *SAS Portman Hotel*, the atmosphere traditional with dark wood panelling, frosted glass and large silver trolleys. This is a sophisticated hotel coffee shop serving above-average-quality food. The most interesting item on the menu is the Portman buffet (£11), a delicious display of cold meat, tomato and mozzarella, marinated aubergine and caramelised onion, chicken terrine *en gelée*, jumbo king prawns plus a hot daily special and many more cold dishes. The à la carte includes traditional steak and kidney

pie (£9.75), fish and chips (£8.50), Caesar salad with poached eggs
(£5.50) and fried calamari (£5.50) and even cheeseburger (£8.50)
and DD's pizza (£7.50). Up-market prices (£10.50 for a three-course
children's meal) are justified by the quality. Three high-chairs are
provided; the spacious Ladies (also on the ground floor) has a vanity
unit for sorting out life's little (two-legged) problems. *Seats 75.*
Open 12-3.30 & 6-11. Access, Amex, Diners, Visa.

WC1   President Hotel   £64

Tel 071-837 8844 Fax 071-837 4653	Hotel
Russell Square WC1N 1DB	Map 18 D2

Large bed and breakfast hotel next door to the Imperial, on the corner
of Guilford Street and Russell Square, catering mainly for tour parties
and exhibition delegates from surrounding sister hotels. Rooms are
currently being renovated. Close to the British Museum. *Rooms 447.*
Coffee shop (10.30am-2am). Access, Amex, Diners, Visa.

SW7   Prince Hotel   £71

Tel 071-589 6488 Fax 071-581 0824	Hotel
6 Sumner Place SW7 3AB	Map 19 B5

A bed and breakfast hotel conveniently located near South Kensington
tube. Bedrooms are well decorated but offer very basic bathrooms,
most of them built into the room. Now under Resort hotel
management, the two Victorian terrace houses could use some
refurbishment. Conservatory and patio garden are pleasant features.
Breakfasts are served at the nearby Alexander hotel. One family room
sleeps four. *Rooms 37. Garden. Access, Amex, Diners, Visa.*

W1   Ragam

Tel 071-636 9098	Restaurant
57 Cleveland Street W1P 5PQ	Map 18 D2

South Indian vegetarian specialities are the main attraction at a popular
little restaurant near Great Portland Street and the Telecom Tower.
Rice and lentil flour, green chilis, semolina, yoghurt, coconut, curry
leaves and tamarind juice all appear in notably good vegetarian dishes
like uthappam (£3.50 – pizza-style rice and lentil pancake with
onions, tomatoes and green chilis) and *avial* (£2.20 – a colourful
Keralan dish made with several vegetables cooked with coconut,
yoghurt and curry leaves). Other interesting dishes range from *masala
dosai* (£3 – pancake filled with potatoes and fried onions, served with
sambar and coconut chutney) to *vadai* (£1.50 portion of two –
savoury gram flour cake served with coconut chutney), banana fritters
and *uppuma* (£1.50 – an unusual light dish of semolina fried with
onions and spices in ghee). Often playing second fiddle to the
vegetarian section are chicken, egg, beef, lamb and prawn in many
curry preparations priced from about £3 upwards. Adjacent NCP car
park. *Seats 36. Open 12-3 & 6-11.30. Closed 25 & 26 Dec. Access,
Amex, Diners, Visa.*

N3   Rani

Tel 081-349 4386	Vegetarian
7 Long Lane Finchley Central N3	Map 16 B1

Stylish red-and-white decor and smart glass-topped tables are not the
norm for Indian vegetarian restaurants, but neither is Rani the norm.

The style of cooking is Gujerati, and even normally mundane dishes
are transformed by interesting use of spices and fresh herbs. Different
days bring different specials, like Wednesday's tiffin or Sunday's
savoury pastry swiss rolls. Regular delights on the menu include
bhajias with wonderful coriander chutney (£2.90), brussels sprout,
courgette and capsicum curry and ripe bananas with fenugreek leaves
and tomato curry (banana mehti £4.90). Some dishes, like aloo papri
chat (chick peas and potatoes served on flat crispy pooris with
tamarind, topped with yoghurt sauce £3.50), and methi thapla (spicy
fenugreek bread roasted and fried £2.40) are near perfect and the
prices could hardly be lower. No eggs, fish, meat or animal fats are
permitted on the premises. Children's set menu for £5.50. There's
no service charge and any money left behind as change or gratuities
will be donated to charity. No smoking area; Saturday is all
no smoking. Buffet lunches (Tues to Fri 12.15 to 3, Sun to 4) and
buffet dinners (Mon-Thur 6 to 10.30). This is one of London's very
best Indian vegetarian restaurant in terms of both variety and cooking.
*Seats 90. **Open** 12.30-2 & 6-10.30. **Closed** L Mon, L Sat, 25 Dec.
Access, Amex, Visa.*

SW11   Ransome's Dock

Tel 071-223 1611	Restaurant

35 Parkgate Road Battersea SW11   **Map 19 B6**

Near the south bank of the Thames midway between Albert and
Battersea Bridges, Ransome's Dock occupies part of a modern dockside
development with the potential for alfresco dining in the summer.
The cooking by Martin Lam, long-time head chef at *L'Escargot*
in Soho, is executed with flair. On offer is a short, modern and
somewhat eclectic brasserie-style menu: globe artichoke and ricotta pie
(£3.95), salad of chargrilled squid (£4.50/£8), chicken leg stuffed
with wild mushrooms and spinach (£8.50) and onion, tomato,
anchovy and olive pissaladière (£7.50). Good puddings. Set lunch
£10.50; brunch on Saturday and Sunday (no roast). Smaller portions
are always available for children; there are two high-chairs. *Seats 60.
Open 12-11 (Sat 12-12, Sun 12-3.30). **Closed** D Sun, D Bank Holidays.
Access, Amex, Diners, Visa.*

W1   Rasa Sayang

Tel 071-734 8720	Restaurant

10 Frith Street Soho W1   **Map 21 A2**

Malaysian/Singaporean restaurant whose prices have not changed for
the past three years. Portions are normally quite generous, so don't
over order dishes and you'll stay within a budget: Char Kway Teow
(broad rice noodles, fried Singapore-style, with mixed vegetables
£4.60), Ayam Limau (boneless chicken pieces cooked in a tangy
lemon sauce £5.90), Gado Gado (popular cooked vegetable salad,
garnished with spicy peanut sauce £4.20), Sotong Goreng (fried squid
with chili dips £4.90). Help-yourself lunchtime buffet on Sunday and
Monday – £5.90 (children £3.50). *Seats 200. **Open** 12-2.45 &
6-11.30 (Fri/Sat to 1am, Sun to 10). **Closed** L Sat. Access, Amex,
Diners, Visa.*
Also at:
38 Queensway Bayswater W2 Tel 071-229 8417   **Map 18 A3**
Open 12-11.15.

NW1   The Regent London   83%   £238

Tel 071-631 8000   Fax 071-631 8080   Hotel

222 Marylebone Road NW1 6JQ   Map 18 C2

This important new addition to the London hotel scene opened last
year in what used to be the Great Central. Three and a half years
of renovation have returned an impressive piece of Grade II-listed
Victorian Gothic architecture to its former glory, creating a luxurious
hotel with a relaxed and informal atmosphere. From the oak-panelled
entrance hall, a majestic staircase leads to the Winter Garden, an eight-
storey glass-covered atrium of breathtaking proportions. Gigantic palm
trees, mezzanine-level Gazebo sitting area and fashionable furniture
contribute to a light modern interpretation of its Victorian ancestry.
Bedrooms are among the largest in London; even the Executive
bedrooms conceived for single businessmen are unusually large. Decor
is identical in all rooms, an elegant mix of smoky green and bronze,
with large custom-made cabinet hiding mini-bar and satellite TV,
relaxing sitting areas with elephant-theme cushions, large desks and
comfortable beds. Rooms overlooking the Winter garden tend
to be darker; two floors of rooms are non-smoking. Marble
bathrooms, equipped with quality towels, bathrobes, Crabtree &
Evelyn toiletries and telephone extension by the bath, are also spacious,
most with separate showers and all with twin wash basins. Well
equipped for families, the hotel provides an endless list of baby
accessories which even includes electric socket guards, playpen and
thermometers; children up to 14 may share their parents' room at no
charge and there are 100 interconnecting rooms. The basement health
club, with a 15m swimming pool, is open from 6am, offering
a complimentary healthy breakfast buffet. Breakfast, also available
in the dining room, extends to frittata, carrot bran muffins and banana
pancakes and is one of the best to be found in London. Light meals and
afternoon tea (3-6pm) are served all day in the Winter Garden.
Lunches and evening snacks are also available in the Cellars, an elegant,
wood-panelled pubby wine bar with its own entrance (closed all Sun
and Bank Holidays). Service handled by young, enthusiastic staff is one
of the hotel's biggest assets. Limited underground car parking. Regent
International Hotels/Four Seasons Hotels. **Rooms** 309. *Indoor swimming
pool, spa bath, gymnasium, sauna, massage, news kiosk, hair salon, coffee
shop (9am-11pm). Access, Amex, Diners, Visa.*

Dining Room   £90

A magnificent room, built on the grand scale with three huge
glittering chandeliers suspended from the ornate plaster ceiling.
Contrasting this classicism is a menu of mostly modish Italian food
which is enjoyably prepared and attractively presented. Only the
desserts from the trolley do not always live up to expectations.
Cosmopolitan but pricy wine list with an accent on Italian wines,
though France and the New World are also well represented.
Seats 100. *Parties* 12. *L* 12-3 (*Sun from* 12.30) *D* 7-11. *Set L* £19.50.

W1   The Ritz, Palm Court

Tel 071-493 8181   Afternoon/Tea

150 Piccadilly W1V 9DG   Map 18 D3

Taking your well-behaved child to tea at the Ritz is a very civilised
thing to do. Taking any other sort of child will entail a tactical
withdrawal of self and progeny, if only for the duration

of unpleasantness. Book at least a week in advance, ask for the sole
high-chair, and enjoy elegant tea sandwiches highly suitable for
children; set tea £14.50 per person. A visit to the splendid Ladies
downstairs is a must for mums. *Seats 150. **Open*** *Tea at 3pm & 4.30pm.*
Access, Amex, Diners, Visa.

W6   Riverside Studios Café

Tel 081-746 3771	Café
Riverside Studios Crisp Road W6	Map 17 A4

A small cafeteria located on the ground floor of the Riverside studio
and convenient for exhibitions, theatre and cinema. A limited menu
offers a healthy, straightforward selection of salads, home-made soup
(£1.65), hot dishes like spinach filo parcels (£3.60), sweet and sour
spare ribs (£3.95) and oven-baked potatoes (from £1.60). Carrot cake
and Danish pastries accompany the speciality teas. Organic wines and
beers are available. The bar, adjacent to the cafeteria, is open from
5.30pm to 11pm. Theatre workshops and children's parties
(up to 12 children); no high-chairs. Children's cinema and theatre
shows are usually at 2.30pm on Saturdays. *Seats 60. **Open*** *12-2.30 &
6-8.30 (snacks 9-8.30, Sun from 10).* ***Closed*** *Bank Holidays.*

W1   Rock Island Diner

Tel 071-287 5500	Restaurant
London Pavilion Piccadilly Circus W1	Map 21 A3

A gleaming '54 Chevrolet is suspended above diners at this whacky recreation of a 50s' American diner on the second floor (via an escalator)
of the London Pavilion. Bobby-soxed waitresses literally dance from
table to table to the sounds of an in-house DJ who plays requests (even
from little Johnny!) and revels in keeping a party atmosphere moving
along at a pace. Burgers, hot dogs, BBQ ribs, five-way chili, BLT
sandwiches, fried chicken salads, Winnie's chocolate brownies, banana
dream cake, waffles and ice cream sundaes arethe order of the day and
everything stops occasionally as the guys'n'gals line up to do a quick
hand jive routine. It's a fun place, best suited to the over-5s who are
guaranteed to love it; they may not serve the 'best burgers in town'
but they certainly serve up enough entertainment to keep a kid happy
for an hour or so. Four high-chairs are provided and there's room
to leave a push-chair by the table cubicles or at the entrance under the
watchful eye of the greeter. Between noon and 5pm at weekends
a child under 10 eats free of charge if accompanied by a "lunch-eating"
adult. Over-10s are expected to eat dishes from the main menu.
Combine a bite here with a visit to Madame Tussaud's rock'n'rolling
Rock Circus next door. A certain very well-known Princess brought
her very well-known little Princes here last year and their much-
publicised visit seems to have been a right royal success. The integral
bar area offers a happy hour from 5.30-7pm (Mon-Fri). Enjoy!
*Seats 160. **Open*** *Noon-11.30 (10.30 Sun).* ***Closed*** *25 Dec & 1 Jan.*
Access, Amex, Diners, Visa.

SW1   Royal Horseguards Thistle   71%   £110

Tel 071-839 3400 Fax 071-925 2263	Hotel
2 Whitehall Court SW1A 2EJ	Map 18 D3

A spacious foyer with beautiful, Wedgwood-style moulded ceilings
sets the tone of elegant public rooms in a comfortable hotel close
to the Thames Embankment. A charming lounge area in cool, pastel

lemon shades boasts chandeliers, oil paintings and a country-house style of furniture. The main restaurant is in the style of a gentlemen's club, and the Terrace Coffee Shop is open all day for snacks and light meals. Bedrooms range widely from a single overlooking Whitehall Court to the Tower Suite on two floors with a panoramic view of the City. The best are grand, spacious rooms with attractive limed oak furniture, elegant mirrors and colourful chintzy fabrics. Superb marble bathrooms are a stunning feature of some rooms. Children up to the age of 12 are accommodated free in parents' room. Good value, considering its grading. **Rooms** 376. *Coffee shop (7am-11.15pm). Access, Amex, Diners, Visa.*

W2   Royal Lancaster Hotel Lounge

Tel 071-262 6737	Afternoon/Tea

Lancaster Terrace London W2 3PF   **Map 18 B3**

One of the rare hotels to welcome children for afternoon teas. They are served in the roomy lounge, where sofas and armchairs are set around low tables, just the right height for children. For younger ones, high-chairs can be borrowed from the café. Their set tea (£10) selection is pleasant but somewhat minimalist: five finger sandwiches, a scone, clotted cream, jam and two pastries like strawberry tartelette and petit chou stuffed with whipped cream. The lounge is on the first floor with easy access via a lift; the anteroom of the toilet nearby is perfect for changing or nursing. A pianist tinkles away on a white grand piano (from 4.30) while one indulges; he'll probably want a large tip to play *Tea for Two*. **Seats** 80. **Open** 3-5.30. **Closed** 25 Dec. *Access, Amex, Diners, Visa.*

SE1   RSJ Brasserie

Tel 071-928 4554	Restaurant

13a Coin Street SE1 8YQ   **Map 20 A3**

On the corner of Coin Street and Stamford Street, RSJ is an ideal stop-off before or after a helping of culture on the South Bank. It comprises a series of rooms below the main restaurant, whose menu and wine list it offers in scaled-down version. Arches link the rooms, decor is white, abstract artwork dots the walls and fresh flowers contribute to a bright Mediterranean feel. New since last year is a ground floor area with a small, fenced-in outdoor section. The simpler brasserie menu offers the quality of the main restaurant at lower prices: kipper paté (£2.95), mushroom risotto (£3.25), fillet of cod served on stock-cooked potatoes and onions (£6.75), calf's liver served with tiny egg dumplings and a vermouth sauce (£8.25). Main courses are served with French fries or a bowl of seasonal salad. Add friendly service and a marvellous selection of wines by glass or bottle (Loire a speciality) and you have the perfect place for Just a Bite. Three-course business lunch at £9.95 is an alternative to the carte. No special facilities for younger children, but if the slightly older ones are ready for the South Bank (or the Young Vic) then they'll probably be ready to enjoy good food. **Seats** 40. **Open** 12-3 & 5.30-11. **Closed** L Sat, all Sun, Bank Holidays & 4 days Christmas. *Access, Amex, Visa.*

SE16   Scandic Crown   £156

| Tel 071-231 1001   Fax 071-231 0599 | Hotel |

Nelson Dock 265 Rotherhithe Street SE16 1EJ   Map 17 D4

A splendid hotel for families, albeit away from the centre of London –
both a positive and a negative factor – with the added bonus of a
borough playground opposite the hotel entrance. Especially popular
with Scandinavian tourists as a London base, the hotel is a clever
conversion of the 19th-century Columbia Wharf, with glass walkways
linking the three bedroom blocks. An old sailing barque moored
in the dry dock between the buildings continues the nautical theme,
and the hotel has its own pier. Some bedrooms have a river view and
include mini bar, trouser press, hairdryer and security locks. Sixteen
rooms have double sofabeds (up to two children under 12 years
sharing the room are free). Cheerful and helpful staff, and an excellent
Scandinavian buffet breakfast, taken in the restaurant beside the river
terrace, starts the day off in fine style; a good evening smörgåsbord
spread is equally impressive. There is a special play area on Sundays
at the buffet lunch (£16.50, £9) and jazz barbecue in summer.
Separate supervised leisure complex, games room and outdoor tennis
court. **Rooms** 390. *River terrace, indoor swimming pool, sauna, solarium,
spa bath, gymnasium, tennis, games room, snooker. Access, Amex,
Diners, Visa.*

SW1   Seafresh Restaurant

| Tel 071-828 0747 | Fish'n'Chips |

80-81 Wilton Road SW1   Map 19 D5

A restaurant for serious fish-lovers, where fish are flown in from
Scotland, on ice and not frozen. They are fried in groundnut oil
or grilled on request. The decor is simple and comfortable: saloon
chairs, fake beams and decorative fishing nets. Cod (£6.45), plaice
(£6.25), skate (£6.75), rock (£5.75), king prawns (£9.45) and
calamari (£7.75) are fried in light batter, served in ample portions
with real potato chips and large slices of pickles. Chicken (£4.25),
pork sausage (£3.15) and spam fritters (£4.15) are also available.
Cheerful service and take-away counter. One high-chair
is provided and there's plenty of storage for push-chairs. **Seats** 100.
Open noon-10.45. **Closed** Sun, 25 Dec-6 Jan. *Access, Amex, Visa.*

NW1   Seashell

| Tel 071-723 8703 | Fish'n'Chips |

49 Lisson Grove Marylebone NW1   Map 18 B2

One of London's best-known fish and chip restaurants, coping
admirably with the crowds who come from all over town to eat
in or take away. The restaurant is on two floors, connected by a spiral
staircase, and is large, smart and comfortable, with a no-smoking area.
Prices may vary according to weight and availability, but cod and
chips costs about £7.90, plaice £7.50, haddock £8.50, Dover sole
£12.90. Set lunch (Mon-Fri £8.75) comprises soup, fish of the day
with chips, sweet and coffee. **Seats** 180. **Open** 12-2 & 5-10.30 (Sat
12-10.30). **Closed** Sun, 25 & 26 Dec, 1 Jan. *Access, Amex, Diners, Visa.*

W1   Selfridges

Tel 071-629 1234	Café

400 Oxford Street W1A 1AB   **Map 18 C2**

A section of the store has been restructured and refurbished, creating
a new direct access to the *Food Garden Café* on the fourth floor.
This new concept emphasises fresh food, and quality that you pay for.
Salads and pies are attractively displayed (£2.95 for a medium size);
hot dishes are prepared to order in large woks. Order the pasta with
mushroom and bacon in tomato sauce (£4.25) in preference to the
rather bland Oriental dishes. Chicken breast (£3.85), pork chops,
hamburgers (£3.25) and assorted vegetables (95p) served in the
griddle section are cooked in advance and kept warm. Breakfast
(£4.95) is available all day. Desserts are a strong point with pastry
display (from £1.60), crepes made to order (walnut and syrup £2.60)
or Häagen-Dazs ice cream (two scoops £2.95). Konig-Pilsener
on pump and a few wines by the glass. This large, airy dining room
(350 seats) is perfect for families; six high-chairs and four booster seats
provided; burger or sausage and chips (£2.50) for youngsters. The
Mother & Baby room is on the third floor. Other more adult retreats
include the *Brass Rail* (42 seats), where you can still get an excellent
salf beef sandwich: a generous portion of beef, freshly carved and
served either on rye bread with a giant pickle and a choice of mustard
and relishes (£4.95) or as a platter with salad and lager (£6.95). The
queue can be daunting but service is efficient. Across from the Brass
Rail and above the Wine shop is the *Balcony Wine Bar* with its
fashionable granite bar, warm colours and decorative Roman
columns – a cosy bar with mainly stools and just a few tables (seats for
28). Along with a varied choice of 25 wines by the glass (from £2.15),
light dishes are offered, freshly prepared with quality ingredients.
*Open 9.30 (Brass Rail from 9, wine bar from 11) -6.45(Thur till 7.45,
Brass Rail till 7.45, wine bar till 7.30). Closed Sun (except Christmas
month), 25 & 26 Dec, Easter. Access, Amex, Diners, Visa.*

SW1   Sheraton Park Tower   79%   £270

Tel 071-235 8050 Fax 071-235 8231	Hotel

101 Knightsbridge SW1X 7RN   **Map 19 C4**

A distinctive, circular, high-rise tower within a stone's throw
of Harrods and with splendid city views from the upper floors.
Bedrooms, apart from the 31 luxury suites, are identical in size and
feature rather pleasing burr walnut-veneered furniture. Thick quilted
bedcovers, turned down at night, match the curtains; TVs and mini-
bars are discreetly hidden away. There are telephones by the bed,
on the desk and in the bathrooms, which have marble-tiled walls,
good shelf space, towels and toiletries. A new messaging system has
recently been installed. Extra services on Executive floors include valet
unpacking, two-hour laundering, a special check-out service and extra
toiletries. 60 rooms are designated non-smoking. Children up to 17
stay free in parents' room; libraries of books, videos and games (even
Super Nintendo machines – very popular with airline crews as well
as kids!) are kept to amuse youngsters; baby-sitting can be easily
arranged (notice needed before 2pm on day). If you forget baby's
nappies, powder, lotion or soap, then housekeeping will happily sell
you supplies. A baby bath and high-chair can also be provided.
Children's menu of favourites (main course £4, three courses £9)
served in the room. *Rooms 295. Beauty & hair salon. Access, Amex,
Diners, Visa.*

Restaurant 101   £50

As we went to press the formal restaurant was in the process of being
renovated and a new-style modern English menu introduced. *Seats 80.
Parties 25. Private Room 150. L 12-3 D 6.30-11.*

W1   Signor Zilli

Tel 071-734 3924	Restaurant
41 Dean Street Soho W1	Map 21 A2

Sunday lunch is the time to visit one of Soho's oldest restaurants, now
actively encouraging families with a traditional Sunday roast (usually
roast beef with Yorkshire pudding – three courses £12.50) alongside
the à la carte menu of Italian dishes. A children's menu (£5) includes
pasta dishes, sausages and mash, burgers or fish with chips and beans,
followed by mixed ice cream and chocolate sauce, fruit salad
or a banana long boat. Desserts from a trolley. The basement room
has a colour television, balloons, activity books and coloured pencils,
plus a magician or clown who entertains diners before the children's
show (and/or disco) at 2.30pm. High-chairs are provided. *Seats 30.
Sunday lunch 12-4. Access, Amex, Diners, Visa.*

W1   Smollensky's Balloon Bar & Restaurant

Tel 071-491 1199	Restaurant
1 Dover Street W1	Map 18 D3

Nothing changes at this basement bar and restaurant with a strong
American feel. The busy split-level dining room is one floor lower
than the bar. It has some quiet corners and a talented piano player who
gets out of the usual rut. As for the food, better stick to what they
do best: steak (eight different types and sauces) and French fries.
A special fixed-price menu (£9.95) offers a salad, entrecote steak and
a glass of house beer, wine or soft drink. Other offerings include
a giant pasta shell stuffed with ricotta cheese, Parmesan, spinach and
basil (£2.95/£6.95), crudités (£3.60), corn-fed chicken (£8.45) and
salmon steak (£8.45). Puddings are of the icky, sticky type – from
Grandma's peanut butter or New York toffee cheesecake to Erna's
chocolate mousse and Keylime pie. Happy hour is between 5.30pm
and 7pm Monday to Friday for some of the best cocktails in London –
try an alcohol-free Pussy Foot (£2.50) or an alcohol-laden Long
Island Iced Tea (£4.95)! Lunchtimes at weekends and Bank Holidays
are dedicated to children who are offered their own menu and
entertainment (face painter, magician, cartoon videos and a clown
on Sundays). Six high-chairs and booster seats are provided,
as is a changing table in the Ladies. Last year's joint winner (with
Smollensky's Balloon) of our Family Restaurant of the Year award; the
Balloon is perhaps better for the over-7s, while the Strand has more
to amuse and distract the under-7s. Dover Street is opposite The Ritz
on Piccadilly; nearby NCP car park. *Seats 220. **Open** noon-midnight
(Sun to 10.30). **Closed** 25 & 26 Dec. Access, Amex, Diners, Visa.*

WC2   Smollensky's On The Strand

Tel 071-497 2101	Restaurant
105 The Strand WC2	Map 21 B3

Here bar and restaurant are both in the basement. The layout is open-
plan with split levels and partitions. The entertainment is loud and the
restaurant popular for big parties. There is live music every night

of the week and Fridays and Saturdays are dancing nights. Sunday
evening is dedicated to jazz, in conjunction with Jazz FM (£3 door
charge). As at its sister restaurant in Dover Street cocktails are perfectly
mixed and steak and fries are what you come for. Aberdeen Angus
cuts are served anywhere from blue (20 seconds per side) to well done.
Don't be put off by the sound of 'Grandma Smollensky's peanut butter
cheesecake' – it's really very good. Happy hour between 5.30 and
7 Monday to Friday. Children's entertainment on weekends with
a magician, clown, children's videos, raffles and a magic show
at 2.30pm. A play area with slide, seesaw and bikes helps the under-7s
through the cooking times of their parents' main courses. Colouring
sheets and pens and cartoon videos help, too. Best of all is the positive
attitude of the staff towards children. There are heaps of high-chairs
and boosters seats available; a changing mat is in the toilet and
a manager's office for breast-feeding in privacy. Joint winner of our
Family Restaurant of the Year award last year. *Seats* 240. *Open* 12-12
(*Fri & Sat to 12.30, Sun to 10*). *Access, Amex, Diners, Visa.*

N16   Le Soir

Tel 071-275 8781	Restaurant
226 Stoke Newington High Street N16 7HU	**Map 16 D2**

Located right at the top of the north end of Stoke Newington High
Street, this is the archetypal neighbourhood restaurant. The
chef/proprietor lives above with his wife. He, of Brazilian, Italian,
German and French origins, cooks while she, of Filipino extraction,
looks after the diners in a very light and cosily decorated two-room
restaurant. Pink paper napkins, candlelight and pretty framed pictures
all contribute to a charmingly informal ambience. Booking
is advisable due to its popularity. There's no minimum charge
on a menu supplemented by daily blackboard specials. Crevettes
mayonnaise (£3.95), choux pastry filled with crab (£2.85) and fried
Camembert with apple and Calvados jelly are typical starters, while
the main courses could include breast of chicken in tarragon sauce,
liver with bacon, caramelised onion and mashed potato (£7.55) and
vegetarian Wellington. There's always a salad and a fish dish of the
day, and crème caramel or profiteroles round off a thoroughly
enjoyable meal. Children are welcome, although there are no special
facilities. *Seats* 46. *Open* 6-midnight, also open for lunch throughout Dec
(*set menu*). *Closed* 25-27 Dec. *Access, Visa.*

SW13   Sonny's

Tel 081-748 0393	Restaurant
94 Church Road Barnes SW13	**Map 17 A5**

The set meal (2 courses and coffee) at £12.50 for lunch and dinner
is quite a bargain, at what is one of the most popular neighbourhood
restaurants around. A typical choice, always including vegetarian
options, could include twice baked artichoke and white truffle soufflé,
salt cod hash with olive bread or mushroom risotto to start, followed
by seared salmon with roasted red onion and saffron or roast lamb
chump with goat's cheese and aubergine purée. Desserts from the carte
could include lemon cheesecake with cream or sticky toffee pudding
(£3.50). Traditional 3-course roast lunch (£14.50) on Sundays.
Simple, unassuming style and informality. The café/bar is open all day
(not Sun) serving light dishes such as goat's cheese, tomato and
tapénade baguette (£2.50), ham hock terrine with home-made

piccalilli, and warm salad of chicken livers, croutons, lardons and frisée
(£3.75). Good value, friendly and "a high-chair can be found" for
popular Sunday lunches when a roast is always offered; ask for
a children's portion if you don't have a budding trencherman in the
family. *Seats 80.* *Open* 12.30-2.30 (Sun to 3) & 7.30-11. Café (hot
dishes noon-4 Mon-Sat). *Closed* D Sun, L Bank Holidays. Access,
Amex, Visa.

N16   Spices

Tel 071-254 0528	Vegetarian
30 Stoke Newington Church Street N16	Map 16 D2

The perfume of burning incense hangs heavily in the air and with
dark, candle-lit tables and Indian music playing in the background
there's a suitably oriental ambience at this South Indian vegetarian
restaurant. To the rear is a more brightly-lit section with booths that
seat four, most unusually, on floor cushions – a novelty that most
children seem to enjoy. This is an ideal location for families as children
are less likely to disturb other diners; the booths also allow a measure
of privacy for nursing. Though the menu features a variety of spiced
dishes made with specially imported fresh herbs and spices, there are
several items suitable for young children such as plain popadums and
pakoras (sliced potatoes and vegetables dipped in gram flour paste and
deep fried £1.70); the waiters will be happy to point out those dishes
that are popular with children. Two children can share a Bombay
tiffin (£2.65) – a starter assortment of delicately spiced gujerati
savouries including samosas, vegetable cutlets and aubergine slices
topped with sour cream (malai baigan). There's always one special
each day (Tuesday brings mushroom and aloo curry served with rice
and salad £4.40) and a thali set of mixed dishes (£6.25). To finish
there are home-made ice-creams with pistachio, mango, almond
or coconut (£1.90) or the unusual kerala payasum made with lentils,
jaggery (palm sugar) and coconut milk. A fresh, nutritious and
delicious drink is either banana or mango lassi (£1.40). Two high-
chairs are provided but a changing area is not; another plus for
families is a car park to the rear with easy pushchair access. *Seats 65.*
Open 12-2.30, 6-midnight. *Closed* 25 & 26 Dec. Access, Amex,
Diners, Visa.

W8   Sticky Fingers

Tel 071-938 5338	Restaurant
9 Phillimore Gardens off Kensington High Street W8	Map 19 A4

The walls of now-retired-Rolling-Stone Bill Wyman's immensely
popular American-style diner are covered with Rolling Stones
memorabilia, but other bands get a share of the sound system. The
food is served in liberal portions by friendly, clued-up staff: starter
helping of ribs £3.85, guacamole and tortilla chips £3.65,
cheeseburger £5.95, Cajun chicken £7.25, steak sandwich £8.25,
frozen yoghurt with honey and almonds £3.15. Half-price drinks
during happy hour 5.30-6.30 (Mon-Fri in the bar only). No bookings
in the evening, but you can boost their coffers by waiting (and
drinking) in the stand-up bar area; bookings are taken for lunch.
Three high-chairs plus four booster seats and clip-on seats; children's
dishes also on the menu; balloons, colouring books and stickers for the
youngsters. A magician magically appears every Sunday. *Seats 140.*
Open 12-11.30. *Closed* 25 Dec. Access, Amex, Diners, Visa.

SE1   Sweeney Todd's

Tel 071-407 5267	Restaurant
Tooley Street London Bridge SE1 2QT	**Map 20 C3**

Located at the back of Hay's Galleria, across from the London
Dungeon, is this two-floor family restaurant with access at street level.
A children's menu offers main course, first fizzy drink and dessert for
£3.45. Main courses include BBQ ribs, chicken nuggets, cheeseburger,
bean burger or pizzas, sundaes, milk shakes or fruit juices – not
exceptional quality but well executed nonetheless. Children are
encouraged to draw their waiter or waitress on the back of their place
mat and may win a T-shirt. Children's parties. Changing shelf in the
Ladies. *Seats 280. Open 11-11. Closed 25 Dec. Access, Amex,
Diners, Visa.*

SW4   Tea Time

Tel 071-622 4944	Café
21 The Pavement Clapham Common SW4	**Map 17 C5**

This institution on the east side of Clapham Common continues
to pull the crowds, particularly at weekends. A window display full
of tempting gateaux and pastries whets the appetite for an all-day 'Tea
Time special' (£6.95), a lavish cream tea with sandwiches, cakes and
a good choice of quality teas. Breakfast, also all-day, includes kedgeree
(£2.95) and scrambled eggs with smoked salmon (£4.95) while other
savoury options include sandwiches, plain, toasted (from £2.30) and
double-decker (£3.85), a daily soup (£1.95) and jacket potatoes
(£3.75). Cosy, civilised ground and basement (no smoking) rooms are
served by cheerful waitresses. Also open evenings 7.30-10.30, set three
course meal £8.95, advisable to book. Unlicensed so bring your own
(corkage £2 Thur-Sat eves). One high-chair; children's portions;
downstairs is favoured by nursing mums but there are no special
changing facilities. *Seats 60. Open 10-6 (Sat & Sun to 6.30) &
7.30-10.30. Closed 25 & 26 Dec, 1 & 2 Jan, Easter. No credit cards.*

SW5   Terstan Hotel   £50

Tel 071-835 1900 Fax 071-373 9268	Hotel
29 Nevern Square SW5 9PE	**Map 19 A5**

Family-owned and run, the Terstan bed and breakfast hotel stands in a
garden square just south of the A4 Cromwell Road (approach via
Earl's Court Road), a couple of minutes from Earl's Court
underground station and Exhibition Centre. Most bedrooms have
private facilities, the exception being some budget singles. Simple
accommodation at a low price. £3 charge for cot provided; good-
value three- and four-bedded family rooms. A high-chair is promised.
Rooms 50. Closed 3 days Christmas. Access, Visa.

SW7   Texas Lone Star Saloon

Tel 071-370 5625	Restaurant
154 Gloucester Road SW7	**Map 19 B5**

Tourists and teenagers file past the wooden Red Indian into this very
busy restaurant inspired by a western saloon. Videos and C&W music
accompany nachos covered with cheese, onion and hot peppers
(£3.85), short-order hickory-smoked BBQ ribs (£3.95), chicken
enchiladas (£6.85), chimichanga with salad and fries (£5.95), chili
(cup £3.65, bowl £4.95), pecan pie (£2.65) and apple pie with

Häagen-Dazs ice cream (£3.65). A noisy place, but fun, and the cocktails (try a virgin colada or coke float) add to the spirit of the occasion. **Seats** 140. **Open** 12-12 (Fri/Sat to 1am). No credit cards.
Also at:
117 Queensway W2 Tel 071-727 2980   **Map 18 A3**
50 Turnham Green Terrace Chiswick W4 Tel 081-747 0001   **Map 17 A4**

N10   Toff's

Tel 081-883 8656	Fish'n'Chips
38 Muswell Hill Broadway N10 3RT	**Map 16 C1**

The Toffalli family's popular fish and chip restaurant is decorated with Edwardian prints of Billingsgate market. Most of their fish now comes from Peterhead, to be coated in batter or egg and matzo meal and fried in groundnut oil. Prices start at £7.25 (cod and chips), with plaice at £7.50, skate at £9.50 and halibut at the top of the range. Nearly everything is also available grilled – which takes a little time and costs £1 more. Add fish soup, fisherman's pie, daily specials, traditional puds and a children's portions and in Toff's you have the ideal family fish restaurant. **Seats** 32. **Open** 11.30-10. **Closed** Sun, Mon, 2 weeks Aug-Sept. Access, Amex, Visa.

W4   Tootsies

Tel 081-747 1869	Restaurant
148 Chiswick High Road W4	**Map 17 A4**

Six branches of this popular burger chain share the same decor of cane bistro chairs and walls covered with enamel signs and colourful mirrors. Aberdeen Angus beefburgers (from £3.95) are offered with a choice of ten different toppings. Salads are made freshly from good ingredients, chicken served grilled or in a sandwich and English breakfast (£5.50) is available all day. 'Tootsies tots' under 10 are given balloons, special plates and a menu of mini hamburger with cheese, egg or beans and fries (under £3); small chicken sandwich or sausage, fries and baked beans; finish with TT's ice cream (£1.20). High-chairs and booster seats are provided. Tables on the pavement in good weather. **Seats** 72. **Open** 12-12 (Sun 12-11.30). **Closed** 5 days Christmas. Access, Visa.
Also at:
147 Church Road Barnes SW13 Tel 081-748 3630.   **Map 17 A5**
48 High Street Wimbledon Village SW19 Tel 081-946 4135.   **Map 17 B6**
177 New Kings Road Parsons Green SW6 Tel 071-736 4023.   **Map 17 B5**
120 Holland Park Avenue W11 Tel 071-229 8567.   **Map 17 B4**
Special breakfast menu at weekends from 9am to noon, then open all day as usual.
115 Notting Hill Gate W11 Tel 071-727 6562.   **Map 18 A3**

N1   Tuk Tuk

Tel 071-226 0837	Restaurant
330 Upper Street Islington N1	**Map 16 D3**

Situated at the Islington Green end of Upper Street, this stylish Thai restaurant is fashioned after the small family shops in South East Asia that sell one-pot dishes to the drivers of tuk tuks (little canopied cycle-taxis). Londoners are encouraged to adopt the familiar Thai tradition of sharing a number of dishes, with perhaps tom yum kung (spicy prawn soup £5.95) or chicken satay (£3.25) to start, then a red curry with rice (kang ped £4.95) or perhaps Thai rice noodles and some vegetable dishes. No particular facilities for families but an interesting, informal restaurant. *Seats 120. Open 12-3 & 6-11. Closed Bank Holidays. Access, Amex, Visa.*

WC2   Tuttons Brasserie

Tel 071-836 4141	Brasserie
11-12 Russell Street Covent Garden WC2	**Map 21 B2**

In the profusion of Covent Garden restaurants, Tuttons Brasserie offers a pretty standard brasserie menu – from full English breakfast (£5.50), Danish pastries (£1.70) and croque monsieur (£3.90) to all-day offerings of onion soup (£2.90), fish cakes (£3.60), hamburger (£6.50), Scotch salmon béarnaise sauce (£8.50) and daily specials. Afternoon tea starts at 3pm with freshly baked scones (£3). In the summer, a large terrace extends on to Covent Garden pavement. Half portions are offered (as are a few booster seats) and a private room can be found for nursing mothers. *Seats 80 (plus 100 outside). Open 9.30am-11.30pm (Fri/Sat to 12.30, Sun to 10.30). Closed 24 & 25 Dec. Access, Amex, Diners, Visa.*

N1   The Upper Street Fish Shop

Tel 071-359 1401	Fish'n'Chips
324 Upper Street Islington N1 2XQ	**Map 16 D3**

Alan Conway set up shop here in 1981, and he's been in charge, with his wife Olga, ever since. When the chips are down, it's quality that counts, something well known to the crowds who come to sit down and eat or take away. Besides the excellent fish and chips (cod, haddock, skate, halibut, even sea bass among the daily specials – prices start at around £6) there are some very tempting starters, including perhaps fish chowder and skewered deep-fried mussels. Look out also for rock oysters from Ireland, fish lasagne and the shellfish plate. Sweets, home-prepared like everything else, are guaranteed to fill any remaining gaps: favourites are bread-and-butter pudding and jam roly-poly. Unlicensed, so take your own wine – there's no corkage. Minimum food charge £7.50. Not suitable for or push-chairs. *Seats 50. Open 12-2 (Sat to 3) & 5.30-10. Closed L Mon, all Sun, Bank Holiday weeks, 1 month Christmas. No credit cards.*

WC1   Wagamama

Tel 071-323 9223	Restaurant
4 Streatham Street off Bloomsbury Street WC1	**Map 21 B1**

'Positive eating, positive living' is the philosophy behind this ultra-modern, fast food Japanese-style noodle bar, conveniently close to the British Museum and five minutes' walk from Tottenham Court Road and the Dominion Theatre. Eleven ways with *ramen* (Chinese-style noodles, not Japanese *soba* or *udon*) in a clear broth and topped with anything from chili beef to teriyaki salmon or prawns and squid, five or so pan-fried noodles dishes and six *donburi* brown rice dishes comprise the main attraction. Chili, lemon grass, carrot, spring onion, aubergine, black bean sauce, garlic mushrooms, tofu, *wakame*, *menma* (pickled bamboo shoots), *kamaboko* (fish cakes), seasonal greens and coriander all appear in various guises, offering an exciting combination of unusual Oriental tastes with more everyday Western flavours. Wonderfully fresh, griddled *gyoza* dumplings (£3), freshly squeezed fruit and vegetable juices (£1.60) and an unusual mixed raw salad (£4) complete the short menu. All main dishes are under £5.50, with many starting at £3.50; three set meals offer even better value. Green tea is served free of charge. No bookings are taken, so expect to queue at peak times. No children's portions or particular facilities but it's such an unusual eating experience that most children who go once can't wait to return; however, it's not the kind of place for a lingering meal – the only lingering is likely to be in the queue at peak times. No smoking. *Seats 104.* **Open** *12-2.30 (Sat 1-3.30) & 6-11.* **Closed** *Sun, 24-26 Dec. No credit cards.*

SW1	**Wilbraham Hotel**	**55%**	**£86**
Tel 071-730 8296 Fax 071-730 6815			Hotel
Wilbraham Place Sloane Street SW1X 9AE			Map 19 C5

Modest Belgravia hotel formed from three Victorian town houses. Bedrooms and bathrooms are generally quite small and spartan, though there are two large suites on the ground floor. Cot or extra bed provided at a small additional charge. The bar is closed Sundays and Bank Holidays. *Rooms 52. No credit cards.*

SW1	**Willett Hotel**	**£97**
Tel 071-824 8415 Fax 071-730 4830		Hotel
32 Sloane Gardens SW1X 8DT		Map 19 C5

Victorian townhouse in the heart of Chelsea converted into a peaceful hotel offering bed and breakfast accommodation, but limited public rooms. Three bedrooms are not en suite. Cot provided at no extra charge. Good-value triple-bedded rooms. Friendly staff. *Rooms 18. Access, Amex, Diners, Visa.*

W5	**Wine & Mousaka**	
Tel 081-998 4373		Restaurant
30 & 33 Haven Green Ealing W5		Map 17 A4

A pair of Greek restaurants serving sensibly priced favourites like taramasalata, houmus (£1.75 each), dolmades (£5.25) and moussaka (£5.25). There's a four-course set menu at £6.95 (weekdays); meze (£9.45) offers 10 dishes, grand meze (£11.95) provides 12 dishes and includes dessert and coffee. *Seats 140.* **Open** *12-2.30 & 6-11.30.* **Closed** *Sun, Bank Holidays. Access, Amex, Diners, Visa.*
Also at:

12 Kew Green Kew Surrey Tel 081-940 5696 Closed Sun.	**Map 17 A6**

W2	**Winton's Soda Fountain**	
Tel 071-229 8489		Restaurant
2nd Floor Whiteleys Queensway Bayswater W2		Map 18 A3

One of the many fast food outlets on the second floor of this vast multi-unit shopping complex: an ice cream soda fountain with marble-topped tables, parquet flooring and a Wurlitzer juke box. There's a range of flavours from a selection of suppliers (as well as their own home-made flavours such as fresh malted banana, Dime bar crunch or pumpkin) from which sundaes such as Monkey Madness (£4.50), Milky Chocolate Fantasy (£4.20), Jolly Giant (£7) and Children's Delight (£2.50) are created. Also available are milkshakes (£2.80), cakes (90p-£1.70) and biscuits. They also make ice cream cakes to order (from £10). No-smoking area. Several high-chairs are shared with other eating outlets; a Mother & Baby changing room is one floor up. The multi-screen cinema is on the same floor, so there's much to keep a teenager happy for an afternoon. *Seats 100.* *Open* 11-10 *(10-10 Sun).* *Closed 25 Dec. No credit cards.*

W1   Woodlands

Tel 071-486 3862	Vegetarian
77 Marylebone Lane off Wigmore Street W1	**Map 18 C2**

A short walk north of Oxford Street, just over Wigmore Street, will find one of a small chain of three restaurants serving Southern Indian vegetarian cuisine. Fresh herbs and spices create clean, distinctive and subtle flavours. Thalis, the set meals, are copious (from £8.95) and give a good introduction to this type of food. From the menu, starters include rasa vada (lentil doughnuts in spicy gravy) and idli (steamed rice cakes served with sambal and chutney £2.75). Main dish specialities are dosas (pancakes) filled with a variety of ingredients – potato and onion, spicy cottage cheese (£3.25-£4.75) – and uthappams (lentil pizzas) with different toppings (£3.75-£4.25). Minimum charge £5. *Seats 70. Open 12-3 & 6-11. Closed 25 & 26 Dec. Access, Amex, Diners, Visa.*
Also at:
37 Panton Street SW1 Tel 071-839 7258   **Map 21 A3**
Open 12-3 & 5.30-11.
402 High Road Wembley Middlesex Tel 081-902 9869   **Map 16 A2**

WC2   World Food Café

Tel 071-379 0298	Vegetarian
First Floor 14 Neal's Yard WC2H 9DP	**Map 21 B2**

Above the herbal shop in the former *Neal's Yard Dining Room*, the café serves a mix of exotic vegetarian dishes at very reasonable prices. Large wooden tables are shared, and there's additional seating around the bar. Presentation isn't a number one priority, but the overall quality of the food is above average. Mexican tortillas (£3.65), Indian samosas or Egyptian falafel could precede Californian raw energy salad, Indian thali or Indonesian gado gado (all main dishes £5). The trip round the globe continues with the desserts (£2.50): American pecan pie, Polish cheesecake, Italian tiramisu, Greek yoghurt with nuts and raisins. No smoking. Bring your own wine (no corkage). One high-chair. *Seats 42. Open 12-8pm (Sat 12-6pm). Closed Sun, 25 & 26 Dec, Bank Holidays. No credit cards.*

SW3   Zia Teresa

Tel 071-589 7634	Restaurant
6 Hans Road Knightsbridge SW3	**Map 19 C4**

Hard by Harrods' west doorway and inevitably packed when the store closes, Zia Teresa is deservedly popular for both its Italian food and its lively atmosphere. Pasta comes in many guises as starter (£3.65) or main course (from £5.75) with ravioli dressed with butter, fresh sage and Parmesan a speciality; traditional veal, chicken and steak dishes abound (veal marsala £8.95, osso buco £9.10, pollo alla cacciatora £8.40) and fresh fish is proclaimed daily on the chalk boards. Limited, though generously topped pizzas, soft Italian cheeses and mostly ice cream-based sweets also pack the voluminous Spaghetti House menu. Three high-chairs. *Open 12-10.50 (Fri & Sat 11.20). Access, Amex, Diners, Visa.*

W1   Zoe

Tel 071-224 1122   Restaurant

St Christopher's Place W1M 5HH   **Map 18 C2**

Modern basement brasserie with a café at street level, both done
in bright and fashionable colours. The atmosphere is hectic and loud.
Two menus, in the brasserie, one Country, the other City, mix
Mediterranean ideas with Latin American ingredients without
neglecting fish and chips and sausage and mash. The menus are
different and spirited, and the cooking is of a good general standard.
The café menu runs a similar gamut, from mushrooms on toast
£3.50/£4.50) or Brie and grape blue corn quesadilla with chili jelly
(£4.95) to home-cured bresaola with caponata and chargrilled
vegetables (£6.95), Rossmore rock oysters (£5.95/£11.50) and grilled
Barnsley chump chop with red pepper and aubergine tart (£8.95). For
dessert, maybe ice cream sandwich (£2.95), almond cream with
blueberries or pan-roasted pear cake (£3.75). Not particularly family-
oriented but a useful place to know as it's one minute off Oxford
Street, almost opposite the top of South Molton Street and Bond Street
underground station. *Seats 80. **Open** 12.30-3 & 6.30-11.30.*
Closed *D Sun, 25 & 26 Dec. Access, Amex, Diners, Visa.*

lifetime™

Lifetime is Cellnet's low cost tariff for people who intend to make most of their calls outside the peak period and at weekends.

With Lifetime you can still receive calls at any time of day. And because you're always in reach, you can be alerted to any sudden changes in plan – to any little surprises life holds in store. You're in touch – wherever life takes you.

Offering all the benefits of the mobile phone to the less frequent user, Lifetime is just perfect on those occasions when you have to contact someone right away. And in emergencies, of course, it really comes into its own.

**Choose Cellnet.
You'll have more choice.**

Call the BIG network for small phones on
0800 21 4000

Lifetime is a registered trademark of TCSR Ltd.

An easy guide to mobile phones

You can't open a paper or turn on the television today without coming across another article or advertisement for mobile phones. There are so many new systems being launched, different call charges on offer and special deals available that it's confusing.

Ford Motor Company Limited has a separate division, Ford Cellular Systems, which specialises in mobile communications.

If you need advice, it's just a phone call away. Dial **0800 52 66 57** and one of Ford Cellular's knowledgeable operators will answer your questions and help you decide on the best phone and the best call tariff to suit your needs. Or call into your local Ford dealer and ask for the Ford phone specialist.

Two basic decisions

In the end it boils down to two decisions, just like buying a phone for home:

1) Which phone do you want?

2) Which tariff should you choose?

1) Your choice of phone depends on what you plan to use it for. Is it for heavy duty use on a building site or do you want something you can slip into a pocket or handbag? Will you use it solely in the car or do you want to carry it around with you as well?

2) Which tariff should you choose, is a much harder question. A tariff is a combination of the monthly rental for the line and the cost of individual calls. If you only want to use your phone in an emergency, then the lowest monthly rental with higher call charges is best for you; if you make all your calls in

London, there are special tariffs designed for use inside the M25.

To help you choose the right tariff, we'll need to know how often you'll make calls, where you're most likely to be when you make them and whether they're more likely to be during the day, at night or weekends.

Ford Cellular can connect you to either of the major companies in the market, Cellnet or Vodafone, so our advice is impartial.

GSM digital or ETACS analogue? - what does it mean?

Most of the mobile phones in Britain today use analogue technology. GSM (Global System for Mobile Communications) is an alternative system which uses digital technology. It has been adopted as an international standard and will replace analogue eventually.

You can already make and receive calls in several European countries on the GSM network. So, if you want the latest technology, with total security, and the ability ultimately to use the same phone almost anywhere in the world, then you should consider GSM.

Currently analogue phones tend to be lighter and less expensive than GSM, and new products and new tariffs continue to make them attractive.

For help, advice and good quality phones at value for money prices, see your local Ford Dealer or phone Ford Cellular Systems on **0800 52 66 57.**

CELLULAR SYSTEMS

England

Abbotsbury   Flower Bowl

Tel 0305 871336	Tea Room
Market Street Abbotsbury Dorset	**Map 13 F2**

Unpretentious tea room found behind the local craft shop where you can enjoy cream tea with home-baked scones (£2.40), ploughman's, sandwiches or home-made soup. In summer sit in the garden, which offers a view of Abbotsbury's 15th-century chapel. One high-chair. Children will be kept amused by a variety of toys made available. *Seats 24.* **Open** *10-6.* **Closed** *End Oct-2 weeks before Easter. No credit cards.*

Alfriston   Toucans Restaurant at Drusillas Zoo

Tel 0323 870234	Restaurant
Drusillas Park Alfriston East Sussex BN26 5QS	**Map 11 B6**

One mile north of the Brighton-Eastbourne road, Drusillas Zoo continues to attract hordes of families and it is rewarding to see them so well catered for when the little ones get hungry. Our 1991 Family Restaurant of the Year has a play corner, designed to combat the long stretches of boredom that visit children at mealtimes, and is always well used. There are bright plastic tablecloths, ample room for prams and push-chairs, excellent nursing and changing areas, high-chairs galore; every facility is provided. The staff are young, friendly and attentive and deliver maximum portions of food, usually with a minimum wait. Baby meals can be ordered, bottles heated and jars warmed. The 'Little Monkeys' menu offers the usual array of children's favourites, from spaghetti bolognese to fish fingers and chips. A roast is offered on Sunday, along with children's entertainment. No smoking; no dogs. The *Inn at the Zoo* next door caters well for adults (from 10-5), offering a short menu of typical pub food and teas. Free car parking. **Open** *weekends and school holidays 10-6 (March-Oct to 5). Zoo open every day (10am-5pm in winter) except 25 & 26 Dec; under-3s free, 3-13s £4.20 inc train and playland (adults £4.80).* **Closed** *Dec 25 & 26. Access, Amex, Visa.*

Allendale   Bishop Field   59%   £76

Tel 0434 683248 Fax 0434 683830	Hotel
Whitfield Road Allendale nr Hexham Northumberland NE47 9EJ	**Map 5 D2**

A mile out of Allendale on the Whitfield road, this former farmhouse was converted in 1985 by Kathy and Keith Fairless and is now run by them with their daughter Bridget, who is also the chef. There's a cheerful, relaxed atmosphere in the lounges, one of which has a cocktail bar; the other is non-smoking. Bedrooms are comfortable and rather pretty, light colour schemes contrasting well with dark-stained furniture. Children are very welcome and although there are not a lot of facilities for them (except a high-chair), the friendly attitude of owners and staff goes a long way to making a family stay a happy one. One of the pretty bedrooms has three extra beds and a cot, and all rooms have neatly-fitted bathrooms (some with shower only). High tea is available or small portions in the dining room; supper trays available. Baby-sitting can be arranged. Children up to 10 stay free in parents' room. **Rooms** *11. Garden, game fishing, shooting. Closed Feb & Mar. Access, Visa.*

Alnmouth   Village Gift and Coffee Shop

Tel 0665 830310	Coffee Shop

**West Tower 58 Northumberland St Alnmouth Northumberland
NE66 2RS**   Map 5 E2

The building dates back to the 1750s and was formerly a Customs
Post Office. The entrance is via a tiny, covered, paved courtyard into
a shop also selling souvenirs, mostly food-based (fudge, biscuits,
preserves). A good menu features some local seafood, especially crab,
served in a salad with pears and walnuts (£2.50), or as part of a lunch
platter alongside smoked mackerel and prawns (£3.95). Cheviot lamb
hotpot, also £3.95 – one of the most expensive items – is ideal on a
cold English summer's day! Equally welcome is a special warmer
of Northumbrian broth (mixed vegetables and pulses), toasted
sandwich (choose from the usual cheese-based range), cup of tea
or coffee, £2.95 the lot. Sweet things are also mostly home-made.
Afternoon tea offers excellent value. Ice cream specials (including
children's at £1) from a soft-freeze dispenser. Some children's specials;
booster seats and beakers. Unlicensed. No smoking. *Seats 33.*
Open 9.30-6.30. *Closed* Mon (*winter only, also some Tues/Wed
in bad weather*). 25 & 26 Dec, 1 Jan. *Access, Visa.*

Alphington   Double Locks

Tel 0392 56947	Pub

Alphington Exeter Devon EX2 6CT   Map 13 D2

The Double Locks isn't easy to find but it's well worth the effort. First
find the Marsh Barton Trading Estate and drive through it to the
council incinerator – don't worry, the pub is some way yet – until you
reach the plank canal bridge, which is made for vehicles, although
it may not appear to be. Once across, turn right, and a single-track
road will bring you to the red-brick Georgian Double Locks in a
splendid canalside location within sight of the Cathedral. Equally
popular with business people and students, this is the perfect summer
pub: there are swans on the canal next to the eponymous lock, a large
garden shaded by huge pine trees, and a barbecue both lunchtime and
evening in summer, weather permitting. There's even a small marquee
in which to shelter from errant showers. Inside is very informal.
Several rooms have black and white tiled floors, draw-leaf domestic
dining-room tables and lots of posters advertising local events – not far
removed from a student bar at University. Chess, draughts, Monopoly,
Scrabble and bar billiards are all keenly played. A huge blackboard
displays the day's offerings, featuring almost as many options for
vegetarians as for carnivores. Start with mushroom and coriander soup
(£1.40), garlic mushrooms and Stilton on toast (£3.40) or a selection
of garlic breads with Cheddar, Stilton or goat's cheese topping (£1.25-
£2.65), followed perhaps by turkey and mushroom pie (£3.30),
lasagne (£3.30), baked potatoes with a variety of toppings (ranging
from £1.25-£3.80) or vegetarian and meat crepes (£3.85). Late
breakfasts here mean a traditional fry-up, either meat or vegetarian,
plus a pint of the beer of your choice at the all-in price of £4. There
is no special children's menu but most things also come in smaller
portions at smaller prces, and several rooms can be used by families,
who are made genuinely welcome. *Bar Food 11-10.30* (*Mon-Sat*),
12-2, 7-10 (*Sun*). *Free House.* *Beer Adnams Broadside, Greene King
Abbot Ale, Marston's Pedigree.* *Riverside garden, outdoor play area, outdoor
eating, summer barbecue. Family room. No credit cards.*

Altrincham   Francs

| Tel 061-941 3954 | Bistro |

2 Goose Green Altrincham Cheshire   Map 6 B2

A French-style bistro in the heart of Altrincham offering a wide
selection of grills, crepes, fish, vegetable and casserole dishes from
a daily-changing menu. A special barbecue menu is on offer for parties
of four or more (up to 60!) – £11.85 a head. There is also a selection
of vegetarian dishes ranging from *omelette maison* (a light herb
omelette with peppers, onion, tomato and cheese £3.75)
to *champignons Bovary* (garlic sautéed mushrooms baked with Brie
and a cheese and parsley sauce £3.25). Pleasant outdoor eating terrace.
Sister restaurant in Chester. **Seats** 85. **Open** 12-3 & 6-10.30 (Sat to 11,
Sun 12-5). **Closed** Bank Holidays. Access, Amex, Diners, Visa.

Altrincham   The French Brasserie

| Tel 061-928 0808 | Brasserie |

24 The Downs Altrincham Cheshire   Map 6 B2

A large bar-brasserie with Provençal-style French cooking; on the
opposite side of the road to the more expensive sister restaurant *The
French*. Typical dishes include wild mushrooms with garlic, parsley
and artichoke (£3.50) or light fish paté with cream and herbs (£2.95)
and main courses like chicken with sherry, tarragon and mushrooms
or lamb with white beans and herbs both at £6.50. For dessert choose
from crème brulée, tarte aux pommes, or mousse au chocolat (£2.50).
Children under 10 eat free Sunday lunchtime and for adults three
courses cost £6.95. Live jazz Wed-Sun eves. **Seats** 160. **Open** 12-12
(*Thur-Sat till 2am*). **Closed** D 25 Dec. Access, Visa.

Alveley   Mill Hotel   72%   £55

| Tel 0746 780437   Fax 0746 780850 | Hotel |

Birdsgreen Alveley nr Bridgnorth Shropshire WV15 6HL   Map 6 B4

From the starting point of a 16th-century mill, whose workings can
still be seen in the pubby public bar, Franco D'Aniello has created
a fine hotel with unusually spacious public areas that include a large,
comfortably furnished lounge and roomy cocktail bar. Beautifully
landscaped grounds provide plenty of photo opportunities – lake, rustic
bridge, gazebo – making this a popular venue for weddings; there are
also a number of well-planned function rooms. Upstairs, dado-panelled
corridors are broad, and well-appointed bedrooms generally large
with freestanding furniture, pleasing fabrics and phones at both desk
and bedside. Superior rooms are particularly large and have either
four-posters or elaborate bedhead drapes plus sofas and armchairs.
Good bathrooms, with either corner or alcoved tubs, boast large bath
sheets, mostly good shelf space, and often have twin basins; five have
separate shower cubicles. A well-run hotel with notable friendly staf,
24hr rooms service and turn-down service in the evenings. Five suites
can be created for families and most rooms can accommodate a cot
(£8) or extra bed (£14.50); baby-listening facilities and baby-sitting
can be arranged. There is no children's menu but high-chairs are
provided and the kitchen will always try to provide whatever
is required. No dogs. **Rooms** 21. Garden. Access, Amex, Diners, Visa.

Ambleside   Rothay Manor Hotel

Tel 053 94 33605	Hotel Lounge
Rothay Bridge Ambleside Cumbria	Map 4 C3

Just two minutes from the centre of Ambleside, Rothay Manor sits
in timeless elegance in a beautiful garden next to Rothay Bridge.
Coffee and home-made biscuits (£1.40) are available until noon when
the buffet lunch (£6-£11) is served in two lounges (one non-
smoking): quiches (leek and almond, broccoli and Stilton), cold home-
cooked ham, pork, lamb, beef, pheasant (or alternative game bird) and
chicken plus 5-6 different salads feature every day. Sunday sees
a traditional roast lunch (3 courses £14) in the restaurant. Tea, also
in the form of a buffet (£6.50), offers sandwiches, vol-au-vents, pork
pies, cakes, scones and jams. Two high-chairs provided. *Seats 50.*
Open 12.30-2 & 3.30-5.30. *Closed* 2 Jan-mid Feb. Access, Amex,
Diners, Visa.

Ambleside   Zeffirellis

Tel 053 94 33845	Café/Pizzeria
Compston Road Ambleside Cumbria	Map 4 C3

Zeffirellis is an unusual complex comprising a shopping arcade,
a cinema, a pizzeria done out in Japanese Art Deco style and a leafy
café. The pizzeria is open in the evenings only (except at weekends)
and is situated above the café. The pizzas have wheatmeal bases rolled
in sesame seeds, and vegetarian toppings; they come in two sizes (plus
one for children), and two different styles, one mozzarella and one
mozzarella and Cheddar (toppings at 40p or three for £1). You can
also get pasta (from £5.65) and desserts. In the café, sweet snacks
(fudge brownies, banana cake, Linzertorte – £1.45) as well as savoury
(soup £1.65, jacket potatoes, salads, quiches, and a dish of the day
at lunchtime – broccoli and Stilton pancakes with sweet and sour
relish, or hazelnut roast £3.85) are available. Scones and jam are
provided at tea time. Children's portions. No smoking. *Seats 80*
(Pizzeria) 50 *(Café).* *Open* Pizzeria: L (Sat & Sun only) 12-2 & 5-9.45.
Café: 10-5. *Closed* Pizzeria: Tue & Wed Nov-Mar. Pizzeria and Café:
25 & 26 Dec. Access, Visa (Pizzeria only).

Ashbourne   Ashbourne Gingerbread Shop

Tel 0335 343227	Coffee Shop
St John Street Ashbourne Derbyshire	Map 6 C3

Gingerbread men (65p plain, 75p chocolate) head the parade of home
baking at a characterful old coffee shop which has been in the same
family ownership since Victoria was on the throne. Staunch support
is provided by scones and teacakes, ginger slab cake (50p) and biscuits,
fresh cream cakes and hot Bakewell tarts and puddings. Small no-
smoking area. *Seats 45. Open* 8-5.30. *Closed* 25 & 26 Dec.
No credit cards.

Ashbourne   Ashbourne Lodge Hotel   66%   £69

Tel 0335 46666 Fax 0335 46549	Hotel
Derby Road Ashbourne Derbyshire DE6 1XH	Map 6 C3

On the A52 from Derby to Leek, this modern redbrick hotel
(previously the Ashbourne Oaks) is lent some old-world style
by rustic-designed public areas. Bedrooms are neat and light but not
over-large, although twelve are suitable for families; five suites have

interconnecting rooms. Cots are provided and baby-sitting can be arranged. Children under five are accommodated free in parents' room. There's a playroom in which children can work up an appetite for the children's menu in the all-day brasserie (The Black Sheep); four high-chairs are provided. No dogs. Convenient for Alton Towers and the American Adventure Theme Park. New owners since last year's Guide. *Rooms 50. Garden. Access, Amex, Visa.*

Ashby St Ledgers   Olde Coach House Inn

Tel 0788 890349	Pub

Ashby St Ledgers nr Rugby Warwickshire CV23 8UN   Map 15 D1

3 miles from Junction 18 of the M1, Ashby St Ledgers is a tiny protected village full of thatched houses and cottages clustered around the manor and 12th-century church, and has a population of just one hundred. An imposing rather than handsome ivy-clad exterior of the Olde Coach House Inn is today mostly reminiscent of the estate farmhouse it once was. Peering through the bow windows, you'll see a rather austere snug bar to one side and a sparsely furnished pool room to the other. But this frontage is very deceptive. Behind these is a cavernous structure incorporating small alcoves, huge log fires and oak beams, which progress past the main interior bar and food buffet to an elevated, beamed dining area beyond and, to the rear, a flat-roofed function and meeting room. Part of the adjoining old stables once housed the village post office, and today the stable yard makes a safe, enclosed area for bored youngsters to explore – as often as not with the McCabe children as resident playmates. Although a new chef arrived as we went to press, the food operation is not expected to change. Cold roast meats, salads, whole Stilton and Brie cheeses are displayed on the buffet, while daily kitchen specials like leek and potato soup (£1.95), rack of lamb glazed with honey and herbs (£7.95), rump au poivre (£8.95), pasta pepperonata (£5.95), a coachman's (2 venison sausages, Stilton and French bread £4.95) or pork Topper (pork chop topped with paté and melted Brie £6.75). A local lady makes several of the puddings such as gingerman cake or banoffi pie (both £2.15). Diverse fishes and cuts of meat are laid out by the nearby patio barbecue, cooked to order and brought out to diners at tables in the garden – quite the most popular of the Coach House's summer attractions. A sense of fun is imbued by the resident landlords, Brian and Philippa McCabe, and their staff, who go out of their way to make visitors welcome. *Open noon-11 Sat, regular hours other days. Bar Food 12-2, 6-9.30 (Sun 7-9). Children's menu. Free House. Beer Boddingtons, Everards Old Original, Flowers Original, IPA, Jennings Cumberland, Morrells, Thwaites, guest beer. Garden, outdoor eating, summer barbecue. Family room. Accommodation 6 bedrooms, all en suite, from £46 (single £39). Children welcome overnight, additional beds and cots available. Access, Amex, Visa.*

Ashford-in-the-Water   The Cottage Tea Room

Tel 0629 812488	Tea Room

3 Fennel Street Ashford-in-the-Water nr Bakewell Derbyshire   Map 6 C2

Everything is home-made in Betty and Bill Watkins' tea shop – brown bread, currant bread, sultana and cheesy herb scones, preserves and cakes. Five different set teas are served on Mondays, Wednesdays, Thursdays and weekends only: Afternoon Tea (£3.50), Derbyshire Cream Tea (£3.25), Tea with Hovis (£2.75), Savoury Scone Tea

($2.60) and Something Light ($2). There's also a choice of leaf teas, herbal infusions and coffees. Coffee and light refreshments are served weekend mornings. Children's drinks and portions available. Special cakes, preserves and low fat items are always provided for customers with diabetic or cardiac problems. Mums should ask to use the owners' private sitting room if they need privacy to nurse or change baby. Children's play area at top of Fennel Street by car park. Feeding the ducks on the river is very popular with youngsters. No smoking.
Seats 20. *Open* 2.30-5, also Sat & Sun only 10.30am-noon.
Closed Tue, Fri, 25 Dec, 1 Jan, 1 week mid Sept.

Ashprington   Waterman's Arms
Tel 0803 732214	Pub
Bow Bridge Ashprington nr Totnes Devon TQ9 7EG	Map 13 D3

Delightfully situated on the banks of the River Harbourne, at the top of Bow Creek, the Waterman's is a favourite summer venue for alfresco riverside imbibing with resident ducks and – if you are lucky – kingfishers to keep you company. Acquired two years ago by enthusiastic owners Phoebe and Trevor Illingworth, it has been transformed from the original small cottage into an efficiently-run and friendly inn with quality overnight accommodation. 'Tardis'-like inside, a series of neatly furnished rooms radiates away from the central servery, all filled with a mix of rustic furniture, old photographs, brass artefacts and other memorabilia. Home-cooked bar food caters for all tastes, from hearty snacks to regular menu favourites like steak and kidney pie ($5.95), rack of Devon lamb ($7.95) and steaks (from $8.95). Fresh authentic pasta dishes and a few Thai dishes represent the more unusual and there's a daily-changing blackboard of specials and puddings. Ten beautifully fitted-out bedrooms have floral, cottagey fabrics and co-ordinating friezes around the walls, attractive dark-stained modern furniture and spotlessly-kept bathrooms with shower cubicles and efficient, thermostatically-controlled showers. Added comforts include telephone, cabinet-housed TV and tea-making facilities. The front rooms overlook the river and surrounding valley sides. Good breakfasts include a selection of fruits and a cooked menu choice that features smoked haddock and kippers. High-chairs provided. *Open* 11-11 *(Sun 12-3 & 7-10.30). Free House.*
Bar Food 12-2.30 & 6.30-9.30 *(Sun 7-9.30).* **Beer** *Dartmoor Best, Palmers IPA, Tetley Bitter. Garden, outdoor eating. Family Room.*
Accommodation 10 bedrooms, all en suite, $53-$57 (single $28.50). Cots and extra beds provided; under-5s free, 5-10s 50%, 11-14s 75% of tariff. Access, Visa.

Ashstead   Superfish
Tel 0372 273 784	Fish'n'Chips
2-4 Woodfield Lane Ashstead Surrey	Map 15 E3

Part of a Surrey-based chain serving above average fish and chips "fried in the traditional Yorkshire way". See Morden entry for more details. High-chairs; fish bites with chips ($2.20) for children.
Seats 56. *Open* 11.30-2 *(Sat to 2.30),* 5-10.30 *(Thu-Sat to 11).*
Closed Sun, 25 & 26 Dec, 1 Jan. No credit cards.

Ashurst   Manor Court Hotel

Tel 0892 740279	Afternoon Tea
Ashurst nr Kent	**Map 11 B5**

Just east of Ashurst on the A264, this pretty tile-hung Georgian
farmhouse is just the spot for afternoon tea on a summer's day. There's
a room indoors, but the garden is the place to be, with its rustic tables
and chairs, a friendly golden retriever and numerous chickens pecking
around. There are lots of lambs to be seen in spring and many
footpaths, including the Wealdan Way, cross the 350 acres of this
working farm that includes woodlands and extends to the River
Medway. Foodwise, the offerings are simple but excellent, cream teas
(£2.95) with delicious scones straight out of the Aga and home-made
jam from a neighbouring farm, a couple of home-made cakes (£1.25)
like chocolate or date and walnut, plus toasted teacakes and cheese and
chive scone (both 75p). Children (and dogs) are most welcome. There
is one high-chair and a bedroom or somewhere private will be found
for nursing mothers and changing baby. B&B accommodation offered
(not inspected). *Seats 25.* *Open 2pm-6pm.* *Closed October-Easter.*
No credit cards.

Avebury   Stones

Tel 067 23 514	Vegetarian
Avebury nr Marlborough Wiltshire	**Map 14 C2**

Still at the forefront of vegetarian cooking with an unstinting mission
to improve the quality of the lives of those who visit, work for, and
supply produce to this exemplary operation. Small local organic
producers are nurtured, herbs and salads come from their own garden
and staff are valued as much as customers. Hilary Howard and Michael
Pitts have created their own monument to which the faithful flock
at this World Heritage site, often serving over 1000 customers a day
from spotless self-service counters in a gentle, civilised atmosphere. All-
day offerings include various home-made light savouries, quiches,
salads (all £2.25), hand-made English and Welsh cheeses with own-
baked breads and crackers and local unsalted butter (£2.25), ginger
people (45p), world-famous date slice (95p) and fruit salad (£2.10).
Noontime choice widens to include delectable inventive soups with
specially baked bread (£2.50), Megaliths, or hot daily specials (£4.75),
the Mason's Lunch, a definitive ploughman's (£3.50) and various hot
and cold desserts (£2). The inimitable afternoon tea (£2.95) is served
from 2.30. No-smoking area. Three high-chairs; changing shelf in the
Ladies. No bookings (except for parties of 6 or more). *Seats 80.*
Open 10-6 (Sat & Sun only Nov-Dec & Feb-Easter 10-5). Closed Jan.
No credit cards.

Bakewell   Chatsworth House,
                   Carriage House Restaurant

Tel 0246 582204	Restaurant
Nr Bakewell Derbyshire	**Map 6 C2**

Behind the great House stands the old carriage house with courtyard
and fountain. The high-ceilinged room has impressive hanging lights
and is decorated with large pictures of the estate; the original arches
have been filled in with plate glass. The 50ft pine self-service counter
displays the food on refrigerated shelves and uniformed staff are
friendly and efficient. Amongst the choice are soup of the day (£1.15),

assorted salads (from £2.90), cottage pie (£3.95), scones and cakes (75p-£1.25), gateaux and treacle tart (from £1.20 to £1.45) and various ice creams (£1.95). There's a roast every Sunday (£4.15) and children's portions are available. Four high-chairs are supplied, baby food is available and mums can change a nappy or breast-feed in a separate room in the Ladies. Visitors to the estate are not obliged to visit the main house in order to eat at the Restaurant, but a £1 car park fee is charged. No smoking area. *Seats 250. **Open** 10.15-5.30. **Closed*** Nov-mid March. *Access, Amex, Visa.*

Baldwin's Gate   Slater's

Tel 0782 680052 Fax 0782 680219	Pub
Maerfield Gate Farm Baldwin's Gate Newcastle under Lyme Staffordshire ST5 5ED	Map 6 B3

Skilful conversion of former outbuildings on a working farm (they still have a 100-head milking herd) has created a stylish new accommodation pub with super facilities for youngsters. In addition to the family room (complete with nappy changing facility in an adjacent ladies' loo) there's a safe, enclosed rear garden full of play equipment (including an abandoned old tractor) and a pair of ducks and geese to talk to. The grown-ups may make time for a game of bowls on the crown green lawn. Set around a cobbled courtyard behind the pub proper, six self-contained cottagey suites contain just about everything for short or long stays: en-suite bathrooms with over-bath showers, fitted kitchenettes and breakfast area, plus extra beds and cots at no extra charge. Breakfast in the dining room if residents prefer: children's meals in pub or garden (all day on Sunday). Bar meals and restaurant (book for Sunday) offer little out of the ordinary. Recommended for B&B only. *Free House.* ***Beer*** *Banks, Boddingtons, Marston's Pedigree. Garden, children's play area.* ***Accommodation*** *6 bedrooms, all en suite, £40 (single £30). Children welcome overnight, additional beds and cots available. Access, Visa.*

Barking   Colonel Jasper's

Tel 081-507 8481	Wine Bar
156 Longbridge Road Barking Essex	Map 11 B4

Hard by Barking Station, below the *Spotted Dog*, this is one of Davy's old ale, port and wine houses, with mahogany furniture, a sawdust-covered floor and candle-light. Specialities are cod, chips and mushy peas, Cumberland sausages with mash and baked beans (£3.50, £4.95) and charcoal grills. Sunday lunch comprises three courses and coffee (£8.95-£11.95). Children's menu. *Seats 100. **Open** 12-3.30 & 5.30-11. **Closed*** L Sat, D Sun-Wed, Bank Holidays. *Access, Amex, Diners, Visa.*

Barnard Castle   Market Place Teashop

Tel 0833 690110	Tea Room
29 Market Place Barnard Castle Co Durham	Map 5 D3

Full of atmosphere and character, this stone-flagged tea room with antique furniture offers much to tempt with good-quality home baking, and a very reasonably priced wine list. Carrot and courgette bake (£2), steak pie (£2.95), quiche and salad (£2.70), sticky toffee pudding and bilberry and apple pie (both £1.85) provide a flavour of what to expect. Children's portions. *Seats 45. **Open** 10-5.30 (Sun from 3). **Closed*** Sun Dec-Feb, 10 days Christmas. *No credit cards.*

Barnard Castle   Priors Restaurant

Tel 0833 38141	Restaurant
7 The Bank Barnard Castle Co Durham	**Map 5 D3**

With tastes to tempt even the most hardened carnivore, Mark Prior's
vegetarian counter-service restaurant and take-away continues to draw
converts and the faithful alike. A blackboard menu might include two
or three soups (spinach and courgette or cauliflower £1), aubergine,
tomato and yoghurt bake (£2.75), sweet and sour courgette and brazil
nut croustade (£2.75) or chick pea and apricot casserole (£2.65), with
blackberry crisp (£1.25) or treacle tart (£1.35) to finish. There's
always a variety of interesting salads (£1) and sandwiches as well
as cakes and tarts – perhaps pecan pie or curd tart (both £1.50).
A few tables outside in fine weather. Good organic wines and beers.
Young families very welcome, children's menu available. High-chair,
cushions, potty and changing mat are all provided. No smoking
throughout. **Seats** 50. **Open** 10-5 (Sat to 5.30, Sun 12-5.30).
Closed 25 & 26 Dec, 1 Jan. Access, Amex, Diners, Visa.

Baslow   Cavendish Hotel, Garden Room

Tel 0246 582311	Bistro
Baslow Derbyshire DE45 1SP	**Map 6 C2**

Set on the Duke and Duchess of Devonshire's Chatsworth Estate, the
building housing the Cavendish Hotel was rebuilt in the early 1970s.
Its original character was retained however and the Duchess selected
the decor and furnishings, some of which came from Chatsworth
House itself. Panoramic views from the Garden Room's conservatory
windows provide the backdrop and the comfortable bistro chairs,
yellow tablecloths, fresh flowers and gentle classical music set the
stage. From mid-morning, chef Nick Buckingham serves 'The Late
Breakfast', followed by lunch, afternoon tea and finally supper. Food
is served in a less formal and more relaxed atmosphere than in the
main restaurant: brown onion soup with toasted cheese bagels
(£4.50), bangers and mash (£8.50), fresh strawberry meringue with
whipped cream (£3.25). Tea offers finger sandwiches (£2 per round),
home-made scones or toasted teacakes (£2.10) and a choice of cake.
In summer guests can eat on the lawn where children are kept busy
with mini-golf and swings. One high-chair; a private area can
be provided on request for nursing or changing baby. **Seats** 32.
Open 11-11. Access, Amex, Diners, Visa.

Baslow   Derbyshire Craft Centre Eating House

Tel 0433 631583	Restaurant
Calver Bridge Baslow Derbyshire	**Map 6 C2**

Craft centre alongside the A623 north-west of Baslow. Paintings of the
Dales and Derbyshire's stately homes hang on the walls. Cakes, tarts
and pies are available throughout the day (lemon meringue pie £1,
Bakewell 95p), while savoury choices include chicken liver paté
(£2.95), nut loaf, pasta bake and quiche (all £4 with a good selection
of salads). There's a play room well stocked with toys. No smoking.
Seats 40. **Open** 10-5.30. **Closed** 25 & 26 Dec, 1 Jan. No credit cards.

Batcombe   The Batcombe Inn

Tel 0749 850359	Pub

Batcombe nr Shepton Mallet Somerset BW4 6HE   Map 13 F1

Tucked away down a web of country lanes in the very rural
Batcombe Vale, this old honey-coloured stone coaching inn
(previously known as the Three Horse Shoes) enjoys a peaceful
position away from the main village, next to the village church. "It's
not difficult to find. . . it's damned near impossible" they admit, but
grid reference 36902 13906 (Lat 51° 39′ 06 N Long 03° 69′ 02 W)
should get you to the front door! Having seen some uncertain times,
the inn has been in the extremely capable hands of Derek and Claire
Blezard (who created the highly successful *Royal Oak* at Over Stratton
near Yeovil) since February last year, and it is clearly evident that the
same formula is being injected with enthusiasm here. The long and
low-ceilinged main bar has exposed stripped beams and is warmly and
tastefully decorated; terracotta sponged walls with ivy leaf stencilling
are hung with several old paintings, creating a relaxed and homely
atmosphere. A mix of individual chairs, deep window seats and
darkwood furniture fronts a huge stone inglenook with log fire.
Adjoining the bar is a newly refurbished dining area, in what used
to be the old barn and toll-house. Bar food is reliably good with
blackboards listing daily-changing specials that might include home-
made soups (£1.95), fresh sardines (£4.25), chili (£5.25), plaice fillets
and a vegetarian dish. The printed menu is better than most, offering
a range of hearty snacks, starters and main dishes, from smoked
chicken and walnut salad (£3.50) and seafood fettuccine (£8.95)
to fish en papillote (£9.95); all the food is home-made. A children's
'booty box' (£2.75) is a wonderful idea – a small sandwich, fruit slices,
yoghurt, crisps and a chocolate bar, all served in a colourful box that
really makes young children feel special; two high-chairs can
be provided. A traditional 3-course Sunday lunch is offered (£8.95).
A big welcome is made to families: children not only have their own
'Kiddies Corner' menu but they also have their own large room
wonderfully equipped with chairs, mini-trampoline, doll's house,
drawing board, books, toys and video recorder with National
Geographic films – enough to pacify any child while relaxed parents
enjoy their meal. For fine weather, children's facilities extend to the
small rear garden, overlooked by the church. If ever there was a pub
worth a detour for families, this is it. **Bar Food** 12-2, 7-10 (to
9.30 Sun). Free House. **Beer** Butcombe, Wadworth 6X, guest beers.
Garden, children's play area. Family room. Access, Visa.

Bath   Bath Puppet Theatre

Tel 0225 480532	Coffee Shop

Riverside Walk Pulteney Bridge Bath Avon   Map 13 F1

Puppeteer-owner Andrew Hume also turns his hand to a variety
of wholesome vegetarian snacks in his coffee shop-cum-puppet
theatre – large ploughman's (£3.70), baked potato with filling (£2),
quiches, pizzas, toasted sandwiches (£2.25), all served with fruit and
salad. Home-made cakes feature scones (in summer), coffee and walnut
cake, chocolate cake, date slice, shortbread (75p-£1.30). There are
daily performances at different times (usually block booked) and since
everything takes place in the same room, visitors are likely to catch
a performance while eating. Children's portions are available, and
on a fine day there's outdoor eating on the terrace overlooking the

river. Good value. Fun atmosphere. Two high-chairs; children's parties
with puppet show; "no space" for changing. No smoking. *Seats 40.*
Open 9.30-5.30 (Summer to 7). Closed 25 & 26 Dec. No credit cards.

Bath	Bath Spa Hotel	87%	£183

Tel 0225 444424 Fax 0225 444006	Hotel

Sydney Road Bath Avon BA2 6JF	Map 13 F1

Without doubt one of Forte's finest hotels with surroundings,
furnishings, a splendid health and leisure spa, and service to match.
Carefully restored and extended, the Georgian mansion stands
in landscaped grounds (visit the grotto at the bottom of the gardens)
and has panoramic views over the city, a ten-minute stroll away.
Behind the elegant porticoed frontage is a good deal of style and
luxury, complemented by super staff. A spacious entrance lobby with
Oriental carpets sets the tone of public areas which include a gracious
drawing room, the neo-classical Colonnade with murals and greenery,
and a clubby bar. Bedrooms (many of which are non-smoking),
including seven suites, are individually decorated in great style with
a striking combination of check fabrics and floral prints; they offer
a high degree of comfort, matched by well-designed bathrooms
in Grecian marble and mahogany, with padded towel seating,
bathrobes and Penhaligon toiletries. Cots, connecting rooms, qualified
baby-sitting (not listening), high-chairs – almost everything you need
for baby or a young family can be supplied; "do not be afraid to ask"
for anything that is not immediately obvious – but do state your
requests when booking. A state-registered nursery (for 16 children,
8.30-6 weekdays, 10-5 Sat, to 4 Sun) has recently been opened in the
grounds; operated by the hotel for 2- to 9-year-olds, it is shared with
non-residents during the week but is exclusive for residents
at weekends and bank holidays. High tea is served from 6-7pm
at weekends in the dining room (or via room service). Extensive 24hr
room service, ample own parking. Dogs (basket and bowls provided)
are welcome: their owners can be accommodated on the ground floor
with easy access to the grounds at the end of the corridor. The Bath
Spa is an adult retreat that caters admirably for youngsters – their
future customers, hopefully. Forte Grand. The hotel is half an hour's
drive from Longleat Safari Park; children may also enjoy visiting the
Cheddar Caves or the *SS Great Britain* and zoo in Bristol. *Rooms 100.*
Garden, indoor swimming pool, gymnasium, sauna, spa bath, solarium,
beauty salon, tennis, valeting, coffee shop (7am-6pm). Access, Amex,
Diners, Visa.

Vellore Restaurant   £90

The original ballroom makes a fine setting in which to enjoy new chef
Jonathan Fraser's excellent cooking. His menus use the best local and
British produce, offering simple but quite robust dishes with style,
variety and a high degree of skilful preparation, as well as pleasing
presentation. The comprehensive wine list has some particularly good
New World wines. Lunches and informal dinners are served in the
Alfresco (Colonnade), with honeyed woodstrip flooring, cane chairs
and picture windows overlooking a patio garden with fountain.
Seasonal dishes with an eclectic cooking style – you can have just
a starter and dessert, or the full three courses. *Seats 100. Parties 8.*
Private Room 120. L (Sun only) 12.30-2 D 7-10; Alfresco 12.30-2 &
6.30-9.30 Set D £34.

Bath   Beaujolais

Tel 0225 423417	Wine Bar/Restaurant
5 Chapel Row Bath Avon	**Map 13 F1**

Philippe Wall and Jean-Pierre Augé run a popular wine bar/restaurant serving French food. A conservatory area and the sunny, secluded small courtyard are popular in summer. The naughty postcards and exotic art that adorn the walls are described by the owners as "wonderfully decadent". The weekly-changing menu offers imaginative dishes – smoked goat's cheese mousse on a red pepper coulis (£3.50), *fromage de tete* (coarse pork terrine set in jelly £3.50), followed by smoked pork cutlet with spicy fruit sauce (£7.90), cheese omelette (£4.80) or pan-fried fillet of red mullet (£8.20), and apricot cheesecake, marbled chocolate terrine and apple crepe for dessert (all £3). The three-course set lunch (£9) could include cream of spinach soup, roast lamb with garlic and fresh herbs, with *chocolat St Emilion* to finish. Children's menu on Saturday lunchtimes (£3.50). **Seats** 70. **Open** 12-2 & 6-10.30 (Fri & Sat 7-11). **Closed** *L Sun, 4 days Christmas, first 2 weeks Jan. Access, Amex, Visa.*

Bath   Café René

Tel 0225 447147	Restaurant
Unit 2 Shires Yard Milsom Street Bath Avon	**Map 13 F1**

Situated in the trendy Shires Yard (former livery stables) alongside small designer shops, Café René is run by an Englishman but everything else about it aspires to be French. The café has its own bakery and patisserie which supplies croissants, brioches, pains au chocolat and traditional French cakes – religieuse, millefeuille (both £1.50) and tartelettes. Continental breakfast (£2.95) is available from 8am and the self-service lunch offers light meals (filled potatoes from £2.95) as well as four hot specials daily: vegetable lasagne (£3.85), broccoli bake (£3.85), fisherman's pie (£4), chicken breast provençal (£4) or beef bourguignon (£4). There's a very large courtyard for alfresco eating which is popular in summer *and* winter. **Seats** 60 (*inside*) 100 (*outside*). **Open** 8-6 (*Thu, Fri, Sat to 6.30, summer only*). **Closed** *Sun (winter only), 25 & 26 Dec. No credit cards.*

Bath   The Canary

Tel 0225 424846	Café
3 Queen Street Bath Avon	**Map 13 F1**

Set in one of Bath's earliest Georgian cobbled streets, The Canary is well worth a stop-off for breakfast (full English £6.75, Continental £3.25) or indivdual dishes such as eggs Benedict (£3.75) or afternoon tea (clotted cream tea £3.25 or the 25th Anniversary Tea £6.75 – minimum two persons). The display of cakes and pastries is matched by a truly remarkable range (50) of Ceylon, Indian, China, fruit and herbal loose-leaf teas. They also serve filled bagels, sandwiches (from £2.10) and various light dishes, appetisers and puddings throughout the day. Children's portions. Traditional Sunday lunch Sep-May £9.95 (three courses). No-smoking area. **Seats** 75. **Open** 9-7 (*Sun 11-5.30*). **Closed** *25 & 26 Dec, 1 Jan. Access, Visa.*

Bath   Fountain House   £120

| Tel 0225 338622   Fax 0225 445855 | Hotel |

9/11 Fountain Buildings Lansdown Road Bath Avon BA1 5DV   **Map 13 F1**

An 'all-suite hotel', Fountain House comprises one, two and three
bedroom suites with sitting room and smart, fully-equipped kitchen,
within a Palladian mansion on the northern edge of the city centre.
The idea is that one gets privacy and space with the level of service
(except room service) one would expect of a conventional hotel – full
maid service with fresh bed linen each day for example. Unfussy decor
and good-quality furnishings are immaculately maintained. A basket
of fresh bread, milk, yoghurt etc and a daily newspaper are delivered
to the door each morning. Reception staff can organise most things
from car hire and theatre tickets to a personal in-room fax or shooting
on the owners' own 750-acre estate. Unlike in a serviced apartment
there is no minimum stay and indeed many guests stay for just one
night. There are no public rooms. *Suites 14. Access, Amex, Diners, Visa.*

Bath   Green Park Brasserie

| Tel 0225 338565 | Brasserie |

Green Park Road Bath Avon   **Map 13 F1**

With free parking at the adjacent Sainsbury's the glass-arched former
Green Park station contains a colonnade of craft shops and Andrew
Peters' family-friendly brasserie under a single roof. Menus are all-
encompassing from cappuccino to a three-course lunch (£7.95),with
sandwiches, salads, snacks and fresh pasta available all day. Popular for
a snack or starter is the grilled goat's cheese salad (£3.95); follow,
perhaps with a vegetarian tartlet (£6.45) served with French fries
or bubble and squeak. English and Continental breakfast (with
newspapers) and traditional roast lunch fill Sunday to the
accompaniment of live jazz in a careful Victorian recreation of the old
Midland Railways ticket office. No-smoking area. *Seats 100.*
Open 10am-10.30pm (Sun/Mon/Tue to 3.30pm). Access, Amex, Visa.

Bath   Number Five Bistro

| Tel 0225 444499 | Bistro |

5 Argyle Street Bath Avon   **Map 13 F1**

A popular, relaxed bistro near Pulteney Bridge. The lunchtime menu
changes daily, offering the likes of club sandwiches (£4.25), chicken
curry and moules marinière. Wednesday evenings bring fish specials,
and there's always something for vegetarians. The place is licensed, but
on Monday and Tuesday evenings you can alternatively bring your
own wine (no corkage). A selection of British cheeses changes each
week. *Seats 40. Open 12-2.30 & 6.30-10.30 (Sat to 11). Closed L Mon,
all Sun. Access, Visa.*

Bath   Pump Room, Milburns

| Tel 0225 444488 | Restaurant |

Stall Street Bath Avon   **Map 13 F1**

The famous Pump Room was built in the late 18th century and was
the haunt of fashionable folk when they came to take the waters. Now
the tourists are attracted in the same way since the tables overlook the
Roman baths; giant Corinthian columns stand guard all around and
a great chandelier hangs overhead. A trio plays morning and
afternoon, bracketing a lunchtime classical pianist. The food ranges

from Continental breakfast (£3.90) to brunch (£6.75), Georgian
Elevenses (hot chocolate, Bath bun, cinnamon biscuits and spa water),
lunch, snacks and four variations on the afternoon tea theme (clotted
cream tea £4.25, high tea £6.25). The lunchtime menu includes soups
(£2.70), pastas (£6.90), salads (warm trout salad £5.90), open-faced
sandwiches (salami and watercress with straw potatoes £3.75)
or breast of chicken with cream and fennel sauce (£7.90). Visitors are
asked to take either a starter with a side dish or main course
at lunchtimes. Mothers will find a pull-down baby-changing shelf
in the Ladies loo. No-smoking area. **Seats** 96. **Open** 10-5 (*winter to* 4).
Closed 25 & 26 Dec. Access, Visa.

Bath   Sally Lunn's House

Tel 0225 461634	Restaurant
4 North Parade Passage Bath Avon BA1 1NX	Map 13 F1

Sally Lunn's brioche-type Bath bun is an acquired taste; famous since
the 1680s, it's served today in her own 15th-century refreshment
house in any number of ways. Twenty of them listed on the menu
include savoury toasts with scrambled eggs (£3.28) or patum peperium
(£2.18), cold with salads of goat's cheese (£5.28), tuna and egg
(£4.98) or prawns (£5.48), and sweet ones with brandy or cinnamon
butter (£1.98) or strawberry jam and clotted cream (£2.88).
Alongside are soup (£2.08) (when the cook thinks it's cold), apple pie,
carrot or banana cake (£1.85), multifarious beverages and speciality
teas. Alone worth the trip is the basement kitchen museum, open every
day. English candle-light dinners from 6pm Tuesday to Sunday (three-
course £12.85). Two high-chairs and children's portions offered.
No smoking. **Seats** 55. **Open** 10-6. **Closed** 25 & 26 Dec. Access, Visa.

Beeley   Devonshire Arms

Tel 0629 733259 Fax 0629 733887	Pub
Beeley nr Matlock Derbyshire DE4 2NR	Map 6 C2

A handy pub for visitors to Chatsworth and Haddon Hall, its rather
dour exterior hiding a maze of interconnecting rooms of apparently
16th-century origin. A rather incongruous dining extension has
picture windows overlooking the village stream where it disappears
under the pub's apron. Families are made especially welcome with
their own space to spread out in, and little bits of virtually anything
from the long, unadventurous menu are offered for youngsters; sticky
sweets from a buffet for those who finish their dinner. *Free House.*
Beer *Theakston Best & XB, Boddingtons. Terrace. Family room.*
No credit cards.

Belton   Belton Woods Hotel   72%   £115

Tel 0476 593200 Fax 0476 74547	Hotel
Belton nr Grantham Lincolnshire NG32 2LN	Map 7 E3

Just off the A607, north of Grantham, a modern complex standing
in 475 acres of grounds, with outstanding sports facilities that are
matched by equally impressive accommodation. A spacious, high-
ceilinged lounge leading off the main foyer is filled with parlour
plants and hanging baskets, and overlooks one of three golf courses
(two 18-hole and one 9-hole). The cocktail bar on the first floor
is more club-like, with easy chairs and rich decor. Spacious bedrooms
have good seating and working areas; plain painted walls lighten
up the use of contemporary fabrics. Ambassador rooms feature extras
like a mini-bar and settee. Excellent facilities for children include

a children's playground and swimming pool, cots and baby-sitting.
The Plus Fours all-day restaurant should be able to cater for out-of-
hours hunger pangs from the children. Now under the group
ownership of De Vere Hotels who, as we went to press, had plans for
40 further bedrooms and even larger leisure facility areas. *Rooms 96.*
Garden, indoor swimming pool, spa bath, sauna, steam room, solarium,
beauty salon, hairdressing, gymnasium, games room, snooker, golf courses
(9 & 18 hole), golf driving range, fishing, tennis, coffee shop (7am-
10.30pm). Access, Amex, Diners, Visa.

Berkhamsted   Cooks Delight

Tel 0442 863584	Vegetarian
360 High Street Berkhamsted Hertfordshire	**Map 15 E2**

A paradise for vegetarians and vegans, both the ground-floor shop and
the restaurant above. Owners Rex and Khai-Eng Tyler are a mine
of information on matters vegetarian, and lecture dinners are held
regularly. Organic produce is used when available on a menu which
could consist of Buddhist monk soup (mung beans, cashew nuts,
pumpkin and sweet potato £2.95), Malaysian curry with stir-fried
vegetables and brown rice (£7.95) and the famous lemon meringue
pie (£2.95) to finish. Rex Tyler keeps an extensive selection of 90
organic wines and over 80 monastic beers, mostly Belgian.
No smoking. Must book for Saturday nights which run on a theme,
usually Malaysian or Chinese (four-course set dinner at £18.95).
Seats 40. Open 12-4 & 7-9.30 (Sat 9-4 & 8-12, Sun 1-3).
Closed D Sun, all Mon, Tue, Wed, 25 Dec. Access, Visa.

Bibury   Jankowski's Brasserie, The Swan Hotel

Tel 0285 740695	Brasserie
Bibury Gloucestershire	**Map 14 C2**

A surprising find in a pretty Cotswold village, this is a genuine
brasserie (rather smart too) with no minimum charge and a wide-
ranging menu that offers everything from crispy filo pastry with
Cerney goat's cheese (£3.95), Bibury trout sausage (£6.95) and home-
made chicken and mushroom pie (£5.95) to spicy Welsh rarebit
(£2.95), fresh fruit parfaits (£2.95)and toasted tea cakes. The menu
has both children's and vegetarian sections and there's espresso coffee
and a good range of loose-leaf teas. The courtyard, with ornamental
fountain, makes a good spot for alfresco eating. Friendly, obliging staff
and two high-chairs add the final touch. *Seats 60. Open 10-10.*
Closed 1 week Christmas. Access, Visa.

Biddenden   Claris's

Tel 0580 291025	Tea Shop
High Street Biddenden Kent	**Map 11 C5**

The Grade I listed building dating back to 1450 that houses Claris's
Tea Shop was formerly part of a long row of weavers' cottages. Brian
and Janet Wingham also run the adjacent gift shop. The simple menu
offers good snacking: ham (£1.75) and prawn sandwiches, tomato
soup (£1.70), creamed mushrooms on toast (£2), poached eggs
on toast. They are well known for their meringues (£2) and other
cakes include coffee walnut cake, fruit cake, lemon Madeira (all £1)
or Cointreau cake (£1.50). Cream tea £2.75. Small patio for outdoor
eating overlooking south-facing garden. Children's portions and
a high-chair provided. Unlicensed. No smoking. *Seats 24.*
Open 10.30-5.30. Closed Mon, 10 days Christmas. No credit cards.

Bingley   Bankfield Hotel   61%   £105

| Tel 0274 567123   Fax 0274 551331 | Hotel |

Bradford Road Bingley West Yorkshire BD16 1TU   Map 6 C1

On the A650 Bradford/Skipton road, a castellated Gothic frontage
that "wouldn't look out of place on a Hollywood film set". Inside,
handsome Victorian day rooms and mainly modern, decent-sized
bedrooms, 29 of which have been recently refurbished. Children
under 15 stay free in parents' bedroom. There are three family suites
and six cots. Baby-sitting and baby-listening services. High-chairs are
provided in the restaurant, where there's a children's menu and small
portions on offer. Conference facilities and winter dinner dances.
Jarvis Hotels. *Rooms 103. Garden. Access, Amex, Diners, Visa.*

Birmingham   California Pizza Factory

| Tel 021-428 2636 | Pizzeria |

42 High Street Harborne Birmingham West Midlands   Map 6 C4

Wood-block floor, brick columns and wall panels and tubular
overhead air-conditioning lend a factory-like feel (and attendant
echoes) to a cavernous pizza house and take-away close to Harborne's
shops. Wood-fired pizzas from an imported Italian kiln are at the heart
of Gary and Tracey Perkins' catering concept and the formula works
a treat. In just two minutes out come flat, crispy pizza bases (hot, too)
with a hint of charcoal flavour and some notably imaginative toppings
from Cajun chicken, bacon and fresh spinach (£6.25) to broccoli, red
onions and courgettes (£4.95) and avocado, smoked bacon and cherry
tomatoes (£5.95). To follow, commendable home-made tiramisu
(£3.50) and Häagen-Dazs hot fudge sundae (£3.25). House wine
weighs in at under £7.50 a bottle (large glass £1.95). No-smoking
areas. *Seats 110. Open noon-10.45. Closed 25 & 26 Dec. Access,
Amex, Visa.*

Birmingham   Chung Ying   £37

| Tel 021-622 5669 | Restaurant |

16-18 Wrottesley Street Birmingham West Midlands B5 6RT   Map 6 C4

The Chinese flock to this well-established, traditionally appointed
restaurant for its long Cantonese menu. The choice extends to well
over 300 dishes, including more than 40 dim sum items and a 'special
dishes' section that covers fried prawn balls with ginger and spring
onion; steamed pork pie with salted egg, diced squid or fresh squid;
and stuffed peppers with black bean sauce. 40-plus range of excellent
dim sum, including one-pot casseroles. Family dining is encouraged
by the provision of at least ten high-chairs, although the tables are
tightly packed. *Seats 220. Meals 12-12 (Sun to 11). Closed 25 Dec.
Access, Amex, Diners, Visa.*

Birmingham   Chung Ying Garden   £37

| Tel 021-666 6622 | Restaurant |

17 Thorp Street Birmingham West Midlands B5 4AT   Map 6 C4

Sister and near neighbour of the original *Chung Ying*, this has more
modern decor, with pillars, plants and murals. The menu is no less
extensive and the chef's specialities include king prawn casserole with
spicy cream sauce, paper-wrapped fillet of beef and quick-fried dry
squid and shredded jellyfish with celery. The menu also lists 40 dim

sum dishes, half of them not available after 5. Don't expect intimate service in an operation of this size. **Seats** *300. Meals 12-12 (Sun to 11pm). Closed 25 Dec. Access, Amex, Diners, Visa.*

Birmingham   Hudson's Coffee House

Tel 021-643 1001	Coffee Shop

City Plaza Centre (1st floor) Cannon Street Birmingham West Midlands   Map 6 C4

The circular City Plaza Shopping Centre with its glass dome makes a splendid setting for a modern recreation of Mrs Hudson's 200-year-old tradition of excellence. Glass-topped tables, crisp white napery and tail-coated butlers greet a loyal clientele on arrival: the morning's press beckons for a quick read (if junior will allow). Served on gold-rimmed bone china, fresh sandwiches and bagels are filled to order – smoked salmon and cream cheese (£3.30); crab, avocado and Brie (£2.95); gourmet seafood and cheese platters (£9.50 and £5.95). Choose from a dozen cafetière coffees, just as many speciality teas and wicked-looking desserts and pastries displayed in the chill cabinet. Light breakfasts all day, set afternoon tea (£4.95) with smoked salmon sandwiches 2 till 6. Two high-chairs; changing facilities in Ladies. No smoking. Outlets also in Coventry and Harrogate. **Seats** *85.* **Open** *8am-6pm.* **Closed** *Sun, Bank Holidays. Access, Amex, Visa.*

Birmingham   Hyatt Regency Hotel, Court Café

Tel 021-643 1234	Café

2 Bridge Street Birmingham West Midlands   Map 6 C4

Behind a striking 25-storey mirrored facade next to the International Convention Centre and Symphony Hall is a stylish, well-appointed and well-run hotel. The main restaurant is the *282 Brasserie*, but equally appealing is the California-themed *Court Café* in the atrium. Here a varied main menu (available from 12 to 2) draws on influences from around the world: Maryland crab cakes (£5.75), tomato broth (£2.90), pasta (£6.95/£9.95), burgers, quesadillas, tacos, Asian chicken salad (£5.75), grilled monkfish (£11), lemon tart, chocolate brownies (desserts £3.50). Sunday brunch is a popular family affair (children under 6 eat free), while afternoon tea (£5.50 for full tea) offers finger sandwiches, scones, pastries and a choice of seven teas. The Court Café opens at 6.30 for breakfast. High-chairs and a short menu of children's favourites (main dishes around £2/£2.50) provided. **Seats** *85.* **Open** *6.30am-midnight. Access, Amex, Diners, Visa.*

Birmingham   New Happy Gathering

Tel 021-643 5247	Restaurant

43 Station Street Birmingham West Midlands   Map 6 C4

Tucked away in a rather run down part of the city (behind New St station) but well worth a visit. A decent selection of dim sum dishes from £2.20. Set dinner £10 (2 diners or more, vegetarian menu £9 available for singles) and for a party of six or more they will prepare a nine-course Chinese banquet at £14 a head. Friendly and informal. No frills. Two high-chairs; changing shelf in Ladies. **Seats** *98.* **Open** *12-2, 5-11.30 (Sat 12-12, Sun 12-11). Closed 25 & 26 Dec. Access, Amex, Diners, Visa.*

Birmingham   Rooftop at Rackhams

Tel 021-236 3333	Restaurant
Corporation Street Birmingham West Midlands	Map 6 C4

A popular shoppers' restaurant six floors up with plain wooden tables, paper flowers and no smoking. Amidst a wealth of commercial patisserie and bakery goods you might find beef and salmon salads, vegetarian quiches and fresh fruit salad. Cooked breakfast (from 99p) is a top early-day seller; there's a popular daily roast (£6.50) and afternoon teas between £1.25-£1.99. Served by three ample lifts, the Rooftop is approached by way of the children's wear and toy department, which might not necessarily be good for harassed parents. Six high-chairs and a mother and baby room provided. No smoking. *Seats 340.* *Open 9.30-6 Closed* Sun, 25 & 26 Dec. Access, Amex, Diners, Visa.

Birmingham   Wild Oats

Tel 021-471 2459	Vegetarian
5 Raddlebarn Road Selly Oak Birmingham West Midlands	Map 6 C4

A fairly basic vegetarian café just across the road from Selly Oak hospital, with rough plastered walls and assorted kitchen tables and chairs. It's simplicity first at Wild Oats, with water carafes on the tables and the day's offering on blackboards. Lunch, perhaps of cauliflower and coriander soup, brown lentil casserole or savoury mushroom tart and damson crumble with yoghurt topping need cost no more than £6. There are healthy fillings for baked potatoes, and salad combinations including carrot and nut, chick pea and Caribbean rice. Unlicensed. No smoking. *Seats 25. Open 12-2 & 6-9. Closed* Sun, Mon, Bank Holidays (except Good Friday), 2 weeks Christmas. No credit cards.

Blackburn   Tiggis

Tel 0254 53135	Restaurant
71 King William Street Blackburn Lancashire	Map 6 B1

Large, slickly-run Italian eatery in the vaulted semi-basement of the neo-Gothic former Corn Exchange in the centre of town. Polished granite table tops over art nouveau cloths and lots of polished brass are features of the pleasing decor. The menu has something for everyone with pizzas (from £4.85), pasta dishes (from £3.95), antipasti like seafood hors d'oeuvre (£3.90), insalata di tonno (£3.90) and old favourites such as pollo cacciatora (£8.80), scampi provençale (£9.80) and chicken Kiev (£9.20). Children get their own Italian-style menu (as do vegetarians) with pizzas, pasta and beefburger, a helium-filled balloon and free birthday cake for birthday boys and girls. Four clip-on high-chairs are available for really tiny tots. Also at Bolton, Preston and St. Anne's. *Seats 150. Open 12-2 & 6-11 (Fri/Sat to 11.30). Closed* Mon (except Bank Holidays), 25, 26 Dec, 1 Jan. Access, Visa.

Blackpool   Harry Ramsden's

Tel 0253 294386	Fish'n'Chips
60/63 The Promenade Blackpool Lancashire FY1 4QU	Map 6 A1

Few of our readers will not have heard of what may be the most famous fish and chip restaurant in the world, but not so many will know that they do a very reasonable children's meal. For those who have not made the trip to Blackpool, Harry Ramsden's has a history stretching back to 1928, and currently feeds one million people a year.

The queues are an inevitable result of its popularity, but the staff are friendly and efficient, and the service is quick. Typical dishes might include haddock fillet and chips (£4.95 including tea, coffee or soft drink plus bread and butter), steamed ginger sponge pudding £1.60; children are tempted by a set meal comprising small haddock fillet and chips, bread and butter, ice cream, soft drink (£2.95). Branches at: Guiseley (Leeds), London Heathrow, Manchester (see entry), Newcastle and Glasgow. *Open 11-11. Closed 25 Dec. Access, Visa.*

Blackpool	**Pembroke Hotel**	67%	£129
Tel 0253 23434 Fax 0253 27864			Hotel
North Promenade Blackpool Lancashire FY1 5JQ			Map 6 A1

A modern conference hotel with facilities for up to 900 delegates (theatre-style) and up to 600 for banqueting. In the main holiday season families are well catered for, with a playroom, baby-sitting and a supervised crèche (9am-9pm) as well as a separate children's menu. Indoor equipment keeps the children amused when they are not taking part in competitions, swimming galas and discos. Children's tea is served at 5.30pm (with a once-weekly barbecue alternative) and there is an excellent menu with out-of-this-world choices like solar soup, orbital omelette and transformer trifle. Youngsters can also join their parents for small portions in the restaurant, poolside snack bar or carvery. The best family rooms have an alcove with fold-down bunk beds, plus scope for a cot. There's a separate games room and bedrooms are equipped with video machines. A large swimming pool and Springs night club are among the leisure amenities. Metropole Hotels. *Rooms 274. Indoor swimming pool, sauna, solarium. Access, Amex, Diners, Visa.*

Blakeney	**Blakeney Hotel**	64%	£112
Tel 0263 740797 Fax 0263 740795			Hotel
The Quay Blakeney nr Holt Norfolk NR25 7NE			Map 10 C1

A family-owned hotel, run in traditional style, on the quayside overlooking the National Trust harbour. Public rooms include a first-floor sun lounge which enjoys to the full the fine views across the salt marshes towards Blakeney Point. Many front-facing bedrooms share the estuary view; there are several mini-suites, four-poster rooms and a ground-floor room suitable for wheelchairs. Some rooms in an annexe have private patios. Children under 16 sharing with two people paying full tariff are charged at £5 per night (plus meals as taken); £10 per day charge for an adjacent bunk room. Children are welcomed but parents are expected "to ensure that their children do not spoil the enjoyment of other guests". Children's high-tea (£4) is served from 5.45-6.30pm in the restaurant or in the bedrooms (£5); favourites include cheese or beans on toast, shepherds pie, beefburgers and jelly; six high-chairs are provided. A baby-sitter may be available if arranged in advance. Large, enclosed garden. One night bookings are not normally accepted on Fri or Sat nights (or Bank Holidays periods). *Rooms 60. Garden, indoor swimming pool, keep-fit equipment, sauna, spa bath, billiard room. Access, Amex, Diners, Visa.*

Blakeney	**King's Arms**		
Tel 0263 740341			Pub
Westgate Street Blakeney nr Holt Norfolk NR25 7NQ			Map 10 C1

Three pleasant knocked-through rooms in a pretty Grade II listed cottage pub not far from Norfolk's only free harbour. Families are made very welcome. *Pub open 11-11 Mon-Sat, 12-3 & 7-10.30 Sun (or 12-10.30 if eating). Free House.* **Beer** *Woodforde's Wherry, Marston, Ruddles, Webster's, occasional guest beer. Garden, children's play area. Family room. Access, Visa.*

Bolham   Knightshayes Court

Tel 0884 259416	Restaurant
Bolham nr Tiverton Devon	Map 13 D2

Amid re-pointed stone walls and polished brick floors, horse brasses and plumes are ready reminders of these former stables' past use. From morning coffee through daily hot lunches to Devon cream teas, waitress service to red-stained wood tables and chairs assures an even flow of fare. Knightshayes ploughman's (£3.95) is a popular choice, so too the buffet salad table with a choice of gammon ham, homity pie or pork and apple pie (£4.95). Full marks for their use of local suppliers of Devon produce (listed on the menu). Admissions to the adjacent National Trust gardens and house are extra, but there's no charge for access to the grounds and café. No smoking. **Seats** *108.* **Open** *10.30-5.30 (1 Nov-19 Dec to 5). Access, Visa.*

Bolton   Tiggis

Tel 0204 397320	Restaurant
63 Bradshawgate Bolton Lancashire BL1 1QD	Map 6 B2

Large airy Italian restaurant in the centre of Bolton with ceiling fans, marble floor and table tops, hanging baskets filled with plants and Italian music in the background. The large menu is divided into Antipasti (di pesce £3.70), pasta (spaghetti alla matriciana £4.60 – bacon, tomato, onion and chili), pizzas (capricciosa £4.60), meat (pollo boscaiola £8.90) and fish, plus a 'vegetarian corner' (penne casalinga – macaroni with mushrooms, cream and a touch of tomato £4.60). In addition, daily special main courses are priced £8-10. The children's menu includes corn on the cob (70p), pizza margherita (£1.60), lasagne al forno (£1.60) and ice cream. If it's a birthday, a complimentary birthday cake is presented in a gold box while lights are dimmed. Three high-chairs, a booster seat, small plates and straws are all provided, and children leave Tiggis clutching a balloon, probably 'well happy'. Also at Blackburn, Preston and St. Anne's. **Seats** *100.* **Open** *12-2, 6-11 (Thu, Fri Sat to 11.30, Sun to 10.30).* **Closed** *L Sun, all Mon, Dec 25 & 26. Access, Diners, Visa.*

Borrowdale   Stakis Lodore Swiss Hotel   71%   £120*

Tel 076 87 77285 Fax 076 87 77343	Hotel
Borrowdale Keswick Cumbria CA12 5UX	Map 4 C3

Holiday hotel set in 40 acres right by Derwentwater; good family facilities and convenient for Keswick ferry (½ mile) and town (3½ miles). Picture windows afford splendid views from the day rooms and the best, front-facing bedrooms. Several splendid family rooms; resident nanny (8am-6pm) in the nursery all year round; baby-listening provided and baby-sitting can be arranged; outdoor playground, high-chairs, children's cutlery; high tea 5-6pm. Charges for children depend upon age (under-1s, 1-6, 6-16). Free golf at Keswick golf club. No dogs. *Half-board terms only.* **Rooms** *70. Garden, indoor & outdoor swimming pools, gymnasium, squash, sauna, tennis, games room, nursery, lock-up garage. Access, Amex, Diners, Visa.*

Bournemouth   Beales Coffee Shop

Tel 0202 552022	Coffee Shop
36 Old Christchurch Road Bournemouth Dorset BH1 1LJ	Map 14 C4

The coffee shop in Beales Department Store can be found on the lower ground floor. The choice is extensive and even the bread and pastries are baked on the premises. Choose from cottage pie, baked potato filled with cheese and ham or curry (all £3.15). Sweet choices include caramel cream (90p), profiteroles (£1.95) or cream tea at £1.85. Three high-chairs and two booster seats provided; plenty of space for changing in the Ladies. The Intermission Restaurant is on the fifth floor. *Seats 130.* **Open** *9-4.45.* **Closed** *Sun, Bank Holidays. Access, Amex, Diners, Visa.*

Bournemouth   Chez Fred

Tel 0202 761023	Fish'n'Chips
10 Seamoor Road Westbourne Bournemouth Dorset	Map 14 C4

Fish and chips 'par excellence' chez Fred – a clever name and a classy product. A lunch special of cod, chips, peas and beverages (£3.75) is unbeatable in the area; daily shopping provides, alternatively, skate wings (£5.95) at competitive prices. Treacle sponge and custard (£1.95) and variously sauced New Forest ice creams (£1.75) turn 'mere' fish and chips into a family meal. Bright lights, lively music and friendly staff mark Fred's out from the crowd: look for Westbourne off the Wessex Way (A35) west of town towards Poole. Two high-chairs; "Small Fry" colouring menu for under-12s. No smoking. *Seats 48.* **Open** *11.30-1.45 & 5-10.* **Closed** *Sun, 25 & 26 Dec. No credit cards.*

Bournemouth   Chine Hotel   65%   £80

Tel 0202 396234 Fax 0202 391737	Hotel
Boscombe Spa Road Bournemouth Dorset BH5 1AX	Map 14 C4

Sister establishment to the *Sandbanks Hotel* (see entry) a bit further around the bay at Poole, the 1874-built Chine has shared the same conscientious family ownership since 1945. Large bedrooms, nearly half with private balcony or patio, have all been refurbished over the last few years with light-oak units and pleasing pale-green colour scheme. Spacious public areas include a cocktail bar open-plan to the large restaurant and a cosy residents' lounge overlooking the pine-fringed outdoor swimming pool; landscaped gardens extend down one side of the Boscombe Chine Gardens to the esplanade and pier below. Business people are attracted by a number of well-equipped conference rooms (in an adjacent building) and families appreciate the playroom, games room, coin-operated laundry room and, during school holidays, a children's activities organiser. Children up to 12 stay free when sharing with two parents. No dogs. **Rooms** *97. Garden, outdoor & indoor swimming pool, sauna, solarium, putting, games room. Access, Amex, Diners, Visa.*

Bournemouth   Norfolk Royale   70%   £138

Tel 0202 551521 Fax 0202 299729	Hotel
Richmond Hill Bournemouth Dorset BH2 6EN	Map 14 C4

Dating from Bournemouth's Edwardian heyday, the Norfolk Royale boasts a splendid two-tier cast-iron verandah as part of its listed facade and the major refurbishment of a few years back was sympathetic to the hotel's origins. Twin conservatories – one having the pool and the other part of the all-day (7.30am-10pm) Orangery restaurant – extend into the pretty garden to the rear and several interconnecting rooms provide plenty of lounge/bar space. Appealing bedrooms, which are properly serviced in the evening, are decorated in a variety of matching fabrics in ribbon and flower-style with limed oak furniture. Good bathrooms come with brass fittings and good-sized towels and robes. Valet parking is a big plus given the hotel's central location. Well-motivated staff. No dogs. Fun pack, baby-sitting, cots, children's menu and high-chairs for families; under-12s free if sharing parents' room. Indoor children's play room and pool parties in July and August. **Rooms** 95. *Indoor swimming pool, sauna, spa bath, steam room. Access, Amex, Diners, Visa.*

Bournemouth	**Royal Bath Hotel**	**73%**	**£140**
Tel 0202 555555	Fax 0202 554158		Hotel
Bath Road Bournemouth Dorset BH1 2EW			Map 14 C4

A splendid Victorian hotel combining traditional values (courteous and helpful staff for example) and modern amenities such as the marvellous Leisure Pavilion which features a heated kidney-shaped swimming pool. The hotel stands in an immaculately-kept three-acre garden with clifftop views out to sea, enjoyed by many of the bedrooms (some with terraces) which vary in style and size but are all smartly furnished with good bathrooms that have large mirrors and decent-sized towels. Excellent housekeeping, including a turn-down service at night, is evident throughout. The vast public areas (bars and lounges), refurbished a few years ago, are comfortable and well appointed, and breakfast in the Garden Restaurant will not disappoint. Children up to the age of 14 years free in parents' room. Supervised crèche daily (10am-6pm) in high season. No dogs. 24hr room service. De Vere Hotels. **Rooms** 131. *Garden, indoor swimming pool, gymnasium, sauna, spa bath, steam room, solarium, beauty & hair salon, putting, snooker, coffee shop (10.30am-8.15pm), children's playground, garage parking (£3.50 per night). Access, Amex, Diners, Visa.*

Restaurant   £60

There are two restaurants in the hotel: the Garden Restaurant is only open in the evenings and for Sunday lunch, serving traditional food, albeit with somewhat grand and flowery descriptions on the menu; regular dinner dances. Oscar's, a more intimate setting with Oscar Wilde memorabilia all round, offers a classical French-orientated menu though the table d'hote set-price meals have an international flavour – typical dishes being a salad of marinated brill fillets, fillet of lamb garnished with fresh pasta, and a hot and sticky toffee pudding. A safe and predictable wine list. Families can eat informally by the side of the pool in the Leisure Club. *Garden: **Seats** 220. L (Sun only) 12.45-2.15 D 7.30-9.30. Set L £14.50 Set D £24. Oscar's: **Seats** 60. L 12.30-2.15 D 6.30-10 Closed Sun & Bank Holidays.*

Bournemouth	**Superfish**	
Tel 0202 426158		Fish'n'Chips
186 Seabourne Road Southbourne Bournemouth Dorset		Map 14 C4

Part of a chain of eight above-average fish and chip restaurants (see also under Morden). Heading the menu is prime fillet of cod – small £2.95, large £3.80, Moby Dick £4.55 – while other choices include huss, plaice (£3.95), children's fish bites (£2.20 with chips) and (as available) skate, haddock, salmon and lemon sole. High-chairs. *Seats 64. Open 11.30-2 & 5-10.30 (to 11 Thurs-Sat), Sun Jul & Aug Closed 25 & 26 Dec. No credit cards.*

Bournemouth   Swallow Highcliff Hotel   70%   £120

Tel 0202 557702 Fax 0202 292734	Hotel
St Michael's Road West Cliff Bournemouth Dorset BH2 5DU	Map 14 C4

An imposing, white-painted Victorian hotel with a splendid clifftop location giving many of the rooms fine marine views. A funicular lift carries guests from hotel to promenade. Good-sized bedrooms in the main house have dark period-style furniture, those in the converted coastguard cottages smart lightwood furniture. Eleven family rooms with cots, baby-sitting and baby-listening are available; supervised crèche in summer (May-Oct from 10am-6pm – check before booking). Cots, baby baths and potties are all supplied and there's a fun pack for rainy days. Children under 14 share parents' room free of charge. Numerous public rooms include a terrace bar, the Plantation Inn (fine for informal eating), a lounge for non-smokers and a night club. Outdoor facilities include a fenced-in outdoor play area with swings, slides and a sandpit; the climbing frame is set on hard ground. The lack of indoor swimming pool, however, makes this more of a summer rather than one-stop winter destination for families; nevertheless, the Bournemouth International Centre has a fun pool with a wave machine and is only three minutes away from the hotel. Easy walking distance to the town-centre shops, Pleasure Gardens and pier. *Rooms 157. Garden, heated outdoor swimming pool, sauna, solarium, all-weather tennis, putting, games room, snooker, brasserie (11am-11pm), night club. Access, Amex, Diners, Visa.*

Bovey Tracey   Devon Guild of Craftsmen, Granary Café

Tel 0626 832223	Café
Riverside Mill Bovey Tracey Newton Abbot Devon	Map 13 D3

Evidence of the Devon Guild of Craftsmen's output abounds throughout the Granary, housed in a restored mill perched on the river Bovey. Watercolours for sale alongside hand-thrown pottery and colourful cookbooks add tone to the bright, airy service counter and dining area. Healthy salads from houmus to mustardy potatoes accompany a wide range of potted meals from steak pie to spinach and ricotta lasagne (£3.50), reheated while you wait. Home baking ranges from poppyseed cake to rich lemon slices (95p); speciality teas and coffee are sold by the mugful; cider and apple juice are organic (as is all the meat used), and wines include Bovey Tracey's own Whitstone (£1.45 glass). Large summer courtyard. Children's portions; one high-chair; changing in Ladies; toys available. No smoking. *Seats 40. Open 10-5 (lunch 12-2.30). Closed 25 & 26 Dec, 1 Jan & winter Bank Holidays. Access, Visa.*

Bowness-on-Windermere   Belsfield Hotel   62%   £112

Tel 053 94 42448 Fax 053 94 46397	Hotel
Kendal Road Bowness-on-Windermere Cumbria LA23 3EL	Map 4 C3

Hilltop Victorian building set in six acres of gardens, overlooking Lake Windermere, Bowness landing piers and the Belle Isle beyond. Accommodation ranges from singles to suites and family rooms (some

with bunk beds, others with adjoining child's room). Good leisure
facilities. Forte Heritage. **Rooms** 65. *Garden, indoor swimming pool,
sauna, solarium, tennis, putting, snooker. Access, Amex, Diners, Visa.*

Bracknell	Coppid Beech Hotel	72%	£140
Tel 0344 303333 Fax 0344 301200			Hotel
John Nike Way Bracknell Berkshire RG12 8TF			Map 15 E2

Of striking Swiss chalet design, the privately-owned Coppid Beech
is Berkshire's newest and largest hotel. A unique feature of the interior
is a triangular shaft extending to the full height of the building, lined
with aquaria (the largest in Europe apparently) and mirrors creating
a mesmerising, watery kaleidoscope. Extensive facilities include a lively
Bierkeller with live entertainment several nights a week, plush state-
of-the-art disco night club and Waves health and fitness centre. Well-
thought-out bedrooms (a significant number are full or junior suites)
are well equipped – there's even an account review and check-out
facility available via the advanced TV system – with large,
comfortable beds. Eight family rooms have an additional bed
in a curtained alcove; free baby pack provided. 24hr room service
is extensive and beds are turned down at night. 3 miles from Junction
10 of the M4, 30 minutes from Heathrow. **Rooms** 205. *Indoor
swimming pool, paddling pool, gymnasium, spa bath, sauna, solarium, steam
room, dry ski slope, ice rink, play area. Access, Amex, Diners, Visa.*

Rowans Restaurant £70

A large solidly comfortable restaurant with a menu that takes its
inspiration from a variety of European cuisines; bouillabaisse-style fish
soup, grilled calf's liver with polenta and Swiss chard, roast partridge
with celery blinis, carpaccio of beef, celeriac and goat's cheese terrine
with Greek-style zucchini. Cooking has a modern, health-conscious
slant and the food is attractively presented. Inventive vegetarian
options. Desserts are chosen from a buffet display. **Seats** 128. *Parties 15.
Private Room 25. L 12-2.30 D 6.30-11. Set L £17.50 Set D £22.50.*

Bradford-on-Avon	The Bridge Tea Rooms	
Tel 0225 865537		Tea Room
24a Bridge Street Bradford-on-Avon Wiltshire		Map 14 B3

A charming 17th-century building, waitresses in mob caps and long
frilly aprons, sepia-tinted Victorian photographs on the walls – all the
makings of a traditional English tea room in fact, with the final
ingredient being Kevin Nye's fine baking displayed on an old
sideboard: plump chocolate roulade, rich fruit cake, frangipane tart (all
at £1.95), coffee and walnut gateau (£2.25) and splendid scones with
jam and thick, yellow clotted cream (£3.95 for a set afternoon tea).
On the savoury side there are salads (from £4.15), sandwiches, baked
potatoes and a hot dish of the day – cottage pie perhaps. A good range
of teas and cafetière coffees completes the satisfying picture. Ask for
children's portions. No smoking. **Seats** 52. **Open** *9.30-5.30 (Sun from
10.30).* **Closed** *25 & 26 Dec. No credit cards.*

Bradford-on-Avon	Woolley Grange	75%	£130
Tel 0225 864705 Fax 0225 864059			Hotel
Woolley Green Bradford-on-Avon Wiltshire BA15 1TX			Map 14 B3

It's difficult not to fall under the spell of Woolley Grange. Partly it's
the charming 17th-century manor house with numerous comfortably
lived-in day rooms full of antiques, pictures, real fires, two spaniels

(Birdie and Henry) and a cat (Toby, or is it Sascha?), but it's also to do with the unstuffy, yet not uncivilised atmosphere created by Nigel and Heather Chapman and their friendly young staff (whose lack of uniform is quite deliberate) who always seem to be around when you need them. Bedrooms vary considerably in size but all have great character with a beamed bathroom here (mostly with Victorian-style fittings), a rugged stone fire breast there (about half have working gas coal fires), brass bedsteads, patchwork bedcovers, antiques and fresh flowers all helping to create an appealing 'country' feel. All bedrooms have double beds, but twins may be substituted by prior arrangement; certain pairs of rooms can be arranged as interconnecting suites for self-contained parties. The Long Room has a TV and video (complete with all 17 episodes of The Prisoner) for bad weather days. Ideal for families, the old Coach House has become 'Woolley Bear's Den' with full-time nanny (10am-6pm) and large games room; both early children's lunch (at noon) and high tea (5pm) are served in the nursery (£5 per head, with a selection that might included everything from pizza, pasta or a fresh daily dish to fromage frais and Rice Krispie cake; orders at least one hour ahead). High-chairs, children's cutlery, baby baths, baby-listening and sitting (by arrangement) are all available on request. Woolley now has a collection of interesting bicycles, including a 20s' tandem, an Indian trishaw (complete with hooded sun-shade) and two specially designed, locally produced Moultons. 14 acres of gardens and paddocks extend beyond the stable yard where there is a play area with outdoor toys, a large sandpit and long grass in which the young ones can romp; riding and golf tuition can be arranged locally. Woolley Grange won our *Family Hotel of the Year* award in 1992 – it's very suitable for parents who want to stay in a civilised, adult hotel with under-8s. One mile north-east of the town on the B3105. **Rooms** 20. *Garden, outdoor swimming pool (Easter-Oct), grass tennis courts, games rooms (snooker, table tennis, video & video games, table football), mini football pitch, children's garden with swing, climbing frame, mini roller coaster and sandpit, laundry service, massage arranged. Access, Amex, Diners, Visa.*

Restaurant   £75

Colin White's uncomplicated yet sophisticated brand of cooking – salmon fish cakes with coriander butter sauce, chargrilled red mullet with griddled polenta and roasted peppers, sauté of guinea fowl with stir-fried vegetables and star anise – is entirely in keeping with the style of the hotel. A good selection of British farmhouse cheeses offers an alternative to puds like baked plums with praline mousse and almond milk. Local produce is used as much as possible and, in summer, they are pretty much self-sufficient in fruit, vegetables and herbs from a one-acre Victorian walled garden. Between noon and 10pm an informal menu – omelette Arnold Bennett, hamburger, focaccia, club sandwich – is served in the conservatory or out on the Terrace – a popular choice with families who need varied feeding times! *Seats* 52. *Parties* 70. *Private Room* 40. *L 12-2.30 (Sat & Sun till 3) D 7-10. Set L £24 Set D £28.*

Branscombe   Bulstone Hotel

Tel 0297 80446	Hotel
Higher Bulstone Branscombe nr Seaton Devon EX12 3BL	Map 13 E2

At the Bulstone you will find everything you might need on a family holiday. Twelve bedrooms (six en suite) have been designed with children in mind and are equipped with cots or extra beds, extra

bedding in case of accidents, changing mats, tea-making facilities, baby-
listening and nappy buckets, if required. Downstairs there
is a playroom with toys and games plus an enclosed outdoor play area
with swings, a climbing frame and a sand pit. The laundry room has
coin-operated washing machine, tumble dryer and there
is a microwave, sink, refrigerator and bottle-steriliser in the guest
utility room. Children take tea together at 4.45pm – lasagne, roast
pork, beans on toast (set price £3.50, under 2s free if parents are
dining, similarly under 5s except during high season). Parents dine
later, by candle-light. **Seats** 28. **Food** No lunches. D 7.45-8.30.
Closed Mid Nov-mid Feb. No credit cards.

Braunston   The Old Plough

Tel 0572 722714 Fax 0572 770382	Pub

Church Street Braunston Leicestershire LE15 8QY	Map 7 E4

Well-regarded local innkeepers Amanda and Andrew Reid have
brought a wealth of experience also to their tastefully modernised inn
on the fringe of the village. Healthy eating options and vegetarian
alternatives (mushroom and walnut cannelloni £6.25) are well
interspersed throughout a menu encompassing 'famous Plough crusties'
(large granary filled rolls from £1.95) through salads and steaks
to chef Nick Quinn's specials. Chicken, leek and bacon pie (£6.25)
or salmon and asparagus filo (£8.25) arrive with chef's potatoes of the
day and crisp, fresh vegetables. Avoid, if you can, predictable fruit and
ice cream concoctions for dessert in favour of the home-made crème
brulée or chocolate rum truffle tarte (£2.50). With light lunches
on the terrace and candle-lit dining in the picturesque conservatory
a sense of occasion is easily engendered. **Bar Food** 12-2, 7-10 (Sun till
9.30). Free House. **Beer** Theakston XB Old Peculier, John Smith's, guest
beers. Garden, outdoor eating. Family Room. Access, Amex, Diners, Visa.

Brent Knoll   The Goat House Café

Tel 0278 760995	Café

Bristol Road Brent Knoll Somerset TA9 4HJ	Map 13 E1

A couple of minutes' drive from Junction 22 of the M5 (stay on the
A38 – don't turn off at the signpost to Brent Knoll). Don't be put off
by the transport caff exterior, inside is bright and airy with pine
fittings, friendly service and a warm welcome for families. There's
room enough to wheel the buggy up to the table if both the high-
chairs are taken. Your kids will be fascinated by their kids –around
a dozen goats and their offspring live in stables across the open-air
paved courtyard where there are a shop and pub-style tables for good
weather. Goat's milk products (including ice cream) are offered
alongside sandwiches, home-made cakes, pastries and pizzas; more
substantial homely fare is also on the menu. Get there before noon and
there are good solid breakfasts to be had. No special changing facilities.
Two no-smoking areas. A really handy place to know about if you're
heading down the motorway. **Open** Mon to Thurs 8-6, Fri, Sat & Sun
8-7.30. **Closed** Dec 25 & 26, Jan 1 & 2. Access, Visa.

Bretforton   Fleece Inn

Tel 0386 831173	Pub

The Cross Bretforton nr Evesham Hereford & Worcester WR11 5JE	Map 16 A1

The atmospheric Fleece Inn was formerly a farmhouse where cider
was brewed for the farmworkers. An annual beer festival takes place

in the barn during the second weekend of July when 50 real ales can be tasted. It is now a National Trust-owned timewarp of a pub with a 19th-century and older atmosphere and a museum-like array of beautiful things, many of them extremely valuable and rare – note especially the priceless collection of Stuart pewter. 60-70 guest ales are on offer during the course of the year. The very big garden is really an "orchard with a play area" – lambs and chickens roam in the paddock. Seating for 200 outside. *Free house.* **Beer** *Hook Norton, Uley Bitter, Everards, Mitchell & Butler's Brew XI. Garden, children's play area. Family room. No credit cards.*

Bridgemere   Bridgemere Garden World Coffee Shop

Tel 09365 381	Coffee Shop
Bridgemere nr Nantwich Cheshire	**Map 6 B3**

A large and very popular garden centre with an equally popular coffee shop in their conservatory. Savoury snacks include Cornish pasties and sausage rolls, lasagne (£3.35), ham and mushroom tagliatelle and the roast of the day (£4.50). For dessert or afternoon tea there is a selection of home-baked fruit pies (£1.60) and cakes from 75p to £1.60. No smoking. *Seats 300.* **Open** *9-7.30 (to 5 in winter).* **Closed** *25 & 26 Dec. Access, Amex, Visa.*

Bridgnorth   Down Inn

Tel 074635 624	Pub
Ludlow Road Bridgnorth Shropshire WV16 6UA	**Map 6 B4**

There's always a friendly welcome at this 250-year-old pub, a couple of miles south of town on the B4364, where rough stone walls and baronial-style leather chairs add to the generally characterful atmosphere. Very much a family affair, with father-in-law behind the bar and the Millingtons' own youngsters about the place – signalling that this is a genuinely child-friendly place (children's menu and portions plus high-chairs available). Paul Millington is the keen cook whose printed menu is almost doubled by the day's blackboard specials which major on his favourite fish and game: ploughman's (£2.95), baguettes (from £2.60), deep-fried potato skins (£2.90), steak and kidney pie (£6.90), vegetable tikka masala (£6.20), marlin steak with herbed olive oil (£7.35), guinea fowl with wine and grapes (£7.85), Spotted Dick and tiramisu (all puds £2.75) show the range. Up to 20 different English farmhouse cheeses on offer too. **Bar Food & Restaurant Meals** *12-2 (Sun to 3), 6.30-9.30 (except Sun) (Fri & Sat to 10). Children allowed in bar to eat, children's menu. Free House.* **Beer** *Constantly changing – five at any one time, plus guest beers. Patio, outdoor eating. Family room. Pub closed Sun evenings. Access, Visa.*

Bridgwater   Nutmeg House

Tel 0278 457823	Café
8 Clare Street Bridgwater Somerset	**Map 13 E1**

Over the last few years Michael Gibson's café and restaurant, in a quiet corner of town just off the High Street, has undergone several improvements. In carefully remodelled dining areas (one for non-smokers) lunch devolves around jacket potatoes and 'pasta corner' snacks, with a roast carvery at lunchtimes (£2.25-£4.50); a typical vegetarian dish could be ratatouille crumble (£3.95). Coffee, cakes, home-made pastries and desserts are sold throughout the day, and

à la carte dinners Friday and Saturday evenings. Two high-chairs
provided. *Seats 45.* **Open** *9-5.30.* **Closed** *Sun, Bank Holidays.*
Access, Visa.

Bridport   George Hotel

Tel 0308 23187	Pub
4 South Street Bridport Dorset	**Map 13 F2**

The George has been spruced up in the past year, yet it still retains the
delightful eccentric air that makes it so popular. A handsome Georgian
building located opposite the Town Hall, it opens its doors at 8.30am
for Continental breakfast – excellent coffee and croissants – served
in the relaxing and informal main bar and tiny dining room. Old-
fashioned in style with Regency-style wallpaper, Victorian-style, red-
painted bar and oil paintings on the walls, it is filled with soothing
classical music during the day and often louder jazz and opera in the
evenings. Reliable bar food is produced from the kitchen – on view –
at one end of the bar. The regular menu lists excellent snacks such
as Welsh rarebit (from £2.50), kedgeree (£4.25), kidneys sautéed
in Madeira (£4.75), mushrooms on toast with garlic (£2.50) and
a variety of omelettes (from £3.75). Daily specials feature fish fresh
from West Bay – lemon sole stuffed with crab in a cream and
vermouth sauce (£3.95) – sausage and tomato pie (£2.75), pork fillet
cooked in cream and paprika sauce (£5.95) and moussaka (£3.75).
Vegetables, salads and potatoes are charged separately (£1.30). The full
range of Palmers ales are dispensed on handpump and, as the brewery
is only just down the road, all are in tip-top condition. Redecoration
(hopefully) will extend upstairs to the four modest bedrooms, all
of which share a bathroom and toilet; one large room will fit
an additional bed. The laid-back atmosphere lends itself well
to families, who are welcome in the small dining room (nicknamed
'Whipsnade'). The residents' bathroom upstairs may be used for
nursing or changing babies. There is no children's menu but the
landlord is always happy to provide smaller portions – "just ask".
Bar Food *12-3, 7-9.30 (No food L Sun, Bank Holidays, winter month
evenings by arrangement).* **Beer** *Bridport Bitter, Palmers IPA, Tally Ho.
Family room.* **Accommodation** *4 bedrooms, £37 (single £18.50).
Children welcome overnight. Cots available (no charge). Access, Visa.*

Bridport   Riverside Restaurant & Café   £36

Tel 0308 22011	Restaurant
West Bay Bridport Dorset DT6 4EZ	**Map 13 F2**

The menu at this friendly, relaxed restaurant (with views out to sea
or over the river) is mostly fish and shellfish, simply prepared
as ordered to bring out all the freshness and flavour. On the regular
side you might find whitebait, grilled sardines, West Bay scallops,
crab, cod, haddock, lemon sole plus lobster heading the luxury stakes
however, daily specials are the most interesting dishes with grilled
black bream, steamed oysters with spinach, red mullet with a spicy
salsa, poached turbot and langoustines showing that the style extends
way beyond fish and chips. Vegetarian dishes are also available:
typically, baked polenta with Gruyère cheese and a rich tomato sauce
or tagliatelle with wild mushrooms and tarragon. Banana and
butterscotch crumble or tiramisu will make a splendid end to a meal.
Also served are late breakfasts, snacks and teas. In good weather eight
tables are set on a patio overlooking the river. Facilities for families;
children's portions attract a 20% price reduction. Hours are extended

in high season. *Seats 80. L 10.30-3 (Sat & Sun to 4) D 6.30-8.30.
Closed D Sun, all Mon (except Bank Holidays & high season), early
Dec-early Mar. Access, Visa.*

Brightling   Jack Fuller's

Tel 0424 82212	Restaurant
Brightling East Sussex	**Map 11 B6**

A mile from Brightling on the Robertsbridge road, a former pub has
been turned into a fine country restaurant by Roger and Shirl Berman.
It's fronted by a well-kept garden, and patio doors lead from the
restaurant to a wide terrace. Oak beams, exposed stone walls and
a huge inglenook give character to the place, and red check tablecloths
lend an air of informality. The menu majors on main courses and
puddings; the former, served in serious portions, could include
gammon and onion pudding, beef stew and dumplings, chicken and
mushroom pie, or prawn and halibut pie (from £5.95-£6.45) with
a wide choice of side dishes – bubble and squelch, poached mushrooms
or Stilton cauliflower (all £1.50). The traditional theme extends to the
nursery puddings – vegetarian Spotted Dick, sticky treacle tart,
mother's bread pudding (all £2.95), all served with cream or lovely
thick custard. Eight high-chairs and children's cutlery provided.
Extensive patio area in the garden overlooking rolling countryside
for alfresco eating. No-smoking area. *Seats 72. Open 12-3 & 7-11.
Closed D Sun, all Mon & Tue, Wed (Oct-April). Access, Amex, Visa.*

Brighton   Al Duomo & Al Forno

Tel 0273 326741	Pizzerias
7 Pavilion Buildings Brighton East Sussex	**Map 11 B6**

It's the genuine, wood-burning pizza ovens that give this pair
of pizzeria/trattorias an edge over the competition. Al Duomo, with
bright yellow awning and rustic interior is next door to the Brighton
Pavilion and Al Forno just 50 yards away with tables spilling out of
a conservatory area into a small square. Near identical menus cover
the full range of standard Italian dishes along with the pizzas (from
£3.80) – prosciutto con melone (£3.95), linguine vongole (£4.50),
fritto misto (£6.75), saltimbocca romana (£7.50). Pizzas available
in children's sizes -"just ask"; the provision of eight high-chairs
indicates the restaurant's popularity with families. The 80-seat
Al Forno is at 36 East Street. Tel 0273 324905. *Seats 120.
Open 12-2.30 & 6-11.30 (Fri-Sun 12-11.30). Al Forno 12-2.30 & 6-11
(Fri-Sun 12-11.30). Closed 25 Dec. Access, Amex, Diners, Visa.*

Brighton   Browns

Tel 0273 23501 Fax 0273 27427	Restaurant
3-4 Duke Street Brighton East Sussex BN1 1AH	**Map 11 B6**

A popular and ultra-busy brasserie near the Lanes offering good-value
traditional food throughout the day, including breakfast. Meat and fish
dishes provide the main bulk of the menu with good old favourites
like fisherman's pie (£6.95), steak, mushroom and Guinness pie
(£6.95) and Scotch sirloin steak (£9.95). This, together with the
hamburgers (£5.95-£7.15) and spaghetti dishes ("seconds of pasta
at no extra charge"), hot sandwiches (from £5.15), salads (Caesar
£6.15, grilled goat's cheese £6.85, avocado, bacon and spinach £6.65)
and a wide range of generous puddings (£2.35), provides for just
about every taste. Vegetarian options are available among the spaghetti
sauces, together with other dishes such as fresh vegetable bake (£5.95)

and vegetables in herb sauce (£6.85). There's also a short but diverse selection of wines (13 sold by the glass) and some 15 cocktails from which to choose. Family-oriented and children-friendly; six high-chairs and a changing table in the loo; short children's menu. Branches in Bristol, Cambridge and Oxford (see entries); this original branch opened in 1973. A separate bar is at 34 Ship Street, Brighton and offers breakfast until noon and freshly-baked baguettes and bagels for lunch. **Seats** 120. **Open** 11am-11.30pm (Sun and Bank Holidays from noon). **Closed** 25 & 26 Dec. Access, Amex, Visa.

Brighton	China Garden	
Tel 0273 325124		Restaurant
88-91 Preston Street Brighton East Sussex		Map 11 B6

A roomy restaurant serving mainly Peking specialities offering a flavourful and varied menu – particularly in the fish department. Braised mussels in black bean sauce (£4.95), king prawns with garlic and spring onions (£2.25 each) and delicately seasoned minced meats, prawns and vegetables served with lettuce (£8 for two) are some of the dishes on offer, together with a juicy array of sizzling dishes on an iron griddle. Dim sum are available until 4. A karaoke room and pianist in the evening make for a good night out. Children are welcome (but no under-9s after 8pm) and the spacious interior helps ease any embarrassment (and dissipate the noise) when junior decides to throw a wobbly! **Seats** 130. **Open** noon-11pm. **Closed** 25 & 26 Dec. Access, Amex, Diners, Visa.

Brighton	Cripes	
Tel 0273 327878		Creperie
Victoria Road Brighton East Sussex		Map 11 B6

This is a small creperie on Victoria Road going towards Seven Dials. Owner Joy Leader offers crepes (from £2.50) and wholemeal buckwheat galettes (from £4.75) with a variety of fillings: chicken livers, spinach and sour cream; smoked salmon, asparagus, cheese and cream; aubergine, Cheddar, pesto sauce and Parmesan; or on the sweet side, bananas in rum with whipped cream, black cherries and ice cream, rum and chocolate (from £2.50). Morning visitors may like to try the scrambled eggs, bacon and mushrooms in a crepe or even the champagne breakfast (£4.95). A choice of French farmhouse ciders is the traditional accompaniment. One high-chair; no-smoking room. **Seats** 50. **Open** 10.30-2.30 & 6-11.30 (Sun to 11). **Closed** 25 & 26 Dec. Access, Amex, Visa.

Brighton	Dig in the Ribs	
Tel 0273 325275		Restaurant
7 Preston Street East Sussex BN1 2HP		Map 11 B6

Clean, airy, informal, noisy and family-friendly, this well-established Tex-Mex restaurant on three floors is just off the main shopping street. An extensive Mexican selection – guacamole (£2.85), nachos (£2.85), burritos, enchiladas (both at £7.25) – shares the menu with hickory smoked ribs (£8.75), Texas T-bone steak (£10.95), chicken wings with sauce dip and (until 5pm) brunch items such as eggs Benedict (£4.25), Texas 'steakwich' (£3.85) and cattleman's vegetable noodle soup (£2.50). Home-made puds range from cinnamon tortillas with honey and cream to jam roly-poly. As well as listing such delights as Sombrero (crisp mini Mexican pizza), Goldfish Toes (golden prawns, fries and tomato ketchup) and Prairie Dog (sausage, beans and buffalo fries) – all at £2.85 including soft drink and fruit or ice cream – the children's menu also includes pages of pictures to colour in, join the dots, spot the difference and other amusements. For the very youngest customers there are plenty of high-chairs, a supply of free emergency nappies and changing facilities in the Ladies. If you would like them to "warm up, sterilise, customise, liquidise or carry out some other childish wish" … just ask. Sundays are particularly busy. **Seats** *110.* **Open** *12-11.30 (to 10.30 Sun)* **Closed** *25 & 26 Dec, Jan 1. Access, Visa*

Brighton   The Dove Hotel

Tel 0273 779222 Fax 0273 746912	Hotel
18 Regency Square Brighton East Sussex BN1 2FG	**Map 11 B6**

On arriving you can expect to be greeted like long lost friends and presented with a welcome drink. Owner Mr Peter Kalinke is happy to do almost anything to keep his junior house guests happy – from the provision of a toy box to a guided tour of the hotel. The hospitality for families is almost second to none: even at breakfast a new selection of toys can be provided for early risers who have already reached the boredom threshold. The atmosphere is informal and low key and in such a small place you feel as if you are in a private home (fire doors notwithstanding). Bedrooms are comfortable and bright with a well-chosen mix of antique furniture and modern fabrics; travel cots and small beds are provided. Room three is the largest (£78) with two double beds and room for a further single; rooms one, five and seven are also family rooms (£65) and front-facing; slightly cheaper, less spacious rooms are also available. Baby-listening and baby-sitting are on offer, the latter only by prior arrangement. Early high teas (either in the dining room or in your room), nappies, potties, baby bottles. Three-course dinner is £13.50, but lighter meals are always available. Mr Kalinke is only too happy to oblige. Sea World, on the sea front by Palace Pier, is a short walk away. **Rooms** *10. From £65 double room; under-2s free, 2-12 £8, 13-17 £15 (reductions for longer stays). Closed 1 week Christmas. Access, Amex, Diners, Visa.*

Brighton   Ed's Easy Diner

Tel 0273 771955	American Diner
16 Prince Albert Street The Lanes Brighton East Sussex	**Map 11 B6**

The Brighton branch of this popular American-style diner is larger than its London counterparts, with a wide circular bar (normally horseshoe in shape at other branches) in the middle of which the friendly staff cook and entertain at the same time. The Original burger costs £2.75, hot dog with sauerkraut £2.45, toasted cheese sandwich £1.95, fries £1 and milkshake £2.10. Children are welcome; although all the 36 seats are high counter stools there is a high-chair that will fit over the top of one – now all you have to do is see if your child's mouth can get round one of Ed's famous burgers! 'Bottomless' cups of coffee are also served. **Seats** *36.* **Open** *12-11.30 (Fri 12-12, Sat 11-1, Sun 11-11.30). Access, Visa.*

Brighton   Food for Friends

Tel 0273 202310	Restaurant
17-18 Prince Albert St The Lanes Brighton East Sussex BN1 1HF	**Map 11 B6**

An informal, cosy establishment furnished with simple pine furniture and potted plants offering an all-vegetarian and wholefood menu in warm and hospitable surroundings. Tasty hot dishes to cheer and warm the belly on a cold winter's day are the masala dosa bake with coconut and coriander dahl and fresh mango chutney (£2.55) or blackeye bean and mushroom stroganoff. Other dishes range from exquisite mushroom and lentil roast to kidney bean and courgette goulash and Turkish falafel. In winter there's a vegetarian Sunday roast. Excellent organic bread selection including croissants and pains au chocolat. Lots of dips and salads. Children are welcome; four high-chairs, children's portions and a changing shelf in the Ladies all provided. No-smoking area. *Seats 55. Open 9.30am-10pm. Closed 25 & 26 Dec. Access, Amex, Diners, Visa.*

Brighton	Old Ship Hotel	65%	£105
Tel 0273 329001 Fax 0273 820718			**Hotel**
King's Road Brighton East Sussex BN1 1NR			**Map 11 B6**

A hotel of considerable charm and history – Paganini played in the ballroom here and a former owner saved the life of Charles II by transporting him to France in his boat – the Old Ship dates in part to the 15th century. A central location on the seafront is a big plus as is the secure parking for 70 cars. Public areas include a surprisingly spacious oak-panelled lobby dotted with antiques, a pair of quiet lounges with Adam-style ceilings and the panelled Tettersell's Bar. About two-thirds of the bedrooms (mostly those in the east wing) are smartly furnished with freestanding darkwood furniture, matching floral fabrics, breakfast table, good armchairs and up-to-date bathrooms. The remainder vary somewhat in age and style but all are at least acceptable; many have sea views. Friendly staff. 24hr room service. Children under 16 stay free in parents' room; supervised indoor play room during school holiday periods; children's menu in restaurant or supper from 6.30pm in the play room. Occasional weekend crèche facilities. *Rooms 152. Access, Amex, Diners, Visa.*

Bristol	Arnolfini Café Bar	
Tel 0272 279330		**Café**
Narrow Quay Prince Street Bristol Avon		**Map 13 F1**

Adjacent to the Arnolfini Gallery in a thriving complex created out of dockside warehouses, this roomy, airy café bar is an ideal stop-off for a light lunch or afternoon tea. The blackboard menu changes daily to offer such dishes as salmon fish cakes with crab sauce (£3.95), rabbit pie cooked in cider and tarragon (£4.20), layered pancake with fresh tomato and pepper sauce (£3.95) and home-made puddings – banana pudding, chocolate pecan pie and chocolate St. Emilion (all £1.95). There's a wide choice of teas and if it's sunny the benches out on the dockside provide a very pleasant place to sit and sip. *Seats 50. Open 12-10 (Sat & Sun to 3pm) & 5-10 (Sat & Sun only). Closed 10 days Christmas. No credit cards.*

Bristol	Aztec Hotel	74%	£96
Tel 0454 301090 Fax 0454 201593			**Hotel**
Aztec West Business Park Almondsbury Bristol Avon BS12 4TS			**Map 13 F1**

A smart, professionally run, purpose-built, modern hotel in the Shire Inns group, owned by brewers Daniel Thwaites. It provides a good balance of facilities between mid-week conferences and weekend family breaks. All bedrooms are of Executive standard with coffee tables, writing desk and fax point; children under 16 are accommodated free in their parents' rooms; 18 rooms are reserved for non-smokers. Syndicate rooms convert to family use at weekends with wall-mounted let-down beds. Day rooms are more than adequate, with lounges on two levels in the central 'lodge' and a smart snooker room. The hotel also has a fine leisure club and its own Black Sheep pub. Light meals and snacks are served in Danby's Bar; more formal dining in Quarterjacks restaurant. Regional specialities at breakfast include Somerset venison sausages and Alderley trout served with scrambled eggs. In a modern business park near Junction 16 of the M5 (south of the M4/M5 interchange), so rather out of the way; there are special B&B rates at weekends. *Rooms 88. Garden, indoor swimming pool, children's splash pool, gymnasium, squash, sauna, solarium, steam room, children's playground. Access, Amex, Diners, Visa.*

Bristol   Browns Restaurant and Bar

Tel 0272 304777	Restaurant
38 Queen's Road Bristol Avon BS8 1RE	Map 13 F1

Housed in the former University Refectory building at the top of Park Street (next door to Bristol Museum and the Wills Memorial Building), this, the fourth in the chain of American-style brasseries has been an instant hit with both students and city types. A busy bar and large dining area still leave room for a central grand piano and ubiquitous aspidistras, amongst which all-day diners choose from pasta, burgers, chargrilled chicken and puddings from pecan to chocolate mousse cake. Start the day with an English breakfast (£4.75) or drop by for cucumber sandwiches and scones at teatime (from £2.05). Children's menu of popular favourites and smaller portions of adult menu on request. At night very much a see-and-be-seen scene with fancy shaken cocktails, and ketchup from Heinz. Live piano music Mon-Thurs 6-8 & Sun 12.30-1.30; jazz quartet Sun 8-10.30pm. Twelve high-chairs and a large mothers' changing area in one of the Ladies (shelf and wipes provided). See also entries under Brighton, Cambridge and Oxford. *Seats 200. Open 11am-11.30pm (Sun & Bank Holidays from noon). Closed 25 & 26 Dec. Access, Amex, Visa.*

Bristol   Café Première

Tel 0272 734892	Café
59 Apsley Road Clifton Bristol Avon	Map 13 F1

The Narimani family's all-day café projects a cosmopolitan air, with its striped awnings and pavement tables clearly visible off Whiteladies Road, just below Clifton Down. Within, the potted plants, ceiling fans and light classical music create a pleasant atmosphere and bustling and generally slick table service keeps things moving. Breakfasts available all day range from Continental (£4.05) to Jack's traditional grill (£6.75); there are also vegetarian strudel, pancakes and casseroles (£5.85) and Eastern-inspired specialities such as fish teriyaki (£8.30) and lamb shashleek (£6.90). Less exotic lunch specials are typified by moussaka and vegetables (£6.20) and baked aubergine with spicy tomato sauce (£4.20). Care is well taken of families a half-floor below, with high-chairs and a booster seat, plastic cutlery and beakers all provided. The children's menu departs from the run-of-the-mill with pasta 'wiggly woos' and kids' breakfast with boiled egg and soldiers (£3.95) inciting not a little jealousy among the adults. Changing mat and emergency nappies provided in the Ladies. *Seats 42. Open 8am-6pm (Sun 9-5). Closed 25 & 26 Dec, 1 Jan. Access, Visa.*

Bristol   Guild Restaurant

Tel 0272 291874	Restaurant
68 Park Street Bristol Avon	**Map 13 F1**

Part of an elegant Georgian shop specialising in crafts and modern furnishings, this restaurant with a covered conservatory offers home-made soups, quiches (£3.70), salads, puddings and cakes as the mainstay. Specials include cashew nut paté (£3.35), wild mushroom and chicken liver terrine (£3.90), chicken with a tarragon sauce (£4.95), farmhouse sausages with baked potato (£3.75), leek bake in Stilton sauce (£4) and apricot and almond fool (£2.25) or trifle with framboise liqueur (£2.45). The 'spécialité de la maison' is chocolate cake (£1.85) baked by their resident *chocolatier*. Children's portions available. No smoking. **Seats** *70.* **Open** *10-4.30.* **Closed** *Sun, Bank Holidays. No credit cards.*

Bristol   Jameson's Restaurant   £50

Tel 0272 276565	Bistro
30 Upper Maudlin Street Bristol Avon BS2 8DJ	**Map 13 F1**

Opposite the Royal Infirmary, Carole Jameson's well-patronised, lively and informal bistro now has earlier evening opening and offers better value menus than last year. The latter now include Sunday lunch (children's portions: large half-price, small £1.50) and imaginative vegetarian selections throughout the week. Listed on a blackboard are the day's fresh fish dishes often featuring sardines, sea bream, monkfish and a Mediterranean fish soup. Otherwise, the style of the menu follows the lines of smoked fish terrine, goat's cheese in filo pastry, fresh soup, beef Wellington, rack of lamb and roast duckling with orange and port wine sauce. Accomplished cooking and an evolving wine list with good Australian bottles. Service is friendly and the music at times equally lively. High-chairs, children's cutlery and storage for push-chairs provided. **Seats** *70. Private Room 40. L 12-2 (to 4 Sun) D 6.30-11.30. Closed L Mon & Sat, D Sun. Set L from £5.50 Set D £12.95/£14.95. Access, Visa.*

Bristol   Rainbow Café

Tel 0272 738937	Café
10 Water Street Clifton Bristol Avon	**Map 13 F1**

This arts-orientated café remains a popular lunchtime favourite with both meat-eaters and vegetarians since the middle of the day brings the greatest choice: green pea and mint soup(£1.30), chicken, grape and tarragon salad (£4.50), mushroom and barley casserole (£4.95), carrot and cashew nut paté (£3.60), quiches (£1.80 – smoked haddock or spinach and bacon). Good fresh salads accompany main courses. You may like to finish with blackberry and apple pie or pear and ginger crumble (both £1.85). Outside lunch hours, the good baking extends to fruit or cheese scones (60p), cakes and slices. Home-made ice cream is always available (coconut and cardamon £1.50). One high-chair provided. No-smoking area. **Seats** *38.* **Open** *10-5.30 (full meals 12-2.30).* **Closed** *Sun. No credit cards.*

Bristol   Redwood Lodge Hotel & Country Club   64%   £85

Tel 0275 393901 Fax 0275 392104	Hotel

Beggar Bush Lane Failand Bristol Avon BS8 3TG   Map 13 F1

Barely ten minutes from the city centre (via Clifton Bridge) Redwood
Lodge offers conference facilities (for up to 175 delegates) and
an impressive choice of leisure activities. Individual residents may lose
out on quiet corners, bedroom space and room service, which
is sporadic at best. Weekenders with families fare better, as there's
plenty to do: an all-day coffee shop, 175-seat cinema (showing one
commercial release per weekend at 8pm) and regular crèche facilities
are available (9am-1.30pm). Children up to 16 stay free in parents'
room. Part of Whitbread's Country Club Hotel group (known for
their golfing facilities, but no golf at this hotel). Special weekend B&B
rates Mar-Aug. *Rooms 108. Garden, indoor, outdoor & children's
swimming pools, keep-fit equipment, sauna, solarium, beauty & hair salon,
tennis, squash, badminton, snooker, cinema, children's playroom &
playground, coffee shop (11am-10.30pm). Access, Amex, Diners, Visa.*

Bristol   Swallow Royal Hotel   77%   £118

Tel 0272 255100 Fax 0272 251515	Hotel

College Green Bristol Avon BS1 5TA   Map 13 F1

Swallow's newly-renovated hotel, faced in Bath stone, dominates
approaches to College Green and Bristol Cathedral. Equally
impressive, on arrival, is the Spanish marble hall flanked by country
house elegance in the drawing room and Club Bar, and a basement
leisure club of Roman bath design. Secure covered parking is a bonus.
Generous space, stylish individual decor and air-conditioning establish
bedrooms high in the comfort category; marble bathrooms are well
lit. Staff are smart, attentive and motivated; company policy,
it appears, is responsible for some lapses in service (no evening turn-
down for instance) which such a standard of hotel deserves. Families
can eat informally in the Drawing Room; Sammy Swallow's
children's menu is served in the Terrace Restaurant. *Rooms 242. Indoor
swimming pool, sauna, solarium, spa bath, beauty salon, hairdressing, keep-
fit equipment. Closed 2 days Christmas. Access, Amex, Diners, Visa.*

Palm Court Restaurant   £65

The grand Palm Court extends up through three floors lined in Bath
stone with curved balustrades and topped by stained-glass skylights.
Menus follow the grand format while the service is formal yet
unfussy. A fixed-price "Concept of the Kitchen" may run through
glazed asparagus with salmon tartare, poached oysters, rosemary-
infused lamb and summer pudding, supplemented by a seasonal
à la carte. The disappointing wine list would benefit from more half
bottles. *Seats 60. Parties 8. D only 7.30-10.30. Closed Sun & Mon,
27-29 Dec. Set D £23 (£25 Fri & Sat).*

Terrace Restaurant   £50

Almost as grand as the Palm Court, the Terrace is surprisingly formal
for a hotel's 'second' restaurant; main courses arrive *sous cloche* and the
sommelier comes complete with *tastevin* hanging from a chain around
his neck. The menu is rather less daunting with the à la carte including
simple grills, liver and bacon with mashed potatoes and onion gravy,
and crispy leg of duck with mushy peas along with the likes of red
mullet glazed with endive and orange, and braised lamb with

aubergine purée and gremolata. Overlooking Cathedral Square. **Seats 150.**
L 12.30-2.30 D 7-10.30. Set L £12.50/£15 Set D £15.50/£19.

Bristol	**Watershed Café-Bar**	
Tel 0272 21435		Café
1 Cannons Road Cannons Marsh Bristol Avon		Map 13 F1

A bright and breezy first-floor café in the Watershed arts and cinema
complex with large windows, wide open in summer, looking down
across the old dock basin. Food orders are made and paid for at a busy
counter and pretty promptly delivered. In addition to soups (£1.70),
sandwiches such as tuna mayonnaise (£2.30) and sticky cakes and
pastries, lunch specials on the board may range from broccoli and
cauliflower cheese (£3.85) to cod fillet with a Mexican sweet pepper
topping (£4). Notably grease-free chips are still a popular choice
of the littlest ones and can come with a child's portion of almost
anything. There's use of a side-entrance lift, on request, for wheelchairs
and buggies (the café's up two flights of stairs); room to change baby
in the disabled loo. While the rafters echo a bit to the sound of jazzy
(though scarcely intrusive) tapes, there are plenty of exhibits to browse
over in the adjacent galleries. Hot food till 4pm only. Two high-
chairs. **Seats 100. Open** 10.30am-9pm (Sun 11-4). **Closed 21-31 Dec.**
Access, Amex, Diners, Visa.

Broadway	**Collin House**	65%	£88
Tel 0386 858354			Hotel
Collin Lane Broadway Hereford & Worcester WR12 7PB			Map 14 C1

A Cotswold-stone house about a mile north-west of Broadway
signposted off the A44 Evesham road (turn right at Collin Lane). John
Mills and his friendly staff offer a warm welcome and plenty of advice
on what to see and do in the neighbourhood (a book of handwritten
notes is placed in each bedroom). Rooms are spacious and have
a cottagey feel with country furnishings and pretty floral fabrics.
In the winter months blazing log fires bring cheer to the lounge and
bar where a lunchtime menu might have mussels in cider, celery and
thyme (£5.25), grilled herrings in a grain mustard sauce (£5.25),
braised oxtails (£6.50), poached breast of chicken with ginger and
spring onions (£6.50) or duck casserole with herb dumplings (£6.20),
all with garden vegetables or salad. For dessert either bread-and-butter
pudding with brandy and whipped cream or treacle tart with home-
made ginger ice cream. Ask for children's portions. On Sundays, the
four-course lunch (£15) starts with a basket of crudités with dips and
breads. Children under 6 are welcome, but "by arrangement"; £20
charge for an extra bed in a room, cots £10. High tea is happily
served from 5pm, as the candle-lit dining room is reserved for adults
at dinner. **Rooms 7.** *Garden, outdoor swimming pool. Closed 24-29 Dec.*
Access, Visa.

Restaurant	£60

In the oak-beamed restaurant great store is set by fresh local
ingredients. Duck is something of a speciality: on a spring menu
it appeared with chicken and pork in a terrine served with quince jelly
and crisply roasted breast with a honey, ginger and kumquat sauce.
On the same menu were pan-fried salmon croquettes, veal Holstein,
grilled halibut steak and carpetbagger steak. Tempting puddings. Bar
and garden lunches are an alternative to the fixed-price menu, and
there's a traditional Sunday lunch (£15, children welcome – charged

according to appetite!). The price of the three-course dinner is shown
against the main course. Short wine list with all areas represented
at fair prices. 'Fine wine' dinners are held every couple of months.
Seats 24. Parties 32. L 12-1.30 D 7-9. Set L £14.50 Set D from £18.

Broadway	Dormy House	69%	£110

Tel 0386 852711 Fax 0386 858636	Hotel

Willersey Hill Broadway Hereford & Worcester WR12 7LF	Map 14 C1

Just off the A44, on an escarpment above Broadway and with views
over the local golf course and the Vale of Evesham, Dormy House
is an extended 17th-century farmhouse. Beams, exposed stonework
and tiled floors set the tone in the main house, whose two homely
lounges have fine bay windows. Converted outbuildings house
cottagey, comfortable bedrooms, many also with timbered ceilings;
two rooms have four-posters. Delegates at the purpose-built conference
centre seem to appreciate the rustic, Cotswold-stone Barn Owl bar
where less formal lunch and dinner menus are available (as well
as afternoon tea). Families welcome; baby-sitting by arrangement;
children's supper menu (£7.50) served from 5pm. **Rooms 49.** *Garden,
table tennis. Access, Amex, Diners, Visa.*

Restaurant   £88

A conservatory overlooks the garden and surrounding countryside,
giving a brighter alternative to the more formal, dimly-lit dining
room, where John Sanderson produces à la carte, table d'hote,
vegetarian and gourmet menus that all display a modern leaning
in both presentation and content. Salad of lamb's tongue, snails,
lardons, button onions and mushrooms with hazelnuts, 'feuillette'
of steamed leeks with pan-fried scallops, steak tartare, pot au feu
of seafood with salmon, turbot and sea bass and salmon and crab
ravioli are all typical of the style. Leave room for the sharp lemon
soufflé served with a lime sorbet in a brandy snap basket – worth the
30-minute wait, or good French cheeses. An improved wine list has
a good selection of half bottles, and plenty of choice under £20.
*Seats 80. Parties 20. Private Room 40. L 12.30-2 D 7.30-9.30 (Fri & Sat
from 7, Sun to 9). Closed L Sat, 3 days Xmas. Set L £14/£16
Set D £25.50/£33.*

Broadway	The Lygon Arms, Goblets Wine Bar	

Tel 0386 852255	Wine Bar

High Street Broadway Hereford & Worcester	Map 14 C1

Part of the world-renowned *Lygon Arms Hotel*, the cosy and
atmospheric Goblets Wine Bar has a beamed interior with leaded
mullion windows and an ancient inglenook fireplace. The seasonal
lunch and supper menu may offer baked English Brie with walnuts
and a country salad (£3.05), smoked mackerel fillets with a rhubarb
chutney (£3), smoked haddock and potato bake with a Welsh rarebit
topping (£5.15), chicken, leek and barley pie (£4.95). Light meals
and daily specials are written up on the blackboard: omelettes (from
£4.20), filled jacket potatoes (£2.70) and casserole of the day. Home-
made puddings are £1.95, cheese and biscuits £2.50. Families are
welcome in the Tankard room; high-chairs provided. *Seats 65.*
Open *11.30-2 & 6-9.30.* **Closed** *2 weeks early Jan. Access, Amex,
Diners, Visa.*

Brockenhurst   Le Blaireau Café/Bar

Tel 0590 23032	Brasserie
Brockenhurst Hampshire	**Map 14 C4**

Set back just off the Brockenhurst-Lyndhurst road, next to the entrance to *Carey's Manor* hotel (and under the same ownership), is a very Gallic brasserie with prix-fixe menus, French-speaking staff led by Jean-Marc Charton and accordion music in the background. High stools at the curving bar (complete with 'pression' beer tap), distinctive posters, a pétanque pitch outside and the rear end of a green Citroen 2CV decorating a wall inside all help perfect the French look! Try a *croissant, pain au chocolat, croque monsieur* (£2.35) or sandwich (made with freshly made baguette) for breakfast, or choose from more substantial offerings like fine pizzas (£3.25-£4.95), omelettes (£3.35-£4.95), *soupe de poissons* served from a tureen (£4.75), *moules marinière* (£6.35), *steak frites* and daily blackboard specials (*légumes à la grecque* £2.25, *boeuf cocotte grand-mère, merlan dugléré, bavarois rhubanné*). Three excellent-value fixed-price menus offer an interesting choice – perhaps *soupe à l'oignon* or *paté forestière* to start, followed by *filet de porc Strogonov* or *filet de dorade bonne femme,* then rich chocolate mousse with rum or *citron givré* to finish (£11.95 dinner/£9.95 lunch). A special promotion as we went to press took £2 off lunchtime prices. A delightful private room – La Rue – to the rear is decorated in the style of a typical shopping street in a small French town and is a most unusual venue for a party. Two high-chairs and changing facilities provided. The hotel's small outdoor play area is round to one side of the restaurant. *Seats 120. Open 10-2.30 & 6-11 (10am-11pm mid-July to early Sept). Closed 24 Dec (eve) & 25 Dec. Access, Amex, Visa.*

Broom   Broom Tavern

Tel 0789 773656	Pub
High Street Broom Warwickshire B60 5HL	**Map 14 C1**

Pretty, timbered village pub dating back to the 16th century, with Virginia creeper clinging to the outside and black beams and brass within. The bar menu, mostly home-made (except for some puds and soups), offers plenty of choice, from ploughman's (£3.75), sandwiches (from £2.50) and starters like duck paté (£3) and prawn cocktail (£3.25) to main dishes such as chicken chasseur (£5), steak and kidney pie (£5.40), lasagne verde (£5.95) and steaks plus omelettes and salad platters. Children are catered for with their own special dishes, a single high-chair and a bouncy castle out in the garden on summer weekends and during school holidays. *Bar Food 12-2, 7-9.30 (Sat 6.30-10, Sun 7-9). Restaurant Meals 12-2, 7-9 (to 9.30 Sat, closed Sun). Beer Whitbread. Access, Visa.*

Burley   Burley Manor   61%   £70

Tel 0425 403522 Fax 0425 403227	Hotel
Burley nr Ringwood Hampshire BH24 4BS	**Map 14 C4**

A Victorian manor house surrounded by 54 acres of parkland in the New Forest. Period decor includes stone fireplaces, a creaky staircase with carved balustrade and unusual commode side-tables. Bedrooms are simply decorated with tiled bathrooms; converted stable-block rooms are the largest and have the best views, plus steps leading on to the lawns and unprotected heated pool (Easter-end of Aug). Riding stables in the grounds offer rides in the New Forest for both novices and experts. Children's high tea served at 6.30-7pm (£5.45) – perhaps a little too late for little ones; high-chairs and cots are provided. Ask about Saturday dinner dances and wedding receptions that may affect the peacefulness of a visit. Dogs welcome. Forestdale Hotels. *Rooms 30. Garden, outdoor swimming pool, hairdressing, putting, coarse fishing. Access, Amex, Diners, Visa.*

Burley   Manor Farm Tea Rooms

Tel 0425 402218	Tea Room
Ringwood Road Burley New Forest Hampshire	**Map 14 C4**

Peter and Kathy Hunt run the archetypal English tea shop, with thatched roof, black beams, wheelback chairs and an open fireplace with a log fire in winter and a display of flowers in summer. Light snacks are served until 1.45 – perhaps a Cornish pastie (£1.05), bacon and mushroom muffin (£1.65) or a piece of fruit cake (80p). The lunch menu, served from midday to 1.45 might offer home-cooked ham, chips and peas (£3.45) or a mushroom omelette (£3.15). Only set afternoon teas are served after lunch but the choice of nine different versions allows for all tastes (£2.40-£4.60). Children's lunches (£1.75) include fish fingers, sausages, chicken nuggets with chips and beans or peas. High-chairs, baby food and bottles can all be provided. No-smoking area. *Seats 84. Open 10-5 (Sun from 10.30, Mon from 2). Closed 25, 26 & 31 Dec. No credit cards.*

Bury St Edmunds   Angel Hotel   66%   £99

Tel 0284 753926 Fax 0284 750092	Hotel
Angel Hill Bury St Edmunds Suffolk IP33 1LT	**Map 10 C2**

In continuous use as a hotel since 1452, the Angel is made up of several adjacent buildings (the oldest part dating back to the 12th century) that gained a unifying facade in Georgian times, now completely covered in Virginia creeper. Public areas are beginning to look a little tired and some of the soft furnishings need attention, but notably friendly staff create a welcoming atmosphere. Bedrooms come in all shapes and sizes from large rooms with four-poster beds and antique furniture to small singles with simple white-painted fitted units; all are in good order and individually decorated – often quite stylishly. 24hr room service. Ample parking. *Rooms 42. Access, Amex, Diners, Visa.*

Bury St Edmunds   Butterfly Hotel   62%   £61

Tel 0284 760884 Fax 0284 755476	Hotel
Symonds Road Bury St Edmunds Suffolk IP32 7BW	**Map 10 C2**

Take the Bury East exit from the A45 to the Butterfly, a modern low-riser with modest accommodation. Under-8s free in parents' room; baby-listening. A useful stop-over. No dogs. *Rooms 66. Access, Amex, Diners, Visa.*

Buxton   Nathaniel's

Tel 0298 78388	Restaurant
35 High Street Buxton Derbyshire	**Map 6 C2**

Situated at the top of the hill in what could be called 'old' Buxton, Nathaniel's glows a welcome with an open coal fire in the small reception/bar area. The restaurant (divided into two rooms) takes

up the ground floor of Andy and Yvonne Coates' home. The rear
room, leading to the kitchen, has a Mediterranean feel with bare
bricks, hanging plants and check tablecloths, while the front room
is painted pink. Three menus feature – à la carte, 'bistro' (evenings
only) and lunchtime. The latter two change daily and are less
expensive than the former: curried mushrooms (£2.45), warm
chicken livers with yoghurt dressing (£3.75), roast rib of beef with
Yorkshire pudding (£8.10), pork chop au poivre (£7.95), tandoori
chicken with rice and salad (£6.75), bread-and-butter pudding
or chilled vanilla soufflé (£1.95-£2.75). Coffee is served with cream.
Traditional 3-course Sunday lunch £9.45. Half portions and high-
chairs are available for children; telephone before visiting with a child
and one of the larger tables will be set aside for you. The owners are
happy for one of their private rooms to be used for nappy changing
or breast-feeding. Not very ideal for a very active toddler, perhaps but
generally friendly and flexible. *Seats* 35. *Open* 12-2.30 & 7-10.30.
Closed D Sun, all Mon. *Access, Amex, Diners, Visa.*

Cadeby   Cadeby Inn

Tel 0709 864009	Pub

Main Street Cadeby nr Doncaster South Yorkshire DN5 7SW	Map 7 D2

This atmospheric old inn was clearly once an elegant country
farmhouse and stands today in a mature orchard garden full
of flowering shrubs. There's plenty of space here for little ones to play
safely, and the picnic tables are especially popular when there's
a barbecue on. In poor weather, children are allowed in the non-
smoking snug, but only until 8pm. Original flagstones and fireplaces
survive in the two bars whose counters are built in brick, while the
walls are hung with horse collars, brasses and webbing. A salad bar
operates at luunchtime, with a hot roast (£4.55) on Sundays. Food,
otherwise, is pretty basic with Yorkshire pudding and onion gravy
(£1.60) and grilled steaks and gammon about the only items not out
of a freezer. Children's burgers and chicken nuggets (from £1.85)
come with mounds of soggy chips. Nonetheless, the Chequers
remains a popular haunt. 200 malt whiskies. *Free House.* **Beer** *Tetley
Best, Burton Ale, John Smith's Best & Magnet, Samuel Smith's Old
Brewery. Garden, children's play area. Family room. Access, Visa.*

Camberley   Frimley Hall   68%   £122

Tel 0276 28321 Fax 0276 691253	Hotel

Portsmouth Road Camberley Surrey GU15 2BG	Map 15 E3

A short distance from Junction 3 of the M3, a turn-of-the-century
Victorian manor house surrounded by splendid grounds that are
floodlit at night. Magnificent stained-glass windows overlook
an impressive carved wooden staircase – Victorian style that is carried
through to the traditionally furnished bedrooms in the main house,
two of which have four-poster beds. However, most of the bedrooms
are located in a modern extension and are smaller, but equally
appealing; 16 are designated non-smoking. Families are well catered
for, particularly at weekends when rates are reduced; fun pack
provided. Children up to 16 stay free in parents' room. Conference
and meeting rooms have Victorian character as well and cater for
up to 60 delegates. Forte Heritage. *Rooms* 66. *Garden. Access, Amex,
Diners, Visa.*

Cambridge   Browns

Tel 0223 461655 Fax 0223 460426	Restaurant
23 Trumpington Street Cambridge Cambridgeshire CB2 1QA	**Map 15 F1**

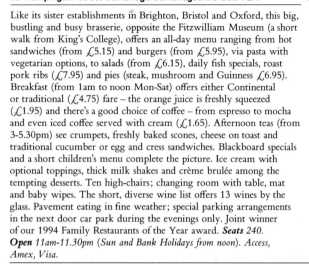

Like its sister establishments in Brighton, Bristol and Oxford, this big, bustling and busy brasserie, opposite the Fitzwilliam Museum (a short walk from King's College), offers an all-day menu ranging from hot sandwiches (from £5.15) and burgers (from £5.95), via pasta with vegetarian options, to salads (from £6.15), daily fish specials, roast pork ribs (£7.95) and pies (steak, mushroom and Guinness £6.95). Breakfast (from 1am to noon Mon-Sat) offers either Continental or traditional (£4.75) fare – the orange juice is freshly squeezed (£1.95) and there's a good choice of coffee – from espresso to mocha and even iced coffee served with cream (£1.65). Afternoon teas (from 3-5.30pm) see crumpets, freshly baked scones, cheese on toast and traditional cucumber or egg and cress sandwiches. Blackboard specials and a short children's menu complete the picture. Ice cream with optional toppings, thick milk shakes and crème brulée among the tempting desserts. Ten high-chairs; changing room with table, mat and baby wipes. The short, diverse wine list offers 13 wines by the glass. Pavement eating in fine weather; special parking arrangements in the next door car park during the evenings only. Joint winner of our 1994 Family Restaurants of the Year award. *Seats 240.* *Open 11am-11.30pm (Sun and Bank Holidays from noon). Access, Amex, Visa.*

Cambridge   Cambridgeshire Moat House   63%   £78

Tel 0954 780555 Fax 0954 780010	Hotel
Bar Hill Cambridge Cambridgeshire CB3 8EU	**Map 15 F1**

The grounds of this well-designed modern hotel on the A604 include a golf course. There's also a leisure centre (including a children's paddling pool) and numerous conference suites, the largest with a capacity of 180, theatre-style. Several bedrooms are suitable for family use, and baby-listening and baby-sitting can be organised in advance. Special mid-week family rates. Snacks in the Gallery bar and lounge; 5.50-6.30pm children's meal time in the dining room at weekends; high-chairs provided; carvery at Sunday lunch. Two children up to 16 stay free in parents' room at weekends. *Rooms 100.* *Garden, indoor swimming pool, keep-fit equipment, squash, spa bath, steam room, solarium, tennis, pool table. Closed 25 & 26 Dec. Access, Amex, Diners, Visa.*

Cambridge   Hobbs Pavilion

Tel 0223 67480	Creperie
Hobbs Pavilion Park Terrace Cambridge Cambridgeshire	**Map 15 F1**

Tucked behind the University Arms and bordering the cricket squares of Parker's Piece, Hobbs Pavilion's substitution of cricket teas with creperie scores steadily with a non-combatant clientele. Owners Stephen and Susan Hill started a family of their own last year but their eminently sensible advice on the menu is unlikely to change: "as you can see from the provision of high-chairs, we are pleased to have children amongst our guests. Out (of) concern for the welfare of everyone, however, we must insist that the child in your care is reasonably quiet. (This does not mean silent). All children have "bad days", but it is unreasonable to expect other customers to have to share the consequences of them. It is also unreasonable to wait for us to tell you when the child in your care is dominating the restaurant's atmosphere and then take offence at that request." Soup (or daily starters on a blackboard) to start, then a choice of 20 or so savoury pancakes cooked to order on circular bakestones; ambitious fillings range from 'Bumper Vegetarian' with cheese, spinach, tomatoes, basil and horseradish through various 'pizza' fillings to 'The Cyclist's' pancake containing chargrilled steak, mashed potato, egg and spinach (£7.50); various fillings are aslo served cold as a salad. A 'menu enfant' offers a bacon sandwich, ice cream with flake and glass of Orangina. Sweeter versions, deftly turned into crispy fans, may contain banana, stem ginger and cream (£3.50) or the perils of 'praline' topped with hazelnut crème (£3.85). Multifarious wines by the glass, fruit juices, speciality teas and coffees. No-smoking area. Outdoor eating for around 24 in good weather. Twitchy toddlers can play outside on the grass while parents wait for their meal on the pavilion steps. Our duck symbol is awarded for one year only for clearly stating the terms on which parents may bring their children; parking may not be particularly easy and there are no changing facilities, but the food is the obvious draw. Clearly the formula is successful as there are usually children in the restaurant on most nights; nevertheless, lunchtime is the best time for youngsters. *Seats 60. Open 12-2.15 & 7-9.45. Closed Sun, Mon, Bank Holidays, mid Aug-mid Sept. No credit cards.*

Cambridge   The Little Tea Room at Perfect Setting
Tel 0223 63207   **Tea Room**
1 All Saints Passage Cambridge Cambridgeshire   **Map 15 F1**

A proper old-fashioned kitchen tea room, nicely decorated in navy blue and lemon with fresh flowers on pine tables, pictures on the walls and classical music – Perfect Setting is the perfect place to feel at home in relaxed and cosy surroundings. Situated in a three-storey house down a pretty passage opposite St John's College, it offers popular teas such as the Post Tutorial Tea which comprises a pot of tea, cucumber sandwiches, home-made scone, jam and cream plus a choice of cake (£3.95). It is perhaps most famous for its hot home-made lemon curd which comes draped over a lemon cake with whipped cream (£1.95). A range of sandwiches with various interesting fillings is available from £1.75: white Stilton and pickle, pastrami, lettuce and mayonnaise and their most popular – egg mayonnaise and cress. Baked potatoes (from £2.25) and the Perfect Breakfast (orange juice, hot drink, croissant, butter, lemon curd or jam £2.75) can be indulged in all day. No smoking. Good selection of teas. *Seats 27. Open 9.30-5.30 (Sun 12-6 Mar to 23 Dec). Closed 25 & 26 Dec. Access, Visa.*

Camelford   Lanteglos Country House Hotel   £100*
Tel 0840 213551   **Hotel**
Camelford Cornwall PL32 9RF   **Map 12 C3**

Lanteglos is set in 15 acres of gardens and woodland and on entering the estate you are immediately made aware of the presence of children, by road signs warning of children at play. In all there are 66 self-catering villas and lodges (sleeping 5 and marketed by Hoseasons) as well as 17 rooms in the 19th-century hotel. Along with 100 cots, they can provide baby baths, potties, safety gates and nappy buckets and a sophisticated baby-listening device. It is an absolute paradise for children, with secret play areas in the woods, four playgrounds, an adventure playground and a games room. The outside pool is well heated and the shallow children's pool has a central island with a fountain. Bedrooms are tastefully furnished, spacious and comfortable. Children's teatime is a carefree affair when children can choose dishes like roast chicken and gravy or Cornish pastie, as well as the usual beefburger and spaghetti bolognese. Don't be late finishing dinner or you'll miss the children's entertainment which starts at 6 o'clock. The minimum stay is two nights and with so much to do this is probably just as well. *Half-board terms only. **Rooms** 17, 66 villas. **Closed** Dec-March. Under-5s free (except in August). Access, Visa.

Canterbury	Ebury Hotel	59%	£60
Tel 0227 768433 Fax 0227 459187			Hotel
65 New Dover Road Canterbury Kent CT1 3DX			Map 11 C5

Two Victorian houses, standing just back from the road, with a large garden, an antique-furnished lounge and a 30'x 15' indoor swimming pool. Light, airy bedrooms have recently been refurbished in mahogany and largely re-carpeted; cots free, extra beds £8. Large garden. Self-catering flats and bungalows in the grounds are let on a weekly basis. Family owned and run. One mile south-east of the city centre; it's an enjoyable walk down to the Cathedral. **Rooms** 15. Garden, indoor swimming pool, spa bath. **Closed** 24 Dec-14 Jan. Access, Amex, Visa.

Canterbury	Falstaff Hotel	£85
Tel 0227 462138 Fax 0227 463525		Inn
8 St Dunstan's Street Canterbury Kent CT2 8AF		Map 11 C5

A centuries-old coaching inn whose day rooms get character from original beams, leaded windows and polished oak tables. Bedrooms are neat and pretty and the majority use solid modern furniture that suits the feel of the place perfectly. Children under 14 are accommodated free – with a full traditional English breakfast – when sharing with an adult. Six rooms are reserved for non-smokers. Within easy walking distance of the town centre, next to the Westgate Towers. No dogs. Part of Whitbread's Lansbury Hotel group. **Rooms** 25. Access, Amex, Diners, Visa.

Canterbury	Il Vaticano Pasta Parlour	
Tel 0227 765333		Restaurant
35 St Margarets Street Canterbury Kent		Map 11 C5

Eat enjoyable Italian fare either in the poster-adorned dining room or the walled garden: start with *gamberetti grigliati* (large grilled prawns in garlic butter £3.95), *patate ripiene* (half a baked potato filled with mushrooms, Cheddar and mozzarella – £2.65) and follow with one of the four pastas: spaghetti, tagliatelle, farfalle and pennette served with one of 14 sauces (*capponata* – vegetables in tomato sauce £4.95, *paradiso* – smoked salmon, prawns in cream and champagne sauce £7.75), or choose a risotto (chicken and prawn in a cream and tomato sauce £6.95) or *alla chitarra* (spicy minced beef and smoked ham in a red wine and tomato sauce). Gateaux (£2.85) to finish. Two high-chairs; changing facilities in Ladies. Walled garden. **Seats** 50. **Open** 11.30-10.30 (Sun 12-10). **Closed** 25 & 26 Dec. Access, Amex, Diners, Visa.

Carlisle   The Grapevine

Tel 0228 46617	Restaurant
22 Fisher Street Carlisle Cumbria CA3 9RH	Map 4 C2

Hanging baskets of greenery and pictures by local artists decorate this friendly, counter-service restaurant in the YMCA building. A varied, all-day menu ranges from hot dishes like Malayan chicken curry (£2.75), lasagne and pitta bread, and vegetable soup to aduki bean, courgette and mushroom bake (£2.75), or filo pastry cheese and nut pasties (£1.15). There's a splendid choice of some 18 salads to accompany and for the sweet-toothed there are various gateaux (£1.25), a moist, buttered teabread (85p) and scrumptious coconut and cherry slice with chocolate. Two evenings a month there's a bookable, eat-as-much-as-you-like, hot and cold buffet at £7.75. Two high-chairs. Upstairs, under the same ownership, is a fully fledged crèche/nursery (with changing facilities) where they will look after the little ones while you eat. **Seats** 70. **Open** 9.30-4.30 (Mon 10-2.30). *Closed Sun, 25 & 26 Dec, 1 Jan, Easter Bank Holiday. No credit cards.*

Carlisle   Hudson's Coffee Shop

Tel 0228 47733	Coffee Shop
Treasury Court Fisher Street Carlisle Cumbria	Map 4 C2

With its William Morris wallpaper, bentwood and wicker chairs, and views across an attractive courtyard and mini garden centre, Steve Hudson's coffee shop is a pleasant place to stop for breakfast, snack lunch or tea. The vegetarian (£2.95) and traditional (£4.05) breakfasts are served all day. Snacks include toasted sandwiches (from £1.30), breaded plaice or battered cod, scampi (£4.95), vegetarian beanburger (£4.25) or lasagne (£4.55) and griddled steak (£8.45). Home baking brings shortbreads, tea breads, spicy carrot cake, cheesecake and scones (from 65p). There's a children's menu, high-chairs, mother and baby room, and toys. The waitress service extends to the courtyard outside on fine days. The Ladies is thoughtfully equipped with a changing bench and a bin for nappies and a courtyard provides space for playing. No smoking. **Seats** 90. **Open** 9-5. **Closed** *Sun, Bank Holidays (except Fri). Access, Amex, Visa.*

Carlyon Bay   Carlyon Bay Hotel   68%   £122

Tel 0726 812304 Fax 0726 814938	Hotel
Sea Road Carlyon nr St Austell Cornwall PL25 3RD	Map 12 B3

Set in 250 acres of sub-tropical gardens and grounds, the hotel enjoys superb views over the bay. It was built in 1930, and while still admirably fulfilling its role of family holiday hotel, it also offers extensive conference/function facilities (for up to 200/250 delegates) and a weekly dinner dance (Saturday). Large-windowed lounges, furnished in traditional style, make the most of the splendid setting, as do most of the light, attractive bedrooms (a supplement is charged for sea-facing rooms). Families are particularly well catered for, with good outdoor facilities and an indoor pool for youngsters. Under-2s stay free in their parents' room during low season (a small charge per day in high season); 2-8s are charged 25%, 9-13s 50% of adult rates. Summer entertainment for children ranges from bouncy castle and fancy dress party magic show during high tea to competitions arranged by a resident entertainer. For the under-5s a childminder can be arranged (at extra cost). Parents can also use the in-house launderette facility on the lower ground floor. A children's menu contains a treasure chest of smuggled goodies (let the baby try the purée of fresh vegetables) and is available each day in the restaurant from 5.30-6.30pm. Outside, an adventure paddock incorporates swings, slides, tree house (and even a pets' corner in summer) within a safe, contained, easily-supervised wooded area. Parents can enjoy the excellent leisure facilities; the restaurant's offerings are not so exciting and gentlemen need a jacket and tie after 7pm. Brend Hotels.

Rooms 73. Garden, 18-hole golf course, 9-hole approach golf course, tennis, helipad, indoor & outdoor swimming pools, spa bath, sauna, solarium, snooker, children's playground. Access, Amex, Diners, Visa.

Castle Cary   Old Bakehouse

Tel 0963 50067	Vegetarian
High Street Castle Cary Somerset	Map 13 E2

Carol Sealey's stone-fronted High Street premises are both wholefood shop and vegetarian café (available in the shop are herbs, spices, organic wheat grains and pure fruit juices). In the café, neatly bedecked with floral cloths and curtains, and hung with watercolours for sale, organically grown produce and wholemeal quiche and pizza bases typify her culinary dedication. A daily-changing lunchtime menu offers carefully chosen seasonal dishes – a lightly curried parsnip and apple soup (£1.40), green lentil cakes with tomato sauce and mixed vegetable lasagne (£3.30). Top sellers to follow include a fine toffee date pudding and apricot and almond tart (with cream £1.60). Cream teas (£2.20) throughout the afternoon accompany the home baking, banana and walnut slice, carrot cake with cream cheese, or Irish tea bread with butter. Children's portions available. No smoking.

Seats 35. Open 9-5. Closed Sun, Mon & Bank Holidays. No credit cards.

Cawsand   Wringford Down

Tel 0752 822287	Hotel
Wringford Down Cawsand nr Plymouth Cornwall PL10 1LE	Map 12 C3

Advertised as a children's hotel, Wringford Down is more realistically described as an extended stone farmhouse offering B&B-quality accommodation, a house party atmosphere and exceptional facilities for younger children – "everything is geared to help you look after your babies and toddlers as you would at home". Run in a committed fashion by Andrea and Harvey Jay, it nestles among the rolling downs of south-east Cornwall, close to Plymouth and the beaches of Whitsand Bay; there are lovely countryside views all around and buzzards fly overhead. Bedrooms are modest (family suites have the best views and are the best value as children's meals are included) and TVs optional, but there is a TV lounge next door to the indoor play room where toys are provided. Young children are likely to be thrilled at the chance of a ride on Barney or Poncho the resident donkeys, stroking an Angora rabbit, meeting Mozart the sheep or just running away from the family of Vietnamese pot-bellied black pigs that live at the end of the garden. The hot swimming pool (open Apr-Nov) is in a separate shed at the end of the garden, so a walk to it in wet weather may be less enthralling! Nevertheless, an enormous play barn will keep youngsters amused for hours if the weather's bad – there's a sand pit, climbing ropes, table tennis, Little Tike push cars, BMX bikes, roller skating, aquarium and a padded playpen for crawlers. Outside there are swings, slides, a toboggan slide and a climbing frame. Food is homely – take a good helping of patience with you, as the only child-free zone (after 8pm) is the small bar at the

end of the dining room. Ideal for under-5s; children's high tea
(£1.50) – the first to finish their main course gets the biggest choice
of wobbly puddings – is served at a long, communal table while
parents enjoy a pot of tea. If you want to investigate before staying,
drop in for afternoon tea – served in a sun-trap extension room. Only
guests with children are accepted; half-board terms during the main
season (1993 prices £170-£210 per person per week; around £30 per
head for nightly terms out of season); under-5s accommodated free
(meals paid for as taken), 5- to 10-year-olds half price. Cots, high-
chairs, booster seats, bibs, small cutlery and beakers all provided. A car
is really needed to make the most of a stay here. Dobwalls Theme
Park outside Liskeard is well worth a visit, offering wooded adventure
play areas, delightful picnic areas and rides on miniature railways –
guaranteed to please. **Rooms** 12. *Garden, indoor swimming & paddling
pool, play barn, laundry room, communal microwave, fridge & steriliser,
baby listening, pool table. No credit cards.*

Chagford	Mill End	63%	£80
Tel 0647 432282 Fax 0647 433106			Hotel
Sandy Park Chagford Devon TQ13 8JN			Map 13 D2

The old flour mill, whose wheel still turns in the courtyard, has been
a hotel since about 1929. It stands on the edge of Dartmoor in the
beautiful valley of the river Teign, on whose banks the hotel has
fishing rights. Shooting is another popular pastime, while for quiet
relaxation the chintzy sitting rooms have the appeal of a well-loved
private house. Bedrooms are furnished with a mixture of traditional,
antique and modern pieces; children can play on grass immediately
outside some rooms. Children up to 15 sharing their parents' room are
accommodated free; good facilities for young families, including
a children's supper menu – from boiled eggs to cottage pie. The hotel
is on the A382 (don't turn off towards Chagford). **Rooms** 17. *Garden,
fishing, shooting. Closed 10 days mid-Dec, 10 days mid-Jan. Access, Amex,
Diners, Visa.*

Chale	Clarendon Hotel/Wight Mouse Inn	
Tel 0983 730431 Fax 0983 730431		Pub
Chale Isle of Wight PO38 2HA		Map 15 D4

This 17th-century coaching inn (on B3399 towards the bottom of the
island) is a perennial favourite, for food, atmosphere, bed and breakfast
and the genuine welcome to children: the Wight Mouse Inn was our
1990 Family Pub of the Year. Parents with children are treated like
first-class citizens both inside and out – hurrah! There are decent
home-made bar meals, too, featuring delicious local fish and seafood
including smoked mackerel paté (£2.30), local crab cocktail (£3.10)
and breaded cod (£3.60), and an astonishing choice of 365 whiskies.
The recently extended dining room has a set five-course dinner menu
for £17 which includes dishes such as deep-fried Brie with raspberry
sauce, chicken kebabs, stuffed trout and turkey escalopes with Jamaican
banana and rum sauce. Nice bedrooms in the Clarendon next door
successfully blend period and modern comforts, excellent family
facilities and pretty views of the sea. One bedroom has a waterbed and
there is also a luxury family suite. Over-6s pay half price, over-13s
two-thirds. Two gardens, one of which overlooks Chale Bay over
to the Needles and the other overlooks St Catherine's Down; a bouncy
castle and entertainment is provided in summer. If your child
is deciding which musical instrument to learn he/she can compare 150

that hang from the ceiling of the bar. *Bar Food & Restaurant Meals*
11.30-10 (12-2.30, 7-9.30 Sun). Children's menu. Free House. **Beer**
Burts, Marston Pedigree, Wadworth 6X. Family room (3 rooms). Garden,
outdoor eating, children's play area. **Accommodation** *15 bedrooms, all*
en suite, £56 (single £28). Children welcome overnight, cots available.
Access, Visa.

Charlbury	Bell Hotel	£75
Tel 0608 810278 Fax 0608 811447		**Inn**
Church Street Charlbury Oxfordshire OX7 3PP		**Map 14 C1**

Once a coaching inn, the Bell stands in the centre of town on the
banks of the Evenlode. Day rooms, including a flagstoned bar (with
open log fire in winter), have a comfortable, traditional appeal, and
bedrooms offer adequate accommodation. Small functions are catered
for (up to 55 people) and the hotel can organise many leisure/sporting
activities in the locality. Children up to 16 stay free in parents' room.
High-chairs are provided. *Free House.* **Beer** *Wadworth 6X, Hook*
Norton. Garden. **Accommodation** *14 bedrooms, all en suite, £75 (single*
£50). Children welcome overnight (under-16s stay free in parents' room),
additional beds and cots supplied. Access, Amex, Diners, Visa.

Charmouth	Fernhill Hotel	£45
Tel 0297 60492		**Hotel**
Charmouth Dorset DT6 6BX		**Map 13 E2**

Whether you stay in the hotel itself, or one of the self-catering
bungalows (not really bungalows but blocks of rooms), Fernhill
is suitable for family holidays. Although the accommodation
is extremely modest, the hotel's fourteen acres have excellent facilities
for children – its own heated swimming pool, paddling pool, games
room, crazy golf and an outdoor play area. There is even a launderette
for when you are forced to remember what you came to get away
from. The bungalows (bring your own linen and towels) have
a double bedroom, separate twin-bunk room, galley kitchen,
bathroom and child-listening service; TVs can be hired although there
is a television room in the hotel, as well as a lively bar. *Rooms 52*
(35 bungalows, 17 hotel). **Closed** *End October-March. Access, Visa.*

Chawton	Cassandra's Cup	
Tel 0420 83144		**Tea Shop**
The Hollies Winchester Road Chawton nr Alton Hampshire		**Map 15 D3**

Directly opposite Jane Austen's house in a pretty Hampshire village,
Cassandra's Cup is a small, bright tea shop with a few outside tables.
The menu covers a range of fruit tarts and teacakes (from 75p),
gateaux and scones, hot snacks on toast, jacket potatoes and breakfast
(bacon, egg and toast £3.20 served till noon). One high-chair. Park
with swings nearby. No smoking. *Seats 40.* **Open** *10.30-5 (Nov-Dec &*
Feb-Jun Wed-Sun only, Jan weekends only). **Closed** *Telephone for winter*
hours. No credit cards.

Cheam	Superfish	
Tel 081-643 6906		**Fish'n'Chips**
64 The Broadway Cheam Surrey		**Map 15 E3**

Part of a Surrey-based chain of above average fish and chip restaurants.
See Morden entry for more details. This, the Cheam branch,

is unlicensed. Unusually, for the chain, no high-chairs (as space
is limited). *Seats 22.* **Open** *11.30-2 (Sat to 2.30), 5-10.30 (Thu-Sat
to 11).* **Closed** *Sun, 25 & 26 Dec, 1 Jan. No credit cards.*

Cheddar   Wishing Well Tea Rooms

Tel 0934 742142	Tea Room
The Cliffs Cheddar Somerset	Map 13 F1

In Cheddar Gorge, this is a long-running family enterprise which
offers original choices in its range of afternoon teas. Plain tea (£1.85)
with bread and butter, cake and tea, cream tea (£2.40, with fresh fruit
salad and cream £2.55) and in season a strawberry tea is served with
clotted cream, scones, cake and tea. Savoury snacks include omelettes,
toasted snacks and freshly made sandwiches. On Sunday the Lewis
family serve a roast lunch (£5.50 for three courses). Two high-chairs;
changing mat and shelf in Ladies. Children's portions of most items.
Unlicensed. *Seats 64.* **Open** *10-6.* **Closed** *all Dec/Jan, Mon-Fri
Oct/Nov & Feb/Mar. Access, Visa.*

Cheltenham   The Retreat

Tel 0242 235436	Wine Bar
10 Suffolk Parade Cheltenham Gloucestershire	Map 14 B1

Food at Michael and Lella Day's friendly wine bar is served
at lunchtimes only and varies daily, with half the menu being suitable
for vegetarians: locally smoked hot chicken salad (£3.50), dolmas
(stuffed vine leaves) with garlic and lemon mayonnaise (£3.95),
chicken supreme in tarragon sauce (£5.50) and seafood risotto
(scallops, squid, prawns and crab claws on saffron rice), with treacle
tart or ricotta timbales and fresh fruit purées to finish. Children's
portions are available; two high-chairs. Alfresco eating is popular
in the enclosed courtyard. *Seats 60.* **Open** *12-2.15 only (for food).*
Closed *Sun, Bank Holidays. Access, Amex, Diners, Visa.*

Chester   Chester Grosvenor Hotel

Tel 0244 324024	Lounge/Brasserie
Eastgate Street Chester Cheshire	Map 6 A2

The Library (open 9.30am-5pm; closed Sun & Bank Holidays)
is a relaxing retreat within the Grosvenor Hotel; its menu is simple
but well done. Morning filter coffee with home-made biscuits and
afternoon tea with sandwiches, scones and pastries (£9.50). At lunch
the choice runs to sandwiches – open or closed (£5.25-£7.25), smoked
salmon, vegetable quiche with carrot and walnut salad and
a predominantly British cheeseboard. **La Brasserie** (open from 7am
for breakfast & noon-11pm) offers an all-day menu and a separate
children's menu with real food: tomato and cheese flan (£2.50),
Grosvenor fish cake with freshly prepared chips (£3.75), ravioli with
beef and a tomato sauce (£3.25), chicken kebab with rice and
barbecue sauce (£3.95); desserts from a trolley (£2.25) and fresh fruit
cocktail with a choc chip ice cream (£2.50). Six high-chairs. "Children
welcome at all times". Changing can be easily managed in one of the
hotel's cloakrooms.

Chester   Francs

Tel 0244 317952	Brasserie
14 Cuppin Street Chester Cheshire	**Map 6 A2**

Chester's busiest, noisy, bustling and chaotic brasserie serves traditional
French provincial fare. Bare floors, wooden tables, timber beams,
ceiling fans and French rock music playing over the loudspeakers set
the scene. The à la carte menu changes every six months and the *plats
du jour* every day (served from noon to 7pm with salad and plenty
of bread) – *noisettine* (£7.35 – hazelnut stuffing with mushrooms and
garlic cheese in butter puff pastry), *crepe aux champignons* (£3.50),
chicken breast stuffed with Boursin £7.35, *boeuf quatro* (£7.85).
Desserts have names such as *daquoise* (nutty meringue topped with
strawberries and cream), *tarte aux pommes* and *crème anglaise à la
mirabelle* all at £2.75. Sundays are family days when part of the first
floor is given over to a play (and dining) area for children (four-course
set menu £7.95, baby meals free) and under-10s eat free
(1 adult = 1 free child) – reservations recommended. Six high-chairs.
Changing facilities include complimentary wipes and nappies.
Seats 100. **Open** *12-11. Access, Amex, Visa.*

Chester   Rowton Hall   64%   £88

Tel 0244 335262 Fax 0244 335464	Hotel
Whitchurch Road Chester Cheshire CH3 6AD	**Map 6 A2**

Built as a private residence in 1779, the hall stands three miles out
of Chester on the A41, on the site of a Civil War battle. There's
a spacious reception area and a lounge bar (serving a snack menu)
looking out on to the smart indoor pool. Rooms in the old house are
stylish and individual, those in the adjoining wing more functional;
under-10s share parents' room free of charge. Good amenities
(Hamiltons Leisure Club – *strictly no children under 6 at any time*) and
conference facilities for up to 200. Baby-listening, high tea (6-7pm
by prior arrangement) and high-chairs provided. Only recommended
for parents with children over 6. **Rooms** *42. Garden, indoor swimming
pool, gymnasium, sauna, spa bath, solarium, squash, coffee bar (9am-11pm).
Closed 25 & 26 Dec. Access, Amex, Diners, Visa.*

Chichester   Clinchs Salad House

Tel 0243 788822	Vegetarian
14 Southgate Chichester West Sussex	**Map 11 A6**

Fresh flowers are always liberally used in the decor of this otherwise
plain and unfussy self-service vegetarian restaurant where the emphasis
is very firmly on the freshness of the food on offer. Alison Ellis, the
owner, insists that nothing is "bought in" and that everything is home-
made in the true sense of the word. The day could begin with the Old
English Breakfast (£2.75) and end with a cream tea (£2.75) but the
choice at lunchtime is varied: parsnip and tomato bake (£2.70), nut
roast with lemon sauce, home-cooked ham, vegetable and cheese layer
bake, mixed vegetable puff (£2.70) and a choice of seven different
salads (from £1.60-£2.20) is worthy of the distinction in the
establishment's name. Fresh baking will bring bread, scones, Bakewell
or treacle tart, blackcurrant cheesecake, and Pavlova (from 45p-
£1.20). Children's portions. No-smoking area. *Seats 48.* **Open** *8-5.*
Closed *Sun, Bank Holidays. No credit cards.*

Chichester   Comme Ca

Tel 0243 788724	Restaurant
67 Broyle Road Chichester West Sussex	Map 11 A6

It's the bar – small with green plush seating, swathes of dried flowers and log fire – of this popular French restaurant that is of particular interest to families. Although the bar menu is set out in courses there's no minimum charge or obligation to have more than a single dish, be it a starter – deep-fried Camembert with a gooseberry brandy sauce (£3.65), eggs bourguignon (£3.60), fresh fish pan-fried à la meunière (£3.85) – or main dish – veal with wild mushrooms in Madeira sauce (£8.95), turbot sautéed and served with a pink berry butter sauce (£8.95). Open from 11 for coffee and biscuits. One high-chair. The restaurant stands north of town on the A286, convenient for the Festival Theatre. *Seats 48. Open 11-2 & 6-10.30. Closed D Sun, all Mon, Bank Holidays. Access, Amex, Visa.*

Chichester   Shepherds Tea Rooms

Tel 0243 774761	Tea Room
35 Little London Chichester West Sussex	Map 11 A6

In a period house just off the main shopping street, Richard and Yvonne Spence set up their lace-clothed tea room to provide a 'haven of peace and tranquillity' some ten years ago and have won many plaudits. Today you may have to queue at busy times to enjoy the home-made cakes – cherry and coconut (£1), chocolate mousse cake (£1.95), sandwiches (from £2.85) and savoury snacks like filled jacket potatoes (from £3.65) and various 'rarebits' (a speciality of the house) including Hawaiian (with pineapple), Stilton and tomato (£4.40), buck (with poached egg), and Shepherd's (with Brie and tomato) as well as the traditional Welsh rarebit (£4.05). There are also teacakes, croissants, muffins and crumpets to accompany the fine selection of loose-leaf teas that include gunpowder (a green tea), Lapsang Suchong, fruit teas and their own special English Breakfast Tea blend – a mixture of Assam, Ceylon and African. One high-chair and one booster seat. No-smoking area. *Seats 50. Open 9.15-5 (Sat from 8). Closed Sun, Bank Holidays. No credit cards.*

Chicksgrove   Compasses Inn

Tel 0722 714318	Pub
Chicksgrove Tisbury nr Salisbury Wiltshire SP3 6NB	Map 14 C3

A timeless air pervades this attractive 16th-century thatched inn, set on a peaceful lane, deep in rolling Wiltshire countryside. An old cobbled path leads to the entrance to the charmingly unspoilt bar, which has a low-beamed ceiling, a partly flagstoned floor and an assortment of traditional furniture arranged in many secluded alcoves. Various farming tools and tackle from bygone days adorn the bare walls and a 100-year-old set of table skittles maintain the old-world atmosphere. A small adjoining dining room/children's room leads out to a sheltered rear garden with rural views. New owners Bob and Ann Inglis have rescued the inn from nearly two years of closure and neglect and are successfully restoring its reputation of being a splendid inn. Ann Inglis is in control of the cooking and takes pride in preparing the short selection of dishes that make up the twice-daily-changing blackboard menus. Ploughman's, sandwiches and macaroni cheese are available at lunchtimes for those wanting a lighter bite and on Sundays a buffet-style lunch is prepared (£4.50-£6.50).

A covered stone stairway leads to the lawned front garden with benches and brollies and to the inn's bedrooms. Three comfortable, neat and spotlessly clean bedrooms (the largest tucked beneath the heavy thatch) radiate off the private, well-furnished sitting room, complete with bookshelves, desk, three-piece chintz sofa, magazines and tea-making facilities. Two of the bedrooms are en suite with shower units, the other having its own private bathroom. Excellent hearty breakfasts, served in the bar, feature home-made marmalade and jam plus locally-made sausages. *Bar Food* (*no food Tue*) *12.20-2.30, 7-10. Free House. Beer Adnams Best, Wadworth 6X, Bass, weekly changing guest beer. Garden, outdoor eating, children's play area. Accommodation 3 bedrooms, 2 en suite, £40 (single £30). Children welcome overnight, additional beds (½ price) available. Pub closed Tuesday. No credit cards.*

Chipping Campden   Kings Arms Hotel, Saddle Room

Tel 0386 840256	Hotel Bar
The Square Chipping Campden Gloucestershire	Map 14 C1

The panelled Saddle Room is the bar at this 16th-century Cotswold-stone hotel in the market square. If the weather is fine, take your lunch out into the walled garden. The choice may include home-made soup (£1.75), sardines fried with garlic and prawns (from £3.75), Cumberland sausage in red wine sauce (£5) and chicken tikka (£5.50) as well as jacket potatoes and sandwiches, with banoffi pie or chocolate lover's delight (from £1.75) to follow. A roast is served on Sundays (£9 for four courses). Two high-chairs provided; simpler favourite dishes for children. *Seats 30. Open 12-3 & 6-9.30. Access, Visa.*

Chipping Norton   Nutters

Tel 0608 641995	Restaurant
10 New Street Chipping Norton Oxfordshire	Map 14 C1

Just off the High Street on the A44 Evesham road, the ground-floor self-service restaurant is part of Nutters Healthy Lifestyle Centre. All the food is basically vegetarian (with ham and fish as further options) and prepared on the premises to special low fat, low sugar, low salt recipes, from salads and hot jacket potatoes to savoury galettes (smoked haddock with mushroom sauce and broccoli (£3.25) or italienne with tomato concassé, oregano and cheese (£2.75). The sweet crepes can all be flambéed with either Grand Marnier, Calvados or orange curaçao (£1 extra); they include the classic with lemon, orange and sugar (£1.25) or parisienne with rich melted chocolate, nuts and ice cream (£1.95). Also cakes, flapjacks and potato scones. The kids (and adults) can have a go on a Rebounder mini-trampoline while Mum and Dad finish their meal. There's a small walled garden. No special family facilities but children are unlikely to leave here unfed or bored! No smoking. *Seats 35. Open 10am-9pm. Closed Sun, Mon, Bank Holidays. No credit cards.*

Church Stretton   Acorn Restaurant

Tel 0694 722495	Vegetarian
26 Sandford Avenue Church Stretton Shropshire SY6 6BW	Map 6 A4

Just off the town's main street, the front door to this first-floor wholefood restaurant is down a tree- and plant-lined passage. Soups (spiced yellow pea £1.90), quiches (onion £1.50), pitta sandwiches (£1.50) and pizzas (cheese, tomato and herb £1.85) are regulars on the menu, and there's always a vegetarian (spinach lasagne and jacket potato £3.50), meat (Persian lamb and brown rice) and fish dish of the day. A selection of 30 teas is available and several home-made puddings (ice creams, crumbles, rice pudding) and cakes to choose from (cider and nut cake, carrot and cinnamon, tea bread, bread pudding, apple strudel from 75p). On fine days the safe, gated garden ("a secluded haven of peace") is open for eating. Three high-chairs and an area "can be provided" for changing baby. Unlicensed. No-smoking area. **Seats** 38. **Open** 10-6 (late Oct-Easter 9.30-5.30). **Closed** Tue, 2 weeks late Nov, 2 weeks Feb, 25 & 26 Dec. No credit cards.

Cirencester   **Brewery Arts Coffee House**

Tel 0285 654791	Coffee House
Brewery Court Cirencester Gloucestershire	Map 14 C2

Pictures adorn the Cotswold-stone exposed walls of this attractive coffee shop specialising, but not exclusively so, in wholefood and vegetarian food. Staff serve the food at the counter where cold dishes prevail in summer and hot meals are available in winter. The choice could be savoury pastry slices (£2.60), home-baked ham with salad (£3), watercress soup (£1.40), spinach, mushroom and rice in Stilton sauce (£3), and hazelnut and celery en croute (£2.60). The resident confectioner bakes over 100 different kinds of cakes for their 'cake-away' service, many of which are available for tea: lemon and mace cake, coffee streusel or sticky fig and almond cake (all 75p). Good choice of teas. No-smoking area. **Seats** 53. **Open** 10-5. **Closed** Sun, 25 & 26 Dec, 1 Jan. No credit cards.

Clare   **Peppermill Restaurant**

Tel 0787 278148	Restaurant
Market Square Clare Suffolk	Map 10 C3

A cottage-style restaurant with origins in the 15th century serving sandwiches (from £1.50) and omelettes (£2.50) as popular lunchtime snacks, with fish pie (£4.50), nut roast or a steak for something more substantial. Bread pudding figures among the sweets. Children's portions available plus crayons and books. The Ladies loo upstairs has changing and nursing facilities. No smoking. **Seats** 20. **Open** 12-2 (& 7-9 Thur-Sat). **Closed** Mon (except Bank Holidays), Tue/Wed following Bank Holidays, 26 Dec & 1 Jan. Access, Visa.

Clavering   **Cricketers**

Tel 0799 550442	Pub
Clavering nr Saffron Walden Essex CB11 4QT	Map 10 B3

200 yards from the cricket green, this recently refurbished pub offers well-prepared home-made food. Tuesdays are seafood evenings (poached strips of salmon on crabmeat sauce (£7.50), deep-fried cod (£6.50), lobster most weeks) and a roast beef carvery (£6.50) is available on Wednesday and Sunday evenings (plus lunchtimes throughout winter). The restaurant has seating for 70, the bar for 120 and 75 can eat outside. Dishes include chargrilled medallions of beef fillet with brandy and paprika sauce (£11.50), supreme of chicken stuffed with mushrooms in puff pastry (£7.50). The restaurant offers a 3-course meal with choice of 10 starters and main courses for £18. 12 desserts are cooked daily – treacle tart, lemon meringue pie, steam puddings (all £2.75). It may all sound rather adult, but youngsters are welcome. **Bar Food** 12-2, 7-10. **Restaurant Meals** 12-2 (Sunday only),

*7-10 (not Sun and Mon). Children's menu. Free House. **Beer** Flowers
IPA, Wethered's, Boddingtons. Terrace, outdoor eating. Family room.
Access, Visa.*

Clawton	**Court Barn**	61%	£70
Tel 040 927 219			Hotel
Clawton Holsworthy Devon EX22 6PS			Map 12 C2

Five acres of garden surround a delightful manor house three miles
south of Holsworthy (follow the A388) and next to Clawton's 12th-
century church. Day rooms like the two lounges and tiny bar are easy
places to relax. The bedrooms are simple but individual in feel with
a number of thoughtful extras. Three rooms are suitable for family
use, and children up to 14 stay free in parents' room. Cots, high-chairs
and baby-listening are available. Bar snacks throughout the day in the
old dining room and bar lunches from 12 to 2. 5 to 12-year-olds are
served their own supper menu between 5 and 6pm and older children
eating with their parents at 8 pm are charged 50%. No smoking. For
adults, the exceptional and somewhat eccentric wine list overshadows
the formal restaurant menu, although there are good afternoon teas
and bar lunches to be had. ***Rooms** 8. Garden, badminton, pitch & putt,
putting, games room. Closed 1 week Jan. Access, Amex, Diners, Visa.*

Clearwell	**Wyndham Arms**	
Tel 0594 833666 Fax 0594 836450		Pub
Clearwell nr Coleford Gloucestershire GL16 8JT		Map 14 B2

John and Rosemary Stanford have just marked their 20th year
as imperturbable hosts at the tranquil Wyndham. Traditional real ales
and the famed malt whisky collection (with over 20 from which
to choose) are indicators of the public bar's civilised style, to which the
menu is entirely apposite. A lunch favoured by many is the 18-dish
hors d'oeuvre trolley (£6.25); the daily special might be creamed
haddock and prawn pie (£7.75), while open sandwiches of grilled
bacon or cheese and herb paté (both £4.95) are practically meals
in themselves. Bar meals, however, may be suspended when the
restaurant (not recommended) is busy. Accommodation is divided
between original bedrooms in the evocative 600-year-old main
building and a newly-built stone extension where room sizes, decor
and comforts are altogether more modern. There's plenty of space for
young children (cots, high-chairs and baby-listening are all readily
available), and the less mobile appreciate use of 6 ground-floor
bedrooms with easy ramps into the pub. Early evening turn-down and
dawn shoe-cleaning patrol aren't found in every pub, but, along
with a hearty breakfast, you'll find it all here. Outside, there's a mature
garden (with access from top of the car park) outside. The Norchard
Steam Railway is nearby. ***Bar Food & Restaurant Meals** 12-2, 7-9.30.
Free House. **Beer** Hook Norton, Bass. Garden and patio. **Accommodation**
17 bedrooms, all en suite, £55 (single £30). Children welcome overnight;
additional beds and cots (including bedding) available at no charge. Access,
Amex, Diners, Visa.*

Cleveleys	**Bay Tree Wholefood and Vegetarian Restaurant**	
Tel 0253 865604		Vegetarian
44 Victoria Road West Cleveleys nr Blackpool Lancashire		Map 6 A1

You will find this pleasant restaurant above a health food shop. The
menu is imaginative – to start you could choose from soup or paté

(£1.65) and main courses could be curried lentil pie, courgette and tomato bake or vegetable goulash (all at £3.90). Desserts might include plum crumble, strawberry almond roulade and gooseberry frangipane. For Sunday lunch there is a special menu £5.50-£6.50 for 3 courses. Children's portions. No smoking throughout. *Seats 36.* **Open** *10-3 & (Fri/Sat) 7-9.* **Closed** *Mon except Bank Holidays, 25 & 26 Dec, 1 Jan. No credit cards.*

Coggeshall	**White Hart**	**69%**	**£82**

Tel 0376 561654 Fax 0376 561789	Hotel

Market End Coggeshall Essex CO6 1NH	**Map 10 C3**

A centuries-old inn that still retains all its character with flagstone floors, low beams, inglenook fireplace and not one but two resident ghosts. Careful renovation and refurbishment in recent years have added style and comfort to the atmospheric surroundings. Individually decorated bedrooms, 12 in a new extension, offer little extras like fresh fruit and mineral water; two family rooms, cots provided. Room service is limited to Continental breakfast. 20% tariff reduction for two-night weekend stays. *Rooms 18. Garden. Access, Amex, Diners, Visa.*

Restaurant   **£60**

A long, low and narrow dining room with sturdy beams and cheerful staff. An Italian menu ranges from a variety of pasta dishes to supreme of guinea fowl flamed in Madeira and cream, and chargrilled steaks. Traditional Sunday lunch and a good selection of desserts – tiramisu is a speciality. *Seats 70. L 12-2 D 7-9.45. Closed D Sun.*

Colchester	**Butterfly Hotel**	**61%**	**£61**

Tel 0206 230900 Fax 0206 231095	Hotel

Old Ipswich Road Ardleigh Colchester Essex CO7 7QY	**Map 10 C3**

Part of a small chain offering practical accommodation (there is separate work space in all the bedrooms) and conference facilities for up to 80 delegates. Located on the A12/A120 near the Business Parks. A handy stop-over. No dogs. *Rooms 50. Access, Amex, Diners, Visa.*

Colesbourne	**The Colesbourne Inn**	

Tel 0242 870376 Fax 0242 870397	Pub

Colesbourne nr Cheltenham Gloucestershire GL53 9NP	**Map 14 C2**

A traditional hostelry alongside the A417, where quietly efficient hotelkeeping from Eric and Mary Bird marks it out from the crowd. Meals in the equally traditional, stone-clad dining room are more the order of the day than any bar snacks, though sandwiches and filled baked potatoes (from £3.50) are readily available. Old English chicken pie (£6.50), home-made lentil loaf (£5.75) and a nightly table d'hote (from £9.95) feature alongside seasonal specials (supreme of guinea fowl with plum sauce £8.50) and a Friday night fish and seafood spectacular. Bedrooms border the car park, well back from the road, in a neatly-planned extension: rear rooms enjoy the best views of rolling country. All have fully-equipped en-suite facilities with bath and shower, and efficient modern accessories, including trouser presses and hairdryers. A lively local atmosphere in the bar awaits those who enjoy some company prior to turning in. *Open 11-11, usual hours Sunday.* **Bar Food** *12-3, 6.30-10 (Sun 7-10).* **Restaurant Meals** *12-3, 7-10. Children's portions. Free House.* **Beer** *Mitchells Best Bitter,*

Wadworth 6X, Farmers Glory. Garden, patio. Family room.
Accommodation *10 bedrooms, all en suite, £49 (single £29).*
Additional beds (£10) and cots available. Access, Amex, Diners, Visa.

Collier Street   Butcher's Mere

Tel 0892 730495	Tea Room

Collier Street nr Marden Kent TN12 9RR   **Map 11 B5**

Stay cosy in Louise Holme's popular beamed tea room or take the sun
in the mature garden, which sports its own duck pond/lake complete
with wisteria-clad wicket bridge. Louise excels in home baking and
jam-making. The light scones, fruit cake, lemon curd sponge,
meringues, chocolate cake, coffee and walnut cake, and apricot log are
some of the most popular choices to have with freshly ground coffee
or a cup of tea. Diabetic cream teas (£3.10) and fat-free sponges are
also available. £1.35 minimum charge. No high-chairs, but Marmite
sandwiches or small portions should satisfy youngsters. Delightful for
families in summer when the garden can be used, but cramped inside
when the weather's not so good. Unlicensed. No smoking. *Seats 32.*
Open *10.30-7 (winter to 6, Thu from 3).* **Closed** *1 week Christmas.*
No credit cards.

Congresbury   White Hart

Tel 0934 833303	Pub

Wrington Road Congresbury Avon BS19 5AR   **Map 13 F1**

Combined quaint village pub and dining venue of particular family
appeal hidden down a long lane off the A370 (follow the Wrington
Road). The business changed hands in mid-1993 and the conventional
line in snacks and salads is now supplemented by some more
promising home-cooked fare: moussaka (£4.75), cauliflower cheese
(£3.75) through to Coronation chicken (£4.25) and poached salmon
(£6.50). An increasing attraction is Sunday lunch (main course
£4.95), especially with families who have use of a neat, fabric-lined
conservatory looking across the large pub garden and away towards
the Mendips. With plastic bottles of pop from the bar youngsters can
amuse themselves in full view on the trampolines, Wendy House and
play equipment and there's an aviary by the terrace. Plans are now
afoot to re-open the former '*Trawlers*' family restaurant housed
separately across the yard. Two high-chairs provided; room for
changing baby in the Ladies. *Beer Butcombe, H & W Badger &
Tanglefoot. Garden. Patio and play area. Family room, children's menu.
Access, Visa.*

Coniston   Bridge House Café

Tel 05394 41278	Café

Coniston Cumbria   **Map 4 C3**

Eat alfresco on the pavement or in the courtyard overlooking the
village. Inside, on two floors, it's cheerful and cottagey with flowered
tablecloths, lamps on the walls, old beams and pictures for sale. Good
baking, including toffee shortbread, fruit cakes, crumbles, scones, slices
(almond or coconut), flapjacks and gingerbread (from 60p),
predominates. A small selection of savoury snacks might include jacket
potatoes (from £2), soup (£1.30 – vegetable or lentil), salads (£3.25),
sandwiches (£1.30) and pizzas (from £3.30). *Seats 50.* **Open** *10-5
(Jul & Aug to 9).* **Closed** *25 & 26 Dec, 1 Jan. No credit cards.*

Constantine   Trengilly Wartha Inn

Tel 0326 4033	Pub

Constantine Cornwall TR11 5RP   Map 12 B4

One mile due south of Constantine down country lanes, the Inn
sits in the beautiful wooded valley of Polpenwith Creek. The
unpretentious main bar is happily unmodernised with games machines
and pool table relegated to a separate room and with another tapestry
upholstered 'lounge' area where families are welcome; there's a small
children's section on the menu too. For summer, there are tables on the
vine-covered patio and in the garden beyond. The bar menu contains
old favourites like chili con carne (£4), home-made soup (£1.95),
quiche (£3.50) and jacket potatoes (from £2.20) with the likes of a
plat de charcuterie, smoked salmon trout with brown bread (£3.60),
local sausages with herbs and garlic (£3) and from the blackboard,
perhaps cod and broccoli strudel or Trengilly cassoulet. Good
vegetarian choice and homely puddings (£2) that come with clotted
cream for an extra 40p. Good range of wines by the glass – either large
or small. Six cosy bedrooms are light and pretty with good modern
carpeted bathrooms and up-to-date conveniences such as remote-
control TV and direct-dial telephones. Beds boast crisp, pure cotton
sheets. *Bar Food 12-2.15 (Sun to 2), 6.30-9.30 (Sun from 7).
Restaurant Meals 7.30-9.30. Free House. Beer St Austell Mild & HSD,
Dartmoor Best, guest beers. Garden. Accommodation 6 bedrooms, 5 en
suite, £55 (single £42). Children welcome overnight, additional beds (£8)
and cots (£2) available. Access, Amex, Visa.*

Cooden   Cooden Resort Hotel   60%   £75

Tel 0424 842281 Fax 0424 846142	Hotel

Cooden Sea Road Bexhill-on-Sea East Sussex TN39 4TT   Map 11 B6

Right on the beach, with views across Pevensey Bay, this 30s' hotel
caters well for both leisure and business guests. There are facilities for
up to 200 conference delegates, a health and leisure club, a modern
lounge, a cocktail bar and a tavern serving real ale. One of the
bedrooms has been adapted for disabled guests; 12 are suitable for
family use. The 'Jolly Jester' menu offers reasonably priced children's
favourites. *Rooms 41. Garden, indoor & outdoor swimming pools, keep-fit
equipment, squash, sauna, spa bath, solarium, beauty & hair salon. Access,
Amex, Diners, Visa.*

Cookham Dean   Inn on the Green

Tel 0628 482638	Pub

The Green Cookham Dean Berkshire SL6 9NZ   Map 15 E2

Tucked away in one corner of the large village green, this interesting
pub has four dining areas but only a small bar – landlord Barry
Ward's cooking seems to take precedence here. Two small drinking
rooms (with just seven tables) lead through to a Swiss chalet-style
rooom where fondues are a speciality (£11), off which the high-
ceilinged Lamp Room restaurant and a small conservatory lead. The
short bar menu is probably the best bet; the range might cover
smoked duck breast (£4.95), steak in a baguette with chips (£5.25),
sausage and mash (£5.25), bacon and three cheese salad (£3.50),
warm goat's cheese salad (£3.25), salmon steak (£8), spring chicken
with chasseur sauce (£5.95), and monkfish with capsicum, peppers

and sherry (£10.35); plus summer pudding, apple crumble, crème caramel or superb treacle tart (all £2.60) to finish. Outside, there's a small patch of grass to the front (plus the enormous green a little further away), a large walled courtyard barbecue area (lit by wall lights and heated by tall gas burners, Apr-Oct) and an acre of paddock behind the car park. It's a wonderful summer pub for families with youngsters: the rear grassed area features a few picnic tables, a tree house, a chalet-style 'Nut House', double slide, climbing frame and rubber tyre swings; however, in winter the inside may be too intimate for anything less than very well-behaved juniors. The sole high-chair was broken when we last visited. Casual food service, but generous portions – stick to the simpler dishes. Easy parking. *Bar Food 12-2.15, 6-9.30 (from 7 Sun). Restaurant Meals 12-2.15, 7-9.45. Free House. Beer Brakspear, Boddingtons, Morland Old Speckled Hen. Garden, terrace, outdoor eating, children's play area. Access, Amex, Visa.*

Corfe Castle   Corfe Castle Restaurant & Tea Rooms

Tel 0929 481332	Tea Room
Corfe Castle Dorset	Map 14 C4

The tea room is suitably old and beamed, with lattice windows and floral drapes. At the back is a garden with views up to the brooding ruins of the castle. Coffee and various cakes are served from 10.30, then at lunchtime come soup (£1.65), salads (from £4), quiche (£3.75) and filled jacket potatoes (from £1.75). There are two choices for afternoon tea, the Dorset cream tea with local home-made jam and Cornish clotted cream (£2.85) or the Purbeck tea, two slices of locally baked bread, jam and a choice of cakes (£2.50). Home-made cakes are also on offer (coffee walnut sponge or rich sticky fruit cake). Sunday roast (£4.75) with a vegetarian alternative. Everything is spot on – a proper job – and they're happy to cater for young children. No smoking. *Seats 100. Open 10.30-5.30 (Nov-mid Feb weekends only, mid Feb-end Mar 11-4). Access, Amex, Diners, Visa.*

Corse Lawn   Simply Corse Lawn

Tel 0452 780771	Hotel Bistro
Corse Lawn House Hotel Corse Lawn nr Tewkesbury Gloucestershire	Map 14 B1

Baba Hine's cooking is as impressive as the splendid Queen Anne house (on the B4211). Baba and husband Denis offer Simply Corse Lawn, their bistro-style section where good food is produced at reasonable prices (all dishes under £10) in a more casual and less formal atmosphere than in the restaurant. There are three sections on their à la carte menu, French, English and vegetarian, but dishes can be chosen from all three at random. Starters or light snacks might be chive and potato soup (£3.95), chicken liver parfait (£4.95), hot French onion tart (£4.95); main courses range from home-made sausages (£5.95) to calf's brains beurre noir (£8.95), millefeuille of wild mushrooms with soy and Madeira (£8.50) or pigeon breasts with red wine (£8.95). Desserts are a must – hot butterscotch sponge pudding (£2.95), elderflower sorbet with gooseberry fool or lemon pancakes. Children's portions on request. There's outdoor seating around the pond. *Seats 35. Open 12-2 & 7-10. Access, Amex, Diners, Visa.*

Coventry   Hudson's

Tel 0203 223800	Coffee House

Cathedral Lanes Broadgate Coventry West Midlands CV1 1LL   **Map 6 C4**

On the top floor of a shopping mall near the cathedral, Hudson's
is part of an, as yet, small group of coffee house restaurants which take
their inspiration from the 1930s, with tail-coated waiters, newspapers
on sticks (old Beanos and Dandys for the youngsters) and a few leather
chesterfields, although most of the seating is bentwood chairs around
white-clothed tables topped with glass. The all-day menu ranges from
breakfast (continental – £5.45, healthy mid-morning cocktail with
milk and honey – £1.95), sandwiches (pastrami on rye £3.15, chicken
tikka – £3.35), New York-style filled bagels (from £3.60), and hot
dishes like beef Wellington (£7.95) and salmon kedgeree (£4.75)
to English afternoon tea (£5.95) and caviar with house champagne
(from £12.50). From noon there's a good-value three-course set lunch
at £5. Small children's menu or small portions of other things from
the menu. Changing facilities in the disabled loo. See also entries under
Birmingham and Harrogate. *Seats 80. Open 9-5.30. Closed Sun &
Bank Holidays (except Good Friday). No smoking. Access, Amex, Visa.*

Crathorne   Crathorne Hall   72%   £110

Tel 0642 700398 Fax 0642 700814	Hotel

Crathorne nr Yarm Cleveland TS15 0AR   **Map 5 E3**

Set in 15 acres of grounds not far from the village centre and a short
distance from the A19, Crathorne Hall was the last of the great stately
houses built in the Edwardian era. Public rooms and the best of the
bedrooms enjoy an elevated view over parkland with not a human
habitation in sight. The drawing room is of classical proportions with
a fine carved overmantel, large portraits in oil and brass chandeliers.
Knoll sofas and buttoned leather Queen Anne style armchairs form
part of the comfortable and very traditional decor. The cocktail bar
has the air of a gentleman's club with its bottle-green walls, mahogany
panelling and pillars and plush red velour chairs. Bedrooms are
splendid though top floor and back rooms are smaller. Furniture
is period style, in keeping with the character of the building and all
rooms are well equipped, superior rooms in particular. Bathrooms,
some with bidets, have quality toiletries and bathrobes. It may sound
rather grand, but families are warmly welcomed with many home
essentials available on request – baby bath, hooded baby towels,
changing mat, bottle warmer, toilet seats and steps, travel cots and
quilts, and wooden cots with bumpers. Baby-changing facilities in the
Ladies. Young guests under the age of 12 (even diners only) receive
the Virgin airline's Kiddies Pack and a comic or magazine along with
their parents' daily newspaper. Under-14s share parents' room free
of charge. Voyager Hotels – part of Richard Branson's Virgin Group.
Rooms 37. Garden. Access, Amex, Diners, Visa.

Cuckfield   Murray's   £55

Tel 0444 455826	Restaurant

Broad Street Cuckfield West Sussex RH17 5LJ   **Map 11 B6**

Several cottagey rooms provide a cosy setting for enjoying Sue
Murray's skilled and imaginative cooking. Influences from Europe and
beyond appear in dishes on the seasonal menu: mussel ravioli, pigeon
casserole in stock and Marsala, salmon baked with raisins, almonds and
ginger in a puff pastry parcel, fillet steak topped with goat's cheese.

Ask for small portions if menu dishes appeal to more adventurous young palates; alternatively, "they can have chicken and chips, if that's what they want". There's a changing area in the Ladies, which should ease a visit with a tiny one, but it's the owners' attitude towards children (they are not considered aliens from another gastronomic world) that warrants inclusion in this Guide. Short wine list with many bottles under £15. One room reserved for non-smokers.
Seats 30. Private Room 18. L 12-1.30 D 7.15-9.30. Closed L Sat, all Sun, Bank Holidays, 2 weeks Feb, 2 weeks Sep. Access, Visa.

Dartington   Cranks Health Food Restaurant

Tel 0803 862388	Vegetarian
Shinners Bridge Dartington nr Totnes Devon	**Map 13 D3**

Cranks continues to cater in fine style for visitors to the ever-popular Cider Press Centre. Service is courteous and efficient at the self-help counter, and seating ample (if closely spaced) at varnished pine tables. Mexican bean broth (£1.70), vegetarian crumble and Boston bean bake (£3.25) are the stuff of lunchtime, amply supplemented by mixed and green salads (£1.30). Baking weighs in with pizza slices and homity pie (£1.90) and a wealth of such sweets as Bakewell slice (£1.65) and lemon cheesecake (£1.90). Especially handy parking and disabled access. Take-away service also. No smoking. No dogs.
*Seats 70. **Open** 10-5. **Closed** Sun in winter, 25 & 26 Dec, 1 Jan. No credit cards.*

Dartmouth   Stoke Lodge   60%   £67

Tel 0803 770523	Hotel
Stoke Fleming Dartmouth Devon TQ6 0RA	**Map 13 D3**

Family-run, and with family holidays very much in mind, the hotel overlooks the village and the sea. There are good views from the large sun terrace which oversees the swimming pool and is a popular spot when the weather's kind. Inside, are homely, unpretentious lounges and neat bedrooms; of the latter, those with sea views attract a small supplement. Under-2s accommodated free (cots available, meals charged as taken), 2-5s 25%, 5-14 50% of adult rate, 14+ 75%. 6pm children's supper (order before noon); high-chairs provided.
Rooms 24. Garden, indoor & outdoor swimming pools, tennis, putting, keep-fit equipment, giant chess. Access, Visa.

Dedham   Dedham Centre Vegetarian Restaurant

Tel 0206 322677	Vegetarian
Arts & Crafts Centre High Street Dedham Essex CO7 6AD	**Map 10 C3**

The former United Reform church in the delightful village of Dedham has been remodelled (but has retained the organ) to house the Arts and Crafts Centre – various open-plan shops selling clothes, jewellery, paintings, pottery plus a toy museum on the first floor – and a vegetarian self-service restaurant. Home-made food includes vegetable soup with wholemeal bread (£1.85), mushroom and cashew roast (£4.95), cheese pancake with filling of the day (£4.25), stuffed jacket potatoes (from £2.75), and toasted cheese or egg sandwich. A daily special (£4.95) may be leek croustade, mushroom crumble or tagliatelle bake, and daily-changing puddings feature fresh lemon tart or apricot and almond tart (both £2.25). A set tea (£2.95) is served all day. Service is brisk and children are well looked after with beakers, two high-chairs and small portions on offer. There are no obvious changing facilities in the small loo, but they say that they "can be made available". Unlicensed. No smoking. *Seats 62.* **Open** *10-5 (Sat & Sun to 5.30).* **Closed** *Mon during Jan-Mar, 10 days Oct, 25 & 26 Dec. No credit cards.*

Dent   The Hop Bine Restaurant

Tel 05396 25400	Restaurant
Dent Crafts Centre Helmside Dent Cumbria	Map 5 D4

Part of Dent Crafts Centre and housed in a converted Dales barn with splendid views across Dent Dale, the Hop Bine restaurant is also a gallery. Pictures line the walls and crafts are displayed in a room with rustic tables and stone-flagged floors. Fourteen 'international platters' are available all day (£2.50-£3.75) – Greek: salad, houmus, tsatsiki, olives and feta cheese. Pizzas start at £2.50 for cheese and tomato and £2.95 for versions such as olive and anchovy or ham and pineapple. Cheese-eaters may like to sample the local varieties (£3.25). Evening meals are available by prior arrangement only and could consist of either a choice from the à la carte menu or the light supper (£5.95 for pasta, salad and garlic bread). There's a set afternoon tea (£4.50) with a choice of ten loose-leaf teas and several home-baked cakes (porter ale cake, lemon whisky buns, coffee kisses, date bars). Outdoor eating in the yard (next to playground). Children's portions. No smoking. *Seats 40.* **Open** *9.30-5.30.* **Closed** *weekdays Jan-Feb. Access, Visa.*

Derby   International Hotel   62%   £55

Tel 0332 369321 Fax 0332 294430	Hotel
Burton Road Derby Derbyshire DE3 6AD	Map 6 C3

On the A5250 south-west of the city centre, the privately owned International, once a Victorian school, concentrates very much on conference and exhibition business, but families might find it handily placed for a weekend stop-over, when rates are considerably reduced (£38.50 per room; suites also available). Under-5s can share parents' room at no charge; cots £5, extra beds £10; baby-sitting can be arranged and high-chairs are provided. Bedrooms offer many extras and the suites boast spa baths. *Rooms 62. Access, Amex, Diners, Visa.*

Devizes   Wiltshire Kitchen

Tel 0380 724840	Restaurant
11 St John's Street Devizes Wiltshire	Map 14 C3

Opposite the town hall, behind a corner shop just off the market square lies a very special eating place. Ann Blunden has been running her popular restaurant for nine years and also specialises in outside catering. Customers help themselves and can sit downstairs, on ground level or outside at a table on the pavement. The day begins with breakfast (full £3.50) and cappuccino with croissant or fresh roll. The menu for lunch changes every day and could include potato and coriander soup (£1.20), seafood roulade (£4.10), roast lamb with garlic herb crust (£4.30), chicken in orange marmalade sauce, spaghetti bolognese or one of the basics, filled jacket potatoes (from £1.95), slice of quiche (Stilton and leek or calabrese from £2.25-£3.10). Leave a space for the home-made puddings (£1.95 with custard or cream) – coffee meringues, fruit crumble, French lemon tart, ginger apple cake. At teatime, choose one of the many teas

available, with a scone if desired. One high-chair. No smoking.
*Seats 48. Open 8.30-5 (summer to 5.30). Closed Sun, 24 Dec-2 Jan.
No credit cards.*

Didsbury   Est Est Est

Tel 061-445 8209	Restaurant
756 Wilmslow Road Manchester Greater Manchester	Map 6 B2

A large and friendly Italian restaurant decorated in light, white
trattoria style and divided across a centre curve giving a raised stage
effect to the rear seating section. The menu has 16 starters (chicken
livers sautéed with Marsala and served on a crouton), and 16 pastas
that can be taken as starters or main courses (penne tossed with tomato,
peperoni and chili £2.25/£4.15), 12 pizzas (£3.95-£5.45) and 15
secondi piatti (scampi in a mild curry sauce £9.65). Tables with
parasols on the pavement in summer. See also entries under Knutsford
and Liverpool. *Seats 200. Open 12-2.30 & 6-11.30 (Sun 12-10.30).
Closed 25 & 26 Dec. Access, Amex, Diners, Visa.*

Diss   Weavers Wine Bar and Eating House

Tel 0379 642411	Restaurant
Market Hill Diss Norfolk	Map 10 C2

This charming restaurant is housed in what was a chapel for the Guild
of Weavers nearly 500 years ago. Some original beams remain and
small alcoves with banquettes are popular for quieter moments. The
lunchtime menu depends on what's in season: soup is the only starter
(£1.45 – apple and parsnip, ham and cauliflower with crispy bacon)
although guests can choose others off the evening menu, followed
by poached breast of pigeon with redcurrant, juniper and sloe gin
sauce (£4.75), wing of skate with prawns and capers, braised oxtail
with red wine, garlic and herbs, seafood tagliatelle (£4.95) or fresh
Cromer crab salad. Home-made puddings (£1.95) are brown bread
ice cream in brandy snap basket, cornflake and apple crunch with
custard or rich chocolate truffle cake. More elaborate evening à la
carte menu. Children's portions; high-chairs, booster seats, children's
cutlery all provided. No smoking during mealtimes. *Seats 80.
Open 12-2 & 7-9.30. Closed L Sat, all Sun, BankHolidays, 6 days
Christmas, last week Aug. Access, Diners, Visa.*

Donnington   Donnington Valley Hotel   74%   £95

Tel 0635 551199 Fax 0635 551123	Hotel
Old Oxford Road Donnington nr Newbury Berkshire RG16 9AG	Map 15 D2

Alongside its own golf course this newly-built, privately-owned hotel
conceals a surprisingly stylish interior behind a rather less remarkable
redbrick exterior. Beneath a vast, steeply-pitched timber ceiling the
main, split-level public areas boast a real log fire, Oriental carpets over
parquet floor and numerous comfortable sofas and armchairs with
intriguing antique knick-knacks dotted about. The effect created is one
of Edwardian elegance (though with modern comfort as the whole
hotel is air-conditioned), a theme that extends to the bedrooms, many
of which have period-style inlaid furniture and hand-painted tiles
in the good bathrooms. There is a turn-down service in the evenings
and extensive 24hr room service. Cots and high-chairs are provided
and baby-sitting is available. Under-12s share their parents' room free
of charge. *Rooms 58. Garden, golf (18), putting, fishing, shooting. Access,
Amex, Diners, Visa.*

Dorchester   Potter In

Tel 0305 260312	Café
19 Durngate Street Dorchester Dorset DT1 1JP	Map 13 F2

There are always fresh flowers on the pine tables and, in winter, a real
fire adds to the welcome at Sue Collier's charming establishment
tucked away down a narrow lane off the main shopping street.
Everything on the menu from traditional English breakfast (£3)
to scones and jam and clotted cream (£1.75) is available all day and
virtually everything, including some 20 or so flavours of ice cream
(served in a cone if requested), is home-made. Help yourself at the
particularly good salad bar to accompany savoury items such
as omelettes (£1.90), locally made Cornish pasties (£1.25), extra-deep
quiches (£1.25) steak or chicken pie and jacket potato (from £1.25).
Various cakes (all at £1) include cider, date, carrot, apricot and
a tangy, moist jaffa cake. Drinks include espresso coffee and their own
special hot spiced apple juice. Two high-chairs and children's drinking
mugs cater for younger customers who can have smaller portions
at reduced prices. A pretty walled patio garden is a popular spot
in summer. **Seats** 60. **Open** 9.30-5 (9-6 in summer). **Closed** Sun
in winter, 4-5 days Christmas. No credit cards.

Dorstone   Pandy Inn

Tel 0981 550273	Pub
Dorstone Golden Valley Hereford & Worcester HR3 6AN	Map 14 A1

The Pandy (located off the B4348) is the oldest inn in Herefordshire.
Built in 1185 by Richard De Brito, a Norman knight, to house his
workers while building Dorstone Church as atonement for his part
in the murder of Thomas Becket. Vegetarians are well catered for
with a variety of dishes to choose from including cheesy vegetable
bake and spinach and mushroom lasagne (both £4.50). Fresh fish from
Cornwall features on Fridays – cod, crab, king prawns (£8.25), sole
fillets (£7.50). Among the 'Light Bites & Starters' on the menu are
crispy whitebait or deep-fried camembert (both £2.95). Follow with
one of the 'House Specialities' – garlic chicken (£4.95), wild rabbit pie
(£5.25) or the 'greedy gammon, with as many eggs as you can eat'
(£6.35). Finally, choose one of the seven desserts on the 'Puddings &
Treats' menu. Lawned garden with swings for children. **Bar Food**
12-2, 7-10. Children allowed in bar to eat/children's menu. Free house.
Beer Bass, Boddingtons, Hook Norton. Garden, outdoor eating, children's
play area. Pub closed Mon lunchtime and all day Tues Nov-Easter.
No credit cards.

Dovedale   Izaak Walton Hotel   59%   £95

Tel 033 529 555 Fax 033 529 539	Hotel
Dovedale nr Ashbourne Derbyshire DE6 2AY	Map 6 C3

A splendidly located hilltop hotel on the Duke of Rutland's estates; its
17th-century farmhouse building, where Izaak Walton once stayed,
affords rolling views of Thorpe Cloud and Dovedale in the Peak
District Park. Fly fishing is available on the River Dove which flows
through the estate. Leather chesterfield sofas and open fires add
comfort and warmth to the public rooms; bedrooms are more
noteworthy for the vistas without than the space within. Five good-
sized bedrooms are suitable for families and there are plenty of cots
and Z-beds available. Baby-listening is provided by means of a two-

way radio, with parents carrying receivers. High tea is served from 5pm in the Buttery; children may also dine in the restaurant with their parents or at tables in the safe garden in summer; high-chairs are provided. The children's menu reflects the interest shown by guests in healthier eating options for their families. A children's fun pack is promised on arrival. Under-16s stay free in parents' room.
Rooms 34. Dinner dance (Sat), helipad. Access, Amex, Diners, Visa.

Downton   White Horse Inn

Tel 0725 20408	Pub
Downton Wiltshire SP5 3LY	Map 14 C3

A handy stop after a day out with the family in the New Forest, or returning from the coast, this rambling 16th-century coaching inn lies a short distance off the busy A338 Bournemouth to Salisbury road. Just off the lively main bar is a dining room for the exclusive use of families; mum and dad can choose from an extensive selection of standard pub fare, which is served fast and efficiently. Children have their own printed menu featuring the usual favourites; smaller portions of adult dishes will also be willingly prepared. A door from the dining room leads to the car park and to the small lawned area beyond, which is dominated by a giant boot playhouse with slide attachments. *Open normal pub hours, but no food Sun eves from Christmas to Easter (or 25 & 26 Dec).* **Beer** Eldridge Pope. Garden. Access, Visa.

Dulverton   Tarr Farm

Tel 064385 383	Tea Room
Tarr Steps Dulverton Somerset TA22 9PY	Map 13 D2

The old English garden is the best place to sit when the weather is kind. Otherwise snuggle up inside this cosy Exmoor farmhouse and enjoy the cream teas. Lunch might include various ploughman's platters, pasties and quiches as well as hot dishes such as lasagne, cottage pie, macaroni cheese, scampi, jumbo sausages and home-cooked ham with salad. Home-made fruit cake or apple pie with clotted cream for pudding. Changing shelf in the Ladies. *Open 11-5.30 & evenings (6-11) by arrangement only.* **Closed** end Oct-end Mar except weekends.

Dunwich   Ship Inn

Tel 0728 73219 Fax 0728 73675	Pub
St James Street Dunwich Suffolk IP17 3DT	Map 10 D2

Well-loved old smugglers' inn overlooking the salt marshes and sea. The delightfully unspoilt public bar offers nautical bric-a-brac, a wood-burning stove in a huge brick fireplace, flagged floors and simple wooden furnishings. There's also a plain carpeted dining room. A fine Victorian staircase leads to simple homely bedrooms, light and clean with pretty fabrics and period touches, but no televisions. Good simple food in generous portions, too: the restaurant menu applies throughout the pub in the evenings; bar meals menu lunchtime only. Choose at lunch from home-made soup (£1.30), cottage pie (£3.25) or steak and mushroom pie (£4.10) and in the evening, hot garlic prawns (£4.95), crispy Camembert parcels (£3.95), rump steak (£7.25), fish of the day (£7.50) or escalope of pork (£7.25), followed by home-made desserts such as boozy bread-and-butter pudding, apple crumble or apple and cider flan (all £2.20). Very secure garden on three levels surrounded by a hedge. **Bar Food & Restaurant Meals**

12-2, 7.15-9.30. Children allowed in the pub to eat. Free House. **Beer**
Adnams Bitter and Broadside, Greene King Abbot. Garden, outdoor eating.
Accommodation *3 bedrooms, 1 en suite, £50 (single £20). Children
welcome overnight, additional beds (£15), cots supplied. Check-in
by arrangement. No credit cards.*

Durham   Station House Hotel and Restaurant

Tel 091-384 6906	Restaurant
High Shincliffe Durham Co Durham DH1 2TE	Map 5 E3

The highly personable Joan McGuiggan has created a lovely, homely
atmosphere at her small hotel (3 rooms) created from an old Victorian
railway station. Good-value eating can be had in the bar area
or restaurant. Starters such as creamy Stilton soup and excellent deep-
fried butterfly prawns with garlic cream and hot crusty bread range
from 95p to £4.50 while main course steaks start at £5.55 and a huge
portion of chicken and bacon en croute costs £5.10. Puddings (all
under £2.50) are rich and delicious. Booking essential for fixed-price
Sunday lunch (roast beef or Cumberland sausage with Yorkshire
pudding £2.99). "Each child is catered for individually on request."
Garden table in fine weather. **Seats** *50.* **Open** *12-3 & 6.30-11.30 (Sun
from 7).* **Closed** *26 Dec. No credit cards.*

Easingwold   Truffles

Tel 0347 822342	Café
Snowdon House Spring Street Easingwold North Yorkshire	Map 7 D1

Crystal chandeliers add a touch of class to this pretty little cottage
tearoom near the market square. Sandwiches (from £1.65), toasties
and cakes like an excellent Victoria sponge (85p) are available all day
with the likes of Cumberland sausage with creamy onion sauce
(£4.20), crunchy vegetable pancake (£4.20), chicken Italian (£5.25)
and omelettes adding to the choice from midday onwards. Sweets
include fresh strawberry sundae and banoffi pie (both £1.90).
Children get their own special menu with all the usual favourites plus
cinnamon toast and mini-meringue with ice cream. There is one high-
chair and a couple of booster seats and nursing mothers seeking
privacy will be offered use of a private lounge. In the evenings (Wed
to Sat) the à la carte supper menu (no minimum charge) offers main
dishes such as pan-fried fillet of beef with mushrooms, grilled gammon
steak and deep-fried scampi (£4.40-£5.85). No smoking. **Seats** *36.*
Open *Mon (12-2), Tues (10-4.30), Wed-Sat (10-8.30), Sun (12-4.30).*
Closed *5 days Christmas. No credit cards.*

East Horsley   Thatchers Resort Hotel   62%   £100

Tel 0483 284291 Fax 0483 284222	Hotel
Epsom Road East Horsley Surrey KT24 6TB	Map 15 E3

Weddings and conferences are the staple business at this attractive
mock-Tudor hotel set back from the road behind a lovely garden. The
main public area is a comfortable open-plan bar/lounge beyond
a spacious parquet-floored reception area. Choose from prettily
decorated accommodation in the main house, smaller motel-style
rooms around the open-air pool and a few more cottagey bedrooms
in an adjacent building. Several family rooms. **Rooms** *59. Garden,
outdoor swimming pool, helipad. Access, Amex, Diners, Visa.*

East Ilsley — The Swan

Tel 0635 281288 Fax 0635 281791	Pub
East Ilsley nr Newbury Berkshire RG16 0LE	Map 15 D2

A well-run, friendly family pub at the heart of an attractive Berkshire village: turn off the A34 just 3 miles north of the M4, Junction 13. The Swan is operated by Morlands, the brewers from nearby West Ilsley, and by the bar is posted a record of their landlords, unbroken since 1865. The pub, however, was a coaching inn in the early 1700s and despite today's open-plan interior many original features remain within its many rooms and alcoves, alongside collections of brewery artefacts, cartoons, local photographs and miniature bottles which have been accumulated over the years. Residents overnight enjoy the best of the old building's charm in carefully modernised bedrooms, all but two with well-appointed en-suite bathrooms. Throughout, all are neatly equipped with beverage trays, colour TVs and direct-dial phones. In summer, the trellised rear patio is a picturesque spot where parents can sit while the children let off steam in the adjacent garden. Food is disappointing – stick to the snacks. Recommended for B&B only. *Beer Morland Original and Old Speckled Hen, guest beer. Family room, patio, garden and play area. **Accommodation** 10 rooms, 8 en suite, £42 (single £32.50). Children accommodated free overnight. Access, Visa.*

East Molesey — Superfish

Tel 081-979 2432	Fish'n'Chips
90 Walton Road East Molesey	Map 15 E2

Part of a Surrey-based chain serving above-average fish and chips "fried in the traditional Yorkshire way". See Morden entry for more details. High-chairs; fish bites with chips (£2.20) for children. *Seats 30. Open 11.30-2 (Sat to 2.30), 5-10.30 (Thu-Sat to 11). Closed Sun, 25 & 26 Dec, 1 Jan. No credit cards.*

Eastbourne — Grand Hotel   75%   £120

Tel 0323 412345 Fax 0323 412233	Hotel
King Edward's Parade Eastbourne East Sussex BN21 4EQ	Map 11 B6

A whitewashed, seafront De Vere establishment that dates back to Victorian times. Marble pillars, crystal chandeliers, vast corridors and high-domed day rooms evoke a more leisurely, bygone age of spacious and gracious hotels. Some of the sea-facing bedrooms have balconies and are huge, with bright furniture and up-to-date fabrics, but not all are as smart or as generous in size. 24hr room service, comprehensive leisure and exercise facilities, themed weekend breaks and children's hostesses (in summer) keep the Grand abreast of its more modern competitors. Families are well catered for; a children's menu is offered in the Garden restaurant and Lounge. De Vere Hotels. *Rooms 164. Garden, indoor & outdoor swimming pools, spa bath, sauna, solarium, beauty & hairdressing salons, keep-fit equipment, snooker. Access, Amex, Diners, Visa.*

Mirabelle Restaurant   £67

Imaginative dishes executed with flair and served in elegant surroundings (more suitable for parents once their youngsters are safely tucked up in bed). Fixed-price lunch and dinner (4-course, priced by choice of main course) menus offer a small choice that includes a daily roast served from a silver trolley. In addition, an à la carte offers classic dishes with modern touches. Cheeses are accompanied by home-made bread and there's a choice of traditional desserts. Longish list of wines includes half a dozen English wines and a choice of 16 brandies. **Seats** 50. *Private Room 20. L 12.30-2.30 D 7-10.30. Closed Sun & Mon, Bank Holidays, 2 weeks Jan, 2 weeks Aug. Set L £14/£17.50 Set D £27.50.*

Eastleigh   Piccolo Mondo
Tel 0703 613180   **Restaurant**

1 High Street Eastleigh Hampshire SO5 5LB   **Map 15 D3**

A long-established Italian restaurant in the central shopping area of town in what was, 20 years ago, a church. Fishing nets, fiasci of Chianti and other Italian bric-a-brac adorn walls and hang from vaulted ceilings, with pine furniture completing the picture. Familiar antipasti, pasta (from £5.75) and pizzas (from £5.25) are joined by veal and steak served various ways, blackboard specials – moules à la Romana (£3.95), sea bass with saffron sauce (£9.50) – and a special lunchtime menu which includes sandwiches and pancakes as well as the usual pizza and pasta. Smartly dressed staff provide quick, efficient service. **Seats** 80. **Open** *12-2.30 & 6.30-11 (Fri & Sat to 11.30).* **Closed** *Sun, Bank Holidays. Access, Amex, Diners, Visa.*

Ebbesbourne Wake   Horseshoes Inn
Tel 0722 780474   **Pub**

Ebbesbourne Wake nr Salisbury Wiltshire SP5 5JF   **Map 14 C3**

The Ebble valley and more especially the village of Ebbesbourne Wake seem to have escaped the hustle and bustle of modern day life, as it nestles among the folds in the Downs, close to the infant River Ebble. This peaceful, unspoilt rural charm is reflected in the village inn which has been in the Bath family for the past 21 years. Its 17th-century brick facade is adorned with climbing roses and honeysuckle, while inside the traditional layout of two bars around a central servery still survives. The main bar is festooned with an array of old farming implements and country bygones and a mix of simple furniture fronts the open log fire. As in the past, in rural inns, well kept real ale is served straight from the cask and both local farm cider and free-range eggs are also sold across the bar. Bar food is homely, the best choice being the freshly prepared dishes that are chalked up on the blackboard menu. The standard printed menu highlights the range of sandwiches, ploughman's and other hot dishes. The set 3-course Sunday lunch (£8.95) is superb value for money, extremely popular and served in the tiny adjoining restaurant – booking necessary. The flower- and shrub-filled garden is perfect for summer alfresco eating and safe for children, who also have access to view the four goats and pot-bellied pig in the pets area. Those wanting to explore this tranquil area further can stay overnight in one of the two modest bedrooms at either end of the inn. Both are decorated in a cottagey style with pretty fabrics and wallpaper and have TVs, tea-making kits and their own private facilities. A peaceful night's sleep is guaranteed. **Bar Food & Restaurant Meals** *12-2, 7-9.30 (except Mon eve). Children allowed in bar to eat. Free House.* **Beer** *Adnams Broadside, Wadworth 6X, Ringwood Best & Old Thumper (in winter). Garden, outdoor eating, pet area.* **Accommodation** *2 bedrooms, both en suite, £32.35 (single £20). Children welcome overnight, additional beds and cots available. No credit cards.*

Edburton   Tottington Manor Hotel

Tel 0903 815757	Pub

Edburton nr Henfield West Sussex BN5 9LJ	Map 11 B6

A 17th-century Grade II listed inn-cum-hotel in its own grounds at the
foot of the South Downs, with lovely views. The bar is simple and
properly pubby, with country furniture and an open fire hogged
by an assortment of animals. Good bar food – jacket potatoes (£4),
sandwiches (£2.60), ploughman's (£3.80); prices are just a little higher
in the restaurant, whose £16, 3-course menu includes half a bottle
of wine. Breast of French duckling with honey and fig sauce, roast
South Down lamb and a wide variety of fresh fish are some of the
main courses, and several vegetarian dishes are always available.
Bedrooms are pretty, with soothing colours and good sturdy furniture,
and en-suite bathrooms have proper guest toiletries. The residents'
lounge is also rather fine. Under-5s not allowed in the restaurant.
20 minutes' drive from Brighton and Worthing. *Bar Food &
Restaurant Meals 12-2, 7-9.15 (Sun to 9 in restaurant). Free House.
Beer Adnams, Bateman, Fuller's London Pride, guest beer. Garden, outdoor
eating. Accommodation 6 bedrooms, all en suite, £50 (single £30).
Children welcome overnight (rate depends on age), additional beds & cot
supplied. Pub closed on Sundays Jan-end March & one week after
Christmas. Access, Amex, Diners, Visa.*

Egham   Bar 163

Tel 0784 432344	Restaurant

High Street Egham Surrey TW20 9HP	Map 15 E2

A friendly welcome helps to dispel initial reservations about the basic
decor, reservations that are finally banished by the wholesome, home-
cooked fare on offer. Typical dishes from the daily-changing
blackboard menu might include parsnip soup (£2.20), moussaka
(£4.50), smoked haddock pancake (£5.50), home-made hamburger
(a regular feature, £5), spicy meatloaf (£4.40) and broccoli and
Stilton lasagne (£5.50). There are always several vegetarian dishes.
Lunchtimes, a couple of snacky dishes like pitta bread filled with tuna
and salad (£3.50) and a bacon club sandwich (£3.50) are added to the
list. It is possible to have just a glass of wine – they started as a wine
bar – but the food side has pretty much taken over and most people
now come here to eat. No particular family facilities, but ask for small
portions. *Seats 76. Open 12-2.30 & 6.30-11. Closed L Sat, all Sun.
Access, Amex, Visa.*

Elland   Bertie's Bistro

Tel 0422 371724	Bistro

7 Town Hall Buildings Elland West Yorkshire	Map 6 C1

Michael Swallow continues to please with his creative flair and skilled
cooking in this Edwardian-style bistro decorated with open
bookshelves and old prints. Start with the likes of cream of wild
mushroom soup with tarragon cream, warm leaf salad of bacon,
sautéed duck's liver and grapefruit, mussels marinière with tomato
and garlic bread, or grilled fillet of mackerel with gooseberry confit
(£1.90-£4.90). There's a regular stew, perhaps beef with celery,
orange and walnuts, or deep-fried monkfish tails in a light Chinese
batter with mangetout. Main courses range from £5.50 to £8.90. For
afters you are spoilt for choice – Bertie's bombe (meringue, brandy

and ice cream with toffee or chocolate sauce), Stilton and Guinness
cake, hot apple dumpling with custard (£2.20-£3.90). Children's
menu. Five high-chairs. *Seats 150. **Open** D only 7-10.30 (Sat 6.30-11,
Sun 5-9).* **Closed** *Mon, Bank Holidays, 25-30 Dec, 1 Jan. Access, Visa.*

Elsted Marsh   Elsted Inn

Tel 0730 813662	Pub

Elsted Marsh nr Midhurst West Sussex GU29 0JT   Map 11 D3

It would be very easy to drive past this unprepossessing Victorian
roadside pub, but that would be to miss out on some good food and
a warm welcome. It was built to serve the railway in the steam age,
when there was a station here, but was later left stranded by Dr
Beeching's 'axe' in the 1950s. This explains the old railway
photographs that adorn the thankfully unmodernised and
unpretentious bars, in what is very much a local community pub,
free of background music and electronic games but with plenty
of traditional pub pastimes like shove ha'penny, darts, cards, dominoes
and even conversation. There are two small bars with lots of original
wood in evidence, original shutters and open fires. A small dining
room, candle-lit in the evening, boast an old pine dresser and colourful
cloths on a few dining tables surrounded by a motley collection of old
chairs. Tweazle Jones and her partner Barry Horton have between
them a varied catering background, the result being a globetrotting
menu – always home-made and based on good local produce – with
the likes of osso buco (£6.50) from Italy, coq au vin (£6) from
France or Mexican tacos (£6). England is also well represented
though, with dishes like braised oxtail, mutton with caper sauce and
sandwiches closely resembling door stops; vegetarians are well served,
too, with lentil bakes and vegetable roulades (both £6). Children can
have half portions at half price, and there's a car tyre hanging from
a plum tree in the shady garden to keep them amused, plus pétanque
for the adults. Dogs are welcome or at least tolerated by the house
hounds, Truffle and Sam, and an area of the garden is fenced off
to keep dogs and children apart. *Bar Food 12-2.30, 7-10 (Sun to 9.30).
Beer Adnams, Ballard's, Bateman, Mitchell's, guest beer. Garden, children's
play area. Access, Visa.*

Elton   Loch Fyne Oyster Bar

Tel 0832 280298	Restaurant

The Old Dairy Elton Peterborough Cambridgeshire   Map 7 E4

The Old Dairy is a stone building standing on its own in a car park
opposite a walled garden, 100 yards from the A605 bypass to Oundle.
The wood-panelled interior (Scots pine and larch from Argyll),
natural slate floor in walkways and aquamarine carpet give
a Scandinavian feel to this predominantly fish (some game) restaurant
which has a retail outlet next door. A pair of kippers served with
sautéed potatoes (£4.95) or Finnan haddock with a poached egg
(£6.95) are breakfast choices. Shellfish include a plate of langoustines
(£9.95), the platter of oysters, langoustines, queen scallops, brown
crab, velvet crab and clams (£14.50) and Loch Fyne oysters (3-£2.25,
6-£4.40, 12-£7.90). Also served is the Loch Fyne speciality
of Bradham rost (hot smoked salmon served with a whisky sauce
£8.95) and a plate of Scottish venison (£5.20). Mull Cheddar,
Dunsyre Blue and Inverlochy goat's cheese are a good alternative to a
pudding, unless of course you cannot resist trifle, sticky toffee pudding,

apple crumble or banoffi pie (all £2.95). Tea with cake and
shortbread is available in the afternoons. A ramp at the entrance makes
access easy for prams and wheelchairs and there's a toilet for the
disabled. Courtyard for outdoor eating. **Seats 85. Open** 9-9 (*Fri & Sat
to 10*). **Closed** 25 & 26 Dec, 1 Jan. Access, Amex, Visa.

Ely   Old Fire Engine House

Tel 0353 662582	Restaurant

St Mary's Street Ely Cambridgeshire   **Map 10 B2**

Good, well-seasoned home-baked food in a traditional and attractive
18th-century house-cum-art gallery. It's open every day with a daily-
changing menu according to what's in season. Dishes include a wide
range of starters such as tomato, onion, Stilton or lovage soup (from
£2.60); mitoon of pork (£3) and smoked salmon paté (£4.80). More
substantial fare weighs in with dishes such as pigeon with bacon and
black olives casseroled in white wine, jugged hare, pork chops
in Suffolk cider, hot game pie, traditional roasts (lamb, beef, pork) and
numerous fish dishes such as lemon sole with prawn sauce and fresh
vegetables (all £10.80). There are puddings to match which include
home-made yoghurt with honey and almonds, fruit pies (£2.40),
or bread-and-butter pudding (£2.90) and coffee meringue or syllabub
(£3.10). There are also a number of ice cream options (£3.65). Try
the afternoon full cream tea, with scones, jam and a slice of cake
(£3.55). Good selection of British cheeses and a choice of some 100
wines. No smoking in main eating area. Tables in the garden for
summer. **Seats 50. Open** 10.30-5.30 & 7.30-9 **Closed** D Sun, Bank
Holidays & 1 week Christmas. Access, Visa.

Eskdale Green   Bower House Inn

Tel 094567 23244	Pub

Eskdale Green Holmbrook Cumbria CA19 1TD   **Map 4 C3**

Despite its out-of-the-way location, the Connors' informal, friendly inn
continues to find favour with a faithful and returning clientele.
Headquarters of the Eskdale cricket team, the bar has a distinctly
clubby feel and opens on to an enchanting, enclosed garden of pine and
shrub, with a tiny wooden bridge traversing the village stream.
Childen can safely play here. Bar menus more reflect the public
demand for steak and kidney pie and scampi (from £4.95) than show
off the kitchen's prowess; however, choices from the specials board
may include spinach roulade (£3), venison in red wine or roast guinea
fowl with cranberry sauce (both £6.25). Table d'hote dinner (£16
per head) served at smartly polished mahogany tables is the preferred
choice of residents. This is a delightful place to stay for peace and quiet
in the Eskdale valley; bedrooms are divided between the main house,
where they are abundant in character, the converted stables and garden
cottages, subtly extended and thoughtfully equipped to meet modern-
day demands. Families are well catered for and there are three large
rooms suitable for family occupation. After a restful night, it's
traditional to tuck into a hearty Lakeland breakfast. **Bar Food** 12-2,
6.30-9.30 (*from 7 Sun*). **Restaurant Meals** 7-9. Free House. **Beer**
Younger's, Theakston Best, Hartleys XB. Garden, outdoor eating.
Accommodation 22 rooms, all en suite, £53.50 (single £42). Children
welcome overnight, extra bed (£5.50) and cot supplied. Access, Visa (75p
surcharge for bar meals).

Evesham	Evesham Hotel	65%	£92

Tel 0386 765566   Fax 0386 765443 — Hotel

Cooper's Lane off Waterside Evesham Hereford & Worcester WR11 6DA

Map 14 C1

A largely Georgian hotel, with Tudor origins, set in several acres of secluded grounds on the edge of town and run in their own jolly style by the Jenkinson family for the last 18 years. The 'Jenkinson' humour breaks out all over the place from the 'seaside postcard' mural by the pool (Evesham-by-the-Sea) to the padlocked perfume in the award-winning public loos that also include magazines and a portable radio in each cubicle. Bedrooms (keys are attached to a teddy bear) have a traditional feel with candlewick bedspreads and all sorts of extras from playing cards and a copy of *Punch* to rubber ducks and washing liquid for clothes in the bathrooms. Some rooms have characterful beams and others a period feel with painted Georgian panelling. Public rooms centre around a comfortable, chintzy bar. "Well-behaved youngsters are as welcome as well-behaved grown-ups" according to the 'Junior à la carte' that also requests no pipes, cigars or bubble gum in the restaurant, and there are all sorts of board games and other amusements about the place to keep younger guests amused, including an outdoor play area with swings, trampolines and slide. There are baby-listening and baby-sitting available (by arrangement) plus cots (the first five come with a pack of nappies and wipes) and extra beds with children changed at £1.50 per year of age (typical of the individual style of doing things here). No room service. Dogs welcome. **Rooms** 40. *Garden, croquet, table tennis, indoor swimming pool. Closed 25 & 26 Dec. Access, Amex, Diners, Visa.*

Restaurant

The jokey menu changes weekly and the setting is elegant (Regency style); results on the plate are quite satisfactory with well-judged dishes like bacon-wrapped breast of chicken filled with tea-steeped prunes on a sherry and tarragon sauce; brochette of tuna marinated in wine, garlic and herbs with a tomato sauce, and slices of pork fillet flamed with brandy and served with Stilton and walnuts. Separate menus provide for vegetarians, children (unpriced, but charged "fairly" according to age) and those looking for simpler dishes – smoked salmon, grills, cold meats and salads. Good puds include treacle tart, a rich chocolate pot and an excellent apple millefeuille. At lunchtime there is a buffet option (£6.65) in addition to the regular menu. Ever idiosyncratic, the long wine list (it comes in five volumes) is strong in New World wines and includes offerings from as far afield as Zimbabwe, Sweden and Peru but none whatsoever from France and Germany; an an almost endless liqueur list runs from 'A' (Almedranda from Mexico) to 'Y' (Ypioca from Brazil). **Seats** 55. *Parties 12. Private Room 12. L 12.30-2 D 7-9.30.*

Ewell	Superfish		

Tel 081-393 3674 — Fish'n'Chips

9 Castle Parade Bypass Road Ewell Surrey — Map 15 E3

Part of a Surrey-based chain serving above-average fish and chips "fried in the traditional Yorkshire way". See Morden entry for more details. High-chairs; fish bites with chips (£2.20) for children. **Seats** 36. **Open** *11.30-2 (Sat to 2.30), 5-10.30 (Thu-Sat to 11). Closed Sun, 25 & 26 Dec, 1 Jan. No credit cards.*

Eyam   Eyam Tea Rooms

Tel 0433 631274	Tea Room
The Square Eyam Derbyshire	Map 6 C2

Situated in a village square in the heart of the Peak District National
Park, the Tea Rooms are family-run and everything is freshly baked
in their own ovens. Snacks include soup (£1.75), sandwiches (from
£2), salads (from £4.25) served with relishes and jacket potatoes
(from £3). Their famous speciality Eyam Cream Tea (£2.75) has two
scones fresh from the oven, cream and jam and a pot of tea. A more
unusual option is the Fruit Cake Tea (£3.25) – fruit cake, served with
Wensleydale cheese, fresh fruit and walnuts plus tea. Children's
portions available. There's no children's menu but half portions are
always available. Two high-chairs are provided and nappy-changing
is feasible in the Ladies loo. No smoking. *Seats 52. Open 10.30-5.
Closed Mon (except Bank Holiday Mons) & Nov-March. No credit cards.*

Eynsham   Newlands Inn

Tel 0665 881486	Pub
Newland Street Eynsham nr Whitney Oxon OX8 1LD	Map 14 C2

A lost corner of the 16th century hides just off the A40 – devoid
of street lamps at night the setting can be magical. Unperturbed by the
two resident ghosts, Nick Godden charcoal grills one of the best steaks
around, and his barbecued hickory-flavoured spare ribs (£5.50) and
Cajun catfish (£5.95) have their fans also. The flagstone floors, candle-
lit dining room and roaring log fires create the draw in winter;
on summer evenings the rear patio with its canvas awning is a pleasant
spot for a snack and occasionally there will be a barbecue in progress.
Among the blackboard specials look for toad in the hole with gravy
or smoked haddock au gratin (both £3.95) and pan-fried king prawns
in garlic butter (£6.25). Despite a lack of space, Christine Godden's
motherly attitude towards children like her own is admirable – no
chicken nuggets here. "If they can't be talked into a small portion
of bangers or bolognese, someone can always manage to boil them
an egg." *Bar Food 12-2, 7-9.30. Beer Greene King IPA, Flowers IPA,
Tolly Original. Outdoor eating, patio, children welcome in dining room
only. Access, Visa.*

Falmouth   Falmouth Hotel   63%   £92

Tel 0326 312671 Fax 0326 319533	Hotel
Castle Beach Falmouth Cornwall TR11 4NZ	Map 12 B4

Solid and imposing Victorian seaside hotel in French chateau style.
Gardens are neat and trim and the day rooms, including
a conservatory, are light and peaceful. Half the bedrooms have a view
of the sea (other rooms overlook the river), and three Executive
bedrooms have balconies and whirlpool baths. There are also self-
catering Manor cottages and Marine Court apartments (let by the
week), and facilities for large-scale conferences and banquets, plus
a leisure centre. Families with young children are admirably catered
for – ask for special children's terms. Video and satellite links to the
bedroom TVs. The beach is literally over the road. *Rooms 72. Garden,
indoor swimming pool, sauna, spa bath, solarium, beauty & hair salon,
putting, snooker, children's games room. Access, Amex, Diners, Visa.*

Falmouth   Royal Duchy Hotel   66%   £99

Tel 0326 313042   Fax 0326 319420   Hotel

Cliff Road Falmouth Cornwall TR11 4NX   Map 12 B4

Originally built in 1893, the hotel sits atop the cliffs between the town
and Gyllyngvase beach commanding fine sea views. Public rooms
range from sun lounge to spacious dining room with live
entertainment during the summer season. A small leisure area has
plenty of facilities, and bedrooms have Regency-style freestanding
furniture and remote-control televisions. Bathrooms are clean and
functional. Under-5s share parents' room free of charge; eight family
rooms, cots provided. Children's evening meal 5.30-6.30pm and
entertainment in summer months. Friendly staff are typical of the
Brend hotel group. **Rooms** 47. *Garden, indoor swimming pool, children's
pool, sauna, spa bath, solarium, games room. Access, Amex, Diners, Visa.*

Fareham   Solent Hotel   75%   £108

Tel 0489 880000   Fax 0489 880007   Hotel

Solent Business Park Whiteley Fareham Hampshire PO15 7AJ   Map 15 D4

In a most unexpected location – a business park adjacent
to Junction 9 of the M27 (10 miles from both Portsmouth and
Southampton) – this modern, gabled hotel has something of the feel
of a New England inn, successfully balancing wood and brick in its
design and happily satisfying the contrasting needs of business and
leisure guests. The functions are separated physically in the building's
design, but high standards of service do not exclude one at the expense
of another. All of the bedrooms are of Executive standard,
in traditional style, with both working and relaxing space plus
comprehensive comforts – from bathrobes to mini-bars. Suites
accommodate syndicate, business and interview requirements in the
week and have ample space for families at weekends (when special
tariff rates apply); children up to 16 are accommodated free in their
parents' room and fun packs are provided. The *Parson's Collar* pub
in the grounds offers Daniel Thwaites' ales and informal eating – a
place for parents to unwind while taking up the hotel's baby-listening
facility. High tea is served in the bar area while Dad can enjoy a good
pint of Thwaites! Older children can happily spend an hour or two
playing hide and seek in the rear woodland before plunging into the
leisure club's fine pool; infants may particularly enjoy the splash pool,
parents the jacuzzi. The leisure club has a private membership, but
access is from within the hotel; a floodlit tennis court is the latest
addition. Plenty of easy parking. Shire Inns. **Rooms** 90. *Indoor
swimming pool, whirlpool bath, children's splash pool, sauna, steam room,
solarium, keep-fit equipment, squash, snooker. Access, Amex, Diners, Visa.*

Woodlands Restaurant   £55

One room in the stone-floored dining area overlooks grass and
woodlands beyond, carefully segregating conference diners when
required, leaving other guests to enjoy the open fire in the main, split-
level room. An enterprising carte and table d'hote offer familiar
favourites with an interesting twist. **Seats** 100. *Private Room 30.
L 12.30-2 D 7-10. Closed L Sat. Set L £14 Set D £18.*

Feock   Trelissick Garden Restaurant & Courtyard Room

Tel 0872 863486	Restaurant
Feock nr Truro Cornwall	**Map 12 B3**

The restaurant is a converted barn overlooking the River Fal
on a superb National Trust estate with a beautiful garden and
parkland. Just three miles south of Truro on the A39, Trelissick
Garden is open for light snacks, lunch and afternoon tea. Salads (beans
with tomato and onions) or a daily hot special (beef, horseradish and
redcurrant pipkin – a 17th century word for an earthenware pot
in which the dish is served – or fruity lamb pipkin and mushroom and
Stilton pancakes) provide the lunchtime choice, preceded by morning
coffee with biscuits and followed by scones, cakes (mixed fruit slice
£1.35, carrot cake £1.30) or cream tea (£2.85). There's a three-course
traditional Sunday lunch (£9.75). For an even lighter bite, The
Courtyard Room, housed in a former farm building, is a self-service
snack bar. Children's portions, easy grip cutlery and bottles or food
warmed; six high-chairs, two booster seats. Changing facilities in the
disabled loo. No smoking. **Seats** 65. **Open** 11-5.15 (Mar & Oct to 4.45,
Nov & Dec to 3.45 L 12-2.15). **Closed** 22 Dec-1 Mar. Access,
Amex, Visa.

Finchingfield   Jemima's Tea Rooms

Tel 0371 810605	Tea Room
The Green Finchingfield Essex	**Map 10 B3**

Finchingfield is situated in North Essex and is probably the prettiest
village in the county. The 900-year-old beamed cottage that houses
Jemima's looks over the picturesque village green alongside other
thatched cottages. A blackboard supplements the very simple menu
of sandwiches (from £1.25), scones and toasted tea cakes (from 85p)
with ploughman's, soups and various locally-made ice creams. Cream
tea £2.95. The scones and generously served cakes are all home-made.
Eating outdoors in the courtyard in the summer. Unlicensed.
No smoking. **Seats** 80. **Open** 10.30-6 (Nov-Feb to 5). **Closed** Mon &
Fri Nov-Feb, 25 Dec. No credit cards.

Fordwich   Fordwich Arms

Tel 0227 710444	Pub
King Street Fordwich nr Canterbury Kent CT2 0DB	**Map 11 C5**

Located next to the smallest, half-timbered medieval town hall in the
country, the Fordwich Arms is a solid Tudor-style village pub, with
a rather handsome but not intimidatingly smart interior featuring
open fireplaces and lovely arched windows. The menu is the same
in the bar as in the restaurant, with dishes like smoked haddock
mornay (£5.75), lamb chops in redcurrant sauce (£5.25) and chicken
fusilli (£5.50). The terrace is a civilised spot, as are the picnic tables
in the garden, safely fenced from the narrow river Stour. **Bar Food**
12-2, 6.30-10 (except Sun eve). **Beer** Boddingtons Pedigree, Fremlins,
Marston, Whitbread.Garden, outdoor seating. Family room. No credit cards.

Fowey   King of Prussia

Tel 0726 832450	Pub
Quayside Fowey Cornwall	**Map 12 C3**

Pride of place on the tiny quay goes to this most unusual three-storey pink-washed building, which overlooks the perpetually busy quayside and river estuary and across to Pont Pill creek, a sheltered inlet filled with sailing craft. It was built by and named after the notorious smuggler John Carter, who operated from Prussia Cove. A clergyman by day and smuggler by night, his ill-gotten gains built the pub and his dual role in life is reflected in the unusual double-sided inn sign. Beyond the lively main bar, complete with juke box and a young crowd, are six delightful en-suite bedrooms, all of which have splendid river views. Neatly refurbished with co-ordinating colours, fabrics and friezes and furnished with modern pine, they are fresh, clean and very comfortable. Usual facilities include TVs and tea-makers, plus in summer months your own colourful window-box of flowers which spill into the room. Bathrooms are compact, well fitted-out and spotless. Breakfast is taken in the tiny pine-furnished restaurant. Recommended for B&B only. *Open 11-11, Sun usual hours.* ***Beer*** *St Austell Bosun's Bitter, Tinners Ale, HSD.* ***Accommodation*** *6 bedrooms, all en suite, £44 (single £22). Access, Amex, Visa.*

Freshwater   Farringford Hotel   57%   £88

Tel 0983 752500	Hotel
Bedbury Lane Freshwater Isle of Wight PO40 9PE	**Map 14 C4**

Once the home of Alfred Lord Tennyson, this 18th-century Gothic-style house is now a peaceful holiday hotel whose neat gardens border National Trust downland. Day rooms include a French-windowed drawing room, a small bar (which also serves snacks) and a library with Tennyson memorabilia. Bedrooms are modest and neat, and there are also a number of self-catering Cottage and Garden suites in the grounds. Families with children are welcome and baby-sitting and baby-listening can be arranged, as can riding at nearby stables. ***Rooms*** *19. Outdoor heated swimming pool, children's pool, children's play area, 9-hole golf course (par 3), putting, bowling green, tennis, croquet, dinner dances (every Sat, plus Wed during July & Aug). Access, Amex, Diners, Visa.*

Frilford Heath   Dog House Hotel   £63

Tel 0865 390830 Fax 0865 390860	Inn
Frilford Heath nr Abingdon Oxfordshire OX13 6QJ	**Map 15 D2**

A ten-minute drive from Oxford, this pleasant 300-year-old tile-hung inn commands a lovely view over the Vale of the White Horse. The bar is spacious, and incorporates a central stone fireplace with a real winter fire. All bedrooms are in contemporary cottage style, with en-suite facilities, remote-control teletext TVs, telephones, hairdryers and pine furniture. Top of the range is the four-poster bridal suite. Bathrooms have smart modern tiling, large mirrors and good lighting. Greatly reduced weekend tariff. ***Beer*** *Morland. Garden, children's play area.* ***Accommodation*** *19 bedrooms, all en suite, £69 (single £60). Children welcome overnight (rate depends on age), additional bed & cots available. Access, Amex, Diners, Visa.*

Frome   Old Bath Arms

Tel 0373 465045	Restaurant
1 Palmer Street Frome Somerset BA11 1DS	Map 13 F1

This is a friendly and informal family affair with a lunchtime buffet
service in cottage-style eating rooms. Main courses: hot £3.40 (roast
lamb, beef and mushroom pie) or salads – cold meat, quiche, pizza,
smoked mackerel or ham and egg pie £2.80-£3.40. A whole array
of traditional English puds (starting at £1) includes apple and
blackberry pie and Bakewell or treacle tarts. Sundays see roast lunches
(bookings taken) at £7.50 for three courses or £6 for 2 courses.
Children's portions (no charge for under-5s); one high-chair and two
booster seats. Changing shelf in the Ladies. *Seats 64. **Open** 12-1.30 &
7.30-9.45. **Closed** D Sun, all Mon, Bank Holidays, 25 Dec-7 Jan.
Access, Visa.*

Frome   Settle

Tel 0373 465975	Tea Room
15 Cheap Street Frome Somerset	Map 13 F1

Leading off Frome's market place, pedestrianised Cheap Street
complete with its central stream is charmingly 'olde worlde'.
In positively cottagey 17th-century tea rooms writer and broadcaster
Margaret Vaughan recreates West Country dishes – Priddie Oggies,
Settle Bobbins and Cotswold Pies – while indulging her 'fruity passion'
for home-produced wines of apple, elderflower and silver birch. Cakes
and bread from the next-door bakehouse range from poppyseed loaf
to an array of richly layered sponges. From breakfast brunch (£5.50)
with Margaret's marmalade through daily lunch specialities (rabbit
cooked in gooseberry champagne), salads and savouries to Somerset
cream tea (£3) and the famous Frome Bobbin (£2.50) of cider-soaked
fruits in wholemeal pastry, her cooking remains unique in its field.
Alongside the fruity wines, beverages range from elderflower cordial
to celebrated Teapot Trail teas. No-smoking area. *Seats 40.*
***Open** 9-5.30 (summer to 6, Thu to 2, Sun 2.30-6). **Closed** Sun Oct-Apr,
Good Friday, 25 & 26 Dec, 1 Jan. Access, Visa.*

Fyfield   White Hart

Tel 0865 390585	Pub
Main Road Fyfield nr Abingdon Oxfordshire OX13 5LN	Map 15 D2

500-year-old ex-chantry house with a 30-foot-high gallery and four
family rooms. The landlord is also the cook. The very large garden
includes a children's play area. *Free House. **Beer** Boddingtons, Hook
Norton, Wadworth 6X, Theakston Old Peculier, Gibbs Mew Bishop's
Tipple, Fuller's London Pride. Garden. Family room. Access, Amex, Visa.*

Gargrave   Anchor Inn

Tel 0756 749666	Pub
Gargrave nr Skipton North Yorkshire BD23 3NA	Map 6 C1

A popular family stop. Whitbread's Brewers Fayre food
is as innocuous as you might expect (stick to the simpler items for
satisfaction) but the beauty is that whether you stop for a sandwich,
chicken masala or Black Forest sundae you won't have a moment's
worry about your children. The huge enclosed outdoor area (seating
300) has two adventure playgrounds – one for the under-5s and one

for 5 to 14-yr-olds. Indoors there is a family room complete with Wendy House, various rides and games machines. Service is impersonal – you collect your tray when your name is called – but with such an array of activities, it doesn't seem to matter that some of the niceties of eating out are lost. Baby-changing facilities in the disabled loo. No dogs. *Bars open 11-11 Mon-Sat, 12-10.30 (3-7 with meals only) Sun. Food served 8am-10pm (breakfast 8-11.30am, £3.50).* **Beer** *Whitbread.* **Accommodation** *5 rooms, all en suite, £39 (single £28); no family rooms. Access, Visa.*

Gateshead **Marks & Spencer Garden Restaurant**

Tel 091-493 2222	Restaurant
Unit 46 Metro Centre Gateshead Tyne & Wear	Map 5 E2

This bright, smart and spotless in-store restaurant in a huge branch of Marks & Spencer is the only one in the country. With wooden walls and tiled floor, the area is divided by large plants and the food is distributed from five areas. The food is familiar to most of us – jacket potatoes (with cottage cheese, chili, or tuna £1.95), quiches, salads, ploughman's, hot dishes (crispy haddock £2.90, meat lasagne £3.05), vegetable dishes (ratatouille £2.40, cauliflower cheese £3.30), pastries, and canned wine. The operation runs very smoothly and efficiently. A cooked breakfast is served from 10 to 10.45 (Sat 9-10). Chiildren's menu and small portions; ten high-chairs. No smoking. *Seats 252.* **Open** *10-6 (Thu to 7, Sat 9-5 (Nov & Dec to 8)).* **Closed** *Sun, 25 & 26 Dec. No credit cards.*

Gerrards Cross **Santucci**

Tel 0753 889197	Restaurant
24 Packhorse Road Gerrards Cross Buckinghamshire	Map 15 E2

A modest-looking pasta restaurant with a tiled floor, pink tablecloths and pretty water-colours on the walls, serving terrific home-made pasta, good desserts and splendid coffee. In other words, a decent neighbourhood trat. Sauces and pastas can be combined to customers' liking, though heartily recommended are dishes like gnocchi alla bolognese, taglioni verdi gratinati and fettuccine all'Alfredo (all £4.50). Grilled sardines and carpaccio are tasty starters; tiramisu, lemon torte and crème caramel satisfying endings (from £2.25). Each day sees an additional 'specials' list of starters and main courses – perhaps fresh asparagus and veal milanese. *Seats 44.* **Open** *12-2.30 & 6.30-10.30.* **Closed** *D Sun. Access, Visa.*

Gittisham **Combe House** 73% £92

Tel 0404 42756 Fax 0404 46004	Hotel
Gittisham nr Honiton Devon EX14 0AD	Map 13 E2

Thérèse and John Boswell are both very much involved in the day-to-day running of their stately Elizabethan mansion. The 3000-acre estate is predictably peaceful, and there are views of the Blackmore Hills, but it's not remote, being less than two miles from the A30 Honiton Bypass. Public rooms have carved panelling in the entrance hall, ancestral portraits in the panelled drawing room, a charming pink sitting room, a cosy bar with pictures of John's horse-racing activities (the hotel owns several racehorses trained nearby – visits to the stables can be arranged), and everywhere architectural features, antiques and personal touches by painter and sculptress Thérèse (and her mother).

Bedrooms vary in size and price, larger rooms tending to have better
views and more interesting furniture and pictures. Two rooms have
four-poster beds. The hotel owns fishing rights on the River Otter,
with a season running from April to the end of September. During
January & February the hotel closes from after Sunday breakfast
to teatime on Tuesday. High-chair and cot provided. *Rooms 15.
Garden, fishing. Access, Amex, Diners, Visa.*

Glastonbury   **Rainbow's End Café**

Tel 0458 833896	Café
17a High Street Glastonbury Somerset	**Map 13 F1**

Approached by a narrow passageway past Pandora arts and crafts, the
busy vegetarian and wholefood Rainbow's End is a jumble of kitchen
tables and chairs extending to a tiny conservatory and walled, paved
garden to the rear. Counter service at lunchtimes offers perhaps mixed
vegetable soup (with roll £1.30), mushroom puff pie or balti and
naan bread (£2.45) with supplementary salads such as wholegrain rice
and beansprouts. Flapjacks, Bakewell slice, carob cake and a creamy
citrus delight (£1.15) are in abundance for puds or simple snacks.
Home-made lemonade and hot spicy apple juice supplement the many
teas and exotic infusions. Two high-chairs, but no changing facilities.
No smoking. No dogs. *Seats 46. Open 10-4.30 (Wed till 2.30).
Closed Sun, Bank Holidays, 24 Dec-2nd week Jan. No credit cards.*

Goathland   **Mallyan Spout Hotel**

Tel 0947 86486 Fax 0947 86327	Pub
Goathland nr Whitby North Yorkshire YO22 5AN	**Map 5 F3**

Goathland village itself is tucked into a fold in the moors two miles off
the A159 and some 9 miles from Whitby. The inn's unusual name
derives from the waterfall which cascades down the wooded valley
just yards from the pub garden; hugging the valley's contours runs the
North Yorkshire Moors Railway. Lunchtime in the Spout Bar can
be a busy occasion with customers regularly overflowing into the
hotel lounge next door. Ever-popular are the ploughman's lunch
of Yorkshire cheeses (£3.95), home-cured gravlax (£4.95), fresh
Whitby cod with chips and plaice goujons in batter (£4.85). Puddings
to follow are of the sticky toffee and summer fruits varieties (£2.45).
Evenings see the hotel restaurant move up a gear, with bar food
restricted to the Spout. Residents and others (who should book)
encounter a three-course table d'hote dinner starting (before extras)
at £18.50 – for fillet steak add another £7.50. Bedrooms, indubitably
upmarket in a purely pubby context, are housed largely to the rear
of the Jacobean-style, ivy-covered hotel with splendid valley views;
small and cottagey in the coach house, spacious and balconied in a
redbrick extension. En-suite bathrooms are generally on the small side.
Negotiate, if you can, a larger room if arriving with a family;
no reduction for children's meals in the restaurant at dinner (when
children under 6 are not welcome); high-tea served from 6-7pm.
*Bar Food 12-2, 6.30-9 (from 7 Sun). Restaurant Meals 12-1.45 Sun
only, 7-8.30. Free House. Beer Malton Double Chance. Accommodation
24 bedrooms, all en suite, from £65 (from £40 single). Children welcome
overnight, cots (£5) and extra beds (£12) available. Garden, patio, family
room. Access, Diners (5% surcharge), Visa.*

Goudhurst   Star & Eagle

Tel 0580 211512	Pub

High Street Goudhurst Kent TN17 1AL   Map 11 B5

Behind the splendid timbered and gabled facade vintage charm and
modern comfort blend harmoniously in a fine 14th-century hostelry
owned by Whitbread. Beams, bricks, vaulted stonework and
inglenooks make great appeal in the public rooms, while creaking
floors and odd angles are the order of the day in the bedrooms. These
vary in size and shape and the majority are furnished in pine, though
the four-poster room has some antiques. In the public areas, period
appeal survives in exposed beams, open brick fireplaces and old settles.
Recommended for B&B only. *Pub open 11-11 Mon-Sat, regular hours
Sun.* **Beer** *Whitbread. Garden. Family room.* **Accommodation**
*11 bedrooms, 9 en suite, £40 (single £30). Children welcome overnight
(if sharing parents' room, under-3s are free, under-12s £15). No dogs.
Access, Visa.*

Grasmere   Wordsworth Hotel   72%   £100

Tel 053 94 35592 Fax 053 94 35765	Hotel

Grasmere nr Ambleside Cumbria LA22 9SW   Map 4 C3

Centrally located in Grasmere village, the Wordsworth's two acres
of well-tended gardens and paddock nevertheless promise calm and
tranquillity. The conservatory bar and adjacent lounge have bold
floral fabrics, some cane seating and the best of the views. The more
active will enjoy the well-equipped leisure centre or the Dove & Olive
Branch pub. Individually decorated bedrooms vary widely in size and
aspect; the best are two suites with whirlpool baths and an antique-
furnished four-poster room. Many rooms are suitable for family use
(cots £10, extra beds £18), and baby-sitting and baby-listening are
available; there's also a children's menu (they're not too proud to offer
'tinned spaghetti' or 'frozen peas') for high-tea in the Drawing Room;
high-chairs are provided. Free golf at Keswick mid-week. **Rooms** *37.
Garden, indoor swimming pool, keep-fit equipment, sauna, spa bath,
solarium, games room. Access, Amex, Diners, Visa.*

Prelude Restaurant   £74

There's a traditional feel to the dining room but many of the variations
on Bernard Warne's menus have a modern ring: terrine of marinated
herring, smoked salmon and potato, chilled two-tone soup, vegetable
and lentil moussaka, baked tenderloin of pork wrapped in brioche
with sage on a coarse broccoli and raisin sauce. To finish, perhaps
a layered trio of chocolate mousses on a pistachio sauce, or cheeses
from the North of England's British Cheeseboard of the Year regional
winner. Note the house selection and bin ends on a well-balanced wine
list which offers plenty under £20. No smoking. **Seats** *60.
L 12.30-2 D 7-9 (Fri & Sat to 9.30). Set L £17.50 Set D £29.50.*

Grassington   Dales Kitchen Tearooms & Brasserie

Tel 0756 753077	Tea Room/Brasserie

51 Main Street Grassington North Yorkshire   Map 6 C1

The marzipan and blueberry pie (£2.45) is not to be missed (someone
in the kitchen has a very cool hand with pastry), the scones are near
perfect and the Black Sheep rarebit (£3.45) very more-ish – in fact
nothing on the menu at this 200-year-old former apothecary's house

in the main street will fail to please. The choices range from sandwich platters (with generous salad garnish – from £2.45), salads and hot dishes like lamb and aubergine moussaka (£4.95) and spinach with feta cheese in filo pastry (£4.45) to toasted teacakes (95p) and scrumptious home-made cakes such as tangy lemon syrup, coffee and walnut or a rich chocolate. Puds include gooseberry fool cheesecake and cinnamon cream (both £2.45). Children are welcomed with a selection of simple sandwiches (from £1.65), small portions of other things from the menu and a couple of high-chairs. A table in the lobby to the loos is convenient for changing baby and they will happily heat baby's bottle or food. No smoking. *Seats 40. Open 10-5. Closed* midweek in midwinter (except Christmas), 25 & 26 Dec. No credit cards.

Grays   R Mumford & Son

Tel 0375 374153	Fish'n'Chips
Cromwell Road Grays Essex	**Map 11 B5**

Long known for its fish and chips, and run by the same family for over 70 years. Ingredients are bought daily from the market. Cod (£5.75, £4.50 at lunchtime), plaice, sole, skate and rock eel are the regular favourites, joined by specials such as halibut. Prawn salad is another popular order, and there's chicken and steak for meat-eaters. Children's menu but no other facilities. *Seats 64. Open 11.45-2 & 5.30-10 (later Fri/Sat). Closed* Sun, Bank Holidays, 25 Dec-6 Jan. No credit cards.

Great Bircham   Windmill Tea Room

Tel 0485 23393	Tea Room
Great Bircham nr King's Lynn Norfolk	**Map 10 B1**

Gina Wagg and her husband Roger bought a derelict windmill in 1975 and have carefully restored it as well as the bakery, which produces bread and rolls daily in the 200-year-old coal-fired oven during the high season. After visiting the mill and bakery museum, Gina's set teas (£2.10 or £2.75), which include delicious light scones, rich fruit cake, ginger cake, shortbread and flapjacks, are very popular. At lunchtime, a few savoury snacks are available – such as rolls (75p-85p), sandwiches (60p) or a ploughman's platter (£2.75). On fine days the patio and small garden are open to customers. The mill, which dates from 1846, stands on the B1155 Bircham-Snettisham road. Changing facilities in the Ladies with a table, mat, wipes and chair. Unlicensed. No-smoking room. Bicycles can be hired and there's an outdoor children's play area (for under-7s) with a small swing, Wendy house and boat. *Seats 70. Open 10-6. Closed* Sat, also end Sep-Easter. No credit cards.

Great Chesterford   Plough

Tel 0799 530283	Pub
High Street Great Chesterford Essex CB10 1PL	**Map 10 B3**

Delightful village pub with a traditional, unspoilt interior. Children enjoy the large adventure playground with its aerial runway, the 9-hole putting green and the playroom complete with pool table and games. There are large patio and lawned areas. *Open 11-11 Sat all year and Mon-Fri during school holidays, regular hours other days. Beer* Greene King. Garden, children's play area. Family room. Access, Diners, Visa.

Great Rissington　　Lamb

Tel 0451 820388/820724	Pub

Great Rissington Gloucestershire GL54 2LP　　　Map 14 C1

Originally a farmhouse, the oldest part of the Lamb dates back nearly 300 years, the newest just a couple of years. That it is difficult to tell the difference is a tribute to the skill and craftsmanship of the appropriately named landlord Richard Cleverly, formerly a builder, who has done all the most recent work himself. The charming restaurant, for instance, with its candles and lacy tablecloths, is housed in a new extension, but makes imaginative use of old timbers and stonework. It fits in well with the stone-walled bar, where incidentally, hangs a plaque to the memory of the airmen who died when their Wellington bomber crashed in the garden here during the Second World War; part of a propeller is displayed above the wood burning stove. Kate Cleverly is no less talented than husband Richard, taking justifiable pride in the fact that everything on the menu is genuinely home-made; even the chicken en croute is cooked to order, starting from scratch with raw chicken breast. The daily-changing blackboard bar menu carries starters like chicken liver paté (£3.25), followed by steak and mushroom pie (£5.50) and sherry trifle (£2.25). The restaurant menu also applies in the bar, giving an even wider choice, such as mushrooms in cream and garlic sauce (£3.50) and duck breast in raspberry sauce (£10.75), and they can usually find some fish fingers or baked beans on toast for children with a hankering for convenience foods. Richard and Kate's skills have combined in the creation of charming bedrooms which include built-in wardrobes made with salvaged timbers, and a splendid four-poster bed, testifying to his skills as a wood carver. Kate's contribution is the pretty decor, each room highly individual in style, with co-ordinating fabrics and wall coverings. Most of the furniture is antique and all but two rooms, which share a shower room, have en-suite bathrooms (five with showers rather than baths). They make a virtue out of not having television or radios in the rooms but addicts will find a television (and a log fire) in the cosy residents' lounge, as well as in the best guest room, a quite luxurious suite. A heated indoor swimming pool (Apr-Oct) in the delightful garden is a luxury all residents can share in the summer months; a separate beer garden is to one side of the pub. Several high-chairs are provided and children are welcome. Dogs (£1.50 per night, not including food) are only permitted in the bedrooms; over eleven years visitors to the Lamb have contributed £22,000 to a Guide Dog fund, providing 22 dogs. Winner of Egon Ronay's Guides' 1994 Pub of the Year award. **Bar Food** 11.30-2 (to 1.30 in winter), 7-9 (to 8.30 Sun). **Restaurant Meals** as per bar meals except: 12-1.30 & 7-8.30 Sun. Children's menu. Free House. **Beer** Morland Old Speckled Hen, Hook Norton, Smiles. Garden, outdoor eating. **Accommodation** 13 bedrooms, all en suite, £48 (four-poster £55, suite £72, 2-room family £76, single £30). Children welcome overnight (under-5s free if sharing parents' room), additional beds (£10.50), cots available (£3.50). Access, Visa.

Great Wishford　　Royal Oak

Tel 0722 790229	Pub

Great Wishford nr Salisbury Wiltshire SP2 0PD　　　Map 14 C3

New owners of this attractive, rambling, ivy-covered pub have maintained the warm welcome that has always been offered to young folk in the past (although the children's play area in the garden was grown over on our last visit). Families are welcome in the bar and in the well-furnished eating areas, where they can choose from a comprehensive menu or from a number of blackboard specials – steak and kidney pie, chili, filled jacket potatoes and steaks. Children can select from their own menu of good-value favourites and a high-chair, beakers and cutlery are all available. Bottles and baby food will be heated on request. *Open 11-3 & 6-11, Sun 12-3, 7-10.30 (food 12-2, 7-10).* **Beer** *Courage, Ushers. Access, Amex, Visa.*

Great Yarmouth	Carlton Hotel	67%	£79
Tel 0493 855234 Fax 0493 852220			Hotel
Marine Parade Great Yarmouth Norfolk NR30 3JE			Map 10 D1

With its fine seafront location directly opposite Wellington Pier and still fresh from refurbishment, the Carlton is the flagship of East Anglia's Waveney Inns Group. An impressive interior now houses conference facilities. Bonuses for individual guests include Penny's café-bar (offering a weekday happy hour and a modern brasserie menu encompassing Tex-Mex) and a hair salon. Bedrooms have bright colour schemes and smart tiled bathrooms. Children under 12 free in parents' room; families are well catered for, with baby-sitting by arrangement and high-chairs for junior diners. **Rooms** *90. Access, Amex, Diners, Visa.*

Gretton	Royal Oak	
Tel 0242 602477		Pub
Gretton nr Winchcombe Gloucestershire GL54 5EP		Map 14 C1

Excellent for people with children in tow, the Royal Oak has a particularly large, safe garden for small people to explore, with a proper play area. At the bottom of the garden is the GWR steam railway, which runs from Toddington a few miles away, and brings a lot of trade. The pub itself is a mixture of ancient and modern, with flagstone floors, beams, stripped oak, pine tables and a conservatory dining room, and visitors are equally diverse, a mix of locals, holidaymakers and day-trippers enjoying varied bar food from a long blackboard list which serves both the bar and restaurant: Cheddar and potato soup (£1.80), mussels grilled with Stilton (£2.95), onion bhajis with mint and yoghurt sauce (£2.95) or baked crab and mushroom pot (£2.95); chicken tandoori curry (£4.75), baked lemon sole with cheese sauce (£7.50) or Arnold Bennett omelette with smoked haddock (£4.50); puddings like gooseberry crumble, lemon torte or chocolate biscuit cake (all £1.95). Live folk music on Wednesday evenings. The huge garden has a tennis court (must book). **Bar Food** *12-2, 7-9.30. Children's menu, children allowed in bar to eat. Free House.* **Beer** *John Smith's, Wadworth 6X, Morland's Old Speckled Hen, Thomas Hardy Country, Marston's Pedigree, Ruddles. Garden, outdoor eating, children's play area, tennis court open to the public. Access, Visa.*

Grimsby	Leon's	
Tel 0472 356282		Fish'n'Chips
Riverside 1 Alexandra Road Grimsby South Humberside DN31 1RD		Map 7 F1

A 'family fish restaurant' serving fish fresh from local boats. Favourites on the short, simple menu include haddock (£4.95), plaice and skate (both £5.40). All served with chips, roll and butter and tea or coffee.

Apple pie and custard or ice cream to finish. Children's portions (around £2.95 including drink). Two high-chairs and two booster seats. **Seats** 80. **Open** 12 (Fri & Sat from 11.30)-2 & 5-10 (Sun 12-8). **Closed** Mon, 2 weeks Christmas, Bank Holidays. No credit cards.

Hailey   The Bird in Hand

Tel 0993 868321 Fax 0993 868702	Pub

Hailey nr Witney Oxon OX8 5XP	Map 14 C2

A delightful 'residential country inn' in a rural setting surrounded by open fields, one mile north of Hailey on the B4022 between Witney and Charlbury. The small, neat, low-walled roadside garden gives an indication of the standards aimed for inside and the large, pebbled car park shows its popularity as a dining pub with a strong local following. A dozen or so picnic tables with umbrellas are set outside on a large patio by the side entrance. Inside, four stone-walled bar rooms include one with a long bar and sofa, plus another with an inglenook where a wood fire burns during winter; the third is darker, leading down to the Dungeon room which, as we went to press, was expected to be changed to offer more lounge-style seating for residents. The emphasis is very much on eating rather than drinking, with a choice of bar and restaurant (charcoal grill and vegetarian specialities) menus supplemented by blackboard specials; fresh fish is a feature of the latter. Regular choices include home-made soup (£2.45), farmhouse paté (£3.45), smoked salmon with citrus fruit salad and melba toast (£6.45) and a choice of interesting fresh pasta dishes; home-made beefburgers with chips (£6.25), avocado, smoked chicken and almond salad with fresh coriander (£5.25), green chicken and coconut curry with poppadums, and rump steak (£9.95) complete the picture. Ploughman's and jacket potatoes with various toppings are among the snackier items. Sunday lunch includes a traditional roast (£5.95). 16 unusually spacious and comfortable, cottage-style bedrooms are in keeping with the original Cotswold-stone former coaching inn, in a U-shaped building on two storeys with wooden balconies; they overlook a quiet, grassed courtyard. Two ground-floor twin roooms have facilities for the disabled; two large family rooms have a double and a single bed plus a double sofa bed and room for the wooden cot provided on request; 4 rooms are twins. Matching floral fabrics, pine furnishings, thoughtful touches like full-length mirrors and cotton wool plus good housekeeping bring all rooms up to an above-average pub standard. Good breakfasts put the icing on the cake. For families with babes in arms or children over five it's a good stopover, particularly for the outdoor tables and big family rooms; two high-chairs are provided and a 'families welcome' sign is displayed outside; if junior diners require high tea before evening bar snack times, they should arrange such when booking. Residential weekday conferences are popular, with one of the restaurant dining rooms doubling as a conference room. Open 11-11 Mon-Sat, regular hours Sun. **Bar Food** 12-2, 7-10 (Sun to 9.30) **Restaurant Meals** 12-2 (Sun only), 7-9.45 (except Sun). Free House. **Beer** Boddingtons, Flowers Original, Bass. Patio, outdoor eating. Family room. **Accommodation** 16 rooms, all en suite, £55 (single £43, family room £80). Children welcome overnight, cot supplied. Check-in all day (except Sun afternoon). Dogs by arrangement. Access, Visa.

Halifax   Holdsworth House   69%   £87

Tel 0422 240024 Fax 0422 245174	Hotel
Holdsworth nr Halifax West Yorkshire HX2 9TG	Map 6 C1

Much period charm has been retained by the Pearson family at their
17th-century manor, which stands two miles from Halifax off the
A629 Keighley road. The impressive oak-panelled restaurant is the
main feature (spreading out over three rooms) and a bar-lounge
provides additional space. The best bedrooms are four split-level suites
and the rest are both neat and comfortable with colourful fabrics and
mainly period furniture. Two rooms specially adapted for disabled
guests. Good facilities for children (under-10s free in parents' room);
the last Sunday of each month sees the Funday Club (£4.95 inc
lunch – a picnic in summer), when young children are "cared for
by experienced nannies" in order that parents may enjoy a peaceful
Sunday lunch (£12.50 adults, £6.50 under-12s). Characterful meeting
rooms hold up to 100. *Rooms 40. Garden.* **Closed** *Christmas/New Year.
Access, Amex, Diners, Visa.*

Harome   Star Inn

Tel 0439 70397	Pub
Main Street Harome nr Helmsley North Yorkshire YO6 5JE	Map 5 E4

The Star is a little gem of a pub. Originally a 14th-century long house,
the single thatched building is picture-postcard pretty outside and
no less delightful within, with its low beamed ceiling, high-backed
settles, 'Mousey' Thompson rustic furniture (somewhere on each piece
he made he carved a small mouse), and, by the fireplace, a rack
of magazines to browse through and a box of Lego and other toys for
those customers not yet of reading age. That the cottage garden to the
rear is just a little unkempt serves only to enhance its charm. Add
a friendly landlady (Victoria Blackburn), good beer, classical music
in the background and good food, and one has what for many would
be the ideal pub. The menu has something to suit most appetites and
tastes from sandwiches (for which they are well known), Stilton paté
(£2.95) and vegetarian crepe (£2.95) to a plate of fresh poached
salmon with chives and cream (£4.95), jacket potatoes (from £2.95)
croque monsieur (£4.95), savoury mince with Yorkshire pudding
(£5.95), Gressingham duck in port, black cherry and cream sauce
(£9.95) and home-made puddings (all at £2.50) like apple crumble
or mincemeat and brandy tart. At night, there is also an especially
attractive restaurant and above in the 'loft' a coffee lounge (also used
by families at lunchtime) that comes complete with playing cards and
board games to keep you amused over post-prandial drinks. Winner
of our Family Pub of the Year award last year. *Bar Food 12-2.30, 7-9
(summer 6.30-9.30).* **Restaurant Meals** *7-9 (exceptSun-Wed). Free
House.* **Beer** *Tetley, Theakston's Old Peculier & Best, Timothy Taylor's
Landlord. Garden, outdoor eating. Family room. Pub closed lunchtime
on Monday. Access, Visa.*

Harrogate   Bettys

Tel 0423 502746	Tea Room
1 Parliament Street Harrogate North Yorkshire	Map 6 C1

Select one of the rare coffees or an unusual tea and enjoy the occasional
morning café concert at this genteel tea room, the first of the Bettys
chain (established 1919). The tea room is divided into two – the

Verandah Café which overlooks the Stray (a grassed area in the centre
of town bedded with flowers) with an airy 1920s' atmosphere and the
Spindler Café which, with its marquetry pictures on the walls, alcoves
and teapot display on the fire surround, has a more cosy feel (closed
in the evenings). The day begins with breakfast – warm Yorkshire
oatcakes (£1.45), mushroom and bacon omelette (£4.98), rösti eiger
potatoes (£5.25) or simply two croissants or brioches with jam and
butter (£1.86). Light lunches bring sandwiches (from £2.55), salads
(corn-fed chicken £5.30), grills, omelettes, hot dishes such as haddock
and prawn croustades and the speciality of the house, rarebit made
with Theakston's Yorkshire Ale served with apple or tomato chutney
(£5.50). Among the summer specialities could be smoked chicken and
green peppercorn terrine or goujons of plaice and scampi (£5.20).
Bettys' famous warm Yorkshire fat rascal (£1.98), buttered pikelets
(£1.02) and banana and walnut loaf (£1.20) are some of the tea
breads. On the evening menu, crudités and prawn and avocado salad
(£3.75) are served as starters and bacon rösti with melted raclette
(£5.25) or mushroom and chestnut roulade with casseroled red
cabbage (£4.55) as a main course. Various ices (from £2.15), desserts
(toffee and brandy snap fanfare) and cakes (from £1.58 – chocolate
brandy roulade, Yorkshire curd tart) to follow. Pianist in the evenings.
Children's menu; ten high-chairs; the Ladies has a playpen, mat, chair
and shelf for changing. No-smoking area. Other branches in Ilkley,
Northallerton and York. *Seats* 174. *Open* 9-9. *Closed* 25 & 26 Dec,
1 Jan. Access, Visa.

Harrogate	**Hudson's Coffee House**	
Tel 0423 506200		**Coffee Shop**
Hudson's Coffee House Station Parade Harrogate North Yorkshire		**Map 6 C1**

On the top floor of a town-centre shopping mall, Hudson's (the name
comes from an 18th-century coffee house in Covent Garden) claims
to recreate an air of 1930s' elegance with its slower pace of life –
waiters have tail coats and there are newspapers and magazines
to read. They sometimes get a bit carried away with the menu
description – 'home-made' carrot and walnut cake, though good,
is actually bought-in and 'freshly sliced ham' is not the good stuff
carved from the bone as one might imagine, but a rather mediocre
product machine-sliced each morning – but the range of coffees and
loose-leaf teas is excellent. The extensive menu ranges from filled
bagels (from £2.15), sandwiches (from £2.85) and hot dishes like beef
Wellington (£8.50) and bangers and mash (£6.50), to cakes and
caviar (Russian Beluga with glass of champagne (£29.50).
Everything – except the set lunch (£5) and set dinner (£7.50) – is
available all day including set breakfasts (from £3.50) and English
afternoon tea (£5.25). No children's menu but small portions, high-
chairs and comics are provided and there are baby-changing facilities
within the mall. No smoking. Branches also in Birmingham and
Coventry (See entries). *Seats* 120. *Open* 9-7.30. *Closed* Sun, Bank
Holidays. Access, Amex, Visa.

Harrogate	**Imperial Hotel**	**65%**	**£95**
Tel 0423 565071 Fax 0423 500082			**Hotel**
Prospect Place Harrogate North Yorkshire HG1 1LA			**Map 6 C1**

In the heart of town, overlooking attractive gardens (and opposite
Bettys – see above), the *Imperial* was once the home of Lord

Carnarvon, discoverer of the Tutankhamen site. A programme
of refurbishment includes the restaurant, day rooms and corridors.
A wood-panelled snooker room has an open fire, leather chesterfield
sofas and a cosy cocktail bar. There are four cots and ten Z-beds
available. Children up to 14 stay free in parents' room. Six high-chairs
are on hand in the restaurant where there's a children's menu offered.
On Sundays, entertainment is laid on in the form of videos. Discounted
tickets for entry to National Trust properties and local cultural and
leisure facilities can also be provided. Principal Hotels. *Rooms 85.
Snooker. Access, Amex, Diners, Visa.*

Harwich   The Ha'Penny Pier at Harwich

Tel 0255 241212 Fax 0255 322752	Restaurant
The Quay Harwich Essex CO12 3HH	Map 10 C3

A modestly priced fish restaurant on the ground-floor with views over
the harbour. Only the freshest fish is served and main courses include
cod and prawn pie, fillet of cod mornay or simple fillet of haddock
or plaice (£4.95-£6.75). Vegetable samosas (£2.85) and prawn
cocktail are among the starters, and sweets on offer could be home-
made lemon cheesecake and chocolate mousse gateau (£2.75).
Children's menu (tomato soup, fish and chips, ice cream – £4.25) and
high-chairs. The Pier Restaurant upstairs provides a more elaborate
and slightly more expensive menu. Within a mile of the ferry port.
*Seats 60. Open 12-2 & 6-9.30. Closed 25 & D 26 Dec. Access, Amex,
Diners, Visa.*

Rooms   £70

The third-floor accommodation comprises six bedrooms of varying
standards. There's a nautical theme and some have views down the
estuary. All have en-suite bathrooms and televisions.

Hatherleigh   George Hotel

Tel 0837 810454 Fax 0837 810901	Pub
Market Street Hatherleigh nr Oakhampton Devon EX20 3JN	Map 13 D2

Dating from 1450, this ancient cob-and-thatch town-centre inn was
once a rest house and sanctuary for the monks of Tavistock. In later
years it became a brewery, tavern, a law court and a coaching inn
before developing into what is now a most comfortable and historic
small hotel. Off the central cobbled courtyard in the converted
brewhouse and coachman's loft is the main bar and family area
extension, while the original inn's bar oozes charm and antiquity with
old beams, an oak-panelled wall, an enormous fireplace and
an assortment of cushioned seats and sofas. It is now largely confined
to residents or waiting diners, as the attractive restaurant is next door.
The Farmers Bar across the courtyard opens only on Thursdays, when
the market is outside in the square. Sloping floors and low 'head-
cracking' doorways lead to eleven individually furnished bedrooms
with pretty chintz fabrics, pieces of old or antique furniture and
generally good clean en-suite facilities. Three rooms have elegant four-
poster beds. TVs, telephones and tea-making facilities are the added
comforts and residents also have the use of a charming lounge and the
outdoor swimming pool. Recommended for B&B only. *Free House.
Beer Bass, Flowers Original, Devon Glory, Boddingtons. Outdoor eating
area. Accommodation 11 bedrooms, 9 en suite, £65-£75 (single £28.50-
£55). Access, Amex, Visa.*

Hatton   Country Café

Tel 0926 843350	Café
Hatton Country World Hatton nr Warwick Warwickshire	Map 14 C1

Treat the whole family to a day at the craft centre, pick-your-own farm, farm shop, rare breeds farm park, adventure playground and garden centre, as well as the café. Baking takes place in full view and the results are good – savoury items include quiches (£1.30) and hot specials such as cottage pie (£3) or filled jacket potatoes (£2.75 to £3), while a changing selection of cakes (around £1) such as coffee and walnut gateau, pineapple and ginger or apple and banana should please the sweet-toothed. Beakers and high-chairs are provided, changing facilities are not. No smoking. *Seats 66.* **Open** *10-5.30.* **Closed** *Dec 25-mid Jan. No credit cards.*
Also at:
Kingsbury Water Park Bodymoor Heath Sutton Coldfield West Midlands
Tel 0827 874823   Map 6 C4

Haywards Heath   Chukka's Café Bar

Tel 0444 416870	Café
59 The Broadway Haywards Heath West Sussex	Map 11 B6

Themed around the 'hectic equestrian ballet' that is polo, a surprisingly light and spacious basement café-bar and restaurant thanks to an attractive rear conservatory overlooking a leafy patio. An eclectic menu offers anything from all-day basket meals (£2.20-£3.75) to roasted poussin with a creamy mustard sauce (£6.95) via guacamole with tortilla chips (£2.95) or tagliatelle marinara (£5.95). Home-made desserts (Baileys and Tia Maria cheesecake) could complete a meal or be had with a good cappuccino for afternoon tea. Early evening special (for orders between 6 and 7pm) includes steak, chips, salad and dessert for £5. Friendly, efficient service. *Seats 75.* **Open** *11am-10.30pm (Mon to 3pm, Sat from 7pm).* **Closed** *D Mon, L Sat, all Sun, Bank Holidays. Access, Amex, Diners, Visa.*

Helmsley   Feathers

Tel 0439 70275	Pub
Market Place Helmsley North Yorkshire YO6 5BN	Map 5 E4

'Elmslac', a Saxon village on the river Rye settled in 600 AD was listed in Domesday, and as Helmsley, renowned for its Norman castle, had a well-documented history throughout the Middle Ages. Feathers was once a merchant's house with the highest rent in town, later it was split into two cottages and now, re-unified by the friendly Feather family, offers some of the best-value accommodation in town. There are, of course, two entrances, two bars – with a unifying theme of the local "Mouse Man" furniture – two dining rooms and two stair-wells. Two floors of bedrooms provide accommodation that is more practical than luxurious; TVs and tea trays are provided, alarm clocks and hairdryers available on request. Family rooms with en-suite bathrooms offer good value, with under-12s accommodated free (meals charged as taken). Several smaller rooms have en-suite wc/shower rooms only, and the three remaining unconverted singles share so-called public, but nonetheless, adequate, ablutions. Recommended for B&B only. *Open 11-11 in high summer, usual hours other periods. Free House.* **Beer** *John Smith's, Theakston Best & Old*

Peculiar. Garden, family room. **Accommodation** *18 bedrooms, 16 en suite,
£53 (£36.50 single). Under-12s stay free, cots and extra beds supplied.
Access, Amex, Diners, Visa.*

Helmsley	Feversham Arms	66%	£70
Tel 0439 70766 Fax 0439 70346			Hotel
1 High Street Helmsley North Yorkshire YO6 5AG			Map 5 E4

Rebuilt in 1855 on the site of a previous hostelry, the inn is in the
capable, friendly hands of the Aragues family. Period appeal lives on,
but the place also moves with the times: the most recent improvement
involves the creating of an additional residents' lounge in the cottage
next door. The other lounge and the bars are named after Aragues
children. Bedrooms (six of which are on the ground floor) all have
little luxuries like personalised toiletries and include some with four-
posters. Children under 16 stay free in parents' room (cots and extra
bed provided). High-chairs and early meal on request. One of the bars
serves as a family room. It may be a historic inn but you'll still find
satellite TV in the rooms. **Rooms** *18. Garden, outdoor swimming pool,
tennis. Access, Amex, Diners, Visa.*

Helmsley	Monets	
Tel 0439 70618		Restaurant
19 Bridge Street Helmsley North Yorkshire		Map 5 E4

John and Heather Dyson's restaurant with rooms, a large private house
just out of the town centre, is the perfect spot (particularly the terrace
in fine weather) for enjoyable daytime snacking. Morning and
afternoon teas with home-made fruit scones (85p), toasted cinnamon
bread (65p) and sandwiches (from £1.70) are joined at lunchtime
by more substantial dishes such as steak and oyster pie (£6.99),
poached salmon with herb butter (£6.75) and vegetable lasagne
(£4.50). Good puds (chocolate sponge pudding £2.25, lemon tart).
More elaborate fixed-price evening meals. No high-chairs but children
are welcome and there's a room provided upstairs for mums who
want to change their charges. No smoking in the dining room.
Seats *22.* **Open** *10-5 (Oct to Mar from 11)* **Closed** *Mon, Bank Holidays.
Access, Visa.*

Hemel Hempstead	The Gallery Restaurant	
Tel 0442 232416		Bistro
The Old Town Hall High Street Hemel Hempstead Hertfordshire		Map 15 E1

A bistro-style restaurant on the first floor of a converted complex
housing an art gallery and theatre. An all-day menu embraces paté
with toast or pitta bread (£2.75), Danish open sandwiches (£2.95-
£3.75), filled jacket potatoes (from £2.60), various cakes and desserts,
perhaps pancakes with maple syrup and cream (£2), and a blackboard
dish of the day – usually pasta such as tagliatelle with roasted
Mediterranean vegetables and fresh Parmesan (£5.95). Particularly
popular for pre-theatre dinners. No-smoking area. **Seats** *60.*
Open *10.30am-11pm (Mon to 4.30pm)* **Closed** *Sun. Access, Visa.*

Henley-on-Thames   Violets & Creme

Tel 0491 412220	Ice Cream Parlour

28 Market Place Henley-on-Thames Oxfordshire   Map 15 D2

Luxury hand-made chocolates and Continental ice creams to take away are on display at the counter, which fronts a smart – darkwood panelling, tented ceiling, waitresses in stin stboaters – *salon glacier* in the centre of town. If eating in (order at the counter) leave the calorie table behind in order to enjoy the likes of a Boatman's special (the "largest banana split in England" £2.75), knickerbocker glory (£3.50), Henley Torte (the richest of chocolate ice cream, chocolate sauce and whipped cream £2.95) and various gateaux and pastries – vacherin, apple strudel, raspberry dome (all at £1.75). On the savoury side there are Italian sandwiches (£3.25), various quiches (£2.95), chicken and asparagus pie (£4.50), salad niçoise (£4.25) and smoked salmon with dill sauce (£6.50). A patio to the rear (the only place where smoking is allowed) is a good spot for summer eating. A full range of beverages includes iced coffee and tea. Seven high-chairs and five booster seats, but no changing facilities for the little ones who are expected to sit in them. *Seats* 48 (*plus 35 outside*). *Open* 9-6 (*Sun 2-6*). *Closed* 25 Dec. Access, Amex, Diners, Visa.

Hereford   Gaffers

Tel 0432 278226	Vegetarian

89 East Street Hereford Hereford & Worcester   Map 14 A1

A friendly, vegetarian co-operative where customers seem more like friends who just happen to have dropped in. The kitchen is within the restaurant so you can see the cooking going on and there's a secondhand 60s' clothes shop in one corner. Italian vegetable stew (£2.50), watercress and cream cheese flan (£1.30), filled rolls (70p), baked potatoes (£1.50), lovely cheesecake (£1.25), carrot cake and poppyseed cake (both 65p) typify the fare. Kids are welcomed with small portions, three high-chairs, comics and books to keep them amused. Changing mat in the Ladies. Smoking is only allowed before 12.30pm. Fenced-in garden. *Seats* 45. *Open* 9.30am-4.30pm. *Closed* Sun, Bank Holidays. No credit cards.

Higham   The Knowle   £68

Tel 0474 822262	Restaurant

School Lane Higham nr Rochester Kent ME3 7HP   Map 11 B5

Set in three acres of secluded gardens, making it a popular wedding venue, Lyn and Michael Baragwanath's large Victorian rectory is both an easy-going restaurant and family home. Sit in the eclectically furnished bar to choose from an equally varied menu of dishes more notable for fresh ingredients and generous portions than modern fads. Cheese soufflé royale, peach Knowle (filled with a mixture of cheese, herbs, brandy and garlic), grilled Dover sole, chicken with ginger, pot-roast pheasant and various sauced steaks show the range. Lunchtimes (except Sunday) and Tues-Thurs evenings there is an additional 'Bistro' menu that is considerably less expensive than the standard carte. No special children's menu but the kitchen is very adaptable and will always find something to suit. Nursing mothers can always be found somewhere private, even if it's the Baragwanaths' own lounge. Four high-chairs are provided. *Seats* 65. *Private Room* 50. *Parties* 14. L 12-1.30 D 7-10. Closed D Sun, all Mon, L Sat. Set L £13.95. Access, Visa.

Highclere   Yew Tree

| Tel 0635 253360 | Pub |

Andover Road Hollington Cross Highclere Berkshire RG15 9SE   Map 15 D3

Just south of the village, on the A343, Jenny Wratten has managed the
trick of improving the Yew Tree without detracting from its old-
world character. Huge logs smoulder in the inglenook fireplace while
old scrubbed pine tables and the odd sofa sit beneath ancient beams.
Several interconnecting rooms comprise the more formal restaurant
but the same menu is served throughout. A seasonally changing menu
(plus dishes of the day) combines simple dishes like grilled lemon sole
(£9.15) and steaks with traditional items – salmon fishcakes (£8.10),
pork tenderloin with apple and calvados sauce (£9.50), steak and
kidney pudding – and more recherché offerings such as crock
of pheasant (£8.10) from an 18th-century recipe and salamagundy
(£3.60), a 15th-century Hampshire dish of meat, cheese and vegetable
sticks with a fruity chutney. Ask for children's portions. Six cottagey
bedrooms offer overnight accommodation with direct-dial telephones,
remote-control TVs, beverage trays and little extras like books and
magazines' all have en-suite bathrooms – half with shower & wc only.
Bar Food 12-2.30, 6.30-10 (7-9.30 Sun). Children welcome in bar to eat.
Free House. **Beer** *Breakspear, Wadworth 6X. Garden, outdoor eating.*
Accommodation *6 bedrooms, all en suite, £55 (single £40). Children*
welcome overnight (under-5s stay free in parents' room), additional beds
available. Access, Visa.

Higher Burwardsley   Pheasant Inn

| Tel 0829 70434 | Pub |

Higher Burwardsley nr Tattenhall Cheshire CH3 9PF   Map 6 A3

The Pheasant is best located by following signs to the candle factory
from the A534. It is tucked into the hillside amongst the Peckforton
hills and on arrival, it's plain to see that the place was once a farm, and
the more surprising, therefore, to find that there has been a pub here
since the 17th century. The oldest part, a half-timbered sandstone
farmhouse, is the venue for the bar, which claims to house the largest
log fire in Cheshire. The adjacent Highland Room, generally known
as the Bistro, was once the kitchen and retains the old cast-iron range.
The most recent addition is an imposing conservatory of striking
modernity, which looks over a tiered patio and, beyond this, right
across the Cheshire plain towards North Wales. The old barn has been
skilfully converted into six very comfortable bedrooms, equipped
to the highest pub standards, with televisions, clock radios, hairdryers,
mini-bars and roomy, if poorly lit, bathrooms. Stonework interiors are
eye-catching, and nights tranquil. Two further bedrooms, housed
in the pub proper, boast original beams and brighter bathrooms,
as well as memorable views. There are three quite distinct aspects
to the food operation. At weekends, a self-service counter in the
conservatory is useful for a quick lunch, perhaps of chicken provençale,
mushroom stroganoff or a Sunday plate of roast beef and Yorkshire
(all at under £5), with a special children's menu (£1.95 main course
and pudding), and extended hours at weekends. In the bar, blackboards
display a daily-changing list for those requiring a little more
adventure. The Bistro, meanwhile, comes into its own at night (and
for Sunday lunch in winter). Space is limited; booking is advised.
Landlord David Greenhaugh has an unusual and passionate interest,
namely his prize-winning herd of pedigree Highland cattle. It's not

surprising therefore to find a certain bias towards meat dishes, amongst
which the steaks are outstanding (sirloin £9.50, fillet £11.95). The
friendly bunch of staff go out of their way to be pleasant and helpful.
Bar Food & Restaurant Meals *12-2 (12-2.30 Sun), 7-9.30 (Fri & Sat
to 10). Children's menu. Free House.* **Beer** *Bass, Worthington. Garden,
outdoor eating. Family room.* **Accommodation** *8 bedrooms, all en suite,
£60 (single £40). Children welcome overnight (0-10 yrs free, over 10 yrs
£10, additional bed & cot available. Dogs by arrangement. Access, Amex,
Diners, Visa.*

Hindon   Lamb Inn

| Tel 074789 573   Fax 07489 605 | Pub |
| Hindon Salisbury Wiltshire SP3 6DP | Map 14 B3 |

Wistaria clings to one corner of this mellow 17th-century coaching
inn. At its height, 300 post horses were kept here to supply the great
number of coaches going to and from London and the West Country.
Prime Minister William Pitt was apparently most put out to find
no fresh horses available when he stopped off in 1786. But there have
also been less reputable visitors: Silas White, a notorious smuggler said
to be leader of the Wiltshire Moonrakers, used the Lamb as the centre
of his nefarious activities. These days, things in Hindon are rather
more peaceful and the Lamb limits itself to providing honest
hospitality to modern travellers who bring their own horsepower
in four-wheeled form. Inside, the long bar is divided into several areas
and is furnished with some sturdy period tables, chairs and settles.
A splendid old stone fireplace with log fire creates a warm, homely
atmosphere, which is also enhanced by an ever-changing collection
of paintings by local artists both here and in the smarter restaurant.
The blackboard bar menu is sensibly not over-long, but still manages
to offer a reasonable choice – seafood au gratin (£5.25), pork chop and
mustard sauce (£5.25), cauliflower and fennel soup (£1.95) and for
pudding chocolate and rum terrine and fresh pineapple sponge (both
£2.10). In the restaurant, a 3-course table d'hote menu (£18.95)
is available. Three high-chairs and children's portions are offered;
breakfast 8-9.30am. Upstairs, there are twelve en-suite bedrooms,
which are furnished and decorated to varying styles and standards.
Open 11-11 Mon-Sat, regular hours Sun. **Bar Food** *12-2, 7-10.*
Restaurant Meals *7.15-9.30. Garden, outdoor eating.* **Accommodation**
*12 bedrooms, all en suite, from £55 (single £30-£38+), four-poster from
£65. Children welcome overnight, additional beds (£10) and cots (£10)
available. Access, Visa.*

Hope   The Hopechest

| Tel 0433 620072 | Tea Room |
| 8 Castleton Road Hope nr Sheffield Derbyshire | Map 6 C2 |

In the heart of the Hope Valley, this little tea room is part of a restored
stable. "Everything is home-made and not just home-baked" – soup
(£1.50), patés (£2.90), hams (£3.10), cakes (Bakewell tart, fruit cake,
carrot cake – all 95p), biscuits (15p) and scones (65p). Set afternoon
tea £3.20. Coffee is ground on the premises. Children's portions
on request and cheaper coffee for senior citizens. Small patio in
walled garden for outdoor eating. No smoking. **Seats** *20.* **Open** *9-5.*
Closed *Sun, Mon (except Aug, Dec & Bank Holidays), 25 Dec, 1 Jan.
Access, Visa.*

Hope Cove   Cottage Hotel   56%   £114*

| Tel 0548 561555 | Hotel |

Hope Cove nr Kingsbridge Devon TQ7 3HJ   Map 13 D3

John and Janet Ireland are the resident proprietors of this popular
family holiday hotel extended, originally, from just one small cottage.
It stands in a fine elevated position in gardens that descend to the sandy
beach. The main lounge is largely in 30s' style, and the cocktail bar
was built from the timbers of a wrecked tall ship, the *Herzogin Cecilie*.
The sun terrace is the place to be in summer, when Devonshire cream
teas accompany the lovely views. Accommodation includes some
rooms with extra accessories like video players; just over half the
rooms have en-suite facilities and some have balconies. A few rooms
at the back miss out on the sea views. Children up to 12 stay free
in parents' room; cots and high-chairs available; children's tea between
5.30 & 6pm – bibs and trainer cups available. Small kiddies'
playground and a games room for rainy days, but the sandy beach and
cliff walks should give them enough fresh air to sleep soundly. Under-
1s £2, 1-3 £5.75, 4-8 £9.75, 9-12 £13.55 daily tariff; child's dinner
£3.10. Dogs £3.25 daily. Gentlemen require a tie for dinner. Special
rates at the Bigbury golf club. *Half-board terms only. ***Rooms** 35.*
Garden, games room. Closed Jan. No credit cards.

Horton-cum-Studley   Studley Priory   64%   £98

| Tel 0865 351203   Fax 0865 351613 | Hotel |

Horton-cum-Studley nr Oxford Oxfordshire OX33 1AZ   Map 15 D2

A striking Elizabethan manor house set in 13 acres of wooded grounds
seven miles from Oxford. Impressive day rooms include a splendid
hall panelled in pitch pine, a lofty drawing room and a Victorian bar
with oak panelling. Six bedrooms are in the main house (antiques and
one with a four-poster dating from about 1700), while the majority
are in the Jacobean wing reached through a labyrinth of corridors –
these rooms are smaller and more modern. There is one family suite
and another four rooms that are most suitable for families; an extra
bed in parents' room is £12. Small conferences are big business here,
so you'll sometimes be sharing the drawing room with the delegates.
Owner Jeremy Parke has three children and is keen to embrace the
European ethic of dining out as a family, especially at Sunday
lunchtime, although children are not allowed in the restaurant after
dark. A cot (£5) and high-chair can be provided. Surrounded by 13
acres of woodland, so there is plenty of space for little legs to run wild
and let off steam after the constraints of being on best behaviour
inside. Imposing, but hopefully not too overpowering for little ones.
***Rooms** 19. Garden, grass tennis court, clay-pigeon shooting, croquet. Access,*
Amex, Diners, Visa.

Hungerford   The Tutti Pole

| Tel 0488 682515 | Tea Room |

3 High Street Hungerford Berkshire   Map 14 C2

Located a few yards from the Kennet and Avon canal, The Tutti Pole
tea room is housed in a cottage dating back to 1634. The name 'Tutti'
derives from the 'Tithing' or 'Tutti' men who still to this day call each
year to collect a penny from all the Common Right houses and a kiss
from the cottage occupants. The men carry a 'Tutti Pole' – a long pole
decorated with flowers and blue ribbon and topped with an orange.
For many years the poles were made in the house where the tea shop

now is. A full English breakfast (£4.15) is served until 11.30am (but the chef can be persuaded to extend the deadline!). Light snacks are available all day – a large assortment of sandwiches (£1.10-£1.45), poached eggs on toast (£2.65), paté on toast (£2.65), salads (from £4.55), Cajun prawns (£4.40). Canal walkers stop by in the afternoon for the Tutti Pole Cream Tea (£3.50) – two home-made scones and jam ("with stones"), Guernsey cream and pot of tea – two crumpets with butter (95p) or perhaps a fresh cream gateau (£1.65). Home-made cakes and meringues are also on sale at the counter. Three-course traditional Sunday lunch £5.95. Children and babies are frequent visitors to The Tutti Pole; they do not have their own menu but the owners try to satisfy children's requests. There's ample storage for prams, high-chairs are provided, food will be blended, bottles can be heated, and nappies can be changed in the loo. No-smoking area. **Seats** 80. **Open** 9-5.30 (Sat to 6, Sun 10-6). **Closed** 25 Dec-1 Jan. No credit cards.

Huntsham	Huntsham Court	68%	£110
Tel 039 86 365 Fax 039 86 456			Hotel
Huntsham Bampton nr Tiverton Devon EX16 7NA			Map 13 D2

A rather gaunt Victorian Gothic pile run in friendly, very casual style by owners Mogens and Andrea Bolwig. Eating is communal, there's an honour system in the bar, and you just wander into the kitchen if you need anything. There's great atmosphere in the day rooms (log fires, a panelled great hall, splendid pieces of furniture) and in the roomy bedrooms, named after composers, there are Victorian beds and baths and pre-war radios with an authentic crackle – not a teasmaid in sight! The hotel is dedicated to music, with the classical variety played *forte* in the evening. The day starts with an excellent buffet breakfast. No dogs. Children are well catered for and under-10s are accommodated free of charge if they share their parents' room; baby-sitting is available. No dogs, however "good" or "small". This is a great place for relaxing – its motto is 'dulce nihil facere' (it's sweet to do nothing). Private house parties and group functions a speciality. Out of the ordinary – you'll probably either love it or hate it. **Rooms** 17. Garden, sauna, solarium, tennis, coarse fishing, shooting, bicycles, snooker. Access, Amex, Diners, Visa.

Restaurant   £72

Five-course dinners (no choice, but variations possible in advance) are enjoyed in leisurely, communal fashion at a convivial candle-lit table. Duck from a local farm, roasted crisp and escorted by a Périgord sauce, is a favourite dish, so too fillet of brill sauce américaine, and for dessert, treacle tart. Guests are welcome to browse around the wine cellars where they'll find the New World and Spain prticularly well represented; fair prices and some wine charged by the glass from bottles left open on the table. **Seats** 30. Private Room 28. D only 8-10.30. Set D £27.50.

Hurtmore	Squirrels		
Tel 0483 860223 Fax 0483 860592			Pub
Hurtmore nr Godalming Surrey GU7 2RN			Map 15 E3

When is a pub not a pub? Possibly when it is converted into a comfortable, brasserie-style 'family' restaurant with the addition of cottagey bedrooms; nevertheless, Squirrels remains a pubby-type operation. Just off the A3 south of Guildford (take the Hurtmore turning), convenient for Godalming, this former pub cleverly offers both a characterful midweek stop-over for businessman and a warm welcome for families at weekends. The terraced garden offers suitable diversions for children: a wooden play house, slide, swings and a grassed area in which to let off steam; children can be supervised by parents from picnic tables in the raised terrace garden or on a patio area, delightfully bedecked with hanging baskets and climbing plants in summer. Inside, the bar area is a mix of comfortable small hotel lounge and country pub styles, with sofas, low tables and squirrels depicted every which way on the walls. Four small dining rooms (including a conservatory) lead off the bar area, as does a small TV room (with satellite) that also offers a few books and games. Simpler bar food seems the best bet, but the "finest home-cooked English breakfast you will ever eat" is promised for those who stay overnight in the bedrooms (some in the main building, 8 in two cottages). Two rooms (both en suite) are particularly suitable for families: one with bunk beds, the other with room for a Z-bed or cot. No changing facilities in the Ladies, but ask general manager Lesley Woodley and "all will be provided". Parents may appreciate the new 'pay-as-you-play' Hurtmore Golf Club nearby; or, for the more adventurous, a hot-air ballon flight from a field to the rear of the main building – where there may be up to five caravans. Occasionally closed at weekends for parties – so maybe it's not a pub after all! No dogs. *Beer Ruddles Best & County, Webster's Yorkshire. Garden, children's play area, patio. **Accommodation** 13 rooms, all en suite, £55-£65 (single £45-£50), weekend reductions. Children welcome overnight, additional bed and cot available, under-12s sharing £5. Access, Amex, Diners, Visa.*

Hythe	Hythe Imperial	71%	£117
Tel 0303 267441 Fax 0303 264610			Hotel
Princes Parade Hythe Kent CT21 6AE			Map 11 C5

A large, family-run hotel set right on the seafront and surrounded by 50 acres of grounds. An imposing, cream-painted exterior of Victorian splendour belies the more classical air within. The polished mahogany reception area is adorned with brown leather chesterfields and leads through to comfortable bars and lounges. All bedrooms have views of the sea or gardens and are mostly of good size with a mixture of quality period furniture, although some have more ordinary darkwood pieces; interconnecting rooms, suites and a bunk-bed room are suitable for families. Excellent, unusually pleasant staff and leisure facilities that include go-karting and a children's play area with Scalextric. Families are particularly well catered for with baby-sitting (by prior arrangement), baby-listening and crèche facilities available on Saturday mornings (10am-1pm, plus additional times over Christmas and New Year); they can eat informally in the leisure centre bistro. The Marston Minor Diner menu offers everything from finger fun food and commercial baby foods to reduced salt and sugar beans on toast, cottage pie, pizza and vegetarian yeast paté sandwiches; puzzles and quizzes at meal times help keep the peace while parents finish their own meal. A new children's playroom is now in use as are two extensions to the conference rooms. Sunday Plus is an interesting idea – extend a weekend stay (keeping the use of your room) until 5pm on Sunday for a nominal charge (£10 in 1993) that includes Sunday lunch. No dogs. Marston Hotels. *Rooms 100. Garden, 45' indoor swimming pool, mini-gym, spa bath, sauna, solarium, steam room, beauty & hair salons, 2 x squash, tennis, games room, 2 x snooker, 9-hole golf course, putting, helipad, coffee shop (8.30am-10.30pm), children's play*

room (weekends and Bank Holidays), outdoor climbing frame. Access, Amex, Diners, Visa.

Ickford   **Waterperry Gardens Tea Shop**

Tel 0844 339254	Tea Shop
Ickford Oxfordshire	Map 15 D2

Self-service tea shop in a horticultural centre. The counter holds a tempting show of baking, all made on the premises: set cream tea (£2.35, 2 scones, jam, cream and tea), cheesecake (£1.60), walnut pie (£1.40), Stilton flan (£2.65), French pastries (all £1.60), chicken, ham and turkey pie (£3.95 per slice). All the cakes are made with free-range eggs. Eat outside and admire the gardens in fine weather. One high-chair (fetch it yourself while juggling trays and buggies), lidded beakers, ramps for easy access, ample room to park buggies at tables and a big green space outside on which children can run about. There is no children's menu but with careful choosing you should be able to select a suitable meal for your child without having to rely on the obvious attraction of cakes and pastries. On a warm day the table in the outside ladies loo could be used for nappy-changing. No-smoking area. *Seats 80. Open 10-5.30 (to 4.30 Oct-end Mar). Closed 1 week Christmas. Access, Visa.*

Ilkley   **Bettys**

Tel 0943 608029	Tea Room
32 The Grove Ilkley West Yorkshire	Map 6 C1

Rarebits made with Yorkshire ale served with apple or tomato chutney and bacon or ham are Bettys' speciality (£5.50-£6.15). Also popular is the Yorkshire cheese lunch with blue, white and smoked Wensleydale cheeses with apple chutney, celery, rolls and butter. Uniformed waitresses will guide you through the cake trolley featuring curd tarts, chocolate brandy roulade, vanilla heart and apple strudel from £1.55. Breakfast grill (£4.45-£5.10). Eight high-chairs, children's menu and portions. Changing shelf with mat, chair and play pen in the Ladies. Part of a very successful and well-run chain with branches in Harrogate, Northallerton and York. No-smoking area. Pay and display parking to the rear of the café. *Seats 110. Open 9-6 (Fri-Sun to 6.30). Closed 25 & 26 Dec. Access, Visa.*

Ipswich   **Marlborough Hotel**   65%   £75

Tel 0473 257677 Fax 0473 226927	Hotel
Henley Road Ipswich Suffolk IP1 3SP	Map 10 C3

Peacefully located north of the town centre, the Marlborough (in the same ownership as the *Angel*, Bury St Edmunds) is run with care and enthusiasm by Wendy and David Brooks. The tasteful public areas and the comfortable bedrooms (the best have antique furniture) are equally well kept. Under-16s share free, extra beds £15, cot and high-chair provided. Pristine garden. No great family facilities, but 24hr room service for late-night requirements. *Rooms 22. Garden. Access, Amex, Diners, Visa.*

Kendal   **The Moon**

Tel 0539 729254	Bistro
129 Highgate Kendal Cumbria	Map 4 C3

A small half-vegetarian bistro-style restaurant in the middle of Kendal opposite the Brewery Arts Centre. Formerly a greengrocery, it has a bar in the central area and linen-clad tables laid out around it. The comfortable and cosy atmosphere is perfect for enjoying good food, much of it made from local produce: warm Camembert on rye bread (£3.25), guacamole with taco chips (£2.75), chicken breast Thai-style, with lime, creamed coconut and coriander (£7.55), courgette, tomato and spinach lasagne (£6.75), Cajun-spiced vegetables in tortillas (£6.75). The Moon hosts a pudding club once a month and consequently the adventurous choice (£2.75) is ever-changing: sticky toffee pudding, steamed puddings, coffee, chocolate and Tia Maria squidge roulade, raspberry and elderflower cheesecake. Children's portions. No smoking. *Seats 38. Open 6.30-10 (Sat from 6).* *Closed 25 & 26 Dec, 1 Jan, last 2 weeks Jan. Access, Visa.*

Kendal   Waterside Wholefoods

Tel 0539 729743	Vegetarian
Kent View Kendal Cumbria	Map 4 C3

Housed in an old converted mill with low ceilings and cottage plaster walls, this wholefood restaurant shares the premises with its adjoining shop. Owner Mrs Dean provides home-baked breads, cakes, puddings and scones (date, sultana, cheese) to accompany lunchtime specials and a large variety of teas (18 herbal). The daily-changing blackboard menu may offer lemon and carrot soup with herb bread roll (£1.80), spicy aubergine paté (£2.95), courgette and mushroom crumble (£4), blue cheese, apple and celery quiche (£3.30) as well as a choice of 10-15 salads (small portion of each £2.70, large £3.40). Puddings feature apple tart and yoghurt, hot sticky toffee pudding and cream, black cherry and chocolate trifle (all £1.60). Tables with parasols are set up outside in summer on the banks of the River Kent. Children are made most welcome with one high-chair provided. Unlicensed. No smoking. *Seats 36. Open 9-4. Closed Sun, 25 & 26 Dec, 1 Jan. No credit cards.*

Keswick   Bryson's Tea Room

Tel 076 8772257	Tea Room
42 Main Street Keswick Cumbria	Map 4 C3

Above Bryson's bakery shop, with its tempting display, is their immensely popular tea room. Hot snacks include Cumbrian ham and eggs (£5.50) and Borrowdale poached trout and Cumberland sausage, and snacky items include filled baked potatoes (from £2.55), omelettes (from £3.95) and salads (£4.70). The output of the bakery is strongly reflected at teatime when you can choose either the Cumberland Farmhouse Afternoon Tea (£3.50) or the Lakeland Cream Tea (£4.15) – served with scones, tea breads and cakes. Children's portions; one high-chair. No smoking. *Seats 84. Open 8.30-5.30.* *Closed Sun, 25 & 26, 1 Jan. Access, Visa.*

Kew   Original Maids of Honour

Tel 081-940 2752	Café
288 Kew Road Kew Surrey	Map 15 E2

Opposite the Cumberland Gate entrance to Kew Gardens is a lovely old-fashioned tea shop which has been in the Newens family since 1853. Round wooden tables, wrought-iron light fittings and bold rose-print curtains make a very atmospheric setting in which to indulge in the results of the hard work in the bakery to the rear. Most famous of the baking are the Maids of Honour (95p), Henry VIII's favourite sweetmeat. Cream cakes, japs, almond slices, eclairs and millefeuilles are other sweet temptations, while savoury items such as steak pie (£2.95) are joined by the daily roast lunch (£5.95 two courses). All the meats are organically produced, as are all the vegetables except peas. Children's portions; one high-chair. No smoking. *Seats 50.* **Open** *10-5.30 (Mon 9.30-1).* **Closed** *Sun, Bank Holidays, 3 days Christmas. No credit cards.*

Keysoe   Chequers Inn

Tel 0234 708678	Pub
Pertenhall Road Keysoe Bedfordshire MK44 2HR	Map 15 E1

Dating back to 1520, the Chequers' one bar is divided into two by an unusual pillared fireplace; log fires in cold weather. The separate lounge opens on to a large, lawned garden complete with a Wendy House, playtree and swing. *Free House.* **Beer** *Hook Norton, Bass. Garden, children's play area. Family room. Pub closed all Mon (except Bank Hols). Access, Visa.*

Kimbolton   The Tea Room

Tel 0480 860415	Tea Room
9 East Street Kimbolton Cambridgeshire PE18 0HJ	Map 15 E1

Home-made and freshly baked are the operative words for this traditional little tea room situated right next to Kimbolton Castle (the very same where Catherine of Aragon spent her last months in exile). The menu offers up sandwiches from tuna mayonnaise with chopped walnuts on iceberg lettuce (£1.85) to turkey Waldorf (£3.25) to beef with horseradish (£1.95). A wide range of salads is available and a generous assortment of chocolate cakes such as fudge, Dundee, coffee, ginger, lemon, passion and cheesecake (made with ricotta) – all home-baked of course, as are the scones (90p). Try also one of the set teas such as Gateaux (£2.70) or Strawberry Cream Tea (£4.25) with one of the ice creams on offer. A lovely courtyard in York stone with redbrick wall and flower baskets comes into its own in summer (20 seats). Good conscientious service in a calm, relaxing atmosphere. Strictly no smoking. *Seats 12.* **Open** *10.30-5.* **Closed** *Mon, also Mon-Wed Nov-Feb. No credit cards.*

King's Lynn   Butterfly Hotel   62%   £67

Tel 0553 771707 Fax 0553 768027	Hotel
Beveridge Way Hardwick Narrows King's Lynn Norfolk PE30 4NB	Map 10 B1

A modern, town-fringe hotel at the A10/A47 roundabout; part of a small East Anglian group aiming at the middle of the market. A useful stop-over; under-16s stay free in parents' room. **Rooms** *50. Garden. Access, Amex, Diners, Visa.*

Kingscote   Hunters Hall

Tel 0453 860393	Pub
Kingscote Tetbury Gloucestershire GL8 8XZ	Map 14 B2

An ideal spot for a family day out, Hunters Hall, standing on the A4135, sports a lovely tree-lined garden with extensive play areas and assault course, while on wet days parents and little ones use the gallery room, almost hidden above the pub's interlinked beamed and flagstoned bars. Bar food is a safe bet, some dishes changing daily (lamb and red wine casserole £5.45) and others with the seasons (smoked bacon and mushroom salad £2.95, salmon with prawn sauce £8.25). A lunchtime buffet in the dining room remains ever-popular, while at night the à la carte rather points up the kitchen's limitations. Standing separately, a Cotswold stone block of recent construction houses the bedrooms, residents' lounge and a conference facility. With roomy en-suite bathrooms, remote-control TVs and dial-out phones, neither space nor comfort is stinted: one ground-floor room incorporates facilities for the disabled, and a large suite with two double bedrooms extends, for some lucky little ones, the day out into tomorrow. Two high-chairs provided. Adventure play equipment, swing, slide, climbing frame in the garden. *Bar Food* 12-2, 7-9.45 (*Sun to 9.30*). *Free House. Beer Bass, Hook Norton Best, Wadworth 6X, Uley Old Spot. Garden, outdoor play area. Family room. Accommodation* 12 bedrooms, all en suite, £58 (single £44). Children welcome overnight (family room for 3 – £68, for 4 – £80). Additional beds (£10) and cots (£4) available. Access, Diners, Visa.

Kingston   La La Pasta

Tel 081-546 6668	Restaurant
141 London Road Kingston Surrey	Map 15 E2

Son of La La Pizza across the road (see below), this friendly, family-run trattoria majors on pasta with some 15 or so sauces served with the pasta of your choice (from £4.75) – although the menu does recommend particular combinations. Starters range from Parma ham with melon (£5.45) and prawn cocktail (£4.20) to grilled sardines (£3.75) and garlic mushrooms with additional daily-changing dishes written up on a blackboard. Decor is informal with bare-board floor and marble-topped tables plus a partially covered courtyard to the rear for summer eating. Children are "always welcome" in typical Italian style and the kitchen will do their best to please their younger customers; three clip-on seats and two booster seats are provided. There is no minimum charge. Booking is essential on Thursday, Friday and Saturday nights but don't be late as tables are only held for ten minutes. *Seats* 70. *Open* 12-3 & 6-12. *Closed* L Sat, all Sun. No credit cards.

Kingston   La La Pizza

Tel 081-546 4888	Pizzeria
138 London Road Kingston Surrey	Map 15 E2

The owners of this cheerful Italian pizzeria continue to add new pizzas to their imaginative range, naming many of them after classical singers or composers: Caruso has smoked cheese, liver sausage, stuffed olives and pine kernels, Verdi includes salami, ham, artichoke hearts and a whole egg. The choice runs to 30 and they range from £3.30 to £6.90; no garlic or capers unless requested. If you can manage a starter as well you could choose from baked dough sticks, borlotti bean and tuna fish salad or Mediterranean seafood salad. For dessert the home-made chocolate mousse (£2.10) is splendidly rich. Four high-chairs; changing shelf in Ladies. "Children are always welcome." Fenced-in garden. *Seats* 50. *Open* D only 5.30-11.30 *Closed* 25 & 26 Dec, 1 Jan, Easter Day. No credit cards.

Kington   Penrhos Court   £65

| Tel 0544 230720   Fax 0544 230754 | Restaurant |

Penrhos Kington Hereford & Worcester HR5 3LH   Map 9 D4

In six acres of grounds, standing on the hill between Lyonshall and
Kington on the A44, Martin Griffiths' and Daphne Lambert's
restaurant is in the beautifully restored 13th-century Cruck Hall,
complete with flagstone floors and heavy beams – a characterful
setting for occasional medieval banquets. Daphne offers daily-changing
menus with a short choice: perhaps queen scallops grilled with
laverbread or grilled goat's cheese to start, followed by pan-fried fillet
of rabbit with oyster mushrooms, garlic and basil or fillet of lamb
with mushroom risotto and a light curry sauce. Simple, but well-
executed desserts such as blackcurrant trifle, lemon tart and chocolate
truffle cake with coffee-flavoured crème anglaise. 4-course Sunday
lunches offer a small choice, but always include a traditional roast.
Plenty of space inside and out for children to let off steam, although
toddlers need to be watched as there's an open pond in the courtyard.
Seats 50. *Private Room* 20. *L (Sun only)* 12.30-3 *D* 7.30-9. *Closed* 25 &
26 Dec, last 2 weeks Feb. *Set L* £12.50/£15.50 *(Sun* £15.50)
Set D £19/£25. *Access, Amex, Diners, Visa.*

Rooms   £110

Nineteen individually-styled bedrooms, named after birds, show some
fine taste. The latest eight rooms are in converted Elizabethan barns;
of a fair size, they use lightwood and mahogany furniture, co-
ordinated contemporary fabrics and bright, clean decor. Bathrooms
(some with shower/WC only) have attractive fittings and quality
toiletries. Limited hotel-style public areas, but high bedroom standards.
The Swallow Room features a four-poster bed and private balcony.
Children up to 10 stay free in parents' room. No dogs.

Kintbury   Bistro Roque

| Tel 0488 58398 | Bistro |

Inkpen Road Kintbury Wiltshire   Map 14 C2

A recent conversion of former school house turned pub just outside
the village (follow Inkpen signs) is energetically run by the Conway
brothers, Jason and Marc. Lively music and bow-tied waiters imbue
a Continental air, reinforced by Mediterranean salads (£3.50)
tagliatelle niçoise (£5.95), Andalucian-style fish soup and halibut
cardinal with shrimp and brandy sauce (£9.95). Chicken cooked three
ways broadens the international theme: chargrilled American-style
with mustard mayonnaise, stir-fried with oyster sauce and tandoori-
style masala are all £7.95 and for vegetarians baked vegetable roll
with tarragon sauce (£6.95). For non-calorie-counters rumpy-pumpy
pie (coffee and chocolate sponge mousse gateau £3.25), fruit crepes
and lemon brulée. Children's portions. Small no-smoking area and
some tables outside. *Seats* 100. *Open* 12-2.15 & 7-10 *(Sun* 9.30).
Closed 24-26 Dec. *Access, Visa.*

Kirkby Lonsdale   Snooty Fox Tavern

| Tel 05242 71308 | Pub |

Main Street Kirkby Lonsdale Cumbria LA2 2AH   Map 4 C4

A smart Jacobean black and white painted inn adjacent to the town
square. Plenty of interest is revealed within the bars: period costumes

adorn the walls amid collections of post horns, farm implements and old beer taps. Food throughout the dining room and three flagstoned bars hits no heights of invention. A warm welcome is given to children, who can play safely in the enclosed rear garden. Overnight, there's space in three larger rooms for a cot or an extra bed and there are TVs for amusement. All five bedrooms are neatly furnished and full of oak-beamed character; three only have full en-suite bathrooms. A hearty English breakfast delivered to the room remains one of the Snooty Fox's attractions. Recommended for B&B only. *Beer Hartleys, Theakston Best & XB, guest beer. Garden, family room. Accommodation 5 rooms, 3 en suite, £46 (single £26). Children under 6 stay free overnight. No dogs. No credit cards.*

Knapp   Rising Sun

Tel 0823 490436	Pub

Knapp North Curry nr Taunton Somerset TA3 6BG   Map 13 E2

Directions here are hard to give and just as hard to follow. Meander down the lanes from the hamlet of Ham, right on the lip of the Somerset levels, and then keep a lookout for the arrows. Built as a Longhouse in 1480 and 'rediscovered' since the arrival of Tony Atkinson in 1991, the Sun attracts its fill of worshippers of fine, fresh fish these days, and diners should mark out their spot especially early at weekends. Separated by a lounge bar with deep sofas in front of a cast-iron stove, two cottage dining areas are now given over to some serious eating with star billing given to fresh fish from Brixham and elsewhere. Star quality is not far off in many of the dishes such as the chunky bouillabaisse (£2.50) and perhaps emperor bream with Creole sauce (£11.50); so popular are the megrims (Torbay sole), lobsters and langoustines that availability cannot be promised to later arrivals. Half portions for children, popular Sunday lunch (from £6.25) with hot fishy bits on the bar and flowery summer patios are all added draws. High-chairs provided. *Bar Food 12-2. Restaurant Meals 12-2, 7-9.30. Beer Boddingtons, Bass, Exmoor Ale. Patio. Family Room and children's portions. Access, Visa.*

Knutsford   Cottons Hotel   65%   £112

Tel 0565 650333 Fax 0565 755351	Hotel

Manchester Road Knutsford Cheshire WA16 0SU   Map 6 B2

Five minutes from the M6 (Junction 19) and just 15 from Manchester Airport, Cottons was designed with a New Orleans theme. There's plenty of free parking, versatile facilities for conferences and a well-designed leisure club to which all guests have free membership during their stay. Two bars provide a choice for the thirsty. Children up to 14 accommodated free in parents' room; cots and high-chairs provided. The Cap'n Feather's Feasts menu should satisfy junior hunger pangs: pizza, baked beans on toast or boiled eggs with Marmite soldiers show an understanding of what most kids seem to enjoy. Shire Inns. *Rooms 82. Indoor swimming pool, gymnasium, sauna, spa bath, solarium, tennis. Access, Amex, Diners, Visa.*

Knutsford   Est Est Est

Tel 0565 755487	Restaurant
81 King Street Knutsford Cheshire	Map 6 B2

Light, bright and spacious, this is one of a small North-West chain
of friendly Italian trattorias. The long menu includes all the traditional
favourites from calamari fritti (£3.55) and some 18 pasta dishes (from
£2.15 as a starter or £3.95 as main course) served with excellent,
freshly grated Parmesan and pizza (from £4.35), to pollo cacciatore
(£8.95) and scaloppine al limone (£10.25). Lunchtimes and until 7.30
at night (except Saturday) there's a good-value set menu at £9.95.
No minimum charge but you're expected to have a main-course dish
at night. Seven high-chairs. Table in the Ladies for changing. See also
entries under Didsbury and Liverpool. *Seats 180*. **Open** *12-2.30 &*
6-11 (Fri to 11.30, Sat 12-11.30, Sun 12-11). **Closed** *25 & 26 Dec,*
1 Jan. Access, Amex, Visa.

Lacock   George Inn

Tel 0249 730263	Pub
4 West Street Lacock nr Chippenham Wiltshire SN15 2LH	Map 14 B2

The virtual epitome of the traditional village pub. The George could
scarcely be in a more ideal spot than the National Trust village
of Lacock. Starting life in 1361 as the *Black Boy* with its own brewery
in farm buildings to the rear, its many modernisations have preserved
and reutilised many of the original timbers. Central to the bar
is a unique mounted dog-wheel built into the open fireplace and used
for spit-roasting in the 16th century (the dog was not roasted, but
trained to rotate the wheel). Today's pub lives well alongside such
idiosyncrasy with its close-packed tables on odd levels set beneath
a wealth of old pictures at many an odd angle. From a menu of firm
favourites, traditional steak and kidney pie (£4.50) is always popular
alongside fresh chicken breast in white wine, cream and garlic
(£5.50), 14oz T-bone steak (£6.95), lemon sole (£4.50) and
a vegetarian spinach and blue cheese crumble (£4.25). Desserts include
bread-and-butter pudding and sticky toffee pudding (both £2.25). The
large garden stretches out on both sides of the rear car park; beyond
it is a safe play area for youngsters, close by an old stocks to restrain
the most troublesome. True to its long-standing identity as a family
concern, the licensees' family not only provides overnight farmhouse
accommodation nearby but also lays on complimentary transport
to and from the pub. Enquires should be addressed to the pub.
Bar Food *12-2, 6-10 (Sun from 7). Children allowed in the bar to eat,*
children's menu. **Beer** *Wadworth. Garden, outdoor eating, children's play*
area. Access, Visa.

Langdale   Langdale Hotel & Country Club   71%   £130

Tel 05394 37302 Fax 05394 37694	Hotel
Great Langdale nr Ambleside Cumbria LA22 9JD	Map 4 C3

An extensive hotel and timeshare complex in 35 acres of woodland
overlooking Great Langdale Beck. Centrally, an open-plan bar-lounge
and restaurant incorporate the old mill stream, while an adjacent pub
bar features slate walls and a log fire. Accommodation comprises
a number of satellite blocks, constructed in Lakeland stone, where
there is plenty of room for families in the former self-catering chalets;
baby-sitting may be available (by advance arrangement) but not baby-
listening, due to the distance between rooms and dining room. Wet-

weather provision includes fine leisure facilities, a Lego table in the bar and coffee shop seating by the large pool. No dogs. *Rooms 65. Garden, gymnasium, indoor swimming pool, children's pool, spa bath, sauna, solarium, keep-fit equipment, beauty & hair salon, tennis, squash, games room, snooker, adventure trail and play equipment, trim trail, bowling green, coffee shop (10am-10pm), news kiosk. Access, Amex, Diners, Visa.*

Lanhydrock   Lanhydrock House Restaurant

Tel 0208 74331	Restaurant

Lanhydrock nr Bodmin Cornwall   Map 12 B3

The former servants' hall of National Trust-owned Lanhydrock House with its oak panelling and bell-boards is now the Restaurant, where uniformed waitresses serve light lunches and teas. The daily hot special might be Elizabethan pork (£5.45) or steak and kidney with Guinness sauce. Other dishes include aubergine and tomato tart with a mixed salad (£4.75), salads (locally smoked mackerel fillet, home-baked ham £5.25). Two puddings feature daily (£2.25 each), one hot (bread-and-butter pudding with fruit sauce) and one cold (fresh lemon tart). The cream tea (£2.85) and the copious Country House Tea (£3.95) are served later in the day with a choice of home-made cakes, scones and splits (Cornish speciality). The wine list extends to elderflower, strawberry and apple wines. Light lunches of jacket potatoes, small salads, soups and puddings are also served in the former housekeeper's and housemaids' sitting rooms in the servants' quarters. Across the courtyard, the Stable Bar serves snacks, drinks, and ice cream throughout the day. Three-course traditional lunch (£9.95) on Sundays. Children's portions; five high-chairs and a fully-equipped mother and baby room. No smoking. *Seats 46. Open 11am-5.30pm. Closed Jan-Mar, limited opening Nov & Dec. Access, Amex, Visa.*

Lavenham   Angel Inn

Tel 0787 247388	Pub

Market Place Lavenham Suffolk CO10 9QZ   Map 10 C3

First licensed in 1420, the Angel looks out on to the market place of one of the best-preserved medieval towns in England. Inside, the bar has been opened up, but without losing its charm, with half set up for eating and the other well supplied with board games, playing cards and shelves of books. There are quiz and bridge nights and on Friday evenings Ray Whitworth (one of the partners) entertains with classical music at the piano. Carrot and coriander soup (£2.25), fresh grilled sardines (£3.25), lamb in paprika and cream (£7.25), duck breast in juniper sauce (£8.50) and steak and kidney pie (£5.95) are typical offerings from the daily-changing evening menu; lunchtime brings similar dishes (at slightly lower prices) plus some more snacky items like ploughman's (£3.95) and cauliflower cheese (£3.50). Good puds (all at £2.45) include excellent fruit pies served with custard in a separate jug. Bedrooms are all en suite (four with shower and WC only) and full of character with old beams, sloping floors and traditional freestanding furniture. All have TV, direct-dial phone and tea and coffee-making kit. Children are made welcome with a couple of high-chairs, free cots and Z-beds, and (although there is no special menu) resident youngsters can be provided with beans on toast or something similar; all children can have small portions of suitable items from the menu. For summer there are tables in a secluded garden plus pavement tables. *Bar Food 12-2.15 (Sun to 2), 6.45-9.15*

(Sun 7-9). **Beer** *Nethergate, Adnams, Courage Directors, Webster's Yorkshire, Ruddles County. Accommodation 7 bedrooms, all en suite, £45 (single £37.50). Access, Visa.*

Lavenham	**Great House**	£45

Tel 0787 247431	Restaurant
Market Place Lavenham Suffolk CO10 9QZ	Map 10 C3

The Great House is 15th-century with a Georgian facade, and stands just opposite the historic Guildhall in this well-preserved medieval town. Frenchman Régis Crépy provides excellent food served in cosy surroundings on rural French and English menus, applying a modern touch to the best local ingredients. "Children are very welcome to have any dish in a smaller helping" – try the deep-fried button mushrooms, lasagne, ravioli with langoustine, chicken fricassee, salmon in pastry or coq au vin. Wide selection of French cheeses. Long brasserie-style lunch menu and both fixed-price and à la carte in the evening. Storage for push-chairs, three high-chairs, one booster seat, toys, garden toys, swings and colouring utensils – what more persuasion does one need? The lawned garden with play area is ideal for letting fidgety feet leave parents to finish their meal in peace. No smoking. **Seats** *40. Private Room 50. L 12-2.30 D 7-9.30 (Sat to 10.30). Closed D Sun, all Mon. Set L £9/£12 Set D £14.95. Access, Amex, Diners, Visa.*

Rooms	£68

There are four charming bedrooms/suites (extra children's bed for under-12s free – breakfast charged as taken – over-12s £10). Thick beams, antique furniture and floral fabrics create the look of village England. Public swimming pool in Sudbury, plus arrangements to use Lavenham tennis club.

Leamington Spa	**Alastair's Bistro**

Tel 0926 422550	Bistro
40 Warwick Street Leamington Spa Warwickshire CV32 5JS	Map 14 C1

A cellar restaurant with bare brick walls, stone floor and antique pine furniture offers a decent meal in a cheerful atmosphere. Steaks (fillet au poivre £12.50) and fresh fish from £6.50 are the specialities here although the blackboard may show other dishes such as taramasalata, tahini dip, squid, boeuf bourguignon or pork normande. Profiteroles, home-made fruit crumbles or chocolate fudge cake (all at £2.25) to finish. One high-chair and one booster seat. Walled patio garden. **Seats** *45. Open 12-3.30 & 7-12. Closed L Sat & Sun and Bank Holidays, 1 Jan.*

Leamington Spa	**Piccolino's Pizzeria**

Tel 0926 422988	Pizzeria
5 Spencer Street Leamington Spa Warwickshire	Map 14 C1

A dependable alternative to the larger high street chains (there's another one in Warwick – see entry). Piccolino's is family-owned and family-friendly, too. Cooked-to-order pizzas (napoletana £4.85; quattro formaggi £5.60) are notably good, pasta alternatives (ravioli di pomodoro £4.95; tagliatelle alla marinara £5.85) richly sauced, and there are steaks (pizzaiola £9.75) for those wishing to splash out more. Two high-chairs and booster seats. **Seats** *85. Open 12-2.30 & 5.30-11 (Fri to 11.30, Sun to 10.30, Sat 12-11.30). Closed 25 & 26 Dec. Access, Visa.*

Ledbury   The Feathers

Tel 0531 5266	Bar Snacks
High Street Ledbury Hereford & Worcester	Map 14 E1

A classic timber-framed former coaching inn and corn exchange
dating from 1564. Original Elizabethan wall-paintings, uneven creaky
floors and drunken staircases characterise the interior. Good snacks and
light lunches are taken in the hop-bedecked Fuggles Bar: Fuggles
home-made soup (£2.75), deep-fried Brie with Cumberland sauce
(£3.45), home-made fish cakes with tomato and herb sauce (£5.25),
mushroom and nut strudel, grilled Herefordshire steaks (from £9.95),
and nutty treacle tart with custard, stuffed baked apple or home-made
profiteroles with chocolate sauce (all £2.75). A traditional Sunday
lunch is served in the restaurant. Small patio at the back for outdoor
eating. One high-chair; no changing facilities. *Seats 50. Open 12-2 &*
7-9 (Sat till 10, Sun till 9). Access, Amex, Diners, Visa.

Leeds   Bibi's

Tel 0532 430905	Restaurant
16 Greek Street Leeds West Yorkshire	Map 6 C1

Squeezed in between city-centre office blocks, there's a certain
incongruity to the classical Roman facade behind which is an
appealingly smart yet informal restaurant. The menu caters to all
occasions from a simple pizza or pasta dish (both around £4.25)
to a comprehensive range of skilfully prepared fish and meat dishes
at all prices from £6.75 to £14. Blackboard dishes of the day might
include fresh asparagus hollandaise, sea bass with aromatic herbs
(£14.75), and veal and pigeon pie. The super-swift lunchtime service
(much appreciated by the local business community) slows down to
a more relaxing pace at night. *Seats 140. Open 12-2.15 & 6-11.15.*
Closed Sun. Access, Amex, Visa.

Leeds   Bryan's

Tel 0532 785679	Fish'n'Chips
9 Weetwood Lane Headingley Leeds West Yorkshire	Map 6 C1

A modestly comfortable fish and chips restaurant serving good fresh
fish fried, in the traditional Yorkshire manner, in pure beef dripping.
Recently extended menu now including grilled fish and seafood when
available. Special children's section; otherwise there's a minimum
charge of £4 per person. Licensed. Own parking. No-smoking area.
Seats 120. Open 11.30am-11.30pm (Sun 12.30-8) Closed 25 & 26 Dec.
Access, Visa.

Leeds   Darbar

Tel 0532 460381	Restaurant
16 Kirkgate Leeds West Yorkshire	Map 6 C1

A modest doorway at street level (opposite Littlewoods) leads
to a large, splendidly grand first-floor restaurant. The shorter than
average Indian menu may explain the above average quality with
notably lean meat in curries (mostly at just under £5) that favour
subtlety rather than 'heat'. Tandoori dishes start at £6.90 and
at lunchtime there is also a self-service hot buffet which, at £3.95,
represents particularly good value and a bargain way of introducing
Indian food to young palates. *Seats 95. Open 11.30-2 (Mon to Sat) &*
6-11.30. Closed L Sun, 25 Dec. Access, Amex, Diners, Visa.

Leeds   Haley's Hotel   74%   £112

Shire Oak Road Headingley Leeds West Yorkshire LS6 2DE   Map 6 C1

Two miles from the city centre, on a leafy lane just off the A660
Otley Road, stands a lovely Victorian house that has been transformed
into a stylish hotel. Although not large, the individually designed
bedrooms are well appointed with smart fabrics in varying styles;
attention to detail extends to a phone on both bedside table and desk,
shoe-cleaning service and antique pieces. Bathrooms are bright and
tiled, and quality toiletries and bathrobes are provided. Smartly attired
young staff; 24hr room service and good breakfasts. Children up to 14
stay free in parents' room. Baby-sitting can be arranged and there's one
cot available. Informal eating for families in the lounge or library;
high-chair provided. Good-value two-night weekend tariff. **Rooms 22.**
Garden. Closed 26-30 Dec. Access, Amex, Diners, Visa.

Restaurant   £52

A serious restaurant with a style and quality unusual for the Leeds area.
The refined, quietly elegant atmosphere is enhanced by neat table
settings, subtle lighting and well-dressed staff. New chef Chris Baxter
offers a straightforward table d'hote and a more involved carte with
dishes like a spicy fish soup under a pastry case, oysters glazed in their
shells with a tagliatelle of vegetables, fillet of beef with Brouilly sauce
and wild mushrooms and duck breasts in pastry with caramelised red
cabbage and plum sauce. Chocoholics can indulge in *la folie de cinq
chocolats*, a speciality of the restaurant. French and British cheeses with
home-made biscuits and walnut bread, plus dessert wines by the glass
(try the unusual Banyuls). **Seats 50. Parties 10. Private Room 25.**
*L 12.30-2 D 7.15-9.45. Closed L Sat, D Sun. Set L £13.95/£16.95
Set D £18.95/£23.95.*

Leeds   Salvo's

115 Otley Road Headingley Leeds West Yorkshire   Map 6 C1

The 'best pizzas in the north' are the claim of this lively pizzeria.
Regulars queue outside in all weathers, their wait made more pleasant
by hot crusty garlic bread served on the pavement. Pizzas include
affumicata with smoked cheese and bacon (£4.75) and Kiev folded
and stuffed with chicken, garlic butter and cheese (£5.35).
Alternatively the menu offers a wide range of pasta dishes and
other savouries including penne arrabbiata with salami (£4.95).
Reservations accepted for lunch only. **Seats 45. Open** *12-2 & 5.30-11.
Closed L Bank Holiday Mons, all Sun, 25 & 26 Dec. Access, Amex, Visa.*

Leek   Primo Piano

2 Sheepmarket Leek Staffordshire   Map 6 C3

A first-floor bistro and pizzeria above the pedestrianised Sheepmarket,
lent authenticity by enthusiastic young owners and by the washing
lines of pristine bloomers where, in Italy, the balcony should be!
Two dozen or so predictable dishes from pizza margherita (£3.95)
to spaghetti carbonara (£4.10) are supplemented by interesting breads
such as rustico (£1.45) and marinara with anchovies (£1.55) and
rather plainer salads (£1.35). Other dishes include pizza quattro
stagioni (salami, ham, tomato and cream (£4.25) and pollo primo

piano (£7.95). Italian sweets and cassata are brought in; children's pizza and pasta offered for £2.50. One high-chair. No smoking. *Seats 60. Open 12-2 & 6-10 (Fri/Sat to 10.30). Closed Sun, Mon (except Bank Holidays). Access, Visa.*

Leominster   Royal Oak Hotel

Tel 0568 612610 Fax 0568 612710	Pub
South Street Leominster Hereford & Worcester HR6 8JA	Map 14 A1

Modest accommodation in an early-18th-century coaching house on the corner of Etnam Street and South Street. Historic relics of its earlier glories are to be found in the Regency Room, complete with chandeliers and minstrel's gallery, and the brick-lined cellar bar which is a cosy spot in the evenings. The main Oak Bar boasts two enormous log fires and serves good real ales and guest beers (Woods Parish Best, perhaps). Bedrooms come in a mixture of sizes and styles with one or two smallish singles, six spacious family rooms and a fine four-poster suite. All have carpeted bathrooms, while room comforts run through TV and intercom (for baby listening and wake-up calls) to tea or coffee makers and electric blankets. Recommended for B&B only. *Open 11-11 Mon-Sat, regular hours Sun. Beer Hook Norton Best, Wadworth 6X, guest beers. Accommodation 18 bedrooms, all en suite, £45 (single £29.50). Children welcome overnight (under-12s stay free in family rooms), additional beds (£4) and cots (£4) available. Access, Amex, Diners, Visa.*

Lincoln   The Plaice

Tel 0522 546124	Fish'n'Chips
St Pauls Lane Lincoln Lincolnshire	Map 7 E2

Just by the Castle car parks on Westgate, John and Debbie Harris have a prime spot for a true family chippy. Cheery waitress service to well-spaced tables serves to emphasise that everything is cooked to order and the quality of daily Grimsby fish supplies speaks for itself. Haddock, chips and peas (green or mushy) at £3.75 is a lunchtime bargain: skate (£5.95), salmon salad (£5.50) and Dover soles attract the more adventurous. Nursery puddings (Spotted Dick £1.75), generous children's portions (from £2.40) and over half non-smoking tables echo family commitment. Two high-chairs, but no changing facilities. *Seats 76. Open 12-2 & 5-9.30 (Sat 12-10). Closed Mon (in winter), two weeks from the 24 Dec. Access, Visa.*

Lindal-in-Furness   Chandlers Country Café

Tel 0229 65099	Café
Lindal Business Park Lindal-in-Furness nr Ulverston Cumbria	Map 4 C4

Look out for the 'candle factory' sign off the A590 to find the factory shop and a large 'designer' country café with its good home baking and exceptionally friendly service from girls in T-shirts and baseball caps. The shortish menu – half a dozen sandwiches like BLT (£2.45) and tuna (£2.75), jacket potatoes (£1.95 to £2.25), salads, a few cookies and cakes like strawberry roulade and chocolate cake (from 95p) plus set tea with egg sandwiches and scones (£2.95) – is supplemented at lunchtime by a couple of hot dishes such as chicken paprikash (£4.25) and there's always a vegetarian and a meat lasagne (both £4.15). Two high-chairs are provided and a separate changing room. Spacious, so plenty of room for buggies. *Seats 82. Open 10-4.30 (Sun from noon). Closed 25 & 26 Dec, 1 Jan. Access, Amex, Diners, Visa.*

Linton   Fountaine Inn

Tel 0756 752210	Pub

Linton nr Skipton North Yorkshire BD23 5HJ   Map 6 C1

An idyllic village green complete with stone bridge over a little
stream is the setting for this charming mid-17th century inn recently
restored in sympathetic style by Francis Mackwood. Several
interconnecting rooms (one for non-smokers and one where children
are made welcome) feature old beams, plus some false ones, but it's
hard to tell the difference, and built-in settles. Foodwise, there are
various open sandwiches (small from £2, large from £3.25), cold
platters such as home-roast ham (£5.50), tuna (£4.75) and chicken
(£5.25) plus the likes of gammon and eggs, lamb cutlets and fresh
local trout, not forgetting the Linton Yorker – a giant Yorkshire
pudding filled with gravy, sausage or casserole of the day. For the
sweet-toothed there are some good home-made puds while for those
with more savoury tastes there's the local Wensleydale cheese that
comes either blue, smoked or in the traditional white style. For
children there are 'turkey aeroplanes', farmhouse sausages, or 'golden
fishes' (£2.75-£3 with chips) plus a single high-chair. "Black Sheep
fine ales and great baa snacks." The village green is well used
in summer although they are not allowed to put out any tables
or chairs. **Bar Food** Noon-2.15 (Sun to 2.30), 7-9.15. Free House.
Beer Black Sheep Best & Special, Jennings Bitter. No credit cards.

Little Cowarne   The Three Horseshoes

Tel 0885 400276	Pub

Little Cowarne nr Bromyard Hereford & Worcester HR7 4RQ   Map 14 B1

Though not immediately obvious, one can still make out the remains
of a tiny two-roomed pub that once stood on this site: the newest
brick is an uneven match with the old and dormers have been added
to the frontage. The Shoes' interior is now a spacious dining pub, with
considerable thought given equally to the needs of children and the
elderly or disabled. The success of Malcolm and Janet Whittall
in attracting both in equal measure is to be commended. Kitchen
production is also prodigious from light bar snacks of haddock and
prawn smokies (£3.50) or devilled kidneys on toast (£3.50) through
to a carvery Sunday lunch (2 courses £6.95). Seasonally changing
main courses offer near endless variety, many flavoured with fresh
herbs from the garden: breast of chicken in tarragon sauce (£6.95)
and fillets of whiting with tomato, basil and chives (£5.50). Among
the home-made desserts rhubarb crumble and sticky toffee cake (both
£1.95) are perennially popular, and the home-made ice creams are
outstanding: brown bread or loganberry, and one made with
damsons – fresh from trees in the paddock, naturally. The recent
additions have included a pair of quiet bedrooms (one double,
one a twin) in appropriate country style with a lovely rural aspect.
Free from intrusive telephones, they're otherwise bang up-to-date with
colour TVs, clock radios, tea-making facilities and small but effective
WC/shower rooms. Disabled loo with exterior ramps; changing
facility in the Ladies. **Bar Food & Restaurant Meals** 11.30-2.30 (Sun
12-2), 6.30-10 (Sun 7-9.30). **Beer** Webster's, Ruddles County. Garden,
patio, barbecue, children's play area. Family room. **Accommodation**
2 bedrooms, not en suite, £31 (single £15.50). Children welcome
overnight (under-5s free), additional beds and cots available. Check-in
by arrangement. Access, Visa.

Little Washbourne   Hobnails Inn

Tel 0242 620237	Pub
Little Washbourne Gloucestershire	Map 14 C1

The licensee's family have run Hobnails for almost 250 years, which
must be some kind of record. The front bar is simply and traditionally
furnished, with a quarry-tiled floor and low beams. There's also
a modernised, carpeted rear lounge and a skittle alley. A printed menu
features a vast selection (32) of intriguingly filled baps (from £1.80),
as well as a choice of 35 puddings! A specials menu carries a short list
of hot specials – home-made curries with real spices, sirloin steak (£6)
and lamb casserole (£5.60); the printed à la carte menu offers further
dishes (wild salmon £7.80). *Bar Food & Restaurant Meals 12-2,
7-10.30 (to 9.30 in restaurant). Beer Wadworth 6X, Boddingtons, Flowers
Original. Garden, outdoor eating, children's play area with swing and slide.
Family room. Access, Visa.*

Liverpool   Casa Italia

Tel 051-227 5774	Pizzeria
40 Stanley Street Liverpool Merseyside	Map 6 A2

Cheap and cheerful decor – painted brick walls and colourful check
plastic cloths over rustic tables – and a noisy bustling atmosphere
at this unbookable 'pizzeria pasta' restaurant in the city centre. All the
reliably cooked pizzas and pasta dishes are between £4.05 and £4.95.
Afterwards, go for the good espresso coffee rather than weak tea
served by the cup. Slick, speedy service. *Seats 120. Open Noon-10pm.
Closed Sun, Bank Holidays. No credit cards.*

Liverpool   Est Est Est

Tel 051-708 6969	Restaurant
Unit 6 Edward Pavilion Albert Dock Liverpool Merseyside	Map 6 A2

Archetypal friendly trattoria, part of a small chain with branches
in Didsbury and Knutsford.The menu steers a familiar course from
minestrone (£2.15) and tonno e fagioli (£3.55) to a long list of pasta
(starter or main course, £2.15-£3.55/£3.95-£6.25) pizzas and
favourites such as scaloppine al limone (£10.25) and pollo principessa
(£8.95). *Seats 95. Open 12-2.30 (Sat to 4) & 6-10.30 (Fri & Sat to 11,
Sun 12-10) Closed 25 & 26 Dec, 1 Jan. Access, Amex, Visa.*

Liverpool   Everyman Bistro

Tel 051-708 9545	Bistro
5-9 Hope Street Liverpool Merseyside	Map 6 A2

One of the most popular bistros in Liverpool, underneath the famous
Everyman Theatre. Painted brick walls are covered with old
advertisements and the menu, which changes twice daily, is displayed
on blackboards. Typical choices run from Turkish lentil soup and tuna
pizza (£1.60) to afelia (£3.95), hot smoked sausage and potato,
spinach and lentil lasagne and to finish Greek custard cake £1.30,
cherry and Kirsch crème brulée or pears in hot fudge sauce (£1.30).
There are no reservations and queues are possible for both lunch and
dinner. Dishes of the day usually finish by 9pm so theatre-goers are
advised to eat before the play. The café/bar is open from 10-2 for
coffee and snacks. Three high-chairs; changing facilities promised
for 1994. No smoking. *Seats 150. Open 12-12. Closed Sun, Bank
Holidays. No credit cards.*

Liverpool   Tate Gallery Coffee Shop

Tel 051-709 0122	Coffee Shop
Albert Dock Liverpool Merseyside	Map 6 A2

The tiny kitchen of this self-service coffee shop is perched on a gallery overlooking the entrance foyer of the Tate Gallery's Liverpool outpost in a refurbished dockside Victorian warehouse. The savoury dishes – one meat (typically corned beef hash £3.75) and one vegetarian (courgette and mushroom lasagne £3.50) are all served with imaginative salads which use fresh herbs from the owner's garden. The likes of carrot cake (£1.20), chocolate cake (£1) and shortbread (60p) come from a good local bakery, plus there are a few filled rolls from 95p. No-smoking. One high-chair; changing facilities "in the public toilets". **Seats** 70. **Open** 10-6. **Closed** Mon (except Bank Holidays), 24-26 Dec, 1 Jan, Good Friday. No credit cards.

Lode   Anglesey Abbey Tea Rooms

Tel 0223 811175	Tea Room
Anglesey Abbey Lode nr Cambridge Cambridgeshire	Map 10 B3

A great advantage here is that the all-day café and National Trust shop are available to all without prior admission to the famous gardens. Counter-served coffee and cakes all day are supplemented by the salad bar (quiche, cooked ham and coronation chicken – all £4.50), hot lunches and vegetarian pulses or pasta (from £3.95) at lunchtime. Afternoon tea remains equally popular, and the enclosed garden and play area is a summer hit with youngsters. Two high-chairs; children's menu (pizza, jacket potato, half portions), scribbling paper and crayons, baby food, bottle warming, children's crockery and cutlery all provided. Non-smoking inside. **Seats** 140. **Open** 11-5.30 Dec-Mar Sat & Sun only, Mar-Dec Wed-Sun only but Jul 12-Sep 7 Mon-Sun. **Closed** 19 Dec-2nd Sat in Jan. Access, Diners, Visa.

Long Melford   Black Lion   65%   £65

Tel 0787 312356 Fax 0787 74557	Hotel
The Green Long Melford Sudbury Suffolk CO10 9DN	Map 10 C3

Count the Toby jugs and admire the maps and copper collection or relax in deep sofas in the charming lounge. Bedrooms are bright and comfortable, attractive fabrics complementing neutral walls and carpets. Each room has antique pine furniture and an easy chair or sofa. High-chairs and cots are provided. **Rooms** 9. Garden. Closed 23 Dec-2 Jan. Access, Visa.

Louth   Mr Chips

Tel 0507 603756	Fish'n'Chips
Ashwell Street Louth Lincolnshire LN11 9BA	Map 7 F2

Just off the Market Square you'll not miss the Hagans' Union Jacks till flying the flag for British fish. A huge, self-service fish and chip restaurant whose specialities are cod and haddock with crunchy chips £2.95/£4.85). Mushy peas sell at the rate of a ton a week! For vegetarians there's a meal of cauliflower, courgettes, onion rings, mushrooms and chips (£4). Families are especially welcomed: a separate mothers' comfort station and disabled persons' toilet are all part of the service. Eight high-chairs and two booster seats provided. The children's meal – for under-13s – offers fish (or sausage), chips, peas or beans for £1.85; ice cream to finish. Facilities for children's parties. No-smoking areas. *Seats 300.* **Open** *9am-11.30pm.* **Closed** *Sun, 25, 26 Dec & 1 Jan. No credit cards.*

Lowsonford   Fleur De Lys

Tel 0564 782431 Fax 05643 782431	Pub
Lowsonford nr Henley-in-Arden Warwickshire B95 5HJ	Map 6 C4

A long, low Whitbread pub with crooked chimneys and wrinkly roof whose canalside position and outdoor tuck shop deservedly attract a family clientele. A score or more picnic tables spread out along the bank, from where parents can watch the longboats while the under-12s master the climbing frames. The garden-side ketchup station of plastic disposable packets suggests quite a lot about the food inside (note table number before ordering); there are plenty of children's meals and a galleried family room, complete with rocking horses and high-chairs indoors. For parents, a toad-in-the-hole (£2.95) may just about fit, without filling out, the bill. More of a family pit stop than a gastronomic destination. **Bar Food** *12-9.30 (closed 3-6 in winter), Sun 12-2, 7-9.30. Children's menu and portions available.* **Beer** *Boddingtons, Flowers Best & Original, Wadworth 6X, guest beer. Garden, outdoor eating, children's play area. Family room. Access, Visa.*

Luccombe Chine   Dunnose Cottage

Tel 0983 862585	Tea Room
Luccombe Chine nr Shanklin Isle of Wight	Map 15 D4

The road winds between Shanklin and Ventnor and on a sweeping left-hand bend is a sharp turn down a narrow road to a hotel and tea rooms. In the cottage, whose walls are adorned with china plates, ornaments and a framed collection of cigarette cards, visitors can enjoy home-made snacks throughout the day. Sandwiches start at £1.60, and there are scones and cakes, ploughman's, salads and jacket potatoes. Lunch brings cottage pie (£4.95), lasagne, home-cooked ham, burgers and basket meals, with roasts on Sunday (Sep-Easter £8.50 three courses). One high-chair. It's a lovely setting and children are asked to respect the 3½ acres of lovely gardens. *Seats 48.* **Open** *10.30-5.* **Closed** *Mon Sept-Easter (exc Bank Holidays).*

Lymington   Passford House   70%   £101

Tel 0590 682398 Fax 0590 683494	Hotel
Mount Pleasant Lane Lymington Hampshire SO41 8LS	Map 14 C4

On the edge of the New Forest between Lymington (2 miles) and Sway, this elegant white house was originally the home of Lord Arthur Cecil. Two bedroom wings and a leisure centre have since been added, but the traditional look survives in the lounges – one oak-panelled with an open fire, another with French windows opening on to a patio and ornamental pool. Upstairs there are bright and airy bedrooms with mostly white furniture; carpeted bathrooms have showers and useful toiletries. There are eight 'de luxe' rooms. The purpose-built Dolphin leisure centre has a good range of facilities. Children are catered for admirably, with cots, high-chairs, an outdoor play area and separate meal times; first child under 12 sharing parents' room is accommodated free. **Rooms** *56. Garden, indoor & outdoor swimming pools, sauna, solarium, spa bath, keep-fit equipment, tennis, putting, games room. Access, Amex, Visa.*

Lympsham   Batch Farm Country Hotel   56%   £56

Tel 0934 750371   Hotel

Lympsham nr Weston-super-Mare Somerset BS24 0EX   Map 13 E1

Mr and Mrs Brown's hotel, with its 50-acre grounds, stands in open
farmland through which the river Axe flows. Origins of the former
farmhouse are evident in the beams which adorn the bar and residents'
lounges, while the neat, practical bedrooms in an extension enjoy
views of either the Mendip or Quantock hills; one good-sized family
room with a double bed and two singles, plus two double rooms with
connecting bunk-bedded rooms. The adjoining Somerset Suite
is a popular venue for functions up to 70. Large lawned gardens.
Lympsham is about 3 miles from Junction 22 of the M5. No dogs.
Rooms 8. *Garden, coarse fishing. Access, Amex, Diners, Visa.*

Lyndhurst   Lyndhurst Park   61%   £70

Tel 0703 283923   Fax 0703 283019   Hotel

High Street Lyndhurst Hampshire SO43 7NL   Map 14 C4

The Forestdale Group's much-extended Georgian mansion set in five
acres of spacious grounds has a popular conference and banqueting
facility (accommodating up to 400). Bedrooms have freestanding
furniture and small, tiled bathrooms. Day rooms include a cocktail bar
and little lounge. Summer activity for families centres round the pool
and a playground with swings. Children up to 15 stay free of charge
when sharing their parents' room. Informal eating in the Inn at the
Park; formal in the Tudor Restaurant and Palm Room. High-chairs
and baby food provided. Playroom with toys. **Rooms** 59. *Garden,
outdoor swimming pool, sauna, tennis, games room, playroom & playground.
Access, Amex, Diners, Visa.*

Lynton   Lee Cottage

Tel 0598 52621   Tea Room

Lee Abbey Lynton Devon   Map 13 D1

Follow the Lee Abbey road from Lynton towards Woody Bar and
although the road seems to stop at the Abbey, keep going until you
find an enchanting cottage run by ladies from the Abbey Christian
Community. The setting of colourful terraced gardens and the views
of the spectacular North Devon coastline are delightful, making the
cottage a marvellous place to pause a while. There is a book in which
prayer requests can be left and the staff offer daily prayers before
opening. Between mid-May and the end of September large numbers
of visitors come to the Cottage to sit on the grass or at benches to taste
Molly Foster's home-made bread rolls (£1.20), scones or "very
inventive" cakes (30p-£1.20 – truffle log, fruit cake with almond
centre, gingerbread men and ladies), cream tea (£2), ploughman's
£2.50 – cheese, pickle and peppers from the garden). Everything
except the doughnuts is home-made – even some herb teas are made
from plants in the garden. Unlicensed. No smoking. Half portions for
children (cakes included). No special family facilities, but a lovely
setting in good weather. **Seats** 200 (mostly outside). **Open** 11-5.
Closed Sun, mid Sep-mid May. No credit cards.

Lytham St Annes   Dalmeny Hotel   60%   £68

| Tel 0253 712236 | Hotel |

19 South Promenade St Annes Lytham St Annes Lancashire FY8 1LX   Map 6 A1

From modest beginnings nearly 50 years ago the Dalmeny has grown into a large family hotel with squash court, indoor pool, games room and no less than three restaurants. For much of the year there are daily events and amusements laid on for children and a well-equipped playroom becomes a crèche. Pine or lightwood fitted furniture with tiled tops features in the large, simply-decorated bedrooms, many with extra beds (some are family suites with several bedrooms) and most with kitchenette. Staff are smart, friendly and helpful. Baby-sitting/listening, cots, high-chairs, children's menu – you name it they've got it! High tea (£3.50) is served in the Carvery between 5 and 7pm; colouring pads and crayons for artistically inclined youngsters who crave an outlet for their art. The hotel is still growing, with a gymnasium and new conference rooms planned. *Rooms 90. Indoor swimming pool, squash, sauna, beauty & hair salon, children's playroom, crèche (supervised, 9-3 high season and holidays), coffee shop (9am-10pm). Access, Visa.*

C'est La Vie Restaurant   £65

The hotel's posh eaterie (there's also a Carvery and a Barbecue restaurant) in a vaulted basement with flagstoned floor. Chef Barry Smith can be seen in his small kitchen giving individual care and attention to each dish from the sensibly limited, French-inspired evening à la carte menu. Lunchtimes, there's a short, keenly-priced table d'hote. No smoking. *Seats 45.L 12.30-2.30 D 7-9 Closed Sun, Mon 24, 25, 26 Dec. Set L £11.50/£13.50.*

Maidenhead   Holiday Inn   66%   £147

| Tel 0628 23444   Fax 0628 770035 | Hotel |

Manor Lane Maidenhead Berkshire SL6 2RA   Map 15 E2

Set in 18 acres of grounds close to Junction 8/9 of the M4 and Junction 4 of the M40. Top-notch, large conference and banqueting facilities include the characterful, reconstructed Elizabethan Shoppenhangers Manor house in the grounds. Straightforward accommodation, but good leisure facilities, including a children's pool. Children's hostess at weekends and an unsupervised playroom; families can eat informally in the poolside café. Children's entertainment most Saturday early evenings, high tea from 6pm on Sat and early breakfast (8-9am) with the hostess on Sunday. Outdoor children's play area. Special tariff reductions at weekends. *Rooms 189. Garden, indoor swimming pool, spa bath, sauna, solarium, squash, gymnasium, snooker, coffee shop (7am-11pm). Access, Amex, Diners, Visa.*

Maldon   Wheelers

| Tel 0621 853647 | Fish'n'Chips |

13 High Street Maldon Essex   Map 11 C4

Long established family-run fish and chip restaurant and take-away in Maldon's high street. In tea-shop surroundings they serve plaice, cod, haddock (£4.20) and rock eel, plus skate and sole when available. Some of the sweets are home-made, including apple pie. No-smoking area. *Seats 52. Open 11.30-1.45 & 6-9.30. Closed Sun, Mon. No credit cards.*

Malmesbury	**Old Bell Hotel**	**64%**	**£98**

Tel 0666 822344 Fax 0666 825145	Hotel

Abbey Row Malmesbury Wiltshire SN16 0BW	Map 14 B2

Hard by the abbey, the Old Bell dates back to 1210 when it was established by the Abbot as a place to refresh his guests. Its wisteria-clad facade is more than a match for its spiritual neighbour. Public rooms comprise two oak-beamed bars and two lounge areas, one with a famous 800-year-old chimney. Bedrooms in the main building come in all shapes and sizes, while those in the converted stables are more uniformly modern. Families are well catered for; children up to 10 stay free in parents' room. The youngest guests are welcomed with the same courtesy extended to more venerable guests. A fun pack keeps children happy while parents unpack in one of the five family rooms. Two cots are available and prams and pushchairs can be stored. Baby-sitting and baby-listening are offered. Bedrooms in the main building come in all shapes and sizes, while those in the converted stables are more uniformly modern. Baby food is available in the restaurant, as is a children's menu and children's portions. There are two high-chairs and any accidents can soon be sorted out by the laundry service. No dogs. **Rooms** *37. Garden. Access, Visa.*

Manchester	**Cocotoo**

Tel 061-237 5458	Restaurant

57 Whitworth Street West Manchester Greater Manchester	Map 6 B2

Run with the enthusiasm expected of Italians, Cocotoo is a large, well-appointed restaurant near the Palace and Green Room Theatres. The menu offers all the usual choices, including pizza, pasta (farfalle al salmone £4.95, green ravioli with minced beef sauce), variations on chicken and veal, steaks from the grill, ice creams and tiramisu. Burgers at lunchtime only. High-chairs "as requested". Small portions prepared at "any time". **Seats** *250.* **Open** *12-2.30 & 5.30-11.30.* **Closed** *Sun & Bank Holidays. Access, Amex, Diners, Visa.*

Manchester	**Greenhouse**

Tel 061-224 0730	Vegetarian

331 Great Western Street Rusholme Manchester Greater Manchester M14 4AN	Map 6 B2

A daily-changing menu with roughly half the items suitable for vegans operates Wednesday to Sunday evenings at the Baxters' popular vegetarian restaurant (booking essential). Starters (from £1.85-£2.35) could include oyster mushrooms in red wine marinade or hazelnut paté with poppyseed toast, mains (£5.25) Stilton and vegetable bake or cashew pilau-stuffed capsicums, puds (£2.25) fresh strawberry pavlova or apple strudel. Matinees on Friday and Sunday (12-2.30) also feature a light meal special of assorted salads with perhaps pizza or samosas for £2.95. Country (elderflower etc) and organic wines. One high-chair; no changing facilities. No smoking. **Seats** *40.* **Open** *12-2 (Wed, Thur, Fri) & 7-11 (Wed-Sun).* **Closed** *L Sat & Sun, all Mon & Tue, 1 week Christmas. No credit cards.*

Manchester   Harry Ramsden's

Tel 061-832 9144	Fish'n'Chips
Water Street Manchester Greater Manchester M3 4JU	Map 6 B2

Purpose-built outpost of the Guiseley original complete with wall-to-
wall carpets, clothed tables and crystal chandeliers. Table service from
swift, friendly staff; the boys in wing collars and waistcoats, the girls
with old-fashioned black and white uniforms. Soups and puds are
bought-in but the fish and chips in between are the real McCoy. All
fish is skinned and filleted on the premises before being battered and
deep-fried in beef dripping to a golden crispness along with real
chunky chips. Haddock (£4.95), parsley fish cake (£3.80), traditional
mushy peas (60p), pickled onions (35p). Children under 12 get their
own special Postman Pat colouring menu (fish or chicken nugget
dishes around £2.95 including bread and butter, soft drink and ice
cream, plus 45p for beans or peas), and there are twelve high-chairs
and a separate baby-changing room with a table, mat, sink and loo.
Room for push-chair storage. See also entry under Blackpool. Also
at Gateshead, Glasgow, Guiseley and Heathrow Airport. *Seats 190.*
Open 11.30am-11pm. Closed 25 Dec. Access, Visa.

Manchester   Henry J Bean's Bar & Grill

Tel 061-832 8900	Restaurant
42 Blackfriars Street Manchester	Map 6 B2

The menu should please most with its mix of Hank's Bar and Chicago
Pizza Pie. Burgers from £4.50, pizzas from £4.35, ribs, burritos and
meat or vegetable fajitas. Side orders of onion rings (£1.30) and garlic
bread will fill any gaps. Finish up with mud pie or chocolate fudge
sundae (desserts £1.50-£2.95). Specialise in cocktails (happy hour
from 5.30-8.30, all night Wed). Children's menu. *Seats 80.*
*Open 11.45am-10.30pm, (Fri/Sat to 11.30, Sun 12-10). Closed 25 &
26 Dec. Access, Amex, Visa.*

Manchester   On the Eighth Day

Tel 061-273 1850	Vegetarian
109 Oxford Road All Saints Manchester Greater Manchester	Map 6 B2

One of the oldest co-operatives in Manchester, a simply furnished
vegetarian and vegan café and shop with, ironically, a picture of a cow
on the wall. A self-service counter displays home-made cakes, and later
in the day, various hot items including soup of the day (£1), filled
baked potatoes (from £1.80), nut roast with tomato and basil sauce
(£2.50), moussaka (£2.50), and desserts such as apple and blackcurrant
crumble (£1.30). BYO licence (no corkage). No smoking. *Seats 58.*
*Open 10-7 (Sat to 4.30). Closed Sun, Bank Holidays, 1 week Christmas.
No credit cards.*

Manchester   Pearl City

Tel 061-228 7683	Restaurant
33 George Street Manchester Greater Manchester	Map 6 B2

A first-floor, sparsely decorated, very popular Cantonese restaurant
in the middle of Chinatown where a pot of tea is put on the table
on your arrival. The special lunch menu (£4.20) served from noon till
2pm offers two courses starting with minced chicken and sweetcorn
soup followed by a choice of five dishes – perhaps sweet and sour cod

or fried sliced beef with pineapple. Other à la carte dishes are priced
from £5.50 to £9. Separate vegetarian menu. *Seats 150.*
Open noon-2am (Sun noon-midnight). Access, Amex, Visa.

Manchester   Royal Exchange Café Bar

Tel 061-833 9682	Café
St Anne's Square Manchester Greater Manchester	Map 6 B2

Smart self-service café in the foyer of the theatre. Stripped pine floors
set off a 1990s' decor with marble-topped tables, stainless steel chairs,
pink walls and a green enamel-effect bar. There's a cold buffet
throughout the day with an extensive choice of salads such as beetroot
and apple, baked bean and sweetcorn, potato and beanshoot (mixed
salad bowl £1.85). Also filled jacket potatoes (from £1.50), soups
(£1.05) and hot dishes typified by beef in red wine, chicken and
mushroom pie or chili con carne (all £3.95). Danish pastries, cream
cakes and biscuits are available at any time of day. No reservations.
No-smoking area. *Seats 95. Open 10-7.30 (Fri & Sat to 8). Closed Sun,
Bank Holidays. No credit cards.*

Manchester   Sannino

Tel 061-236 5532	Pizzeria
35 Fountain Street Manchester Greater Manchester M2 2AF	Map 6 B2

Next door to Lewis's store. Plush pizza/pasta saloon with urban prices,
dark polished wood, gleaming brass and Tiffany-style lamps. A simple
but popular format centres around pizzas (from £4.50, 16" for sharing
£8.50), with pasta variations (starter or main course), of fish, chicken
and steak dishes (from £8.25) in the Italian manner and liqueur-
soaked ice cream desserts (£2.95) to finish. Good, strong espresso.
Half-portions for children; two high-chairs. Branches also in Glasgow
and Leeds (78 Merrion Street Tel 0532 454312). *Seats 164. Open 12-3
& 5-11 (Fri till 12, Sat all day 12-12). Closed L Sun. Access, Amex,
Diners, Visa.*

Manchester   Victoria and Albert Hotel, Café Maigret

Tel 061-832 1188	Café/Bistro
Water Street Manchester Greater Manchester	Map 6 B2

A cleverly converted Victorian warehouse between their TV studios
and the river Irwell. Beside the main restaurant – the *Sherlock
Holmes* – is an all-day French style café/bistro serving an interesting
variety of dishes from spinach and tomato soups (two soups in one
bowl £2.50) and hot salmon fishcake salad (£4.25) to seafood risotto,
sausage and mash with onion gravy, ragout of beef (£6.95) and a stir-
fry of three cabbages with apple and raisins. British bulldog puds – rice
pudding, crumble and sponge, apple pie with thick custard, Yorkshire
pudding filled with ice cream and treacle (£2.50). Baby food
or bottles will be warmed and the separate Ladies powder room
is large enough for keeping the little one in good order. A vacant
bedroom or a quiet corner of the private lounge will be offered for
nursing – just ask. Four high-chairs and small cutlery are supplied.
Buggies may be left with the concierge. No-smoking area. The hotel
is recommended in our Hotels & Restaurants Guide and the Granada
Studios Tour is just across the road. *Seats 70. Open 10am-10.30pm.
Access, Amex, Diners, Visa.*

Manchester   Yang Sing

Tel 061-236 2200	Restaurant
34 Princess Street Manchester Greater Manchester	**Map 6 B2**

Still the best 'Chinese' in town with an enormous Cantonese menu that
includes such exotic offerings as stewed duck's web and fish lips, and
several varieties of bird's nest soup along with more familiar dishes.
Tanks of live carp, eels and lobster testify to the importance
chef/proprietor Harry Yeung places on freshness and quality
of ingredients. Some 40 different dim sum (even more on Sundays.
£1.80-£2.40) can be chosen from trolleys parked in the middle of the
restaurant or ordered from the waiting staff lest as the menu puts it,
'you have difficulty making yourself understood in Cantonese to the
trolley girls'. Unusually the dim sum are also available throughout the
evening – coming direct from the kitchen after 4.30pm. A selection
of pastries (from their own kitchen) or fresh fruit to finish. There's
a simple three-course set lunch and dinner menu (£13.20). Recently
opened on the ground floor is a Chinese Fondue Restaurant where
dishes are cooked in a stock (rather than oil) that is drunk as a soup
after the main ingredients of the dish have been eaten. Six high-chairs
available. *Seats 140. Parties 40. Private Room 200. Meals 12-11.30.
Closed 25 Dec. Set meals from £26.50 for two. Access, Amex, Visa.*

Marlborough   Polly Tea Rooms

Tel 0672 512146	Tea Room
26 High Street Marlborough Wiltshire	**Map 14 C2**

For many years now the West family and the manageress have been
running these traditional tea rooms. Beams, pine dressers, pretty lace
cloths and uniformed waitresses create a splendidly traditional air and
there's a mouthwatering display of wonderful gateaux (tiramisu,
Baileys Irish coffee cream, lemon and redcurrant cheesecake) at the
entrance while inside, croissants, brioches, Danish pastries, strudels,
excellent sausage rolls, muesli scones, rows of biscuits and pastries
(from 95p) are laid out – all baked on the premises. The full Polly
breakfast starts the day (2 eggs, bacon, Wiltshire sausages, mushrooms,
tomatoes, sautéed potatoes, toast, marmalade and coffee – £5.95).
Lunch offers parsnip and apple soup (£2.50) with home-made bread,
fish mousse (£5.75 with salad), locally smoked trout and specials such
as beef and Guinness pie with dauphinois potatoes (£5.50), chicken
provençale with noodles, or spinach, cream cheese and mushroom
roulade (£5.50). On weekend afternoons only, a savoury set tea is now
offered (£3.75 – quiche and salad with a drink). Set afternoon teas
include the Polly Tea (three scones £3.75) and Special Gateaux Tea.
Children's portions. No-smoking area. *Seats 100. Open 8.30-6 (Sat
8-7, Sun 9-7). Closed 25 & 26 Dec, 2nd & 3rd Fri & Sat in Oct. Access,
Amex, Visa.*

Marshside   Gate Inn

Tel 0227 860498	Pub
Marshside Chislet nr Canterbury Kent CT3 4EB	**Map 11 C5**

Delightfully set, with a duckpond in the garden. Indoors, it's rustic and
wholly unpretentious, and prides itself on still being "a talker's pub",
in tandem with a thriving bar meal trade. Fresh, local produce is used
to produce homely, honest English fare (spicy sausage hot pot £3.90,
garlic mushrooms £1.75), along with burgers and a famous black

pudding sandwich (£1.25) served with mango chutney. Free-range
eggs and local vegetables are also sold over the bar. A good log fire
in winter. Live jazz every Tuesday; quiz night is Thursday night
(when there's also a special menu). *Bar Food all open hours. Beer
Shepherd Neame. Family room. Riverside garden, outdoor eating.
No credit cards.*

Matlock   The Strand

Tel 0629 584444	Bistro
Dale Road Matlock Derbyshire	Map 6 C2

Judith and Julian Mason run a very friendly, genuine bistro
in a former Victorian draper's shop. The high-ceilinged panelled room
is lit with replica gas lamps and attractive cast-iron pillars and
balustrades lead up to more seating on the gallery. During the day, the
menu offers a variety of light, inexpensive dishes with ten different
daily specials – chef's paté (£3.25), prawns aioli (£3.50), vegetarian
stuffed vine leaves and salad (£3.25), chicken tandoori with yoghurt
and cucumber (£3.95), gravad lax and prawn salad (£4.50), cottage
pie with a cheese topping (£3.75), Brooklyn tuna bake (£3.75). The
more comprehensive evening menu changes every day. Starters are
priced between £1.95 and £4.50, and main courses £6.95 to £12.50.
Children's portions available on request; special lunch dish (£2.25) for
under-12s – perhaps a sandwich with french fries or baked beans
on toast followed by ice cream. Two high-chairs; large Ladies loo.
Live music is played three evenings a week, piano (Tue), jazz (Thur &
Fri). Only well supervised children in the evening. *Seats 64.
Open 10-2 & 7-10. Closed Sun, Mon (winter only), 25 & 26 Dec, 1 Jan.
Access, Visa.*

Matlock   Tall Trees

Tel 0629 732932	Café
Oddford Lane Matlock Derbyshire	Map 6 C2

Part of a garden centre a couple miles north of Matlock on the A6.
Open throughout the day for light snacks, it offers the best variety
at lunchtime with dishes such as home-made soup, cheesy leek and
mushroom pasta (£4.10), barbecued chicken with rice and assorted
quiches. The sweet-toothed will relish orange and apricot mousse,
butterscotch tart and chocolate roulade (£1.75 each). No smoking
lunchtimes. *Seats 40. Open 9-5.30 (winter to 5). Closed 25 & 26 Dec,
1 Jan. No credit cards.*

Mawgan   The Yard Bistro

Tel 032 622 595	Bistro
Trelowarren Estate Mawgan nr Helston Cornwall	Map 12 B4

Part of a stately home, the attractive Yard Bistro is housed in the old
coach house on one side of the stable yard. Being the headquarters
of the Cornish Craft Assocation, there's also a working pottery,
weaving studio and art gallery as well as outdoor theatre and garden
nursery. The bistro is open plan with granite stanchions, a bar at one
end and an open log fire at the other. Coffee only until noon, then the
changing menu may offer Cornish crab broth (£2.20), rich smoked
salmon and scrambled eggs (£3.95), fresh green tagliatelle with stir-
fried vegetables (£4) or grilled goat's cheese (£3.25) as well as a
choice of four hot dishes of the day (roast duck with raspberry and
port sauce £5, smoked chicken and prawn biryani with red chilis

£4.50). Clotted cream accompanies puddings such as warm chocolate and walnut brownies or treacle tart (both £2). A three-course roast lunch features on Sundays (£7). In summer, the stable yard provides an outdoor alternative for lunch or tea (Cornish Cream Tea in high season only £2.25). More elaborate evening meals. Children's portions. *Seats 46.* **Open** *11-2 & 7-9.* **Closed** *Low season: D Sun-Wed, all Mon, all Jan & Feb, 25, 26 & 31 Dec. No credit cards.*

Melbourn **Pink Geranium**	**£100**
Tel 0763 260215	Restaurant
Station Road Melbourn nr Royston Hertfordshire SG8 6DX	**Map 15 F1**

Steven Saunders' delightful 16th-century thatched cottage in the village centre is all a country restaurant ought to be. Low, black-beamed ceilings characterise the cosy, intimate ground-floor rooms (there's a lofty upstairs private dining room which has a wide brick chimney breast at its heart). Decor is of palest pink plaster walls, with curtains and upholstery in geranium pink. The pretty floral theme extends throughout, from the comfortable bar which comprises several, small interconnecting rooms, to the split-level dining room with its sunny conservatory overlooking an attractive, well-tended garden. It's a smart restaurant – perhaps only for parents with really young ones or for youngsters who can guarantee to be on best behaviour. Steven is the author of a book on children's food; he scorns sausages and other fast food but gladly serves small portions of exquisitely presented main-menu items to young visitors. Food will be puréed for babies and bottles warmed, beakers filled and customer's own food warmed on request. The Ladies is equipped with a chair for nursing, changing table and nappy bin. Fenced garden. *Seats 72. Private Room 16. L 12-2 D 7-10 (Sat to 10.30).* **Closed** *L Sat, D Sun, all Mon. Set L £13.95/£16.95 Set D £24.95. Access, Amex, Visa.*

Mellor **Millstone Hotel**	
Tel 0254 813333 Fax 0254 812628	Pub
Church Lane Mellor Blackburn Lancashire BB2 7JR	**Map 6 B1**

Daniel Thwaites, the Blackburn brewers, operate the Shire Inns chain; its original flagship, the Millstone remains true to its roots and is closest to the brewery. Pub first and foremost it has a thriving local trade and is consistently busy for bar food. Baked queen scallops (£3.95/£6.90), salad niçoise (£3.50/£5.75) and smoked Scottish salmon (£5.20/£8.50) are offered as starters or main courses. More substantial offerings are the Cumberland sausage and Bury black pudding with creamed potatoes and brown onion sauce (£5.25) or a brochette of pork and peppers served with a salad (£6.95). By comparison, the à la carte restaurant and en-suite bedrooms are decidedly 'hotel' and priced accordingly. Rooms, in fact, come in both standard and executive grades with satellite TV, trouser presses and hairdryers throughout. Executive rooms receive rather more space, towelling bathrobes and top-drawer toiletries. Of great benefit to the less active is the wing of nine ground-floor bedrooms (there is no lift) which are also appreciated by parents of very little ones. *Open 11-11 Mon-Sat, regular hours Sun.* **Bar & Restaurant Food** *12-2, 7-8.45 (Restaurant till 9.30).* **Beer** *Thwaites Mild, Bitter and Craftsman. Patio. Family room.* **Accommodation** *21 bedrooms, all en suite, £74 (single £56). Children welcome overnight (under-16s free if staying in parents' room), additional beds and cots available. Access, Amex, Diners, Visa.*

Melmerby   Shepherds Inn

Tel 0768 881217	Pub

Melmerby nr Penrith Cumbria CA10 1HF   Map 4 C3

After a dozen years as tenants here, Martin and Christine Baucutt have
had the good fortune (and good sense) to buy from Marston's brewery
the business for whose fine reputation they have worked so hard.
Subsequent installation of Jennings beers from Cockermouth has
proven an added bonus. At the heart of the operation, though,
is Christine's cooking and it's no exaggeration that regulars cross and
re-cross the Pennines simply to sample the variety on offer. On any
one day, creamed mushroom soup (£1.80), Stilton and walnut pasta
bake (£3.20), cheese, onion and courgette quiche (£3.95) and lamb's
liver lyonnaise are just the 'Specials'; regular favourites, meanwhile,
include bowls of chili (£3.40), lamb rogan gosht (£6.80) and baked
aubergine Parmesan (£5.40). There's a traditional Sunday roast (main
course £4.80). Up to a dozen sweets displayed on the counter (from
£2.15) come with lashings of local Jersey cream, while cheese
enthusiasts can choose from a dozen or more, including interesting
North Country varieties. A sensible, no-nonsense attitude towards the
young enables grown-up meals as they'd like. No fish fingers here, but
chips possible and scrambled eggs, even, on request; high-chairs, too.
Beer *Jennings Bitter, Cumberland Ale and Sneck Lifter. Family room.*
No smoking area and cobbled patio. Access, Amex, Diners, Visa.

Melmerby   Village Bakery

Tel 0768 881515	Restaurant

Melmerby nr Penrith Cumbria   Map 4 C3

On the A686 Alston road, ten miles from Junction 40 on the M6, the
Village Bakery is in a converted barn with a bright airy conservatory
and old pine furniture. Andrew and Lis Whitley organically grow
their own ingredients and bake the breads and cakes in a brick oven.
Vegetarians will be pleased to know that they now offer a 'vegetarian
full fried breakfast': aduki bean pattie, potato and vegetable cake, egg,
grilled mushrooms, tomato and fried bread (£6.25). Raspberry
porridge (£2.50) and oak-smoked Inverawe kippers (£5.45 a pair) are
alternatives. Lunch brings courgette and fennel soup (£2.50) or garlic
and pine kernel tartlet (£2.50) as starters and as main courses, grilled
Cumberland sausage served with apple sauce (£6.25) or an organic
tomato tart (organic tomatoes, basil, French mustard and olive oil
(£6.25). Another option is the baker's lunch (£5.45) – bread from the
oven with cheese from the north country. Home-made puddings
include summer pudding (£2.50) or chocolate and almond cheesecake
(£1.65) and popular biscuit slices such as a peanutter, chocolate chip
cookie or Westmorland parkin should be tasted. **Seats** *45.* **Open** *8.30-5*
(Sun 9.30-5). **Closed** *25 & 26 Dec, 1 Jan, Sun in Jan & Feb. Access,*
Amex, Diners, Visa.

Mere   Old Ship Hotel   £52

Tel 0747 860258 Fax 0747 860501	Inn

Castle Street Mere Wiltshire BA12 6JE   Map 14 B3

A splendid 17th-century inn with flagstones, exposed brick and
stonework, log fires, panelling and beamed ceilings. Period oak
furniture in the three characterful bars (good Badger's beers) and the
quiet residents' lounge complements the ancient fabric of the building.

Bedrooms in the main house have traditional furnishings (one features a four-poster) while ten in the annexe are more compact and modern; eight bedrooms not en suite share three bathrooms. Characterful, gabled and beamed restaurant. This is a popular base for touring, walking and riding; children are welcome in the lounges. The small garden has a slide and small tables and chairs for children. *Beer Badger Best & Tanglefoot. Garden, children's play area. **Accommodation** 23 bedrooms, 16 en suite, £52 (single £39). Children welcome overnight (under-2s stay free in parents' room), additional beds (£10) and cots available. Access, Visa.*

Middle Wallop	Fifehead Manor	61%	£85
Tel 0264 781565 Fax 0264 781400			Hotel
Middle Wallop nr Stockbridge Hampshire SO20 8EG			Map 14 C3

On the A343 in the centre of the village (between Andover and Salisbury), the manor house stands in 3½ acres of land and has origins going back to the Middle Ages. Central to the house is the medieval dining hall with its mullioned windows and there is a small bar plus a lounge. Large bedrooms in the main house have good-size bathrooms; smaller singles (with showers only) are in an annexe, but have the attraction of leading out on to the rear lawn. Subdued fabrics and colour schemes are used throughout, and the furniture is mostly modern, although a few antiques help contribute to the friendly and informal atmosphere. Fine cooked breakfasts and a restaurant menu that tempts more than it delivers; however, good bar snacks are served in the bar and lounge area: home-made soup (parsnip £2.50), sandwiches (from £2), cold platter with salad (£5.50), and two hot dishes – maybe sausages (£5.50), escalope of salmon (£8.50) or omelette (ham £5) – with a trio of chocolate mousse or stuffed apples with almonds and apricots in an apricot sauce (both £3.50) to finish make up the short menu. Scones, cakes (banana loaf, caramel shortcake, fruit cake), teas and coffee are served at any time. Outdoor eating (and playing) on the lawn. No charge for under-5s if sharing parents' room (over-5s £15). *Rooms 16. Garden. **Closed** 2 weeks Christmas/New Year. Access, Amex, Diners, Visa.*

Midsomer Norton	Mrs Pickwick	
Tel 0761 414589		Tea Room
70 High Street Midsomer Norton Avon		Map 13 F1

Mrs Pickwick is a friendly tea room with a patio for fair-weather snacking. Owner Pauline Towler has just built an extension on to the back of the house thus increasing the seating capacity. Hot lunches are taken upstairs: omelettes, cottage pie, chicken curry, macaroni cheese (all £2.55), whilst downstairs is available for snacks, toasted sandwiches (from £1.20) and gateaux. Clotted cream tea with home-made scones £1.90. Children's portions available. No smoking. *Seats 44. **Open** 9-5.30. **Closed** Sun, Bank Holidays.*

Milton Keynes	Friendly Hotel	57%	£79
Tel 0908 561666 Fax 0908 568303			Hotel
Monksway Two Mile Ash Milton Keynes Buckinghamshire MK8 8LY			Map 15 E1

Practical, modern low-rise hotel at the junction of the A5 and A422. Twelve Premier Plus suites with small kitchenette and fax machine in a small lounge are favoured by both business people and families.

Televisions offer satellite channels and in-house movies, and there are
tea and coffee-making facilities; a cot can be provided at no extra
charge. At meal times, children are given snakes & ladders place mats
and a stuffed snake with foot measurements is held up against the child
who is then charged accordingly per foot for his/her meal.
On Sundays, the conservatory area is converted into a play area
showing children's videos. There's a playground outside but children
will need to be supervised. Baby food is not available on the premises
but staff are happy to heat bottles. The children's menu includes fish
snakelets, forked tongue burger and a slithering snake cake. Children
stay free in parents' room. **Rooms** *88. Indoor swimming pool, gymnasium,
sauna, spa bath, steam room, solarium. Access, Amex, Diners, Visa.*

Minstead   The Honey Pot

Tel 0703 813122	Tea Room

Minstead nr Lyndhurst Hampshire   **Map 14 C4**

The Honey Pot is housed in a building in the garden behind the
thatched cottage where the owners also run The Honeysuckle Cottage
Restaurant. Various set teas are featured on the menu – Honey
(£1.95), Beehive (£2.95), Drones (£2.55) and Queen Bee (£3.95)
with scones, walnut and coffee cakes and buttery shortbread. For
savoury, there's a show of salads (smoked chicken £5.25), quiches,
ploughman's and a hot dish such as lasagne (£4.75), steak & kidney pie
(£4.95) or deep-fried cod fillets. Puddings might be pear frangipane,
rum and chocolate mousse or Bakewell tart (all £1.80). A more
expensive evening menu is served in the restaurant (7.30pm onwards).
The Honey Pot is closed during the winter but teas and light snacks
are served in the restaurant from Wednesday to Sunday from 11am
to dusk. Two high-chairs and an outdoor play area with a Wendy
House and toys. Outdoor eating on fine days. **Seats** *35.* **Open** *10.30-6.*
Closed *November-Easter. Access, Visa.*

Monksilver   Notley Arms

Tel 0984 56217	Pub

Monksilver Taunton Somerset TA4 4JB   **Map 13 E1**

The experienced Sarah and Alistair Cade have brought inimitable flair
to this white-painted roadside village pub and in just a few short years
built up a formidably good reputation. The interior is charmingly
simple: an L-shaped bar with plain wooden furniture, black and white
timbered walls, candles at night, and twin wood-burning stoves;
a small but bright and cheery family room leads off, and there's
a stream at the bottom of the trim, cottagey garden. The big attraction
here, though, is the bar food, which roughly divides into three
categories – the traditional, the Eastern or exotic, and the vegetarian –
all given equal thought, the finest fresh ingredients, and cooked with
sure-handed skill. Old favourites and four or five daily hot specials are
chalked up on the blackboard. For a light but satisfying lunch, choose
one of the delicious pitta bread sandwiches with garlic butter, tender
meats and good crispy salad. Local scrumpy cider in summer. Despite
the crowds at peak times, all runs effortlessly smoothly and with good
humour. **Bar Food** *12-2 (Sun to 1.45), 7-9.30 (Sun to 9).* **Beer** *Ruddles
County, Theakstons Best, Ushers Best, Wadworth 6X. Riverside garden,
outdoor eating. Family room. Pub closed 2 weeks end Jan-early Feb.
No credit cards.*

Monkton Combe   Combe Grove Manor   71%   £168

Tel 0225 834644 Fax 0225 834961	Hotel

Brassknocker Hill Monkton Combe Bath Avon BA2 7HS   Map 13 F1

Perched high up above the Limpley Stoke valley and set within its
own 68 acres of wooded grounds, the manor has extensive leisure
facilities belonging to the associated country club. Elegant day rooms
and the best of the bedrooms – individually decorated in some style
with reproduction period-style furniture – are in the original Georgian
house beneath which, in the old cellars reached via some external steps,
is an informal bar and bistro decorated in ancient Roman style. The
majority of more standardised bedrooms are some 50 yards away
in the Garden Lodge, designed to take full advantage of the splendid
view across Limpley Stoke Valley (just four rooms are rear-facing)
with most having a private patio or balcony. Beds are turned down
at night. 24hr room service. 2 miles from the centre of Bath.
Rooms 41. *Garden, outdoor swimming pool, gymnasium, sauna, spa baths,
steam room, solarium, beauty salon, tennis, golf (5-hole), putting, golf
driving range. Access, Amex, Diners, Visa.*

Morden   Superfish

Tel 081-648 6908	Fish'n'Chips

20 London Road Morden Surrey   Map 15 E2

Part of a Surrey-based chain serving "delectable fish and chips fried
in the traditional Yorkshire way". All dishes are served with well-
cooked chips, French bread, pickles or sauces and "hopefully a smile".
Beef dripping is used for frying in the traditional manner and a fillet
of cod may be small, large or a Moby Dick (£3.35, £4.25 or £5.05).
Huss, scampi and fillet of plaice are other regulars, while salmon,
lemon sole, haddock, skate and whole plaice are on the menu
according to availablity. A children's platter of fish bites with chips
costs £2.20. No reservations. Another quote from the menu:
"We admire your decision not to smoke". *Seats* 42. *Open* 11.30-2
*(Sat to 2.30, 5-10.30 (Thu-Sat to 11). Closed Sun, 25 & 26 Dec, 1 Jan.
No credit cards.*

Motcombe   Coppleridge Inn

Tel 0747 51980 Fax 0747 51858	Pub

Motcombe Shaftesbury Dorset SP7 9HW   Map 14 B3

The Coppleridge Inn is a splendid example of how to convert an 18th-
century farmhouse and its adjoining farm buildings into a successful
all-round inn. Set in 15 acres of meadow, woodland and gardens
it enjoys a lofty position with far-reaching views across the Blackmore
Vale. The old farmhouse forms the nucleus of the operation,
comprising a welcoming bar with stripped pine tables, attractive prints
and a small gallery with seating. There's a comfortable lounge with
flagstoned floor and inglenook fireplace and a delightful light and airy
restaurant with open country views. In the bar a comprehensive
blackboard menu lists the daily selection of reliable home-cooked
dishes that are on offer. Begin with a good choice of soups – carrot and
coriander, celery and Stilton and a thick and hearty guinea fowl
broth(£1.75) – or artichoke with lemon mayonnaise (£2.50) and
smoked trout paté (£4), followed by an interesting and varied range
of main courses – all at £4.50 – such as John Dory in Cambozola
sauce, lamb rogan josh, venison and wild mushrooms in red wine,

kidneys in cider and Dijon mustard or haddock and mushroom gratin. Home-made pizzas are a speciality on Tuesday and Friday nights. Restaurant fare is more elaborate. Across the lawned courtyard with benches and fountain are ten well-appointed, en-suite bedrooms, all superbly incorporated into the single-storey old barns. Tasteful, attractive fabrics, pine furniture, mini-bars, TV, telephones, radios, sparkling clean bathrooms with bidet and rural views characterise these comfortable rooms. Also part of the complex is a hair salon and a magnificent 18th-century barn that has been converted into a conference and function room. High-chairs are provided. Safe, enclosed play area with fort, climbing frame, swings, scramble net and Wendy house. **Bar Food** 11-10.30 (Sun 12-2.30 & 7-10). **Restaurant Meals** 6-9.30. Afternoon Teas 3-6. Free House. **Beer** Fuller's London Pride, Hook Norton Best Bitter, guest beer. Garden, outdoor eating area. Children's play area. **Accommodation** 10 bedrooms, all en suite, £55 (single £35). Cots (£5) and extra beds supplied (£10). Access, Amex, Visa.

Mullion	Polurrian Hotel	66%	£164*
Tel 0326 240421 Fax 0326 240083			Hotel
Mullion Helston Cornwall TR12 7EN			Map 12 B4

Large, white clifftop hotel from which a path winds down past tennis court and cricket practice net – there's a keenly contested game between staff and guests each week in high season – to a sheltered sandy cove 300 feet below. It's the epitome of a traditional English holiday hotel with friendly staff and children well catered for with their own special events arranged during school holidays and plenty to do in the area. Flambards theme park is nearby and the Cornish Seal Sanctuary just a short trip away at Gweek. Comfortable lounges take full advantage of the view and excellent breakfasts include locally caught mackerel with horseradish butter and honey from breakfast chef David's own hives. Bedrooms are comfortable rather than luxurious with well-kept bathrooms. Children under 14 stay free in parents' room with meals 'as taken' charged for those over 6 years. Indoor children's play room for under-7s – limited supervision on request; adventure playground in the garden. Baby-sitting is also available, as are baby baths, potties and nappies – the business! High tea is served 5.30-6.30pm (order before noon) and changes daily: perhaps home-made fish pie or deep-fried chicken followed by fresh fruit, jelly, yoghurt or banana custard; there are at least a dozen high-chairs in the restaurant, but tea can be served in your room. Informal eating in the Aqua Bar and Brasserie. *Half-board terms only, plus self-catering family apartments. **Rooms** 40. Garden, indoor & outdoor swimming pools, keep-fit equipment, squash, badminton, sauna, spa bath, solarium, tennis, badminton, putting, sea fishing, boating, snooker, brasserie (7.30am-8.30pm). **Closed** Nov-Mar. Access, Amex, Diners, Visa.

Nettleton	Nettleton Arms		
Tel 0249 782783			Pub
Nettleton nr Chippenham Wiltshire SN14 7NP			Map 14 B2

This old mellow Cotswold-stone inn dates from around 1500 and enjoys a peaceful rural setting, yet it is only a few miles from the tourist honey-pot of Castle Combe. It was once the Manor House for the Codrington family and despite much modernisation over the years, it still retains some ancient timbers at a fine minstrel's gallery in its welcoming and neatly furnished bar. A quiet and comfortable night's sleep is ensured in the four bedrooms that have been incorporated into the medieval barn across the courtyard, complete with original rafters and two-foot-thick walls. Each room has cottage-style fabrics, practical modern furnishings, TVs, direct-dial phones, tea-making kits and good en-suite bathrooms with tubs and showers. Standard of housekeeping is good throughout. The large safe garden has a slide, swings and wooden climbing apparatus. High-chairs provided. Recommended for B&B only. *Children not allowed in bar in evening. Free House. Beer Bass, Archers Village, Wadworth 6X, guest beers. Garden, outdoor play area. Accommodation 4 bedrooms, all en suite, £43.50 (single £30). Additional beds and cots available at no charge. Dogs welcome by arrangement. Access, Amex, Visa.*

New Alresford	Hunters	£52
Tel 0962 732468		Restaurant
32 Broad Street New Alresford Hampshire SO24 9AQ		Map 15 D3

Wine bar/brasserie with two distinctive bow-fronted windows, awnings and candle-light within, run by the Birmingham family. A dozen or so light dishes at lunchtime range from pan-fried quail breast with watercress salad to bacon-wrapped fillet of pork with pesto and basil cream sauce. Dinner dishes are more involved: black pudding and chicken livers with creamed potatoes and Madeira sauce, cassoulet, grilled halibut with leeks, tomatoes and chives. Local watercress makes regular appearances, as above or in a dish of grilled fillet of salmon on a bed of watercress with pesto cream sauce. Hot apple tart with caramel citrus sauce, and hot chocolate soufflé with warm orange cream sauce complete the picture. Friendly, laid-back service and good-value wines. Children are made welcome with high-chairs and smaller portions; convenient for the nearby Watercress Line preserved steam railway. *Seats 30. Parties 15. Private Room 80. L 12-2 D 7-10. Closed D Sun, 24-27 Dec. Set L £7.95/£9.95 Set D £9.95/£11.75. Access, Amex, Diners, Visa.*

Rooms £48

Three rooms in an old Georgian building, all with shower and WC en suite. Children under 5 free if sharing a room with parents; extra bed £10.

New York	Shiremoor House Farm	
Tel 091-257 6302		Pub
Middle Engine Lane New York Tyne & Wear NE29 8DZ		Map 5 E2

This imaginative conversion of derelict farm buildings stands in open ground at the edge of a small industrial estate in a new town suburb five minutes from the Tyne tunnel. Courage and vision in unlikely circumstances have paid off, and the pub has luckily won many friends. Lunchtimes bring local trade from the industrial estate, while in the evening it's more of a drive-out-from-Newcastle crowd. Inside this mellow stone building, a large open-plan bar is subtly lit, with stripped walls. Flagstones support a mix of tables and chairs – wicker, upholstered, wing, country and banquette-style. The only modern intruder in an otherwise jukebox- and fruit machine-free zone is the computerised till. Blackboard-listed dishes feature mostly fresh produce, like a tasty pork casserole in a Dijon mustard-flavoured cream sauce (£3.75), accompanied by a generous array of fresh, crisp vegetables. Old favourites from the English tavern repertoire appear alongside re-interpreted classics. Honest, capable cooking at very competitive prices. The flagged and grassed garden is the former farmyard. *Open 11-11 Mon-Sat, regular hours Sun.* **Bar Food** *12-2.30 (Sat to 9), 6-9 (Sun from 7).* **Restaurant Meals** *12-2, 7-9.30. Free House.* **Beer** *Bass, Stones Best, Theakston Best & Old Peculier, Timothy Taylor Landlord, weekly-changing guest beer. Garden, outdoor eating. Access, Amex, Diners, Visa.*

Newport	**God's Providence House**	
Tel 0983 522085		Restaurant
12 St Thomas' Square Newport Isle of Wight		Map 15 D4

Legend has it that this property, now largely Georgian but with earlier elements, was delivered from several visitations of the plague. Now it's a haven of good-quality baking and healthy eating with an Upstairs Parlour offering wholefood dishes – quiche (£2.35), filled baked potatoes (from £2.30), open sandwiches (£2.95) and salads (£2.30) from 11-3, and a counter-service restaurant on the ground floor. Morning coffee (9-12) and afternoon tea (2.30-5) are bisected by lunch (12-2) offering soup of the day (£1.35), home-made steak pie (£4.30), a roast of the day (£4.60) and traditional puddings such as trifle and fruit pies (from £1.30). Four high-chairs; changing shelf in Ladies. Most areas are non-smoking. **Seats** *100.* **Open** *9-5.* **Closed** *Sun, Bank Holidays. No credit cards.*

Newquay	**Hotel Riviera**	**63%**	£78
Tel 0637 874251 Fax 0637 850823			Hotel
Lusty Glaze Road Newquay Cornwall TR7 3AA			Map 12 B3

Popular for family holidays, functions and conferences (for around 150), this well-appointed modern hotel overlooks a lovely stretch of coastline. Three bars, a lounge and a garden provide plenty of space to relax, and in summer there's evening entertainment. Most of the bedrooms enjoy sea views. Children's supper 6-6.15pm in La Piazza 'night spot' area or at 7pm with their parenmts in the restaurant. **Rooms** *50. Outdoor swimming pool, squash, sauna, games room, snooker, racquetball, children's playroom and play area.* **Closed** *few days Christmas. Access, Amex, Visa.*

Newton	**Red Lion**	
Tel 05297 256		Pub
Newton nr Sleaford Lincolnshire NG31 0EE		Map 7 E3

In a quiet hamlet tucked away off the A52, this is a civilised, neatly kept pub with shaded rear garden and play area. Popular unchanging formula is the cold carvery/buffet of fish and carefully cooked cold meats, from pink beef ribs on the bone to Lincolnshire sausages. Price depends on size of plate and the number of meats chosen (small – three choices £6.95, medium – four choices £7.95 and large with unlimited choice £8.95): help yourself from a dozen or more accompanying salads. Limited choice of starters (soup, home-made paté £2.25, prawn cocktail £2.45) and ever-changing array of home-made desserts £2.25). Children's prices and eating areas; informal, easy-going atmosphere. **Bar Food** *12-2, 7-10 (Sun to 9). Free House.* **Beer** *Bass, Bateman's XXXB, John Smith's. Garden, outdoor eating, children's play area. Family room. No credit cards.*

Norden   The Manor

Tel 0706 50027	Pub
Edenfield Road Norden nr Rochdale Lancashire OL12 7TW	**Map 6 B2**

On the A680 between Rochdale and Edenfield, one of Whitbread's
Brewers Fayre family-themed chain of pubs. Children have their own
menu and there is a handful of high-chairs. Indoor fun factory
(admission 50p) for children. Good changing facilities. Fenced garden
with picnic tables and outdoor play equipment. Children's party
facilities. No-smoking area. A handy pit-stop for bored children on the
move, but no great gastronomic destination! *Open Bar Food 11.30-10
(Sun from 12).* **Beer** *Whitbread. Access, Visa.*

Northallerton   Bettys

Tel 0609 775154	Tea Room
188 High Street Northallerton North Yorkshire	**Map 5 E3**

In a long terrace of houses, Bettys is the traditional tea shop that every
town deserves. The day begins with breakfast – warm Yorkshire
oatcakes (£1.45), mushroom and bacon omelette (£4.98), rösti
potatoes (£5.25) or simply two croissants or brioches with jam and
butter (£1.86). Light lunches bring sandwiches (from £2.55), salads
(corn-fed chicken £5.30), grills, omelettes, hot dishes such as haddock
and prawns au gratin and the speciality of the house, rarebit made
with Theakston's Yorkshire Ale served with apple or tomato chutney
(£5.50). Bettys' famous warm Yorkshire fat rascal (£1.98), buttered
pikelets (£1.02) and banana and walnut loaf (£1.20) are some of the
tea breads. Cream tea £3.66. Various ices (from £2.15), desserts
(toffee and brandy snap fanfare £4.25) and cakes (from £1.55 –
chocolate brandy roulade, Yorkshire curd tart). Rare coffees and
a selection of teas. Children's portions; four high-chairs. Changing shelf
with mat, chair and playpen in the Ladies. No-smoking area. *Seats 58.
Open 9-5.30 (Sun from 10). **Closed** 25 & 26 Dec, 1 Jan. Access, Visa.*

Norton   Hundred House Hotel

Tel 095271 353 Fax 095271 355	Inn
Norton nr Shifnal Shropshire	**Map 6 B4**

A creeper-covered, red-brick, Georgian inn with enormous charm,
alongside the A442 Bridgnorth to Telford road. Personally run by the
Phillips family, the characterful interior features mellow brick walls,
stained glass, colourful patchwork leather upholstery and dozens
of bunches of dried flowers and herbs (all from Sylvia's splendid
garden which one is encouraged to visit) hanging from the ceiling
beams. Son Stuart's cooking combines traditional and more modern
influences, and makes good use of Sylvia's herb garden; salmon fish
cakes with tomato and cumin sauce (£6); savoury pancake stuffed
with red peppers, mushroom and coriander (£3.50 as a starter, £6.50
as a main dish with vegetables), Black Country griddled black
pudding with apple sauce (£2.75), spiced chicken and bacon salad
with mint vinaigrette. If you find it difficult to choose from the menu
of excellent desserts (shared with the separate restaurant) then try the
'ultimate dessert' (£7.50) which brings a selection all on one dish with
fresh fruit and home-made ice cream. It may all sound very adult but
children's favourites (burgers, fish fingers and sausages with chips) are
happily served up for youngsters. Three high-chairs and storage for
push-chairs provided; Mothercare baby-changing facilities in both
Ladies and Gents. Enchanting antique-furnished bedrooms have nice

:ouches like patchwork bedcovers (often on antique brass beds), fresh
flowers, pot-pourri, iron and ironing board, plus some even boast
a swing. All have good en-suite bathrooms and throughout the day
and evening there is room service of drinks and light snacks. Family
rooms have one extra bed and room for a further Z-bed. The hotel
is perfectly situated for a visit to Ironbridge Gorge museums or the
Severn Valley steam railway. Close to Junction 4 of the M54. *Bar
Food & Restaurant Meals* 12-2.30, 6.15-10 (7-9 Sun). *Children
welcome in bar to eat, children's menu. Free House.* **Beer** *Phillips Heritage
Ale, Ailrics Old Ale, Flowers Bitter, Brains Dark Mild. Garden, outdoor
ating.* **Accommodation** *10 bedrooms, all en suite, £69 (family room
sleeping four £79; single use of double £59). Children welcome overnight,
additional beds and cots provided at no extra charge. Access, Amex,
Diners, Visa.*

Norwich   Britons Arms Coffee House

Tel 0603 623367	Coffee House
Elm Hill Norwich Norfolk	Map 10 C1

Built in 1420 from second-hand materials by seven women, this
ancient half-timbered house is a popular all-day restaurant/coffee house.
It's on two floors, with three rooms (two non-smoking) and alfresco
ating (lunchtime only) in the garden terrace off the first-floor room.
Coffee, tea and light snacks are served until 12.15. There's one hot dish
er day – baked stuffed tomatoes served with turmeric rice and garden
alad (£3.90), pork, spinach and herb terrine with salad (£3.50),
anchovy, caper and Gruyère tart (£3.40) as well as quiches (£3.45),
ies (£3.65 – chicken and leek, Norfolk pork and apple) and jacket
otatoes (£2.70). Working partners Gilly Mixer and Sue Skipper
make their own puddings (gooseberry and elderflower fool or lime
and lemon meringue pie – both £1.95) as well as scones and cakes
lemon and honey, Greek walnut and cinnamon) – from 95p
 £1.20. £2.50 minimum charge between 12.15 and 2pm. *Children
under 8 not allowed in stepped garden. Children's portions; one high-
hair. No-smoking area.* **Seats** *65.* **Open** *9.30-5.* **Closed** *Sun, Bank
Holidays. No credit cards.*

Norwich   Café La Tienda

Tel 0603 629122	Vegetarian
St Gregory's Alley Norwich Norfolk	Map 10 C1

at at simple pine tables and benches and tuck into some deliciously
wholesome fare at this unfussy little lunch-only restaurant. Blackboard
ecials such as black-eyed bean and vegetable cottage pie or cheese and
ushroom savoury, both with salad (£3.90) back up the short regular
enu of soup (cream of leek £2), vegetable and cashew nut paté
£3.20) and hot filled pitta breads (houmus, spicy bean £3.20). Finish
ith ice creams, apple and apricot crumble or pecan pie (from £2-
2.50). *Children's portions; one booster seat. No smoking.* **Seats** *38.*
pen *11-2.30 (Sat 10-3).* **Closed** *Sun, Bank Holidays. No credit cards.*

Norwich   Norwich Sport Village Hotel   63%   £65

Tel 0603 788898 Fax 0603 406845	Hotel
rayton High Road Hellesdon Norwich Norfolk NR6 5DU	Map 10 C1

actical, roomy bedrooms are at the centre of a very extensive sports
omplex situated just off the outer Norwich ring road on the A1067
 Fakenham. All the rooms have en-suite facilities, half showers, half

tubs. Children up to 14 share parents' room free. Sporting facilities are the most impressive feature. They include seven squash courts and no less than a dozen tennis courts, seven of them indoors. Hotel guests share the lively open-plan bar, bistro and restaurant with the other users of the complex. The Aquapark swimming complex includes a competition pool, a shallow, warm, playpool with two slides and rapids and a paddling pool for toddlers. There's a soft play area for the very young. All the rooms are suitable for families and cots, potties, nappies, high-chairs and baby food can be provided; supervised crèche for six hours a week. Hotel guests share the lively open-plan bar, bistro and restaurant with the other users of the complex. No dogs. Conference facilities for thousands. Dinosaur Park (open mid Apr-Nov) is 9 miles away on the A1067 Fakenham road. *Rooms 55. Garden, indoor swimming pool, gymnasium, squash, sauna, steam baths, solarium, whirlpool bath, multi-sports hall, aerobics, beauty & hair salon, tennis, badminton, snooker, coffee shop (7am-10.30pm). Access, Amex, Diners, Visa.*

Norwich Airport — Ambassador Hotel — 65% — £76

Tel 0603 410544 Fax 0603 789935	Hotel
Cromer Road Norwich Airport Norwich Norfolk NR6 6JA	Map 10 C1

Modern redbrick hotel whose aeronautical associations include the Concorde Bar and a replica Spitfire in the garden. Practical accommodation in decent-sized bedrooms; the honeymoon suites feature four-poster beds and jacuzzis; video players in all rooms. Purpose-built facility for conferences and banquets (up to 350/500). *Rooms 108. Indoor swimming pool, gymnasium, sauna, steam room, whirlpool bath. Access, Amex, Diners, Visa.*

Nottingham — Higoi

Tel 0602 423379	Restaurant
57 Lenton Boulevard Nottingham Nottinghamshire	Map 7 D3

Japanese chef Mr Kato, assisted by his English wife, educates the locals in the delights of his native cuisine. Helpful and informative staff will explain all the specialities and menus, including good-value vegetarian, children's and *dombure* one-pot lunches and a bento box dinner. Set lunch starts at £6.90 (a bargain, by all accounts, as set dinners run from £17 to £25). One for the budding gourmet? Simple decor, lightwood tables and an assortment of Japanese artwork. On the Nottingham-Derby road (turn left at the Savoy cinema). *Seats 35. Open 12-2 & 6.30-10. Closed L Mon & Tue, all Sun & Bank Holidays. Access, Amex, Diners, Visa.*

Nottingham — Loopers Restaurant

Tel 0602 632175	Restaurant
Model Aviation Centre Goosedale Farm Moor Rd Bestwood Nottingham Nottinghamshire	Map 7 D3

A converted 17th-century barn housing the country's largest collection of working model aircraft and, separated by a windowed partition, a popular daytime restaurant and bakery, the latter also supplying local businesses. Large hot scones (60p) and vine-fruit-packed cake (£1) are joined at lunch by traditional fare ranging from prawn cocktail (£2.25) and soup of the day (£1.70) to chicken Kiev (£7) and plain grilled steaks (from £7.50). Self-service with friendly, helpful staff. Popular with families, especially for the traditional Sunday roast.

No smoking. Open evenings table d'hote or à la carte menus (£12 for
three-courses). Letting rooms and flats. Sign-posted from the A60
Nottingham-Mansfield road. **Seats** 150. **Open** 10-5.30 & 7-9 (last
orders). **Closed** Tues from Jan-Mar, 25 & 26 Dec. No credit cards.

Nottingham   Nottingham Knight

Tel 0602 211171	Pub
Loughborough Road Nottingham Nottinghamshire NG11 6LS	Map 7 D3

Scottish and Newcastle's first excursion into the themed family pub
market ('Homespreads') introduces the indoor 'Funky Forest' (which
parents may liken to a padded playroom; for those under 4 foot tall),
but the majority of youngsters will probably prefer to ape around
outdoors. Don't expect wonders from the hot, quick, vegetarian and
sandwich 'spreads', but the tables are suitably spaced and there's plenty
of room to spread out. No children in the bar. Also at The Foxhunters,
Prestongate, North Shields, Lawns, Yate, nr. Bristol, and Darrington,
nr. Pontefract, West Yorkshire. Pub open 11-11 Sat (and Bank Holidays
except Good Friday and Christmas), usual hours other days. **Bar Food**
11-2.30, 5-10.30 (Sun 12-10.30). **Beer** S & N Home Bitter, Theakston.
Garden, outdoor eating. Family Room. Access, Visa.

Nottingham   Punchinello's

Tel 0602 411965	Bistro
35 Forman Street Nottingham Nottinghamshire	Map 7 D3

Good cooking, good prices, jolly staff and long opening hours in a
bistro/restaurant opposite the Nottingham Playhouse. Breakfast starts
the day (either Continental or poached eggs or Boston baked beans)
and the Bistro menu comes on stream at 12; a blackboard announces
the likes of cottage pie (£2.65), chili (£2.65) and assorted quiches
with salads (£3.25). Dinner in the Balcony Restaurant is served in a
slightly more formal atmosphere. **Seats** 100. **Open** 8.30am-10.30pm.
Closed Sun, Bank Holidays. Access, Amex, Visa.

Nottingham   Sonny's

Tel 0602 473041	Restaurant
3 Carlton Street Hockley Nottingham Nottinghamshire	Map 7 D3

Chef Andy Poole brings the influences of France, Italy, Asia and
further regions to the open kitchen of this popular and successful
restaurant. Classic French fish soup with Gruyère, rouille and croutons
(£3.75), warm salad of duck, cloudear mushrooms and coriander
(£4.75) are starters with a modern ring while main courses such
as prawn and chorizo gumbo with sweetcorn and Cheddar hush
puppies (£8.50) or vegetarian rösti, ratatouille and goat's cheese
sandwich (£7.45) are no less fashionable. Desserts are something of a
speciality, with sticky toffee pudding a firm favourite alongside
chocolate and polenta cake, banana praline baskets and baked citrus
cheesecake. There's a two-course lunch at £9.95, three courses £12.95.
Crèche facilities on Sundays. **Seats** 80. **Open** 12-2.30 & 7-10.30 (Fri,
Sat to 11). **Closed** Bank Holidays. Access, Amex, Visa.

Nunton   Radnor Arms

Tel 0722 329722	Pub
Nunton nr Salisbury Wiltshire SP5 4HS	Map 14 C3

This welcoming ivy-clad village pub dates from the 17th century and
part of it once served as the village stores and post office. Locals come

now purely for the well-kept ale and for the honest home-cooked selection of meals that are served in its low-ceilinged and simply furnished main bar and neat opened-out dining areas. Traditional lunchtime favourites can be found on the printed menu, while the changing blackboard menu advertises the lunch specials and evening choices. Fresh fish dishes and rib-eye steak are regulars on the board, which may also include salmon paté (£2.50), herrings in Madeira (£3.25), calf's liver in garlic butter and herbs (£7.95), rack of lamb with port and redcurrant (£7.95) and salmon steak with white wine and dill (£6.25). Treacle and walnut tart (£2.25) and spiced apple pie (£2) are popular puddings. The large rear garden has fine rural views, plenty of picnic benches and much to amuse energetic children: climbing ropes, bikes, a Wendy house and an old tractor provide the entertainment. Children can eat inside where they are offered a short menu or smaller portions. The large disabled loo is fine for changing. *Bar Food 12-2 (Sun to 1.30), 7-9.30. Children allowed in side room away from bar to eat, children's menu. Beer Hall & Woodhouse. Garden, outdoor eating, children's play area. Family room. No credit cards.*

Oakham   Whipper-In Hotel   70%   £80

Tel 0572 756971 Fax 0572 757759	Hotel
Market Place Oakham Rutland Leicestershire LE15 6DT	Map 7 E3

Standing in the market square of Rutland's old county town, this relaxed, rural hotel dates back to the 17th century. A flagstone-floored foyer leads through to a low-beamed bar-lounge that is popular with the locals. Bedrooms, two of which boast four-poster beds, are neat and individually decorated with comfortable seating areas and a few antiques. Children up to 12 free in parents' room. High-chairs, cots, baby-listening, baby-sitting and room service are all offered. Room service available for all meals; informal eating in the Market Bar. Good-value two-night weekend breaks. Sister hotel to the *Royal Oak* in Sevenoaks, Kent. *Rooms 25. Access, Visa.*

Odiham   Blubeckers

Tel 0256 702953	Restaurant
The Mill House Odiham Hampshire RG25 1ET	Map 15 D3

Blubeckers is in a magnificent old mill house where in the restaurant, you can still see the huge wheel churning round. Half of the restaurant is set aside for families. The children's menu is excellent value and features cocktails for youngsters. Adults are offered char-grilled steaks and burgers, and 'old favourites' like chicken and Stilton crumble or smoked haddock and spinach pie. The long list of puddings ranges from Baileys hot chocolate cake to grandma's hot walnut pud and maple syrup mountain; ask for at least a couple of spoons! High-chairs are set with baby cutlery and a helium balloon is tied to all children's chairs, threatening to pull them up, up and away. Children are invited to enter the menu-colouring and awful joke contest and prizes are awarded each month. At one end of the room there is a 'dungeon' where children can escape to when mealtime formality becomes too much. Outside there is boating on the pond (supervision needed), a Wendy House, climbing frame, swings and a vast, green lawn. This outlet of Blubeckers won our 1992 Family Restaurant of the Year award. See also entry under Shepperton. Also Blubeckers at the White Hart in Chobham (Tel 0276 857580). *Seats 150. Open 12.30-2 (Sat until 2.15, Sun until 3) & 6.30-9.45 Fri until 10.45, Sun from 6, Sat 6-10.45). Closed Christmas. Access, Amex, Diners, Visa.*

Onecote   Jervis Arms

Tel 0538 304206 Fax 0538 304514	Pub
Onecote nr Leek Staffordshire ST13 7RU	Map 6 C3

Positioned just at the edge of the Peak National Park, the pub stands
on one bank of the Hamps river; park on the opposite bank and cross
a footbridge into the garden. While the picnic tables, play area (with
swing, slide and tree house) and ducks are super, parents should
be mindful of the littlest ones by this fast-flowing stream. Food has
improved here, though the ordering and delivery systems appear
faulty at peak times. (A tip, here: choose your table and stick with it!)
Vegetarian and children's meals both feature prominently on the
printed menu (curried nut, fruit and vegetable pie £4.50; egg, chips
and beans £1.95), alongside pretty standard pub grub. A little more
adventure emanates from the blackboard: lamb rogan josh, chicken
korma and vegetable masala (all £4.50) spice things up a little –
though not a lot. Adjacent to the pub is holiday accommodation in a
converted barn, available for rent by the week. *Bar Food 12-2, 7-10.
Children's menu. Free House. Beer Theakston Best, XB & Old Peculier,
Bass. Riverside garden, children's play area. Family room. Access, Visa.*

Orford   Old Warehouse

Tel 0394 450210	Tea Room
The Quay Orford Suffolk	Map 10 D3

A fine old warehouse on Orford Quay, with tea rooms on the ground
floor offering a range of tasty home-prepared food: Stilton soup
(£1.95), Welsh rarebit (£2.65), potted shrimps, quiche, spaghetti
bolognese (£3.95). On Sunday comes a roast beef lunch (£6.95) with
all the trimmings and a drink. Two high-chairs. *Seats 42. Open 10-6
(in winter 10-5 Sat & Sun only). Closed 25 & 26 Dec. Access, Visa.*

Ormesby St Margaret   Ormesby Lodge   58%   £46

Tel 0493 730910 Fax 0493 733103	Hotel
Decoy Road Ormesby St Margaret nr Gt Yarmouth Norfolk NR29 3LG	Map 10 D1

A small family-run hotel five miles north of Great Yarmouth and
within a mile or so of several beaches. The building is Victorian, and
some of the original feel survives in the bar/lounge. Bedrooms vary
in their decor and furnishings but all are in good order and all have
private bathroom facilities. *Rooms 9. Garden. Access, Amex,
Diners, Visa.*

Oswestry   Wynnstay Hotel   68%   £83

Tel 0691 655261 Fax 0691 670606	Hotel
Church Street Oswestry Shropshire SY11 2SZ	Map 8 D2

In the town centre opposite St Oswalds church, this is a typical
Georgian building with stylish day rooms. Besides the restaurant and
lounge there are conference facilities for up to 180, plus a 200-year-old
crown bowling green as an unusual leisure offering. Best of the
bedrooms have whirlpool baths. Informal eating in the bar; high-
chairs provided, baby sitting by arrangement. Children up to ten free
in parents' room. *Rooms 27. Garden, bowling, coffee shop (9.30am-
10pm). Access, Amex, Diners, Visa.*

Otley — Chevin Lodge Country Park Hotel — 64% — £87

Tel 0943 467818 Fax 0943 850335	Hotel

York Gate Otley West Yorkshire LS21 3NU   Map 6 C1

Set "in the heart of Emmerdale Farm country", in fifty acres
of birchwoods by a private lake and built of Finnish pine, the Lodge
is the largest log construction in the country. Bedrooms are in either
the main building or smaller log Lodges scattered among the trees.
Despite the rusticity, rooms have all the usual modern conveniences.
Executive lodges have separate lounges; some have their own kitchen;
some have more than one bedroom – £16 per person charge per
night if second room is used. Children under 12 sharing their parents'
room are charged only £5 (inc breakfast) per night. High-chairs and
cots can be supplied. The well-equipped Woodlands Suite has facilities
for up to 120 conference delegates. Guests have free membership
of nearby Manor private leisure club, 5 minutes, drive away; this
offers gymnasium with indoor running track, indoor swimming pool,
full-size snooker tables and a supervised crèche (for over-4s only). The
room price comes down at weekends (Fri & Sat only). *Rooms 52.
Garden, sauna, solarium, all-weather tennis, fishing, games room, jogging
trails, free cycle hire. Access, Amex, Visa.*

Over Stratton — Royal Oak

Tel 0460 40906	Pub

Over Stratton nr South Petherton Somerset TA13 5LQ   Map 13 F2

This row of three 400-year-old thatched cottages merges with its
neighbours in the main street of the village and, but for the pub sign,
it would be easy to miss altogether; at the South Petherton roundabout
(A303) take the old Ilminster town-centre road. Cottage atmosphere
is still the secret of an interior with a real sense of style. Original
features like old beams, hamstone and flag floors (as well as a couple
of stone pillars that look to have been there for ever but were actually
salvaged from the cellars of a nearby house a couple of years ago)
blend successfully with dark rag-rolled walls, scrubbed wooden tables,
a polished granite bar counter and extensive displays of dried flowers,
hops and strings of garlic. A Booty Box (£2.75) is on the children's
menu, full of goodies including a wholemeal sandwich, cheese, fruit,
crisps and a Crunchy bar – all served in a special box that children can
take away with them. The adult equivalent is a barbecue pack (£8.50)
containing a pair of lamb cutlets, sausage, gammon steak and a chicken
drumstick (along with salad and jacket potato) that, weather
permitting, is cooked on the grill outdoors. Beyond the barbecue,
there are swings, a junior assault course and trampolines to keep the
kids amused. Very much a recommendation for good days, when
outdoors is the place to be. Inside, readers have reported a cold
reception. *Bar Food & Restaurant Meals 12-1.45, 7-10 (7-9.30 Sun).
Children allowed in the dining room to eat. Beer Hall & Woodhouse.
Garden, outdoor eating, children's play area. Access, Visa.*

Oxford — Blue Coyote

Tel 0865 241431	Restaurant

36 St Clements Street Oxford Oxfordshire   Map 15 D2

Bare-board floor, bentwood chairs and plain wooden tables, each
sporting a cactus in a pot, set the informal tone here. The menu is a
veritable cook's tour of American cuisine with Maryland crab cakes
on a tomato and basil sauce (£3.95), New York deli-style marinated

salmon (served in a bagel with cream cheese £4.25), Sausalito pasta (with goat's cheese and sun-dried tomatoes £6.95), enchiladas (£6.75), Cajun blackened duck (£8.45), Yucatan sausages (veal, flavoured with bay and green chilli £8.45), BLT (£4.25) and much else besides. Side orders include some yummy sweet potato fritters. Two high-chairs provided, but no changing facilities. Ask for half-price children's portions. No minimum charge. To the east of the town centre, there's a pay and display car park to the rear. **Seats** 68. **Open** 12-3 & 6-11 (Sat/Sun noon-11). **Closed** 25 & 26 Dec, 1 Jan. Access, Visa.

Oxford — Browns

Tel 0865 511995 Fax 0865 52347 — **Restaurant**

5 Woodstock Road Oxford Oxfordshire OX2 6HA — Map 15 D2

Close to Little Clarendon Street turning, almost next door to Radcliffe Infirmary. Light, airy restaurant and bar with a lively, informal atmosphere, immensely popular since opening in 1976; chef Eamonn Hunter has been here since opening. Bumper hot sandwiches remain a favourite sustaining snack (Vera's double egg and bacon £5.15, toasted tuna on wholemeal bread with melted cheese £5.55), along with hamburgers, salads and pasta (spaghetti or a daily-changing pasta with a choice of four sauces, £5.95 includes garlic bread and a mixed salad – "seconds at no extra charge"). Country chicken pie (£6.85), steaks and fish specials for serious main courses, banana cream pie and chocolate mousse cake among the puddings (around £2.35). Typical blackboard specials might be baked monkfish wrapped in bacon on a bed of spinach with a fresh lime sauce (£6.35 inc vegetables) or beef tomatoes stuffed with spinach and wild mushrooms and topped with a fresh herb sauce (£5.75). Traditional English breakfast (11-12 Mon-Sat, £4.75), plus equally traditional cucumber or egg and cress sandwiches at tea time (3-5.30pm); roast Sunday lunch (£8.25). Ten high-chairs and a changing room with table, changing mat and baby wipes are all provided; short children's menu or smaller portions. Other branches in Brighton, Bristol and Cambridge. Joint winner of our Family Restaurants of the Year award for 1994. As we went to press further improvements to both restaurant and bar were getting underway. **Seats** 240. **Open** 11am-11.30pm (Sun and Bank Holidays from noon). **Closed** 25 & 26 Dec. Access, Diners, Visa.

Oxford — Gourmet Pizza Company

Tel 0865 793146 — **Pizzeria**

100-101 Gloucester Green Oxford Oxfordshire — Map 15 D2

A branch of the popular and successful pizza group based in London. Children's menu of pizza and pasta (£1.75-£2.25). Separate changing facilities in the disabled loo lobby, complete with emergency supplies. See London entry for further details. **Seats** 60 (plus 40 outside). **Open** 12-10.45 (Fri/Sat to 11). **Closed** 25 & 26 Dec, 1 Jan. Access, Amex, Visa.

Oxford — St Aldate's Coffee House

Tel 0865 245952 — **Coffee House**

St Aldate's Oxford Oxfordshire OX1 1BP — Map 15 D2

There are seats for 72 in this self-service coffee house opposite Christ Church, plus outside seating on the patio or on the grass in front of St Aldate's church. Sandwiches (from £1.35) and home baking (scone and butter 75p, rock cake 65p, chocolate truffle cake £1.40)

are always available, joined at lunchtime by jacket potatoes, soup
(£1.40) and daily hot specials (£3.50 upwards). Two high-chairs;
table and chair provided in the Ladies. No smoking. *Seats 72.*
Open 10-5. Closed Sun, Bank Holidays. No credit cards.

Padstow   Old Custom House

Tel 0841 532359	Pub
South Quay Padstow Cornwall PL28 8ED	**Map 12 B3**

Proudly set on the quayside with picturesque views across the bustling
harbour with its colourful boats and beyond over the Camel estuary,
the Old Custom House began life as the Customs and Excise building
in the 1800s. St Austell Brewery have invested money in refurbishing
the inn, resulting in spacious, well-decorated and neatly furnished
public areas, which display a good collection of prints. A new light and
airy conservatory (suitable for families) added to the front of the
building has a quarry-tiled floor and good cushioned cane furniture
and is a popular spot from which to watch harbour life. Of the 27
tastefully furnished and well-equipped bedrooms, over half enjoy
harbour and estuary views. Modern in style with fresh co-ordinating
fabrics and wallpapers, they all have excellent spacious and sparkling
bathrooms with good fixtures and fittings, plus fluffy towels and
hairdryer. The honeymoon suite has an elegant four-poster, a double
shower and a large deep jacuzzi set in the floor. Telephones, beverage-
making facilities and satellite TV are standard throughout.
Recommended for B&B only. *Open 11-11, Sun usual hours. Cream teas
3-5 in summer. Beer St Austell Bosun's Bitter, Tinners Ale.*
*Accommodation 27 bedrooms, all en suite, £42-£69 (single £27-£52).
Extra beds and cots supplied (under-3s free, 3-12s half price). Access, Amex,
Diners, Visa.*

Painswick   St Michael's Restaurant and Guest House

Tel 0452 812998	Restaurant
Victoria Street Painswick Gloucestershire	**Map 14 B2**

Opposite the village church, which boasts no less than 137 clipped
yew trees in the churchyard, St Michael's Restaurant and Guest House
(there are four well-kept bedrooms) offers good home baking –
chocolate cake (£1.40), fruit cake, scones – plus snacks on toast and
sandwiches, either side of a varied lunch menu. This offers some half
a dozen main dishes – lasagne al forno, beef chasseur, vegetarian
crumble – at prices from £5.25-£6.95. There's a pleasant walled
garden for summer eating. A traditional roast is served on Sundays
(£10.50, under-12s £6.25). More expensive evening meals (£15.95
fixed-price menu). One high-chair; light snacks are available from 10-
noon and 2-5 – ideal for high tea. *Seats 36. Open 10-5 & 7.30-9 (Sun
12-2). Closed Mon (except Bank Holidays), 24-26 Dec. No credit cards.*

Penistone   Cubley Hall

Tel 0226 766086	Pub
Mortimer Road Penistone Barnsley South Yorkshire S30 6AW	**Map 6 C2**

This unusual conversion from Edwardian country house to what
is almost a 'stately pub' passed its tenth anniversary in July 1993.
It echoes a bit when empty and hums along busily when full. With
sizeable parties accommodated in the conservatory, there can be a
scrum for tables to eat at. Food follows generally predictable lines
from beefburger and onions (£1.40) through to the steak and grill
range (mixed grill £6.95), but the daily specials come to the rescue:

lamb korma (£4.75), Cubley game pie (£4.95) and beef stroganoff (£6.25) are better indicators of a capable kitchen which also produces weightier weekend fare for the adjacent Workhouse Carvery (check opening times). The extensive gardens and grounds with play areas (including a tree house) and drinking patios are a major draw for families through the summer. *Free House. **Beer** Tetley Best, Burton Ale, Marston's Pedigree. Garden and patio, children's play area. Family room. Access, Visa.*

Penrith	North Lakes Hotel	71%	£108
Tel 0768 68111 Fax 0768 68291			Hotel
Ullswater Road Penrith Cumbria CA11 8QT			Map 4 C3

A stern-looking hotel, by Junction 40 of the M6, which comfortably divides its time between mid-week conferences and a weekend base for Lakeland visitors. Facilities for both categories are purpose-built around a central lodge of local stone and massive railway-sleeper beams, which houses bar, lounges and coffee shop. Newest Executive-style bedrooms have raised work areas with fold-away beds, while interconnecting syndicate rooms convert handily for family use at holiday times. A welcoming pack on arrival will keep the children happy; if they finish the quiz and crossword they could win a baseball cap. Children up to 12 stay free in parents' room. *Shire Inns.* **Rooms** 85. *Garden, indoor swimming pool, sauna, spa bath, solarium, gymnasium, squash, snooker, coffee shop (9am-11pm). Access, Amex, Diners, Visa.*

Penshurst	Fir Tree House Tea Rooms	
Tel 0892 870382		Tea Rooms
Penshurst nr Tonbridge Kent TN11 8DB		Map 11 B5

Mrs Fuller-Rowell's traditional tea room with a delightful cottage garden (with a swing) is still a firm favourite with both families and those after straightforward afternoon teas from a past era. Home-baked tea breads (40p a slice), an array of delectable cakes (from 75p), sandwiches (£1) and, whenever possible, home-made jams continue to please, with set cream (£2.50) and traditional (£4.25) teas as popular as ever. A good selection of loose-leaf teas too. No smoking. *Seats 45. **Open** 3-5.45 Apr-Oct, 2.30-5.30 Sat & Sun only Jan-Mar. **Closed** Mon except Bank Holidays, Tue following Bank Holidays, all Nov & Dec. No credit cards.*

Peterborough	Butterfly Hotel	63%	£70
Tel 0733 64240 Fax 0733 65538			Hotel
Thorpe Meadows Longthorpe Parkway Peterborough Cambridgeshire PE3 6GA			Map 7 E4

One of a small chain of modern, low-rise brick-built East Anglian hotels (the others are in Bury St Edmunds, Colchester and King's Lynn). Peterborough's Butterfly sits at the water's edge, overlooking Thorpe Meadows rowing lake. Neat, practical accommodation ranges from studio singles to four suites and double or family rooms will be supplied with cots and Z-beds on request (children up to eight stay free). Baby-sitting and baby-listening can be arranged in advance and Walt's place, the open-plan, pine-clad restaurant overlooking the lake, offers a simple children's menu. Good breakfasts. No amusements in the hotel, but nearby Belvoir provides good family entertainment. **Rooms** 70. *Access, Amex, Diners, Visa.*

Plymouth   Moat House   70%   £118

| Tel 0752 662866   Fax 0752 673816 | Hotel |

Armada Way Plymouth Devon PL1 2HJ   Map 12 C3

Day rooms at this high-rise hotel, in particular the penthouse
restaurant and bar, command spectacular views of the Hoe and
Plymouth Sound. So do many of the good-sized, picture-windowed
bedrooms, which have double beds (twins have two double beds),
seating areas and plenty of writing space. On the ground floor the
large, bright reception area includes the relaxing International Bar.
Usually a busy business hotel, but occasionally transformed into
a haven for children, for example on the Baby & Toddlers Delight
weekends – ring them for details of special arrangements for families.
Children under 16 are accommodated free if sharing their parents'
room. Children will love a ride on the Shuttle Train that runs right
past the hotel in summer. *Rooms 212. Indoor swimming pool,
gymnasium, sauna, steam room, solarium, games room. Access, Amex,
Diners, Visa.*

Polkerris   Rashleigh Inn

| Tel 072681 3991 | Pub |

Polkerris Fowey Cornwall PL25 3NJ   Map 12 C3

Literally on the beach in a tiny isolated cove and known locally as the
'Inn on the Beach', the Rashleigh is well worth seeking out for its
magnificent setting. Once the old lifeboat station, until becoming
a pub in 1924, it is a popular refreshment spot for coast path walkers
and for families using the beach. Summer alfresco drinking
is unrivalled in this area, for the table-filled terrace is a splendid place
from which to watch the sun set across St Austell Bay. On cooler days
the sea views can still be admired from the warmth of the main bar,
especially from the much sought after bay-window seats. Parents
enjoying a drink on the terrace can keep an eagle eye on their children
playing on the beach. Food is predictable. *Free House.* **Beer** *St Austell
HSD, Dartmoor Strong, Burton Ale, Dartmoor Best (Bolsters). Outdoor
eating area. Pub closed Tues eve Jan-Mar. Access, Visa.*

Pontefract   Parkside Inn

| Tel 0977 709911   Fax 0977 701602 | Pub |

Park Road Pontefract West Yorkshire WF8 4QD   Map 7 D1

A haunt of racegoers – opposite the racecourse – and a haven for
families with its enclosed gardens and play area, the Parkside appeals
to many tastes. In a layout reminiscent of a Western ranch, it contains
a host of bar areas with conservatory and sun lounge, a carvery and
à la carte restaurant. Accommodation has been carefully incorporated
and added to over the years. Of most character is the old farmhouse,
connected now by an arched walkway, where the old front door and
stairs can still be seen, and what is now a residents' lounge retains the
original kitchen sinks and shelves. A large family room and sets
of connecting twins are especially popular with weekending families;
baby-listening is all part of the service. Accoutrements run through
TV and phones to hairdryers and trouser presses; ask, though,
for a room with full bath, as some of the shower rooms are, to say the
least, cramped. Recommended for B&B only. *Free House.* **Beer** *John
Smith's Best & Magnet, Wilson's Mild. Garden, children's play area.*

Family room. ***Accommodation*** *28 bedrooms, all en suite, £57 (single £45). Children welcome overnight (large family room £50), additional beds (£10) and cots (no charge) available. Access, Diners, Visa.*

Poole	**Sandbanks Hotel**	59%	£110

Tel 0202 707377 Fax 0202 708885	Hotel

15 Banks Road Sandbanks Poole Dorset BH13 3PS	Map 14 C4

Ideal for families, with an attractive patio and garden leading straight on to the surprisingly clean sandy beach, and complete holiday services that include organised activities, a children's restaurant (the Kiddy Bar) and a nursery with changing facilities; baby sitting can be arranged. Four tiers of balconied bedrooms look either out to sea or across Poole Bay and the open-plan bar, vast sun lounge and dining rooms also enjoy panoramic views over the sea. 20 larger rooms in the original hotel building are designated as family rooms. Adult guests may use the leisure facilities at the *Haven Hotel* nearby. Special out-of-season two-day break half-board tariff. No dogs. ***Rooms*** *105. Garden, indoor swimming pool, sauna, steam room, solarium, spa bath, gymnasium, crèche (daily during school holidays, full supervision during lunch 1-2), entertainers in the morning and 6-9pm in the ballroom, children's outdoor play area. Access, Amex, Diners, Visa.*

Porth	**Trevelgue Hotel**	

Tel 0637 872864 Fax 0637 876365	Hotel

Porth nr Newquay Cornwall TR7 3LX	Map 12 B3

With the rolling downs of north Cornwall behind and a 180° sea vista to the front, the Trevelgue has a head start with its position. Self-styled as a "parents' haven" and "children's paradise", aiming fairly and squarely at becoming "the no. 1 hotel in the UK for childcare", its continued success (after 12 years) is achieved by providing almost everything that families with young children actually need in order to have a peaceful stay away from the comforts of home. Some hotels are described as a 'home-from-home' because they are, quite simply, homely, but there is so much more here to satisfy not only the requirements of demanding children – from babes in arms to energetic teenagers – but also parents who need a break from the incessant routine that is inherent in bringing up children. You can hire a toddler's tricycle or take the whole family on a bike ride along a six-mile disused railway line; you can purchase a youngster's daily pint of milk over the counter in the tea room (and keep it fresh in your bedroom fridge) or indulge yourself at dinner with a bottle from the distinctly ungreedily-priced wine list; you can even have a full top-to-toe beauty treatment while the children are looked after in carefully arranged groups. You name it, they've generally thought of it, and they bring it off with panache; particularly impressive are the arrangements for children's high tea and for parents to enjoy their evening meal: the very young are looked after in the fully supervised Teddy Bears Club for a quiet time before bed, while older children (3-7s) can expend their final energies in an indoor playroom; constantly monitored baby-listening. The list of activities is too long to list, but there is sufficient to keep everybody happy in both good and bad weather; cots, high-chairs, bunk beds, bikes, buggies, back packs, baby walkers, baby baths, sterilisers, bottle warmers and bouncy chairs can all be booked in advance. Surprisingly, although the Trevelgue attracts young families like Pooh to the Hunny Pot, the hotel is spacious enough never to feel like a nursery and the management is clever enough to make the adult attractions as inviting as those for their junior guests. A very large, sandy beach is just down the hill. Lastly, and by no means least, the tariff is incredibly reasonable for all the activities provided and accommodation in the identical family suites is unusually spacious. Half-board terms only: 1994 prices £224-£336 per person per week, shorter breaks out of season with free under-7s offers; children are charged on a sliding scale according to age – under-1s 10%, under-3s 20%, under-7s 50%, 7-14s 65% of adult rate. Winner of our 1994 Family Hotel of the Year award (see page 9). *Rooms 42 family suites, 28 rooms. Garden, tennis & organised sports in high season (football, rounders, volleyball), squash, golf practice net, 3-hole golf course, mini-golf, giant chess, croquet & boules, skittles, air rifle range, adventure playgrounds, sandpit, Wendy houses, outdoor & indoor swimming pools, health and beauty salon, mother & baby room, table football, pool table, disco, table tennis. Hotel closed Nov-end Mar (booking office open). Access, Visa.*

Powerstock   Three Horseshoes Inn

Tel 0308 485328/229	Pub

Powerstock Bridport Dorset DT6 3TF	Map 13 F2

The inn was rebuilt in 1906 after a devastating fire, but solidly old-fashioned in style, with its stone and thatch, simple country furnishings, open fires and a delightful garden. But people come to this reliable old favourite for the chef/licensee Pat Ferguson's food; not cheap, certainly, but fresh and delicious, specialising in fish, for instance fresh crab with melon (£4.50), grilled sardines with garlic butter (£2.75), John Dory deauvillaise (£9.50) or fillet of sea bass on a julienne of vegetables with garlic sauce (£12.50). The blackboard menu can also include anything from grilled lobster to fish pie, bourride and sea bass cooked in a paper bag. Meat and game dishes, too: garlic-studded rack of lamb, kidneys turbigo, venison pie. Desserts include summer pudding, sticky toffee pudding and sunken chocolate soufflé (£2.50-£3.50). Must book for busy Sunday lunches (£12.50) in winter. Tables in the garden for summer eating. Bedrooms are large and traditionally styled with central heating, en-suite bathrooms and lovely views. Delightful garden. Families with children are welcome in the restaurant. *Bar Food & Restaurant Meals 12-2 (Sun to 3), 7-10. Beer Palmers Bridport, IPA & Tally Ho. Garden, outdoor eating, children's play area with swings and climbing frame. Accommodation 2 bedrooms, both en suite, £45 (single £24). Children welcome overnight, additional beds and cots supplied. Check-in by arrangement. Access, Visa.*

Repton   Brook Farm Tea Rooms

Tel 0283 702215	Tea Room

Brook End Repton Derbyshire DE65 6FW	Map 6 C3

Brook Farm is a working dairy and arable farm and the Tea Rooms are housed in an old sandstone and brick barn beside a trout brook. There's a large, lawned and walled garden which has bench seating for summer eating. The lunchtime menu is written up on the blackboard and offers such choices as sweet and sour pork, asparagus pancakes or salmon, cod and mushroom pie (all £3.70) and home-made cakes and puddings (treacle sponge and custard, apple crumble both £1.15). The Brook Farm Cream Tea (£2 – two scones with jam, cream and pot of tea) and Farmhouse Tea (£2.20 – round of sandwiches, scone with butter and jam, pot of tea) are tea-time options or there's a choice of toasted teacakes (65p), crumpet (45p) or 10 flavours of locally-made

dairy ice cream (£1). Children's menu (£1.10) or portions available.
One high-chair; children's changing mat and child's seat provided;
walled garden and lawn away from road. No smoking inside. After
tea, take a stroll by the brook or explore Repton, whose history goes
back to 653AD. **Seats 54. Open** *10.15-5.* **Closed** *1 week Jan.*
No credit cards.

Richmond	**Refectory**	
Tel 081-940 6264		**Restaurant**
6 Church Walk Richmond Surrey TW9 1SN		Map 15 E2

Martin and Harriet Steel understand the needs of children and provide
four high-chairs, a booster seat, storage for prams and pushchairs
and a changing area in their ever-popular cottagey restaurant and
coffee shop. Conveniently located just off the high street by the
church, most of the tables are likely to be taken by families and the
babble and chatter is reassuringly vigorous without ever becoming
intrusive. When the sun shines the pretty little paved courtyard comes
into its own, but more often you will opt to sit inside at the mellow
pine tables. The food is served speedily but it is certainly not fast food.
Children may have small, half-price portions of the traditional British
dishes like cottage, steak and kidney or fish pie (around £4.30, adult
portion); generous portions of vegetables (£1.20, choice of four) can
be shared; a vegetarian option is always offered (leek, broccoli and
courgette bake £4.10). Steamed puddings (£2.45) and Loseley ice
creams (£1.65) to finish if you've still got room. Fruit juices, straws
in glasses (try the elderflower cordial 95p). Normal menu (no roast)
on Sundays. Pleasantly informal; no bells, no whistles, just a sensible
place to eat out en famille. Booking advised. No smoking. **Seats 44.**
Open *from 10am for coffee, lunch 12-2, teas 2-5 (not Sun).* **Closed** *all
Mon, 1 week Christmas.* Access, Visa.

Richmond	**Richmond Harvest**	
Tel 081-940 1138		**Vegetarian**
5 The Square Richmond Surrey		Map 15 E2

Ten years on and this small semi-basement vegetarian restaurant in the
centre of town is still as popular as ever. The secret is the constantly
changing menu with starters, served with their own brown bread, like
guacamole (£1.95), green pea and mint soup (£1.95) and black bean
and basil paté (£1.95). Main courses – marrow and ginger bake,
Spanish chickpea casserole, cauliflower sweet and sour – are all
at £5.50 with a few snackier items, such as jacket potatoes (from
£1.95) and cheese and vegetable pie (£3.50), served at lunchtimes.
Composite salads are nicely varied and puds include hot fruit crumble
(£1.95) and banoffi pie (£2.25). No facilities for youngsters. **Seats 38.**
Open *11.30-11 (Sun 1-10).* **Closed** *25 Dec. No credit cards.*

Richmond	**River Terrace**	
Tel 081-332 2524		**Restaurant**
11 Bridge Street Richmond Surrey TW9 1TQ		Map 15 E2

Great location in a Georgian building right on Richmond Bridge. Eat
inside or out on the large terrace from a short menu offering the likes
of corn chips with guacamole, potato tortilla with caponata, salmon
with a light, creamy curry sauce and strawberry cheesecake with
raspberry coulis. Reasonable food at not unreasonable prices. Lunch
is good value (2 courses £10, 3 £12.95). Inside has an outdoor feel,

too, with a cream and green theme. The sign for Baby Changing
Facilities is larger than the sign for the Ladies, so you're unlikely
to miss it. Despite the steps it's reasonably negotiable for push-chairs.
*Seats 300. Open 12-3 (Sat & Sun till 4) & 7-10 (Sat till 11). Access,
Amex, Diners, Visa.*

Romsey   Cobweb Tea Room

Tel 0794 516434	Tea Room

49 The Hundred Romsey Hampshire SO51 8GE   **Map 14 C3**

Angela Webley's tea room is a homely place with beams, green
tablecloths, cheery service and a little patio at the back. Temptingly
displayed baking includes old-style madeleines (80p), rum truffles and
a delicious apricot Bakewell tart (£1.50), plus various sponge gateaux.
Light lunches offer toasted sandwiches (from £1.25), baked potatoes
with special fillings (cottage cheese and prawn or bolognese at £3.75)
or hot dishes such as wheat and walnut casserole, vegetable stroganoff,
steak and mushroom pie or chicken curry (all £3.75). Pavlova, date
and apple crumble and tiramisu are popular puddings (all £1.50).
Cream teas £2.50. Children's portions; three high-chairs; small toy
box. No smoking (except in walled garden). *Seats 32. Open 10-5.30
(Bank Holiday Mon from 12, Sun prior to Bank Holiday Monday from
2.30). Closed Other Sun, Mon, 1 week Christmas, 2 weeks end Sep/early
Oct. No credit cards.*

Romsey   Latimer Coffee House

Tel 0794 513832	Coffee House

11 Latimer Street Romsey Hampshire   **Map 14 C3**

Lots of old beams and timbers tell of the Tudor origins of this coffee
house in a side street near the town centre. Order at the counter,
where the good home baking is displayed (lemon drizzle cake,
chocolate cake, cherry coconut slice – all at 70p) from a selection
of sandwiches (from £1.65), jacket potatoes (from £2.75) and good-
looking quiche plus, from noon, the likes of cottage pie and lasagne
(both £4). At night, in addition to the above snacks, there is a
waitress-service supper menu with mostly pasta-based main dishes (all
about £5). High-chairs provided; baby food heated up on request;
large Ladies for changing. A small terrace to the rear, decorated with
hanging flower baskets, is a peaceful spot for a summer snack. *Seats 75.
Open 9.30-5 (Sun 11-4) also 7.30-11. Closed D Sun & Mon.
No credit cards.*

Ross-on-Wye   Fresh Grounds

Tel 0989 768289	Coffee Shop

Raglan House 17 Broad Street Ross-on-Wye Hereford & Worcester   **Map 14 B1**

A Queen Anne town house is home to Norma Snook's refined coffee
shop/restaurant. There's plenty for just-a-biters throughout the day
from filled jacket potatoes (from £2.20), open sandwiches (from
£2.80) and various salads to scrambled eggs with smoked salmon
(£3.75) and cream teas (except between 12-2pm when there are
lunchtime specials like braised beef (£4.95) and Spanish chicken with
rice). Scrumptious home-made cakes include hazelnut meringue,
Victoria sponge and lemon cake – from £1.35. There are also things
like freshly baked croissants and cinnamon toast plus (although it's not
on the written menu) a full English breakfast at £4.50 served until

10am, or sometimes a bit later. Friday and Saturday evenings (7-9) there's a fixed-price dinner menu at £15.25 (four-courses). Seven en-suite letting bedrooms (not inspected). **Seats 40. Open** 9-5 & 7-9. **Closed** D Mon-Thu, all Sun, 25 & 26 Dec, 1 Jan. Access, Diners, Visa.

Ross-on-Wye	Meader's Hungarian Restaurant	
Tel 0989 62803		Restaurant
Copse Cross Street Ross-on-Wye Hereford & Worcester HR9 5PD		Map 14 B1

Hungarian-born Andras Weinhardt offers hearty lunchtime dishes from his native land like ham and bean soup (£1.50), layered cabbage (£4.50), pork or beef goulash and beef stroganoff with rice (£5.50). The set evening menu (£19 for two – not Saturday – including a bottle of Hungarian wine) comprises a main course and dessert: chicken in paprika or mushroom goulash could be followed by apple trudel or a pancake with lemon, sugar and cottage cheese. The evening carte offers starters at £2.50, main courses at £7.50 and desserts at £2. Children's evening menu £3.50; "please ask if you want something else for your child"; favourite dishes for under-10s at lunchtime. Two high-chairs; folding table and changing mat in the ladies. No-smoking area. **Seats 45. Open** 10-2.30 & 7-9.30. **Closed** Sun, Mon (except D Bank Holidays), 25 & 26 Dec, 1 Jan. No credit cards.

Ross-on-Wye	Pengethley Manor	67%	£114
Tel 0989 87211 Fax 0989 87238			Hotel
Pengethley Park nr Ross-on-Wye Hereford & Worcester HR9 6LL			Map 14 B1

Fifteen acres of estate with a par 3 golf course, trout lake, vineyard and landscaped gardens enhance Pengethley's tranquil country setting. Plenty of activity for the sporting, and the garden offers plenty of space in which youngsters can let off steam; high-chairs and baby food are provided at mealtimes. There are purpose-built, family rooms in converted stables, some with their own lounges and sofa beds. Baby-sitting/listening and a laundry service are all available. Banqueting for up to 90 and conference rooms accommodating 75 kept discreetly separate. Purpose-built bedrooms for disabled guests; children up to 16 stay free in parents' room. **Rooms 24.** Garden, outdoor swimming pool, golf (9-holemm), fishing, snooker, outdoor chess. Access, Amex, Diners, Visa.

Rowlands Castle	Coffee Pot	
Tel 0705 412538		Tea Room
4 The Green Rowlands Castle Hampshire PO9 6BN		Map 15 D4

Mrs Lomer, who has written a short history of Rowlands Castle, provides a popular service, both eating in and taking away, at her cottagey tea room overlooking the village green. Millionaire shortbread, flapjacks, macaroons and gateaux (55p-£1.80) are part of a good range of home baking, and at lunchtime there's a variety of light meals such as quiches (from £1.35), steak pies (£1.50), jacket potatoes (from £1.50) and lasagne. Vegetarian options, too (vegetable bakes from £3.25 and vegetable pasties £1.20). The full English breakfast is £4.25 and the Sunday roast £5.95. Evening meals for groups by arrangement only. No smoking. Garden. **Seats 40. Open** 9-5 (Sun 10-6). **Closed** 25 & 26 Dec. No credit cards.

Rugby   Summersault

Tel 0788 543223	Vegetarian
27 High Street Rugby Warwickshire CV21 3BW	Map 7 D4

Eileen and Michael Jeff's unusual High Street emporium with
an Edwardian flavour purveys an uneven assortment of goods from
designer-label clothes to soaps and shampoo, confectionery, teas and
coffee; it's 30m from the entrance to Rugby School. There's a mellow
air also in the pine-furnished café (to the rear) which is Rugby's
vegetarian Mecca. Daily lunchtime dishes are typified by leek
croustade, chestnut pie, mushroom and apple spaghetti bake and
ratatouille pancakes (all at £3.95) with any three of the colourful,
tasty salads that adorn the self-service counter. Outside main meal hours
there's a creditable array of sandwiches and home baking (apple and
hazelnut crumble pie £1.25, pecan, toffee and apple flan £1.60) that
can be enjoyed with an assortment of beverages including speciality
and herb teas. Two high-chairs; pizzas and jacket potatoes always
popular with junior diners. Marble-topped washstand for changing
in the Ladies. *Seats 50. Open 9-4.30. Closed Sun and Bank Holidays.
Access, Visa.*

Ryton-on-Dunsmore   Ryton Gardens

Tel 0203 303517	Café
Wolston Lane Ryton-on-Dunsmore Warwickshire	Map 6 D4

A larger restaurant/café opened in July last year. Wholefood dishes
using organic ingredients are the speciality: not unsurprisingly, as it
is part of the National Centre for Organic Gardening owned by The
Henry Doubleday Research Association since 1985. A typical menu
lists tomato soup (£1.50), cider and lentil loaf, French onion tart
(£4.25 with salad), organic chicken in white wine and cream sauce
(£4.25). Sweeter things include sticky prune cake, carrot cake, vegan
fruit cake and ginger cake from 80p. No smoking throughout. Two
high-chairs; changing facilities. Tables outside (for 86) in fine weather.
Outdoor play area with swing, slide and climbing frame. On the road
to Wolston, off the A45, 5 miles south-east of Coventry. *Seats 75.
Open 10-4 Oct-Mar, 10-5 Apr-Sept. Closed 25 & 26 Dec. Access, Visa.*

St Agnes   Driftwood Spars Hotel

Tel 0872 552428	Pub
Trevaunance Cove St Agnes Cornwall TR5 0RT	Map 12 B3

Constructed in the 17th century of huge ship's timbers and spars
(hence the name), with stone and slate, the hotel is 100 yards from one
of Cornwall's best beaches. Seven of the ten rooms are en suite and one
is a family room with bunk beds. Rooms are equipped with TVs,
telephones, tea and coffee-making facilities and hairdryers. Guests are
treated to the sound of waves on the beach and live music from West
Country bands on Fridays and Saturdays. Beer garden across the road.
Recommended for B&B only. *Open all day Mon-Sat, usual hours Sun.
Free House. Beer Tetley, Burton. Family room. Children's Menu. Garden.
Accommodation 10 bedrooms, 7 en suite, £58 (single £29). Children
welcome overnight, cots supplied, under-2s no charge, 2-6 years half price.
Access, Amex, Diners, Visa.*

St Albans   Kingsbury Mill Waffle House

Tel 0727 853502	Waffle House
St Michael Street St Albans Hertfordshire	Map 15 E2

The building is an old water mill, in use until 1936 and restored in 1973. You can eat inside or in the pretty garden/terrace. What you eat will be plain or wholewheat waffles, Belgian style, using free-range eggs and organic flour. Savoury varieties include ratatouille (£3.65) and ham, cheese and mushroom (£4.20), while sweet choices range from coconut (£1.70) and spiced fruit to chocolate mousse (£2.50). Four high-chairs; no children's portions; fenced-in garden. "No service charge – it's our pleasure." *Seats* 80. **Open** *11-6 (Sun from 12).* **Closed** *Mon except Bank Holidays, Tue after Bank Holiday Mon, 25 & 26 Dec. Access, Visa.*

St Albans   Sopwell House Hotel & Country Club   65%   £108

Tel 0727 864477 Fax 0727 844741	Hotel
Cottonmill Lane Sopwell St Albans Hertfordshire AL1 2HQ	Map 15 E2

The country club is the centrepiece of this much extended 18th-century house. There are plenty of ways to pamper yourself – indoor pool plus toddler pool, supervised gymnasium, beautician and hairdressing. The grand marble entrance hall sets a good impression and efficient staff are genuinely welcoming to families. The Brasserie (7am-10pm) offers informal meals in a conservatory setting and the kitchen will gladly fulfil orders of boiled eggs and soldiers for smaller diners, as well as small portions of most dishes on the menu. Cots and high-chairs are supplied and baby-sitting and baby-listening can be arranged. *Rooms* 92. *Garden, gymnasium, indoor swimming pool, sauna, solarium, spa bath, steam room, beautician, hairdressing, snooker. Access, Amex, Diners, Visa.*

St Dominick   The Edgcumbe Arms at Cotehele Quay

Tel 0579 50024	Tea Room
The Quay Cotehele St Dominick nr Saltash Cornwall	Map 12 C3

A stretch of woodland, containing a chapel built by Richard Edgcumbe during the Wars of the Roses, separates Cotehele Quay from Cotehele House (near the village of Callington). Along the quayside, amid a row of 18th and 19th-century houses, The National Trust's Edgcumbe Arms is sited in a former lime worker's cottage which became a public house. It looks out on to the *Shamrock,* the sole surviving stone-carrying Tamar barge, and the River Tamar. Drinks and light refreshments are available all day: home-made soup (£2.25), paté, ploughman's, fisherman's lunch (£3.90 – smoked mackerel fillet), jacket potatoes (£2.75), home-made fruit pie and clotted cream (£2.25), various cakes and biscuits, and traditional Cornish Cream Tea (£2.85) with Cornish splits (soft white yeast buns). A quarter of a mile up the hill at the late-medieval Cotehele House, the converted barn in the terraced grounds is now **The Barn** restaurant serving a variety of inexpensive hot and cold dishes. (In season, visitors are required to pay a grounds only entrance fee (£2.50) to eat at the restaurant). Licensed with meals. Children's portions. No smoking. *Seats* 76. **Open** *11-5.30 (Apr-Oct), 11-4 (Sat & Sun only in Nov, Wed-Sun in December, Sun only Jan, Feb, Mar). Access, Amex, Visa.*

St Ives   Slepe Hall   61%   £60

Tel 0480 463122 Fax 0480 300706	Hotel
Ramsey Road St Ives Cambridgeshire PE17 4RB	Map 10 B2

A Grade II listed building dating from 1848 and originally a private
boarding school for girls. Now a small, comfortable hotel, it's kept
in excellent order by Jan and Colin Stapleton. Several bedrooms
feature four-poster or half-tester beds, and among the public areas
is the Brunel Suite, which can cater for 220 conference delegates
or banqueters – weddings receptions may dominate at weekends, so ask
in advance. Cots, extra beds, high-chairs and half portions are offered
for youngsters. 10 minutes from the town centre. *Rooms 16. Closed 25
& 26 Dec. Access, Amex, Diners, Visa.*

St Martin's   St Martin's Hotel   69%   £178*

Tel 0720 22092 Fax 0720 22298	Hotel
St Martin's Isles of Scilly TR25 0QW	Map 12 A2

Hotel launch and Suzuki 4-wheel drive provide transport for arrivals,
so make your travel arrangements when booking. St Martin's, 28
miles out in the Atlantic, provides the ultimate escape for solitude
seekers, an equally novel activity centre for families (under-14s stay
free in parents' room), and the last word in privacy for a conference
(max 100) or private dinner (up to 80). Public rooms include the first-
floor sunset lounge which affords wonderful views westward towards
Tresco. High-chairs, baby-sitting and a funpack on arrival help make
a visit to this informal hotel a joy for children – as they say: "in a place
where they call hedges of escallonia 'fences' and the drystone walls
'hedges', you just know you're somewhere different". *Half-board
terms only. *Rooms 24. Garden, indoor swimming pool, fishing, snooker,
sailing and scuba-diving instruction. Closed Nov-Mar. Access, Amex,
Diners, Visa.*

Restaurant   £55

Table d'hote dinners make good use of fish and shellfish, game and
home-grown vegetables. Typical items on a high-summer menu range
from prawn and lobster salad and grilled skate on a bed of steamed
courgettes to broccoli soufflé and pan-fried strips of pork in a brandy
sauce, garnished with pears. No smoking. Lighter bar lunches.
Seats 80. Private Room 14. L in bar only D 7.15-9. Set D £25.

St Mawgan   Falcon Inn

Tel 0637 860225	Pub
St Mawgan Newquay Cornwall TR8 4EP	Map 12 B3

In the heart of holiday land where good unspoilt traditional pubs are
an endangered breed, the Falcon survives and is a haven for the
discerning pub-goer. Nestling in a most attractive village, deep in the
Vale of Lanherne and a stone's throw from its tiny stream, this 16th-
century wisteria-clad inn is a popular summer destination with those
escaping the bucket-and-spade brigade on the beach. Inside, the main
bar is neatly arranged and decorated with pine farmhouse tables and
chairs, trellis wallpaper and decent prints and is thankfully music and
game-free. The adjacent dining room has a rug-strewn flagged floor,
a pine dresser and French windows leading out into the bench-filled
cobbled courtyard. Beyond a rose-covered arch there is a splendid
terraced garden, ideal for enjoying some summer refreshment.
Children are welcome in the dining room where they can choose

from their own menu or enjoy smaller portions of adult fare. The garden is very safe, with plenty of space for youngsters to run around and a modern climbing frame and slide is available for the even more energetic. The wishing well should appeal to most children's imagination. B&B is also offered, but is not recommended.
Beer *St Austell Tinners, HSB, XXXX Mild. Garden, outdoor eating area. Access, Visa.*

St Michael's Mount   The Sail Loft Restaurant

Tel 0736 710748	Restaurant
St Michael's Mount Marazion Cornwall	Map 12 A4

Take the ferry at high tide or walk across a cobbled causeway for a meal at The National Trust's converted boat store and carpenter's shop. Hot lunches – with local fish a feature – include the Hobbler's Choice (the island ferrymen are known as Hobblers), grilled whole plaice with savoury butter served with parsley potatoes and green salad (£4.95), jacket potatoes (from £2.95) and nutty rice and mushroom loaf with mushroom sauce and side salad (£3.95). Salads (from £4.25-£4.50) include vegetarian Cheddar and savoury seafood cheesecake. Good choice of home-made cakes, biscuits and puddings with the traditional Cornish Cream Tea (£2.85) featuring splits (soft white yeast buns) instead of scones. Four high-chairs; changing shelf in Ladies. No smoking. ***Seats*** *88.* ***Open*** *10.30-5.30.* ***Closed*** *Nov-Mar. Access, Amex, Visa.*

St Neots   Chequers Inn

Tel 0480 472116	Pub
St Mary's Street Eynesbury nr St Neots Cambridgeshire PE19 2TA	Map 15 E1

A lovely old English country pub, where you can sit in the main bar with its roaring winter fires and highly-polished dark furniture or at tables with green tablecloths for bar food, or in the dining area for more substantial meals. The changing blackboard bar menu offers home cooking by landlord David Taylor: cauliflower and broccoli soup (£1.85), steak and mushroom pie (£5.50) or steak and ale pie (£7.25), a substantial ploughman's (£3.95), crispy cauliflower with Provençal sauce (£3.95), pasta with chicken (£5.25). The restaurant proposes the likes of prawn dishes, pork tenderloin in mushroom and pepper sauce (£11.20), creamed mushroom stroganoff (£11.20), lamb's liver and diced bacon in Marsala sauce (£8.50). Children are kept amused in the outdoor play area in the fenced off garden.
Bar Food *12-2, 7-9.45 (Sun to 9.30).* ***Restaurant Meals*** *12-1.45 (Sun to 1.30), 7-9.30 (Sat to 9.45). Free House.* ***Beer*** *Webster's, Sam Smith's. Garden, outdoor eating, children's play area. Access, Amex, Diners, Visa.*

St Neots   Eaton Oak

Tel 0480 219555 Fax 0480 407520	Pub
Crosshall Road Eaton Ford St Neots Cambridgeshire PE19 4AG	Map 15 E1

The completely renovated Charles Wells brewery's Eaton Oak is located at the junction of the A1 and A45 but the bedrooms are happily undisturbed by traffic – you can expect a comfortable overnight stay. The rooms in the motel extension are large and warm, with fitted units, colour TVs, tea-makers, direct-dial telephones and well-fitted bathrooms. In the main building (once a farmhouse) the bar has been extended along with the restaurant and a conservatory added which leads on to the garden. Families are well looked after

(even a free kiddies menu) and an outdoor play area is provided.
Recommended for B&B only. **Beer** *Charles Wells.* **Accommodation**
*9 bedrooms, all en suite, £40 (single £35). Children welcome overnight
(rate depends on age), additional bed available. Check-in by arrangement.
Access, Amex, Visa.*

Salcombe	Soar Mill Cove	66%	·	£128
Tel 0548 561566 Fax 0548 561223				Hotel
Soar Mill Cove nr Salcombe Devon TQ7 3DS				Map 13 D3

Spectacular coastal location and unrivalled sea views make for
a memorable holiday hotel. The closeness of 14 bedrooms, all
at ground level with neighbouring patios, readily engenders a house
party atmosphere, much in keeping with the Makepeace family's
philosophy, and to which the staff contribute willingly. Thoroughly
comfortable bedrooms, close-carpeted through to equally adequate
bathrooms (some new bathrooms have recently been built), provide
essential ingredients for a peaceful stay. The National Trust sandy
beach and cliff walks prove highly popular daytime activities. Families
with young children are admirably catered for (ages 1-6 charged 20%
of tariff, 6-15 30%); high tea at 5pm is designed to leave adult residents
in peace in the dining room during dinner. An ongoing upgrading
programme has recently seen a new entrance hall, and enhanced
bedroom and restaurant decorations. Breakfast includes the option
of Salcombe smokies (kippered mackerel). **Rooms** *14. Garden, indoor &
outdoor swimming pools, tennis, putting, games room, laundry room. Closed
Nov-early or mid-Feb. Access, Amex, Visa.*

Salcombe	South Sands	60%		£136*
Tel 0548 843741 Fax 0548 842112				Hotel
Cliff Road Salcombe Devon TQ8 8LL				Map 13 D3

Under the same ownership as the *Tides Reach Hotel* nearby, but even
closer to the shore with the sandy beach reaching right up to the
terrace walk, the South Sands caters more for younger children.
Parents can sit and have a drink on the terrace while the children play
in full view on the beach just below. There are ten family suites
and a special high tea for youngsters served in the terrace bar/coffee
shop anytime up to 7.30pm. Main public room is a spacious,
comfortably leather-furnished bar/lounge with splendid views over
the bay. Generally good-sized bedrooms, half with freestanding pine
and half with white melamine fitted furniture, are uncluttered, with
carpeted, fully tiled bathrooms. Friendly staff. No room service. A fine
location for a classic British seaside holiday without the promenade
and day-trippers; a small ferry goes directly from the beach into town
regularly and there are wonderful cliff-top walks over the Bolt Head –
the children will really feel that they've had a holiday here. *Half-
board terms only, but B&B in early and late season. **Rooms** *30. Indoor
swimming pool, spa bath, steam room, solarium, moorings, children's
playroom, coffee shop (noon-8.30 high season only). Closed Nov-around end
of Mar. Access, Visa.*

Salisbury	Harpers		
Tel 0722 333118			Restaurant
6 Ox Row Market Place Salisbury Wiltshire			Map 14 C3

Providing you order something more than just tea or coffee, there's
no minimum charge at this friendly first-floor restaurant overlooking

the Market Square. Various set and à la carte menus offer good value
and a wide choice that ranges from fish soup (£3.30) to mild-cured
pork loin marinated in sage, orange mustard and honey (£8.50),
breadcrumbed sole with tartare sauce (£4.70), beefsteak casseroled
in vegetables with parsley dumplings (£4.70) and Harpers nut loaf
(£7.90) – there are always plenty of vegetarian options (pasta
diavola – tossed in a tomato-based sauce with fresh chili and ginger
£4.10 or lentil, mushroom and tomato lasagne with mozzarella
£4.70). Everything is home-cooked with Adrian Harper in the
kitchen and wife Ann running front of house. No-smoking area.
*Seats 60. Open 12-2 & 6.30-10 (Sat to 10.30). Closed Sun (except
for D in summer), 25 & 26 Dec, 1 Jan. Access, Amex, Diners, Visa.*

Salisbury   Michael Snell Tea Rooms

Tel 0722 336037	Tea Room
8 St Thomas's Square Salisbury Wiltshire SP1 1BA	Map 14 C3

Michael Snell's splendid establishment is a former school, tucked
between St. Thomas's church and a rushing weir. In addition to the
two rooms and outside eating areas, there's a shop selling cakes and
chocolates. The regular snacks on the substantial menu are
supplemented by a dish of the day such as steak and kidney pie (£5.25
with vegetables) or moonraker vegetable pie (£5.45). Michael bakes
the ham for salad (£5.95) as well as the many gateaux and pastries
(95p-£2.70). A Wiltshire Cream Tea is served (£3.35) with
a selection of teas or home-roasted coffee. At busy lunchtimes, there's
a £4 minimum charge in the school tea room. Under-10s have their
own menu; two high-chairs; tiny Ladies. No-smoking areas.
*Seats 112. Open 9-5 (Sat from 8.30). Closed Sun, Bank Holidays.
No credit cards.*

Salisbury   Old Castle

Tel 0722 328703	Pub
Old Castle Road Salisbury Wiltshire	Map 14 C3

Having taken the family on a stroll around the ruins of Old Sarum,
carefully cross the main road into the safe confines of the Old Castle,
which welcomes children of all ages. Active youngsters enjoy jumping
around in the summer bouncy castle or careering down the long
slippery slide in the large garden. During inclement weather facilities
are welcome in the wicker furnished garden Room, where there are
high-chairs, a mechanical train ride and baby-changing facilities (with
mat and wipes) in the adjoining Ladies. Food is of very average
quality; children have their own menu of favourites: Wam, Bam,
Boom (sausage, beans and chips), Gold Digger (chicken nuggets),
Fishing Trip (fish fingers, chips and beans) – all £2.50 – plus filled
jacket potatoes (£2.25). Two high-chairs. The terraced garden has
picnic tables and fine views of Salisbury; youngsters need to be
watched as the road below the pub is busy. Forte Trencherman
Restaurant. *Pub open 11-3 (from 12 Sun) & 5.30-11 (from 6 Sat,
7 Sun), plus 11am-11pm Fri, Sat & Sun in summer. Beer Courage Best
& Directors, Ruddles County. Garden, outdoor eating. Access, Amex, Visa.*

Salisbury   Redcoats Tea Rooms

Tel 0722 414536	Tea Room
58 The Close Salisbury Wiltshire	Map 14 C3

Within the ancient museum of The Duke of Edinburgh's Royal
Regiment in the north-west corner of the cathedral close, this tiny tea
room offers a good range of sandwiches (from £1.35), salads (from
£3), ploughman's and light lunches such as home-made soup, pasties,
quiche (£4) and, from noon, jacket potatoes with various fillings
(from £2). Home baking includes banana cake (70p), passion cake
(£1.10), and various slices. In summer, eat out on the charming,
walled patio or picnic (with food purchased from the tea room only)
on the extensive lawns that reach down to the river. No smoking.
Seats 30 *(plus 30 outside)*. **Open** *10-4.15 (Fri to 4)*. **Closed** *most Dec/Jan.
No credit cards.*

Satwell   The Lamb Inn

Tel 0491 628482	Pub
Satwell nr Shepherds Green Henley-on-Thames Oxon RG9 4QZ	Map 15 D2

An untypically tiny Thames Valley inn, tucked away off the B841,
two miles south of Nettlebed. Beneath a weird agglomeration
of unevenly pitched roofs, it contains only two small rooms within;
floors are quarry tile and the tables are assorted. Every nook and
cranny seems taken up with collectables: old beer bottles (glass and
earthenware) dating back to the last century; an old dog grate, butter
churn and mangle. There's extra room to spread out in the garden,
while very little ones can frolic on a swing or a slide. Young tenant
licensees, less than sartorially elegant in appearance, seem otherwise
eager to please. **Beer** *Brakspear Best, Special, Old Ale. Garden.
Children welcome indoors to eat. No credit cards.*

Saunton   Saunton Sands   67%   £120

Tel 0271 890212 Fax 0271 890145	Hotel
Saunton nr Braunton Devon EX33 1LQ	Map 12 C1

An ideal, family-oriented resort hotel, where you may park your car
for a week and never need to use it; Saunton Sands commands
panoramic views over the North Devon coastline. Five miles of golden
sands stretch past the door; within, the leisure facilities are as abundant
as the sporting and aquatic activities without. Bedrooms are neat, light
and airy, with Laura Ashley-style fabrics. Children's facilities
include a crèche, play areas, plenty of cots, baby-sitting, baby-listening
and high teas. Three conference suites accommodate 20-200. No dogs.
Rooms 96. *Garden, tennis, squash, indoor & outdoor swimming pools, spa
bath, sauna, solarium, snooker, hairdredressing. Access, Amex, Diners, Visa.*

Seaton Sluice   Castaways Antique & Teashop

Tel 091 237 4548	Tea Shop
32 Collywell Bay Road Seaton Sluice Tyne & Wear	Map 5 E2

Whilst seated in the midst of a vast array of china and glassware bric-
à-brac, most of which is for sale, you can choose from a selection
of home-made sweets and savouries. Quiche and salad, hot beef stotty,
cheese scones (45p) or scone, jam and cream (75p). Cakes include fresh
cream sponge (95p), lemon meringue and cheesecake. A very well-
known place, and very popular in the area. One high-chair, four
booster seats; "bathroom facilities". **Seats** 40. **Open** *11-5.30 (Sat & Sun
from 10.30)*. **Closed** *Mon, Tues, 4 weeks Christmas. No credit cards.*

Seaview   **Seaview Hotel**   **62%**   **£73**

`Tel 0983 612711   Fax 0983 613729`   Hotel

High Street Seaview Isle of Wight PO34 5EX   Map 15 D4

The epitome of a small, family-run seaside hotel – incredibly busy
in high season (Jul, Aug & school holidays), quietly charming at other
times. Nicholas and Nicky Hayward run their popular hotel-cum-
local inn set just back from the sea front with a most appealing
efficiency. A small patio with pub-style white iron tables and chairs
at the front of the hotel is a delightful sun trap from which one can
watch the world (and his wife) go by; it leads into a narrow hallway,
either side of which are a busy bar and a restaurant. Enjoyable bar
snacks (12-2 & 7-9.30 inc D Sun) range from chilled fennel gazpacho
with crusty bread (£1.95), pork and parsley terrine (£3.50) and
herring roes on toasted muffins (£3.60) to two herb sausages and chips
(£2.60), seafood quiche topped with prawns and cheese (£4.95) and,
on Sundays, roast beef with Yorkshire pudding and all the trimmings
(£5.95); treacle sponge (£2.75) or apple pie and cream (£2.40)
to finish. To the rear are two snug lounges (one for non-smokers),
another popular nautically-themed bar with bare boards and an open-
air yard. Public rooms buzz in season, yet are snug in winter. Upstairs,
the bedrooms (some with views over the Solent) are all individually
decorated with predominantly blue and yellow colour schemes and
feature interesting pictures, objets d'art and spotless bathrooms. High
season (July & August) can see the hotel very busy, with literally
dozens of teenagers in the rear courtyard 'sunshine bar'. **Rooms** 16.
Sea fishing, family apartment. Access, Amex, Diners, Visa.

Restaurant   £50

An intimate dining room with close-set tables, candle-lit in the
evenings. Local crab might feature in a creamy soup or a hot ramekin
with tarragon, and oak-smoked Island garlic is used in garlic bread and
to season a salad of mussels and mushrooms. Main courses are
becoming more adventurous. Two sittings in high season and
on Saturday nights. Short, realistically priced wine list. High-chairs
provided "as needed", but not after 7.30pm. **Seats** 32. L 12-2
D 7.30-9.30. *Closed D Sun.*

Sedbergh   **Ye Olde Copper Kettle Tea Room**

`Tel 053 96 20995`   Tea Room

43 Main Street Sedbergh Cumbria   Map 5 D4

Ann Forshaw does the baking – apple pie (£1.45), Yorkshire fruit
cake with Wensleydale cheese (£1.15), sticky toffee pudding (£1.65),
real Yorkshire parkins – while partner Wendy Barry looks after the
savoury side of things with the likes of carrot and orange soup
(£1.35), Cumberland sausage with a baked apple and baked potato
(£3.95), salads with good home-cooked beef or ham, filled granary
rolls (from £1.65), ploughman's (£3.65), Brie fruit salad with
mayonnaise dip and French bread (£3.75), various snacks on toast and
a real trencherman's portion of ham and eggs at £3.95. Everything
is available all day, including the full English breakfast. The setting is a
tiny, cottagey tea room in the cobbled main street of town. Two high-
chairs, baby plates, mugs, cups with Winnie the Pooh designs and
children's favourites (Marmite soldiers, banana butties etc) are
provided. There are baby-changing facilities and an upstairs room has
books, crayons and colouring books. Friday and Saturday evening

there's a short fixed-price dinner menu (£9.50), for which prior booking is required. No smoking. *Seats 32*. *Open 10-6 (winter-5)*. *Closed Tue, one week Nov. No credit cards.*

Shaftesbury   Royal Chase Hotel   60%   £84

Tel 0747 853355 Fax 0747 851969	Hotel
Shaftesbury Dorset SP7 8DB	Map 14 B3

This former monastery, owned by George and Rosemary Hunt for 21 years, is set back from the A30/A350 roundabout on the eastern side of Shaftesbury. Families are well catered for, particularly in holiday periods, and children up to 16 stay free in their parents' room. Some family rooms are close to the pool where parents can sit at tables and watch their water babies. Flexible eating arrangements; high-chairs are provided and there's a mix of children's favourites and smaller main-course portions from which to choose. Outside meal times, there's a large garden plus videos and games indoors to keep the youngsters amused. Purpose-built conference facilities. *Rooms 35. Garden, indoor swimming pool, steam room, solarium. Access, Amex, Diners, Visa.*

Shanklin   Cliff Tops Hotel   64%   £70

Tel 0983 863262 Fax 0983 867139	Hotel
Park Road Shanklin Isle of Wight PO37 6BB	Map 15 D4

One of the Isle of Wight's largest hotels enjoys panoramic views from its position on the cliff 300 feet above Sandown Bay (a public lift down to the seafront is right alongside). There's a choice of bars, a leisure club, conference rooms for up to 250 delegates and plenty of facilities for children. Most of the bedrooms have balconies. Children up to 14 stay free in parents' room (50% discount in their own room). Following a period of uncertainty, the hotel changed hands last summer and the tariff has now been reduced; good-value weekly and two-day half-board rates now apply in high season. All children join the Sammy Seagull Club on arrival and are given a fun case and badge; high tea (5-6pm), separate dining area with video entertainment, supervised crèche (9am-1pm) during school holidays, aquaglide in the indoor pool, baby-listening and high-chairs are all on offer. *Rooms 88. Garden, indoor swimming pool, gymnasium, sauna, spa bath, steam room, solarium, beauty & hair salon, snooker, children's play area. Access, Amex, Diners, Visa.*

Shanklin   Hambledon Hotel

Tel 0983 862403	Hotel
Queens Road Shanklin Isle of Wight PO37 6AW	Map 15 D4

A home from home is what Beryl and Norman Birch aim to provide at their comfortable family hotel close to the beach; guests can use the leisure facilities (swimming pool, water slide, sauna, spa bath, steam room and gym) at the nearby (50yds) Cliff Tops Hotel for a nominal charge. Two suites and five large rooms have ample space for the cots (with linen) provided and amenities include high-chairs, boosters, toys and children's books. Nappies and baby clothes placed in a special bucket in the bedroom will be washed, dried and returned the same day and by night there is a baby-listening service and patrol by 'Aunty' Beryl, a qualified nursery nurse. All bedrooms have en-suite showers but a bathroom is provided for children who prefer something in which they can sail a rubber duck. Children may eat with parents or take early tea at 5pm. Special diets are catered for and food will

be puréed for babies. Outside is a safe garden, with slide. £179 half
board per person per 7 day, high-season stay. Under-1s £2.50 per day;
1-3s £46, 4-10s £90, 11-14 £134 per week. **Rooms** 11. *Access, Visa.*

Shepperton Blubeckers Eating House

Tel 0932 243377	Restaurant
Church Square Shepperton Middlesex TW17 9JY	Map 15 E2

Not quite matching the stylish country mill setting of its sister outlet
in Odiham, Hants (our 1992 Family Restaurant of the Year), this well-
established restaurant is right on a bend in the road opposite
Shepperton's pretty church square. The old building contains a warren
of rooms filled with check tablecloths and high-chairs with balloons
tied to them. Almost as soon as one sits down the helpful, efficient staff
produce a jokey children's menu, along with a cup of wax crayons.
A new children's menu now offers fish sticks, junior burger, cheesey
potato skins, roosters' chicken, ribs, chicken on a stick and scampi
(£1.95-£3.75), all served with fries or baked potato, baked beans
or fresh vegetables. There's a long list of tempting puddings (£1.45-
£1.95) for adults; Smartie smacker topped with a sparkler (£1.45),
bananas and shark-infested custard (£1.25), chocolate dipper and
pancakes with soft ice cream for children; oddly-named children's
cocktails (humdinger, slime juice, Dracula's dribble £1.25) should also
raise a laugh. Sunday lunch is a real bargain – £7.95 for three courses
with a choice of any starter or pudding from the normal dinner menu.
Good ribs, burgers, haddock and spinach potato-topped pie plus
desserts that should test even the finest of trenchermen! There is no
room in the Ladies to change a baby, but otherwise this a fine
destination for a family outing, albeit a little cramped and underlit.
After lunch a short stroll past the Warren Lodge Hotel will take you
to the edge of the Thames where ducks will delight younger children.
See also entry under Odiham. **Seats** 85. **Open** *L Sun only (also every
day during December 12-3) 12.30-9.30, D 6.15-11 (from 6 Fri & Sat,
to 11.30 Fri & Sat).* **Closed** *3 days Christmas.*

Sherborne Eastbury Hotel 67% £98

Tel 0935 813131 Fax 0935 817296	Hotel
Long Street Sherborne Dorset DT9 3BY	Map 13 F2

Built in 1740, the Eastbury is a fine Georgian town house with well-
proportioned rooms. Public areas comprise an elegant entrance hall,
a comfortably furnished lounge, a library and an intimate cocktail bar
with an ornately carved counter. Bedrooms, named after English
flowers, have smart polished-wood furniture and pretty fabrics.
Bathrooms offer showers and tubs, plus good soaps and toiletries.
No dogs. Families are well catered for – children up to 10 stay free
in parents' room. Large conservatory restaurant overlooking the
garden; high-chairs provided. Clipper Hotels. **Rooms** 15. *Garden.
Access, Visa.*

Sherborne Oliver's

Tel 0935 815005	Café
19 Cheap Street Sherborne Dorset	Map 13 F2

On one of Sherborne's characterful main streets, Oliver's is a former
delicatessen with its original tiled walls, little pine tables, plants and
rustic ornaments. The self-service counter displays a tempting range
of croissants from 80p, gateaux from £1, deliciously rich treacle tart

£1.50, sandwiches and rolls from £1.70, quiche £1.50, pizza £2, cold meats and salads from £2.50. In the winter there are hearty hot dishes like casseroles (from £2.50), whilst filled baked potatoes are served all year round. A choice of teas, espresso and iced coffee. Children's portions. Mostly non-smoking. **Seats** *55.* **Open** *9-5 (Sat to 5.30, Sun 10-5)* **Closed** *25 Dec. Access, Amex, Visa.*

Shrewsbury The Good Life

Tel 0743 350455	Vegetarian

Barracks Passage Wyle Cop Shrewsbury Shropshire Map 6 A3

A narrow passage off Wyle Cop leads to this informal vegetarian restaurant in three rooms of a restored 14th-century building. Upstairs is the no-smoking area and downstairs offers counter service providing fresh food throughout the day: various quiches – asparagus, sweetcorn and cheese (from £1.50) or hot specials like lasagne, spinach moussaka or savoury cheese vegetable bake (all £2.05). Home-made puddings (£1.50), cakes and scones are also available. **Seats** *65.* **Open** *9.30-3.30 (Sat to 4.30).* **Closed** *Sun, Bank Holidays. No credit cards.*

Sidmouth Victoria Hotel 67% £120

Tel 0395 512651 Fax 0395 579154	Hotel

The Esplanade Sidmouth Devon EX10 8RY Map 13 E2

Named after Queen Victoria, a frequent visitor to her neighbouring residence, the hotel was actually opened early in the reign of Edward VII. Lounges are roomy and relaxing, and most of the well-appointed bedrooms face the sea (many have French windows leading to private balconies). Families are well catered for with good leisure facilities, baby-sitting and considerations for children in the dining room. Room service is available at any hour. Only really suitable for children during Christmas and high summer season (when entertainment is provided), as the rest of the year sees mainly elderly folk enjoying the sea breezes. No dogs. **Rooms** *65. Garden, indoor & outdoor swimming pools, keep-fit equipment, squash, sauna, spa bath, solarium, hairdressing, tennis, putting, snooker & games room, lock-up garages. Access, Amex, Diners, Visa.*

Sissinghurst Granary Restaurant

Tel 0580 712850	Restaurant

Sissinghurst Castle Sissinghurst Kent TN17 2AB Map 11 C5

Part of the National Trust-run Sissinghurst Gardens, there is free parking and no entrance fee if just visiting the restaurant although it would be a pity to miss Vita Sackville-West's garden with its famous 'outdoor rooms'. Formerly a cow-shed, the self-service restaurant is full of exposed beams, and picture windows look out across neighbouring farmland. Almost everything on a fairly extensive menu is made on site with main dishes like steak and kidney pie, chicken à la king (both £5.95) and ratatouille with rice (£5.50), and light lunches – jacket potatoes (from £1.35), salmon mousse, ploughman's (£4.25), cottage cheese ploughman's (£3.50), salads (from £5.50) – served until 3 or 3.30pm after which the cakes and pastries take centre stage: caramel slice (95p), chocolate éclair (£1.10), caramel and banana pie (£1.85); croissant, cream and strawberries (£1.40), meringue Chantilly (£1.35) and much else besides including scones and a traditional Kentish cream tea (£2.95). Be prepared to queue at busy times. Licensed to serve alcohol only with full meals. Four high-chairs are available and most things are available in small portions and reduced prices. On sunny days children can play on a grassy area outside. No smoking (or changing facilities). **Seats** 300. **Open** 12-5.30 (Sat & Sun from 10). **Closed** all Mon, Oct-Good Friday (except Oct 27-Dec 24 when open Wed-Sat 11-3). Access, Visa.

Skelwith Bridge   Chesters
| Tel 05394 32553 | Café |

Kirkstone Galleries Skelwith Bridge nr Ambleside Cumbria   Map 4 C3

Enjoying a pretty riverside setting next to Skelwith Bridge, this appealing café shares space with the showroom and shop of a restored slate works – Kirkstone Galleries. An impressive array of home baking (55p-£1.80) includes chocolate fudge cake, John Peel pie, tiffins, carrot cake with fudge topping, lemon yoghurt cake, orange and coconut cake, date slices, flapjacks and several puddings (banana toffee or apple and passion fruit flan – £1.80 or Chesters meringues £1.40). Given the popularity of Karen Lawrence's cakes, the savoury menu is kept small – home-made soup (curried parsnip or mushroom and split pea – £1.75), quiches (leek, cheese and broccoli £2.95), selection of rolls (from £1.75) or walnut and Stilton paté (£2.25). Terrace in front for summer days. Children's portions of savoury items; one high-chair provided. Changing facilities in Gallery staff toilet. Chester is a rather old, extremely stubborn and particularly unattractive English bull terrier, but don't let that put you off! No smoking inside. **Seats** 50. **Open** 10-5.30 (winter to 4.45). **Closed** 24-26 Dec, 1 Jan, 1 week Jan. No credit cards.

Skipton   Randell's Hotel   65%   £78
| Tel 0756 700100   Fax 0756 700107 | Hotel |

Keighley Road Snaygill Skipton North Yorkshire BD23 2TA   Map 6 C1

A purpose-built hotel, just south of the town centre, standing by the Trans-Pennine Waterway. Spacious bedrooms are light and contemporary with fully-tiled private facilities. Day rooms include an open-plan lobby and a first-floor bar. There's also a well-equipped leisure centre that offers splendid facilities for over-7s in the form of the Young Adventurers' Club as well as a baby pool. The hotel's Playzone supervised nursery/crèche (shared with non-residents) for under-7s is open from 8am-6pm weekdays, 10-2 Sat and 11-3 Sun and is equipped with table toys, games, house corner and paints; "...we've qualified and experienced staff who like to play and love to laugh – there's water, dough, paint and sand, home corner and messy play to hand...". Babies can rest in a separate quiet room. Changing facilities (including baby wipes and nappies) are also provided. Children can either eat in the nursery or with their parents and can choose from the children's menu. Ten high-chairs are provided together with booster seats, beakers and cutlery. The hotel's restaurant has a fenced-off terrace overlooking the canal. Children up to 16 stay free in parents' room; 7 to 14-year-olds have free membership of the Young Adventurers club ("for fun and frolics") every Saturday and during school holidays. **Rooms** 61. Indoor swimming pool, gymnasium, squash, sauna, spa bath, solarium, hair & beauty salon, coffee shop (7am-10pm). Access, Amex, Diners, Visa.

South Holmwood   Gourmet Pizza Company

| Tel 0306 889712 | Pizzeria |

Horsham Road South Holmwood nr Dorking Surrey   **Map 15 E3**

The pizzas (if not the puds) live up to the name with generous
amounts of topping – made from fresh ingredients – in some unusual
combinations. Chinese duck (£7.95) with Peking duck and plum
sauce, smoked Edam, broccoli, spring onions, coriander and ginger;
English Breakfast (£5.25) with Cumberland sausage, smoked bacon,
tomatoes, mushrooms and two eggs; and Cajun prawn and chicken
with spinach, roasted yellow peppers, roasted garlic, ginger and sweet
pickle (£7.95) among other more classic varieties. There are also some
good salads and a handful of pasta dishes. Six high-chairs, crayons
provided at the table for colouring the kids menu (child-size pizzas
and pasta ribbons or twirls £1.75-£2.25; lollipops for those who
finish all their food); baby changing room. Children's parties. Purpose-
built adventure playground and lawned, fenced garden outside. Part
of a small chain, this one is about two miles south of Dorking on the
A24. Ample parking (for 60 cars). No-smoking area. **Seats** 85 (*plus
30 outside*). **Open** *noon-11pm (Fri & Sat to 11.30).* **Closed** *25 & 26 Dec.
Access, Amex, Visa.*

South Molton   Corn Dolly

| No telephone | Tea Shop |

115a East Street South Molton Devon EX36 3DB   **Map 13 D2**

Tracy Dodd and her friendly crew continue their commendable
reliance on local produce, free-range eggs and fine home baking at her
'Real Tea Shop' attached to a tiny craft and gift centre where speciality
teas, coffees and Devon relishes are also sold. By keeping the menu
selection simple, the quality is assured: King's Ransom (£4.25) –
a grilled stilton-covered teacake – is a perennial favourite; Seafarer's
Tea (£3.45) features locally smoked mackerel; also ham and cheese
grills – ham topped with red Leicester and mature Cheddar and grilled
until bubbling (£3.40). Two high-chairs and a bouncer chair
provided. Children's teas (£1.55) include Little Bo Peep (buttered
scone and jam, jelly, ice cream and juice), Little Jack Horner (Marmite
soldiers, fruit cake and juice) or Humpty Dumpty (boiled egg and
soldiers plus juice). **Seats** 20. **Open** *9.30-5 (Mon from 10, Wed to 2,
Sat 10-5.30).* **Closed** *Sun. No credit cards.*

Southwold   The Swan   65%   £88

| Tel 0502 722186   Fax 0502 724800 | Hotel |

Market Place Southwold Suffolk IP18 6EG   **Map 10 D2**

The ancient Swan (rebuilt in 1660 and remodelled in the 1820s) faces
the market place of a most charming seaside town. An old long-case
clock and fresh flowers grace the flagstoned foyer and an abundance
of sofas the period drawing room. Main-house bedrooms are
traditional in style with freestanding furniture, including the odd
antique, while simpler chalet-style rooms surround a garden to the
rear. An adjacent brewery can occasionally disturb the peace during
the day. Good bar snacks. **Rooms** 45. *Access, Amex, Visa.*

Restaurant   £65

An elegant, pink dining room and a choice of fixed-price only menus.
Chef David Goode offers an interesting mix ranging from salmon and
lemon sole mousse cake with saffron mayonnaise to braised Norfolk

duck breast with an apple and ginger compote; leave room for puds: lemon meringue pie, praline millefeuille with chocolate sauce and poached pears in a mulled wine syrup are typical. Good British cheeses. Sunday lunch offers a wide choice including vegetarian options. Wines from Adnams, who also own the hotel. *Seats 50. Parties 10. Private Room 20. L 12.15-1.45 (Sun to 1.30) D 7-9.30 (Sun to 9). Closed D 3rd Sun in Jan. Set L £12.50/£16.95 Set D £17.50-£30.50.*

Sowerby Bridge   The Hobbit

Tel 0422 832202 Fax 0422 835381	**Pub**

Hob Lane Sowerby Bridge West Yorkshire HX6 3QL	**Map 6 C1**

Standing in the hamlet of Norland, on the very lip of the moor (follow directions carefully), the Hobbit enjoys panoramic views over the Pennines and Sowerby Bridge far below. Formed out of three old stone cottages, it's a relaxed and welcoming place – a haven for families, with Bilbo's bistro open all day, every day: youngsters receive a fun pad on arrival. The extensive menu covers a range from sandwiches (from £1.95), pasta dishes (from £4.50) and pizzas (£4.25) to grills, chicken grandmère (£6.95), salmon in dill and vermouth sauce (£6.95) and home-made puds. There are also various set menus including a special Early Chick menu for children (£2.65 served between 4 and 6.30pm; £5.95 for adults Mon-Fri only), who are well looked after with high-chairs and booster seats. Bedrooms are modestly furnished, well-kept and spotlessly clean. Connecting bedrooms are available for families, with special weekend rates, while a thoughtful array of accessories appeals equally to the mid-week business traveller (well-lit table, chair, direct-dial phone, radio alarms). Satellite TVs, for instance, include a video channel and fresh milk is conveniently kept in a corridor fridge. A cottage annexe across the road contains splendidly-furnished executive bedrooms which also benefit from the finest views down the valley. No-smoking areas in bistro and restaurant. Pub activities range from quiz nights and murder mystery evenings to charity race nights and in-house discos at the weekends (with the landlord spinning the discs). Half of the spacious bistro is reserved for non-smokers. Expect to book for Saturday nights. *Open 11-11 (up to 2am with meals). Bar Food 12-10.30 (to 11 Fri & Sat, 10 Sun). Beer John Smith, Courage Directors, Ruddles Best. Garden. Family room. Accommodation 21 rooms, all en suite (15 with shower/WC only), £57 (single £39); reduced rates at weekends. Under-5s accommodated free overnight, cots provided, extra beds £10. Access, Amex, Visa.*

Sparsholt   Plough

Tel 0962 776353	**Pub**

Sparsholt nr Winchester Hampshire SO21 2NW	**Map 15 D3**

A delightful flower- and shrub-filled garden complete with children's playhouses, wooden garden chalet, chickens and donkeys is a popular summer feature at this much extended 200-year-old cottage, located on the edge of the village. It has been smartly refurbished by the new tenants, the old 'pub-style' furniture being replaced by pine tables, a dresser and comfortable cushioned chairs, with plenty of attractive prints brightening up the walls and an open brick fireplace for cooler days. Plans are afoot for more improvements to both bars and garden. The bar food on offer is promising as well:

a weekly-changing blackboard menu lists some 12 interesting dishes
that are freshly prepared to order, such as mackerel and gooseberry
paté (£5.25), spaghetti with peppers and Polish sausage (£5.50),
smoked salmon and dill tart (£6.50), guinea fowl with anchovies and
capers (£6.25) and regular favoured specialities like curries, steak and
kidney pudding and various steaks. Vegetarians are not left out, with
at least three choices offered. A short snack menu offering
ploughman's, omelettes and sandwiches is available for both lunch and
supper. Children welcome in the bars if eating. *Bar Food* 12-2, 7-9.30.
Free House. Beer Wadworth IPA, 6X, Farmer's Glory, guest beers.
Garden, children's play area. No credit cards.

Spetisbury   Marigold Cottage

Tel 0258 452468	Tea Room

High Street Spetisbury Blandford Forum Dorset   Map 14 B4

Marigold Cottage is a thatched, whitewashed building dating from the
16th century. The menu covers breakfast (£3.35), roasts at lunchtime
and cream teas £2.75. Home bakes include New Zealand carrot cake
(£1.30) and Afghan chocolate cookies (65p). More elaborate meals
Friday and Saturday evening. Children's portions. No smoking.
Seats 40. Open 9.30-5.30 also *(Fri & Sat only)* 7.30-9.30. *Closed* Mon,
25 Dec-1 Feb. Access, Visa.

Stafford   Soup Kitchen

Tel 0785 54775	Tea Room

Church Lane Stafford Staffordshire   Map 6 B3

Tucked away down a cobbled lane between St Mary's Grove and Mill
Street, the Sandy family's cottagey, 16th-century tea rooms reveal
within a veritable warren of comfortable interlinked rooms, with
plenty of no-smoking areas. Production of home baking through the
day is prodigious, and the choice of lunches – from three soups
(£1.05) through cottage pie and vegetable lasagne (£3.55) to daily
roasts and pies – is both extensive and predictable. "Families welcome:
children and grannies adored" is their highly appropriate motto;
children's favourites (around £1.65), six high-chairs, bibs, toys and
feeder cups plus changing facilities with mat all provided. *Seats 170.*
Open 10-5 (Sat from 9.30). Closed Sun and Bank Holidays.
No credit cards.

Stafford   Tillington Hall   63%   £80

Tel 0785 53531 Fax 0785 59223	Hotel

Eccleshall Road Stafford Staffordshire ST16 1JJ   Map 6 B3

Half a mile from the M6 (J14), this modern De Vere hotel adds good
leisure and conference facilities to decent bedrooms that range from
singles to four-poster rooms. Children up to 14 share adult
accommodation at no charge, with breakfast included. Its main
attraction for families is obviously the proximity of Alton Towers;
packed lunches can be provided. Fun pack given to children on arrival,
entertainment during holiday periods and children's channels on the
satellite TV. *Rooms 90. Garden, indoor swimming pool, gymnasium,
sauna, spa bath, solarium, beauty salon, tennis, snooker, coffee shop (10am-
10pm). Closed 28 & 29 Dec. Access, Amex, Diners, Visa.*

Stamford   George of Stamford, Garden Lounge

Tel 0780 55171	Lounge Snacks

St Martin's High Street Stamford Lincolnshire   Map 7 E3

The bright and airy Garden Lounge of this grand old coaching inn
(recommended in both our Hotels & Restaurants and Pubs & Inns
Guides) offers a good choice of snacks. The buffet offers a large
selection of meats (£9.50) or cold salmon (£9.50), whilst the menu
has various hot dishes: fresh baked mussels (£5.95), whole grilled
plaice with tartare sauce (£9.45), Gruyère cheese fritters with quince
jelly (£6.95), vegetarian fritto misto (£6.45) or chargrilled lamb's
liver (£6.95). In addition, the Pasta Menu offers seven choices (all
£6.95). Puddings (£3.45) include summer pudding, pavlova, pecan
pie and lemon meringue pie. Sandwiches, scones and teacakes are
available at tea time. Set tea £6.50, set breakfast £10. There are
several tables on the pretty cobbled patio for alfresco eating; five
high-chairs; ask for children's portions. *Seats 100.* **Open** *7am-11pm*
(Sun to 10.30). Access, Amex, Diners, Visa.

Stanstead Abbots   Briggens House   70%   £106

Tel 0279 792416 Fax 0279 793685	Hotel

Stanstead Road Stanstead Abbots nr Ware Hertfordshire SG12 8LD   Map 15 F2

A large, stately home-from-home, a few miles off the M11, set in 45
acres of grounds with its own 9-hole golf course. High standards
of service are typified by the smart, uniformed doormen.
A magnificent carved wood staircase leads up from the entrance hall
with its glass chandelier to 22 bedrooms in the main house; 32 more
are in the converted coach house and have lower ceilings, but all are
equally tastefully decorated with a good range of extras included
as standard. Swagged drapes and stylish reproduction antiques give
an elegant air. In summer, tables are set on the expansive lawns outside
the French windows leading off the lounge. A fun pack is provided for
children and there are four cots, with bedding, for the five family
rooms. Baby-listening/sitting is offered. Children may have high tea
in the restaurant (high-chairs/half portions) or eat in their rooms but
they are not allowed in the dining room at night. Large gardens
with a pond and an unheated swimming pool. Laundry service.
Children under 12 free in parents' room. Queens Moat Houses.
Rooms *54. Garden, outdoor swimming pool, tennis, 9-hole golf course,*
bowls, fishing. **Closed** *1 week Christmas. Access, Amex, Diners, Visa.*

Stapleford   Stapleford Park   86%   £142

Tel 057 284 522 Fax 057 284 651	Hotel

Stapleford nr Melton Mowbray Leicestershire LE14 2EF   Map 7 E3

"19th-century hospitality backed up by 21st-century technology" is the
stated aim at *Chicago Pizza Pie* entrepreneur Bob Payton's sumptuous
country house hotel and "sporting estate"; set in a majestic stately
home surrounded by 500 acres of mature parkland, they bet that "the
former (hospitality) is easier to deliver than the latter (technology)". Its
welcoming air of informality in a formal setting, freshness and
spontaneity owe much to its larger-than-life creator, who with his
carefully chosen young staff idiosyncratically cuts out the snobbery;
he also obviously enjoys taking coals to Newcastle! The result is casual
luxury at its best, evident throughout day rooms that exude quality

and style and in wonderful bedrooms individually designed by such
eminent names as David Hicks and Turnbull & Asser. The splendid
library, lounge and galleried salon abound with beautiful fabrics, oil
paintings and ornaments; each bedroom shares this comfortable style
with wonderful marble-tiled bathrooms and numerous thoughtful
extras. Children up to 10 stay free in their parents' room; cots
provided and baby-sitting can be arranged. If you have a basketball-
mad child and want to get away to a country-house hotel with
a difference then look no further! Golf, horse-riding and hunting can
be arranged nearby. Dogs welcome. ***Rooms** 35. Garden, croquet, fishing,
tennis, pitch & putt, basketball. Access, Amex, Diners, Visa.*

Restaurant   £70

Stapleford's restaurant style is light-hearted and isn't afraid to serve
French fries when appropriate. Lunch menus might feature Caesar
salad, grilled chicken (with French fries) and cheeseburgers.
At dinnertime the menu extends to incorporate popular
Mediterranean flavours. Twelve tables are set on a terrace for alfresco
dining in good weather. A 'casual menu' is also served all day.
In certain respects the hotel and restaurant may be laid back, however
"ties are not required in the evening but men are requested to wear
a jacket". No smoking. ***Seats** 70. Parties 10. L 12-3 (Sun to 3.30)
D 7-10 (Sat to 10.30, Sun to 9.30). Set D £19.92.*

Stockport   Boutinot's Bistro

Tel 061-477 0434	Bistro
8 Vernon Street Stockport Cheshire	Map 6 B2

Friendly bistro run by two sisters. An all-day bumper breakfast ·
(£2.80) offers bacon, sausage, egg, tomato, mushrooms and toast.
Other choices include sandwiches, jacket potatoes, mushroom
pancakes, omelettes and main dishes such as chili con carne, steak
and ale pie and chicken in red wine. Small portions and children's
favourites (sausage, burger or fish fingers with chips and beans plus
ice cream £1.80). Three high-chairs; small area in the Ladies for
changing. No-smoking area. ***Seats** 85. **Open** 8.30-5. **Closed** Sun &
Bank Holidays. No credit cards.*

Stonor   Blades at Stonor Arms

Tel 0491 638345	Brasserie
Stonor nr Henley-on-Thames Oxfordshire RG9 6HE	Map 15 D2

There are two levels of food in this attractively converted former
pub and it's the bar menu that will appeal to snackers. There's
no minimum charge and guests can have as many or as few courses
as they wish. Some typical dishes and prices: tomato and apple soup
(£3.15), chicken liver parfait with quince jelly (£4.25), chargrilled
tuna served on a French bean, olive and mixed leaf salad (£9.15),
crisply roasted leg of duck (£8.65). To finish, perhaps hot pear tart
with caramel sauce and clotted cream or iced Drambuie parfait on an
orange salad. One high-chair; ask for children's portions – although the
dishes are generally rather 'adult' there is usually pasta, fish and chicken
on the menu, but nonetheless it's not really suitable for youngsters.
Only over-10s in the evening. Pleasant conservatory and gravelled
garden with pond in fine weather. ***Seats** 40. **Open** 12-2 & 7-9.30 (Sun
to 9). Access, Amex, Visa.*

Stow-on-the-Wold   Fosse Manor   60%   £95

Tel 0451 830354 Fax 0451 832486	Hotel
Fosse Way Stow-on-the-Wold Gloucestershire GL54 1JX	Map 14 C1

Resident proprietors Bob and Yvonne Johnston (21 years at the helm) and their loyal staff run a family haven that attracts many repeat visits. Built in the style of a Cotswold manor house, it stands in its ivy coat in grounds set back from the A429 (originally the Fosse Way). Bedrooms (including ten equipped for family use – cots provided) overlook colourful gardens and the bright look of the day rooms is enhanced throughout by potted plants, fresh flowers and spotless housekeeping. Family facilities include supervised play times for children in a playroom and playground on high days and holidays; children's menu of firm favourites. *Rooms 20. Garden, sauna, spa bath, solarium, beauty salon. Closed 22-30 Dec. Access, Amex, Diners, Visa.*

Stratfield Turgis   Wellington Arms

Tel 0256 882214 Fax 0256 882934	Inn
Stratfield Turgis Basingstoke Hampshire RG27 0AS	Map 15 D3

Hard by the A33 between Basingstoke (M3 Junction 6) and Reading M4 (Junction 11), behind a handsome white Georgian facade, a charming former coaching inn with a mix of old and new. The cosy, pubby L-shaped bar features a polished flagstone floor, a characterful mish-mash of wooden tables and chairs laid for bar snacks, stained-glass detail around the bar itself and swagged heavy drapes above the tall, windows; it leads directly round into an informal drawing room in country-house style with open fire, sunken-cushioned sofas, gilt-framed oil portraits and glass-cased stuffed birds. French windows open on to a small lawned area where picnic tables are set. Light meals and snacks are served in the bar, while the traditional restaurant offers a table d'hote (£14.50) and à la carte; a wooden high-chair is provided. Fifteen bedrooms in the original building include two luxury doubles' (one a suite with a heavily-carved four-poster and spa bath); these are larger and will accommodate a Z-bed. 20 further rooms are in a two-storey modern extension to the rear, uniformly decorated with Laura Ashley pastel blues and yellows plus modern light oak furniture suites, and overlook a grassed area; a travel cot just fits in an alcove. Hotel room facilities like a comfortable armchair, remote-controlled TV, powerful showers and tea/coffee-making facilities are standard; high tea can be ordered from room service (burgers, fish fingers and chips (£2.25) – ask for vegetables, yoghurt etc.). A couple of modern suites serve as family rooms with pull-down additional beds in the sitting room. In winter families may feel cramped, but in summer it's a useful spot to stay. Next door to the Duke of Wellington's estate (Stratfield Saye House, where river fishing can be arranged; open May-Sept) and close to the 550-acre Wellington Country Park (miniature steam train rides, boating on a lake, adventure trail – ideal for family outings, open Mar-Oct). Busy Mon-Thurs with businessmen; restful at weekends, when reduced rates apply. Badger Inns. *Bar Food and Restaurant Meals 12-2.30 & 6.30-10. Closed L Sat, D 25 Dec. Beer Hall & Woodhouse Badger Best. Garden, outdoor eating. Accommodation 35 bedrooms, all en suite, £58 single £48), weekend £45 (single £35). Children welcome overnight, additional cot & extra beds available. Access, Amex, Diners, Visa.*

Stratford-upon-Avon   **Windmill Park**   **64%**   **£98**

Tel 0789 731173   Fax 0789 731131   Hotel

Warwick Road Stratford-upon-Avon Warwickshire CV37 0PY   Map 14 C1

Four linked blocks provide practical accommodation in a modern
redbrick hotel on the A439 (leave the M40 at Junction 15). Fully-
equipped leisure centre; conference facilities for up to 360; many large
family and interconnecting bedrooms, with under-12s staying free
in parents' room. Baby-listening service and a baby-sitter can
be arranged. Children have their own menu (or smaller portions), but
bring your own baby food, which is willingly reheated; high-chairs
provided. *Rooms 100. Indoor swimming pool, gymnasium, sauna, spa
bath, steam room. Access, Amex, Diners, Visa.*

Stretton   **Ram Jam Inn**   **£59**

Tel 0780 410776   Fax 0780 410361   Inn

Great North Road Stretton nr Oakham Leicestershire LE15 7QX   Map 7 E3

Hard by a service station nine miles north of Stamford on the
northbound lane of the A1 (southbound drivers take the B668 exit
to Oakham and follow signs), the Ram Jam Inn provides a comforting
respite from the usual commercial hotels and fast food outlets dotted
along the A1. All the bedrooms overlooking the garden and orchard
are individually and tastefully decorated with limed pine furniture,
and surprisingly quiet considering the proximity to the road. Public
rooms are devoted completely to informal, yet smartly furnished
eating areas (bar, snack, outdoor terrace and restaurant). Popular, quick
snacks include one-inch-thick home-made burgers and giant granary
baps; children's favourites include spaghetti on toast, fish fingers, egg
and chips and chicken fingers. For more substantial fare, one can also
try hot dishes such as poached Polish sausage with warm potato,
shallot and watercress salad (£4.50), stir-fried duck and Oriental
vegetables in ginger and soy sauce (£5.95), half pint of shell-on
prawns with crusty bread and mayonnaise (£4.25) or tortilla chips
with melted cheese and tomato salsa (£3.40). Desserts to tempt even
the most stoically diet-conscious range from rich chocolate mousse
cake with vanilla sauce (£3.95) to French style lemon tart with
blackcurrant coulis (£3.50). Open all day, the Inn also offers
a selection of home-baked cookies and scones for tea. Traditional
Sunday lunch £7. Outdoor terrace overlooking an orchard for
snacking in good weather. Two high-chairs and booster seats
provided; pull-down changing shelf in the Ladies. No-smoking area.
*Rooms 10. Garden, coffee shop (7am-10pm). Closed 25 Dec. Access,
Amex, Visa.*

Restaurant   **£35**

Served in a pleasingly light dining room overlooking the orchard,
an interesting range of dishes runs from prawns with mayonnaise and
spiced confit of duck leg with green lentils, bitter lettuce and sherry
vinegar to Cajun-style lamb steak and a vegetarian Mediterranean
platter. Breakfast is served from 7-10.30. *Seats 40. Private Room 25.
L 12-2.30 D 7-10 (light meals 7am-10pm).*

Strinesdale   Roebuck Inn

Tel 061 624 7819	Pub

Brighton Road Strinesdale nr Oldham Greater Manchester OL4 3RB	Map 6 C2

A family welcome from Sue, Mark, John, Mary and Peter, and a prodigious choice from the menu await those who venture up the moor to the Howarth and Walters families' imposing hillside pub; the pub's not easy to find on a map – it's about a mile off the A672, taking Turfpitt Lane south of Denshaw. While the little ones can choose from fish fingers, beefburgers or sausages (£1.70), a specials board can help buck the otherwise chip-and-peas mentality. Go, perhaps, for avocado with cottage cheese and crabmeat (£2), stir-fry of pork and prawns (£5.50) and cream-soaked sticky toffee pudding (£2). From bookable tables by the picture windows, views down the moor's edge end in an urban skyline; in the foreground a paved yard beckons animal-loving youngsters whose parents don't mind them getting mucky. *Pub open noon-10 for food on Sundays, regular hours other days.* **Bar Food** *12-2.30, 5.30-10 (Sun 12 noon-10). Children allowed in the bar to eat, children's menu.* **Beer** *Whitbread, Boddingtons, Castle Eden. Garden, children's play area. Family room. Access, Amex, Visa.*

Stroud   The Old Lady Tea Shop

Tel 0453 762441	Tea Shop

Threadneedle Street Stroud Gloucestershire	Map 14 B2

The Walker family have owned the bakery below this pleasant first-floor tea shop for over 30 years. There's a small menu of light snacks (toasted sandwich from £1.30, pizza £1.50, ploughman's £2, jacket potato from £1.75) and an understandly good choice of cakes, flapjacks, lardies, cream cakes, doughnuts, gingerbread men, iced buns and excellent light scones (cream tea £2). Unlicensed. *Seats 32. Open 9.30-4.30 (Mon & Thu to 4). Closed Sun, Bank Holidays. No credit cards.*

Studland Bay   Knoll House   63%   £165★

Tel 092 944 251 Fax 092 944 423	Hotel

Studland Bay nr Swanage Dorset BH19 3AH	Map 14 C4

100 acres of land near Studland Beach provide the setting for this friendly hotel, run since 1959 by the Ferguson family with families very much in mind. There's a large adventure playground with a pirate ship, indoor play rooms, family suites with interconnecting rooms and even a children's dining room (strict times: breakfast from 8am, lunch 12.30-1.15, supper 5-6pm; under-5s eat here, as do all under-8s for supper) with a separate kitchen to keep the little ones happy. The health spa is designed for adult relaxation, open from 10.30-1 & 3.30-7.15, but children's hour (for accompanied children under 14) is between 11am and noon. Wooded grounds, a nearby bird sanctuary and a safe, sandy National Trust beach (300yds away) provide other diversions. There's plenty of comfortable lounge space, and bedrooms – neither large nor small – are plain and practical. TVs may be hired. Supervised crèche from 1-2pm for peaceful parents' lunches; picnic lunches are also provided. Baby-listening and sitting can be arranged, as can riding lessons for over-7s at nearby stables. Coach House games room with table-tennis and board games; nursery playroom; self-service laundry. ★Half-board terms, except in high summer season when rates are full board only. Fircone battles are

frowned upon. Winner of our 1991 Family Hotel of the Year award.
Children are charged on a Junior Tariff at a % of the adult rate
according to their age: 13-100%, 5-50%, 6mths to 2-20%. **Rooms** 80.
*Garden, indoor outdoor swimming pool (end May-mid Sept), children's
paddling pool, keep-fit equipment, sauna, steam room, solarium, whirlpool
bath, two tennis courts, golf (9-hole, par 3), boutique.* **Closed** *Nov-Easter.
No credit cards.*

Swindon	Blunsdon House	69%	£93
Tel 0793 721701 Fax 0793 721056			Hotel
Blunsdon Swindon Wiltshire SN2 4AD			Map 14 C2

A farm guest house in 1958, a country club in 1960, and a fully
licensed hotel since 1962 – and the Clifford family have been here
from the beginning. It's a popular conference rendezvous (up to 300
delegates) with extensive leisure club facilities that even extend to a
toddler's splash pool; children are allowed in the Leisure Club until
7pm. Guests are provided with a good standard of comfort in the form
of gardens, formal and casual bars, a residents' lounge, two restaurants
and porterage; younger guests have their own play room and whizz
kids can relax in the Big Lad's computer room. All the bedrooms are
reasonably roomy and many have pleasant views. Decoration and
appointments are of smart modern business standard, and bathrooms
all have shower attachments and ample toiletries; some have spa baths.
A nine-hole golf course opened last year. Families are well catered for;
baby-sitting/listening available (arrange in advance); children up to 16
stay free in parents' room. Plenty of high-chairs and children's tea
is provided by room service; informal eating for families in Carrie's
Carverie; children's menu. No dogs. From Junction 15 of the M4 take
the A419 Cirencester road. After about 7 miles turn right to Broad
Blunsdon. **Rooms** 88. *Garden, indoor swimming pool, gymnasium, squash,
sauna, spa bath, steam room, solarium, beauty & hair salon, all-weather
tennis, 9-hole golf (par 3), putting, games room, snooker, crèche (9am-noon;
parents must stay in hotel), outdoor children's playground, one-mile
woodland jog/walk circuit, skittles.* Access, Amex, Diners, Visa.

Tewkesbury	Tewkesbury Park	62%	£98
Tel 0684 295405 Fax 0684 292386			Hotel
Lincoln Green Lane Tewkesbury Gloucestershire GL20 7DN			Map 14 B1

Built around an 18th-century mansion, but the atmosphere today
is more country club than country house and conferences (up to 150
people) are big business. Well-appointed bedrooms afford views of the
Malvern Hills. Good facilities for families with a supervised crèche
(10-noon) in the leisure club seven days a week and informal eating
arrangements. Children's playroom and playground. No dogs.
Country Club Hotels. **Rooms** 78. *Garden, indoor swimming pool, keep-fit
equipment, squash, sauna, spa bath, solarium, beauty salon, tennis, golf,
snooker, coffee shop (10am-10.30pm).* Access, Amex, Diners, Visa.

Thelbridge Cross	Thelbridge Cross Inn	
Tel 0884 860316		Pub
Thelbridge Cross nr Witheridge Devon EX17 4SQ		Map 13 D2

Attractive white-painted inn, isolated high up in a very rural part
of Devon with views across to Dartmoor. The recently extended and
much modernised interior is carpeted and open-plan in layout with
some comfortable settees and a couple of log fires and is delightfully

free of live music, juke box or pool table. The adjacent barns have been well converted to provide a comfortable block of seven bedrooms and a large self-catering apartment. Bedrooms are rather compact with pretty matching fabrics and modern units but room is found for a telephone, TV, tea-makers and a small fully-tiled shower room. Housekeeping is of a good standard. An occasional attraction is the original 'Lorna Doone' stagecoach which brings extra Sunday lunch trade. A separate family room has a TV and children are offered their own menu of favourites. One high-chair provided. Youngsters will enjoy clambering over the 'enchanted tree' in the garden. Recommended for B&B only. *Free House. **Beer** Bass, Butcombe Bitter, Wadworth 6X. Garden, outdoor eating area. **Accommodation** 7 bedrooms, all en suite, £60 (single £30). Access, Amex, Diners, Visa.*

Threshfield	Old Hall Inn	
Tel 0756 752441		**Pub**
Threshfield nr Grassington North Yorkshire BD23 5HB		Map 6 C1

A lovely stone-built Dales inn, based on a Tudor hall from which comes its name, the Taylors' pub gains further character from its idiosyncratic individuality. An eccentric mix of flagstone floors, classical music and chamber pots suspended from the ceiling is accentuated by the "Brat Board" at ankle height by the fireplace: chicken nuggets and chips followed by two scoops of multi-flavoured ice creams (£2.75) seem fairly brat-proof. Adult choices mix the almost banal Late Breakfast (£5.45) and jumbo fish and chips (£5.95) with the basic Yorkshire puddings (£1.75), Wensleydale ploughman's (£3.25) and the popular seafood bake (£5.95). In the daily specials line, notably fresh market fish predominates, as in queen scallops with cheese and garlic crumbs (£3.85) and baked hake in a tomato and basil sauce (£5.95); for a spicier palate, perhaps, Tuscany chicken (£5.95) or nasi goreng (£5.75). A perennially hectic place; ordering and paying at the bar can be a little chaotic, though for a little peace and quiet the garden is a delightful alternative. A self-contained cottage is let out at around £150 per week. Vanity unit in the Ladies for changing. No high-chairs. Kilnsey Park, with its trout farm, adventure playground and large aquarium, is nearby. *Bar Food 12-2, 6.30-9.30 Tue-Sat). Children's menu. Free House. **Beer** Younger's Scotch, Theakston XB, Timothy Taylor Best. Garden and family rooms. Inn closed all day Monday & Sun eve. No credit cards.*

Thurlestone	Thurlestone Hotel	69%	£160
Tel 0548 560382 Fax 0548 561069			**Hotel**
Thurlestone Kingsbridge Devon TQ7 3NN			Map 13 D3

The elegance of the '20s combines with the amenities of the '90s in a handsome family-owned hotel in a lovely setting with spectacular sea views and close to sandy beaches. Splendidly geared to family holidays (it has an excellent leisure club), particularly at Easter and half-term times with special programmes organised that include magician, film shows, outdoor sports, cartoons, cabaret and competitions (including crosswords!). Baby-sitting/listening can be arranged to allow parents flexibility to enjoy the adult facilities; early-evening children's suppers are also offered. Children up to 16 can stay free of charge in their parents' room. Extensive gardens with swings, climbing frames and climbing net. Riding and sailing can be organised locally for older children. Toddlers will enjoy the indoor paddling pool, nursery menus, cots in family bedrooms and high-chairs. The hotel also has an off-peak trade in small conferences (for up to 100). Day rooms make the most of the location, likewise half the smart, well-equipped bedrooms. Children up to 12 can stay free of charge in their parents' room. *Rooms 68. Garden, indoor & outdoor swimming pools, keep-fit equipment, squash, sauna, sun bed, beauty salon, hairdressing, tennis, golf (9-hole), putting, badminton, games room, coffee shop (8am-10pm). Access, Visa.*

Tickton   Tickton Grange   62%   £56

Tel 0964 543666 Fax 0964 542556	Hotel

Tickton nr Beverley Humberside HU17 9SH   Map 7 E1

A family-owned Georgian house standing just off the A1035 east of Beverley in 3½ acres of rose gardens, where afternoon teas are served in the summer. Day rooms retain a traditional appeal, and bedrooms are decorated in a fresh, light style. There are two suites, one with a Georgian four-poster bed. Tickton truffles are offered on arrival. The Whymant family run the hotel along friendly and informal lines, offering a particularly warm welcome to families. There are four family-size rooms and baby baths, potties, nappies, bottles, a changing mat and baby food are all stocked; a cot is provided free of charge and an extra child's bed is £9.75. In addition, there are swings, a nursery slide and a climbing frame on the lawn and there's a safely enclosed courtyard where the owners' dogs and friendly ducks hold court for interested youngsters. Plenty of lawned areas for letting off steam. *Rooms 16. Garden. Access, Amex, Diners, Visa.*

Tivetshall St Mary   Old Ram

Tel 0379 676794 Fax 0379 608399	Pub

Ipswich Road Tivetshall St Mary Norfolk NR15 2DE   Map 10 C2

Conveniently situated off the A140, between Norwich and Ipswich, the Old Ram dates back to the 17th century. Five 'luxury' en-suite rooms are on offer at this popular roadside family dining pub, and in one of the larger rooms there are two bunk beds for family use. On the eating side, the entire pub is occupied by diners – the bar, the no-smoking area or in the Coach House room which is set up in pew style with refectory-type tables. Try the daily seafood specials like the Billingsgate pot (six varieties of market fresh fish served in a creamy sherry and paprika sauce £7.50), lobster platter (1lb lobster with king prawns £11.95) or jumbo cod in batter (£6.50), skate sautéed in lemon butter sauce (£7.95), Dover sole (£11.95). Non-fish eaters may prefer steak and kidney pie (£6.50), moussaka (£6.50) or chicken in mushroom and parsley sauce (£6.95). Good traditional features and a warming fire in the main bar, which has other nice rooms leading off. Open from 7.30am for breakfast every day and stays open all day until 11pm. *Free House. Bar Meals 7.30am-10pm. Free House. Beer Adnams, Webster's, Woodforde's, Ruddles County. Garden, outdoor eating. Children allowed in the Coach House room to eat. Accommodation 5 bedrooms, all en suite, £59.50 (single £39). Children welcome overnight (£10), but no cots or extra beds provided. Guide dogs only overnight. Access, Visa.*

Tolworth   Superfish

Tel 081-390 2868	○	Fish'n'Chips

59 The Broadway Tolworth Surrey   Map 15 E2

Part of a Surrey-based chain serving above-average fish and chips "fried in the traditional Yorkshire way". A few steps away from the large Marks & Spencer underneath the distinctive tower block by the A3 underpass. See Morden entry for more details. High-chairs; fish bites with chips (£2.20) for children. **Seats 36. Open** 11.30-2 (Sat to 2.30), 5-10.30 (Thu-Sat to 11). **Closed** Sun, 25 & 26 Dec, 1 Jan. No credit cards.

Topsham	**Georgian Tea Room**	
Tel 0392 873465		Tea Room
Broadway House High Street Topsham Devon EX3 0ED		Map 13 B3

Only the bread is not home-made at this tea room in a large Georgian house that you can't miss as you enter town. Decor does not really complement the building but pretty embroidered cloths over the tables add a certain charm. Cakes and cookies – Victorian sponge, fruit cake, date and walnut slice (all at 70p), flapjacks (50p) – are joined at lunchtime by a good range of savoury items ranging from beef lasagne (£3.50), gammon platter (£3.20) and various quiches (from £2) to jacket potatoes, sandwiches and beans on toast. Some dishes, including the cream tea with its home-made jam and clotted cream to go with the excellent scones still warm from the oven, come in smaller portions at a reduced price not only for children but also for the elderly – a nice touch. You'll need to book for lunch on Tuesdays and Thursdays when, in addition to the regular menu, there is a special roast lunch. Feeding cups, bibs and a couple of high-chairs help with the feeding of little ones and there's a box of toys to keep them amused once fed. Unlicensed. No smoking. **Seats 26. Open** 9.30-5. **Closed** Sun, 4 days Christmas. No credit cards.

Tormarton	**Compass Inn**	
Tel 0454 218242		Pub
Tormarton nr Badminton Avon GL9 1JB		Map 13 F1

Creeper-clad in summer; the oldest part of the inn dates back to the late 17th century and the not-entirely-unspoilt bars boast some old timbers and exposed stonework. The Orangery, a glass-roofed courtyard, is a good spot in summer, also a nice, informal room for families. Most of the generally good-sized bedrooms are in a newer wing. Darkwood fitted furniture is the norm with wing armchairs and the usual amenities – beverage tray, trouser press (some with iron and ironing board attached), hairdryer etc. Most of the well-kept bathrooms have tubs (just a few have shower and WC only), many with shower above. Recommended only as a B&B stop-over; food was disappointing on our last two visits. Less than ½ mile from M4 Junction 18. Large, lawned garden. Free House. **Beer** Bass, Smiles, Archers. Garden, terrace. **Accommodation** 31 bedrooms, all en suite, £79 (single £63). Children welcome overnight, additional beds and cots available. Access, Diners, Visa.

Torquay	**Livermead Cliff Hotel**	**60%**	**£80**
Tel 0803 299666 Fax 0803 294496			Hotel
Sea Front Torquay Devon TQ2 6RQ			Map 13 D3

Right by the sea, with direct access to the beach and popular for family holidays. From the M5, take the A379 to Torquay, follow the A3022 through town to the seafront; turn right for Paignton and the hotel is 600 yards along on the seaward side. It's geared up to the conference trade (for up to 70 delegates), so it's quite a busy place all

year round. Picture windows in the lounge look out to sea. Parents
with offspring are well catered for with cots, baby-sitting, baby-
listening and children's high tea available. Good housekeeping, friendly
staff. Lovely outdoor pool and garden overlooking the bay. **Rooms** *64.*
Garden, outdoor swimming pool, solarium, laundry room. Access, Amex,
Diners, Visa.

Torquay	Palace Hotel	68%	£110
Tel 0803 200200 Fax 0803 299899			Hotel
Babbacombe Road Torquay Devon TQ1 3TG			Map 13 D3

Once the home of the Bishops of Exeter, the Palace, set in 25 acres
of gardens and woodland stretching down to the sea, opened in 1921
as a hotel offering some of the finest sporting facilities in the land.
It still provides admirably for the active guest (golf, swimming, tennis
and squash professionals on hand), but the roomy and elegant lounges
hold equal appeal for moments (or hours!) of quiet relaxation. Music
or entertainment is provided nightly, and families are very well
catered for; a supervised crèche operates from 10-1 & 2-7 with a full-
time nanny; high-chairs, cots, extra beds are all provided; baby-
listening is offered and baby-sitting can be arranged; high tea from
5.30pm. Out of season the hotel is often busy with conferences
(handling up to 450 delegates theatre style and offering a full range
of services). Six large bedroom suites have splendid views, individual
decor and good-quality furniture; other rooms are simpler but
comfortable with handsome period bathrooms. No dogs. A large
operation, with tremendous sporting facilities for active teenagers;
younger families might prefer more intimacy. **Rooms** *140. Garden,*
indoor & heated outdoor swimming pools, squash (2), sauna, hairdressing,
indoor (2) & outdoor (4) tennis, 9-hole (par 3) golf course, snooker, table
tennis, children's playroom. Access, Diners, Visa.

Totnes	Willow		
Tel 0803 862605			Vegetarian
87 High Street Totnes Devon			Map 13 D3

Fran Goldsworthy, Paul and Sasha Roberts boldly fly the vegetarian
and vegan flag from the Willow masthead. Their cakes and pastries
throughout the day range from the 'relatively healthy' to the 'luscious
but naughty', with organic milk ices and soya ice cream always
to hand. Daily-changing lunch menus ensure a steady stream
of regulars to sample French Canadian green split pea soup (£1.20),
red wine, olive and tofu dip (£2.20) and perhaps cheese and nut
rissoles baked in ratatouille (£2.95). Evening dishes served with salads
might be Moroccan couscous royale (£5.10), broccoli and tofu
in spicy peanut sauce (£5.40) and mushroom strudel (£5.95).
Wednesday night is exclusively Indian, and Friday live music night.
Organic wines and bottled beers; take-away also available. Children's
menu and safe, enclosed garden. One high-chair and a family room
to the rear. Toys, books and a rocking horse should keep the little ones
occupied after feeding time. All no-smoking (except in garden).
Seats *60.* **Open** *10-5, 6.30-10.* **Closed** *D Mon/Tue, also Thu Sep-Jul,*
all Sun. No credit cards.

Trent   Rose & Crown

Tel 0935 850776	Pub

Trent nr Sherborne Dorset DT9 4SL   Map 13 F2

Initially two separate thatched cottages, the Rose & Crown
is refreshingly unpretentious within, simply furnished, with a rug-
strewn stone floor and roaring log fires in winter. No pub games, fruit
machines or music, but children's play things in the garden. There's
a great emphasis on good fresh food, though, making good use of local
gardens and farms. The 40-seat conservatory restaurant serves dishes
such as smoked pigeon breast with kiwi and lime sauce (£2.95) and
half a roast duck with apricot and ginger sauce (£7.95). Regular bar
food is also all home-made. Sustaining snacks could include a cheese
and sirloin steak sandwich (£4.95) or prawn and garlic pizza (£4.25).
Excellent local cheeses. Families are well catered for; one high-chair
provided and facilities in the Ladies for changing. **Bar Food &
Restaurant Meals** 12-2, 7-9.30 (to 10 Fri/Sat). Children's menu/portions.
Beer Boddingtons, Fuller's London Pride, Hook Norton. Garden, outdoor
eating. Family room. Access, Visa.

Tresco   Island Hotel   67%   £170*

Tel 0720 22883 Fax 0720 23008	Hotel

Tresco Isles of Scilly TR24 0PU   Map 12 A2

Tresco, England's "Island of Flowers", is privately owned and
maintained, its lanes free of traffic. Guests arriving at the quay
or heliport (from Penzance) are transported by tractor-drawn
charabanc to the island's only hotel, set in beautifully tended gardens
by the shore. It's "totally unlike hotels on the mainland, with
a different pace of life prevailing". Picture windows make the most
of its spectacular location and the panoramic sea views: should the
mists close in there's a Terrace Bar and a Quiet Room stacked with
books, magazines and games. Six high-chairs, cots, baby-
listening/sitting, high tea from 6pm. The Terrace Bar offers a selection
of Children's Delights – from beefburgers to the Tresco picnic (cheese
or ham sandwich, apple or orange, fruit yoghurt, crisps, chocolate
biscuit and a can of drink £3.95). Special holiday packages for
gardeners, bird-watchers and others. Bicycles can be hired for both
children and adults (there are no cars – or banks – on the
island). Bucket and spade essential for youngsters. *Half-board terms
only. **Rooms** 40. Garden, outdoor swimming pool (heated May-end Sept),
fishing, boating, bowling green, games room. **Closed** Nov-Feb. Access,
Amex, Visa.

Restaurant   £60

Table d'hote and à la carte menus place strong emphasis on local
seafood (Scillonian scallops, Bryher crab), and there's Devonshire beef
from the grill and a cold buffet. Traditional farmhouse cheeses.
Luxurious Sunday buffet (including lobster). Children under 12 can
eat half-price from the carte. No smoking. **Seats** 95. Private Room 10.
L 12-2 D 7-9.30. Set D £24.

Ullswater   Old Church Hotel   67%   £90*

Tel 076 84 86204 Fax 076 84 86368	Hotel

Watermillock Ullswater Cumbria CA11 0JN   Map 4 C3

A stylish water's-edge hotel (on the A592) where residents are greeted
very much as Kevin and Maureen Whitemore's house guests; with

five children of their own they certainly understand the problems of travelling with a brood. Both lounges are built for relaxation and packed with board games and periodicals. Maureen's bold colour schemes brighten the bedrooms (priced according to the view), with crown canopies and half-testers framing really comfortable beds. By contrast, bathrooms are on the cramped side. Breakfasts deserve to be taken seriously, ranging from Lakeland yoghurts and home-made muesli to Manx kippers, Cumberland sausage and mixed grill with black pudding. Every need is covered for a visit with a young baby: backpack, baby relax chair, children's cutlery, feeding cup, crockery, cot, playpen, high-chair and steam bottle steriliser are all provided. "For the comfort and consideration of fellow guests", children are requested not to appear in the bar or dining room after 7pm. No dogs. ★Half-board terms. *Rooms 10. Garden, fishing, boating. Closed Nov-Mar. Access, Visa.*

Restaurant	**£60**

The smaller lounge doubles as an aperitif bar where guests gather prior to dinner (availability is limited for outside diners). The short-choice menu (order by 7.30) might start with mushrooms and crispy bacon with garlic butter, or prawns and avocado with salad leaves, and progress via soup to salmon, rack of lamb or sirloin of beef béarnaise. Choice of puds, then cheese, coffee and fudge. Fair prices and helpful tasting notes on a concise wine list. Note that the restaurant is no longer open for lunch – "everybody wants to go out for lunch in the Lake District"; if guests want a packed lunch they will be happy to provide one; similarly, children's teas and early suppers with "wholesome" food will be accommodated – just ask. No smoking. *Seats 30. D 7.30 for 8. Set D £20.*

Ventnor	Royal Hotel	60%	£66
Tel 0983 852186 Fax 0983 855395			Hotel
Belgrave Road Ventnor Isle of Wight PO38 1JJ			Map 15 D4

Neat gardens front a large Victorian sandstone hotel owned by Forte. The rattan-furnished conservatory entrance hall and the cosy bar are favourite areas to sit and relax. Bedrooms have lightwood fitted units and colourful floral curtains. *Rooms 54. Garden, outdoor swimming pool, games room. Access, Amex, Diners, Visa.*

Ventnor	Spyglass Inn	
Tel 0983 855338		Pub
The Esplanade Ventnor Isle of Wight PO38 1JX		Map 15 D4

Stephanie and Neil Gibbs have done a marvellous job of totally rebuilding the Spyglass Inn after the disastrous fire of just a few years ago. Wandering around the warren of interconnecting rooms, which include two reserved for non-smokers and several where children are welcome, it is difficult to believe that the pub is not hundreds of years old. The bar counter is built of old pews and the whole place is full of old seafaring prints and photographs, as well as numerous nautical antiques, ranging from a brass binnacle and ship's wheel to old oars and model ships in glass cases. The setting could not be better, at one end of the seafront with a front terraced area stretching right to the edge of the sea wall. In winter, the waves break right over the wall and more than one customer has been known to get a soaking by mis-timing their exit from the pub. In summer, there's an outside bar and kiosk selling shellfish and ice cream. Food is straightforward with some particularly good fish straight from fishermen who land it on the beach right next door to the pub. In winter, there are home-made soups (£1.95) from a blackboard menu, and on Saturday nights a candlelit dinner, for which booking is advisable, complete with pianist. In the season, there is entertainment nightly (less frequently in winter). Two neat little flatlets with upholstered rattan furniture and a sea-facing balcony offer accommodation for up to two adults and two children; a small kitchenette is provided for you to cook your own breakfast (as provided). A public car park is just 50 yards away, but check your brakes before venturing down here – the road to the seafront has hairpin bends and a gradient of 1 in 4. *Open 11-11 Mon-Sat May-end Sept, regular hours Sun and other times. Bar Food 12-2.15, 7-9.30 (7-9 Sun). Children's menu. Free House. Beer Burton, Ansells. Patio/terrace, outdoor eating. Family room. Accommodation 2 en-suite flatlets, sleeping 4, £45 (single £30). Children welcome overnight, cot available. Check-in after midday. No credit cards.*

Waddesdon   Five Arrows Hotel

Tel 0296 651727 Fax 0296 658596	Pub

High Street Waddesdon Buckinghamshire HP18 0JE   Map 15 D2

A delightful Victorian confection built by the Rothschilds to house the architects and artisans working in nearby Waddesdon Manor (NT) – itself worth a visit. The name comes from the family crest with its arrows representing the five sons sent out by the dynasty's founder to set up banking houses in the financial capitals of Europe. Recently restored from top to toe and bedecked with flowers (there's a fine garden to the rear) the hotel/inn is now run in a friendly, family-orientated fashion by Gaynor Hitchcock and Terence Jackson. One enters straight into the bar from which open several rooms with antique tables, colourful upholstered chairs plus the odd settee and armchair with pictures from Lord Rothschild's own collection on the walls along with numerous photos of old Waddesdon – charmingly un-pub-like. Food is important (and good) here with the likes of mousseline of salmon with basil butter sauce (£5.95), Roquefort salad (£3.50), sautéed lamb with honey and garlic (£6.95), oyster mushroom tart with fresh herbs and sour cream (£4.95) and lovely desserts like fresh raspberry tart (£2.95) supplemented at lunchtimes by more snacky items. Afternoon teas (£2.50 per person) are served at weekends. At least a dozen wines are available by the glass. Six good-sized bedrooms are individually decorated with matching en-suite bathrooms (two with shower and WC only) and boast extra large beds (with pure Egyptian cotton sheets) and antique Victorian washstands along with modern comforts: remote-control TV, direct-dial phones and tea/coffee-making facilities. No smoking in the bedrooms. *Open 11-3 & 6-11, Sat 11-11, Sun 12-3 & 7-10.30. Bar Food 12-2.30, 7-9.30 (to 10 Fri & Sat). Afternoon teas 3-6 Sat & Sun. Free House. Beer Fuller's London Pride, Hook Norton Old Hooky & Hock Mild, guest beer. Garden. Accommodation 6 bedrooms, all en suite, £65 (single £45). No dogs. Access, Amex, Visa.*

Walberswick   Mary's Restaurant

Tel 0502 723243	Restaurant

Walberswick Suffolk IP18 6UG   Map 10 D2

There's a distinctly nautical theme to this neat, family-run restaurant and tea shop in a small coastal village on the opposite side of the river Blyth to the better known Southwold. Things like toasted tea cakes

(75p), sandwiches (from £1.40) and cream teas (£2.75) are available
all day while the blackboard lunch menu features local fish (caught
by the only full-time fisherman left in Walberswick) such as grilled
slip sole (£7.95), brill (£5.95) and cod (grilled or fried £5.10) along
with the likes of steak and kidney pie (£5.50) and chicken in barbecue
sauce. Starters include home-made soup (£1.95), brandied liver paté
(£2.75) and grilled banana with Stilton and cream. In the afternoons
there are also high teas (last orders 5.30pm Fri & Sat) – scrambled eggs
(£3), cheese on toast with bacon (£3.75) or ham, egg and chips
(£4.95). For well-behaved children there are small portions of suitable
dishes plus a single clip-on high-chair. Booking is advisable, especially
for weekends and the fixed-price dinner (£15) served on Fri, Sat and
Sun nights. Changing shelf in the Ladies. No smoking in the twin
eating rooms, but it's allowed in the small bar or outside in the
secluded garden with its tables set out around the Union Jack-sporting
flag pole. *Open 10-6 Tues-Sun Easter to October, plus Mon spring Bank
Holidays & late July-early Sept. Nov-Easter open Fri, Sat & Sun only.
7.15-9pm Fri & Sat all year. No credit cards.*

Wallingford   Annie's Tea Rooms

Tel 0491 836308	Tea Room
79 High Street Wallingford Oxfordshire OX10 0BX	Map 15 D2

Jean Rowlands' tea room is a cosy, relaxed little place in the high
street. Speciality teas come in a wide variety to accompany scones,
teacakes and other home baking (scone and butter with jam and cream
95p). These are available all day, and at lunchtime there are open
sandwiches (egg mayonnaise £1.55, rollmop herring £1.75), jacket
potatoes (chili £2.85) and a hot dish of the day, perhaps beef hot pot
(£3.85) or tuna and mushroom pizza with salad. No smoking,
including the walled garden. One high-chair. *Seats 31. Open 10-5
(Summer to 5.30, Sun 2.30-5.30). Closed Sun (in winter) & Wed.
No credit cards.*

Wansford-in-England   Haycock Hotel Lounge

Tel 0780 782223	Hotel Lounge
Wansford-in-England nr Peterborough Cambridgeshire	Map 7 E4

In a lovely 17th-century coaching inn (now a 51-roomed hotel) just
off the A1, the main lounge and Orchard Room provide good,
familiar food all year round. The most popular dishes include chicken
liver paté (£4.25), grilled sardines in garlic butter (£4.20), lasagne
(£6.95) and steak and kidney pie with old-fashioned pastry and chips
(£7.75); ask for children's portions. Set afternoon tea with scones and
Devonshire cream costs £3.50. There's a no-smoking section in the
Orchard Room, which looks over the gardens. Five high-chairs;
changing facilities in a separate bathroom. In summer, tables and chairs
are set out on the terrace – a lovely setting. Walled garden. The
Tapestry Room restaurant is distinctly more adult. Poste Hotels.
Seats 90. Open 12-11. Closed 25 Dec. Access, Amex, Visa.

Wantage   Vale & Downland Museum Centre

Tel 0235 771447	Café
Church Street Wantage Oxfordshire OX12 8BL	Map 14 C2

A museum of past and present local life set in a 17th-century cloth
merchant's house. In the coffee shop, good home baking is the
showpiece, from chocolate cake, date slice and Boston brownie at 50p,

down to ginger animals at 3p each. The lunchtime menu runs from
soup to jacket potatoes, quiche, lasagne and cottage pie (£2.25).
Lidded beaker, bib and baby food can all be provided on request.
Patio with seating, lawn area with children's play facilities (play house,
hopscotch). Two high-chairs and a booster seat. Pull-down changing
shelf in the disabled loo. Unlicensed. No smoking. *Seats 50.*
Open 10.30-4.30, Sun 2.30-5. Closed Mon, 25 Dec, 1 Jan.
No credit cards.

Ware   Sunflowers

Tel 0920 463358	Vegetarian
7 Amwell End Ware Hertfordshire	Map 15 F2

Wholefood shop and, above it, a little vegetarian restaurant of modest
appearance. The food choice is simple and healthy, with organic
produce to the fore. Pizza with salad £1.95, moussaka, apple pie, nut
slices. Steep stairs; one high-chair – but if your child's vegetarian and
over 5 then you'll probably find this a haven of healthy eating.
No smoking. Unlicensed. *Seats 28. Open 9-5. Closed Sun, Bank
Holidays. No credit cards.*

Warmington   The Wobbly Wheel

Tel 0295 89214 Fax 0295 89354	Pub
Warwick Road Warmington Banbury Warwickshire OX17 1JJ	Map 14 C1

Rapidly-expanding operators Premier House have converted and
extended the old Wobbly Wheel (on the B4100, between Junction 10
& 11 of the M40) into the grand prix version of a family
entertainment pub. Set in its own garden and play area, the 'Jungle
Bungle' is a self-contained fun-house (admission £1) for all who can
pass beneath the gorilla's outstretched palm; more funds will
be required for pop and candy. Pub food from the next door, chain-
themed 'Millers Kitchen' is ground out by the barrow-load – hardly
a gourmet destination. Fifteen new bedrooms look out over open
country, promising a restful night once the fun factory's finished.
Recommended as a children's pit-stop (there are dozens of other outlets
in the chain, not all offering accommodation). *Pub open 11-11 Mon-
Fri, 12-10.30 Sun. Bar Food 12-2.30, 6-9.30 (to 10 Fri & Sat), Sun
12-9.30. Children's menu and portions available. Beer Davenport Best,
Boddington, Flowers Original. Garden, outdoor playing area. Family room.
Accommodation 15 bedrooms, all en suite, £47.95 (single £42.95).
Children welcome overnight, additional beds and cots available (both £5).
Access, Amex, Diners, Visa.*

Warwick   Brethren's Kitchen

Tel 0926 492797	Tea Room
Lord Leycester Hospital Warwick Warwickshire	Map 14 C1

Tea room in the heart of Lord Leycester Hospital. The menu
is short and simple. Home-baked cakes, fruit loaf, slices and flapjacks
throughout the day. Oaken oatcakes and Leycester's loaf are
specialities. Also plain or toasted sandwiches (from £1.25),
ploughman's, salads and sardines on toast. Jacket potatoes (£2.25-
£3.25) come filled with coleslaw, cheese, tuna or prawns. Dish of the
day could be salmon in tarragon sauce (£3.95) or cauliflower and
broccoli bake with jacket potato (£2.95). Service is friendly and
informal. Children's menu (£2) offers beans or spaghetti shapes
on toast, mousse or ice cream an a small glass of squash or lemonade;

one high-chair. The hospital loos can be used for changing baby. No smoking. *Seats 40.* **Open** *10-5.* **Closed** *Mon & end Oct-1 week before Easter. No credit cards.*

Warwick   Piccolino's Pizzeria

Tel 0926 491020	Pizzeria
31 South Street Warwick Warwickshire CV34 4JA	Map 14 C1

A dependable alternative to the larger high street chains (there's a branch also in Leamington Spa – see entry). Piccolino's is family-owned and family-friendly too. Cooked-to-order pizzas (*napoletana* £4.85, *quattro formaggi* £5.60) are notably good, pasta alternatives (*ravioli di pomodoro* £4.95, *tagliatelle alla marinara* £5.85) richly sauced, and there are steaks (*pizzaiola* £9.75) for those wishing to splash out more. Despite somewhat functional decor, suggesting that the heart of the operation lies firmly in the kitchen, service is typically relaxed and informal. "Children are always welcome" and two high-chairs and booster seats are provided. *Seats 70.* **Open** *12-2.30 & 5.30-11 (Fri to 11.30, Sun to 10.30, Sat 12-11.30).* **Closed** *25 & 26 Dec. Access, Visa.*

Warwick   Racehorse

Tel 0926 496705	Pub
Stratford Road Warwick Warwickshire CV34 6AP	Map 14 C1

One of a small Midlands chain of family-orientated theme pubs owned by Everards, stronger on ideas to keep the kids happy than on anything to do with imaginative food for adults. A jokey children's 'Meal Wheel' offers the likes of scampi, fish fingers and burgers, and includes a pudding, all for £1.99; there's an airy conservatory in which to consume it, high-chairs and smaller portions also provided. Wait, if wise, for a summer's day when little ones can let off steam in the garden and playground. Changing room. Recommended only as a children's pit-stop (there are eight others in Leicestershire in the chain, but not listed in this Guide). *Bar Food 12-10.15 (Sun 12-2, 7-10). Children's menu and portions are available.* **Beer** *Everards Beacon, Tiger, Old Original, guest beers. Garden, outdoor play area, barbecue area, patio. Family room. Access, Amex, Diners, Visa.*

Welbeck   Dukeries Garden Centre, Welbeck Coffee Shop

Tel 0909 476506	Coffee Shop
Welbeck nr Worksop Nottinghamshire S80 3LT	Map 7 D2

Situated in the walled gardens of historic Welbeck Abbey, the coffee shop is housed in restored Victorian greenhouses with exposed beams and bare brick walls. All the food is made on the premises and may include daily specials such as fisherman's pie (£3.75), chicken and mushroom pie or beef hot pot. Cakes and gateaux (45p-£1.85) or hot toffee pudding (£1.55). Roast Sunday lunch £5.15. Children's portions, two high-chairs and an adventure playground in the garden centre complex. *Seats 140.* **Open** *10-5.30.* **Closed** *4 days Christmas. Access, Visa.*

Wells   Cloister Restaurant

Tel 0749 676543	Restaurant
Wells Cathedral Wells Somerset BA5 2PA	Map 13 F1

Self-service restaurant in the cloisters of the cathedral. A daily choice of savoury specials may see Somerset chicken casserole, salmon and

asparagus flan, nut roast with Brie, spinach and cottage cheese lasagne
or vegetable stroganoff (all £3.25). Quiche (£1.35) and salads (£1.40-
£1.95) are always available. For pud apple and orange meringue
or sticky toffee (both £1.25). Scones, cream and jam 90p, tea and
coffee served all day. Children's portions. Three high chairs and
a mother & baby room in the cathedral toilets. Profits from the
restaurant go towards the upkeep of the cathedral. **Seats 96. Open** 10-5
(*Nov-Feb to 4.30, Sun 2-5*). **Closed** *Good Friday, 2 weeks Christmas.
No credit cards.*

Wells	**Good Earth**	
Tel 0749 678600		Vegetarian
Priory Road Wells Somerset		Map 13 F1

A wholefood shop at the front and a restaurant at the back. Lunchtime
savouries include home-made soup (lentil 95p), cheesy Scotch egg with
potato (£2.25), mixed salad platter (£1.40) and pizza with a light
bread base and a choice of tasty toppings from £1.55. Fruit cake,
carrot cake, flapjack and a vegan cake from 75p. Leafy courtyard with
children's play area. No smoking inside. **Seats 80. Open** 9.30-5.30.
Closed *Sun & Bank Holidays. Access, Visa.*

West Bexington	**Manor Hotel**	**59%**	**£76**
Tel 0308 897785 Fax 0308 897035			Hotel
Beach Road West Bexington nr Bridport Dorset DT2 9DF			Map 13 F2

An old manor house just a short walk from Chesil Bank, with stone-
walled cellar bar, leafy conservatory and residents' lounge. "Where
country meets coast", says their literature, and indeed Richard and
Jayne Childs' manor house stands in a garden on a gentle slope near the
famous shingle beach. Within, stone walls and oak panelling are much
in evidence; day rooms include a lounge/reading room, Cellar Bar,
restaurant and conservatory. Pretty, cottagey bedrooms, most with sea
views, are furnished with old pine and enhanced with books and
ornaments; magazines and dried flower arrangements add a homely,
welcoming feel; tea and coffee-making kits, TVs, direct-dial phones,
sherry, elderflower water and goodnight chocolates are the finishing
touches. Snacks and teas (3-6pm, also to non-residents) in the Cellar
Bar, the pretty no-smoking conservatory or the garden, which offers
a view of the sea. Families are very well catered for with high tea
on request, high-chairs and baby food indoors, Wendy House and slide
outdoors. No dogs. **Rooms** 13. Garden, children's playground. Access,
Amex, Diners, Visa.

West Byfleet	**Superfish**	
Tel 0932 340366		Fish'n'Chips
51 Old Woking Road West Byfleet Surrey		Map 15 E3

Part of a Surrey-based chain serving above-average fish and chips
"fried in the traditional Yorkshire way". See Morden entry for more
details. High-chairs; fish bites with chips (£2.20) for children. *Jane's
Upstairs* restaurant offers a wider choice of dishes and wines plus
home-made sweets in more stylish surroundings. Booking at Jane's
is essential: 0932 345789. **Seats 30. Open** 11.30-2 (Sat to 2.30), 5-10.30
(Thu-Sat to 11). **Closed** Sun, 25 & 26 Dec, 1 Jan. Access, Visa (only
Upstairs).

Westcliff-on-Sea   Oldham's

Tel 0702 346736	Fish'n'Chips
13 West Road Westcliff-on-Sea Essex	Map 11 C4

Licensed fish restaurant opposite the Palace Theatre. Specialities are
plaice, salmon, sole, scampi, cod cuts and 'supreme fish special' with
a selection of fried fish (£5.50). Ice creams and home-made apple pie
to finish, or the daily special. Children's portions. *Seats 80.*
Open 11-9.30 (Sun to 9). Closed 25 & 26 Dec. No credit cards.

Weston   Otter Inn

Tel 0404 42594	Pub
Weston Honiton Devon EX14 0NZ	Map 13 E2

Situated 400 yards off the busy A30 and beside the River Otter, this
much-extended 14th-century cottage is a popular refreshment stop
en route to and from the West Country, and a particular favourite
with families. The original old cottage interior is delightfully unspoilt
with a vast inglenook fronted by comfortable armchairs and old tables.
Plenty of prints, books and various bric-a-brac make this a cosy and
relaxing spot in which to sit. The main bar extension is very much
in keeping with heavy beams, a real assortment of old sturdy tables
and chairs, an unusual chamber pot collection hanging from the beams
and the added touch of fresh flowers on each table. Beyond some
double doors is a skittle alley and games room. A printed bar menu
highlights many of the usual snacks such as salads (from £2.70),
ploughman's (£3.50), filled jacket potatoes (from £2.70), steaks (from
£6.95) and main course specialities include chicken pillows (£8.95),
rack of lamb (£9.65) and steak and oyster pie (£7.50), all
accompanied by fresh vegetables and potatoes. Daily special dishes are
chalked up on a board with more involved, well-executed dishes
(perhaps monkfish £9.20) during the evening. The Ducklings Menu
offers a good choice of 'dindins, delights and drinkipoos' and a lollipop
for ducklings with a clean plate (and even for those who can't make
it through to the end of a generous portion of Sunday lunch – £3.50
main course and ice cream). Two high-chairs are provided along with
a changing mat in the Ladies. Children who have been cooped
up in the car for long periods will relish the space in the splendid
riverside garden, which offers youngsters the chance to paddle in a
very safe shallow section of the river. In one corner there is an animal
enclosure, with a notice on the gate inviting children in to study and
learn about the rabbits and guinea pigs that live in this wild and
peaceful part of the garden. There is also a swing and in summer
months supervised children's archery is a well-attended event. Children
will also be entertained outisde by the resident ducks and chickens;
inside, landlady Sue Wilinson, if she's not rushed off her feet, will treat
them like Kings and Queens, providing a toy box and crayons
to colour the menu. *Bar Food 12-2 & 6.30-10 (Sun 7-9.30). Free
House. Beer Eldridge Pope Hardy Ale. Garden, outdoor eating.
Access, Visa.*

Whitby   Elizabeth Botham & Sons

Tel 0947 602823	Tea Room
35/39 Skinner Street Whitby North Yorkshire YO21 3AR	Map 5 F3

Situated up a steep flight of stairs, above a bakery that provides much
of the produce available on the large menu, this is a traditional, rather
old-fashioned seaside tea shop "in the style of the old Lyons Corner

Coffee Houses". An all-day breakfast (£3.50), cinnamon toast (58p), filled baked potatoes (from £1.30), home-made pork pie and tomato chutney (£3.05), fish and chips (£4.35-£4.60) and a wealth of fresh cream cakes and gateaux paint the picture. Best value is the special meal of the day (£4.95) which includes soup or a sweet. Children's meals (£1.25) offer baked beans or spaghetti on toast followed by a scoop of ice cream and a wafer (75p). Two high-chairs, a Lego table for youngsters and a changing shelf in the Ladies. *Seats 100.* *Open 9.30-4.30 (9-5.30 high season). Closed Mon (except highseason), Sun, Bank Holidays.*
Also at:
30 Baxtergate Whitby North Yorkshire. Tel 0947 602823.
A contrastingly modern branch with smaller menu but same food. More suitable for young children. One high-chair and a changing shelf with roller paper cover.

Whitby   Magpie Café

Tel 0947 602058	Fish'n'Chips
14 Pier Road Whitby North Yorkshire	**Map 5 F3**

A lovely café overlooking the fishing quay, from where much of the superb fresh fish is delivered. The McKenzie family have run it for over 40 years, and still go about their daily tasks with enthusiasm. It's on three floors (there's a view of the harbour from the second) with autographed celebrity photographs decorating the white walls and uniformed waitresses providing very friendly and efficient service. Fish can be fried, grilled or poached – try Whitby crab, cod (in cream and tarragon sauce £5.25), haddock, plaice, sole, lobster (£8.95), salmon, monkfish (grilled skewers £8.95) – you name it, they serve it. There are five set menus at lunchtime (£7.75 to £10.95) – the Magpie de Luxe Lunch offers Whitby crab and prawns, lemon sole, pudding and cheese. Vegetarian meals are always available (mushroom and butter bean stroganoff (£4.35) and there's a children's menu at £2.95. 27 home-made puddings (Jamaican fudge slice, bread-and-butter pudding, sticky toffee pudding, Yorkshire curd cheesecake, sherry trifle – all £1.95) include gluten-free, wholefood, fat-free and vegetarian. The home baking is again emphasised at teatime with biscuits, cakes and fruit cakes (cream tea £1.75, afternoon tea £3.25). Most tables are no-smoking. *Seats 80. Open 11.30-6.30. Closed 3rd week Nov-1st week Mar. Access, Visa.*

Whitby   Trenchers

Tel 0947 603212	Fish'n'Chips
New Quay Road Whitby North Yorkshire	**Map 5 F3**

Down by the harbour this large, bright, bustling eatery is immaculately well kept – the marble loos are particularly impressive – and well run by brother and sisters team Terry, Judy and Nicky with the help of numerous smartly kitted-out staff who combine friendliness and efficiency to a high degree. Good fresh fish (much locally landed) and chips (cod and chips £5.75), cooked in pure beef dripping in true Yorkshire style, are the mainstay of a menu that also offers plenty of alternatives including lasagne (£5.45), home-made steak pie (£5.65), traditionally roasted ham (£5.65), various sandwiches (made with white or the same good granary bread that comes with the fish and chips) and a wide range of puds. After 6pm there are also 'starters' like fresh Whitby crab (£3.95) and egg mayonnaise (£1.95). Children are well catered for with their own

Junior's Choice of seven meals (all at £3.55 – from cottage pie to cod
and chips, served with bread and butter), some 20 clip-on high-chairs
and proper baby-changing facilities in the Ladies loo. Surprisingly
good, short wine list. *Seats 180. Open 11-9 (mid Mar-mid Nov).
Closed Mon-Thur evenings Mar and Nov. No credit cards.*

Whitney-on-Wye   Rhydspence Inn

Tel 0497 831262	Pub

Whitney-on-Wye nr Hay-on-Wye Hereford & Worcester HR3 6EU	Map 9 D4

Set in the heart of Kilvert country, on the A438 about a mile out
of Whitney-on-Wye, this is a well-loved, reliably entertaining inn
with a delightful timbered interior, two attractive bars with real fires,
old furniture and beams aplenty. Nice touches include magazines and
newspapers, creating an atmosphere in keeping with the old library
chairs. The charming dining room and restaurant overlook the garden.
Five comfortable bedrooms have beams, sloping floors, plus
an armchair at the least; some rooms are more romantic; one has
a four-poster. Bar food suggestions include spinach and mozzarella
crunch (£4.95), braised liver and onions (£5.75), and vegetable and
nut pie (£5.50). The longer restaurant menu is as varied: chargrilled
scallops (£5.95), avocado and chestnut millefeuille (£5.75), turbot
roasted with seaweed in vermouth (£11.50) and supreme of duck
with honey and mustard sauce (£12.95), plus an excellent choice
of farmhouse cheeses. A 3-course traditional Sunday lunch is available
in the restaurant (£11.50). Summer lunchers can enjoy the view over
the Wye Valley from the terraced garden. *Bar Food & Restaurant
Meals 11-2 (12-2 Sun lunch in restaurant), 7-9.45. Children allowed
in bar to eat. Beer Bass, Robinson, Hook Norton. Garden, outdoor eating.
Family room. Accommodation 5 bedrooms, all en suite, £55 (single
£27.50). Children welcome overnight, additional beds (£12.50). No dogs.
Access, Visa.*

Willerby   Grange Park   67%   £87

Tel 0482 656488 Fax 0482 655848	Hotel

Main Street Willerby nr Hull Humberside HU10 6EA	Map 7 E1

Adjacent to the A164 and Willerby Shopping Park, Grange Park is a
much-extended Victorian house standing in 12 acres of grounds.
Besides comfortable modern accommodation it offers extensive
purpose-built conference facilities (for up to 550) and extensive leisure
facilities. Families are quite well catered for with a children's
playground and (limited) crèche arrangements; children up to 10 stay
free in parents' room. Cots and baby-listening are provided, baby-
sitting can be arranged. There's a children's menu in the Cedars
Restaurant. *Rooms 104. Garden, indoor swimming pool, gymnasium,
helipad. Access, Amex, Diners, Visa.*

Wimborne   Cloisters Restaurant

Tel 0202 880593	Restaurant

40 East Street Wimborne Dorset BH21 1DX	Map 14 C4

Teas, coffees and snacks make up the menu in a cheerful little
restaurant behind a shop front. Breakfast starts the day, and a crisp,
freshly prepared BLT (£4.25) is a popular morning snack. Filled
jacket potatoes, ploughman's and curry pancake rolls with coleslaw are
other savoury possibilities, while daily specials might include braised
liver and onion (£3.95) or fisherman's pie (£4.25). Sweeter things run

from flapjacks (55p) and shortbread (65p) to bread pudding and home-made Dorset apple cake with fresh cream. Good espresso coffee. Children's portions and favourites (chipolatas, fish fingers, scampi, chicken nuggets £1.30-£2.10); two high-chairs. No-smoking area. **Seats** 54. **Open** 9-5. **Closed** Sun & Bank Holidays. No credit cards.

Wimborne Minster	**Quinneys Coffee House**	
Tel 0202 883518		Coffee Shop
26 West Borough Wimborne Minster Dorset BH21 1NF		Map 14 C4

A tea and coffee shop on two floors offering a good selection of teas and coffees, home-made cakes and sandwiches. A few more traditional home-cooking dishes like pies, quiches or liver and bacon now complete the picture. No particular family facilities, but useful to know about for a break. No smoking. **Seats** 44. **Open** 9-5.15. **Closed** 10 days early Jan. No credit cards.

Winchester	**Lainston House**	75%	£145
Tel 0962 863588 Fax 0962 72672			Hotel
Sparsholt Winchester Hampshire SO21 2LJ			Map 15 D3

63 acres of majestic parkland surround Lainston House, an elegant William and Mary building dating from 1668; $2\frac{1}{2}$ miles from Winchester on the A272. That it's an impressive establishment is clear from the moment you enter the parquet-floored foyer, which is dominated by a large fireplace decorated with fine Delft tiles. Flowers, paintings, books and ornaments make the comfortable lounge homely and relaxing and there's a splendid bar panelled with carved cedar. Main-house bedrooms are of grand proportions, with quality soft furnishings, period furniture and harmonious colour schemes; annexe rooms in Chudleigh Court are smaller. The old stable block was converted last year to provide six smart new bedrooms; these overlook a rose garden. Swings and see-saws in the grounds; high-chairs and high tea in the dining room. Grand, but hopefully not too overbearing for families. Exclusive Hotels. **Rooms** 38. Garden, tennis, coarse fishing, helipad. Access, Amex, Diners, Visa.

Windermere	**Miller Howe Kaff**	
Tel 05394 46732		Café
Alexandra Buildings Station Precinct Windermere Cumbria LA23 1BQ		Map 4 C3

Within Lakeland Plastics (a large kitchenware store near the railway station) the in-store café is now wholly owned by Ian Dutton – formerly head chef at the eponymous Miller Howe Hotel. The printed menu offers a few snacky items – jacket potatoes (from £1.75), cheese and herb paté (£2.95), summer salad with mini wholemeal loaf (£2.95) – and three regular main dishes – bobotie (an African dish of spiced, minced lamb), local Cumberland sausage and locally cured ham – all at £4.95, but the real variety is to be found on the extensive, daily-changing blackboard menu that might include tripe with fennel and celery in a cream sauce (£5.95), guinea fowl in red wine (£5.95) and devilled mushrooms along with more familiar chili con carne and soup and quiches of the day plus puds – strawberry brulée, rhubarb fool – cakes, pastries and batch-baked scones. Everything is available all day and there's no minimum charge but there is often a queue as space is limited. Two high-chairs, changing facilities and an indoor children's play area. **Seats** 45. **Open** 9-5 (Sun 10-4). **Closed** Sun, 25 & 26 Dec, 1 Jan. Access, Visa.

Windsor   Oakley Court Hotel, Boaters Brasserie

| Tel 0628 74141 | Brasserie |

Windsor Road Water Oakley nr Windsor Berkshire   **Map 15 E2**

A grand Victorian manor hotel three miles west of Windsor on the
A308, with landscaped gardens that slope down to the banks of the
river Thames. Part of the dining room has been set aside for informal
eating, and though not a brasserie in the true sense of the word, there's
a nod to that style – you can select just one course or several. Decor-
wise there's a blackboard menu, gingham tablecloths, boaters on the
wall and a real punt, plus whatever matches the programme of themed
weeks (French, Greek, American, Taste of India) when any two
courses will cost £9.95 per person. On the regular menu some dishes
appear with two prices indicating both starter and main-course
portions, such as salmon and crab cakes served with a tomato sauce
(£3.75/£5.50), or pitta bread parcels filled with finely diced chicken,
ham and grated cheese (£3.90/£5.50). Plainer dishes – steak and
kidney pie with mash and peas (£7.50) or grilled black pudding,
lamb's kidneys and bacon (£8.50) – are also available. Decent choice
of desserts and coffee, plus a fine selection of good wines by the glass
and excellent fresh French baguette bread. Five high-chairs are
provided along with half portions. Last year saw a Teddy Bears lunch
at the end of June when children under 10 ate free with their parents.
In fine weather tables are set out on the terrace. *Seats 32.*
Open 12.30-2 & 7.30-10. *Access, Amex, Diners, Visa.*

Winterton-on-Sea   Fisherman's Return

| Tel 0493 393305 | Pub |

The Lane Winterton-on-Sea Norfolk NR29 4BN   **Map 10 D1**

Small it may be, but this prettily-kept row of former fishermen's
cottages is an ideal hang-out for locals and visitors alike, be they
fishermen or not. Built in traditional brick and flint, the buildings are
probably 16th-century, and unaltered over the last quarter century
or more. The public bar is lined in varnished tongue-and-groove
panelling and hung with sepia photographs and prints of Lowestoft
harbour, the Norfolk Broads and the pub itself. Centre stage, the cast-
iron wood-burner opens up in winter to add a glow of warmth to an
already cheery atmosphere. A smaller and possibly older lounge, low-
ceilinged, with a copper-hooded fireplace and oak mantel, is carpeted
these days and ideal for a quick, if cramped, snack. Families will more
likely head to the "Tinho", a timbered rear extension of pool table and
games machines which leads mercifully quickly to a lovely enclosed
garden and adventure playground. The menu's pretty comprehensive.
Individual savouries and omelettes, generously garnished, are the
popular choices; there are pasta dishes at £4.75 and sea trout with
herb dip and new potatoes at £5.75. Overnighters, too, are in for
a treat. A tiny flint-lined spiral staircase leads up under the eaves
to three cosy bedrooms, which share the house television (propped
up on a seaman's trunk) and two bathrooms (one with shower only).
The largest, family room also has a sitting area with its own television.
Modest comforts, maybe, but entirely adequate for a brief stay,
a stone's throw from the beach and long walks over the dunes. Visitors
are made truly welcome by John and Kate Findlay, and seen on their
way with the heartiest of seafarer's breakfasts. *Bar Meals 11.30-2,
6-9.30 (winter from 7). Children's menu. Beer Adnams. Garden, outdoor*

eating, children's play area. Family room. **Accommodation** *3 bedrooms, sharing 2 bathrooms, £40 (single £28). Children welcome overnight. Check-in by arrangement. No credit cards.*

Wirksworth   Crown Yard Kitchen Restaurant

Tel 0629 822020	Restaurant
Crown Yard Market Place Wirksworth Derbyshire	Map 6 C3

Look for the Heritage Museum sign (an old silk mill now showing the history of lead mining in the area), walk through the arch and up the winding slope where you will find this bright, airy restaurant. In addition to the menu which features home-made pies (from £3.50), pizzas (£3), lasagne (£3.70) and curries (£3.50) are jacket potatoes (from £1.30), sandwiches (80p) and salads (£3). Having visited the Heritage Centre, a cup of one of the several teas available (45p) together with a home-made biscuit or cake, toasted teacake (55p) or set cream tea (£1.75) is most refreshing. Children's portions available; two high-chairs provided, but no changing facilities. Seating on terrace in summer. Smoking is not allowed between 12 and 2. *Seats 32.* **Open** *9-5 (Sun from 10).* **Closed** *25 & 26 Dec, 3 weeks Jan. Access, Visa.*

Wisley   Conservatory Café & Terrace Restaurant

Tel 0483 225329	Café
The Royal Horticultural Society's Garden Wisley Surrey GU23 6QA	Map 15 E3

Everything in the garden is lovely, and that includes the Conservatory Café (run by Cadogan Caterers) which manages to maintain creditably high standards despite serving upwards of 4,000 customers on a busy day. Virtually everything in the light, airy café with its large terrace, is made on site – light sponges oozing fresh cream (from £1.65), tea cakes, Chelsea buns (both 60p), almond florentines (70p), lemon meringue pie (£1.55), salads, sandwiches (from £1.60), well-filled Cornish pasties (£1.65), quiches (£1.50) and, at lunchtime, various hot vegetarian dishes at £3.75. The table-service Terrace restaurant offers traditional English breakfasts until 11.30 then (from noon) set lunches (£11.75) and, in the afternoon, a choice of set teas from £3.95. Within The Royal Horticultural Society's Garden (adult entrance fee will be £4.20 until April 1994), the café and restaurant are open from 9.30am on Sundays, but only to RHS members. Children's portions; fifteen high-chairs and a table available for changing in the Ladies. *Seats 400.* **Open** *10-5.30 (winter to 4).* **Closed** *Sun (except to RHS members) mid Dec to first Fri in Jan. Access, Visa.*

Wolverhampton   Healthy Way

Tel 0902 772226	Vegetarian
87a Dartington Street Wolverhampton West Midlands	Map 6 C4

A small, informal counter-service wholefood restaurant in the town centre serving hearty, healthy dishes such as cheese, egg and potato pie (£1.65), broccoli roulade, vegetarian crumble, pizzas with salads from £1 and sandwiches made to order. Carrot cake and fruit flan are a couple of the home-made sweet alternatives. No-smoking area. *Seats 30.* **Open** *8.30-5.* **Closed** *Sun & Bank Holidays. No credit cards.*

Woodbridge   Seckford Hall   68%   £90

| Tel 0394 385678   Fax 0394 380610 | Hotel |

Woodbridge Suffolk IP13 6NU   Map 10 D3

Look out for the hotel sign on the A12 Woodbridge by-pass (don't
turn off into the town) to find this imposing Elizabethan manor house
set in extensive gardens which include an ornamental fountain and
lawns leading down to a willow-fringed lake. Inside, period features
abound with linenfold panelling and heavily beamed ceiling in the
Great Hall (lounge), huge stone fireplaces and carved doors. Bedrooms
are comfortably furnished more in private house than hotel style, four
have four-poster beds (one dates back to 1587) and some are in a
courtyard complex that includes an inspired conversion of an old tithe
barn into a delightful heated swimming pool. Children's menu with
everything from Marmite sandwiches to a Coke float. Adjacent 9-hole
pay-and-play golf course. *Rooms 35. Garden, indoor swimming pool,
solarium, spa bath, keep-fit equipment. Closed 25 Dec. Access, Amex,
Diners, Visa.*

Woodstock   Brothertons Brasserie

| Tel 0993 811114 | Brasserie |

High Street Woodstock Oxfordshire   Map 14 C2

The informal, relaxed atmosphere of this popular town-centre brasserie
is perfect for enjoying a morning coffee, lunch, tea or evening meal.
The printed menu keeps regular favourites like Brothertons smokies
(£3.95), deep-fried Brie with cranberry sauce (£3.25), large
Mediterranean prawns with garlic (£4.85) and crepes (chicken with
mushrooms and parsley £6.95), supplemented by specials that change
daily like chicken supreme with mustard sauce (£8.25) or mushroom
stroganoff (£5.95). Traditional English puddings to finish. Scones and
jam for tea (£1.70) and a roast dish on Sundays (£5.95-£6.50).
*Seats 65. Open 10.30am-10.30pm. Closed 25 & 26 Dec, 1 Jan. Access,
Amex, Diners, Visa.*

Woolacombe   Woolacombe Bay Hotel   65%   £172*

| Tel 0271 870388   Fax 0271 870613 | Hotel |

South Street Woolacombe Devon EX34 7BN   Map 12 C1

Family summer holidays, winter breaks and conferences (for up to 200
delegates) are the main business at this imposing Edwardian hotel,
whose lawns and gardens reach down to three miles of lifeguard-
patrolled golden sands. Public rooms are fairly grand, bedrooms bright
and roomy, with mostly modern furnishings. There are self-catering
suites, apartments and flats. Cots, baby-sitting/listening, 50 high-chairs,
children's menu and baby food are all provided; the basement contains
a cavernous playroom. Children's supper (for up to 8s) 5.15-6pm and
supervised crèche/playtime (7.30-9.30pm) during holiday periods.
Informal eating in Maxwell's Coffee Shop & Bistro (open 10am-10pm,
to 4pm in winter). Reduced rates at nearby Saunton golf club.
No dogs. *Half-board terms only. *Rooms 61. Garden, indoor & outdoor
swimming pools with long slide, keep-fit equipment, squash, sauna, spa bath,
steam room, solarium, hairdressing, floodlit all-weather tennis, pitch & putt,
bowling, billiards room, children's playroom and organiser in high season.
Closed Jan. Access, Amex, Diners, Visa.*

Worthing   Fogarty's

Tel 0903 212984	Tea Room
10 Prospect Place off Montague St Worthing West Sussex BN11 3BL	Map 11 A6

A mother and daughter team, Marjorie Denney and Jane Ambridge, is responsible for the home baking both sweet – honey, banana and walnut loaf (90p), caramel slice (70p), banoffi pie (£1.50) – and savoury – various quiches all at £2.20 – on offer at this neat little tea room between the seafront and the main shopping street. Even more popular are the lunches that always include fresh plaice (either grilled or mornay at £4.90) and gammon steak with pineapple (£4.90) together with daily specials like stuffed marrow topped with a cheese sauce (£4.90). No specific facilities for mother and baby, but they are always welcome. *Seats 40.* **Open** *9-5.* **Closed** *Sun, Mon, 2 weeks Feb, 2 weeks Sep. No credit cards.*

Worthing   Seasons

Tel 0903 236011	Vegetarian
15 Crescent Road Worthing West Sussex	Map 11 A6

Located in the old part of the town, Seasons is a bright, clean self-service wholefood restaurant with pine furniture and several prints hanging on the pale green walls. Sheila Boyle and Georgina Fincher-Jones offer a variety of dishes from 11.30 onwards: filled jacket potatoes, spiced almond risotto, leek and mushroom savoury potato top in a peanut sauce, buckwheat slice with a bean and vegetable casserole (all £3), as well as eight different salads every day (60p-£2). Home-made puddings and cakes. Unlicensed but you can bring your own. One high-chair; ask for children's portions. No smoking. *Seats 40.* **Open** *9-4.30.* **Closed** *Sun, 1 week Christmas, 1 Jan. No credit cards.*

Wybunbury   Swan Inn

Tel 0270 841280	Pub
Main Road Wybunbury Cheshire CW5 7NA	Map 6 B3

Few signs remain here of the 18th-century farmhouse with an unusual bow-front opposite St Chad's church, where only the 15th-century leaning tower survives today. The Church was abandoned in 1972, and the tower's last vertical correction occurred in 1989. Even more recent straightening-out of the Swan divides the interior into alcoves separated by curtains, brass rails and banquettes, and warmed by real fires in winter. The menu is equally traditional and unchanging, supplemented by daily specials boards: filled baguettes of steak and onions (£3), beef and ale casserole (£4.50) and home-made summer fruit pavlova (£2) are not untypical. Outside in summer are a 'Pop Shop', and plentiful new children's play equipment and neatly-spaced picnic tables on a lawn by the lychgate. *Bar Food* *12-2, 6.30-9.30 (except Sun eve). Children's menu.* **Beer** *Boddingtons, Jennings, Tetley, Greenall Original, Marston's Pedigree, guest beers. Garden, children's play area. Family room. Pub closed Sunday evening. Access, Visa.*

Wyre Piddle   Anchor Inn

Tel 0386 552799	Pub
Wyre Piddle nr Pershore Hereford & Worcester WR10 2JB	Map 14 B1

Standing low and white-painted at the roadside, bedecked with fairy lights and flower baskets, the Anchor reveals its wealth of talents

on further investigation. This is one of the region's premier summer
pubs with its grassy terraces and rolling lawn graduating down to the
Avon river bank where holidaymakers may moor their narrowboats.
Views across the river take in the verdant Vale of Evesham whence
come the asparagus and strawberries that enrich the summer menus.
Menus change daily in any case: popular for snacks are the Greek dips
with olives and pitta bread (£2.75) and home-made fresh salmon paté
(£2.95). Chicken tikka (£6.25), savoury pork and mushroom pie
(£5.75) through to a cold seafood platter at £7.25 are substantial bar
meals, with strawberry shortcake or chocolate pudding and chocolate
sauce (£1.85) to follow. An elevated dining room has possibly the best
view; the restaurant menu offers steaks with fowl and fishy
alternatives and a family Sunday lunch. Children welcome away from
the bar serveries. **Bar Food & Restaurant Meals** 12-2.30 (Sun to 2),
7-9.30 (Sun to 9 in bar, no food Sun eve in restaurant). **Beer** Whitbread,
Banks's Best. Garden, children's play area. Family room. Access, Visa.

Yarm   The Coffee Shop

Tel 0642 791234	Coffee Shop
44 High Street Yarm Cleveland	Map 5 E3

A haven of wholesome, home-prepared food on the first floor
of a small family-run department store. Wholemeal flour is used
in scones (69p) and in the home-made bread for sandwiches (from
£2.45, £2.55 and £4.65 for plain, toasted and open varieties
respectively). Hot dishes, which gradually appear throughout the
morning, include mini-quiches, perhaps prawn and mushroom
(£4.59), lasagne verdi (£4.99) and broccoli bake (£3.79), and there
are equally tempting desserts like hazelnut meringue (£2.25) and hot
chocolate fudge cake (£1.99). There's a courtyard for fine weather.
Seats 50. **Open** 9-5.30. **Closed** Sun (except July & Dec), some Bank
Holidays, 25 & 26 Dec. Access, Visa.

Yarmouth   Jireh House

Tel 0983 760513	Tea Room
St James's Square Yarmouth Isle of Wight	Map 14 C4

Cosy, comfortable tea rooms in a 17th-century building. The
atmosphere is homely and relaxing, making it a popular spot for
enjoying a range of straightforward snacks that are available all day
long. Coconut and cherry slice, rock cakes, gateaux and crumbles are
priced from 55p, and there are two afternoon teas, one with scones,
jam and clotted cream (£2.75), the other adding sandwiches and cake
(£4.95). Also on the menu are ploughman's, jacket potatoes, salads and
hot specials such as macaroni cheese, shepherd's pie and vegetable bake.
Three set menus (from £8.95 – £12.50), include soup and sweet with
one of grilled salmon, fillet steak or half a lobster. Cooked breakfast
(£3.50) is served way beyond breakfast hours. No high-chairs, but
an eminently civilised, satisfyingly straightforward place for a light
bite while touring the Island or waiting for a ferry. No smoking.
Seats 72. **Open** 8.45am-10pm. **Closed** end Oct-Easter. No credit cards.

York   Bettys

Tel 0904 659142	Tea Room
6 St Helens Square York North Yorkshire	Map 7 D1

Unashamedly old-fashioned dishes, made with quality ingredients, are
served by neatly uniformed waitresses. Ceiling fans humming leisurely

to the strains of the evening pianist evoke a bygone era. The days begins with breakfast – warm Yorkshire oatcakes (£1.45), mushroom and bacon omelette (£4.98), rösti potatoes (£5.25) or simply two croissants or brioches with jam and butter (£1.86). Light lunches bring sandwiches (from £2.45), salads (corn-fed chicken £5.30), grills, omelettes, hot dishes such as haddock and prawns croustades and the speciality of the house, rarebit made with Theakston's Yorkshire Ale served with apple or tomato chutney (£5.50). A wide choice of teas and rare coffees accompanies buttered pikelets (£1.02), banana and walnut loaf (£1.20) or a warm Yorkshire fat rascal (£1.98) at tea time. On the evening menu, prawn and avocado salad (£3.75) and haddock and prawn croustade (£3.60) are served as starters and a chicken and mushroom brochette (£5.85) or mushroom and chestnut roulade with casseroled red cabbage (£4.55) as a main course. Various ices (from £2.15), desserts (toffee and brandy snap fanfare) and cakes (from £1.55 – chocolate brandy roulade, Yorkshire curd tart) to follow. Children's menu; six high-chairs. Changing shelf with mat, chair and playpen in the Ladies. No-smoking area. **Seats** 174. **Open** 9-9. **Closed** 25 & 26 Dec, 1 Jan. Access, Visa.

York   Four Seasons

| Tel 0904 633787 | Café/Restaurant |

45 Goodramgate York North Yorkshire — Map 7 D1

Dating back to the late 15th century this splendid old timber-framed building in the centre of town is full of character – ask about the resident ghost. The extensive all-day menu is full of interest too – coriander mushrooms in olive oil (£3.15), potted devilled ham (£2.95), pork and plum pie (£6.40), Glamorgan sausage (a vegetarian sausage of cheese and leeks with home-made chutney £5.35 – one of a number of vegetarian options), various salads (from £5.10), jacket potatoes, sandwiches, desserts like pavlova with apricot sauce (£3.15) and Boodles orange fool (£2.45), cakes and much else besides with yet more dishes written up on a blackboard – warm bacon and mushroom salad (£3.95), pasta and bean bake (£4.75), rump steak (£10.45), chicken supreme (£7.25). The menu can also call upon the 40-odd British farmhouse cheeses that are sold (along with wines and many of the menu items) at the shop counter near the entrance. Children can choose from their own menu of half portions of most things. A large area on the first floor (overlooking the pretty courtyard/garden) has a comfortable settee where mothers can nurse baby and there's a changing table with mat and wipes; emergency nappies can be provided, but don't rely on them. **Seats** 90. **Open** 10am-10pm. **Closed** 25 & 26 Dec, 1 Jan. Access, Amex, Diners, Visa.

York   Grange Hotel   74%   £98

| Tel 0904 644744   Fax 0904 612453 | Hotel |

Clifton York North Yorkshire YO3 6AA — Map 7 D1

A fine Regency town house, carefully restored from a group of flats, just 400 yards north of the city walls on the A19 road to Thirsk. The relaxed, homely atmosphere is exemplified by the elegant morning room – plump cushions on the couches, a fine open fire, oil paintings hanging on the walls and fresh flowers. The bedrooms may not be large but are individually furnished with fine-quality fabrics, antique furniture and English chintz. The young management and friendly staff have high hotel-keeping standards and help make this a good alternative to uniform, commercial rivals. Baby-sitting can be arranged in advance and there's a high-chair in the Brasserie (easiest access is via the rear car park). Under-4s share parents' room free of charge. *Rooms 29. 24hr lounge service. Access, Amex, Diners, Visa.*

Ivy Restaurant   £70

Chef Cara Baird's interesting fixed-price lunch and dinner menus might include salmon and asparagus terrine with dill yoghurt, salad of lamb's kidneys or chicken livers to start, followed by carbonnade of beef, a selection of seafish or roast lamb stuffed with apricots and rosemary. The carte is slightly more involved, with good vegetarian options, and written in a refreshingly unpretentious style, matching the kitchen's intentions. Simpler fare, but equally well executed, is offered (except Sun) in the brick-vaulted Brasserie converted from the old cellars. From the charcoal grill come lamb kebabs (£6), garlicky king prawns, mixed grill and sirloin steak (£10.50), wild boar sausages, mash and pear chutney (£5.25), chicken pie and salmon fish cakes. Available as starters and mains are moules marinière (£3.50/£6.50), watercress pasta (£3.50/£5.50) and mushroom and Stilton beignets with a tomato and basil sauce (£2.80/£4.80); also salads and sweets. *Seats 55. Private Room 60. L 12.30-2.30 D 7-10 (Brasserie 6-10.30, closed Sun). Set L £12.50 Set D £21.*

York   Miller's Yard Vegetarian Café

Tel 0904 610676	Vegetarian
Gillygate York North Yorkshire	**Map 7 D1**

A workers' co-operative with wholefood bakery, takeaway and a sparsely decorated, counter-service split-level vegetarian and vegan café. Hearty portions of wholesome produce draw the crowds. Filled jacket potatoes (£1.60), pizza (£1.50), vegan items such as mushroom and nut pasty (80p) and tofu burger (60p), and a daily hot dish, perhaps cashewnut loaf with an asparagus-based sauce (£2.70), use organic produce wherever possible and offer excellent value for money. Equally filling sweets such as Tassajara cake (95p) to finish. No smoking. BYO licence (no corkage). Pavement tables in fine weather. *Seats 60. Open 10-4 (summer to 4.30, Sat to 5). Closed Sun, 25 & 26 Dec. No credit cards.*

York   National Trust Tea Rooms

Tel 0904 659282	Tea Room
30 Goodramgate York North Yorkshire YO1 2LG	**Map 7 D1**

Round the corner from the National Trust shop and about 200 yards from the minster, the tea rooms are well kept and efficiently run. Profits from the catering contribute to the upkeep of the Treasurer's House (qv). The menu covers morning coffee and afternoon tea (cheese scone 80p, cakes from 90p); all-day breakfasts, open sandwiches, salads, savoury snacks, and dishes of the day such as cod, cheese and broccoli bake (£4.95). Plenty of children's choices. Note the selection of Yorkshire fruit wines (to be consumed with meals only). Two high-chairs; changing mat, mobiles, children's pictures, wipes and bibs in the Ladies. No smoking. *Seats 50. Open 9.30-5.30 (Sun 12-4.30 Jul-Aug). Closed Sun, 25 & 26 Dec. Access, Visa.*

York   Spurriergate Centre

Tel 0904 629393   **Restaurant**

St Michael's Church Spurriergate York North Yorkshire YO1 1QR   **Map 7 D1**

Spiritual food in a carefully renovated and converted redundant
church by one of York's most historic crossroads. Paved stone and
notable 15th-century stained glass lend bags of atmosphere, and there's
plenty of wholesome food to feed the body. Home-made cakes and
scones are supplemented by hot daily specials (from 11.30) such
as filled Yorkshire puddings (£2.20), mushroom stroganoff (£3.45)
or harvest pie (£3.45), with sandwiches, filled jacket potatoes and
generously portioned puddings the mainstay of the menu. No smoking
throughout. **Seats** 90. **Open** 9.30-5. **Closed** *Sun, 2nd Tue of each month.*
No credit cards.

York   Taylor's Tea Rooms & Coffee Shop

Tel 0904 622865   **Tea Room**

46 Stonegate York North Yorkshire YO1 2AS   **Map 7 D1**

Quintessential tea rooms, part of the estimable Bettys group, at the top
of steep stairs in a listed city-centre building. An exceptional range
of fine teas and coffees, available here by pot or cafetière, has been sold
on lower floors for over 100 years. There is also much good-quality
eating to be had, from an all-day breakfast grill (£5.10 for the works)
or cream tea (£3.66), via various sandwiches – plain from £2.45 – to
salads (£1.98 per portion) and hot dishes such as omelettes (£4.80)
and rarebits (£5.50). Sweet things include a myriad of gateaux and
tarts, and the speciality Yorkshire fat rascal (£1.98), a warm, thick
scone packed with vine fruits and smothered with butter.
Traditionally attired staff provide quick, friendly service. Unlicensed.
Children's menu for under-12s offers half portions plus Welsh rarebit
(£2.98), omelettes (£3.55) and breakfasty items. Preservative and
additive-free foods for small babies are offered; they are happy to heat
up milk as well. Three high-chairs, beakers and bibs provided;
changing shelf with mat, chair and play pen in a separate facility next
to the Ladies; nappies are available for emergencies. Three rooms no-
smoking. **Seats** 65. **Open** 9-5.30. **Closed** *25 & 26 Dec, 1 Jan.*
Access, Visa.

York   Treasurer's House

Tel 0904 646757   **Tea Room**

Minster Yard York North Yorkshire   **Map 7 D1**

A National Trust property, originally home to the medieval treasurers
of York Minster and largely rebuilt in the 17th century, with the
basement cellars converted into a neat and tidy tea room. Friendly,
helpful staff dispense good-quality home baking such as ginger parkin,
date and walnut cake and treacle tart (from 80p), with savoury choices
ranging from mushroom stroganoff (£3.95) to York ham sandwich
(£2). Round things off with a delicious sticky toffee pudding
or various cheesecakes. Five Yorkshire fruit wines available by the
glass. No smoking. **Seats** 60. **Open** 10.30-5. **Closed** *Nov-end Mar.*
No credit cards.

York	**Viking Hotel**	69%	£113

Tel 0904 659822   Fax 0904 641793   Hotel

North Street York North Yorkshire YO1 1JF   Map 7 D1

Tall, modern Queens Moat Houses hotel standing in a convenient
central location by the river Ouse. Style and comfort are not lacking
in the brick-walled reception, the lounge and the bar, the last two
with river views. Leisure facilities include a well-equipped, supervised
gymnasium. Handily placed for the Jorvik Viking Centre and the
Waxwork Museum, the Viking welcomes families with open doors.
Most of the spacious double rooms, which are well lit and amply
furnished, will accommodate a cot or extra bed; seven suites serve
larger families. The restaurant, which offers high-chairs, a children's
menu and small portions, opens at 5.30pm for parents who prefer
to get their charges fed and bedded early. No dogs. *Rooms 188.*
*Gymnasium, sauna, spa bath, solarium, golf practice net. Access, Amex,
Diners, Visa.*

Recommended by

EGON RONAY'S GUIDES

1994

primetime™

Primetime is the tariff for those who use a mobile phone frequently during the day. The fixed costs (connection charge and monthly subscription) are higher than Lifetime but calls are cheaper during peak business hours.

Primetime features a wide range of useful call handling services and information lines that can help you to increase business efficiency and productivity, and enables you to make international calls.

Choose Cellnet.
You'll have more choice.

Call the BIG network for small phones on
0800 21 4000

Primetime is a registered trademark of TCSR Ltd.

Every Mondeo i. packed with features we hop you'll never use.

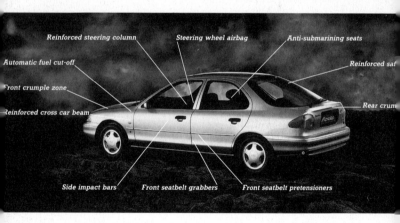

Reinforced steering column

Steering wheel airbag

Anti-submarining seats

Automatic fuel cut-off

Reinforced saf

Front crumple zone

Reinforced cross car beam

Rear crum

Side impact bars

Front seatbelt grabbers

Front seatbelt pretensioners

The Ford Mondeo is the only car with Dynamic Safety Engineering. None of the safety features are optional extras, they are all fitted as standard.

In a crash, side impact bars and crumple zones immediately absorb the force, the fuel supply from the tank is automatically cut off and sensors instantly the severity of collision.

If the force of impact is great enough, within a tenth of a second the steering wheel airbag will inflate and seatbelt "grabbers" and "pretensioners" will operate to hold you tight

in the seat. Specially designed "anti submarining" also stop you sliding under the belts.

Before an accident you wouldn't even know features were there, thankfully after one, you'll be a appreciate why they were. For more information on Mo schemes and details of your nearest Ford Motability dealer, call free (quoting M24) on: **0800 111 222.**

Everything we do is driven by

Scotland

Aberdeen   Henry J Bean's Bar & Grill

Tel 0224 574134	Restaurant

Windmill Brae (almost under the bridge) Aberdeen Grampian   **Map 3 D4**

Of the plethora of American-themed burger joints, this is up with the
best, success due severally to relaxed but lively surroundings, slick
service, good value (particularly during daytime hours) and a better
than average product, namely burgers grilled to order 'without cheese,
no extra charge' – the chili version (£4.65), BBQ ribs and bibs
(£4.75) and Cajun chicken (£4.35) and garlic mushrooms (£2.55).
Hot fudge sundae or American style apple pie (both £1.75) to finish.
Happy hours bring prices down further. Drink coffee from
'bottomless' mugs, or designer beers. **Seats** 50. **Open** *11am-10.30pm*
(Sun 6.30-11). **Closed** *L Sun, 25 Dec. No credit cards.*

Aberfeldy   Farleyer House

Tel 0887 820332	Bistro

Weem by Aberfeldy Perthshire   **Map 3 C4**

Originally a 16th-century croft and later dowerhouse to nearby
Menzies Castle, Farleyer House hotel enjoys a fine position
overlooking the Tay valley to the west of town on the B846. Make
for the Scottish Bistro, open for lunch and supper, with a menu that
runs from Swiss potato cake and bacon (£2.95) and egg mousse with
prawn salad to gratin of stuffed fennel (£5.50), Italian meatballs with
pasta, ragout of monkfish, venison steak with redcurrants (£6.20) and
honeyed mutton bridies. Ice creams, sorbets, hot chocolate pudding
and old-fashioned lemon tart feature among the desserts (£3/£3.25).
Small no-smoking area. **Seats** 52. **Open** *10-2 & 6-9.30. Access, Amex,
Diners, Visa.*

Alexandria   Cameron House   81%   £150

Tel 0389 55565 Fax 0389 59522	Hotel

Loch Lomond Alexandria Strathclyde G83 8QZ   **Map 3 B5**

An extended Georgian house turned into an elegant hotel with most
impressive leisure facilities. Just off the A82, it enjoys a splendid
location by Loch Lomond on a large estate that includes time-share
lodges. Peaceful, country house-style day rooms in the original house
contrast with the more lively bar that overlooks the leisure club.
Spacious bedrooms are individually decorated with stylish fabrics and
boast comfortable armchairs; there are huge, soft towels and bathrobes
in the bathrooms. Smiling staff offer a warm welcome and high
standards of service. Families are well catered for, with a daily crèche
(normally to 5pm, but extended to 9pm on Thurs & Fri) and baby-
sitting available. Supervised children's activities such as nature trails,
treasure hunts and day trips can also be organised. The Brasserie
provides high-chairs, a children's menu (melon boats with orange sails,
beans, burgers, spaghetti hoops, corn on the cob, omelette, milk shakes,
banana split etc) and there's a changing/breast-feeding area. No dogs.
*Rooms 68. Indoor swimming pools, steam room, sauna, solarium, spa bath,
squash, badminton, snooker, gymnasium, hairdressing, beauty salon, crèche,
kiosk, 9-hole golf course, tennis, watersports centre, marina, fishing,
mountain bikes. Access, Amex, Diners, Visa.*

Georgian Room   £75

Sparkling chandeliers, rich drapes and quality silverware create
a luxurious setting for serious, sophisticated cooking; the short

à la carte menu seems to have learned something from the decor.
Casserole of langoustines with woodland mushrooms and black,
ginger-flavoured noodles and a lobster and lentil sauce; supreme
of chicken with leek and truffle ravioli; and geranium and
blackcurrant parfait served with a praline basket of fruits are indicative
of the involved style. An imaginative, six-course Celebration menu
is also offered – for those wishing to become even more involved –
plus fixed-price daily menus. *Seats 60. L 12-3 D 7-10.*
Set L £12.95/£15.50 Set D £29.50.

Almondbank   Almondbank Inn

Tel 0738 83242	Pub

Main Street Almondbank Tayside PH1 3NJ	Map 3 C5

Just off the A85 to the west of Perth, on the village main street, the
whitewashed Almondbank Inn enjoys fine views over the River
Almond from its small well-kept rear garden. It's not a quiet pub:
a juke box in the bar regularly pumps out the latest hits, and there's
a pool table on the first floor. Food is taken fairly seriously, however,
and the Birdcage Bistro, despite some rather gimmicky, tacky
descriptions (a "galaxy of titbits", "salad days are here again") produces
generally pleasing food, the majority of it from fresh produce,
including some first-rate home-made chips. All the beef used
is Aberdeen Angus from the licensee's own family butcher, and even
the scampi is fresh and crumbed on the premises. The uniformed staff
are friendly and approachable and the locals, gathered on stools at the
bar, are also only too willing to chat. Two high-chairs and toys in the
family room; changing facilities. *Open 11-11.30 Fri & Sat, 12.30-11
Sun, regular hours other days.* **Bar Food** *12-2.15 (Sun from 12.30),
5-8.30 (Fri/Sat 6.30-10). Children's menu. Free House.*
Beer *Greenmantle. Riverside garden, outdoor eating. Access, Visa.*

Ardentinny   Ardentinny Hotel   59%

Tel 036981 209 Fax 036981 345	Hotel/Pub

Ardentinny Loch Long nr Dunoon Strathclyde PA23 8TR	Map 3 B5

35 miles from Glasgow, on the A880, this west-coast droving inn lies
on a small promontory in Loch Long surrounded by the Argyll Forest
Park. The Viking and Lauder Bars have stunning views and access
to the gardens and beach (50yds away). Lots of local produce –
particularly strong on venison, lamb, salmon, lobster and crab.
Popular dishes from the bar are West Coast clam chowder (£2.25),
crab cakes (£3.95), venison sausages with onion sauce (£4.25), and
lemon sole on the bone (£8.50); ask for children's portions. The
restaurant table d'hote menu (£19.50) offers the likes of seafood crepe
with cream and herb sauce, Musselburgh pie or poached fillet
of salmon Glayva and a choice of Scottish cheeses or puddings (boozy
bread & butter pudding or McCallum – shortbread, ice cream and jam
sauce). Good wine list. Popular with Clyde yachtsmen at weekends
and fishermen. Comfortable bedrooms are good-sized, neat and bright,
with white units or period furniture; some have showers only; there
are stunning views of the loch and surrounding forests and mountains
from those designated 'Fyne'. The hotel has a guest boat to journey
up Lochs Long and Goil. No real ales. *Pub open 11-11 all week,*
Bar Food *12-2.30, 6.30-9.30 (Sat & Sun noon-10).* **Restaurant Meals**
*7.30-9. Children's menu, children allowed in bar to eat. Seaside garden,
outdoor eating. Family room.* **Accommodation** *11 bedrooms, all en suite,*

from £50 (single from £25). Children welcome overnight, additional beds (£8), cots supplied (£3). Fishing, hotel boat, mountain bikes. Hotel closed Nov-mid March. Access, Amex, Diners, Visa.

Arisaig   Old Library Lodge & Restaurant

Tel 068 75 651	Restaurant

Arisaig Highland PH39 4NH   **Map 3 A4**

Alan and Angela Broadhurst have completed ten years at the Old Library, a 200-year-old stable converted into a restaurant and guest house. It stands in an area of great natural beauty, commanding fine views over Loch Nan Ceall and the Inner Hebrides. Lunchtime is the time for snacking, from a menu typified by mussel and lentil soup with home-baked bread (£1.60), smoked trout salad (£4.70), coq au vin (£4.95) and fresh Mallaig cod with mushrooms (£4.95). Toasted sandwiches are £1.50 a round. The evening table d'hote menu is more expensive. There are three tables out on the patio and two high-chairs. **Seats** 28. **Open** 11.30-2.30. **Closed** *end Oct-week before Easter. Access, Visa.*

Auchmithie   But'n'Ben

Tel 0241 77223	Restaurant

Auchmithie by Arbroath Tayside   **Map 3 D5**

Margaret and Iain Horn's simple, friendly cottage restaurant, 3 miles north-east of Arbroath, offers good local produce with a distinct Scottish flavour from midday, with mussels in wine and garlic (£3), poached salmon salad (£4.20), Angus sirloin steak (£6.80) and sweets from the trolley, but those turning up early will always get a welcoming cup of coffee. A hearty Scottish high tea from 4 to 5.30 brings a choice of perhaps Grandma Horn's meat-roll salad, Arbroath smokie pancake or local haddock fried in oatmeal, with wholemeal bread, home-made scones, cake and tea for £6.50. The choice widens in the evenings when more substantial dinners are served. Smoking in the sitting rooms only. **Seats** 40. **Open** 12-9.30 (*Sun to 5.30*). **Closed** *Tue. Access, Visa.*

Auchterarder   Gleneagles Hotel   86%   £205

Tel 0764 662231 Fax 0764 662134	Hotel

Auchterarder Tayside PH3 1NF   **Map 3 C5**

Jack Nicklaus's name has now been added to the famous sportsmen who have given their names to the outstanding sporting facilities at this renowned resort hotel. The latest 18-hole golf course, the Monarch's course, was designed by Nicklaus and opened in May 1993, adding to the famous King's and Queen's and Wee Course facilities; clubs may be hired (even by under-14s) and professional tuition is offered. Gleneagles may be synonymous with golf but it has many further sporting attractions: a Health Spa in the leisure centre, Jackie Stewart's Shooting School, the Mark Phillips Equestrian Centre, the British School of Falconry and an arcade where one can shop (considered an equally professional sporting activity by some) in such famous names as Harvey Nichols, Mappin and Webb, Burberry's and even a branch of the Bank of Scotland. The hotel is grand in every sense of the word with large, high-ceilinged public rooms featuring numerous faux-marble fluted columns and pilasters, and decorative plaster ceilings. The cocktail bar and restaurant boast pianists and there is dancing to a live band in the drawing room each evening. The grading of bedrooms depends largely on size and outlook; all are individually decorated to the same high standards from the smallest single room to the twenty full suites. Good family facilities; informal eating in the Country Club or Equestrian Centre; formal dining has been a disappointment on recent visits. With equal staff to guest ratio, levels of service are kept high. *Rooms 236. Garden, indoor swimming pool, sauna, solarium, whirlpool bath, gymnasium, hairdressing, tennis, squash, golf courses, pitch & putt, jogging trails, bowling green, riding, clay-pigeon shooting, coarse and game fishing, mountain bikes, children's playground, snooker, valeting, shopping arcade, bank, post office. Access, Amex, Diners, Visa.*

Auchterhouse	Old Mansion House	68%	£95
Tel 082 626 366 Fax 082 626 400			Hotel
Auchterhouse by Dundee Tayside DD3 0QN			Map 3 C5

Seven miles from Dundee on the B954, a 16th-century, whitewashed Scottish baronial house has been skilfully converted by Nigel and Eva Bell to a charming and relaxed hotel. Some nice architectural features include the vaulted entrance hall, an open Jacobean fireplace and a splendidly ornate 17th-century plasterwork ceiling. Pleasantly furnished bedrooms – two are family suites with separate children's bedrooms – have good bathrooms well stocked with toiletries. Baby-sitting can be arranged, baby-listening is offered; 7pm curfew for children in the bar and restaurant. The heated outdoor pool is fenced. Informal eating in the courtyard bar. *Rooms 6. Garden, outdoor swimming pool, squash, tennis. Closed Christmas, 1 week Jan. Access, Amex, Diners, Visa.*

Restaurant £66

Much local produce is used for the varied carte that is supplemented by a separate vegetarian menu. Cullen skink, smoked Tay salmon, prawn tails in a curried apple and cucumber cream sauce, medallions of venison, and raspberry crème brulée with a nut crust are typical dishes. Good-value lunches. No under-10s at night. No smoking. *Seats 50. Private Room 22. L 12-2 D 7-9.30 (Sun to 9). Set L £11.95/£13.95.*

Aviemore	Stakis Coylumbridge Resort Hotel	62%	£96★
Tel 0479 810661 Fax 0479 811309			Hotel
Aviemore Highland PH22 1QN			Map 3 C4

Skiing is the thing at Aviemore, but this sprawling modern hotel caters admirably for all sorts of activities for both adults and children. New since last year are a sports hall for children, a fun house and an outdoor play area. It's also geared up for large conferences (maximum 750 delegates). Most of the bedrooms are big enough for family use, and baby-sitting, plus (at busy times) a crèche are provided. A couple of rooms are suitable for disabled guests. ★Half-board terms preferred. *Rooms 175. Two indoor swimming pools, sauna, spa bath, steam bath, solarium, beauty & hair salon, tennis, archery. Access, Amex, Diners, Visa.*

Ayr	Fouters Bistro		
Tel 0292 261391			Bistro
2a Academy Street Ayr Strathclyde			Map 4 A1

Laurie and Fran Black have been running this cheerful bistro in a converted vaulted basement originally owned by the British Linen

Bank (1720) since they took it over in 1973. Scottish produce
is cooked in French style with consistently enjoyable results. There are
three good-value lunchtime menus at £4.95-£8.50 for 1-3 courses.
Starters may include West Coast mussels, Fouters country terrine
served with Cumberland sauce or home-made soup followed
by navarin of lamb, confit of duck with herbs and spices or vegetarian
lasagne. Home-made ice creams feature on the dessert menu along
with their popular bread-and-butter pudding with sherry and brandy
or an iced Grand Marnier soufflé. A variety of British and French
cheeses on the board – ploughman's with loaf, fresh fruit and nuts
£4.95. More robust Provençal food is served in the evenings and the
two-course bistro menu is a reasonable £9.90. Children's menu and
portions; two high-chairs and beakers provided; changing shelf in the
Ladies. One no-smoking room. *Seats 38.* *Open 12-2 & 6.30-10.30.*
*Closed L Sun, all Mon, 2 days Christmas, 2 days New Year. Access,
Amex, Diners, Visa.*

Ayr   The Hunny Pot

Tel 0292 263239	Coffee Shop
37 Beresford Terrace Ayr Strathclyde KA7 2EU	**Map 4 A1**

Sunny yellow walls, old pine tables and lots of bears at this Winnie the
Pooh-oriented coffee shop on the edge of the town centre. Everything
on the menu is home-made and available all day (except for
breakfast – till noon); smackerels (Pooh's word for all those delicious
things which wreck the diet/wasitline) are always on offer, but
so is an abundance of wholesome, healthier offerings! The choice
is wide taking in various baked potatoes (from £2.20), sandwiches –
including banana delight and French cinnamon – (from £2.40),
omelettes and all sorts of home-baked goodies – crunchy lemon
sponge, coffee walnut (mostly at £1), tray bakes – and daily
blackboard specials like butter bean and cider casserole (£4.15),
fisherman's pie (£4.25) and haggis, neaps and tatties (£4.15). Pooh's
Old Fashioned Afternoon Tea comes at £4.40 or for smaller appetites
there's Piglet's Cream Tea at £2.65. Good range of teas and fresh
ground coffees including espresso and Austrian (with whipped cream
and Swiss chocolate shavings). Sandwiches, soups, cakes and teas only
on Sundays. The window seat is the best for families. *Seats 32.*
Open 10-10 (Sun 11-5.30). Closed 25 & 26 Dec, 1 & 2 Jan.
No credit cards.

Ayr   The Stables

Tel 0292 283704	Coffee Shop/Wine Bar
Queen's Court 41 Sandgate Ayr Strathclyde	**Map 4 A1**

A characterful wine bar-cum-coffee shop in a charming shopping area
formed out of a group of Victorian and Georgian buildings near the
town centre. The all-day menu, which has a strong Scottish flavour,
offers everything from a scone (freshly baked each morning 50p)
or a bowl of soup (84p) to a full meal – one of their speciality pies
perhaps, like ham and haddie (£5.45) or Tweed kettle pie (casserole
of salmon, mushroom, celery, spring onions and mace (£5.85).
In between come such snacks as haggis (£3.60), macaroni cheese
(£3.30), chicken stovies (£3.60) and crofters (from £2.60 – granary
cottage loaves or baked potatoes with various fillings). Smoked
salmon, eel, venison and duck breast come from the family's own
smoke house and there is always a small selection of Scottish farmhouse
cheeses. The wine list includes a selection of traditional country wines

(silver birch, elderflower, blackberry) and there is a good range
of single malt whiskies, including a malt of the month. No-smoking
area. There is no special children's menu but a few dishes come
in junior portions (as do their own ices). A couple of high-chairs cope
with the really young ones (for whom they will liquidise something
in the kitchen or heat up customers' own baby food and bottles) and
there is a little menagerie of toy animals and some picture books
to keep the little ones amused. Outdoor eating for 26. *Seats 52.*
Open 10-5. Closed 25 & 26 Dec, 1 & 2 Jan. No credit cards.

Ballachulish	**Ballachulish Hotel**	**60%**	**£75**
Tel 085 52 606 Fax 085 52 629			Hotel
Ballachulish Argyll Highland PA39 4JY			Map 3 B4

An imposing inn set below rugged mountains which sweep down
to Loch Linnhe, on the A828 Fort William-Oban road. Impressive
views are shared by restaurant, cocktail bar and baronial residents'
lounge. There's a "local" atmosphere in the Ferry Bars. Bedrooms are
called Lairds or Chieftains, the latter enjoying the best of the light,
space and views. Guests have free use of the leisure centre at the sister
hotel *The Isles of Glencoe* about two miles away. Families are well
catered for by child-friendly staff; the garden's farm area is an added
attraction. Under-16s free if sharing, cots £4.50, extra beds £25.
Supervised crèche (in the village, but owned by the hotel –
arrangements need to be made in advance) from 9am-3pm; high-chair
provided. *Rooms 30. Garden, sea fishing. Access, Visa.*

Banchory	**Raemoir House**	**71%**	**£110**
Tel 033 02 4884 · Fax 033 02 2171			Hotel
Raemoir Banchory Grampian AB31 4ED			Map 3 D4

$2\frac{1}{2}$ miles north of Banchory on the A980. Three generations of the
Sabin family have built friendly hospitality into the fabric of their
hotel, an 18th-century mansion set in a 3500-acre estate. Rich red
brocade chairs, panelled walls and valuable antiques enhance the
traditional look of the morning room, and the bar is fashioned from
a Tudor four-poster. Bedrooms are all different in size and character,
but most have inviting chaises longues, day beds or armchairs. Six
rooms are in the historic 16th-century Ha'Hoose immediately behind
the mansion. There are five self-catering apartments (from £325+
electricity per week) converted from the original coach-house and
stables. Bar and picnic lunches plus informal family eating in the
Music Room, Morning Room or private sitting room; high tea from
5-7pm. Very much a family hotel, with nearly all mother and baby's
requirements provided on request – from potties and baby baths
to baby-listening and laundry. A delightful, rather special hotel –
staying here is more like spending time in a country house as a
personal guest of the owners; one of those special places to which
one always promises to return. *Rooms 25. Garden, sauna, solarium,
keep-fit equipment, tennis, game fishing, 9-hole mini golf, shooting,
helipad. Closed 1 week Jan. Access, Amex, Diners, Visa.*

Restaurant	**£68**

Top-quality produce is cooked without undue elaboration and served
in generous portions by friendly staff. Crab paté, cream of lettuce and
pea soup or venison consommé, devilled whitebait, honey-roast
duckling with a Grand Marnier and kumquat sauce, grilled rack
of lamb with a redcurrant tartlet, and poached salmon from the river

Dee typify chef Derek Smith's style. Both table d'hote and à la carte are offered, plus a long choice for vegetarians, individually-presented sweets (from a piquant lemon tart to a chocoholic's delight) and a fine Scottish cheese trolley. *Seats 64. Private Room 32. L by arrangement on Sun 12.30-2 D 7.30-9. Set L £13.50 (Sun) Set D £23.50.*

Banchory	Tor-na-Coille Hotel	66%	£85
Tel 033 02 2242 Fax 033 02 4012			Hotel
Inchmarlo Road Banchory Grampian AB3 4AB			Map 3 D4

Built as a private house in 1873 and a hotel since the turn of the century, Tor-na-Coille retains much of its Victorian character. The programme of refurbishment instituted by owner Roxanne Sloan most recently involved the foyer and stairs. The function room can accommodate 90 people for a banquet, 80 for a conference. Bedrooms are furnished with antiques. The hotel copes very well with children (under-10s stay free in parents' room) with cots, baby baths, potties, changing mats, baby-sitting and baby-listening. Baby food, children's menu and cutlery are also provided; a small charge is made for cots and under-15s. Further facilities are offered during Summer school holidays (ring for details). Laundry service on site. *Rooms 25. Garden, squash, playground, crèche (8-4, Mon-Fri). Closed 25-28 Dec. Access, Amex, Diners, Visa.*

Busta	Busta House Hotel		
Tel 080622 506 Fax 080622 588			Pub
Busta Brae Shetland Islands ZE2 9QN			Map 2 D1

This 16th-century former laird's home overlooking the sea is a tremendously civilised hotel in a wild place, simply furnished in Scottish rural style. Open to non-residents for good home-cooked bar lunches and suppers – smoked Shetland salmon (£3.95), pork and pepper terrine (£2.95), stuffed courgettes with tomato and fresh chili sauce (£4.85), peppered chicken and pork fillet with rice (£5.95), followed by bramble Cranachan or orange and lemon cheesecake (both £2.05). The restaurant offers a 5-course daily-changing fixed-price menu (£20.50) which could include deep-fried fresh local squid with spicy tomato sauce, roast breast of duck with hazelnut and orange sauce, followed by home-made toffee and Malibu ice cream. All fresh vegetables, and Raven Ale from 'nearby' Orkney. 136 malt whiskies on offer! Four acres of walled garden, small private sea harbour, and holidays arranged of the fly/sail and drive kind too. *Bar Food 12-2 (Sun 12.30-2), 6.30-9.30 (6.30-9 winter, except Fri & Sat). Restaurant Meals 7-9. Children are allowed to eat in the bar. Beer Orkney Raven Ale. Garden, outdoor eating. Accommodation 20 bedrooms, all en suite, £80 (single £60). Children welcome overnight (if sharing parents' room £10), additional beds and cots available. Bar and accommodation closed 22 Dec-3 Jan. Access, Diners, Visa.*

Cairndow	Loch Fyne Oyster Bar		
Tel 049 96 264			Restaurant
Clachan Farm Cairndow Highland			Map 3 B5

West Highland produce including oysters from their own fishery and fish smoked in house such as hot smoked mackerel with a gooseberry sauce (£4.95) or the local speciality Bradhan Rost – hot kiln-smoked salmon with a whisky sauce (£8.95) – at this family operation with

branches in Elton (Peterborough) and Nottingham. Top of the bill
is still the shellfish platter of oysters, langoustines, queen scallops,
brown crab, velvet crab and clams (£14.50), washed down perhaps
with a copita of Manzanilla or a bottle of champagne. Ask for
children's portions of poached Finnan haddock or salmon cakes.
Two high-chairs; new toilets "will include a changing facility".
Seats 80. **Open** 9-9. **Closed** 25 Dec, 1 & 2 Jan. Access, Amex, Visa.

Carbost   Old Inn

Tel 0478 640205	Pub
Carbost Isle of Skye Highland IV47 8SR	Map 2 A3

Next to the loch, and near the Talisker distillery, a charming, chatty
little island cottage, popular as a walkers' base. *Family Room. Lochside
patio/terrace, children's play area. Children welcome overnight.*
No credit cards.

Crieff   Crieff Hydro   64%   £104★

Tel 0764 655555 Fax 0764 653087	Hotel
Crieff Tayside PH7 3LQ	Map 3 C5

An enormous, Victorian building, now a family hotel par excellence
with an impressive range of leisure activities to keep everyone busy
and fit – from indoor cinema and table tennis room to outdoor riding
school and golf course. Apart from singles, most of the bedrooms are
of a decent size, furnished with either lightwood units or more
traditional or antique pieces; some family rooms have bunk beds
in a separate alcove; family suites, baby-listening and cots (free for
under-2s) are also available; nine two-storey family chalets are in the
woods behind. Banqueting and conference facilities for up to 400
delegates keep the place busy during the week; some sporting facilities
are reserved for competitions during bowls and tennis weeks.
Breakfast, lunch and supper for the under-10s are taken in the nursery
where high-chairs, and baby food are provided; a playroom adjoins
the nursery. Nine whitewashed two-storey family apartments are also
close to the hotel; the sitting rooms here include two single bed-
settees. ★Half-board terms only. No dogs, except in the self-catering
Hydro Chalets on a wooded hillside above the hotel (easy access for
cars); a few kennels are available but require prior booking. All
accommodation has free use of all the leisure facilities: young children
might particularly enjoy the outdoor adventure playground and the
children's swimming pool with chute, while adults may like to take
a breather by using the facilities of the supervised children's nursery
(for over-3s only) during meal times, relax in the hot tub by the
children's pool or jog around the outdoor nature trail. Special teenage
activities week in July includes free coaching. Table licence only,
no bar. The Crieff Hydro has been family-run for over 125 years and
they know that "happy children mean happy parents...". Winner
of our Family Hotel of the Year 1993 award. **Rooms** 199. Garden,
croquet, indoor swimming pool, children's pool, outdoor paddling pool,
whirlpool, spa bath, sauna, steam room, sunbeds, boutique, hairdressing and
beauty salon, coffee shop, tennis, squash, badminton, basketball, volleyball, 9-
hole golf course, putting, all-weather bowling green, snooker, riding school,
football pitch, cinema, playroom, playground, dinner dancing, supervised
crèche (7-9pm). Access, Amex, Diners, Visa.

Crinan   **Crinan Coffee Shop**

Tel 0546 83261	Coffee Shop
Crinan by Lochgilphead Strathclyde PA31 8SR	**Map 3 B5**

An idyllic setting for this characterful coffee shop, a stone's throw
from its parent hotel, by the lock basin at the end of the 200-year-old
Crinan Canal. Eager girls run things with great enterprise and a no-
nonsense approach producing king-size sausage rolls (£1.65), quiche
and salad (£2.65), scones, doughnuts, lemon or caramel slice (£1),
chocolate or cream gateau (£1.50/£1.65), date flapjacks and the
speciality cloutie dumpling (£1.20). Two high-chairs. *Seats 50.*
Open 9-5 **Closed** *end Oct-Easter. No credit cards.*

Cromarty   **Royal Hotel**

Tel 0381 600 217	Pub
Marine Terrace Cromarty Highland IV11 8YN	**Map 2 C3**

Formed out of a row of 18th-century coastguards' cottages facing the
Cromarty Firth, the black and white painted 'Royal' is now under the
hospitable Morrisons, and is a hotel of considerable charm. Except
in the warmest of weather a real fire burns in the homely lounge off
which a Lloyd Loom-furnished sun lounge looks across the road to the
water beyond. The lounge bar features armchairs along with
banquettes or you can challenge the locals to a game of pool or darts
in the Public Bar. Immaculate, individually decorated bedrooms, each
with a sea view, have traditional furniture and crisp pure cotton
bedding. Bar open all day. Recommended for B&B only. *Free House.*
Beer *Belhaven Best. Garden, children's play area. Family room.*
Accommodation *10 bedrooms, 8 en suite, £50 (single £28). Access, Visa.*

Dirleton   **Open Arms Hotel**   67%   £110

Tel 0620 85241 Fax 0620 85570	Hotel
Dirleton nr North Berwick Lothian EH39 5EG	**Map 3 D5**

A good name for a friendly, characterful hotel in a charming position
overlooking the village green and the ruins of 16th-century Dirleton
Castle. It's been in the same family for nearly half a century, and
there's a relaxed, domestic warmth to the lounge, which has
comfortable armchairs and sofas, a log fire, magazines and newspapers;
the bar is tiny but full of character. Bedrooms are mostly bright and
airy, with floral curtains; each has an easy chair and personal touches
such as flowers and fruit. Children up to 10 stay free in parents' room;
baby-sitting by prior arrangement. Good light meals in the lounge
(Mon-Sat) offer fresh local produce in many dishes: soup of the day
(£1.50), mussel and onion stew (£2.20), grilled fillets of lemon sole
with chive and white wine sauce (£5.40), mushroom-sauced vegetable
crepe, pan-fried escalope of pork with tomato and basil sauce.
Traditional Sunday lunch (£14.75); more elaborate evening meals;
afternoon tea. A high-chair can be provided (as can children's portions)
and there's a safe garden. *Rooms 7. Garden. Closed 1 week Jan.*
Access, Visa.

Dulnain Bridge   **Muckrach Lodge**   59%   £78

Tel 0479 85257 Fax 0479 85325	Hotel
Dulnain Bridge nr Grantown-on-Spey Highland PH26 3LY	**Map 2 C3**

Considerably improved by the Watsons over the last couple of years,
this former Victorian hunting lodge sits in ten acres of its own

rounds with fine views of the Dulnain valley all around. If you stay
or more than one night, or have stayed before, you are rewarded
ith miniatures of malt whisky and fresh fruit in bedrooms furnished
ith good-quality freestanding furniture and decorated in a variety
f soft colour schemes. Carpeted bathrooms offer good towelling and
l sort of bits and bobs from cotton wool balls to a nail brush. The
ormer steading (stables) now houses two full suites, one especially
dapted for wheelchair-bound guests. Magazines and fresh flowers add
o the comfort and relaxation in the lounge. Hearty home-made soups,
ibstantial sandwiches and a handful of hot dishes (for 'Muckrach
Iinors') should satisfy hungry families; two high-chairs are provided.
he cosy panelled bar overlooks 10 acres of grounds and tables are
o be found on lawns and terrace in fine weather. Children up to five
e accommodated free in five good-sized family rooms (cot free
f charge, extra bed £5); baby-listening is available. Straightforward
mily facilities, but the willingness of hotel staff to accommodate
iildren more than makes up for the absence of hot and cold running
owns! No dogs. **Rooms** *12. Garden, fishing. Closed 3 weeks Nov.
ccess, Amex, Diners, Visa.*

---

umfries	**Opus Salad Bar**	
el 0387 55752		Café
5 Queensberry Street Dumfries Dumfries & Galloway DG1 1BH		Map 4 B2

or a quarter of a century the Halliday family have been running
. unpretentious salad bar that's part of a first-floor store in a cobbled
eet just off the shopping square. There's a rapid lunchtime turnover
 the self-service counter, where plenty of hot and cold dishes are
i offer for both carnivores and vegetarians. All the food is made
i the premises and covers a range of wholesome dishes like vegetable
umble (£2), shepherd's pie (£2.10), lasagne and a selection of salads
0p per portion). Assorted cakes (lemon, chocolate, banana pie 85p),
ones, carrot cake, biscuits. Non-smoking area. Breakfast 9-10.30. One
ooster seat and room for changing in the Ladies. "Children are
commodated in any way." **Seats** *44.* **Open** *9-4.30 (Thur to 2.15).
osed Sun. Access, Visa.*

---

undee	**Raffles Restaurant**	
el 0382 26344		Restaurant
Perth Road Dundee Tayside		Map 3 C5

hind the ruffled net curtains is a motley collection of old dining
airs and tables where a good crowd gathers to enjoy a wide range
 wholesome dishes at keen prices. Apart from the main menu
lmon and prawn pot £2.90, Madeira-sauced guinea fowl £7),
 all-day snack menu offers open sandwiches, jacket potatoes (grated
eese £1.75), spaghetti bolognese, savoury pancakes (from £3.10),
eet pancakes and home-baked bread. Children's portions; two high-
airs and a large area in the Ladies for nursing mums. **Seats** *70.*
en 12-2 & 6-9 (Fri to 10.30, Sat all day 11.30-10.30). **Closed** *Sun,
on, 1st 2 weeks Jan, 2 weeks Jul/Aug. No credit cards.*

---

dinburgh	**Caledonian Hotel**	79%	£192
el 031-225 2433 Fax 031-225 6632			Hotel
nces Street Edinburgh Lothian EH1 2AB			Map 3 C6

fectionately known as 'the Caley', the hotel stands on the site of the
l Caledonian railway station (demolished in 1965), one mile from

the current Waverley station at the end of Princes Street overlooking Edinburgh Castle. The carpeted foyer leads to a grand, gracefully proportioned and elegant lounge, furnished with plush shot-silk sofas. Carriages restaurant and bar retains the redbrick former station entrance as an inside wall. Bedrooms are individually styled, featuring well-chosen furniture and luxurious drapes; 5th-floor rooms are smaller than some of the others; 41 rooms are reserved for non-smokers. De luxe rooms and those with a view of the Castle attract a supplement; there are also 22 suites. Towelling robes are provided in all the bathrooms, which include a TV/radio speaker; elegant antique-style fittings in Executive bathrooms. Plus factors are the number of telephone extensions in the rooms, 24hr lounge service and a turn-down service. Families are particularly well catered for; a children's menu is served either in the restaurant or in your room – high tea is suggested to be served at 6.30pm. Generous afternoon tea (3-5.30pm: £8.50) and all-day snacks in the Lounge. No baby-listening, so arrange baby-sitting before arriving should you require it. Children up to 12 stay free in parents' room. No dogs. Own free parking. Queens Moat Houses. **Rooms** 240. *News kiosk. Access, Amex, Diners, Visa.*

Pompadour Room £100

The Pompadour is elegant and formal; ornate plasterwork frames large wall paintings of delicate flowers, a pianist plays soothing music and excellent staff provide impeccable service. Chef Tony Binks offers an interesting lunch menu and a long evening carte with modern French dishes – from parfait of quail with watercress and glazed oranges or langoustines wrapped in smoked salmon with vegetable blinis to roast fillet of sea bass with crispy leeks and a caviar butter sauce and grilled fillet of Angus beef with a claret sauce and braised onion hearts. A *menu dégustation* offers five well-balanced light courses. Good French and Scottish cheeses. The wine list is well chosen but offers little choice under £20. *Seats* 50. *Private Room* 160. *L* 12.30-2 *D* 7.30-10.30. *Closed L Sat & Sun, also D Sun Nov-Mar. Set L £27 Set D £35*

Carriages Restaurant £60

The hotel's second restaurant is open for breakfast, lunch and dinner seven days a week, serving familiar dishes like chicken liver paté, choices from a salad bar, lamb hot pot and pasta shells with seafood and a lobster sauce, along with a few Scottish favourites such as Musselburgh pie and haggis with neeps and tatties. There are also daily-changing table d'hote lunch and dinners, plus traditional Sunday lunches. Exemplary staff and high-chairs for the wee ones. Dinner dance every Saturday night when the band plays until past midnight. *Seats* 150. *B 7-10 (Sun 7.30-10.30) L 12-2.30 (Sat & Sun from 12.30 D 6.30-10. Set L £13.75/£17.25 (Sun £14.75) Set D £23.50.*

Edinburgh	Carlton Highland	68%	£13
Tel 031-556 7277 Fax 031-556 2691			Hotel
North Bridge Edinburgh Lothian EH16 6XY			Map 3 C

Despite its granite vastness, the Carlton is a welcome oasis for families. Besides well-equipped bedrooms (all with satellite TV) and comfortable day rooms the Carlton Highland (located between Princes Street and the Royal Mile) has a fine leisure club (including supervised daytime play room; ask about children's hours in the club), conference facilities for up to 350, two restaurants and a night club

(the Minus One) with dancing and live entertainment several nights
a week. Children up to 16 stay free in their parents' room (15 rooms
suitable for family use). Baby-sitting only requires one hour's notice,
but check when booking that this is still the case. Good children's
menu in the restaurant where you'll also find high-chairs and small
portions; high tea at 5pm in Court's Carvery, Grill & Salad Bar.
Carlyle's Coffee Shop is open from 10am-6pm Sept-May, to 9pm
May-Sept. *Rooms* 199. *Indoor swimming pool, gymnasium, sauna, spa
bath, steam room, solarium, squash, snooker, hair & beauty salon, coffee shop
(Court's: 7am-10.30pm). Access, Amex, Diners, Visa.*

Edinburgh	The Engine Shed Café	
Tel 031-662 0040		**Vegetarian**
9 St Leonard's Lane Edinburgh Lothian		Map 3 C6

As the name would suggest, this vegetarian café is on the first floor
of an old stone building that was formerly an engine shed (for
a standing engine that pulled other engines up the hill). On the ground
floor there's a bakery (wholesale) which interestingly makes its own
tofu. The café is run by Garvald Community Enterprises, a charity
employing people with special needs. The bright, airy room has stone
walls displaying up-and-coming artists' works and there's a large public
notice board. There's always a home-made soup (parsnip and apple,
leek and potato 65p) and the hot dishes of the day may include spicy
chick pea stew (£2.75) or nut roast with tomato sauce (£2.75); there
is always at least one vegan choice. Otherwise home baking dominates
with carrot cake, chocolate brownies, scones, millionaire shortbread
(from 40-70p) or filled rolls. Children are made particularly welcome
since access is easy, the café is spacious and they love the tofu whips
(yoghurt-style dessert); high-chairs, beakers, good changing facilities
and a lift for buggies indicate a caring attitude towards mums and wee
ones. Unlicensed. No smoking. *Seats 55. Open 10.30-3. Closed Sat,
Sun, 1 week Christmas, 1 week Easter, 2 weeks summer. No credit cards.*

Edinburgh	Fishers	
Tel 031-554 5666		**Pub**
The Shore Leith Edinburgh Lothian EH6 6QW		Map 3 C6

Fishers is a jewel cast up from the sea, an outstanding seafood speciality
bar which serves full meals all day, noon to 10.30 pm. It's taken root
in a renovated corner building at the end of The Shore, at the foot
of what looks like an ancient bell-tower or lighthouse. The bar area,
in which you can also eat, groups high stools around higher-still tables.
Up a short flight of steps, the main eating area features light-wood
panelling with night-sky blue tables and chairs, windows half
of frosted glass, half giving a view to the harbour and beyond, and all
presided over from a great height by a bejewelled mermaid figure.
The pricing structure and the variety of food on offer are admirably
suited to most appetites and pockets, whether for serious eating
or quick snacking. It's worth going the full three rounds from starter
to pudding, and make an evening of it, when it's also wise to book;
word is spreading. In addition to the photocopied handwritten menu,
a blackboard of daily specials offers a host of starters and main courses
which should appeal to more than fish fans alone. The creamiest, most
deeply delicious salmon soup (£2.95) competes for attention with fish
patés and oatcakes (£2.85), mussels in white wine, garlic, tomato and
herbs (£2.50), seafood platter (£9) or one of the day's specials;

a sheep's cheese and olive salad (£5.50) in a creamy sauce fills a whole platter, with little room left for the new potatoes, garnished with mint. Salads are crunchy, fresh and in plenty – endive, Chinese leaves, tomatoes, radishes, mangetout and spring onions. Chose your dressing from a piquant selection of onion, hazelnut or raspberry vinaigrette, or mix your own combination from the bottles of Spanish olive oil and French champagne vinegar thoughtfully provided on each table. If any room remains, there are simple home-made fruit flans, pies and crumbles (£2.85). Altogether excellent quality and value for money. *Open all day 11am-10pm. **Bar Food & Restaurant Meals** 12-10 (from 12.30 Sun). Children's portions. Free House. **Beer** Caledonian 80/-, Tartan Special. Riverside, outdoor eating. Family room. Access, Visa.*

Edinburgh   Helios Fountain

Tel 031-229 7884	Vegetarian
7 Grassmarket Edinburgh Lothian EH1 2HY	**Map 3 C6**

Jos and Mei-Lian Bastiaensen's vegetarian and vegan coffee house at the rear of a crafts and book shop continues to draw the crowds, particularly students and academics, who appreciate the relaxed, unpretentious surroundings and very keen prices. From 10am scones (75p) and cold savouries such as lentil pie with tomato sauce (£1.20) are gradually joined by a selection of 9 or 10 cakes – Dorset apple (£1.10), banana yoghurt (£1.50) – and biscuits – tollhouse cookie (60p), date slice (50p) – and six salads such as red cabbage and tomato or curried chick pea, priced from 75p. Lunch brings a hot quiche (£1.85), soups (spicy cauliflower £1.10) and perhaps a casserole (plantation £1.90). Normally closed on Sunday except during the Festival and August (open 11-6) and December (11-5). One high-chair, toy box and a changing area outside the loos. Non-smoking throughout. *Seats 40. **Open** 10-6 (to 8 duringFestival). **Closed** 25 & 26 Dec, 1 & 2 Jan. Access, Visa.*

Edinburgh   Henderson's Salad Table

Tel 031-225 2131	Vegetarian
94 Hanover Street Edinburgh Lothian EH2 1DR	**Map 3 C6**

Here for more than 30 years, the Henderson family continue to preside over their hugely popular counter-service vegetarian restaurant, in a large basement below the family fruit shop. The day starts at 8 with organic fruit juices, yoghurt and wholemeal croissants (50p) and the counter display gradually fills up with cold savouries such as felafel, salads (from 80p) and spinach and rice balls (£1.10), and various cakes including some sugar-free items such as apricot slice and cashew nut (60p). Hot items, chalked on a blackboard (which also highlights vegan options) are available from 11.30 to 2.30 and again from 4.30 to 10.30 and could include lentil and butterbean bake (£2), broccoli and Brie crumble (£2.20) and Bravastouriana – aubergine and vegetable fritters in wine (£3.20). To finish, Scottish cheese and desserts such as trifle (£1.50), citrus cheese cake (£1.50) and dried fruits with soured cream and ginger (£1.50). Prices are extremely reasonable, but ask for a child's portion if you require one. Four high-chairs and changing facilities in both Ladies and Gents. *Seats 180. **Open** 8am-11pm. **Closed** Sun (except during Festival – open 9am-10pm), Bank Holidays. Access, Amex, Visa.*

Edinburgh   Kalpna

Tel 031-667 9890	Vegetarian
2-3 St Patrick Square Edinburgh Lothian EH8 9ES	Map 3 C6

After many years of excellence, Kalpna still holds its reputation as one of the best vegetarian Indian restaurants in the country. Focus here is strictly on food in clean but basic surroundings. Service is helpful and charming, and the owner will happily give advice. Tasty ingredients and freshly ground spices are used to produce superior-quality dishes which all have their own identity and specific flavours. Aneer kadhai are home-made cheese cubes cooked in a rich sauce flavoured with tomato, garlic and fenugreek leaves. Sabzi kufta are potato and vegetable balls served in a sweet and sour sauce yoghurt sauce. Khoya kaju is a mix of cashew nuts, khoya, sultanas, nutmeg and fresh coriander. The lunch time buffet starts at £3.50 and thali at £7. Booking is essential but you still might wait. Two high-chairs and two booster seats. No smoking. *Seats 65.* **Open** *12-2 & 5.30-10.30.* **Closed** *L Sat, all Sun (except during the festival), 25 & 26 Dec, 1 Jan.* Access, Visa.

Edinburgh   Lazio

Tel 031-229 7788	Restaurant
95 Lothian Road Edinburgh Lothian	Map 3 C6

Run by the Crolla family since 1981, this long, narrow restaurant with a mural of the owners' home village on the end wall offers authentic pasta and pizzas for around £5 – spaghetti carbonara, rigatoni Vincenzo, lasagne al forno, Lazio and margherita pizzas. More substantial dishes are steaks (£8.90), pollo Cleopatra (£7.50) and scampi Lorenzo (£7.70). Desserts include around 20 variations on an ice cream theme. *Seats 55.* **Open** *noon-2am (weekend to 3am).* **Closed** *25 & 26 Dec, 1 Jan.* Access, Amex, Diners, Visa.

Edinburgh   Lune Town

Tel 031-220 1688	Restaurant
38 William Street Edinburgh Lothian	Map 3 C6

A long-standing Cantonese restaurant with cosy ground and basement rooms and sound, sometimes spectacular cooking. Dim sum and soups are £1.80, the wun tun soup being one of the best around, while main courses include beef in black bean (£5.80), aromatic duck (£10.50), and king prawns in hoi sin sauce (£9.80). A discretionary minimum charge of £10 can apply when busy. Small no-smoking room downstairs. *Seats 75.* **Open** *12-2.30 & 6-11.30 (Fri to 12, Sat 4pm-1am, Sun 4pm-11pm).* **Closed** *L Sat & Sun, 25 Dec, 1 Jan, 3 days Chinese New Year.* Access, Amex, Visa.

Edinburgh   Scottish National Gallery of Modern Art, Gallery Café

Tel 031-332 8600	Café
Belford Road Edinburgh Lothian EH4 3DR	Map 3 C6

Located in the museum basement, this is a popular café worth queueing for. The dining area is bright but the most attractive setting is the outdoor terrace where the metallic tables and chairs match the style of the modern sculptures exhibited on the lawn; children are asked to be closely supervised in this very special garden. The self-service café has a limited but unusually inventive menu. Soups could

be lettuce and mint or cauliflower and caraway (£1.15). Hot dishes
might include pepper and cabbage stuffed with lentils (£3.60). Salads
(90p a portion) are creative and delicious, the likes of shredded carrot,
cabbage and mint, broccoli, cauliflower and blue cheese. Farmhouse
cheeses (£2.20 for a selection) are attractively displayed and sliced
to order. All pastries are home-made using free-range eggs, lemon cake
(£1), peanut biscuit (55p), shortbread (85p), scones (65p) and even
home-made preserves. Children's portions and baked potatoes always
available; one high-chair and baby cups provided. No-smoking area.
*Seats 50 (plus 60 outside). Open 10.30-4.30 (Sun from 2). Closed 25 &
26 Dec, 2 days New Year, May Day. No credit cards.*

Elie   Ship Inn

Tel 0333 330246	Pub
The Toft Elie Fife KY9 1DT	Map 3 C5

Recent rebuilding of the Ship, part of a terrace of old cottages down
by the harbour, has, to the relief of the locals, left the original bar very
much as it was before with wooden benches around the dark-painted,
boarded walls, beamed ceiling and back room with booth seating.
What has been added is a pair of restaurant rooms with old dining
tables, sturdy kitchen chairs and, on the first floor, a small balcony
with coin-operated binoculars for scanning the harbour. Limited
snacks – soups, burgers and toasted sandwiches – are served in the bar
while more substantial meals are available in the restaurant where one
can have just a single dish (or children's portions) from the printed
menu if one wants. Cakes and biscuits are served with tea and coffee
throughout the day. In July and August, tables on the sea wall opposite
the Ship are served by an open-air barbecue. When the tide is out
a vast expanse of sand is revealed where, twice a year, the Ship's own
cricket team plays a match against a visiting side. Two high-chairs.
*Restaurant Meals 12-2.30 (to 3 Sun), 6-9.30 (Fri/Sat to 10, Sun to 9).
Free House. Beer Belhaven 80/-, Courage Directors. Family room (separate
area at back of bar). Access, Visa.*

Falkirk   Coffee Cabin

Tel 0324 25757	Coffee Shop
23 Cockburn Street Falkirk Central	Map 3 C5

Fiona Marshall does her own baking in her tiny coffee shop tucked
away behind the main shopping area. Cream scones (60p), sponges
with butter icing (40p) and fruit slices (40p) are typical items, with
apple pie (90p) and spicy fruit crumble (90p) among the sweets. For
savoury palates there are filled rolls (from 60p), toasted sandwiches
(£1.10), flans (£1) and jacket potatoes with fillings ranging in price
up to chicken curry (£1.80). Soup (80p) comes with wholemeal bread
and butter, breakfast costs £2.20. Children's portions. Unlicensed.
Seats 30. Open 9.30-5. Closed Sun, 25 & 26 Dec, 1 Jan. No credit cards.

Fochabers   Gordon Arms

Tel 0343 820508 Fax 0343 820300	Pub
High Street Fochabers Grampian IV32 7DH	Map 2 C3

Antlers decorate the exterior of a former coaching inn standing
alongside the A96 and a short walk away from the River Spey, while
the public bar sports a variety of fishing bric-a-brac – including stuffed
prize catches. Simple overnight accommodation is provided by 13
well-equipped bedrooms (TVs, tea-makers, hairdryers and direct-dial

telephones), which include both older rooms with large carpeted bathrooms and a number of smaller but quieter ones in the extension. Open all day 11-11. Free house. **Beer** McEwan's 80/- & Export, Tartan Special. Garden. Family room. **Accommodation** 13 bedrooms, all en suite, £70 (single £43). Children welcome overnight, additional beds (from £10), cots supplied. Access, Visa.

Forfar	**Royal Hotel**	57%	£65
Tel & Fax 0307 62691			Hotel
Castle Street Forfar Tayside DD8 3AE			Map 3 C4

A modest entrance conceals a thriving, compact, well-kept hotel complete with leisure centre, ballroom and roof garden. A cheerful welcome and real fire greet guests in the tiny tartan reception area with cosy bar and rattan-furnished lounge nearby (changes are planned to the day rooms). Bedrooms, apart from one four-poster room, are small, but neat and practical. Children can eat in the informal Pool bar (where there are toys and a children's menu offered 10am-11pm) rather than in the more formal first-floor Royal restaurant (traditional Scottish high teas served on Sundays); nevertheless, two high-chairs are provided in the restaurant at breakfast and lunch. Cots £5, extra beds £15. No dogs. **Rooms** 19. Indoor swimming pool, sauna, spa bath, solarium, hair salon, coffee shop (10am-11pm). Access, Amex, Diners, Visa.

Garve	**Inchbae Lodge**	57%	£56
Tel 099 75 269			Hotel
Inchbae by Garve Highland IV23 2PH			Map 2 B3

About three miles north of Garve on the A835, this old stone-built (now white-painted) hunting lodge is a very friendly, convenient sort of place. The small, rustic bar is also the 'local' and in the lounge, where a real fire burns most of the year, the modern low-backed settees are arranged so as to encourage conversation among guests. There are board games and jigsaw puzzles for the occasional rainy day. Bedrooms, half in the main house and half in an adjacent red cedar chalet, are modestly appointed – no TV, radio or telephone and all but three have shower and WC only – but well-kept and quite attractive with pine furniture and a plum and pale green colour scheme. The pubby bar features blue-cushioned banquettes around the panelled walls, rustic tables and some exposed stonework. Good bar food (12-2, 6-8.30, Sun from 12.30 and 6.30), from a daily soup with home-made bread to honey-baked gammon salad, casserole and pasta dish of the day. Triple-decker sandwiches, filled baked potatoes, omelettes and steaks complete the picture. Breakfast choices include locally smoked haddock. Children are made very welcome with their own high tea from 5pm or smaller portions in the bar or at dinner; two high-chairs and children's cutlery provided. In the grounds are hens and the family's pet rabbits; watch out for the pond and unfenced river Blackwater at the end of the garden. Children stay free in their parents' room regardless of age. **Rooms** 12. Garden, fishing. No credit cards.

Restaurant

The menu is short, just two choices at each stage plus a soup course, but changes daily and allows chef-proprietor Les Mitchell to concentrate on dishes that make good use of some excellent local ingredients: perhaps a really peaty smoked salmon stuffed with poached wild salmon and mayonnaise, loin of wild venison cooked pink and served with a tarragon sauce or corn-fed chicken with bacon and a Stilton cream sauce. Charlotte is responsible for the puds – perhaps raspberry and peach brulée or a delicious chocolate brioche pudding – and sweeties served with good coffee in the lounge. No smoking. *Seats 24. D only 7.30-8.30. Set D £19.50.*

Gatehouse of Fleet   Murray Arms Inn   £79

| Tel 0557 814207   Fax 0557 814370 | Inn |

Anne Street Gatehouse of Fleet Dumfries & Galloway DG7 2HY   Map 4 B2

A warm, friendly old posting inn (established over 300 years) whose hospitable day rooms include the Burns Room, where the poet reputedly wrote *Scots Wha Hae*. There's also a little cocktail bar. Bedrooms, all centrally heated, are by no means grand but lack nothing to provide a good night's rest. These, and the bathrooms, are kept in very good order. In the garden there's a cottage suite with its own bedroom, sitting room, bathroom and a bed settee for additional children. Children up to 14 free in parents' room, plus special family room deals during July and August. Very much part of the local community, the inn also acts as the town's pub and coffee shop; of the three dining rooms the Lunky Hole is open all day. Cardoness Castle and Castramon Wood Wildlife reserve are close by. The inn stands on the A75 Dumfries to Stranraer road. *Rooms 13. Garden, coffee shop (noon-9.45pm). Access, Amex, Diners, Visa.*

Gifford   Tweeddale Arms

| Tel 062 081 240 | Pub |

High Street Gifford Lothian EH41 4QU   Map 3 D6

Probably the oldest building in the village, the black and white Tweeddale Arms lies alongside a peaceful village green. The comfortable, mellow lounge features some old oil paintings while the bar has recently been refurbished with tapestry-style upholstery and baskets of dried flowers hanging from the old beams. The bar menu, which changes every few weeks, offers a good selection of carefully cooked dishes; high-chair provided. Good, clean bedrooms have either light or darkwood freestanding furniture and modern en-suite bathrooms; two family rooms. All have TV, direct-dial phone and a tea/coffee-making kit. A nice old inn, family run in friendly fashion. Outdoor play area with swing, slide and climbing frame. *Pub open all day (to midnight Sat). Bar Food 12-2, 7-9. Free House. Beer Burtons, Tetley. Children's play area. Accommodation 18 bedrooms, all en suite, £60 (single £47.50). Children welcome overnight, additional cots and beds provided. Access, Visa.*

Glasgow   Café Gandolfi

| Tel 041-552 6813 | Brasserie |

64 Albion Street Glasgow Strathclyde   Map 3 B6

Rustic wooden floors, walls and designer furniture in this bustling café (once a Victorian pub) in the old Merchant district. The day begins at 9am with croissants (£1.40), fruit scones (95p) and eggs en cocotte (£2.40), the choice widening at lunch to include soup (£1.95), salads (£2.10-£3.60), gravad lax (£4.25) and hot dishes such as Finnan haddock (£7), Italian sausages (£6.60) and a couple of daily blackboard specials, perhaps chicken with coriander (£7.60) or baked fish pie with potatoes (£7). There is always a vegetarian choice, and

puddings include home-made ice creams (£2.80) and crème brulée
(£2.80). No under-14s after 8pm. **Seats** 70. **Open** 9am-11.30pm.
Closed Bank Holidays. No credit cards.

Glasgow   Caffé Qui

Tel 041-552 6099	Café
17 John Street Glasgow Strathclyde	Map 3 B6

Between Giorgio Armani and Gianni Versace in the Italian Centre,
this Italian café is (not surprisingly) rather smart. Savoury offerings
include toasted focaccia with various fillings (from £2.50), open
sandwiches and croissants (from £2.50), a few pizzas and *piatti grandi*
like pasta carbonara (£3.95) and seafood pasta (£4.95). A supper
menu is introduced at around 7pm each night until last orders.
Pavement tables, and others in a courtyard beyond the conservatory
area, add to the Continental atmosphere. Three high-chairs for little
ones; storage of push chairs is no problem. **Seats** 150 (*plus 70 outside*).
Open 10am-9.45pm (*Sun from 11*). **Closed** 25 & 26 Dec, 1 & 2 Jan.
Access, Amex, Diners, Visa.

Glasgow   Chapter House

Tel 041-221 8913	Café
26 Bothwell Street Glasgow Strathclyde	Map 3 B6

Set in the heart of of the business district, this light, airy café at the
rear of Christian bookshop *Pickering & Inglis* does a roaring trade over
its 'we-serve-you' counter, offering a simple but consistently good
selection of healthy, home-made products. Business people can browse
through the day's papers at breakfast, snacking on tray-bakes (from
75p), coffee, and bacon or scrambled egg rolls (£1.25), while at lunch
the choice expands to include soup with roll and butter (£1.35), salads
(£1.10), quiche (£1.30) and a daily casserole (£2.99-£3.50). Finish
with trifle, fruit salad or perhaps rhubarb tart (£1.30). Particularly
popular with families on Saturdays – even a toy box for children.
Pavement café during fine weather. Unlicensed. Non-smoking section.
Seats 60. **Open** 8.30-4.30 (*Sat from 9*). **Closed** Sun, Bank Holidays.
Access, Visa.

Glasgow   Janssen's Café/Restaurant

Tel 041-334 9682	Café/Restaurant
1355 Argyle Street Glasgow Strathclyde	Map 3 B6

Dutchman Jan Leenhoutts and his Glaswegian wife preside over their
informal café-restaurant offering a formula that allows most items
to be had as full meals or in smaller tapas-style portions. Specials such
as swordfish or Italian meatballs (from £7) join more permanent items
including Cajun chicken (£7.30) and grilled gambas (£8.75),
vegetarian lasagne or satay (£6.40), salads (£4.50), houmus (£3.60)
and deep-fried mussels (£3.15). Cakes and desserts all come from
an Italian pasticceria, save the apple bowl, made with cinnamon and
wrapped in puff pastry. **Seats** 50. **Open** 12-10.30 (*Fri & Sat to 11, Sun
to 9*). **Closed** 25 & 26 Dec, 1 & 2 Jan. Access, Visa.

Glasgow   The Jenny Traditional Tea Rooms

Tel 041-204 4988	Tea Room
18 Royal Exchange Square Glasgow Strathclyde	Map 3 B6

The Jenny is a recreation of one of the Victorian tea rooms for which
Glasgow was once as famous as Vienna for its coffee houses. Cottagey

decor and waitresses in floral print dresses create a charming
atmosphere in which to enjoy one of the set teas (from £2.75),
a savoury brioche bun with various toppings, or a 2-in-1 pie (£4.45)
in which half an earthenware dish is filled with a pie, steak and
mushroom or turkey and sweetcorn perhaps, and the other half with
either cauliflower cheese or sauté potatoes. A sideboard (from which
one helps oneself) is laden with all sorts of home-made cakes and
biscuits. In addition to the all-day menu there is a choice of breakfasts
(till 11am) from a traditional fry-up (£4.45) to warm croissants with
preserve (£2.45). On Thursday, Friday and Saturday (from 6-9),
a special "Taste of Scotland" dinner is served (main courses £7.95).
Four high-chairs and good baby facilities. *Seats 110. Open 7.45am-7pm
(Sun 11-6), also Thur/Fri/Sat 6-9. Closed 25 Dec, 1 Jan. Access, Amex,
Diners, Visa.*

Glasgow   Joe's Garage

Tel 041-339 5407	Restaurant
52 Bank Street Glasgow Strathclyde	Map 3 B6

American diner-themed restaurant in the West End area serving slick
Mexican, American and Italian dishes, with vegetarian options in each
category. Tagliatelle funghi prosciutto (£5.75), chicken gumbo
(£8.80), pizzas (£5) and enchiladas (£7.40) are typical. American late
breakfasts with pancakes and maple syrup on Sundays. Good family
atmosphere. *Seats 67. Open 12-3 (Sun from 11) & 5-12 (Sat & Sun
12-12). Closed 25 Dec, 1 Jan. Access, Diners, Visa.*

Glasgow   Loon Fung

Tel 041-332 1240	Restaurant
417 Sauchiehall Street Glasgow Strathclyde	Map 3 B6

Formerly a cinema, then a dance hall, and for the past 25 years a very
busy and popular Cantonese restaurant. Dim sum (from £1.80) are
favourites for snacks or light meals, and the rest of the menu provides
plenty of variety, with chef's recommendations ranging from quail egg
and meat dumpling (£1.80) and crunchy stuffed crab claw (£5.50)
to stuffed aubergine, bean curd and green pepper (£7.50), lamb and
spring onion hot pot (£7.90) and lobster in either garlic or cheese
sauce. Good-value business lunches. Two high-chairs; small changing
shelf in the Ladies. *Seats 200. Open 12-11.30. Access, Amex, Visa.*

Glasgow   October Café

Tel 041-221 0303	Restaurant
The Rooftop Princes Square Glasgow Strathclyde	Map 3 B6

Princes Square's shopping centre is trendy and upmarket and the
October Café has a prime location at the top, light wood and black,
in a semi-circular setting, and the whole bathed with light. The bar
menu sticks to simple fare of freshly made soup (£1.75), carrot and
Gruyère quiche (£3.75), steak and kidney pie (£3.95) or vegetable
and cheese enchiladas (£3.95) of satisfying quality but somewhat small
portions; the main menu offers restaurant dishes at a considerably
higher price. "Ask for a children's portion." One high-chair and
changing facilities within the shopping centre downstairs. *Seats 120.
Open 12-6 (for food). Closed Sun, 25 & 26 Dec, 1 & 2 Jan. Access,
Amex, Visa.*

Glasgow   Sannino Pizzeria

Tel 041-332 8025	Pizzeria

61 Bath Street Glasgow Strathclyde   Map 3 B6

In the city centre, opposite British Home Stores. The decor
is darkwood panelling, Tiffany-style lamps and heavy brass rails, the
menu lists reliably good pasta (£4.95-£5.95) and pizzas. Pizza platters
offer a portion of pizza with coleslaw and potato salad while the full
16-inch pizza (£8.10-£9.90) serves two – with different toppings
on each half if you like. Good value business lunch (£4.90). Three
high-chairs and half portions provided. **Seats** 150. **Open** 12-2.30 &
5-11 (Thur/Fri/Sat/Sun to 12). **Closed** L Sun. Access, Amex,
Diners, Visa.
Also at:
61 Elmbank Street. Tel 041-332 3565.
This branch offers a pre-theatre menu.

Glasgow   Ubiquitous Chip

Tel 041-334 5007	Restaurant

12 Ashton Lane Glasgow Strathclyde   Map 3 B6

Friendly staff provide exemplary service that's entirely appropriate
to the surroundings at this popular bar above the more formal
restaurant. A daily-amended menu keeps pace with current trends and
offers much to excite even the most jaded palate. Starters include
macerated Scotch beef with tapénade (£2.95), pan-fried langoustine
tails (£4.95), and vegetarian haggis (£2.95), main courses range from
whole roasted Perthshire wood pigeon with a rich vegetable and game
sauce (7.95) to crab with mayonnaise (£6.95), and desserts from bread
pudding and cream to tropical fruit sorbet (£2.50). A balcony with
seven tables overlooks the restaurant courtyard below. Children's
portions. Saturdays are particularly popular with families. Excellent
Scottish cheeses and some 12 wines by the glass. **Seats** 40. **Open** 12-11
(Sun from 12.30). **Closed** 25 Dec, 1 Jan. Access, Amex, Diners, Visa.

Glasgow   Warehouse Café

Tel 041-552 4181	Café

61-65 Glassford Street Glasgow Strathclyde   Map 3 B6

Stylish, bustling designer café on the third floor of the Warehouse
clothes store. Deep-fried Brie (£1.95), grilled tomatoes with
mozzarella (£1.95), lasagne (£3.95), pastrami on rye bread (£4.50),
filled potatoes and croissants (from £3.50) and vegetarian wholemeal
quiche (£3.75) are joined daily by specials such as chicken and
vegetable terrine (£4.25) or poached salmon (£4.95). Home-made
puddings include sticky toffee and bread-and-butter (£1.50). The
ground-floor sandwich bar offers a good selection of filled sandwiches
and salads. No facilities, but a useful place to know (as long as you
don't get caught short by junior!). **Seats** 60. **Open** 10-6. **Closed** Sun,
Bank Holidays. Access, Amex, Diners, Visa.

Glasgow   Willow Tea Room

Tel 041-332 0521	Tea Room

217 Sauchiehall Street Glasgow Strathclyde   Map 3 B6

A glorious example, immaculately restored from the 1904 original,
of Charles Rennie Mackintosh art deco design. Old-fashioned cream

teas (£5) are served all day (naturally they use cake stands) as are
scones, locally-baked cakes – millefeuille, choc fudge, carrot, lemon
meringue pie – and savoury items such as home-made soup, quiche and
salad (£3.25), filled baked potatoes (from £2.50), lasagne (£3.25),
muffins, toasts and open sandwiches. Typical daily specials could
include cauliflower cheese, steak pie and mushroom-stuffed haggis.
Excellent selection of teas and coffee. Children's options include
spaghetti hoops on toast, macaroni and sausage and beans (all £1).
Two high-chairs, but no changing facilities. *Seats 50. Open 9.30-4.30.*
Closed Sun. No credit cards.

Glenelg   Glenelg Inn

Tel 059 982 273 Fax 059 982 373	Pub

Glenelg by Kyle of Lochalsh Highland IV40 8JR   Map 3 B4

With an idyllic location on the shore of Glenelg Bay, the inn combines
a rustic bar with a civilised restaurant and, created out of the old stable
block, six spacious bedrooms which have been individually decorated
and charmingly furnished with antiques. All have good bathrooms but
that with the master bedroom is particularly sybaritic. The bar menu,
for residents only on Sunday, offers a varied selection of main dishes
with the addition of soups (£1.50), sandwiches (£1.50) and pastries
(scones 50p) only at lunchtime. In the restaurant, the fixed-price
dinner menu (£19 for non-residents) majors on the loch-fresh seafood
along with hill-bred lamb or, perhaps, local venison. After dinner,
residents repair to the comfortable, antique-furnished 'morning room'
(the first to arrive puts a match to the log fire on cool evenings) where
the atmosphere lends itself to conviviality. Trips can be organised
in either the inflatable boat or the inn's motor yacht. A large, walled
and fenced-in garden overlooks the sea and is safe for children. Baby-
sitters on hand. Half-board terms only. *Bar Food (no food end-Sept-
Easter or Sun in season for non-residents) 12.30-2, 7-8.45. Restaurant
Meals 7.30-9. Free House. Garden. Accommodation 6 bedrooms, all
en suite, half-board terms only £110 (single from £60). Children welcome
overnight (rate depends on age), additional beds and cots available. Dogs
by arrangement. Access, Visa.*

Glenrothes   Balgeddie House   65%   £87

Tel 0592 742511 Fax 0592 621702	Hotel

Balgeddie Way Glenrothes Fife KY6 3ET   Map 3 C5

Until recently surrounded by farmland, this 18th-century Georgian
house was only converted to a hotel in 1989 and is now part
of a suburb of Glenrothes new town. The whole place is well kept,
from lounge and oak-panelled bar to the bedrooms; those on the first
floor are superior and spacious, with fine modern bathrooms, those
on the second floor are twins, with sloping ceilings. Two separate bars
with juke box, fruit machine and pool tables set the tone inside; outside
there's a lawn the size of a football pitch and eight acres
of landscaped gardens to explore. Bar snacks and suppers served
informally in the Paddock bar. Children under 12 stay free in their
parents' room. Tariff reductions for two nights' minimum stay
at weekends. *Rooms 18. Garden. Access, Amex, Diners, Visa.*

Gollanfield   **Culloden Pottery Restaurant**

| Tel 0667 462 749 | Restaurant |

Gollanfield nr Inverness Highland   **Map 2 C3**

On the A96 halfway between Inverness and Nairn, the restaurant
is above a craft and gift shop where Bob can be seen at work on his
potter's wheel. Essentially vegetarian although there is also some fish
on the menu, everything is made on the premises using free-range eggs
and organic produce wherever possible. Soup (£1.60), nut paté
(£1.95) and houmus (£1.95) all come with crusty wholemeal bread
and there is a good selection of composite salads to go with the day's
hot dishes (from noon) like pepper and baby corn crumble, vegetable
lasagne and shepherdess pie (all at £4.50). Sandwiches and filled jacket
potatoes cope with lesser appetites. The sweet-toothed might enjoy
their fruit pies (£1.60) and cakes like a delicious, moist lemon cake
(£1.05). For babies there are clip-on seats and they will happily heat
up baby's bottle and food or liquidise something in the kitchen.
A small, safe play area outside has swings, a slide, scramble net and
rustic play house. Nappy-changing facilites, including wet wipes, are
available in the ladies loo. For the disabled there's a special loo on the
ground floor and a stair lift up to the restaurant. Children have their
own section on the menu. No-smoking area. *Seats 42.* **Open** *9.30-7.30
(closes earlier out of season, open to 9pm Fri & Sat all year).* **Closed** *25 &
26 Dec, 1 & 2 Jan. Access, Visa.*

Greenlaw   **Castle Inn**

| Tel 03616 217   Fax 03616 500 | Pub |

Greenlaw Borders TD10 6UR   **Map 3 D6**

Greenlaw is a small town on a major road, not far from Hume Castle
and other attractions. The handsome Georgian Castle Inn is the sort
of place you could take a variety of people for lunch and feel confident
that they would find something to their taste. It is expensive for bar
meals, by local standards, and falls into the middle ground of bar meal
and restaurant. The Mirror Room, where drinking and dining take
place, has a large mirror above a marble fireplace transforming what
would otherwise be a hall into a splendid room, with a comfortable
sitting area by the fireplace and elegant Georgian windows through
which there's a view to well-kept gardens. The octagonal room and
the small library are excellent spots in which to take coffee, and the
bar itself is popular with locals on Friday nights and weekend
lunchtimes. The welcome is friendly but not intrusive. Family facilities
are excellent: high-chairs, baby foods, a Freddy Fox children's menu,
books in the library and cheerful, tolerant staff. The printed menu,
supplemented by blackboard specials, is very varied. A 2-course
traditional Sunday lunch is served (£6.95) with a choice of ragout
or roast. The local cheese is good and always features Kelsea and
Stichell (cheese platter £2.50), and house wine very drinkable. Fenced
and hedged-in garden. **Bar Food** *12-2.30, 6.30-10. Children allowed
in bar to eat, children's menu. Free House.* **Beer** *Caledonian, Broughton
Greenmantle Ale. Garden.* **Accommodation** *6 bedrooms, 1 en suite £40
(single £20). Children welcome overnight (family room £45/£48),
additional beds and cots available. Access, Diners, Visa.*

Innerleithen   Traquair Arms

Tel 0896 830229 Fax 0896 830260	Pub
Traquair Road Innerleithen Borders EH44 6PD	**Map 4 C1**

Off the main road (well signposted) which runs through Innerleithen
and five minutes' walk from the River Tweed is the Traquair Arms
Hotel, a handsome stone building on the road leading to St Mary's
Loch, which is, incidentally, a delightful journey across country roads
to one of the most picturesque parts of the Borders. The bar leads off
the hotel reception area; dine here, or in the more comfortable dining
room, or, if weather permits, in the garden. A choice of dining areas
and a wide choice of freshly prepared meals is typical of the admirable
flexibility of the Traquair Arms, where children are positively
welcomed, even the most boisterous; three high-chairs are provided.
There are changing facilities in the Ladies. For adults, a well-stocked
bar features the Traquair's own Bear Ale, with a teddy bear-clad
pump. The pub opens at 7.30am in order to serve a full breakfast (£6).
Afternoon teas and high teas are also available. Service is genuine and
informal, the atmosphere convivial. One benefit of dining in the bar
is that the glass doors lead off into the garden, which is enclosed and
safe for energetic children. The linen-laid dining room proper, though
pleasant in the evenings, is rather too formal for lunchtime. Diners are
offered 3- and 4-course table d'hote menus (£14.50, £18). Bed and
breakfast is recommended – particularly the handsome Scottish
morning meal, complete with superb kippers. Traquair House, next
door, is well worth a visit too, a romantic old house with pretty
grounds and its own ancient brewhouse; the front gates of Traquair
are firmly shut, and will never open again until a Stuart returns to the
throne of Scotland. *Bar Food 12-9. Restaurant Meals 7-9. Children
allowed in bar to eat. Free House. Beer Traquair Bear Ale, Broughton
Greenmantle Ale, occasional guest beer. Garden, outdoor eating.*
*Accommodation 10 bedrooms, all en suite, £54 (single £35). Children
welcome overnight (0-4 yrs free, 4-12 yrs 50% adult rate if sharing parents'
room), additional beds and cots available. Access, Visa.*

Inverness   Bunchrew House   70%   £115

Tel 0463 234917 Fax 0463 710620	Hotel
Bunchrew Inverness Highland IV3 6TA	**Map 2 C3**

From Inverness follow the signs to Beauly/Drywall on the A862.
A mile from the outskirts of Inverness you'll find the entrance to 16th-
century Bunchrew House (opened as a hotel in 1987), which stands
in 15 acres of landscaped gardens and woodland on the shores
of Beauly Firth. New owners took over last year and promised further
improvements. *Rooms 11. Garden, fishing. Access, Amex, Visa.*

Kenmore   Kenmore Hotel   62%   £88

Tel 0887 830205 Fax 0887 830262	Hotel
Kenmore by Aberfeldy Tayside PH15 2NU	**Map 3 C5**

The Kenmore claims to be Scotland's oldest inn, dating from 1572,
in a lovely Perthshire village overlooking the River Tay; at the east
end of Loch Tay on the A827. The Poet's Parlour bar, devoted
to Burns, is cosy, with green tartan seats; Archie's Bar is simpler, with
glorious views of the river. Bedrooms, 14 in a Victorian gatehouse
opposite, vary considerably in decor and furnishings with everything
from melamine to antiques. Guests have free use of the swimming

pool and leisure facilities at the nearby Kenmore Club. Kenmore attracts both fishermen (they have 2 miles of private beats on the Tay) and golfers. No real ales. Recommended for B&B only. *Riverside garden. Family room.* **Accommodation** *38 bedrooms. Children welcome overnight (under 14yrs free if sharing parents' room), additional beds and cots available. Dogs welcome in annexe only. Access, Visa.*

Kentallen of Appin	Holly Tree	65%	£75
Tel 063 174 292 Fax 063 174 345			Hotel
Kentallen of Appin Highland PA38 4BY			Map 3 B4

An old railway station which has been cleverly converted into a civilised hotel, the Holly Tree stands on the edge of Loch Linnhe, three miles south of Ballachulish Bridge. The little bar was once the station tea room, and there's a delightful lounge with a central fireplace and comfortable seating. Bedrooms are equally appealing, with floral fabrics and pine furniture; bathrooms are up-to-date and attractively tiled. The restaurant is non-smoking. Children under 5 stay free in parents' room; families are well catered for in the ten family rooms; three cots and three high-chairs are available for toddlers. A wee dram of Drambuie in your breakfast porridge should set you up for exploring the West Coast. **Rooms** *11. Garden, fishing. Access, Amex, Visa.*

Kilberry	Kilberry Inn		
Tel 08803 223			Pub
Kilberry by Tarbert Strathclyde PA29 6YD			Map 3 A6

This single-storey white cottage in an isolated, pretty little hamlet is located half a mile from a glorious coastline, and reached by an invigorating 16-mile drive down a winding, hilly, single-track road from the north, with superb views of Jura and other islands. John and Kath Leadbeater, English chef-proprietors, are vigorously interested in good food, and justifiably proud of their achievements here, in an out of the way spot where the vegetables come via van and taxi, and fresh fish is peculiarly hard to get. It's very much a dining pub, though locals and others are equally welcome to drop in for a drink. The building was originally a crofting house, and the snugly comfortable little bar, with a peat fire at one end and a wood-burning stove at the other, still has an unpretentious rural style. Leading off at the left, the brighter, plainer dining and family room has good-sized pine dining tables and a genuine welcome for children; John's Donald Duck impression certainly breaks the ice. The daily blackboard-listed short menu (perhaps only four or five main courses at lunchtime), genuinely home-made and morning-planned, is cheerfully annotated for ditherers with lively accounts of how each was made, and what's particularly recommended that day. This is very much John's role, circulating, chatting, advising, gossiping and occasionally quacking, in between stints in the kitchen and bar; Kath is very much behind the scenes, doing the hard work at the stove! The house speciality is home-made meat dishes of an old-fashioned country sort, often with a modern reinterpretation, and delicious: perhaps a hearty sausage pie (£7.25), roast loin of pork stuffed with "locally caught haggis" (£13.50), beef in Old Peculier casserole (£12.50), rumpsteak and kidney pie (£7.50); Kath has a famously light hand and the pastry is superb. She also makes the bread, and pickles, jams and chutneys on sale at the bar. Fish isn't really their interest, but the salmon fish pie (£8.25), layered with sliced potato, is creamy and satisfying. Whatever you do, make sure you leave room for one of Kath's delicious fruit pies (£3.25), which are laid out on the counter as soon as they come out of the oven. Equally scrumptious are the bread-and-butter pudding, fresh lemon cream, grapefruit cheesecake and chocolate fudge. Though there's no real ale, the Greenmantle range from Broughton Brewery in the Borders is available by the bottle, and the wine list includes a few offered by the glass. Accommodation is also now available in two "luxury" en-suite bedrooms (£50 double, £30 single) – opened after our press deadline. Note that the pub is closed in winter and never opens on Sundays. One high-chair is provided, as are children's portions. *Bar Food 12.15-2, 6.30-9. Free House. Beer No real ale but large range of Scottish bottled beers. Family room (no smoking). Inn closed Sun, also mid October – Easter (open at New Year for 10 days). Access, Visa.*

Kilfinan	Kilfinan Hotel	£68
Tel 070 082201 Fax 070 082205		Inn
Kilfinan by Tighnabruaich Strathclyde PA21 2AP		Map 3 B5

A delightful Swiss/Scottish couple, Rolf and Lynne Mueller, run this remote whitewashed stone former coaching inn amid magnificent scenery on the east shore of Loch Fyne, reached down a single-track road (B8000, off the A886) between Strachur and Tighnabruaich. The Dunoon ferry is less than an exhilarating hour's hair-raising drive across the moors. Purchased about ten years ago by the Laird of Kilfinan, so that it would not fall into the hands of developers, the inn has exclusive access to beautiful Kilfinan Bay (about 20 minutes walk through the garden and the estate) and is well placed for traditional outdoor pursuits. Two cosy bar/lounge areas complete with open fires are good spots for the whole family to enjoy snacks ranging from simple soups, sandwiches and paté to venison burgers (£4.50), steak and stout pie (£5) and Otter Ferry salmon fishcake (£4.70); puddings (from £2) include treacle tart and fruit crumble. Breakfast is served from 7.30 (earlier if required), afternoon teas from 2 to 6. Bedrooms – some antique-furnished – offer all the usual little luxuries, including good-quality toiletries in the carpeted en-suite bathrooms; one room overlooks St Finnan's graveyard, a surprisingly pleasant view. Incidentally, don't be alarmed by the brown peat-coloured water – 'at least it hasn't been filtered seven times by humans!'. Good walking country begins right outside the door. *Rooms 11. Garden, fishing. Closed all Feb. Access, Amex, Visa.*

Restaurant £55

Crisp table linen, cutlery and glassware gleaming in the candle-light, and a glowing log fire make the twin dining rooms particularly appealing. Rolf brings Swiss precision into his cooking, exemplified in the fixed-price-only dinner menu that offers a small choice at each of the four courses: a recent menu offered salad of duck breast with orange and pink peppercorn sauce, ragout of wild mushrooms and asparagus or grilled smoked halibut with sherry butter sauce to start, followed by potage valaisanne and then langoustine-stuffed supreme of chicken with a champagne sauce, fondant of lamb in a rosemary jus or steamed fillets of brill in a port and beetroot sauce. Tarte tatin with apple, chocolate marquise with a mint anglaise or a selection of local cheeses to finish, plus good coffee served with petits fours. Lighter lunches are served in the recently refurbished Lamont Room. Outdoor eating in the garden in good weather. *Seats 22. D only 7.30-9.30. Set D £22.*

Killiecrankie   **Killiecrankie Hotel**   **64%**   **£92**

Tel 0796 473220 Fax 0796 472451	Hotel

Killiecrankie by Pitlochry Tayside PH16 5LG   Map 3 C4

Four acres of landscaped gardens overlook the river Garry and the Pass
of Killiecrankie (turn off the A9 north of Pitlochry). There's
something of the feeling of an inn about the little hotel, which was
built as a manse in 1840. The reception hall and small panelled bar
(which has a suntrap extension) have displays of stuffed animals and
an upstairs lounge offers various board games plus a variety of books
as distractions. Pine-furnished bedrooms are fresh and bright. Under-5s
free of charge if sharing parents' room (cot supplied); 5-16s charged
50% of adult rate if sharing a room of their own. Children's menu
of popular favourites (from fish cakes and pizza to syrup sponge
pudding and Pooh Bear crunch ice cream) served in the Sun Lounge;
under-5s requested not to eat in the dining room in the evening.
Rooms *11. Garden, putting. Closed Jan & Feb. Access, Amex, Visa.*

Killin   **Clachaig Hotel**

Tel 05672 270	Pub

Falls of Dochart Killin Central FK21 8SL   Map 3 B5

18th-century ex-smithy and coaching inn, once closely linked with
the McNab clan, and beautifully set overlooking the spectacular Falls
of Dochart with the River Tay a five-minute walk down the road;
very Richard Hannay-ish. Rather basic inside, though, its bar usurped
by juke box and pool table, but bar food is plain and decently
cooked – Scotch broth (95p), home-made steak pie (£3.75), haggis
(£2.95), Highland crumble (£1.50); and the dining room seats 48 in
the evenings – Clachaig paté (£2.95), Highland venison (£8.95) and
steaks, trout Rob Roy (£8.95), Loch Tay salmon (£9.25), sweet and
sour vegetables (£4.25) and home-made puddings (£1.50). Restaurant
meals are also available during the day in the bar. The clean and
modest bedrooms are good value for the area, equipped with TVs,
tea/coffee-making facilities and hairdryers on request. The best of them
have dramatic views over the Falls. ***Bar Food*** *12-4, 5.30-9.30.*
Restaurant Meals *6.30-9.30. Children's menu (£1.50 per dish). Free
House. Beer McEwan 80/-, Tartan. Garden, outdoor eating. Family room.*
Accommodation *9 bedrooms, 8 en suite, £36 (single £18). Children
welcome overnight, additional beds (£9), cots supplied. Access, Visa.*

Kincraig   **Boathouse Restaurant**

Tel 0540 651 272	Restaurant

Loch Inch Kincraig Highland   Map 3 C4

Watch the watersports on Loch Inch (or the curling when it freezes
over in winter) from the balcony of this log-cabin restaurant while
enjoying the home-made fare on offer. During the day it's self-service
of toasted sandwiches (from £1.95), jacket potatoes (from £2.25),
hamburger in a roll (£3.25), lasagne (£4.25) and steak pie plus
a vegetarian section – quiche (£4), vegetable lasagne (£4) – and home-
baked scones, flapjacks and shortbread. After 6.30pm it becomes
waitress service with main dishes such as fettuccine (£8), salmon steak
with noodles and herb cream sauce (£9) and filet mignon (£11.95).
A couple of high-chairs, bottle-heating and children's menu (of the
chicken nugget, hamburger and pizza variety) should keep the little
ones happy. £3 children's meal includes a main dish, soft drink and ice

cream in a cone. No special facilities for baby changing. No smoking
in the evenings. *Seats 30. Open 10-9. Closed* early Nov-Dec 26.
Access, Visa.

Kinlochbervie	**Kinlochbervie Hotel**	**64%**	**£84**
Tel 0971 521275 Fax 0971 521438			Hotel
Kinlochbervie by Lairg Highland IV27 4RP			Map 2 B2

Built 25 years ago, the hotel sits above Kinlochbervie harbour almost
at the northernmost tip of mainland Scotland. Picture windows
on two sides of the hotel lounge and dining room overlook loch and
ocean from high up on a hill. Six bedrooms (and a first-floor residents'
lounge crammed with literature for walkers and fishermen) enjoy
these views to the full. All rooms have showers as well as baths. Third
persons (be they little ones or nay) share a room free of charge (for
B&B). The public bar is a favourite with local fisherman, while in the
lounge and Garbet Bar visitors can enjoy a good choice of worthy
snacks and moresubstantial dishes; high-chairs available. Gateaux,
sandwiches and scones are available for afternoon tea, and although
advertised as closed during winter, those braving the far north
of Scotland in winter will often find the door open and food available.
No smoking in the restaurant. 47 miles from Lairg. *Rooms 14. Sea
fishing and loch fishing. Closed 1 Nov-end April. Access, Amex,
Diners, Visa.*

Kippen	**Cross Keys**	
Tel 0786 870293		Pub
Main Street Kippen Central FK8 3DN		Map 3 C5

A simple, welcoming Scottish pub with rooms, rather than an inn
proper, set in a pleasant rural village not far from Stirling. The entire
pub has recently been refurbished. The locals' public bar is large and
basic, with pool table, fruit machine and television; a smaller, long and
narrow lounge is where most of the food is served, and a larger family
room has high-chairs primed and ready for use; there's also a small
restaurant with seating for about 20. Most of the walls are of exposed
stone, colour-washed white, and the furnishings a collection of old,
polished tables and chairs. The restaurant is more modern. Bar food,
which is well cooked rather than exciting, is chosen from a standard
enough printed menu. The restaurant is open in the evenings and
offers more elaborate dishes. If staying the night, ask for one of the
rooms under the eaves, which have sloping ceilings and fine views.
Bedrooms are simple and homely, with the usual tea and coffee kits,
and wash handbasins. Towels of good quality are provided, and there
are extra blankets in the wardrobe. Housekeeping in the rooms
is usually good. There is no residents' lounge, just the main bars
downstairs, busy even midweek with diners and locals. Breakfasts,
served on linen-laid tables in the restaurant, are hearty traditional fry-
ups and service is pleasant and helpful. There's a beer garden at the rear
with access from both the public and lounge bars. One high-chair;
changing facility (with emergency nappies) provided. *Bar Food 12-2
(Sun from 12.30), 5.30-9.30. Restaurant Meals 7-8.45. Free House.
Beer Broughton Greenmantle, Younger's No.3. Garden, outdoor eating.
Family room. Accommodation 3 bedrooms, sharing a bathroom, £42
(single £21). Children welcome overnight. Access, Visa.*

Kirkcaldy — Hoffmans

Tel 0592 204584	Pub
435 High Street Kirkcaldy Fife KW1 2SG	Map 3 C5

Hoffmans is an extraordinary place. Situated to the east of the town centre (don't be confused by the High Street address), it's an unlikely looking venue for a pub serving imaginative food, but first impressions can deceive. Owned in partnership by Vince and Paul Hoffman, it opened in March 1990, after Vince returned to his home town and set up at a previous pub just down the road. The building they subsequently decided on to set up on their own was unpromisingly seedy; they smartened up the interior with subtly toned wall covering, brown upholstered bench seating, polished tables, a large central ceiling fan, angled mirrors, and fake greenery. The attractive seascape and still life oils are courtesy of Hoffman sisters, and rather fine colour photographs from a couple of regulars. But the food is the thing here, and so popular that booking is advised for lunch as well as dinner. And rightly so. Vince Hoffman is so confident in the quality of his raw ingredients that local suppliers are listed at the front of the menu, which is handwritten and changes daily. Often it's not even decided on until just before opening time, when suppliers and fishmongers have been visited and produce assessed. Fish is a particular interest of Vince's. A three-course lunch can be had for as little as £6.50! In the evening, the room is partitioned, half the space reserved for drinkers, the other run as an à la carte bistro, when tables are laid and candle-lit, and there's waitress service. Capable service is also genuinely friendly, thanks to the Hoffman teamwork. There are two high-chairs for children; ask for small portions. *Open 11am-midnight.* **Bar Food** *12-2, 7-9 (Wed-Sat).* **Restaurant Meals** *7-9 (Wed-Sat).* Children allowed in bar to eat. Free House. **Beer** *McEwan's No. 3, 70/- and Theakston XB. Pub closed all Sun. No credit cards.*

Kirkton of Glenisla — Glenisla Hotel

Tel 057 582 223	Pub
Glenisla nr Blairgowrie Tayside PH11 8PH	Map 3 C4

This old coaching inn is set high up in Glenisla, one of the 'Angus Glens', and dates back over 300 years to the days before the Jacobite rebellion. A warm welcome avails today's travellers in the split level, beamed bar with its real fire (even in summer on chilly days) and posies of heather and wild flowers on the tables. Afternoons bring cream teas with scones fresh from the oven and home-made jam. Good bar food; a pretty restaurant opens for both lunch and dinner at the weekends (Friday, Saturday and Sunday). Older children have their own games room (pool, snooker); three high-chairs provided. *Open 11-11 Mon-Sun.* **Bar Food** *12-2.30, 6.30-9 (In winter to 8.30).* **Restaurant Meals** *(Fri, Sat & Sun) 12-2.30, 6.30-9.* **Beer** *Theakston's Best, McEwan's 80/-. Garden, outdoor eating. Family room. Access, Visa.*

Kyle of Lochalsh — Wholefood Café & Restaurant

Tel 0599 4388	Vegetarian
Plockton Road Kyle of Lochalsh Highland	Map 2 B3

Take the Plockton Road out of town to find this wholefood/vegetarian restaurant set in the Highland Design Works, once the village school. Counter service through the day offers rock buns (75p), carrot cake (£1.30), banana bread (85p) and the like to be joined at midday by hot dishes such as aduki bean burger (£2.95), spiced

chick peas and rice (£3.65) and cauliflower and courgette casserole
(£3.25). Everything is prepared on the premises using local and
organic produce where possible; there is always a small collection
of local cheeses served with oatcakes (£1.75). Evenings bring a short,
à la carte, waitress-service menu that adds seafood dishes like smoked
seafood platter (£3.75) and wild Loch Duich salmon roulade with
fennel and parsley sauce (£8.50) to the vegetarian choices. The café
is especially busy between 5.30 and 6.30pm when children (and
parents) can try breaking the burger habit. There are two high-chairs
and nursing mums have a folding chair in the Ladies. Out of high
season the hours may be curtailed and they might close completely
on Saturday and/or Monday so it's worth checking in advance.
No smoking. *Seats 50. Open 10-9. Closed* mid Oct-Easter. Access, Visa.

Largs   Nardini's

Tel 0475 67455	Café/Restaurant
The Esplanade Largs Strathclyde	**Map 3 B6**

To enter Nardini's seafront 'Continental lounge café' is to step back
in time – a huge room with gold-painted wicker chairs and glass-
topped tables, parlour plants and numerous waiters and waitresses
in smart red waistcoats providing swift, friendly service. It's still run
by theNardini family, who first set up in Largs in 1890. Their own
award-winning, real dairy ice cream comes in some 48 different
flavours and speciality sundaes with names like amarena delight (£4),
semi freddo (£4) and Valentino special (£9.50) whilst the bakery
provides bread for the sandwiches – parma ham (£2.45), fresh salmon
(£2.45), pizzas and a wide range of patisserie from a scone (at 60p)
to gateau St Honoré and double fresh cream torte (both £1.40).
Breakfasts are served until 11am, a separate restaurant offers a wide
range of Italian and English dishes – locally landed fish are
a speciality – and a confectionery shop in the foyer boasts an impressive
range of luxury chocolates. The children's menus for lunch and high
tea in the restaurant are unusually extensive – not just burgers and fish
fingers (although they are also on the menu) – and the special Sunday
Family Lunch comes at a reduced price for under-12s and
is completely free for under-fives. There's a special Junior Choice
section on the café menu 'for discerning under-12s only' and plenty
of room for buggies, numerous high-chairs and baby-changing
facilities are available in the Ladies loo. One should not leave Largs
without visiting Nardini's, a veritable institution. No-smoking area.
*Seats 260 (plus 80 outside). Open 8am-10.30pm (in winter to 9, weekdays
only). Closed 25 Dec. Visa.*

Letham   Fernie Castle   60%   £75

Tel 033 781 381 Fax 033 781 422	Hotel
Letham by Cupar Fife KY7 7RU	**Map 3 C5**

On the A914, one mile north of A91 junction, 12 miles south of the
Tay Bridge. The castle was first recorded in the mid-14th century, and
later additions have not spoilt its charm; the latest owners have
instigated a programme of refurbishment. Best of the public rooms
is the first-floor drawing room in a Georgian extension and the most
atmospheric the medieval Keep Bar with its rough-stone vaulted
ceiling. Bedrooms vary from a small single to a few spacious rooms
with reproduction antique furniture; most fall somewhere between
the two. Children under 4 stay free in parents' room; high-chairs,
children's menu (see if they can resist banana and custard with 100s &

1000s), laundry and baby-sitting/listening can all be provided – state your requirements when booking. No dogs. **Rooms** 15. *Access, Amex, Visa.*

Linlithgow	**Champany Inn Chop & Ale House**	£50
Tel 050 683 4532		**Restaurant**
Champany Linlithgow Lothian EH49 7LU		**Map 3 C5**

The same outstanding Aberdeen Angus steaks (though less expensive and cut a bit smaller) as at its sister restaurant, together with various burgers, deep-fried Scottish prawn tails (scampi), char-grilled grain-fed chicken and a cold buffet with help-yourself salad bar are among the offerings at this much less formal eaterym. For afters go for the home-made, hot malted waffles or Champany's own cheesecake served with apricot purée. A few high-chairs are provided for trainee trencher-persons and extra plates happily produced for parents to share a meal with their offspring. The pleasant courtyard is lovely in good weather (ten tables are set there) but it opens on to a side road and is thus not suitable for active toddlers. The biblical wine list here is extraordinary – 10 own-label house wines, burgundies by the bucketful, an enormous South American selection and a good worldwide choice at fair prices. No children under eight in the main Champany Inn restaurant. **Seats** 32. **Parties** 6. L 12-2 (*Sun 12.30-2.30*) D 6.30-10. Closed 25 & 26 Dec. *Access, Amex, Diners, Visa.*

Loch Eck	**Coylet Hotel**	
Tel 036 984322		**Pub**
Loch Eck nr Kilmun Strathclyde PA23 8SG		**Map 3 B5**

It's the setting that makes the Coylet really special: just the west coast road to Dunoon, shrouded in trees, separates the pretty white building from the glorious beauty of Loch Eck and the hills beyond. Not another house can be seen in any direction; be early for a window seat in the bar or dining room. Inside it charms in an unaffected way. The public bar is handsome and cosy, and friendly local ghillies and others gather on bar stools to pass the time of day. The beer's good too. Through the hall is an attractively simple little dining bar, where families (even tiny babies) are welcome; one high-chair is provided. Through into the dining room proper are half a dozen tables (one, large group size, in the prize window spot), wheelback chairs and piano. The food is a mix of standard bar menu stuff, from sandwiches (even in the evening) and ploughman's to vast, well-cooked platefuls of haddock and chips, or sizzling steaks; the quality draws both locals and tourists. But it's worth choosing off the specials board – a twice-daily changing short blackboard list. Puddings, all home-made, are also good, and come in hefty portions. Upstairs are three tiny little bedrooms which offer simple comfort. All have sash windows with views over the loch, and pretty cottagey print paper and fabrics. The twin is a bit bigger than the two doubles. The shared bathroom, a very attractive, immaculately clean, carpeted and pine-panelled room, is bigger than any of them. Breakfasts are ungreasy and commendably accommodating of personal preferences. Service is genuinely friendly from both the resident owners and their few, able staff. Lochside garden. **Bar Food & Restaurant Meals** 12-2 (*Sun from 12.30*), 5.30-10 (*Sun 7-9*). Free House. **Beer** Younger's No. , McEwan's 80/-, Deuchars IPA, occasional guest beer. *Garden, outdoor* *eating. Family room.* **Accommodation** *3 bedrooms, sharing facilities, £35 (single £17.50). Children welcome overnight, cots available. Check-in by arrangement. No dogs. No credit cards.*

Melrose   Burts Hotel

Tel 089 682 2285 Fax 089 682 2870	Pub

Market Square Melrose Borders TD6 9PN   Map 4 C1

Located 200 yards from the River Tweed – "Scotland's favourite salmon river" – is the imposing 18th-century inn at the heart of still-fairly-sleepy, affluent Melrose. Bar food shows an appetising balance of the comfortingly traditional and modern aspirational – and this philosophy could be said to sum up the whole hotel. The bar is comfortable rather than quaint. Good Scottish produce is featured on two table d'hote menus in the rather smart restaurant – 'Menu de la Semaine' dinner £18.50 and lunch £13.75, in addition to à la carte dishes. A choice of eight cheeses is always on offer including locals such as Bonchester, Teviotdale and Lanark Blue. Two high-chairs are provided. The bedrooms are light, contemporary and in pristine order; five have just shower/WC. Two acres of fenced-in garden at the back of the building. *Bar Food 12-2, 6-9.30 (Fri/Sat to 10.30).* *Restaurant Meals 12.30-2, 7-9 (Fri/Sat to 9.30). Children allowed in bar to eat. Free House.* **Beer** *Belhaven 80/-, Courage Directors. Garden, outdoor eating.* **Accommodation** *21 bedrooms, all en suite, £68 (single £40). Children welcome overnight (0-3yrs free), additional beds (£15 for 3-12s) and cots (£2) available. Access, Diners, Visa.*

Moffat   Black Bull

Tel 0683 20206 Fax 0683 20483	Pub

Churchgate Moffat Dumfries & Galloway DG10 9EG   Map 4 C2

Modernised 16th-century street-side local with a beer garden outside and duckpond nearby in a curiously old-fashioned, isolated little spa town, whose life blood is coach party tourism. It has been recently refurbished, but the proper local bar survives. There is now a total of eight bedrooms – four look on to the courtyard and four on to the churchyard opposite. Each bedroom has a different colour scheme and is fully equipped with TV, telephone (in en-suite rooms), and tea/coffee-making facilities. Recommended as a convenient B&B stop-over only. *Open 11-11 (Sun from noon). No evening meals Mon-Thurs from Nov-Feb.* **Beer** *Theakston's Best, Marston's Pedigree, two guest ales changing weekly. Garden, outdoor eating. Family Room.* **Accommodation** *8 bedrooms, 6 en suite, from £39 (single £29). Children welcome overnight, additional bed or cot in room at no extra charge. No dogs. Access, Visa.*

Monymusk   Grant Arms Hotel

Tel 046 77 226	Pub

The Square Monymusk Inverurie Grampian AB51 7HJ   Map 3 D4

With 6,000 acres of rough and driven shooting and 10 miles of salmon and trout fishing on the river Don this is very much a sporting inn as the decor of the panelled bar – antlers, stag's head, stuffed bird and old fishing rods – confirms. A typically solid, unspectacular 18th-century Scottish inn on the village green, the bedrooms are clean and bright if not luxurious. All have radio alarms, telephones and tea/coffee-making facilities but no televisions (there is one in the residents' lounge). The bar menu offers something for most tastes, whether traditional – fresh oysters (£7 per 6), game soup with lentils and sherry (£1.95), farmhouse mixed grill (£5.95) and steaks, or more exotic – chicken gumbo with rice and crackers (£4.45) and crayfish tails with crab claws in a thermidor sauce. *Pub open 11-3, 5-11 (11.45 Fri), 11-11.45 Sat, Noon-11 Sun.* **Bar Food** *Noon-2.30, 6.30-9 (to 9.45 Fri-Sun). Free House.* **Beer** *S&N 80/-. Garden, children's play area. Family room.* **Accommodation** *15 bedrooms, 7 en suite £62 (single £43). Access, Visa.*

Nairn	Golf View Hotel	65%	£99
Tel 0667 52301 Fax 0667 55267			Hotel
Seabank Road Nairn Highland IV12 4HD			Map 2 C3

Built at the very end of the last century, the hotel stands on the shores of the Moray Firth, overlooking Black Isle. It's a great place for family holidays, with a games room, pool, a children's play area and weekend evening entertainment. A golf course is just around the corner and there's a children's leisure park a short walk away. Nearly half the bedrooms are suitable for family occupation and children are charged according to age (under-4s free). Baby-listening and baby-sitting can be arranged. Day rooms were refurbished in last year. Considerably lower tariff out of main season (Jun-Sept). **Rooms** *47. Garden, outdoor swimming pool, tennis, putting, games room. Access, Amex, Diners, Visa.*

Netherley	Lairhillock Inn	
Tel 0569 30001 Fax 0569 31175		Pub
Netherley Grampian AB3 2QS		Map 3 D4

Standing alone surrounded by fields, the Lairhillock is easily spotted from the B979, thanks to the large white INN daubed on its roof. The closest major village to the inn is Peterculter, some four miles to the north; Netherley's a mile to the south. Formerly a farmhouse, the original building is 17th-century, extensions are in sympathy, and the interior is full of old rustic atmosphere. The large lounge is dominated by a central log-burning fireplace; walls are half-panelled, and exposed floorboards covered with numerous rugs. The public bar, in the oldest part, is by far the most characterful room, with its exposed stone, panelling, open fire, old settles and bench seating, every kind of horse tack, polished brasses and numerous other bits and pieces. Bar food is certainly taken seriously at the Lairhillock, where only fresh produce is used, cooked to order. The menu carries a fair choice, changing daily. It gets extremely busy, especially on Friday and Saturday evenings. Across from the main building, in the old stables, is the evening restaurant, with its high beamed ceiling, stone walls, red-tiled flooring and solid polished tables. There's candle-light and a pianist plays nightly. Service is pleasantly informal but always efficient. A recently-built conservatory with panoramic views furnished with Lloyd Loom tables and chairs provides an ideal room for families to eat. **Bar Food** *12-2, 6-9.30 (6-10 Fri/Sat).* **Restaurant Meals** *12-2 (Sun only), 7-9.30 (7-10 Fri/Sat). Children's portions. Free House.* **Beer** *Courage Directors, Thwaites, McEwan's 80/- and Export, Boddingtons, guest ale every week. Patio/Terrace. Access, Diners, Visa.*

New Abbey   Abbey Cottage

Tel 038 785 377	Tea Room

26 Main Street New Abbey by Dumfries Dumfries & Galloway   Map 4 B2

Next to the ruined abbey, from which the town takes its name, the
original part of this charming Victorian cottage is given over to the
sale of local arts and crafts – the no-smoking tea room
is in an extension to the rear, which includes a special loo for the
disabled. Mrs McKie's all-day menu ranges from home-baked cakes
(60p), fruit loaves, scones and toasted teacakes (75p) to savoury items
like sandwiches (from £1.35), salads and baked jacket potatoes (plain
£1.50, cheese and onion £2.40). The ploughman's lunch (£3.60)
features an award-winning vegetarian Cheddar from the nearby Loch
Arthur Creamery (a Camphill Village Trust). Daily specials could
include quiche and lasagne (£3.25). For good weather there is a neat
little brick-floored patio garden. Children are always welcome and
there's a high-chair, books to read and toys with which to play;
toddlers can have their food heated up. *Seats 46. Open 10-5.30.*
Closed Weekdays Nov & Dec, all Jan/Feb/Mar. No credit cards.

New Abbey   Criffel Inn

Tel 038 785 305	Pub

2 The Square New Abbey by Dumfries Dumfries & Galloway   Map 4 B2

Located five miles from the coast, an unassuming inn on the village
square, with a small garden for summer sipping and letting off juvenile
steam. The McCullochs are the most welcoming of hosts (and have
been for 37 years!) at their solid Victorian pub where things don't
change much from year to year. There's an unpretentious 'locals' bar,
slightly smarter lounge bar and dining room with red banquettes.
Upstairs, the residents' lounge has a domestic feel and bedrooms, with
wood-effect melamine fitted furniture, go in for a medley of floral
patterns. Two bedrooms are now en suite, one has a 'tin' shower
cubicle in the room and two others share an immaculate bathroom.
There are two cots (under-5s free), additional beds and two family
rooms. Jenny McCulloch keeps the customers well fed with a good
variety of wholesome home cooking using local products and
vegetables from her garden. Lunchtime brings soup – perhaps
a warming vegetable broth – and a daily special like roast pork with
apple sauce or savoury mince pie, supplementing toasted sandwiches,
salads, fish and roast beef. You'll need a real appetite for the high teas
(served from 4.30-7pm) when the main event is local Solway salmon
(£7) or home-cooked York ham and salad (£6), gammon steak and
pineapple (£7) or sausage, bacon and eggs (£6); whichever you
choose it comes with bread and jam, home-made cakes, scones and
a pot of tea. Similar main dishes appear on the bar lunch (12-2pm) and
supper (from 7pm) menus. It's worth leaving room for the day's
special sweet, which could be bread-and-butter pudding or a tart
of locally picked fruit. Children are offered baby food, fish fingers,
burgers, sausages and so on, but palates eager to learn can be easily
satisfied – particularly by the puds; two high-chairs are provided.
There is a 3-course roast lunch on Sunday. No smoking in the lounge.
*Bar Food 12-2, 4.30-7. Children's menu. Free House. Beer Broughton
Bitter. Patio, outdoor eating. Accommodation 5 bedrooms, 2 en suite, £44
(single £22). Children welcome overnight (rate depends on age), additional
beds and cots available. Access, Visa.*

Newcastleton   Copshaw Kitchen

Tel 0387 375250	Coffee Shop

4 North Hermitage Street Newcastleton Borders   Map 4 C2

The charming original fittings have been left in place in this converted
grocer's shop, even the range, which still warms the restaurant/coffee
shop on cold days. The restaurant features Mrs Elliot's collection
of china washstand sets, which requires careful negotiation by toddlers.
The adjoining tea room is better suited to your little missiles, and mum
can relax while they enjoy home-made beefburgers from the children's
menu. Adults can enjoy a choice of sweet and savoury snacks to satisfy
all tastes. Savouries include paté with oatcakes, Scotch pie and scampi
(all £3.75). Sweets and cakes on offer could be chocolate brandy
mousse, apple crumble (both £1.75), millionaire shortbread, almond
slice and mint cake (from 45p). Full afternoon tea £3. Now also open
Wednesday to Saturday evenings (7-9, 3 courses around £12). Full
afternoon tea £2.85. The reception area provides a convenient space
for nursing mothers when it's quiet; it is often busy on Sundays and
Bank Holidays. **Seats** 18. **Open** 9.30-6 (winter 10-5 Jan/Feb weekends
only, March Friday to Sunday). **Closed** Tue, 26 Dec. Access, Visa.

Newton Stewart   Creebridge House Hotel

Tel 0671 2121 Fax 0671 3250	Pub

Newton Stewart nr Minnigaff Dumfries & Galloway DG8 6NP   Map 4 A2

Formerly home to the Earls of Galloway, the 18th-century, stone-built
Creebridge House, set in pretty gardens, is a hotel rather than an inn
but there's a pubby bar offering a good range of bar meals. 'Snacky'
lunchtime menu plus various blackboard specials. Bedrooms, which
include a couple of family suites, feature fairly modest freestanding
furniture in a variety of styles but all are well kept and equipped with
TVs (some remote-controlled), telephones, hairdryers and tea/coffee-
making kits – although room service is also available throughout the
day and evening. Good, modern en-suite bathrooms, all with shower
and tub plus the normal toiletries. Day rooms include an elegantly
proportioned Georgian lounge. £1 charge on credit card payments.
Bar Food 12-2, 6-9 (Sat to 10, Sun from 7). Free House.
Beer Theakston's XB, Belhaven 80/-. Garden, outdoor eating. Family
room. **Accommodation** 20 bedrooms, all en suite, £70 (single £35).
Children welcome overnight (under-12s free if sharing in parents' room),
additional beds and cots supplied. Access, Visa.

Onich   Onich Hotel   61%   £74

Tel 085 53 214 Fax 085 53 484	Hotel

Onich nr Fort William Highland PH33 6RY   Map 3 B4

Fine views of Loch Linnhe, well-maintained gardens and multifarious
activities for all ages make the Onich hotel a popular year-round
choice. Iain Young has put his personal stamp on the place for over 30
years, developing an atmosphere of friendly informality where guests
and locals chat together in the bars. It lies on the A82 two miles north
of Ballachulish Bridge and ten miles south of Fort William, making
it a splendid base from which to explore the West Highlands and
islands (the hotel can recommend many walks and day tours). The
best front bedrooms (let on a half-board basis only) have lochside
balconies. None is denied a fair share of the view, but some suffer
slightly from proximity to the road. Easily sloping gardens lead down
to the pebble beach; impress the children by skimming with fool-

proof Ballachulish slates. Cook is on duty all day for nipper's nosh and
there's a coin-operated laundry for longer stays or mishaps. Under-2s
£2.50 per day, 2-5 25%, 6-12 50%, 13-16 25% of adult tariff;
cots, high-chairs and play areas are all provided. *Rooms 27. Garden,
spa bath, solarium, pool table. Access, Amex, Diners, Visa.*

Peebles   Cringletie House   65%   £86

Tel 0721 730233 Fax 0721 730244	Hotel
Peebles Borders EH45 8PL	Map 4 C1

Set well back from the A703, three miles north of Peebles on the
A703, this Scottish baronial-style mansion offers peace and quiet and
enjoys views of the distant Meldon and Moorfoot Hills. Open fires,
fresh flowers from the gardens and antiques enhance the traditional
decor. Most impressive of the day rooms is the panelled drawing room
with fine painted ceiling. Well-kept bedrooms offer considerable
comfort and excellent bathrooms boast big soft towels; there's a long
climb to those on the third floor at the top of the house; cots, extra
beds and high-chairs are provided for wee ones. Children's play area
in the many acres of grounds. Around twenty miles from Edinburgh.
*Rooms 13. Garden, tennis, croquet, putting green. Closed 2nd week Jan-1st
week Mar. Access, Visa.*

Restaurant   £60

A two-acre walled kitchen garden provides much of the fresh produce
served in the lofty twin dining rooms. Cooking is soundly based, with
dishes such as prawn and dill roulade, poached sole with ginger and
chives, spinach-sauced vegetarian pancakes and medallions of beef with
bacon and mushrooms. Prices are extremely favourable on a sound
wine list. No smoking. *Seats 56. Parties 12. Private Room 28. L 1-1.45
D 7.30-8.30. Set L £14 Set D £23.50.*

Peebles   Kailzie Gardens

Tel 0721 22807	Restaurant
Kailzie Gardens Peebles Borders	Map 4 C1

A cottagey restaurant housed in converted stables in Kailzie Gardens
beside the river Tweed. Grace Innes offers good things to eat
throughout opening hours, with the widest choice at lunchtime: soup
with home-baked bread (£1.25), fresh peach with cottage cheese
(£1.95), roast gigot of pork (£4.35), beef and mushroom casserole
(£4.35), vegetarian quiche (£3.55). Afternoon tea (£3.25) features
home baking, and the bread for the open sandwiches is also home
produced. Traditional Sunday lunch (£5.20). Courtyard with
outside eating for 16. No-smoking area *Seats 50. Open 11-5.30.
Closed Oct-mid March. No credit cards.*

Peebles   Peebles Hotel Hydro   70%   £103

Tel 0721 720602 Fax 0721 722999	Hotel
Innerleithen Road Peebles Borders EH45 8LX	Map 4 C1

A fine and majestic holiday hotel overlooking the Tweed valley, run
by energetic Pieter van Dijk, manager for over 20 years. Formally
a hydropathic hotel, its extensive sports facilities in the 30 acres
of grounds are a major attraction, keeping even the most active guests
fully occupied. Public rooms of grand proportions are both attractive
and comfortable; in the bar there's a good selection of malt whiskies.
A sun room overlooks the valley, as do some of the good-size
bedrooms, which are charmingly furnished and well kept. 25 rooms

are designated for families and 22 have a small, separate children's bedroom. Families are well catered for with the likes of baby-sitting and baby-changing facilities in Bubbles leisure centre; a small charge for children covers breakfast and high tea. An outdoor adventure playground can keep older children busy and hostesses ('not nannies') organise high-season activities such as treasure hunts and painting and drawing competitions. 24hr laundry service and an ironing room in the first-floor launderette. The hotel also offers adaptable conference and function facilities for up to 400 delegates. Weekend dinner dances. **Rooms** 137. *Garden, indoor swimming pool, sauna, solarium, spa bath, gymnasium, beautician, hairdressing, tennis, squash, badminton, pitch & putt, putting, riding, games room, snooker, coffee shop (10am-11pm), kiosk, children's playground & playroom.* Access, Amex, Diners, Visa.

Peebles   Sunflower

Tel 0721 22420	Restaurant
4 Bridgegate Peebles Borders EH45 8RZ	Map 4 C1

Just behind the high street, at Veitch's Corner, Sunflower is friendly and intimate behind its distinctive green-and-yellow shop front. Lunches and tasty snacks are served throughout the day. For lunch you can enjoy filled baguettes, croissants or baked potatoes (£3/£3.50) or something like Brie and smoked bacon tart or garlicky king prawns from the menu. Speciality cheeses. In the evening the menu is changed and dining becomes slightly more expensive with main courses priced at around £7. Over-14s only in the evenings. One high-chair; room in the Ladies for changing. Safe garden. **Seats** 30. **Open** 9-5.30, also Tue-Fri 7.30pm-9pm. **Closed** D Mon, D Tue/Wed in winter, all Sun & Bank Holidays. No credit cards.

Peterhead   Waterside Inn   67%   £89

Tel 0779 71121 Fax 0779 70670	Hotel
Fraserburgh Road Peterhead Grampian AB42 7BN	Map 2 D3

At Inverugie, two miles outside Peterhead on the Fraserburgh road, surrounded by fields and the banks of the winding River Ugie. A large, low-rise modern hotel which is comfortable and efficiently run. There's a series of bars to suit every taste, and several conference rooms (maximum capacity 250). 40 studio bedrooms in a separate block are compact and functional, while those in the main building are more spacious and luxurious; children stay free (no age restriction) in parents' room. Six family rooms have bunk beds. Greatly reduced rates at weekends when conference delegates are thin on the ground. All-day 'kiddies menu' and high-chairs provided; informal eating in the grill room or lounge. A few miles away, the Aden Park Agricultural Heritage Centre brings the rural past of Buchan to life. Turn left at a grassy roundabout as you approach Peterhead from Aberdeen (A92) and follow signs to St Fergus. **Rooms** 110. *Garden, indoor swimming pool, keep-fit equipment, sauna, spa bath, solarium, snooker, grill oom (7am-10pm Tue-Sat).* Access, Amex, Diners, Visa.

Pitlochry   Luggie Restaurant

Tel 0796 472085	Restaurant
Rie-Achen Road Pitlochry Tayside	Map 3 C4

The old stone barn, which used to be a dairy, is now a roomy self-service restaurant with rough-stone walls and a beamed ceiling. The cold selection includes ham, beef (£3.95), fresh salmon steaks (£4.95),

smoked trout and a decent selection of salads, plus fruit cake, fruit pies
(from 85p), scones (85p) and shortbread. Pork and apple paté (£2.25)
and smoked venison platter (£3) are among the starters, and daily hot
dishes, from 11.30-5, include lasagne and chili (both £3.75). Evening
candle-lit carvery (£7.95) with cold buffet. Traditional roast
on Sundays (£4.95 for 2 courses). Breakfasts throughout winter
(from £3.75). Children's portions. Large terrace. Small no-smoking
area. *Seats* 90 (*plus 70 outside*). *Open* 9-5, *also* (*summer only*) 6-9.30.
Closed Feb. Access, Visa.

Port William	Corsemalzie House	61%	£75
Tel 098 886 254			Hotel
Port William by Newton Stewart Dumfries & Galloway DG8 9RL			Map 4 A3

A popular and unpretentious hotel in a 19th-century stone mansion
surrounded by the secluded setting of forty wooded acres. Among its
many sporting attractions, fishing is a major activity (rights
on stretches of the Rivers Bladnoch and Tarff, plus nearby lochs) and
there's good rough shooting and arrangements with local golf courses.
The lounge and bar provide easy relaxation, and bedrooms are
generally of a decent size; all have private bath or shower. Children
under 13 in parents' room are charged at £3 a night; high tea served
in the bar 5-6.30pm, with high-chairs and small portions provided.
Outdoor playground. *Rooms* 14. *Garden, putting, game fishing, shooting.*
Closed 25 & 26 Dec, 14 Jan-mid Mar. Access, Visa.

Portpatrick	Crown Hotel		
Tel 077 681 261 Fax 077 681 551			Pub
Portpatrick Wigtownshire Dumfries & Galloway DG9 8SX			Map 4 A2

Right down by the harbour, the blue-and-white-painted Crown
is a bustling, friendly place where the several unpretentious rooms that
form the bar – with a real fire even in summer on chilly days, and
a motley collection of prints above dado panelling – contrast with
a stylishly informal restaurant and smart, appealing bedrooms. The
latter have loose rugs over polished parquet floors, a variety of good
freestanding furniture and attractive floral fabrics along with pristine
bathrooms and the standard modern necessities of direct-dial phone
and TV. Restaurant and bar share the same menu (except for the
basket meals and sandwiches that are served in the bar only), which
majors on seafood. Chef Robert Campbell knows that the lobster and
crabs are fresh as he's out in his boat at 6 o'clock each morning
to collect them. Much of the other fish is bought direct from the
Fleetwood trawlers that call in at Portpatrick to unload their catches.
Bar Food & Restaurant Meals 12-2.30, 6 (6.30 Sun)-10. *Children's
portions. Free House. Beer* S&N 80/-, Tartan Export. *Family room.*
Accommodation 12 bedrooms, all en suite, £62 (single £33). *Children
welcome overnight, additional beds* (ages 4-10 £10), cots supplied. Access,
Diners, Visa.

Ratho	Bridge Inn		
Tel 031-333 1320			Pub
27 Baird Road Ratho Lothian EH28 8RA			Map 3 C6

Starting life as a farmhouse and becoming a hostelry when the Union
Canal was built alongside, the Bridge Inn fell into decline along with
the canal and was almost derelict when taken over by the irrepressible
Ronnie Rusack some 22 years ago. Not content with just reviving the

Inn, Ronnie has been instrumental in making some seven miles of the canal navigable again and runs two restaurant barges, specially adapted barges to give the disabled trips along the canal (a charity he founded and which has now spread to other Scottish canals), a boat for short pleasure trips and other smaller craft for hourly hire (picnic hampers can be provided); he has even established a duck breeding programme! Inside, the original inn features boarded walls and a collection of the many old bottles found when clearing the canal; a new family-orientated extension (the 'Pop Inn') features wheelback chairs and views over the water. One can choose form the Pop Inn's informal menu throughout the day – Bargee's broth (£1.25), curried egg and apple mayonnaise (£2.50), steak and kidney pie (£5.75), home-made burgers (£5), salmon mayonnaise (£5.25) and various locally made puds (all at £2.75) – or from the à la carte menu (main courses from £11 to £15) served lunch and evening in the bar, which becomes fairly restaurany in the evening with cloths on the tables. Steaks are a good bet here with good Scottish meat cooked on an open grill in full view but the daily roast suffers from being machine-sliced and re-heated. Children have thier own special menu of favourites (two courses £2.85, three courses £3.35) with the likes of fish fingers, chicken drumsticks and fruit jelly and ice cream. There's an 'adult-powered' carousel on the patio, a 'pirate boat' play area in the grounds, proper baby-changing and nursing facilities (that come complete with complimentary nappies and baby powder etc) and plenty of high-chairs and booster seats. There is hardly room to list everything that goes on here, the annual Scottish Open Canal Jump Competition is held each June and before Christmas there are special 'Santa Cruises' to a 'grotto' built each year on an island by the local art college. The Bridge Inn won the *Egon Ronay's Pubs & Inns Guide* Family Pub of the Year award for 1994. *Pub open noon-midnight all week.*
Bar Food *Noon-9.30.* **Restaurant Meals** *12-2.30, 6.30-9.30.*
Free House. **Beer** *Belhaven 80/-, Best. Garden. Children's play area.*
Family room. Access, Diners, Visa.

Ringford   **Old School Tea Room**

Tel 0557 22250	Tea Room
Ringford Dumfries & Galloway	Map 4 B2

Old class photographs look down from the walls of this former school-house on the main A75 and 'daily specials' have replaced the alphabet on the blackboard of what is now a welcoming craft shop-cum-tearoom. The all-day menu includes super home-made soups like tattie and parsnip or chicken and rice (£1.20), open sandwiches such as home-cooked ham and mayonnaise (£3), and lentil and mushroom paté (£2.85) made with excellent wholemeal bread, along with club sandwiches (from £3.20), baked tatties with various fillings (from £2.35) and good home baking – brides tart (65p), carrot cake (75p), shortbread, flapjacks and butterscotch fruit slice. Ask for children's portions; high-chairs available; baby food heated on request. No-smoking area. **Seats** *40.* **Open** *10-6 (11-5 in winter).*
Closed *Mon in winter. No credit cards.*

St Andrews   **Brambles**

Tel 0334 75380	Restaurant
5 College Street St Andrews Fife	Map 3 D5

A splendid little eating house which for the past five years has been owned by dedicated husband and wife team Paul and Pauline Rowe.

It's popular with townsfolk, tourists and students. Decor is clean and simple, with plain wooden tables. A blackboard lists the daily fare, all fresh and tasty and mainly with a traditional ring: French onion soup (£1), mushroom and lentil au gratin (£3.95), lasagne, omelette Arnold Bennett (£4.65), salmon en croute (£5.65), chili con carne (£3.85). Half the menu is vegetarian. Good baking, too, including maple syrup cake (55p), carrot cake (65p) and fudge cake (£1.45). Tables outside in the garden. No smoking. *Seats 45.* **Open** *9-5 Mon-Sat, also 12-5 Sun Easter-mid Sep.* **Closed** *2 weeks Christmas. Access, Visa.*

St Fillans	Four Seasons Hotel	60%	£70
Tel & Fax 0764 685333			Hotel
St Fillans nr Crieff Tayside PH26 2NF			Map 3 C5

The setting for the Scott family's agreeable little hotel, in four acres of grounds, is one of outstanding natural beauty, with Loch Earn in the foreground and the mountains beyond. Simple but comfortable public rooms take advantage of the location: there are several small lounges, the Tarken Bar (where Andrew Scott's good snacks are served in hearty-sized or children's portions), restaurant and coffee shop. Much redecoration has taken place over the last few years. Bedrooms are also unfussy in their appointments and include six chalets on a wooded hillside behind the main building; families with dogs should choose the chalets. Children up to 7 stay free in parents' room. **Rooms** *18. Garden, water-skiing. Closed Christmas-end Feb. Access, Amex, Visa.*

Selkirk	Philipburn House	60%	£99
Tel 0750 20747 Fax 0750 21690			Hotel
Linglie Road Selkirk Borders TD7 5LS			Map 4 C1

Set back from the A707/A708 junction, a mile from the town centre on the Peebles road, this extended 18th-century house has been turned into a delightful family hotel with a Tyrolean-style interior. Jim and Anne Hill, owners since 1971, cater for all kinds of visitors – business, fishing, tourist, family – and friendly hospitality is their watchword. Bedrooms – in the house, by the pool or in the 'log cabin' – feature pine, pretty fabrics and a host of extras. Parents will appreciate the privacy provided by many separate but connecting children's rooms. An interesting 'Quick Bite' menu is served in the characterful pine-panelled bar which features an open fire and garden outlook (sit outside in fine weather). Lighter bites include crayfish bisque with aïoli (£1.85) and queenie scallops in garlic butter (£4.85), while more substantial offerings range from the old favourite rösti topped with bacon, mushrooms and melted Swiss cheese (£6.95) to Tiroler Grostle – fried potato, onions and ham topped with two fried eggs (£4.95). Vegetarians have their own menu which features Pithiviers with a range of fillings (perhaps Brie and broccoli £6.50) and avocado, egg and Gruyère gratin, and desserts include hot lemon tart with cream and ice cream or two chocolate iced parfaits (£2.95). Six high-chairs and booster seats are provided. High tea at 5.30pm. Squash club nearby. **Rooms** *16. Fenced-in garden, outdoor swimming pool, games room with table tennis, badminton, pool, children's outdoor playground with sand pit, swing & slide, climbing frame, trampoline, woodland 'action man centre', tree house, crèche. Access, Visa.*

Skeabost Bridge	Skeabost House	60%	£86

Tel 047 032 202 Fax 047 032 454	Hotel

Skeabost Bridge by Portree Isle of Skye Highland IV51 9NP	Map 2 A3

Twelve acres of woodland and gardens surround a former hunting lodge on Loch Snizort. It's a comfortable place, with the same family owners since 1970, and relaxation is easy in the lounges, the flagstoned sun lounge, the cosy bar and the billiard room. Pretty bedrooms include one with a four-poster and a few in the nearby Garden House. One is a large family room. The hotel owns eight miles of the river Snizort, which runs through the grounds, and has a boat on a nearby loch. **Rooms** 26. *Garden, golf (9-hole), fishing, snooker. Closed mid Oct-mid Apr. Access, Visa.*

Spean Bridge	Letterfinlay Lodge	55%	£68

Tel 0397 712622	Hotel

Spean Bridge Highland PH34 4DZ	Map 3 B4

Here since 1963, the Forsyth family have created a comfortable and very Scottish atmosphere in a ruggedly beautiful setting on the banks of Loch Lochy (seven miles north of Spean Bridge). The public rooms include a cosy little bar, a homely TV lounge and a sun lounge with glorious views. Bedrooms furnished in various styles are named by colour and decorated accordingly; all have private bathrooms, three not en suite. Five rooms are considered suitable for family use. *Rooms* 13. *Closed Nov-mid Mar. Access, Amex, Diners, Visa.*

Stonehaven	Marine Hotel		

Tel 0569 62155	Pub

The Shorehead Stonehaven Grampian AB3 2JY	Map 3 D4

Down by the harbour, the ground-floor bar of the Marine Hotel very pubby with boarded walls, copper-topped tables, games machine, juke box, pool table and a changing selection of real ales. The same menu (with the addition of a few bought-in items like steak pies) is served here as in the more family-oriented, first-floor dining room with its blue nautical decor and waitress service. Varied offerings range from Mexican nachos (£2.25) and onion barjee and vegetables samosa (£1.95) to golden fried haddock (£4.65), chili with garlic bread (£4.45), steaks and salads. For children there are the usual fish finger/pizza offerings and a couple of high-chairs; children are not allowed in the bar to eat. Six modest but clean bedrooms (the two largest are family rooms with cots available) all have harbour views and are furnished with fitted white melamine units and matching duvets and curtains, have shower cabinets in the rooms but share two loos. All have phones, televisions and beverage kits. *Bar open all day. Bar Food 12-2, 5-9.30 (to 9 in winter). Free House.* **Beer** *Bass, Taylor. Children's play area. Family room.* **Accommodation** *6 bedrooms, £37.50 (single £27.50). Access, Visa.*

Stornoway	Cabarfeidh Hotel	64%	£85

Tel 0851 702604 Fax 0851 705572	Hotel

Manor Park Stornoway Isle of Lewis Highland PA87 2EU	Map 2 A2

An early-70s hotel with a rather faceless exterior (belying the inviting interior) on the edge of town, a brisk walk from the Ullapool ferry terminal. The Viking Bar, a cocktail bar and a restaurant divided into three differently styled areas comprise the public rooms. Cheerful

bedrooms, all en suite. There are four adjoining rooms suitable for
families, with cots available. Baby-sitting and baby-listening can
be arranged and baby baths, potties, nappies, high-chairs and baby food
provided if you prefer to brave the Islands unprepared! For visitors
not staying at the hotel there is an area for nappy changing and breast
feeding. The restaurant keeps children happy with their own menu (or
small portions) and parents happy with a wee dram at the Viking Bar
where a longship makes up the counter. Open all year round.
***Rooms** 46. Garden. Access, Amex, Diners, Visa.*

Strathblane   Kirkhouse Inn

Tel 0360 770621 Fax 0360 770896	Inn
Glasgow Road Strathblane Central G63 9AA	**Map 3 B5**

Ten miles north of Glasgow on the A81 Stirling and Aberfoyle road,
this roadside inn is at the foot of the Campsie Fells and thus popular
with walkers. It's an ideal touring centre as Loch Lomond, the
Trossachs, Glasgow and Stirling are all within 30 minutes by car.
Sprucely kept public areas include a busy public bar and quieter
lounge and restaurant. Pastel colours are used in the bedrooms, which
include a honeymoon suite with a sunken bath. All rooms have TVs,
radios, telephones and beverage trays. *Bar open 11-11 Mon-Thu, 11am-
midnight Fri & Sat, 12.30-11 Sun. Free House. **Beer** Maclay's 80/-.
Garden. **Accommodation** 15 rooms, all en suite, £72 (single £55.25).
Children welcome overnight (under-12s free if sharing parents' room),
additional beds and cots available. Access, Diners, Visa.*

Strathcarron   Carron Restaurant

Tel 052 02488	Restaurant
Cam-Allt Strathcarron Highland	**Map 2 B3**

On the A890, this is an agreeable modern restaurant next to a craft
shop and adjoining pottery, with views out over Loch Carron. Open
in season for 11 hours a day it serves tea, coffees, snacks and light meals
(toasted sandwiches from £1.70, quiche £3.80), plus a selection
of Scottish steaks, salmon, pork chop and venison cooked on the
chargrill (sirloin steak £10.30, salmon £8.90). Children's menu and
portions plus one high-chair and two booster seats. Safe, large grassed
area for letting off steam. All no-smoking in 1994. *Seats 43.*
***Open** 10.30-9.15 **Closed** Sun & end Oct-1 Apr. Access, Amex, Visa.*

Stromness   Hamnavoe Restaurant

Tel 0856 850 606	Restaurant
35 Graham Place Stromness Orkney	**Map 2 C1**

An attractive little restaurant in an alley off the High Street. The
dinner menu offers a good choice ranging from white crab
in a whisky sauce (£3.75) and breaded farmhouse cheese with
cranberry and orange sauce (£2.50) to carrot and almond loaf
(£6.50), grilled steaks (£9) and puff pastry of scallops and mussels in a
lobster sauce (£8.50). Daily specials usually take the form of fresh
grilled fish – halibut, turbot, monkfish – purchased from the fishing
boats berthing at Stromness harbour. To finish, perhaps apple pie with
hot fudge sauce or a medley of home-made ice creams. Families with
older children are welcomed, but there are no special facilities.
***Seats** 36. **Open** 7pm-midnight. **Closed** mid Oct-May. No credit cards.*

Swinton   **Wheatsheaf Hotel**

Tel 0890 860257	Pub

Main Street Swinton Borders TD11 3JJ	Map 3 D6

The village of Swinton is six miles north of Coldstream, on the way
to nowhere, and is easy to miss. The Wheatsheaf, dominating this
simple Scots farming hamlet, overlooks the plain little village green
and has very limited parking; at busy periods, the main street is full
up with cars. This is very much a dining pub (drinking goes on in the
pool-tabled, fruit-machined public bar at the back, so separate from
the food operation that most visitors aren't even aware it exists)
with a very well-regarded restaurant, the Four Seasons, and it's wise
to book even for bar meals, such is the reputation of the pub in the
Borders. The emphasis is on fresh food: a menu reproduced on one
blackboard, daily specials listed on another. Tables are laid with cloths
and place mats; freshly baked wheaten rolls are presented as a matter
of course, and butter comes in a slab on a saucer, with no foil packets
or sauce sachets in sight. Salads are imaginative and fresh. Service
is assured from uniformed waitresses. One high-chair; sings in the
garden. *Bar Food* (*except Mon*) *11.45-2* (*Sun from 12.30*), *6-9* (*Sun
6.30-8.30*). *Children allowed in bar to eat until 8pm. Free House.
Beer Broughton Greenmantle Ale, Special Bitter. Garden, outdoor eating,
children's play area. Family Room. **Accommodation** 4 bedrooms, 1 en suite,
£38-54 (single £25-40). Children welcome overnight, additional beds
(charged) & cots (no charge) available. Pub closed all Mon, 1 week Feb &
1 week Nov. Access, Visa.*

Tayvallich   **Tayvallich Inn**

Tel 05467 282	Pub

Tayvallich by Lochgilphead Strathclyde PA31 8PR	Map 3 A5

This simple white-painted dining pub – though it's fine to pop in for
a drink, most people come for the food – is in a marvellously pretty
location at the centre of a strung-along-the-road, scattered village
stretching around the top of Loch Sween. Sit outside, on the front
terrace, at one of the five parasolled picnic tables, and enjoy the view
of a dozen little boats, and low wooded hills fringing the lochside; the
word Tayvallich means "the house in the pass". Inside, the Tayvallich
is surprisingly modern – smartly pine-clad, with a little bar and larger
adjoining dining room proper. The bar is tile-floored, with raffia back
chairs and little wood tables, the dining room similar, but spacious and
relaxing, with a woodburning stove, attractive dresser, and bentwood
chairs around scrubbed pine dining tables. The star of the handwritten
menu is the freshest local seafood; so local that oysters (half a dozen
£6) come from just yards away in Loch Sween itself, and scallops
from the Sound of Jura (£9.50) just round the coast. Portions are
generous, and the whole atmosphere is very informal and relaxed.
Holidaymakers turn up in shorts, and babies are commendably
tolerantly treated, with clip-on chairs and specially rustled up toddler
food – they'll even find chips if the kids scream the house down!
Puddings (all £2.50), made by the landlady, are of the chocolate nut
flab and banoffi pie sort; few dedicated seafood lovers, having
munched through two courses already, get that far though! Non-fish
choices as well. *Open 11-midnight Monday-Sunday July & August,
regular hours other days. **Bar Food** 12-2, 6-9. **Restaurant Meals** 7-9.
Children only allowed in no-smoking area of the bar to eat. Free House.
Beer Tetley. Patio/grassy foreshore, outdoor eating. Inn closed all Monday
from 1 November to 31 March. Access, Visa.*

Troon	**Marine Highland Hotel**	**67%**	**£138**

Tel 0292 314444 Fax 0292 316922	Hotel
Crosbie Road Troon Strathclyde KA10 6HE	Map 4 A1

This handsome Victorian sandstone structure overlooks the 18th
fairway of Royal Troon championship golf course. Accommodation
options are standard, de luxe or top-of-the-range Ambassador suites.
Families welcome, with entertainment during festive periods, baby-
sitting, baby-listening and high-chairs offered. All-day informal eating,
including a children's menu, in Crosbie's brasserie. Leave the A77 and
follow the B789 to Troon. *Rooms 72. Indoor swimming pool,
gymnasium, squash, sauna, spa bath, steam room, solarium, beauty salon,
putting, snooker. Access, Amex, Diners, Visa.*

Turriff	**Towie Tavern**

Tel 08884 201	Pub
Auchterless nr Turriff Grampian AB53 8EP	Map 2 D3

Long a favourite for its satisfying, wholesome food, this is a roadside
pebbledash pub on the A497, some four miles south of Turriff and
a short distance from the National Trust's 13th-century Fyvie Castle.
Seafood is featured at the Towie and a different daily menu assures
very fresh produce. The 'Fisherman's choice' offers whatever
is available that day: plaice, herring, mackerel or perhaps haddock
(poached or deep-fried £4.95). The food is more elaborate in the
restaurant. Vegetarian options and home-made puddings. Smartly
rustic decor within and room outside to let off steam. Music in the
non-smoking dining room. *Bar Food 12-2, 6-9 (5-8.30 Sun).
Restaurant Meals 6-9. Children's menu (£1.95-£2.50 per dish).
Children allowed in bar to eat. Free House. Beer McEwan's Export,
Theakston, guest beer. Patio/terrace, outdoor eating. Access, Visa.*

Tweedsmuir	**Crook Inn**	**59%**	**£52**

Tel 089 97 272 Fax 089 97 294	Hotel
Tweedsmuir nr Biggar Borders ML12 6QN	Map 4 C1

Standing on the A701 Moffat-Edinburgh road and set in the ruggedly
beautiful Tweed valley, the Crook is a good base for walking,
climbing and touring holidays. Guests can also enjoy free fishing on 30
miles of the River Tweed. Burns wrote *Willie Wastle's Wife* in what
is now the bar, and locally-born John Buchan set many of his novels
in the area. Neat bedrooms are simple in their appointments, with
no TVs or telephones; a Z-bed or cot will fit in the larger rooms (£5
charge for under-8s). There are a few Art Deco features in the lounge
and some of the bathrooms. Two high-chairs in the family room. Bar
open all day, seven days a week. Lawned garden away from the road.
A craft centre (glass-making a speciality) has recently been created
from the old stable block. *Rooms 7. Garden, fishing, putting. Access,
Amex, Diners, Visa.*

Ullapool	**Ceilidh Place**	**£90**

Tel 0854 612103	Inn
14 West Argyll Street Ullapool Highland IV26 2TY	Map 2 B2

Jean Urquhart presides with wit, charm and efficiency over
an establishment long renowned as a centre for good company and

good food. Located 200 yards from Loch Broom, this is a celebrated northern community centre, which started as a coffee shop, and, like Topsy, just growed; three cottages in this seaside village were knocked into one to create it. Literally meaning 'Meeting Place', Ceilidh Place is much more: bookshop, arts centre, coffee shop, evening restaurant and venue for theatre, music and poetry all housed in a cosy collection of welcoming rooms. Such is the extent of the live entertainment that the single little TV is more than adequate. The pretty bedrooms are comfortable and spotless; ten rooms now have en-suite facilities. Eleven additional rooms in a separate building across the street offer more spartan, budget accommodation with shared facilities (not really suitable for families). Food is displayed at and served from a counter, and includes sandwiches (£1.50), salads (85p), wholemeal scones (60p) and cakes, widening at lunchtime and in the evening to include soup(£1.25), lasagne, vegetable crumbles, even mince and tatties (from £5); children's portions and high-chairs are provided. If it's available, try the rich, sticky, cherry chocolate truffle cake (£1.95). There's a terrace for open-air snacking, and a no-smoking area. **Rooms** 13. *Coffee shop (9.30am-9pm), children's play area. Closed 25 Dec, 2 weeks Jan. Access, Amex, Diners, Visa.*

Weem	Ailean Chraggan Hotel	
Tel 0887 820346		Pub
Weem by Aberfeldy Tayside PH15 2LD		Map 3 C4

Delightful little cottage inn, beautifully located against a steep woodland backdrop, and with two acres of gardens overlooking the Tay valley. The bright, sunny, well-kept bar has a central log-burning stove, with a dining area beside the picture windows. Simple, well-cooked food is highlighted by superb local seafood; try the Loch Etive mussels (£6.50), served in huge steaming portions with garlic bread or the Sound of Jura prawn platter (£11.95). Bedrooms are also recommended: spacious and light with nice pieces of old furniture, armchairs, and, in two rooms, small dressing areas. All are equipped with TVs, hairdryers and tea/coffee-making facilities. Ask for one of the front bedrooms, which have inspiring views to wake up to. Patio and lawned garden to front and side. *Open 11-11 Monday-Sunday April-end October, regular hours other days.* **Bar Food** *12-2, 5.30-10 (In winter to 9). Children allowed in bar to eat. Free House.* **Beer** *No real ales. Garden, outdoor eating.* **Accommodation** *3 bedrooms, all en suite, £52 (single £26). Children welcome overnight (under-10s half price, babies free), additional beds and cots available. Closed two weeks in January. Access, Visa.*

Whitehouse	Old School Tea Room	
Tel 0880 73215		Tea Room
Whitehouse nr Tarbert Strathclyde PA29 6XR		Map 3 B6

Five miles south of Tarbert on the A83, this neat little tea room has long been distinguished by the excellent baking of Heather Howe and Ken Pryor. Kenneth specialises in cheesecakes, two of the favourites being dark chocolate and rum, and Cointreau and white chocolate (each £1.50). Among the savoury choices could be rolls and sandwiches, salads (from £3.80), ploughman's platters and smoked salmon mousse. Hot dishes, too, such as burgers and poached salmon. Children's portions offered. Tables on the lawn in summer. *Unlicensed.* **Seats** *30.* **Open** *10.30-6.* **Closed** *Tues & Oct-Easter. No credit cards.*

citytime™

Citytime is a new national service offering users lower charges for calls made in the London and M25 area. However, unlike other regional services, Citytime customers will be able to use their phone anywhere on the Cellnet network.

Choose Cellnet.
You'll have more choice.

Call the BIG network for small phones on
0800 21 4000

Mondeo from Ford. World class safety

Mondeo is the first car with Dynamic Safety Engineering, providing the ultimate in integrated driver and passenger safety.

Every Mondeo features: Steering wheel airbag • Front seatbelt pre-tensioners and grabbers • Anti-submarine seats • Reinforced bodyshell • Side impact bars.

For more information on Mondeo, available safety features and the location of your nearest dealer call free on **0800 111 222**

Everything we do is driven by you.

Wales

Aberaeron   Hive On The Quay

Tel 0545 570445	Café

Cadwgan Place Aberaeron Dyfed SA46 0BT   Map 9 B4

Fourteen years continuous *Egon Ronay's Just a Bite Guide* stardom
perhaps says suffficient about the Holgates' flawless summertime café.
It's part of a family-run concern which includes the unique honey-bee
exhibition and a fresh fish shop which sells the catch from their own
boat. In the café with its quayside conservatory there's so much
to be enjoyed from a simple chicken and leek soup (£1.30) and home-
made quiche with an array of salads (self-served from £3.60) to local
lobster and crab and cucumber sandwiches. All day there are bara
brith and honey spice cake, banana sandwiches for the little ones;
boiled egg and soldiers (£1.30) at tea-time. Cheeses are local
farmhouse varieties and ice creams from honey and hazelnut
to nectarine are home-made (a speciality) and quite delicious. Suppers,
waitress-served in the restaurant from 6pm in summer, weigh in with
cod steaks in green peppercorn sauce (£7.25), spicy cauliflower with
nan bread and apricot chutney (£6.25) and home-baked American
cheesecake. Licence with full meals only. Two high-chairs and a safe
courtyard in which to feel free of any restrictions; children may
be fascinated by the exhibition (admission fee charged, open 11-1 & 2-
5 from May 22-mid Sept) with its observation hives and instructive
video. **Seats** 55. **Open** 10.30-5 (*Jul, Aug to 9.30*). **Closed** 1 Oct-Spring
Bank Holiday. *Access, Visa.*

Aberdovey   Penhelig Arms Hotel

Tel 0654 767215 Fax 0654 767690	Pub

Aberdovey Gwynedd LL35 0LT   Map 8 C3

Unrivalled views across the Dyfi estuary to Ynyslas make a splendid
setting for Robert and Sally Hughes' smart black and white-painted
pub by the A493. Some disadvantages are inherent in a situation
where no pavement exists 'twixt front door and double yellow lines,
nor greater space, almost, between the single rail line at Penhelig halt
and the hotel's gable end. Road noise and BR's occasional arrivals
notwithstanding, the sea wall opposite makes a marvellous spot at any
state of the tide to enjoy a leisurely alfresco lunch, while the tiny
Fisherman's Bar provides a relaxing, and shady, alternative. Fan-cooled
on the hottest summer days, and heated by two open fires in winter
(set back-to-back beneath a central stone chimney), here's an ideal place
to enjoy a pint of good beer and catch up on some local gossip. The
bar's the focal point of lunches from Monday to Saturday, and, when
the weather's inclement, eaters soon overflow into the restaurant next
door. By night, bar meals are suspended in favour of a set-price dinner
(3 courses £16.50) offering diverse daily choice. Sunday lunch, rather
more economically priced (3 courses £10.50), has a more limited
choice, but brings cooking of equally consistent quality. Booking
is advisable. The lengthy wine list offers around 200 wines. Plump for
a room with a view : in fact, only two of the bedrooms lack a seascape.
All have a cottagey feel and benefit from an individual approach
to decor which makes the best of their higgledy-piggledy layout.
Private bathroom, television and radio, and beverage trays are
included throughout, but for a truly special stay ask for one of the
three superior rooms, with balconies and sea views. Residents' lounge.
One high-chair provided. **Bar Food & Restaurant Meals** 12-2 (*Sun
12.15-2*), 7-9. *Free House.* **Beer** *Tetley Traditional, Ansells Mild,*

Greenalls Original, guest beer. Seawall patio, outdoor eating.
***Accommodation** 10 bedrooms, all en suite, £64 (single £38), superior
£78. Children welcome overnight (no charge if sharing parents' room).
Additional beds and cots supplied. Access, Visa.*

Aberdovey	**Trefeddian Hotel**	58%	£88★
Tel 0654 767213 Fax 0654 767777			Hotel
Aberdovey Gwynedd LL35 0SB			Map 8 C3

Trefeddian stands back from the A493, half a mile north
of Aberdovey, with fine views across Cardigan Bay. Day rooms,
which include lounge, reading room and bar, offer a choice of peace
and quiet or conviviality. Neat, practical bedrooms include several
with balconies; six family suites and four family rooms; cots and extra
beds charged according to season. ★Half-board terms only in the hotel.
Self-catering accommodation is also available in a house, flat and
bungalow. No under-5s in the dining room during dinner, but supper
is arranged for children in the bedrooms between 5.45 and 6.30pm.
***Rooms** 46. Garden, indoor swimming pool & paddling pool, tennis, putting,
snooker. Closed end Dec–mid Mar. Access, Visa.*

Abergavenny	**Llanwenarth Arms Hotel**	
Tel 0873 810550 Fax 0873 811880		Pub
Brecon Road Abergavenny Gwent NP8 1EP		Map 9 D5

A roadside inn (on the A40) some 3 miles west of Abergavenny
standing on an escarpment above the Usk valley. Chef/landlord
D'Arcy McGregor's creative cooking leaves little to chance, his bar
menus making full use of the best local produce available. Stilton and
watercress soup (£2.50), smoked chicken and fresh pineapple with
honey and nut dressing (£4.50) for a lunchtime bite, or a half rack
of Welsh spring lamb with leeks and cream sauce, boiled new potatoes
and fresh vegetables make a truly hearty meal. Seasonally revised
menus are equally well balanced, served throughout the two bars,
family dining area and splendid summer terrace set some 70 feet above
the river with views across to Sugar Loaf Mountain. Residents enjoy
the use of their own lounge, and a Victorian-style conservatory
furnished with comfortable cane furniture. Bedrooms, approached
by way of a sheltered courtyard, are attractively furnished and
immaculately kept, each one enjoying its fair share of the view across
to Sugar Loaf Mountain. TVs, telephones, trouser presses and
hairdryers are all standard; bathrooms also have over-bath showers
and ample supplies of toiletries. Four high-chairs provided along with
a children's menu or portions. ***Bar Food & Restaurant Meals** 12-2
(Sun to 1.30), 6-9. (Sun 7-9.30). Children's menu. Free House.*
***Beer** Bass, Worthington, Wadworth 6X. Garden, outdoor eating. Family
room. **Accommodation** 18 bedrooms, all en suite, £59 (single £49).
Children welcome overnight (under-16s half price), additional beds (£5),
cots supplied. No dogs. Access, Amex, Diners, Visa.*

Abergorlech	**Black Lion**	
Tel 0558 685271		Pub
Abergorlech nr Carmarthen Dyfed SA32 7SN		Map 9 B5

At the heart of one of Wales's best-kept villages, the white-painted
Black Lion stands between a tiny stone chapel and the Gothi River
bridge; private fishing beats are nearby. The single bar with flagstone
floors and high settles leads to a flat-roofed dining extension. On the

main menu local sewin, fillet steaks and generous salads satisfy the heartiest appetites, while blackboard daily specials might feature chili con carne, chicken Kiev and vegetable lasagne (all under £6). Opposite the pub, a scenic riverside garden with picnic tables features regular summer barbecues. Children welcome to eat in the restaurant (not the bar). Safe garden. *Pub open 11-11 Mon-Sat in summer, usual hours Sun.* **Bar Food & Restaurant Meals** *12-2.30, 7-9.30. Free House.* **Beer** *Felinfoel Double Dragon. Riverside garden, outdoor eating. Family room. Access, Visa.*

Abersoch	**Porth Tocyn Hotel**	69%	£94
Tel 0758 713303 Fax 0758 713538			Hotel
Bwlchtocyn Abersoch Gwynedd LL53 7BU			Map 8 B3

Once a row of lead-miners' cottages, the hotel stands high above Cardigan Bay. It's about 2½ miles south of Abersoch, through the hamlets of Sarn Bach and Bwlchtocyn. The Fletcher-Brewer family have guarded their reputation for attentive hospitality for three generations, and the chintzy lounges contribute just the right degree of homeliness. A sitting room with TV, videos, toys and games is set aside for children; children's high tea is also served there. Bedrooms, though generally small, are individually furnished in a similar style, many with restful sea views, all with private bathrooms and showers. Families with children are well catered for (children stay free in parents' room); youngsters can let off steam in the 25 acres of grounds. Riding stables are just outside the hotel grounds. *Rooms 17. Garden, outdoor swimming pool, tennis. Closed mid Nov-week before Easter. Access.*

Restaurant £60

The focal point of Louise Fletcher-Brewer's culinary output is her short-choice two-or five-course dinner menu, completely changed each day. Salmon and cucumber mousse, venison brochettes with port and rosemary sauce, onion and thyme leaf soup, prawn-stuffed baked bream and veal escalopes with cassis sauce show the style. Steamed Snowdon pudding with gin sauce is a tempting dessert. Lunch is casual, maybe alfresco by the pool, with a hot and cold buffet on Sundays. An evolving and sensibly priced wine list includes good-value wines from around the world. House selection offers terrific value. *Seats 50. L 12.30-2 D 7.30-9.30. Set L (Sun) £14 Set D £17.50/£23.*

Afonwen	**Pwll Gwyn Hotel**		
Tel 0352 720227			Pub
Afonwen nr Mold Clwyd CH7 5UB			Map 8 C2

Formerly a 17th-century coaching inn of some renown with an unusual remodelled Victorian frontage (on the A541), Pwll Gwyn's fortunes are being revived today by enthusiastic and energetic young tenants Andrew and Karen Davies. Andrew provides the brains (and the brawn) behind an intelligently run kitchen whose output is much dictated by his shopping from Liverpool's markets. Best bets for the bar food, therefore, come from the daily blackboard: avocado, chicken and curry mayonnaise (£2.90), liver and smoked bacon with gravy and potato cake (£4.95) or fillets of brill with mushrooms, wine and cream (£6.40). Desserts, too, are impressive: cappuccino cake (£2.30) and toffee crunch cheesecake (£2.40) feature on a long list of home-made delights. More substantial cooking with a classical base comes à la carte in the two separate dining rooms (one for non-smokers); special event evenings (Italian, Chinese, Indian) and summer barbecues are a regular feature. Four large double bedrooms are currently in use, one with a full bathroom; installation of WC and shower rooms by the owning brewery is currently in hand, and extra beds for family use are promised for the coming year. Swing, climbing frame and tree house in the garden. *Bar Food 12-2.30, 7-10 (Sun to 9.30).* *Restaurant Meals 12-2 (Sun only), 7-10 (except Sun). Children's menu. Garden, outdoor eating. Family room. Beer Greenalls.* *Accommodation 4 bedrooms, £30 (single £15). Children welcome overnight. Check-in by arrangement. No dogs. Access, Visa.*

Barry	Mount Sorrel Hotel	59%	£85
Tel 0446 740069 Fax 0446 746600			**Hotel**
Porthkerry Road Barry South Glamorgan CF6 8AY			**Map 9 C6**

Converted from two Victorian houses 30 years ago, with more recent additions for extra accommodation, meeting rooms and leisure facilities. Comfortable day rooms, very acceptable bedrooms (children up to 12 stay free when sharing with parents); two suites have interconnecting rooms and six other rooms are suitable for families. High-chairs and a children's menu in the restaurant. *Rooms 43. Indoor swimming pool, keep-fit equipment, sauna, coffee shop (7am-8pm). Access, Amex, Diners, Visa.*

Bodfari	Dinorben Arms	
Tel 0745 710309		**Pub**
Bodfari nr Denbigh Clwyd LL16 4DA		**Map 8 C2**

Landlord Gilbert Hopwood marks his 35th anniversary this year at the 17th-century Dinorben Arms, which you'll find off the A541, taking the B5429 and sign to Tremeirchion, on a hill in the village below the church. Today's pub, much developed from days of yore, enjoys a prodigious output. Lunchtimes concentrate on the self-served smörgåsbord (£7.50) and in the evenings both cold starters and sweets are mostly served buffet-style in the Well Bar. The "Chicken Rough" (£4.45), originally presented to be eaten with fingers, lives on since being introduced in 1961; the Farmhouse Buffet (Wed/Thu £8.95) and Carverboard (Fri/Sat £12.95) are more recent evening additions. Special dishes nightly may include salmon with prawn sauce (£8.50), chicken Amsterdam with melted Dutch cheese (£7.95) and beef stroganoff (£8.95). However, there are plenty more snacky items, children's and vegetarian choices (aubergine moussaka £4.75) and families are well catered for in their own room and on the smart, flower-decked, tiered patios. At the top of the extensive hillside gardens is a children's adventure play area with swing, slide and climbing frame. High-chairs are provided and there's a changing table in the spacious Ladies. *Bar Food & Restaurant Meals 12-2.30, 6-10.30 (Sun to 10.15). Free House. Beer Thwaites. Garden, children's play area. Family room. Access, Visa.*

Burton Green	Golden Grove Inn	
Tel 0244 570445		**Pub**
Llyndir Lane Burton Green nr Wrexham Clwyd LL12 0AS		**Map 8 D2**

Best found by turning off the B5445 at Rossett, by the signs to Llyndyr Hall; at the end of a lane seemingly leading nowhere stands

a group of black and white timber-framed buildings which comprise
the pub and its many outhouses. Within is a treasure trove of antiquity
with some splendid 14th-century oak beams and magical old
inglenooks and fireplaces. A modern extension housing a carvery
dining-room leads to drinking patios and a large, safe garden replete
with swings and play equipment, justifiably popular in the summer
months. Following a period of crisis in early 1993, the Golden Grove
is now operating under new management and flies the flag
of Marston's Brewery. Recommended for its atmosphere rather than
food. Families welcome: swing, slide, climbing frame and activity
house in the garden. *Free House.* **Beer** *Marston's Best & Pedigree.
Garden, outdoor play area. Family room. Access, Visa.*

Cardiff   **Chapter Kitchen**

Tel 0222 372756	Café
Chapter Arts Centre Market Road Canton Cardiff South Glamorgan	**Map 9 D6**

Make for the Chapter Arts Centre in Market Road, Canton, to find
an art gallery, a theatre and two cinemas. The minimalist all-day café,
whose metal chairs and hardwood tables set up constant echoes, serves
up wholefoods, hearty soups and hefty salads at rock-bottom prices.
Cooking of the vegetable curry (£2.95), nutburgers and chicken and
mushroom pies (£3.50) may best be described as average, but scores
on value. Filled baps and baked potatoes; flapjacks and mince slice
alongside fruit crumble (£1.25) and cheesecake. Coffee, herb teas,
organic wine and bottled beers to drink. No-smoking area. *Seats 80,
28 outside.* **Open** *9am-10pm.* **Closed** *Bank Holidays, 1 week Christmas.
No credit cards.*

Chepstow   **Castle View Hotel**   £60

Tel 0291 620349 Fax 0291 627397	Inn
16 Bridge Street Chepstow Gwent NP6 5EZ	**Map 9 D6**

Originally a private house, much of the stone used in construction 300
years ago came from Chepstow Castle which commands the huge
riverbank opposite. Ivy-covered today and genuinely welcoming, it's
immaculately kept by Martin and Vicky Cardale. The original stone
walls and timbers enhance the setting for a snack. Through both 'light
and bigger bites', the bar menu encompasses omelettes and steak
sandwiches, vegetables crepes and hazelnut and mushroom fettuccine
(£3.95), with turkey, ham and sweetcorn (£4.95) or steak, kidney
and Tetley pie (£5.95) as carnivorous alternatives. In the dining room,
an evening table d'hote (2-courses for £11.95) is supplemented by a
short à la carte on which the local Wye salmon is a regular feature.
Sunday lunch also (main course £5.95). Over a two year period, most
bedrooms have been systematically upgraded and refurbished with
smart mahogany furniture. En-suite bathrooms (two with shower/WC
only) are neatly kept; radio and TV (with use of videos), mini-bars,
direct-dial phones and beverage trays are standard throughout. The
cottage suite (sleeping up to four) incorporates a quiet residents'
lounge; and overlooking the garden, a restful spot, are two spacious
family rooms. **Bar Food and Restaurant Meals** *12-2, 6.30-9.30
(Sun 7-9). Children allowed in the bar to eat. Free House.* **Beer** *Tetley,
Marston's Pedigree, Butcombe. Garden, outdoor eating.* **Accommodation**
*11 bedrooms, all en suite, £60 (single £40). Children welcome overnight,
additional beds and cots available. No dogs. Access, Diners, Visa.*

Chepstow   St Pierre Hotel   66%   £100
| Tel 0291 625261   Fax 0291 629975 | Hotel |
St Pierre Park Chepstow Gwent NP6 6YA   Map 9 D6

Three miles from the Severn Bridge, take exit 22 off the M4, then
A48 away from Chepstow. The heart of the hotel is a much-extended
14th-century mansion standing in 400acres complete with an 11-acre
lake. An extensive leisure club, two golf courses and a conference area
make it a fine base for work or leisure. Among the day rooms are
spacious lounges, three restaurants and a poolside bar. Bedrooms, many
with splendid views, include 30 of Executive standard and 43 in the
Lakeside village, where there are also multi-roomed lodges. Children
up to 16 stay free in parents' room. Direct reservations line 0291
624444. Country Club Hotels. **Rooms** 147. *Garden, indoor swimming
pool, squash, badminton, sauna, spa bath, solarium, beauty salon, tennis,
bowling, coffee shop (10am-10pm). Access, Amex, Diners, Visa.*

Clytha   Clytha Arms
| Tel 0873 840206 | Pub |
Clytha nr Abergavenny Gwent   Map 9 D5

Clytha stands on the old main road (now the B4598) between
Abergavenny and Usk. Two years ago, it was closed and close
to dereliction; today it is decidedly a pub for eating in, and chef-
patron, Andrew Canning, certainly knows how to cook. His
beautifully balanced starter of oysters in their shells with leeks and
Caerphilly (£3.95) could rightly become a signature dish; or plump
for the Glamorgan sausages with plum and orange chutney (£2.75).
Main courses deliver some fine fresh fish (monkfish with pink
peppercorns £9.50) and country-style cooking from rabbit Portuguese
hunter style (£7.50) to osso buco with mushroom risotto (£8.95).
Results may be variable, though the intent is serious. In lighter mood,
bar snacks are typified by home-made fish soup (£2.50), laverbread
with bacon and cockles (£3.45), faggots with peas and beer gravy
(£2.45) and treacle sponge and custard (£1.95). The flagstoned public
bar with its dartboard and skittles table may present unforeseen
hazards – to which the tree-lined garden provides a serene summer
alternative. There is a wooded area with a duck pen, a few outdoor
toys and small trees to climb. **Bar Food & Restaurant Meals**
*12.30-2.30, 7.30-10 (restaurant to 9.30) (no food Sun eve). Children's
menu. Free House.* **Beer** *Hook Norton, Courage Directors, Wadworth 6X.
Garden. Family room. Pub closed L Mon. Access, Visa.*

Cowbridge   Off The Beeton Track
| Tel 0446 773599 | Restaurant |
1 Town Hall Square Cowbridge South Glamorgan CF7 7DD   Map 9 C6

Alison and David Richardson's little town-centre restaurant with
courtyard provides much to tempt all tastes and pockets. The day
starts at 10 for coffee and home baking – Welsh cake (40p), bara brith
(55p) – then from midday choose from either the quick snack menu –
soup (£1.40), open sandwiches (£2.10), filled jacket potatoes
(£2.10) – or lunch menu, with starters such as mushrooms in herb
butter (£3.20) or paté (£1.80), main courses such as navarin of Welsh
lamb (£4.85) or goujons of plaice (£4.25) and there is always a daily
vegetarian dish, perhaps mushroom stroganoff or tomato and
gorgonzola ravioli (both £4.25). Puddings such as white chocolate
truffle cake or trifle are £2.50. Afternoon teas are served from 3-5,

then comes an early dinner three-course menu from 6.45-8 (£8.50
Tue to Fri only) and more elaborate and expensive à la carte until 10.
Traditional Sunday lunch (£8.20). Good Welsh cheeses. Children are
welcome at lunchtime. *Seats 30. **Open** 10-2, 3-5 & 6.45-10.*
Closed D Sun & Mon, 1 week Jan. Access, Amex, Visa.

Criccieth   Prince of Wales

Tel 0766 522556	Pub
High Street Criccieth Gwynedd LL52 0HB	**Map 8 B2**

Busy pub, right on the square, and a lively local: live music
on Tuesday nights, and a piano in the bar (impromptu performances
encouraged). Family-orientated: children are positively welcomed, not
just tolerated. *Open daily in summer (except Sun). **Beer** Whitbread.*
Family room. Pub closed Sundays. No credit cards.

Crickhowell   Bear Hotel   £59

Tel 0873 810408 Fax 0873 811696	Inn
Brecon Road (A40) Crickhowell Powys NP8 1BW	**Map 9 D5**

One of the original coaching inns on the London to Aberystwyth
route, the Bear today bristles with personality and honest endeavour.
Front bars, a hive of activity, are resplendent with oak panelling,
ornamental sideboards and welcoming log fires. Refurbishment
of three of the inn's oldest bedrooms has revealed open stone fireplaces
which date it back to 1432. Further top-grade bedroom
accommodation is housed in a modern Tudor-style courtyard
extension, and in a garden cottage containing two bedrooms and
a suite with its own spa bath. Four-poster beds and antique furniture
abound. Meals in the bar are hearty and traditional by design. Winter
favourites include faggots and mushy peas (£4.95) or perhaps bubble
and squeak with bacon, replaced in summer by salmon béchamel pie
(£5.50) and Welsh lamb casserole with cumin and apricots (£5.95).
House speciality bread-and-butter pudding and lemon crunch pie
(£2.50) are available all year round. Plenty of standards (paté, filled
pancakes and pork pie) served in small portions for little people; filo
parcels of Brie (£3.60) and aduki bean and peanut rissoles (£5.50) for
vegetarians. A la carte restaurant in the evenings. 2-course Sunday
lunch £7.95. One high-chair; children's portions provided in the
restaurant (they are not allowed in the bar). *Bar Food 12-2, 6-10 (Sun
7-9.30). **Restaurant Meals** 7-9.30 (except Sun). Free House. **Beer** Bass,
Ruddles Best & County. Garden, outdoor eating. Family room.*
*Accommodation 28 bedrooms, all en suite, £59 (single £49). Children
welcome overnight, additional beds and cots available (under-5s £5, over-5s
£10). Access, Amex, Visa.*

Eyton   Plassey Bistro

Tel 0978 780905	Bistro
Eyton nr Wrexham Clwyd	**Map 8 D2**

At the centre of a complex of unique Edwardian farm buildings
housing traditional craft workshops, Plassey Bistro is a remarkable
conversion of the former shippen. Bar snacks range from giant filled
rolls through home-made burgers and mushroom stroganoff to some
imaginative blackboard specials including glazed prawn and Brie-filled
pear (£2.95), chicken sauté in mild curry cream (£6.95) and pasta
shells with Madeira and sweet peppers (£5.95). Plassey's speciality is a
half shoulder of lamb slow-roasted with redcurrant and rosemary

(£7.95). In addition to Plassey's own real ale bottled beers from 18
countries worldwide are a novel feature, as is the new wall of wine
which contains over 400 varieties all priced at either £6.95 or £9.95
for the customer to choose from. This isn't a pub, though, despite the
look and the beers: it only has a restaurant licence. Children
particularly welcome on Sundays, but not on Saturday nights.
Seats 100. **Open** *12-2.30 & 7-10.* **Closed** *Mon. No credit cards.*

Felindre Farchog   Salutation Inn

Tel 0239 820564	Pub

A487 Felindre Farchog nr Crymych Dyfed SA41 3UY   Map 9 B5

Felindre, a dot on the map where the A487 road bridge crosses the
Nyfer, *is* the Salutation. Well-tended lawns slope down to the river,
and there are gardens and terraces for a peaceful drink. The single-
storey bedroom wing is neat and well-appointed. Bright duvets set the
tone, with satellite TV, radio alarms, tea-makers and hairdryers
providing up-to-date refinements. Three family rooms have bunk
beds, and cots are also provided free of charge. High-chair available.
Recommended for B&B only. **Beer** *Federation Bitter.*
Riverside garden, outdoor eating. Family room. **Accommodation**
*9 bedrooms, all en suite, £52 (single £32). Children welcome overnight,
additional beds (from £5 up to 16 yrs) and cots (under-2s free) available.
Access, Visa.*

Hay-on-Wye   Old Black Lion

Tel 0497 820841	Pub

26 Lion Street Hay-on-Wye Powys HR3 5AD   Map 9 D5

That it may be strangled these days by its own success should not
reflect unkindly on the unstinting efforts made over the last six years
by John Collins and his effervescent wife, Joan. Notoriety, it seems,
draws its own adverse comment: yet, in premises so small,
an ambitiously large menu possibly overstretches the kitchen.
Following starters ranging from ham and lentil soup to moules
marinière, main courses on any given day may encompass venison
bourguignonne, veal cordon bleu, a casserole of wild boar and Wye
salmon in herb butter sauce (priced in the £9-£10.50 range).
An entire menu section is devoted to steaks, sauced or plain, and
another to vegetarian options: there's a sense of inevitability that
mistakes will occur. Restaurant reservations give due preference
to residents, and booking for tables in the bar is advised. Nonetheless,
if arriving (announced or not) at peak periods, be prepared to wait.
Bedrooms within the main building, of 17th-century origins, render
the Black Lion justifiably famous. Refurbishment has generally
enhanced the building's character and comforts of high degree include
direct-dial phones, TVs, radios, beverage trays and bright duvets
(traditional bedding provided on request). Rooms in the Annexe are
more modern, though no less comfortable; all rooms (with the
exception of one single with a private bathroom) have entirely
acceptable en-suite facilities. Families particularly enjoy the Cromwell
Room with its gallery and two additional beds. The whole pub
is candle-lit at night. **Bar Food** *12-2, 7-9 (In winter to 8.30).*
Restaurant Meals *12-2 (Sun only), 7-9. Children are allowed in the bar
to eat. Free House.* **Beer** *Flowers Original, Fuller's London Pride. Small
patio.* **Accommodation** *10 bedrooms, 9 en suite, £40 (single £18.95).
Children welcome overnight (under-12s £12.50, over-12s £13.50),
additional beds and cots available. Access, Visa.*

Hay-on-Wye   Kilverts

Tel 0497 821042 Fax 0497 821580	Pub

Bull Ring Hay-on-Wye Powys HR3 5AG   Map 9 D5

Co-proprietor and food buff Colin Thomson has come a long way:
much further, in fact, than the 150 yards from his Lion's Corner
House which was praised by our *Just a Bite* Guide in the mid-1980s.
With him has come his inimitable hat collection, Victorian Spy
cartoons and the nightly-played baby grand which imbue the bar with
such character. Still a top seller in his new-found location is the home-
made 6oz beefburger, alongside daily specials ranging from laverbread,
bacon and cockles on toast (£3.70) to salad of freshly grilled sardines
(£4.95). Increasingly popular with visitors and locals alike is Colin's
Bistro, still exhibiting the Lion logo, where relaxed informality
remains the key. Seasonal à la carte menus are again supplemented
by daily specials: Evesham asparagus hollandaise (£4.50), skate wing
with black butter and capers (£7.85) and Wye salmon with samphire.
Desserts of tiramisu, crème brulée and summer pudding (£3) also live
up to expectation. Residents' accommodation is both comfortable and
stylish with brass bedsteads, smoked glass tables and attractive floral
bed linen. In addition to tea trays, direct-dial phones, TVs and radios
(incorporating a baby-listening service), accoutrements include
hairdryers and trouser presses. Bathrooms are a little utilitarian,
nonetheless incorporating powerful showers and copious amounts
of hot water. Two high-chairs provided. *Bar Food 12-2, 7-9.30.*
*Restaurant Meals 7-9.30 (Fri & Sat to 10 plus Sun in July & Aug only
and occasional Bank Holidays). Children allowed in the bar to eat, children's
menu available on request. Free House.* **Beer** *Boddingtons, Castle Eden,
Bass.* **Accommodation** *11 bedrooms, all en suite (5 with shower only), £48
(single £34), £38 Oct-Easter. Children welcome overnight, additional beds
and cots available. Patio, garden and barbecue. Access, Visa.*

Letterston   Something's Cooking

Tel 0348 840621	Café

The Square Letterston Dyfed SA62 5SB   Map 9 A5

Recent additions here of a bright, airy conservatory and full restaurant
licence have helped develop Trevor Rand's roadside fish-and-chip take-
away (by the A40 at its junction with the B4331) into the area's
premier chippy. A warm family welcome is the added bonus, while
senior citizens benefit from keenly-priced mid-week lunches.
In addition to a plethora of lightly battered fresh fish, specials add
perhaps shrimps and herrings marinated with dill, with Southern fried
chicken, BBQ spare ribs and vegetarian spring rolls for those of less
aquatic persuasion. Three high-chairs; ask for children's portions.
No dogs. No smoking. *Seats 48.* **Open** *11-2 & 5.30-10.30 (Sun 6-10,
Sat 11-10.30). Closed L Sun (all Sun in winter), 1 week Christmas.
Access, Visa (minimum charge £10).*

Llanarmon Dyffryn Ceiriog   West Arms Hotel   £78

Tel 069176 665 Fax 069176 622	Inn

Llanarmon Dyffryn Ceiriog nr Llangollen Clwyd LL20 7LD   Map 8 D2

In a picturesque hamlet at the head of the Ceiriog valley, this 16th-
century former farmhouse stands to the front of well-manicured, safe
gardens which run down to a fence by the river bridge. Black and
white painted outside and bedecked with creeper and summer flowers,
it's a haven of cosy comfort within, the tone set by open log fires,

flagstone floors, blackened beams and rustic furniture. Tucked round
the back, the Wayfarers' Bar serves a modest selection of well-prepared
snacks in chintzy surroundings with an adjacent family lounge and
patio. Following soup (£2.75), smoked mackerel paté (£3.25) and
herb mushrooms with garlic mayonnaise (£3.50), local Ceiriog trout
(£5.75) heads a list of main meals which might include John Cope's
sausages (£4.95), tagliatelle with peppers, mushrooms and cream
(£4.95) or spinach and Stilton pancakes (£4.25). Jam roly-poly and
bread-and-butter pudding (both £2.85) are typical of the traditional
puddings. Bedrooms retain the period comfort afforded by handsome
antique furnishings alongside modern fitted bathrooms: homely extras
include pot pourri and quality toiletries. Five rooms are reserved for
non-smokers and the two suites have plenty of space for family use.
Table d'hote dinner is available to residentsand others, priced around
£21 per head. Two high-chairs provided; changing mat in the Ladies.
Open 11-11 Mon-Sat, regular hours Sun. **Bar Food** *12-2.30, 6-9 (Sun
from 7).* **Restaurant Meals** *12-2.30 (Sun only), 7-9.30. Children allowed
in the bar to eat. Garden, outdoor eating.* **Accommodation** *14 bedrooms, all
en suite, from £78 (single (from £49). Children welcome overnight,
additional beds (£21) and cots (£5) are available. Dogs welcome
by arrangement. Hotel closed last week Jan and first two weeks Feb. Access,
Amex, Diners, Visa.*

Llanbedr   Llew Glas Brasserie Restaurant

Tel 0341 23555	Restaurant
Llanbedr Gwynedd LL45 2LD	Map 8 B2

Marj and Trevor Pharoah have moved premises from Harlech
to an old beamed cottage-style restaurant three miles away with
parking and easier access. As before, they're only open for dinner, and
the menu of home-cooked dishes runs from paté, seafood chowder
(£3.65) and baked eggs on chicken livers to spinach and Gruyère
pancake (£4.50), sole dugléré (£7.05), ratatouille crunch and lamb
steak with braised leeks (£7.50). Griddled steaks with a traditional
garnish of onions, mushrooms and tomatoes are also popular. Desserts
include speciality sundaes (£3.65). Minimum charge for food and
drink £10.50 (apart from children, who have their own blackboard
menu with the likes of soup, melon and orange salad, cheese and
tomato pizza, deep-fried lemon sole with rösti or salad – wholesome
food). No-smoking area. **Seats 40. Open** *D only 6.30-10 (winter
Thur-Sat from 7pm).* **Closed** *Sun. Access, Amex, Diners, Visa.*

Llanbedrog   Glyn-y-Weddw Arms

Tel 0758 740212	Pub
Abersoch Road Llanbedrog nr Pwllheli Gwynedd LL53 7TH	Map 8 B2

Attractive, completely refurbished, popular pub close to a delightful
beach; the garden can get very hectic in summer, when the whole
village is a sheltered sun-trap. Children welcome (but no under-14s
in the bar area 'by law'); swings and climbing frame in the garden
play area. Inside, nipper's nosh features on the menu; six high-chairs
are provided. Vanity unit in Ladies should suffice for changing baby.
Patio with around 20 tables outside. *Open all day daily in summer, all
day Sat only Nov-Mar.* **Beer** *Robinson's, Hartleys. Garden, children's play
area. Family room. Access, Visa.*

Llanbedrog   Ship Inn

Tel 0758 740270	· Pub
Bryn-y-Gro Llanbedrog nr Pwllheli Gwynedd LL53 7PE	Map 8 B2

Cosy and traditional inn with a popular outside sitting area. High-
chairs and booster seats provided, along with a nappy changing facility
in the Ladies. *Open all day in summer (except Sun).* **Beer** *Burtonwood.
Family room. Pub closed all day Sunday. No credit cards.*

Llandudno   St Tudno Hotel   69%   £104

Tel 0492 874411 Fax 0492 860407	Hotel
The Promenade Llandudno Gwynedd LL30 2LP	Map 8 C1

The enthusiastic Blands have been welcoming guests to their charming
seafront hotel for over 21 years now with a winning combination
of friendliness and professionalism. Either side of the entrance hall the
bar/lounge and sitting room (reserved for non-smokers) are Victorian
in style – parlour plants, original fire places – in contrast to a bright
coffee lounge to be found behond the reception desk where fresh
flowers compete with the receptionists' smiles. A small bottle
of sparkling wine greets guests in bedrooms that, though generally not
large, are individually decorated in pretty co-ordinating fabrics and
wall coverings with a good eye for detail. Rooms are properly serviced
in the evenings as are the bathrooms with their generous towelling
and good toiletries. High tea is served in the coffee lounge where high-
chairs are provided. In 1861 Alice Liddell, later to be immortalised
in Lewis Carroll's *Alice's Adventures in Wonderland,* spent a holiday
here. Limited parking (for up to eight cars). **Rooms** *21. Patio, indoor
swimming pool. Access, Amex, Visa.*

Garden Room Restaurant   £65

Painted greenery and trellis work on the walls together with potted
plants and conservatory-style furniture provide the garden atmosphere
while David Harding in the kitchen provides competently cooked
dishes for the fixed-price menus that offer some half-a-dozen choices
at each stage. Smoked haddock and leek tart with butter sauce, chilled
fresh orange or grapefruit juice, tomato and basil soup, Welsh lamb
cutlets with plum and port wine sauce, and poached halibut with
prawns and parsley sauce demonstrate the range. There's a good house
selection on the comprehensive wine list, which has an expanded New
World section this year. Plenty of good drinking under £25.
No under-5s; no smoking. **Seats** *60. L 12.30-2 D 7-9.30.
Set L £11.50/£13.50 (Sun £14.50) Set D £19/£22/£25.*

Llangammarch Wells Lake Country House Hotel 68%   £98

Tel 05912 202 Fax 05912 457	Hotel
Llangammarch Wells Powys LD4 4BS	Map 9 C4

Standing in 50 acres of parkland with sweeping lawns, rhododendron-
lined pathways and riverside walks, enjoying genuine tranquillity
in the heartlands of Brecon, a mainly Edwardian building run along
personable lines by Jean-Pierre and Jan Mifsud. Grandly proportioned
day rooms include a handsome parlour lounge that retains much of the
period character by using traditional furnishings and fabrics. Bedrooms
have fine views and are individually styled with a combination
of antiques and restful colour schemes. Smart, efficient staff mirror the
owners' enthusiasm. Popular with fishermen as the river Irfon runs
through the grounds. Traditional Welsh teas are served in the drawing
room (3.30-6pm) beside log fires and in summer beneath a mature

chestnut tree overlooking the river. Children's high tea at 6pm.
Rooms *19. Garden, pitch & putt, tennis, fishing, snooker. Access, Amex, Visa.*

Restaurant   £65

Fixed-price, five-course dinners with a choice of three or four dishes at each stage are typified by cream of celery and apple soup, wild mushroom-filled saffron ravioli with avocado, roulade of chicken with pistachio nuts, sweet peppers, tomatoes and chestnuts, panaché of fish (including hake, monkfish, salmon and red mullet), and *langue du chat* basket filled with orange and cardamom ice cream and cinnamon sauce. Table d'hote lunches are served in the restaurant, lighter lunches in the lounge; good choice at Sunday lunchtime. No children under 12 in the dining room. Plenty of choice on the varied wine list.
Seats *50. L 1-2 (non-residents by arrangement only) D 7-8.45. Set L £15.50 (Sun) Set D £24.50.*

Llangorse   **Red Lion**

Tel 0874 84238	Pub
Llangorse nr Brecon Powys LD3 7TY	**Map 9 D5**

Just a mile from Llangorse Lake, at the heart of the village by St. Paulinus Church, stands the Rosiers' welcoming local. Picnic tables in front by the village stream make it a picturesque spot. Riding, fishing and water skiing (mid-week only), all available locally, draw many regulars to the Red Lion. Accommodation in neat pastel-shade bedrooms with attractive duvets is practical rather than luxurious, though TV, radio-alarms and tea-makers ensure an acceptable level of comfort. Five have well-kept bathrooms en suite, the remainder (with showers and washbasins only) share a couple of adjacent toilets. Built into the hillside, all rooms have level access to a rear garden reserved for residents. Recommended for B&B only. *Free House.* **Beer** *Flowers Original, Marston's Pedigree, Brains SA and Boddingtons. Riverside terrace/patio. Family room.* **Accommodation** *10 bedrooms, 5 en suite, £48 (single £24). Children welcome overnight. Additional beds (no charge under 12 yrs) and cots supplied. No credit cards.*

Llangurig   **Blue Bell Inn**

Tel 05515 254	Pub
Llangurig nr Llanidloes Powys SY18 6SG	**Map 9 C4**

A welcome in the hillside – courtesy of Diana and Bill Mills – awaits you in their charming 16th-century fishing inn in Wales's highest village. An old black iron range stands on the slate floor of the simple, friendly bar. Enjoy a game of darts or dip into a book in the homely residents' lounge. Compact, rustic bedrooms have modern units and co-ordinated decor. One has en-suite facilities; the others share two modern public bathrooms. Popular with walkers and caravanners. Recommended for B&B only. *Free House.* **Beer** *Tetley's Bitter, Flowers Original. Family room.* **Accommodation** *10 bedrooms, 1 en suite, £33 (£30 not en suite, single £16). Children welcome overnight. Additional beds and cots available. Check-in by arrangement. Access, Visa.*

Llanwrtyd Wells   **Drover's Rest**

Tel 059 13 264	Café
The Square Llanwrtyd Wells Powys	**Map 9 C4**

Nestling by the Irfon river bridge at the heart of Wales's smallest town (population 600) is Peter James's delectable café. He cares about his customers and his catering: local suppliers provide the produce, his sister is the proud patissière. Start the day with a substantial Welsh breakfast (£3.80), or choose at lunchtime between fresh filled sandwiches and baked potatoes, local trout (£6.95) and lamb cutlets (£5.95) or the daily changing vegetarian menu (provencale nut wellington) and pasta with vegetable cream sauce (£5.60 – £6.50). The popular Welsh Afternoon Tea (£3.65) includes buttered *bara brith* and Welsh cakes. Book for family Sunday lunches (£7.50) and gourmet Friday, Saturday and Sunday dinners, which are more expensive. **Seats** 34. **Open** 9.30-5 *(Sun from 10), also Fri-Sun 7-10.30.* **Closed** *Mon, 25 Dec. No credit cards.*

Llwyndafydd   Crown Inn

Tel 0545 560396	Pub
Llwyndafydd nr New Quay Dyfed SA44 6FU	Map 9 B4

A large, rather handsome 18th-century inn which dominates the tiny valley (just off the A487) running down to the National Trust bay at Cwmtudu. It's the massive patio, landscaped gardens and well-equipped children's play area, however, which draw the crowds equally in the summer months. For little pub-goers, food is of the baby pizza and chicken nuggets genre, and there are voluminous adult snacks to choose from: chicken curry (£4.75), lamb pie (£4.95) or vegetarian and peperoni pizzas (£3.75). Daily specials are generally more adventurous: leek and potato soup (£1.85), baked cod forestière or plaice roulade with cheese sauce (£5.35) and Welsh lamb cutlets (£5.95). Restaurant à la carte. One high-chair. **Bar Food** 12-2, 6-9 *(Sun 7-9).* **Restaurant Meals** 7-9. Free House. **Beer** Bass, Whitbread Flowers IPA & Original. Garden. Family room. *Pub closed Sun eve Oct-Mar. Access, Visa.*

Llyswen   Griffin Inn

Tel 0874 754241 Fax 0874 754592	Pub
Llyswen Brecon Powys LD3 0OU	Map 9 D5

Mythically speaking, the griffin is a creature of vast proportions, half lion, half dragon, its whole being considerably less awesome than its constituent parts. No such problems exist for Richard and Di Stockton, for their Griffin is nothing short of splendid in all departments and conspicuously well run. That locally-caught salmon and brook trout feature so regularly on the menu is scarcely surprising as the Griffin employs its own ghillie, and fishing stories abound in the bar, which is the centre of village life. It's hung with framed displays of fishing flies and maps of the upper and lower reaches of the Wye valley, and dominated by a splendid inglenook fire. Beer is also taken seriously and kept in tip-top condition, summerbrews giving way to sturdier guest beers in winter. In the adjacent lounge, low tables, high-backed Windsor chairs and window seats make a comfortable setting for either a light snack or one of the daily-changing hot dishes, perhaps cream of mushroom soup (£2.90), deep-fried whitebait (£2.90), ratatouille pasta (£4.50), fisherman's curry & rice (£6.25) or braised oxtail in Irish Stout (£6.75). Evening meals provide a wider choice of more substantial fare, either in the no-smoking restaurant or the bars, as space allows. Plenty of space in the Ladies for non-resident mums to change a nipper's nappy. The eight bedrooms, all but one with en-suite facilities, revert to the fishing theme: Alexandra Durham Ranger and Green Highlander, for instance, being named after salmon flies. To say that they are cottagey is not to decry the pretty floral curtains and bed-covers; they are wonderfully tranquil, and though there are telephones, television is considered superfluous. The splendid residents' lounge on the upper floor of the inn's oldest part is dramatically set under original rafters dating, it is thought, back to its origins as a 15th-century sporting inn. Children stay in parents' room free and there's no charge for additional beds or cots. There is no garden but children may eat in the bar and small portions are served. Two high-chairs. *Bar Food* 12-2, 7-9 *(except Sun – cold supper for residents only)*. *Restaurant Meals* 1-3 *(Sun only – £11.50)*. *Children allowed in bar to eat. Free House.* *Beer* *Boddingtons, Flowers IPA, Bass, Brains, Marston's Pedigree. Patio, outdoor eating.* *Accommodation* 8 bedrooms, 7 en suite, £50 (single £28.50). Children welcome overnight. Additional beds and cots available. Access, Diners, Visa.

Machynlleth — Centre for Alternative Technology
Tel 0654 702400 — Vegetarian Restaurant/Café
Pantperthog Machynlleth Powys SY20 9AZ — Map 8 C3

A co-operative-run vegetarian restaurant and coffee house that forms part of a fascinating complex at the forefront of alternative technology. It's 3 miles north of Machynlleth, just off the A487 to Dolgellau and has been built in the old converted slate quarry engine shed. The counter service selection is slightly restricted in winter months, but in the busy summer season offers tempting cakes – carrot or *bara brith* (70p), a salad bar (£1.50-£1.95 per portion), vegetarian pasties and sausage rolls and, from midday onwards, hot foods ranging from soup (carrot and red lentil £1.75) and baked potatoes with cheese (£1.80), to homity pie (£1.95) and red dragon pie (aduki beans, vegetables and potatoes – £2.50). Try the trifle (£1.50) to finish. Always a vegan soup and main course, and plenty of organic produce from local sources – "the greenest meal available in Wales". Picnic area next to the children's adventure playground area. No smoking. Good children's facilities: six high-chairs, undercover play area for younger children, changing facilities in both Gents and Ladies – hurrah! *Seats 80.* *Open* 10-5 *(summer to 6)*, 11-3 *Nov-Mar*. *Closed* *Dec-Easter except for group bookings. No credit cards.*

Machynlleth — Quarry Shop
Tel 0654 702624 — Café
13 Maengwyn Street Machynlleth Powys — Map 8 C3

Part of the same co-operative that runs the Centre for Alternative Technology, a friendly counter-service café with pine furniture, and wholefood shop. Various cakes – carrot and coconut, carob, ginger and date ripple, apricot slice – are 65p, salads are 95p per portion, or there's a daily soup (£1.10), pizza (£1.75) and hot daily specials, perhaps sweet and sourvegetables and tofu, strudel parcels or moussaka (all £3.20). Breakfast, from 9 to 11am, includes muesli, toast, yoghurt and fruit. Pavement tables. Good children's facilities. No-smoking area. *Seats 35. Open* 9-5 *(winter to 4.30 and Thu to 2) Closed* Sun *(except Jul/Aug)*. No credit cards.

Marford — Trevor Arms Hotel
Tel 0244 570436 — Pub
Marford nr Wrexham Clwyd — Map 8 D2

Quaint 17th-century architecture is a feature of Marford's original buildings, which all incorporate a cross to ward off evil spirits. The

Trevor Arms, built later as a coaching inn, echoes these features and also plays its full part in village life. Bar food is served in the oldest part of the inn (and can get very busy), with more elaborate meals served in a quieter dining extension. From the blackboard, choose pancakes of bolognese, seafood or vegetarian varieties (£3.75 to £6.50), pork chop au poivre (£4.95) or the "Cock and Bull", a chicken and steak mixture (£7.95) which is quite another story. Saturday lunch carvery (12-2 £5.25). In addition to a children's play area, the garden's latest attraction is a covered barbecue patio complete with freestanding gas heaters for use on chillier evenings. Overnight accommodation is divided between the main house and former stable block where the pick of the bedrooms are housed in the hayloft. All have up-to-date appointments including TV, radio and phones; there are five full bathrooms while the remainder offer shower/WCs en suite with impressively powerful showers, if rather small stalls. *Pub open 11-11 Mon-Sat, usual hours Sun. Bar Food 12-2.30, 6-9.30 (Sun from 7). Restaurant Meals 12-2 (Sun only), 6-9.30 (Sun from 7). Garden, outdoor eating. Family Room. Accommodation 16 bedrooms, all en suite, £32.50 (single £26). Children welcome overnight, additional beds and cots available. No dogs. Access Visa.*

Miskin	Miskin Manor	70%	£100
Tel 0443 224204 Fax 0443 237606			Hotel
Penddylan Road Pontyclun Miskin Mid Glamorgan CF7 8ND			Map 9 C6

A handsome stone mansion in 20 acres of garden and woodland, Miskin Manor was built in 1858. Day rooms are very comfortable and deep sofas in floral fabrics invite guests to relax and gaze out over the gardens. The bedrooms are vast – even singles have sofas – and are luxurious without being ostentatious. Some have four-posters and there are two suites. Children stay free in parents' room. The Fredericks sports and leisure complex (open 10am-11pm) offers informal eating and relaxing areas; conference facilities handle up to 180 delegates. Parents with children may feel engulfed by mid-week conference delegates or even by weekend weddings; nevertheless, the Manor can be a haven of tranquillity – enquire when booking about large gatherings. A supervised crèche (from 9am-3pm) operates Monday to Friday for children up to the age of five. The hotel is undergoing an extensive programme of refurbishment. M4 Junction 34, 8 miles from the centre of Cardiff. *Rooms 32. Garden, indoor swimming pool, gymnasium, spa bath, steam room, sauna, solarium, beauty salon, badminton, coffee shop (10am-10pm), crèche (9am-3pm Mon-Fri). Access, Amex, Diners, Visa.*

Nevern	Trewern Arms Hotel		
Tel 0239 820295			Pub
Nevern nr Newport Dyfed SA42 0NB			Map 9 B5

The hidden hamlet in a valley on the B4582 is a world all on its own with historic pilgrims' church and Celtic cross, nurseries, cheese dairy and cake shop. Across the stone bridge over the Nyfer (or "Nevern"), the Trewern Arms is creeper-clad with sparkling fairy lights, exuding a magical air. Bedrooms, carefully added to the original 18th-century stone building, are furnished in cane and pine with floral curtains and matching duvets. The bathrooms are all en suite (7 with shower/WCs only); TVs and tea-makers are standard. There are three spacious family rooms. A foyer lounge upstairs has plenty of literature for walkers and fishermen, and the lounge bar below sports comfortable armchairs and sofas. Unambitious bar food and à la carte restaurant. Children's room; garden and play area. Recommended for B&B only. *Free House.* **Beer** *Whitbread, Flowers Original, Boddingtons, guest beers. Garden, children's play area. Family room.* **Accommodation** *9 bedrooms, all en suite, £45 double (single £28), £55 family room. Children welcome overnight, additional beds and cots supplied. Access, Visa.*

Newport   Cnapan

Tel 0239 820575	Restaurant

East Street Newport Dyfed — Map 9 A5

The charming Lloyd and Cooper families are well known by other families for having created a lovely country-house setting with pretty garden in which to enjoy inventive, vegetarian-biased food. The day starts with coffee but at noon the main interest arrives with the light lunch menu which offers thick vegetable soup with soda bread and Llanboidy cheese (£1.95), the Cnapan cheese platter with home-made chutney (£3.25) and oat-based flans, the boozy carrot, cashewnut and cream cheese or flaked smoked fish, horseradish, mustard seed and mango versions, served with jacket potato and salad (both £3.75) among the most popular. A blackboard lists puddings, perhaps treacle tart, fruit crumble or old favourite piggy's delight (all £2.25). Special children's burgers (children welcome at lunchtime only); booster seats provided; baby-changing area; safe garden. Popular family Sunday lunch. Smoking in the bar area only. More elaborate evening meals and five letting bedrooms. **Seats** *48.* **Open** *10-2.* **Closed** *Tue, all Feb and Nov-Easter (except L Sun). Access, Visa.*

Nottage   Rose & Crown

Tel 0656 784850 Fax 0656 772345	Pub

Nottage Heol-y-Capel nr Porthcawl Mid Glamorgan CF36 3ST — Map 9 D6

Just a mile from Royal Porthcawl Golf Club and the town's West Bay stands this white- painted row of stone-built former cottages at the heart of a tiny hamlet. In an area short of good pub accommodation, its friendly village bar and neat cottage bedrooms are justly popular. Redecoration in pastel shades with fitted pine furniture, practical bathrooms and room comforts including phone, TV and trouser press promise a restful and comfortable stay. Recommended for B&B only. *Chef & Brewer. Pub open 11-11 Sat, usual hours Sun.* **Beer** *Courage, Ruddles County & Best, Webster's Yorkshire. Garden, children's play area.* **Accommodation** *8 bedrooms, all en suite, £29.95 for room. Children welcome overnight (£2.50 up to 12 yrs), cots available (no charge). No dogs. Check-in by arrangement. Access, Diners, Visa.*

Old Walls   Greyhound Inn

Tel 0792 39014	Pub

Old Walls North Gower nr Swansea West Glamorgan SA3 1HA — Map 9 B6

Attractive, well-run free house in the middle of the unspoilt Gower peninsula. Fenced children's play area with swings. Go down to the astonishingly dramatic Rhossili beach for a walk. Local fish and Welsh cheeses feature on the unusually interesting menu; 'Skinny Dog Kids menu' covers snacks, big bites and treats. **Beer** *Regularly changing real ales. Garden, children's play area. Family room. Access, Visa.*

Penmaenpool   George III Hotel   £88

Tel 0341 422525   Inn

Penmaenpool nr Dolegellau Gwynedd LL40 1YD   Map 8 C3

The new owners, John and Julia Cartwright, are now well settled in.
Most bedrooms and the restaurant have been redecorated, central
heating and curtains renewed and the garden is gradually being
improved. In a memorable location hedged between the road (A493)
and former railway line, the George III, hugging the bank of the tidal
Mawddach estuary was once an integral part of the Penmaenpool
railway station. Today's inn was created in the 1890s from two 17th-
century buildings, one the original pub and the other a ship's
chandler's which serviced the adjacent boat builder's yards. Far from
sharing with locals and visitors the stone-flagged cellar bar, residents
might prefer the rather dated air of the Welsh Dresser bar and its cosy
lounge with striking copper-hooded inglenook. Main house bedrooms
echo the period feel with creaky floors and some fine exposed roof
timbers. The Victorian lodge, which, prior to the railway's closure
by Dr Beeching in 1964, housed the station waiting room and ticket
office, has been converted to provide six quite stylish bedrooms, all en-
suite; these enjoy residents on the pick of the views. Free fishing permits are
available to residents on the reservoir and 12 miles of the Mawddach
River. Recommended for B&B only. *Open 11-11 Mon-Sat, regular
hours Sun. Free House. Beer Ruddles, John Smith's. Garden.*
Accommodation *12 bedrooms, all en suite, £88 (single £45). Children
welcome overnight (under-12s £12.50, babies free if sharing parents' room),
additional beds an cots available. Access, Visa.*

Penybont   Severn Arms Hotel

Tel 0597 851224   Fax 0597 851693   Pub

Penybont nr Llandrindod Wells Powys LD1 5UA   Map 9 C4

A white-painted former coaching inn by the junction of the A488 and
A44, at the heart of the Ithon Valley. Loved by JB Priestley for its
creaky floors, old oak beams and sloping ceiling, it has some of the
best family rooms around, tucked under the eaves of the pub's top
storey, with pastoral views down the garden to a wooden bridge over
the river. Caring management by Geoff and Tessa Lloyd has extended
over ten years and the bedrooms are both immaculately kept and well
equipped; all en suite, most have trouser presses and all have TV,
radio, direct-dial phones and tea-making facilities. From the flagstoned
entrance there's access to the village bar festooned with local football
trophies, a more sedate lounge bar and extensive dining room.
Residents enjoy us of their own quiet TV lounge on the first floor.
Recommended for B&B only. *Free house. Beer Bass, guest beer. Garden.*
Accommodation *10 bedrooms, all en suite, £50 (single £28). Children
welcome overnight, additional beds £10 (over 10yrs), cots available £2.
Accommodation closed one week Christmas-New Year. Access, Visa.*

Pisgah   Halfway Inn

Tel 097084 631   Pub

Devil's Bridge Road Pisgah Aberystwyth Dyfed SY23 4NE   Map 9 C4

650 feet up overlooking the Rheidol Valley below, this is a marvellous
country pub in a lovely setting with magnificent views. Well known
as a beer-lovers' favourite, with its choice of six beers. Never
modernised or extended, this 250-year-old Inn retains its traditional

feel – candle-lit in the evenings and log fire in winter. Families use the Stone Room bar (walls made of stone). Recommended for its setting and pub atmosphere. *Pub open 11-11 Mon-Fri mid-July to end Aug, 11-11 Sat all year, usual hours Sun and other times. Children allowed in bar to eat, children's menu. Free House.* **Beer** *Felinfoel Double Dragon, Flowers Original, Castle Eden, Wadworth 6X, Bateman 3XB, guest beers. Garden, children's play area. Family room. No credit cards.*

Pont-ar-Gothi   Cresselly Arms

Tel 0267 290221	Pub

Pont-ar-Gothi nr Nantgaredig Dyfed SA31 7NG   Map 9 B5

Tucked off the A40 by the Gothi River bridge, this friendly pub makes full use of a riverside summer garden (no unaccompanied children, please) and dining room with restful river views. In the two spacious bars hung with fish nets and horse brasses, snacks encompass sandwiches, hot platters (fish bake £4.75), pot meals (steak and mushroom £4.50) and standard vegetarian and children's fare. Daily specials weigh in with local sewin salad (£4.75), minty lamb fricassee (£3.95) and vegetarian options such as mushroom goulash (£4.30). *Free House.* **Bar Food** *12-2.15, 6.30-9.30 (Sun 7-9).* **Restaurant Meals** *12-1.30, 7-9.30 (Sun 7-9). Children's menu.* **Beer** *Whitbread. Riverside garden, children's play area. Family room. Access, Visa.*

Red Wharf Bay   Ship Inn

Tel 0248 852568	Pub

Red Wharf Bay Anglesey Gwynedd LO75 4RJ   Map 8 B1

Landlord Andrew Kenneally has been running the low, white-painted limestone Ship Inn for 22 years. Right on the shore at Traeth Coch and overlooking the sweep of the bay, it is fronted by hanging baskets and sports a fine pair of Lloyd and Trouncer cast-iron street lamps at its entrance. A depiction of *SS Royal Charter* is inlaid in the upper wall, and a Silver Jubilee replica of the royal yacht *Britannia*'s wheel is mounted in the bar. Customers come early at mealtimes, so at busy summer peak times delays are unavoidable, yet the menu remains sensibly short and with it comes a guarantee of freshness. Stick around a while and see the local fishermen delivering their catch. The menu includes a selection of light meals, described as snacks: paté and toast (£3.70), smoked salmon trout and stuffed mushrooms (£4.05), all of which come with salad. Main meals, accompanied by chips or baked potato, start with spicy monkfish casserole (£5.65), chicken stuffed with Stilton and wrapped in bacon (£5.65) or the grilled catch of the day in the £7-£9 range. The board may change at a moment's notice – braised lamb hearts (£4.80), mushroom and parsnip stroganoff (£4.75). Desserts include crème brulée and rhubarb crumble (all £2.40). Quarry-tiled floors, genuine exposed beams and stonework, plus a mish-mash of maritime memorabilia and chiming clocks all make for an interesting interior; look too for the Tom Browne snooker cartoons and the fine Toby jug collection, whose rarest specimens are glass-encased. Children can enjoy their own menu in the little back family room, or, while parents keep a constant eye on the treacherous tide, they can romp in the garden on the shore line. At weekends, a no-smoking room is opened upstairs for diners. *Pub open all day (except Sun) from Jun-Sep.* **Bar Food** *12-2.15, 7-9.15 (Sun 12-2, 7-9). Children's menu. Free House.* **Beer** *Marston's Pedigree, Tetley Bitter and Dark Mild, guest beer. Garden, outdoor eating. Family room. Access, Visa.*

Red Wharf Bay   Old Boathouse Café

Tel 0248 852731	Café
Red Wharf Bay Anglesey Gwynedd	**Map 8 B1**

Typical seaside fare at the Griffiths' summer café remains
commendable more for freshness than originality. To great advantage
are the home-cooked steak and kidney (£3.95) and cottage pies,
chicken tikka masala (£4.95) and lasagnes piled with chips which
make for substantial inexpensive eating, with children's portions
of almost anything available on request. Start off the day with an all-
morning Welsh breakfast (£3.50) or snack on sandwiches and baked
potatoes (from £1.50) through the day, or scones with jam and cream
(75p) and dependable home baking. The tiled floor and pine tables
are neat and tidy within and there's a spacious front patio.
Unlicensed, so bring your own (no corkage). *Seats 30. Open 10-7.
Closed Nov-Easter. No credit cards.*

St David's   St Non's Hotel   56%   £73

Tel 0437 720239 Fax 0437 721839	Hotel
St David's Dyfed SA62 6RJ	**Map 9 A5**

A friendly family hotel half a mile from the town centre offering
some of the best children's terms around: under-6s stay free in parents'
room and enjoy free breakfast and high tea; over-6s are charged £12
half board. Other bonuses include five ground-floor bedrooms for the
less mobile, and free golf at the picturesque St David's 9-hole course.
Rooms 24. Garden. Access, Amex, Diners, Visa.

Swanbridge   The Captain's Wife

Tel 0222 530066	Pub
Beach Road Swanbridge nr Penarth South Glamorgan CF64 2UG	**Map 9 D6**

As a welcome change from the fleshpots of Barry Island, the pub,
reputedly haunted by the "Captain's Wife", stands right on the coast
just outside the village of Sully. Very popular with families, it sports
an extensive play area with pirate ship, a safe rear courtyard and
seating right on the sea wall overlooking Sully Island. Smugglers
Haunt char-grill dining-room; family Sunday lunches in Mariners
Restaurant. Recommended for atmosphere only (not food) in our
1994 Pubs & Inns Guide. *Pub open all day Mon-Fri in summer; all day
Sat all year, Sun usual hours. Free House.* **Beer** *Courage Directors & John
Smith's, guest beer. Garden, outdoor eating, children's play area.
Access, Visa.*

Swansea   Langland Court Hotel   £78

Tel 0792 361545 Fax 0792 362302	Inn
31 Langland Court Road Langland Swansea West Glamorgan SA3 4TD	**Map 9 C6**

Take the A4067 from Swansea to Mumbles, head for Caswell, turn
left at Newton Church, and follow the sign to this comfortable old
clifftop Tudor hotel. Beyond the impressive entrance hall are two
bars, the cocktail bar and 'Polly's Wine Bar' which commemorates
Dylan Thomas. Accommodation ranges from bow-windowed Tudor-
style rooms with four-posters (and some with views over the Bristol
Channel) to attic rooms with third-bed alcoves and convertible
couches. Rooms in a coach house across the road are smaller but
equally bright, clean and well-equipped; dogs are allowed in these
rooms only. Children up to 16 stay free if sharing their parent's room.

Popular for conferences and functions. Hairsalon. Recommended for B&B only. *Open 11-11 Mon-Sat, regular hours Sun. Free House.* **Beer** *Webster's, Ruddles. Garden.* **Accommodation** *21 bedrooms, all en suite, £78 (single £55). Children welcome overnight (under-16s £12), additional beds & cots supplied. Check-in by arrangement. Access, Amex, Diners, Visa.*

Tintern Abbey	Royal George	59%	£67
Tel 0291 689205 Fax 0291 689448			Hotel
Tintern Abbey nr Chepstow Gwent NP6 6SF			Map 9 D5

Tony and Maureen Pearce offer a warm welcome at their friendly hotel set at the foot of a lovely wooded hillside. A trout stream runs alongside, and the ruins of Tintern Abbey are just a short walk away. There's ample bar and lounge space (one lounge is stocked with board games) and a large function room. Some of the bedrooms have balconies overlooking the gardens. One child under 14 free in parents' room; ten rooms are suitable for family occupation; three cots are provided and baby-sittign can be arranged in advance. 'Good grub for mini tots' includes mermaid's favourite fish fingers and cowboy's allnighter. **Rooms** *19. Garden, fishing. Access, Amex, Diners, Visa.*

Trellech	The Village Green	
Tel 0600 860119		Pub/Brasserie
Trellech nr Monmouth Gwent NP5 4PA		Map 9 D5

Saved from dereliction five years ago by Bob and Jane Evans, the 450-year-old, creeper-clad Village Green comprises restaurant (recommended in our 1994 *Hotels and Restaurants* Guide as a Restaurant with Rooms) and bistro as well as pub and there are even a couple of small bedroom suites with kitchenette-cum-lounge and bedroom with en-suite shower room (they are let either on a self-catering or bed and breakfast basis) in an adjacent stable conversion. The two small, carpeted bars display rugby paintings by Richard Wills, one of Wales's best known artists who lives locally, and the stone-walled bistro is festooned with bunches of dried flowers hanging from the rafters. In the bistro a long, wide-ranging, blackboard menu changes frequently and might include whole grilled lobster (£11.50), beef teriyaki (£7.75), loin of pork in cider (£7.75), a tender, winey beef bourguignonne (£8.50) and chicken niçoise (£8.50). A separate bar menu offers more traditional pub fare with sandwiches (from £2), jacket potatoes (£2.50-3.50) and various ploughman's (from £3.50) that come with their own excellent home-made bread. **Bar Food** *(no food Mon) 12-1.45, 7-9.45 (Sat to 10, closed Sun eve). Children allowed in the bistro to eat, children's portions. Free House.* **Beer** *Worthington Best, Bass. Patio, outdoor eating.* **Accommodation** *2 bedrooms, both en suite, £45 inc continental breakfast only (single £35). Children welcome overnight (free if sharing parents' room), additional bed available and cots supplied. Pub closed Sun eve, all Mon (except for D on Bank Holidays) & 10 days in Jan. Access, Visa.*

Welshpool	Powis Castle Tea Rooms	
Tel 0983 555499		Tea Room
Powis Castle Welshpool Powys		Map 8 D3

You needn't pay admission to the famous gardens to enjoy a snack at this National Trust restaurant, and the drive past ponds and peacocks is draw enough. A spacious hall, refectory-style, adjoins the

castle keep; from morning coffee through light lunches to afternoon teas it's a bustling place. Most notable are the assorted Welsh cheeses of theCoachman's Choice (£4.95), a Powis Welsh Cream Tea (£2.85) and imaginative alternatives for youngsters (£1.60-£1.75). There are daily hot lunches and salads; licensed also with main meals.
No smoking. The tea rooms are open Wed to Sun from April to end June and September/October; Tue to Sun July and August; also Bank Holiday Mondays. *Seats 80. Open 11-5.30. Access, Visa.*

Wrexham   Bumble

Tel 0978 355023	Café
2 Charles Street Wrexham Clwyd LL13 8BT	**Map 8 D2**

This long-standing favourite, upstairs from Bumble's multi-faceted gift shop, continues to offer all-day snacks for all tastes and pockets. Following morning coffee and biscuits, filled jacket potatoes, Welsh rarebit, freshly cut sandwiches and ploughman's, fisherman's and coachman's platters are supplemented by home-made quiche lorraine (£3.50), and perhaps cod and mushroom bake or prawn and bacon pasta bake, or nut roast with mixed salads £2.95. Bumble blend tea with Welsh cakes (£1.15) remains a popular afternoon choice, while assorted cakes, meringues and pies lie temptingly in the display cabinet. Two high-chairs provided; ask for children's portions. *Seats 60. Open 9-5. Closed Sun. Access, Amex, Visa.*

Recommended by

EGON RONAY'S GUIDES

1994

Hotels & Restaurants   Pubs & Inns
Just A Bite   Oriental Restaurants
.... And Baby Comes Too   Ireland
Paris Restaurants & Bistros   Europe

Egon Ronay's Guides are available from all good bookshops or can be
ordered from Leading Guides, 73 Uverdale Road, London SW10 0SW
Tel: 071-352 2485/352 0019 Fax: 071-376 5071

There are times when the Mondeo's fuel supply will suddenly cut out.

In a crash the fuel supply from the new Ford Mondeo's reinforced tank will automatically cut off.

This is just one of the car's many integrated safety features. Safety features which, by the way, are all fitted as standard, not as optional extras.

The new Ford Mondeo is the only car with Dynamic Safety Engineering.

In a crash side impact bars and crumple zones immediately absorb the force and sensors instantly detect the severity of collision.

If the force of impact is great enough, within a tenth of a second the steering wheel airbag will inflate and seatbelt "grabbers" and "pre-tension will operate to hold you tight in the seat. Spec designed "anti-submarining" seats also stop sliding under the belts.

Before an accident you wouldn't even k. these features were there, thankfully after one, y be able to appreciate why they were. For more mation on how Mondeo can put safety at the top of your fleet's agenda call **0245 344 856**.

Everything we do is driven by y

Channel Islands
& Isle of Man

Alderney

Braye	First & Last	£30
Tel 0481 823162		Restaurant
Braye Alderney		Map 13 E4

The only restaurant on the island to benefit from the sea view with a panoramic dining room on the first-floor. The blue decor is strongly marine. Fish is of course a speciality with a beautiful crab bisque made from local crab and simply prepared catch of the day. Vegetarians and meat-lovers are also well catered for. In the evening, red lanterns are lit for a more romantic atmosphere. *Seats 65. Parties 40. L 12.15-1.30 D 7-10.* **Closed** *Mon, Oct-Apr. Access, Amex, Diners, Visa.*

St Anne	Gannets	
Tel 0481 823094		Café
6 Victoria Street St Anne Alderney		Map 13 E4

Attractive little café with a patio feel and garden furniture. Pleasant for afternoon teas with home-made cakes (from £1.20) or cream tea (£2.80). They are open all day long and through the evening on Friday and Saturday. The menu offers full English breakfast (£4.50), open sandwiches (from £1.20), burgers (£3.95) and a daily special. A "mini menu for small people" offers the usual favourites – from "fresh" fish fingers to spaghetti hoops and small jacket spuds with a variety of fillings. Three tables outside, but no high-chairs. *Seats 30.* **Open** *8.30am-5pm (Sun-Thur), 8.30am-midnight (Fri/Sat & all August).* **Closed** *Jan/Feb/Mar. No credit cards.*

St Anne	Inchalla Hotel	64%	£73
Tel 0481 823220 Fax 0481 823551			Hotel
The Val St Anne Alderney			Map 13 E4

Small hotel located on the heights of St Anne which benefits from a pleasant view of the town roofs with the sea in the background. Bedrooms are bright and well maintained with colour TV and well-stocked mini-bar. The surrounding gardens are peaceful and restful and the owner Valerie Willis will take care of the smallest details like ordering a cab for airport transfer. The use of jacuzzi, sauna and solarium is by appointment only with a £5 charge. *Rooms 10. Garden, sauna, spa bath, solarium.* **Closed** *10 days Christmas. Access, Amex, Visa.*

Restaurant	£52

The simply decorated dining room matches the well-executed, unpretentious cooking. The evening table d'hote menu offers simple fare of cauliflower and Stilton soup, almond trout and boeuf bourguignon where excellent ingredients are brought to their best. From the more extensive à la carte menu, choose the catch of the day cooked to your liking or fresh Alderney crab and lobster. Good-value bottles on the short wine list. *Seats 35. L (Sun only) 1-1.45 D 7-8.30.* **Closed** *D Sun. Set D £12.*

Guernsey

Castel	La Grande Mare	73%	£134*
Tel 0481 56576 Fax 0481 56532			Hotel
Vazon Bay Castel Guernsey			Map 13 E4

Set in 100 acres of land with a 9-hole golf course, La Grande Mare is an unusual hotel which has the feel of a country inn and caters mainly for families. Although a few double bedrooms are available, most are studios or suites, which can accommodate up to 8 guests. Bedrooms, although with four poster beds, are minimally furnished. Suites have breakfast bar and comfortable sitting areas. All bedrooms have satellite TV, trouser press and hairdryer. Bathrooms are particularly large and agreeable. *Half-board terms only. **Rooms** 27. *Outdoor swimming pool, spa bath, golf (9), fishing. Access, Amex, Diners, Visa.*

Restaurant   £70

With a comfortable open-air layout and picture windows looking out on to the golf course, the restaurant has a strong country club atmosphere. The service has a bygone *je ne sais quoi* with waiters in white gloves and flambé trolleys. A new chef had just taken over as we went to press. Particular attention is given to the wine selection both on the wine list and through a set dinner menu which offers a different glass of wine with each course. Simple but well-executed desserts. **Seats** *75. L 12-2 D 7-9.30.*

Castel	Hougue du Pommier	
Tel 0481 56531 Fax 0481 56260		Inn
Castel Guernsey		Map 13 E4

'Hougue du Pommier' means 'apple-tree hill' and the apples from the ten acres of orchards surrounding this fine old Guernsey farmhouse were once used to make local cider. Now a lovely inn, the building dates back to 1712. The Tudor Bar features a traditional atmosphere, with beams and an inglenook fireplace. Quiet bedrooms overlooking the particularly well-kept gardens are comfortable, with remote-control colour TVs, telephones and beverage trays. The solar-heated outdoor swimming pool is in a secluded spot surrounded by trees. Nearby is a 10-hole pitch-and-putt golf course and an 18-hole putting green. The restaurant, a succession of small dining rooms, retains the charm of the farmhouse, although food was a disappointment on our last visit. The sandy beaches of Grandes Rocques and Cobo are ten minutes' walk away. **Beer** *Guernsey Brewery. Garden. Sauna, solarium, games room.* **Accommodation** *38 bedrooms, all en suite, £71 (single £35.50). Children welcome overnight (0-5 yrs £5, 5-11 yrs 50% adult rate), additional beds and cots available. No dogs. Access, Amex, Diners, Visa.*

L'Erée	The Taste of India	£35
Tel 0481 64516		Restaurant
Sunset Cottage L'Erée Guernsey		Map 13 E4

One of the few Indian restaurants on the island, it is well located at the end of Rocquaine Bay near Lihou island. No sea view but an attractive intimate decor. The menu is strong on tandoori. Dishes are prepared with quality ingredients and a delicate mix of spices. There is a branch in St Peter's Port (Tel 0481 723730). *Seats 52. L 12-2 D 6-12. Set L £6.95 (Sun £9.95) Set D £12. Access, Amex, Diners, Visa.*

Forest   Deerhound Inn Hotel

Tel 0481 38585	Inn
Le Bourg Forest Road Forest Guernsey	Map 13 E4

Located off a main road, not far from the airport, this converted old Guernsey farmhouse is situated above Petit Bot valley and beach and offers a particularly warm welcome and basic accommodation. Next to the small bar is Poachers Restaurant with additional tables outside in the garden. The menu is strong on chargrilled meats with the addition of chef's specials like Cumberland pie (£4.25), chicken Kiev and daily specials of red lentil soup (£1.50) and braised lamb casserole (£4.25). Good reliable cooking. One of the bedrooms is a family room with bunk beds; the TV lounge can act as a children's playroom and there are swings in the garden. Generous breakfasts. *Bar Food & Restaurant Meals 12-1.45, 7-9.30. Beer Tetley, Theakston. Garden, children's play area. Family room. Accommodation 10 bedrooms, 2 en suite, £40 (single £20). Children welcome overnight (0-4 years 25% adult rate, 5-12 years 50%), additional beds and cots (no charge) available. Access, Diners, Visa.*

Forest   Mallard Hotel   67%   £63

Tel 0481 64164 Fax 0481 65732	Hotel
Forest Guernsey	Map 13 E4

Conveniently located near the airport, the hotel offers good accommodation at kind prices. Public rooms are particularly large and the big attraction is of course the outdoor solar-heated swimming pool with plenty of sun beds and outdoor tables. Bedrooms are comfortable with trouser press, hairdryer, colour TV, tea/coffee facilities. Rooms overlooking the swimming pool have balconies facing south. Rooms facing the back of the building are quieter. Perfect for families. *Rooms 47. Garden, outdoor swimming pool, keep-fit equipment, sauna, spa bath, solarium, tennis, games room, 2 cinemas. Access, Amex, Visa.*

Kings Mills   Fleur du Jardin

Tel 0481 57996 Fax 0481 56834	Inn
Kings Mills Castel Guernsey	Map 13 E4

The 16th-century inn was tastefully refurbished two years ago, keeping the traditional country feel. Several low-ceilinged dining rooms interconnect, creating a quiet atmosphere. The cooking is the highlight here. While the extensive menu offers the usual pub fare, the daily specials are strong on fish and game: oven-baked lemon sole with basil and lemon butter (£6.50), John Dory with deep-fried leeks (£5.50) or roast pheasant with caramelised onions £6.50). Also a popular place for a Sunday roast lunch (£5.65 on bar menu or 4-courses £9.50 in the restaurant). The bedrooms are attractive and amenities include remote-control TVs, telephones and tea/coffee-making facilities; some rooms have trouser presses and small refrigerators. There's a beautiful view of the surrounding countryside from the heated outdoor swimming pool. *Bar Food 12-2, 6.30-9.30 (Sun 7-9). Restaurant Meals 12-2, 7-9.30. Beer Guernsey Brewery. Garden, children's play area. Accommodation 17 bedrooms, all en suite, £70 (single rate varies according to season and availability, £35+).*

Children welcome overnight (0-4 years rate varies; 4-11 50% adult rate with high-tea included Jun-Aug, free at other times of the year), additional beds and cots available. No dogs. Access, Amex, Visa.

Pleinmont   Imperial Hotel

Tel 0481 64044 Fax 0481 66139	Inn
Pleinmont Torteval Guernsey	Map 13 E4

Attractive little hotel ideally located at the south end of Rocquaine Bay. Bar, restaurant and most of the bedrooms benefit from a beautiful view of the bay. Ongoing refurbishment is improving the clean and bright accommodation with tea and coffee-making facilities, TVs and direct-dial telephones. Four rooms have attractive balconies with patio furniture. Children are welcome if well behaved (50% discount for children under 11). Special rates include car hire. Safe garden and a short walk from the beach. **Bar Food** *12-2, 7-9 (except Sun eve).* **Restaurant Meals** *6.30-9 (Summer to 9.30).* **Beer** *Randalls, Worthington. Garden.* **Accommodation** *17 bedrooms, all en suite, £57 (single £28.50). Children welcome overnight (0-2 years free, 2-11 50% reduction), additional beds and cots available.* **Closed** *Nov-Apr. Access, Visa.*

St Martins   Old Grape House Café & Lakeside Tea Garden

Tel 0481 36538	Café
Sausmarez Manor St Martins Guernsey	Map 13 E4

A Visit to Sausmarez Manor in St Martins will provide an afternoon of entertainment with its doll's house and train rides. The little café/tea shop is right next to the lake and offers toasties, freshly made sandwiches (from 90p) and a Guernsey speciality not to be missed, the gache melée (a light apple cake 70p). Scones and cakes are home-baked daily by one of the owners (and granfather decorates cupcakes for the kids!). Burgers and pizzas look less inviting. **Seats** *36 (plus 50 outside).* **Open** *10-5.30.* **Closed** *weekends (Nov-Easter).*

St Martin   La Trelade Hotel   61%   £70

Tel 0481 35454 Fax 0481 37855	Hotel
Forest Road St Martin Guernsey	Map 13 E4

A holiday hotel in three acres of grounds off the main airport road. Two split-level lounge areas (one non-smoking) have modern brown leather-look seating, and the bar has smart and comfortable salmon-pink upholstery. Bedrooms are decent-sized and are equipped with simple white built-in units and clean bathrooms, some with shower and bath, others with shower only. Friendly staff. Families are well catered for with a children's playground and baby-listening available. Children up to 16 pay for meals but not accommodation in parents' room. **Rooms** *45. Garden, outdoor swimming pool, putting, games room. Access, Amex, Diners, Visa.*

St Peter Port   St Pierre Park   71%   £130

Tel 0481 728282 Fax 0481 712041	Hotel
Rohais St Peter Port Guernsey	Map 13 E4

Located in a quiet setting of 45 acres of parkland, away from the town's activity, it provides the island's most impressive leisure complex, with Tony Jacklin-designed 9-hole golf course, three outdoor tennis courts, a 25m indoor swimming pool and a fully-equipped health suite. Recently renovated public rooms are airy and elegant. The lounge/bar and some bedrooms overlook the garden and ornamental lake. Bedrooms, some yet to be redecorated, offer comfortable accommodation with up-to-date accessories. Children under 11 stay free in their parents' room. **Rooms** *134. Garden, indoor swimming pool, gymnasium, sauna, spa bath, solarium, beauty & hair salons, tennis, 9-hole golf course, snooker, coffee shop (10am-10pm). Access, Amex, Diners, Visa.*

St Peters   The Tea Garden

Tel 0481 63486	Tea
Braye du Lihou St Peters (St Pierre du Bois) Guernsey	Map 13 E4

Follow signs for Lihou island, but be careful: there are no signs to advertise it on the main road. The tea garden is one of the most charming settings on the island. Tables are set outside on a flowery terrace of a private house; but what about when it rains? – "it never lasts in Guernsey", they say. The kitchen has been converted into a self-service counter. Beautiful scones and cakes are lovingly baked by the lady owner, who treats her customers like friends. Coconut and lime sponge, toffee fudge and coffee walnut are among the ten cakes baked daily. Sandwiches are freshly made and the soup of the day might be carrot and tarragon, weather permitting! Ample parking. **Seats** *50 (outside only).* **Open** *10.30-5.30 (Easter to mid October).*

Herm

Herm	White House	64%	£116*
Tel 0481 722159 Fax 0481 710066			Hotel
Herm			Map 13 E4

The only hotel on the island, the White House offers comfortable accommodation for those who want to escape the hurly-burly of mainland life. The hotel produces its own electricity and there are no televisions or telephones in the bedrooms; a small butane cooker is used to heat up the kettles. The best bedrooms have sea view and balcony; some newly refurbished ones are brighter with brand new bathrooms. The hotel is self-contained with a succession of homely lounges, an elegant sea view restaurant and the Ship Inn, a pub with a Carvery dining room. Children are very welcome and there are many family rooms; children under 6 stay free (if sharing with parents) in low season. In addition to the fair weather attractions of the outdoor pool, tennis courts and the island's beaches, the hotel provides both adult and children's games. High tea is served between 5 and 6pm in the dining room. *Half-board terms only. Self-catering cottages and flats also available.* **Rooms** *38. Garden, outdoor swimming pool, tennis.* **Closed** *mid Oct-end Mar. Access, Visa.*

Restaurant   £40

Meals are served in an elegant dining room where smoking is not allowed. No à la carte, but a tempting four-course menu proposing the likes of duck liver risotto, cream of mushroom soup or grilled whole plaice with herb butter and fresh lime as well as vegetarian alternatives. The gourmet menu, well priced with a choice of five courses is only available on Saturday nights. **Seats** *100. Parties 50. L 12.30-1.30 D 7-9. Set D £14.45.*

Ship Inn & Captain's Coffee Shop

A small bar area connects to the first-floor Captain's coffee shop, a carvery-style restaurant. 'To pipe you aboard' are the likes of crab cocktail (£3.50) or Herm oysters (6 for £3.50!); continue with 'the daily catch' (perhaps fresh plaice £6.85), bosun's burgers (£3.75), 'midshipman's main courses' (steaks £6.75-£10.75 or vegetarian salad £5.75) or the lunchtime carvery (daily roast £4). Children are offered their own young sea dogs' menu (king-size sausage, fish fingers, chicken nuggets, all £2.75). Afternoon teas. **Open** *9am-5pm.* **Closed** *Sun.*

Jersey

Gorey	The Jersey Pottery Restaurant	
Tel 0534 51119		**Restaurant**
Gorey Village Gorey Jersey		**Map 13 F4**

One of Jersey's most popular and busy tourist attraction where the pottery-making process can be watched, from throwing to glazing. Next to the attractive conservatory restaurant is the self-service café, which fills up rapidly for cold luncheon and afternoon teas. Seafood is a speciality, as in the restaurant, and ranges from a simple prawn cocktail (£4.50) to the copious plateau de fruits de mer (£16). A selection of pastries made on the premises offers fresh fruit tarts, chocolate and cherry gateau (£1.75) or scones with jam and cream (£1.60). There are tables set outside near the conservatory restaurant, which has an extensive à la carte menu. Children's portions and eight high-chairs provided; storage for push-chairs. No-smoking area. **Seats** *220 (plus 120 outside).* **Open** *9-5.30.* **Closed** *Sat, Sun, 10 days Christmas. Access, Amex, Diners, Visa.*

Grouville	Grouville Bay Hotel	62%	£80
Tel 0534 51004 Fax 0534 57416			**Hotel**
Grouville Jersey			**Map 13 F4**

Located right next to the Royal Jersey Golf course, the hotel has no golf concession but enjoys attractive views over the greens. Outdoor heated swimming pool and footpath to the nearby beaches are pluses. Comfortable public rooms and basic bedrooms (40% for family use) with colour TV and tea/coffee facilities. **Rooms** *56. Garden, outdoor swimming pool, children's swimming pool, games room.* **Closed** *2nd week Oct-2nd week Apr. Access, Amex, Diners, Visa.*

Havre des Pas	Hotel de la Plage	66%	£84
Tel 0534 23474 Fax 0534 68642			**Hotel**
Havre des Pas St Helier Jersey JE2 4UQ			**Map 13 F4**

A well-run modern hotel on the seafront, with picture windows to enhance the views. Day rooms are in various styles: subdued and modern in the split-level lounge-bar, tropical in the Caribbean Bar, bamboo in the sun lounge. Sea-facing bedrooms have balconies; inland-view rooms are cheaper. Snacks are served all day in the lounges, in the bedrooms or on the terrace. No dogs. **Rooms** *78. Keep-fit facilities, solarium, games room.* **Closed** *end Oct-early Apr. Access, Amex, Diners, Visa.*

Portelet Bay   Portelet Hotel   66%   £100

Tel 0534 41204 Fax 0534 46625	Hotel
Portelet Bay St Brelade Jersey	Map 13 F4

A well-kept modern hotel open only in summer. Most popular of the
public rooms is the sun lounge overlooking the pool to St Brelade's
Bay beyond. Elsewhere there's a quiet residents' lounge and a 70s'-style
cocktail bar. Many of the bedrooms have private balconies. Free early-
morning tea or coffee and paper, mini-bus to town. No dogs.
Rooms 86. Garden, outdoor swimming pool, tennis, putting, games room.
Closed Oct-Apr. Access, Amex, Diners, Visa.

St Brelade   Old Smugglers Inn

Tel 0534 41510	Pub
Ouaisné Bay St Brelade Jersey	Map 13 F4

Two 13th-century fishermen's cottages were rebuilt from their ruins
in 1721 by local fishermen and remained as such until the early 1900s
when they were enlarged and developed into a small residential hotel
retaining most of the original granitework, beams and fireplaces. After
the German occupation the property underwent further changes and
the Old Smugglers emerged. Today, it is one of the few 'genuine' free
houses on the island. A succession of small dining rooms (one non-
smoking) serve food from 'The Treasure Chest' menu. Food is taken
seriously and there's an extensive selection of tempting dishes – Yankee
fried potato skins (£2.25), home-made fish soup (£1.75), king prawns
won ton with sweet chili sauce (£3.95), chef's spicy BBQ-style baby
back ribs (£4.50), Smugglers' ocean bake (£4.75), cottage pie (£4.50)
or baked veggie crumble (£4.20). One high-chair and changing
facilities provided. Children welcome until 8pm (Jersey law). *Bar*
Meals 12-2, 6-8.45 (+ all day Sun). Children allowed in bar to eat. Free
House. *Beer Bass, Boddingtons, Theakston. Terrace. Family room.*
No credit cards.

St Brelade   La Place Hotel   67%   £110

Tel 0534 44261 Fax 0534 45164	Hotel
Route du Coin La Haule St Brelade Jersey JE3 8BF	Map 13 F4

Once a farmhouse but now much enlarged by modern extensions,
La Place is for those who like rural surroundings. The main public
rooms are part of the original, 400-year-old building. There's
a delightful open-air seating area in a south-facing courtyard, a bright
bar with green bamboo furniture and two lounges, one of which has
a black-beamed ceiling, a pink granite fireplace, antique furniture and
polished brass ornaments. Bedrooms include seven around the pool.
Children up to seven stay free in parents' room; children's high tea
is offered. *Rooms 40. Outdoor swimming pool, sauna. Access, Amex,*
Diners, Visa.

St Brelade's Bay   St Brelade's Bay Hotel   70%   £140

Tel 0534 46141 Fax 0534 47278	Hotel
St Brelade's Bay Jersey JE3 8EF	Map 13 F4

This smartly whitewashed, low-level hotel bears evidence of the long-
term care and pride heaped upon it b the Colley family. Behind
it is a lovely garden set with sun-loungers where parents can relax
while a lifeguard teaches their children to swim; inside, an airy,
spacious foyer leads you to the elegant and comfortable lounge, with

antiques, chesterfields, parquet floors and beautiful rugs. There's live
music in the cocktail bar, and a club room and games room for
younger guests. First- and second-floor rooms are traditional, while
those on the third floor are more modern; all are attractively and
tastefully decorated and furnished. Families are well catered for.
Rooms 82. *Garden, outdoor swimming pool, keep-fit equipment, sauna,
solarium, games room, tennis, putting.* **Closed** *mid Oct-end Apr.*
Access, Visa.

St Helier	Apollo Hotel	63%	£88
Tel 0534 25441 Fax 0534 22120			Hotel
9 St Saviour's Road St Helier Jersey JE2 4LA			Map 13 F4

A modern two-storey hotel built round a courtyard. Public areas
provide plenty of space to relax: there are two bars (one in pub style),
a coffee shop serving snacks throughout the day, an indoor leisure
centre and a sun-trap terrace. Bedrooms, some with balconies, include
many suitable for family occupation. **Rooms** 85. *Indoor swimming pool,
gymnasium, sauna, spa bath, solarium, coffee shop (11am-9pm). Access,
Amex, Diners, Visa.*

St Helier	Grand Hotel	68%	£120
Tel 0534 22301 Fax 0534 37815			Hotel
The Esplanade St Helier Jersey JE4 8WD			Map 13 F4

The long, gabled frontage of the Grand is a distinctive feature on the
seafront and the entrance is appropriately impressive, with ornate,
coloured pillars and a marble floor. The smart period-style bar and
lounge have fine views and so do balconied front bedrooms, which
attract a hefty surcharge. It's a busy hotel catering for both holiday and
business visitors (conference/banqueting facilities for 180/250).
Families are well provided for with free accommodation for under-14s
in their parents' room, plus baby-sitting and special children's meals
also available. De Vere Hotels. **Rooms** 115. *Indoor swimming pool, keep-
fit equipment, sauna, spa bath, solarium, beauty salon, hairdressing, snooker.
Access, Amex, Diners, Visa.*

Victoria's   £70

Formal elegance and a traditional French/British à la carte menu.
There's a second restaurant, the Regency. **Seats** 250. *L 12.15-2.15
D 7-10 (Sun to 9.30). Set L £14 Set D £19.50.*

St Helier	Hotel de France	71%	£120
Tel 0534 38990 Fax 0534 35354			Hotel
St Saviour's Road St Helier Jersey			Map 13 F4

Located in the northern part of St Helier, on St Saviour's Road, the
hotel has the elegance of a mid-nineteenth century palace spoiled
by the construction of modern conference and leisure buildings. The
extraordinary conference facilities include a 600-delegate auditorium,
the 1,200 sq. ft. Skyline Hall and a profusion of banqueting suites and
boardrooms. To accommodate the 320 bedrooms, a large conservatory
restaurant and two bars are adequate – unlike the tiny indoor and
outdoor swimming pools. Bedrooms in the old wing are large
although not as well equipped as the smaller rooms in the new wing.
The hotel caters for families particularly well. Children under 12 stay
free in their parents' room between April and October. **Rooms** 320.

Terrace, outdoor and indoor swimming pool, keep-fit equipment, squash, sauna, spa bath, solarium, beauty & hair salon, games room, snooker, news kiosk (8-12, 4-7). Access, Amex, Diners, Visa.

St Lawrence   British Union Hotel

Tel 0534 861070	Pub
St Lawrence Main Road St Lawrence Jersey	Map 13 F4

Across the road from St Lawrence Parish Church, this is a pleasant pub with a good atmosphere and warm welcome. It has the same owners as the Star & Tipsy Toad Brewery but is under licence to the Mary Ann Brewery and serves Guernsey Brewery beers. A central bar divides two lounges with an additional family/games room to the rear. Well prepared daily specials like steak and kidney pie (£5), lemon or spicy chicken (£5.50), or cod with beer batter (£4.10); ice cream is the only dessert offered. Good for families: a small 'children only' rear patio has a Wendy House. *Pub open 9am-11pm Mon-Sat, 11-1, 4.30-11 Sun.* **Bar Food** *(except Sun) 12-2, 6-8.30. Children's menu/children allowed in bar to eat.* **Beer** *Guernsey Brewery. Children's play area. Family room. No credit cards.*

St Ouen   The Lobster Pot   £65

Tel 0534 482888 Fax 0534 481574	Restaurant
L'Etacq St Ouen Jersey	Map 13 F4

A popular spot with tours and coaches where booking is recommended for weekends. The location is attractive, overlooking St Ouen's Bay. The speciality is of course locally caught lobster served grilled, à la nage, Newburg or Thermidor, but an extensive menu will please all tastes. Well-prepared flambé desserts. Next to the main restaurant is the **Coach House Bar**, a pubby bar with a beautiful flowery terrace looking out onto St Ouens Bay. Here a small selection from the restaurant menu is served, with the likes of bisque de homard (£2.75), salads (£4.95) and even cream teas (£2.60), plus simpler snacks such as baked potatoes, mussels and beef burgers. Children are welcomed throughout, with meal times to satisfy hunger pangs at any time of day. *Seats 90. Restaurant: L 12.30-2.15 D 7.30-10. Set D £14.50. Access, Amex, Diners, Visa.*

Rooms   £88

Thirteen large bedrooms with the usual modern amenities of TV, trouser press, hairdryer and even a small bar area with tea and coffee facilities and a small refrigerator. The best rooms naturally have a sea view. Good for families, with under-14s staying free if sharing their parents' room. Rooms are large enough to accommodate an extra bed.

St Peter   Mermaid Hotel   64%   £92

Tel 0534 41255 Fax 0534 45826	Hotel
Airport Road St Peter Jersey JE3 7BN	Map 13 F4

A modern hotel located near the airport and built next to a natural lake. Bedrooms all have the expected facilities and though not large they benefit from south-facing balconies with a lake view. The hotel is self-contained with restaurants, bar, pub and impressive leisure facilities. No dogs. *Rooms 68. Garden, outdoor & indoor swimming pools, keep-fit equipment, sauna, spa bath, tennis, putting. Access, Amex, Diners, Visa.*

St Peter's Village   **Star & Tipsy Toad Brewery**

Tel 0534 485556	**Pub**
St Peter's Village Jersey	**Map 13 F4**

Right on the A12, in St Peter, the only pub on the island with its own brewery. The attractive decor retains some character with the granite walls, old coat stoves and oak wood panelling. Young, enthusiastic staff prepare good basic pub food like steak and ale pie (£4.95), chicken Kiev (£4.50) or fresh cod in beer batter (£4.50). The brewery can be visited on arranged tours. Indoor and outdoor play areas in addition to the 'Little Toadies' menu and baby-changing facilities make this a perfect pub for families. *Pub open 10am-11pm Mon-Sat, 11-1, 4.30-11.30 Sun. Bar Food (except Sun) 12-2.15, 6-8.15. Children's menu. Free House. Beer Tipsy Toad Brewery: Jimmy's Bitter, Horny Toad, Cyril's. Beer garden, outdoor play area. Family room, indoor play area. No credit cards.*

St Saviour   **Merton Hotel**   60%   £86★

Tel 0534 24231 Fax 0534 68603	**Hotel**
Belvedere St Saviour Jersey	**Map 13 F4**

Located right outside St Helier, on a sloped street off the A3, a spacious hotel with basic accommodation and the amazing Aquadome complex of indoor and outdoor swimming pools. Good for children, with entertainment for them in the evening. ★Half-board terms.
Rooms 330. Garden, indoor and outdoor swimming pool, children's swimming pool, squash, spa bath, tennis, bistro (10.30-2, 3-6, 9.30-12). Access, Amex, Diners, Visa.

Sark

Sark   **Aval Du Creux Hotel**   57%   £63

Tel 0481 832036 Fax 0481 832368	**Hotel**
Sark Channel Islands	**Map 13 E4**

Eight miles east of Guernsey is the island of Sark, a peaceful retreat with forty miles of coastline, bracing walks and no traffic. Peter and Cheryl Tonks' friendly little hotel, originally a farmhouse, is a good place for family holidays, with four of the bedrooms of a suitable size for families. There are two lounges and a small bar hung with local pictures. *Rooms 12. Garden, outdoor swimming pool, boules. Closed Oct-Apr. Access, Visa.*

Restaurant   £52

Seafood plays the leading role here, with local crab served hot in a shell with cheese glaze, plus oysters, lobster (surf'n'turf) and monkfish. Fresh asparagus from Guernsey (in season) and pan-fried pigeon breast with gingerbread sauce, and guinea fowl in filo pastry with sweet red peppers show that care is taken not only in preparation but also in obtaining quality ingredients. *Seats 40. Private Room 15. L 12-2 D 7-8. Set D £15.95.*

Sark   Stocks Hotel   61%   £102*

| Tel 0481 832001   Fax 0481 832130 | Hotel |

Sark Channel Islands   Map 13 E4

Peace and relaxation come without too much trouble at the Armorgie
family's granite-built hotel, which lies in a wooded valley 20 minutes
walk from the harbour. There's a homely atmosphere in the lounge,
and comfortable, unfussy bedrooms are decorated with darkwood
furniture and floral fabrics. No TVs in the rooms. *Half-board terms
only. *Rooms 25. Garden, outdoor swimming pool, coffee shop (10am-
10pm). Closed mid Oct-Easter. Access, Diners, Visa.*

Cider Press Restaurant   £50

Both table d'hote and à la carte menus are offered, with local fish,
shellfish and meat always featuring. Mussels Catalan-style, crab and
smoked bacon soup, roast shoulder of veal, grilled turbot and lobster
prepared several ways all use Island produce. Coffee, lunch, cream teas
and light evening meals are served in the *Courtyard Bistro*, with
alfresco tables in summer adjacent to the swimming pool; children's
supper menu served here from 5-7pm. *Seats 60. Private Room 12.
L 12-2.30 D 7.30-9 (Sun to 9). Set D £12.50/£15.50.*

Isle of Man

Douglas   L'Expérience

| Tel 0624 623103 | Restaurant |

Summerhill Douglas Isle of Man   Map 4 B4

An informal seafront restaurant whose authentic onion soup served
under a crust of melted cheese is claimed to have become famous across
the island. If this is not your choice there are queenies (scallops with
bacon or in a brandy sauce £4.50), croque monsieur £2, omelette,
cassoulet £4.25 or champignons aux paprika £3.25. Sweets include
French apple flan, chiffons or a real chocolate mousse. Ask for
children's portions. Patio. *Seats 65. Open 12-2 & 7-11. Closed L Sun &
Tue in summer, all day Sun & Tue in winter, 25 & 26 Dec, 1 Jan.*

Peel   Creek Inn

| Tel 0624 842216 | Pub |

The Quayside Peel Isle of Man   Map 4 B4

The industrious and friendly landlords, Robert and Jean McAleer,
of this bustling pub right by the quayside of Peel harbour offer seafood
specialities from the fish yard in their large, bright and unpretentious
bar. Home-made Manx kipper paté (£3.25), fresh crab salad (£4.80),
Manx scallops ('Queenies') served on the shell in a mornay sauce
(£4.95), avocado sunrise (fresh crab, prawns and pineapple £4.95)
might all feature on the menu or among the blackboard specials.
Other offerings range from open sandwiches (£1.95-£3.95) to curries,
home-made pizzas and steak and kidney pie (£3.95). Several fruit tarts
(£1.50) or home-made gateaux to follow. Junior diners pay £1.50
or £1.75 for their portions. Full selection of Irish spirits. Easy parking.
*Pub open 11-10.45 Mon-Sat & 12-1.30, 8-10 Sun. Bar Food 11-10.45
(Sun 12-1.15, 8-10). Children's menu. Beer Worthington, Okells Bitter &
Mild. Outdoor eating on the quayside. Children welcome in bar 12-1.30
only if eating. No credit cards.*

Ramsey	**Harbour Bistro**	
Tel 0624 814182		**Bistro**
5 East Street Ramsey Isle of Man		**Map 4 B4**

Informal eating in a friendly bistro near the quay. Seafood is quite
a feature on the menu: local queenie scallops cooked with Mornay
sauce, with a garlic sauce on a bed of spinach, or with bacon, onion
and black pepper; deep-fried or baked plaice, fisherman's pie, lobster
and Dover sole. There's also plenty of choice for meat-eaters, plus
indulgent desserts. **Seats** *46. L 12.15-2.30 D 6.30-10.30.* **Closed**
Christmas, 5 July, 2 weeks Oct. Set L (Sun) £9.95. Access, Visa.

St John's	**Shuttle Stop Café**	
Tel 0624 801600		**Café**
Tynwald Mills St John's Isle of Man		**Map 4 B4**

The café, formerly the *Tynwald Mill Patisserie*, is now licensed and has
been moved downstairs to the ground floor in this complex of craft
shops near the seat of the Manx Parliament. Staff are helpful, serving
an all-day menu with good home-made sweets like lemon meringue
pie and apple pie. Children will find colouring books and crayons,
high-chairs and their own Little Weavers menu of favourites (pizza,
jumbo fish fingers, home-made meatballs, chicken nuggets – all £2.25
including a fizzy drink or ice cream). Traditional three-course Sunday
lunch is £7. Outside, there is further seating for 30 people
and a children's receational area with swings, slides, a tunnel
and a picnic area. **Seats** *95.* **Open** *10-6.* **Closed** *25 & 26 Dec, 1 Jan,
Good Friday. Access, Visa.*

It may be your car,
but it's still our baby.

When you need a little attention it's nice to know there's always someone you can trust to turn to. That's why Ford's commitment to their vehicles doesn't stop when they drive off the dealer's forecourt.

Today, more than ever they are involved in helping their dealerships set the highest standards of service and customer care.

Most dealerships have now installed 'Fault finding diagnostic computers' that can spot at a glance when something is wrong.

And thanks to Ford's investment in training, their engineers can remedy any concerns quickly and expertly

TRAINING

Modern cars are sophisticated pieces of machinery, often with complicated electronics, so Ford send over 5,000 engineers a year to their special schools, and send them back again when they bring out something new

But as everyone knows an expert workman needs expert tools. Each dealership has more than 200 specialist tools designed just for Fords, and they use only those parts which are designed especially for Fords.

They also have over 2,000 different shades and mixes of paint, and the special ovens required to treat it properly, so they can match the colour of your Ford perfectly

SPECIALIST TOOLS

But Ford haven't forgotten that servicing the car is only half the job, so they've introduced things like menu pricing where the cost of the job is estimated before any of the work takes place, so that the price you see is the price you pay

We feel we've come **SERVICE** a long way in trying to make the servicing of your car as efficient and friendly as possible.

After all, it may be your car, but it's still our baby

Hotel Groups
listed in county order

Overleaf is a listing of major hotel groups each of which has to a lesser or greater extent a definable corporate identity. We have included budget hotel chains (some coming under the banner of the major groups) which, while not given our normal percentage grading, nevertheless offer a convenient stop-over.

A brief description of the main characteristics of each group is given as well as head office addresses, and phone and fax numbers for general enquiries and central reservations.

Prices quoted are for high season and include a cooked breakfast for two adults. Research conducted November 1993.

0800 telephone numbers are freephone.

Campanile Hotels

**Reservations (from UK): Tel 010 33 1 64 62 46 46   Fax 010 33 1 64 62 46 61
Weekdays 8am-7pm, Saturdays 9am-12pm (French time).**

A chain of 14 modern, purpose-built, functional hotels; part of a 350-strong group throughout Europe. All are open 365 days. Liverpool has 24hr reception. All bedrooms are either twin or double, have remote-control colour TV, fully fitted bathrooms, radio-alarms. Each hotel has rooms designed for the disabled. A standard tariff of £35.75 per room (£29.50 at weekends) applies though there is a third person supplement of £7.50 (children under 12 are free, cots available). Two sets of communicating rooms per hotel (no extra charge). Bistro-style restaurants feature a children's menu (£2.95 for under-12s), themed around *Campi* their green bear 'chef's helper' mascot – stickers, games on paper, balloons, poster and table mat should keep the children interested; children's parties arranged at 2 days' notice. No early evening meal before 7pm; 2-course meal £7.35, buffet £8.35, bistro £9.45. Buffet breakfasts, either Continental or full English, are £4.25 per person, from 7-9am (from 8 at weekends). Each hotel has conference facilities for 30. Most hotels have swings in the garden (not Liverpool, Washington, Rotherham or Wakefield). Cardiff has the largest garden and a little more outdoor play equipment. All major credit cards accepted. Last check-in time 11pm.

Copthorne Hotels

Reservations: 0800 414741

Primarily a business hotel group, but locations may be convenient for family weekend breaks; Plymouth is an example, London good value. Standard rooms (Classics) offer good-sized bedrooms each with a double bed, colour TV with movie and/or satellite channel (only the hotel in Slough/Windsor has the children's channel), en-suite bath and shower as well as the other usual facilities that are expected of a modern hotel. Executive rooms (Connoisseur) have larger more comfortable bedrooms and, usually, a better outlook. Extras include fresh fruit and magazines, while bathrooms offer bathrobes and better-quality toiletries. Under-16s share parents' room free of charge, except at the Copthorne Tara in London. Dogs are generally not welcome in rooms. *Weekends Away* brochure for two-night breaks; prices (1993: £129 UK, £149 London) include entrance tickets to local attractions; children £15 per night including breakfast and ticket. Breakfast from £8.50, 50% for children. Copthorne Kids Menu ('designed by children under 12 for children under 12') offers a good choice of standard favourites; jars of proprietary baby food (along with plainly cooked meat or fish and vegetables plus a complimentary yoghurt) are provided and baby's bottle will happily be heated. Effingham Park, Gatwick Airport has a crèche facility as part of its leisure centre, also an outside play area. Baby-sitting can sometimes be arranged in advance. All major credit cards accepted.

De Vere Hotels

Reservations: Tel 0925 265050   Fax 0925 601264

On the whole, these are quite distinctive hotels, some grand, others not so, each with its own style and character based on comfort and tradition. Properties range from the Grand hotels on the seafront in Eastbourne and Brighton to the Belfry in Wishaw, North Warwks and the Belton Woods Hotel (complete with crèche – not Thurs – and supervised 'splash time' – Fri & Sat – in the leisure centre) near Grantham in Lincolnshire with their magnificent golf courses. Standards of service are generally high. Leisure clubs are free to guests; many have splash pools (no children under 8 in the spa baths). Under-14s share their parents' room at no charge, but meals are charged as taken (except at Tillington Hall where breakfast is included). Tillington Hall in Stafford is convenient for Alton Towers; packed lunches (£4.50/£6.50), children's entertainment at holiday periods, satellite TV with children's channel all provided. Fun pack on arrival, complete with colouring book. All major credit cards accepted.

Edwardian (Radisson) Hotels

Reservations: Tel 081-564 8888   Fax 081-759 8422

A London-based group of hotels ranging from the Hampshire in Leicester Square and the Edwardian International (the only one with a swimming pool) at London Heathrow to the more modest but still comfortable Kenilworth and Grafton Hotels. Mainly aimed at the business and group markets (only babies can share their parents room at no charge), but the convenient locations may suit families with babes in arms or slightly older children. Baby-sitting can be arranged. The most recent refurbishment in the group has been at the Savoy Court Hotel, Granville Place, Marble Arch, W1 Tel 071-408 0130. All major credit cards accepted.

Forte Hotels

Reservations (local call cost): Tel 0345 404040   Fax 0296 81391

Trusthouse Forte was rebranded a couple of years ago and this vast network of hotels now offers six categories of hotels ranging from the Exclusive, Grand and Heritage brands down to the budget Travelodges. The Forte Crest and Forte Posthouse brands are the two primarily aimed at the businessman; the latter offers probably the best all-round value-for-money accommodation in the UK for families on the move. In 1993 a 'School Holiday Special' promotion offered a free room (meals charged as taken) for up to two children when booking a 3 or 4 night holiday in all Crests and selected Posthouses; early suppers and organised activities at some Crests and a playroom set aside in Posthouses at weekends. Heritage hotels are mid-priced and of mixed appeal; they are generally situated in small towns and more rural locations, often with a coaching inn history. Free parking (for up to 15 days) at Forte's 15 airport hotels. Children under 16 stay free (plus under-5s eat free) when sharing with their parents at all Forte hotels; at Crest hotels up to three children under 16 may stay in a separate room when accompanied by two adults. 25% reduction on Leisure break prices for children occupying their own room at other hotels. Bumper Fun Pack (with postcards, colouring book, colouring pencils, puzzle, games and magic scribble pad), complimentary soft drink, cots, high-chairs, Heinz baby food, baby-listening and baby-sitting are provided in almost all Forte hotels when booking a Leisure break for two or more nights.

Forte Crest

Reservations: (local call cost) 0345 404040

Incorporating some of the best former Posthouses and most of the original Crests, this is a chain of around 28 modern business-orientated hotels. Over half have fully-equipped business centres. All offer 24hr room service for both executive and standard rooms. All major credit cards accepted.

Forte Posthouse

Reservations: 0800 404040

A leading UK chain of around 65 mostly purpose-built modern hotels. Many have health and fitness centres. Rooms have lost the starkness of the early 80s but currently the chief attribute of this chain is the room rate – from Sunday to Thursday the daily 'room only' rate is £53.50, dropping to £41.50 for Friday and Saturday (prices exclude breakfast). Some family rooms have up to four beds; cots and Z-beds available. The midweek room price including cooked breakfast for two people is £67.40. Unsupervised children's playroom at weekends. Half the sites have indoor swimming pools. Outside play area at almost all sites. Under-5s eat free, 5-16s can choose from either the Junior Diner menu or have half-price, half-size portions from the adult menu. The latest hotels to open within the group are

at Colchester and Hemel Hempstead; Stevenage, in contrast, was extended from a 15th-century building. Executive rooms are sometimes available for a small supplement. Forte's Bumper Fun Pack (see above) is given to all junior guests. All major credit cards accepted.

Forte Travelodge

Reservations: 0800 850 950

Roadside budget accommodation offering simple but modern rooms in 93 locations conveniently sited along major routes. Room rates, payable in advance, are currently £31.95 per room. All have en-suite bathrooms with shower, colour television, radio/alarms and tea- and coffee-making facilities. Rooms sleep three adults, a child under 12 on a sofa bed and a baby in a cot (but cots not supplied). Every Travelodge has a room equipped for the disabled. The lodges have either 27 or 56 bedrooms, but no restaurant as almost all are adjacent to a Little Chef, Happy Eater, Harvester or Welcome Break restaurant (all also owned by Forte). Access, Amex and Visa cards accepted.

Friendly Hotels

Reservations: 0800 591 910

A small chain of mixed-quality hotels. Featured in our county list are a couple of purpose-built hotels in Norwich and Milton Keynes; the latest openings in Boston, Cardiff and Loughborough have not yet been inspected and are not included. Modest accommodation, but children under 14 stay free (meals charged as taken). Friendly Freddy's colouring menu offers a three-course children's meal for £2.95 and an opportunity to exercise budding artistic talent. Considerable tariff reductions at weekends. Late-night supper trays delivered to your room if ordered before 9pm. Premier Plus Rooms offer a higher standard with welcome drink, trouser press, teletext TV, mini-bar, hairdryer and personal toiletries. All major credit cards accepted.

Granada Lodges

Reservations: 0800 555 300

A chain of around 21 budget hotels located close to major routes. All rooms are doubles or twins and have private bath and shower, colour TV with satellite channels, radio/alarm and tea- and coffee-making facilities (no phones). In-room continental breakfast is available, otherwise meals are taken in the adjacent service area restaurant (*AJ's* at Leicester, Saltash, Warminster, Grantham and Edinburgh or *Burger King* at Toddington and Exeter – a Granada Hotel). Family rooms are available and 2 children under 16 sharing with 2 adults are accommodated free (excluding breakfast). Every lodge has rooms for the disabled. Prices are from £37.95 (Sun-Thurs, £34.95 Fri & Sat) for twin, double or family rooms; exceptions are Heston (London Heathrow) and Thurrock (Dartford Crossing) which are £46.95 (Sun-Thurs, £43.95 Fri &Sat). Special prices (£24.95) to the end of 1993 (ring for 1994 price) at Grantham on the A1/A151. Payment is on arrival; cot supplied at no extra charge (as are non-allergenic pillows). 50% of lodges have outdoor play areas for children. No dogs. All major credit cards accepted.

Hilton Hotels

Reservations: Tel 0923 238877   Fax 0923 815594

The Hilton Hotel group is now a mix of Hilton International (London-based), 23 Hilton National and a further eight associate hotels around the country. Although mainly aimed at the business market, a Short Break brochure is produced offering special deals for activity and special interest (eg theatre, racing) visits. A teddy bear symbol in the brochure indicates hotels where up to four children can stay free in their own room; at other hotels two children under 16 can stay free if sharing with their parents (£5 charegd for breakfast if taken); in the latter locations up to four children can share a room for £14 per head including breakfast. The Hilton National in Croydon features an American diner (complete with pink Cadillac on the wall). Croydon, Basingstoke, Bracknell, Watford, Southampton, Newbury, East Midlands/Nottingham, Leeds, Leeds Garforth, Newport and Swansea are designated as Happy Family Hotels, many with 3- or 4-bedded rooms. Hilton International and Hilton National hotels have superior rooms designated either Executive or Plaza – these are to a higher specification than standard rooms. They include large teletext TVs, a welcome tray with miniature spirits, chocolates, bathrobes, additional toiletries and lounge seating. Apart from the London hotels, the majority of Hilton hotels have leisure centres that include swimming pools, fitness rooms and saunas. All major credit cards accepted.

Holiday Inns

Reservations: Tel 0800 897 121   Fax Tel 010 31 20 606 5491

One of the leaders in the field of luxury business hotels in the 70s and early 80s, but many of the newer hotel groups have now caught up. Top of the Holiday Inn range are the Crowne Plazas in Aberdeen, Bristol, London Heathrow and Manchester. Standard Holiday Inns offer large double beds and good bathrooms as well as free accommodation for children and young adults (*up to the age of 19*) when sharing with parents. All have good leisure facilities and well-equipped conference rooms. Children's menu (monster meals for under-12s!); breakfast free for under-3s, half price for under-12s. Baby-sitting can be arranged with registered childminders if organised in advance at certain locations. The most family-orientated outlets are at Birmingham, Cambridge, Heathrow, Maidenhead (where a hostess is available at weekends; unsupervised play room Sat am/pm & Sun am, magician most Sat pm, high tea Sat 6pm & Sun breakfast with hostess 8-9am, outdoor play area, separate children's pool and videos), Sutton and Telford. Holiday Inn Weekender breaks offer special rates for weekend and longer stays (eg five nights for the price of four). All major credit cards accepted.

Holiday Inn Garden Courts

Central Reservations: 0800 897 121

Under Bass plc the original Holiday Inn concept has been expanded to include Holiday Inn Garden Courts, an economy version offering excellent value accommodation but more limited hotel facilities. Outlets in Ashford, Edinburgh, Nottingham and Warrington/Chester; the latest one opened in Brent Cross, north London at the end of 1993, but it's the only one without a garden. All major credit cards accepted.

Jarvis Hotels

Linkline Reservations: Tel 0345 581237   Fax 071-589 8193

A nationwide network of 39 middle-range hotels – a mixed portfolio, but usually dependable. A few have leisure clubs (free to guests) and 27 have purpose-built Summit meeting rooms. Trouser presses and hairdryers are standard to all rooms; Executive bedrooms have a better standard of decor and additional amenities such as fruit and chocolates plus extra toiletries in the bathrooms. Children are charged 50% of the adult rate if occupying their own room – this charge includes meals; Jarvis Juniors menu offers a good choice (it's only for juniors because "grown-ups just don't understand what good food is all about!"- from boiled egg with bread and butter to chicken nuggets and chips, toasties and a knickerbocker glory; Heinz baby food for babies and toddlers. Up to two children under 16 may share their parents' room at no charge (meals charged as taken). Embassy Leisure Breaks offer special rates for weekend and longer stays. The Jarvis Junior Fun Pack might include an "I'm a Jarvis Juniors monster" badge, giant colouring book, join-the-dots book, crayons and magic slate. 10 of the hotels have leisure clubs, five with children's splash pools. Great Danes in Hollingbourne, Kent is near Leeds Castle and features a Sebastian Coe Health Park plus an outdoor play area. Clayton Lodge in Newcastle-under-Lyme is convenient for Alton Towers. All major credit cards accepted.

Marriott Hotels:

Reservations: Tel 0800 221 222   Fax 071-287 0271

The Marriott corporation run the London Marriott and Cheshunt Marriott, while the remainder are operated under franchise by Scott's Hotels who were previously associated with Holiday Inns. Many millions of pounds have since been spent upgrading all aspects – from landscaping, exteriors and interiors to staff uniforms – of the former Holiday Inns. Staff have been trained to the high corporate standards demanded by Marriott, the aim of the group being to attract senior management in the business market during the week and family and leisure business at weekends. Bedrooms are spacious, with large desks and comfortable sofas. The Bristol, Heathrow/Slough, Marble Arch and new Leeds Marriott (recently opened and not yet inspected) have Executive floors with private lounges and complimentary canapés. There are 18 hotels in the group including four **Courtyard by Marriott** (Leamington Spa, Lincoln, Northampton, Slough) outlets, which offer more moderately priced accommodation but still have good-sized rooms with separate seating and dressing areas, plus mini-gyms. All major credit cards accepted.

Mount Charlotte Thistle Hotels

Central Reservations: Tel 071-937 8033
Highlife Shortbreaks Reservations: 0800 700 400

Next to the Forte Hotels group, Mount Charlotte Thistle hotels are the most widespread throughout the country with hotels from Plymouth in Devon to Wick in the north of Scotland, and including 24 in London from the enormous Tower Thistle at Tower Bridge to the country house-style Cannizaro House in Wimbledon. Overall, the quality of bedroom accommodation is good for the price; children are accommodated in a variety of ways – from Z-beds and sofa beds to additional single beds; under-14s share their parents' room during the week (subject to availability of suitable rooms at the time of booking, with meals charged as taken). Under-16s stay free during weekend breaks – it varies because the weekend breaks offer special travel rates with BR (who offer concessions to under-16s). The majority of hotels offer Executive bedrooms: these are larger rooms, more recently decorated and each having a number of useful extras. Lady guests have specially designated rooms. The overall corporate attitude towards families is hard to define as the group is so diverse; however, at least one restaurant in each hotel should offer Monty Lion's corporate children's menu (or a variation on it) with popular favourites – fish fingers, chicken drum sticks, omelettes, ice cream boats and so on; Heinz baby food is offered for wee ones and boiled egg with soldiers for getting those first teeth into. Monty's Super Funpack – complete with cardboard curlytop cap, card game, puzzle, colouring and join-the-dot book and crayons – is offered to junior guests. The large, modern Hospitality Inn in Brighton has a seafront location, convenient for the Lanes; the Golden Valley Thistle in Cheltenham is a good base from which to tour the Cotswolds (although there are leisure club restrictions for under-14s; three-course room service children's menu £5.25). Motor racing enthusiasts could head for the modern Castle Donington or Brands Hatch Thistle hotels. All major credit cards accepted.

Novotel

Resinter Reservations: Tel 071-724 1000   Fax 081-748 9116

A multinational hotel chain with properties located on the outskirts of cities and close to motorway junctions. 14 Novotels are listed in our county listings; there are also hotels at London Heathrow, Belfast, Sheffield and Wolverhampton. York is a good base for visiting the Viking Centre and National Railway Museum; there's an indoor swimming pool and the children's three-course menu (£3.25) even includes bubble gum ice cream or Thunderbirds fromage frais. Children can expect to receive a model of 'Dolfi' the Novotel mascot, puzzle and matching game cards. Rooms, if somewhat plainly decorated, are large and functional. The standard is identical in all and is designed for practical comfort and rest. Each has a bed/settee as well as a double bed. There is ample writing space among the usual modern facilities offered. Accommodation and breakfast are free for two children under 16 sharing their parents' room. Food and room service are available at any time from 6am to midnight and most bars follow the same hours. 1993 special weekend rates (two nights minimum) offered half board at £35 per night per person with 'free newspaper, free soft drink and cookie daily for the kids, and free baby-listening' – no great incentive, merely a level of service that many other hotels consider as standard. Only Newcastle, Sheffield and York hotels have indoor swimming pools; Bradford, Manchester, Nottingham, Plymouth, Preston, Stevenage and Wolverhampton have outdoor pools. Birmingham, Newcastle and Sheffield have fitness centres. Major credit cards accepted in most Novotels but not all.

Principal Hotels

Reservations: Tel 0800 454 454 (7 days a week)

A group of 23 hotels (not all listed in our county listings), most located in town or city centres, that are characterised by an attractive, traditional style and decor. Standard rooms are well equipped, with all the usual amenities. Executive rooms have bathrobes and a trouser press. Under-12s stay free if sharing their parents' room. Sky TV (with the cartoon channel) in most hotels. Special 'Flexibreak' half-board rates for stays of two nights or more (can be spread over more than one hotel). All major credit cards accepted. Under-4s free; 4-14s free when sharing with two adults; half price if sharing own room.

Queens Moat Houses

Reservations: Tel 0800 289 331   Fax 0708 761 033

With properties as diverse as the Royal Crescent in Bath, Eastwell Manor in Ashford, the Rose and Crown in Salisbury and the Newmarket Moat House, there is no longer a characteristic pattern to the 100+ UK hotels currently in the Queens Moat Houses directory (one of the largest three hotel groups, alongside Forte and Mount Charlotte Thistle). It was only a relatively short time ago that the group name was synonymous with pleasant enough but, on the whole, rather lacklustre hotels offering acceptable standards of accommodation. With its newest acquisitions Queens Moat Houses has moved firmly into the luxury hotel league as well. 25 of the hotels have swimming pools. Bournemouth, Plymouth, Stoke on Trent (convenient for Alton Towers) and Telford (Ironbridge Museums and Gorge) are the most 'family-friendly'; Plymouth even offer a Baby & Toddlers Delight weekend with all the necessary accoutrements provided. Weekend breaks offer free accommodation and food for under-6s; 6-15s inclusive stay free with their parents (£3 breakfast, £9 breakfast and dinner); under-16s in a separate room charged 50% adult rate (meals charged as taken). Check when booking for availability of three- and four-bedded rooms, children's menu, special meal times and so on – not all hotels are geared up particularly well for families or offer the special weekend deals (some, such as Eastwell Manor in Ashford, Kent and the Elms Hotel in Abberley near Worcester are delightful adult retreats). Nottingham's

Savoy Steak Bar has a toy box available until 7.30pm and one child under 13 eats free from the children's menu when dining with an adult before 7pm. Many QMH hotels near airports give free car parking (except Gatwick where only a reduced rate is offered and Stansted where it's only free while resident) for up to 15 nights – Shepperton (Heathrow 5 miles), Manchester (4 miles), Birmingham (7 miles), Glasgow (3 miles), Edinburgh (5 miles); enquire about courtesy transfer facilities. All major credit cards taken.

Resort Hotels

Reservations (local call charge): Tel 0345 313 213

Based in the South of England; there are now 52 hotels in this group. They vary from a 12th-century coaching inn near Maidenhead to modern purpose-built hotels, some with leisure clubs. These clubs are free to overnight guests. Cooden in East Sussex has an outdoor pool, and many have a health club with indoor swimming pool. Most offer baby-listening and baby-sitting can be arranged in advance at some hotels. It is hard to define corporate policy within such a disparate group, but there is a Fido Dido's mega mountain bike menu and brain buster game card/colouring sheet to keep up the interest of children. Under-16s stay free if sharing their parents' room. Kirtons Resort Hotel and Country Club at Pingewood near Reading is sited around 33 acres of lake on which many international watersport events take place; a morning crèche facility operates six days a week. Randell's Hotel in Skipton (a Henry the Duck award winner) is now an associate Resort hotel. All major credit cards accepted.

Shire Inns

Head Office: 0282 414141 (no central reservation number)

A small group of elegant hotels owned and run by Daniel Thwaites brewers, thus many have a separate pub in their grounds. The range, from south to north, covers Fareham, Bristol, Kettering, Knutsford, Blackburn, Burnley (nr Brierfield), Penrith and Carlisle. Some are extended from older properties, while others – like Kettering, Bristol and Fareham – are modern, custom-built hotels cleverly sited to attract a good business clientele. Adjacent health clubs (open to hotel guests as well as a private membership), often with squash and tennis courts, help enliven the hotels at weekends when Weekend Refreshers offer reduced tariffs for two-night stays (if one night is a Saturday then a third night is given free of charge). Children under 16 share their parents' room at no charge (breakfast included); if they occupy their own room they are charged 50% of the adult tariff. Some family rooms include bunk beds. Children's menu, cots, high-chairs and baby-listening are all offered; some hotels offer a welcoming pack on arrival (particularly noteworthy is that at the North Lakes in Penrith (Cumbria), which includes a quiz and games to win a baseball cap, colouring pencils, postcard and badge; a children's club operates at weekends; high teas served 6.30-7.30pm. A Teddy Bears Picnic weekend was offered at the Millstone Hotel in Blackburn, Lancashire (the only hotel without a leisure club) during the late May and August bank holiday weekends in 1993; visits to the Museum of Childhood and Sabden Treacle Mines were arranged as well as a treasure hunt in Witton Country Park. The Crown at Carlisle, Cumbria also organised an Adventure Weekend (karting, archery, horse riding, quad bikes etc) in mid June and a Hallowe'en Horror weekend at the end of October; a third night's half-board stay was offered at no extra charge. The latest purchase by the group is the Four Seasons hotel near Manchester Airport (68% grading in Egon Ronay's Cellnet Guide 1994 Hotels & Restaurants Guide, Tel 061-904 0301). The Montcalm in Marble Arch, London is an associate hotel. Bristol, Kettering Park, Penrith and Fareham feature children's splash pools as a part of their indoor swimming pools. Dogs welcome. All major credit cards accepted.

Stakis Hotels

Reservations: 0800 262 626   Fax 041-304 1111

Located close to major business centres and trunk routes as well as in country settings, the hotels offer spacious, comfortable accommodation and 10 currently have a self-contained business centre. Guests have free use of the sports and leisure facilities. Originally based in Scotland but now with over 30 hotels scattered throughout the UK. The Stakis Lodore Swiss wins a Henry the Duck award. In 1993 Stakis Aviemore Coylumbridge Resort Hotel offered Toddlers' weeks in Jan, Mar & May, family break weekends (early Feb and end Apr), family stress breaks and a teenagers' week in April; two swimming pools, tennis courts, carpet bowls, full-time entertainment staff, Cyril the Squirrel Club and fun house (with nets, slides, tower, inflatable castle, ball pond, mirrored tunnels), breakfast parties, high teas, film shows, competitions, games, 12-16 club with special teenage activities – you name it they've thought of it. The Coylumbridge is exceptional within the Stakis Group, but it caters admirably for family holidays. Short Breaks and Family Holiday brochure highlights those group hotels that offer Cyril the Squirrel Club facilities (they vary from hotel to hotel) – several have a special Sunday morning programme of entertainment for under-12s from 8-9.30am. All major credit cards accepted.

Swallow Hotels

Reservations: Tel 091-529 4666   Fax 091-529 5062

Based in the North East but with new hotels and acquisitions in the south this is a chain of hotels that continues to improve its image. Hotels of the standing of the Birmingham Swallow are to be much admired. 28 of the 35 current hotels have leisure clubs; most include an indoor heated swimming pool (children's splash pool at Grantham and Waltham Abbey), sauna and/or steam room, solarium and spa bath (not for under-12s). Mini-gyms also feature in many (not available for under-15s). The facilities are free to overnight guests. Dundee, Newcastle and Carlisle have outdoor play areas. Children of 14 years and under sharing a room with two adults are accommodated and served a cooked breakfast free of charge. Some family rooms have three or four beds (bunks). Sammy Swallow looks after the children with a seriously corny menu ("the chef has to go a long way for our Chinese Chicken – but we think it's worth it!"), but, jokes aside, it is likely to succeed with its mix of popular favourites – omelettes, pasta, baked potatoes, pizza, yoghurt, cakes and more. The Swallow Highcliff at Bournemouth gains a Henry the Duck award; it features a fully supervised outdoor swimming pool, games room and family cottages plus Sky TV's Children's Channel, slip mats in the bathrooms and fresh milk in all rooms – unusual attention to detail. All credit cards accepted.

Voyager Hotels

No central reservations number

Part of Richard Branson's Virgin Group, Voyager Hotels are a mixture of interesting properties: Norton House in Ingliston 6 miles from Edinburgh (Lothian), Crathorne Hall near Yarm in Cleveland (North Yorkshire border) and Rhinefield House in Brockenhurst (Hampshire); there is one additional hotel outside the UK – La Residencia in Deia, Majorca. Each offers Shortbreak Holidays at special half-board tariffs for stays of two nights or more. Children under 14 stay free in their parents' room (one child per paying adult – special rates for single parent families); meal are charged as taken; children in their own room are charged 75% of adult rate. Baby-listening is offered and baby-sitting can be arranged in advance (when you should also book a high-chair and a proper cot). Due to the characterful old style of buildings it is not always possible to provide suitable family rooms, so ring some way in advance of your stay – if only to avoid (or join in as is your wont) the Whisky (hangover), Victorian, Murder Mystery and Wine appreciation weekends! Virgin Atlantic children's fun pack is offered to younger guests under the age of 12 (even diners only); at Crathorne Hall (the most family friendly) children's special meals are offered, along with toddlers' toys in the bedrooms; there are changing facilities in the Ladies and supplies of young babies' everyday requirements – from toilet steps and seats to changing mat, baby bath and hooded baby towels. Only Rhinefield House has a swimming pool (both indoor and outdoor); hotel amenities are shared with occupants of their time-share facilities. The Close in Tetbury, Glos is now under a management contract to Voyager (not listed in the following county round-up). At one stage in 1993 late bookings for the same night attracted a very low standby rate – a nice touch from the owners of the Virgin airline. All major credit cards accepted.

Whitbread Hotels

Head Office: Tel 0582 422994   Fax 0582 405680

Country Club Hotels

Reservations: Tel 0582 396969   Fax 0582 400024

A feature of the 10 hotels currently in this group is that all but two (Redwood Lodge, Bristol, Avon and Broughton Park, Lancashire) have at least one 18-hole golf course. Additionally, all feature a comprehensive range of leisure and sports facilities including swimming pools, saunas, solarium, tennis and squash courts and fitness studios. Tudor Park, Bearsted (Kent), St Pierre Park, Chepstow (Gwent, Wales) and Tewkesbury Park, Gloucestershire feature a children's play area. Redwood Lodge has a cinema; Forest of Arden, Meriden (W Midlands) has a dance studio. Some leisure clubs also offer a limited-hours crèche facility and informal eating (Splash the Dolphin's colouring and games menu) in their poolside restaurants. Under-16s stay free if sharing parents' room; occupying their own room they are charged 70% of adult rate; Z-beds and cots provided at no charge. All major credit cards accepted.

Lansbury Hotels

Reservations: Tel 0582 396922   Fax 0582 400024

43 in the group last year, but now only 19 remain as Lansbury-branded hotels. The character is fairly traditional, but they differ considerably in style ranging from old coaching inn (The Falstaff, Canterbury) to mock Tudor (Chimney House Hotel, Sandbach, Cheshire) and purpose-built modern buildings. No particular family facilities, mainly business-orientated hotels. Under-16s stay free if sharing with parents; a Z-bed or cot can be supplied. Prices are reduced for two-night B&B stays at weekends. All major credit cards accepted.

Travel Inns

Reservations: Tel 0582 482224   Fax 0582 405680

There are now 43 Travel Inns (plus 20 more expected to open in 1994), all located next to separate popular themed eating chains (Brewers Fayre – no bookings – or Beefeater – bookings advised), where breakfast is served (7-9am weekdays, 8-10am weekends and Bank Holidays). All rooms have bath and shower, always a double bed with duvet, remote-control TV, tea- and coffee-making facilities, radio/alarm and adequate writing/work space. Travel Inns currently operate a price of £33.50 per room irrespective of whether taken as a single, double or for family occupancy. Two children under 16 are accommodated free when sharing with adults. Payment is on arrival and reception closes at 11pm. Every Travel Inn has a specially adapted room for the disabled. Family-size rooms are not available at Basildon and Harlow (Essex), Birmingham (W Midlands), Cannock (Staffs), Cardiff (Wales), Longford (Gloucester), Northampton (Northants) and Tring (Herts) at these locations a second room can be booked (at weekends only – Fri, Sat & Sun) for under-16s at a charge of £16.50. "All junior beds and cots are subject to availability." No-smoking rooms are available in all locations. No dogs except guide dogs. Only Access and Visa credit cards accepted.

LONDON GROUP HOTELS

Key: QMH (Queens Moat Houses), MtCT (Mount Charlotte Thistle).
Note: This information comes from Egon Ronay's Cellnet Guide 1994 Hotels & Restaurants. Lodges (Forte Travelodge, Travel Inn, Granada, Campanile) and Inns are ungraded; the latest openings (not listed in the above Guide) are marked as NEW.
The price quoted is for a double room for two occupants with private bath and cooked breakfast in high season.
'Pool' refers to an indoor swimming pool only; prices may be considerably cheaper at weekends and for stays of more than one night.
We recommend that you call to confirm family facilities before staying at the hotels listed.

Location	Establishment	Group	Grade	Price	Tel	Rooms	Pool	Address
E1	Tower Thistle	MtCT	66%	£176	071-481 2575	808		St Katharine's Way E1 9LD
EC1	New Barbican Hotel	MtCT	51%	£100	071-251 1565	470		Central Street Clerkenwell EC1V 8DS
N1	Great Northern Hotel	Compass	60%	£83	071-837 5454	89		King's Cross N1 9AN
NW1	Kennedy Hotel	MtCT	63%	£102	071-387 4400	360		Cardington Street NW1 2LP
NW2	Holiday Inn Garden Court	Holiday Inn	NEW	£80	081-452 5001	153		Tilling Rd Brent Cross NW2 3DS
NW3	Clive Hotel	Hilton	64%	£64	071-586 2233	96		Primrose Hill Road NW3 3NA
NW3	Forte Posthouse	Forte	65%	£68	071-794 8121	140		215 Haverstock Hill NW3 4RB
NW3	Regent's Park Marriott Hotel	Marriott	73%	£192	071-722 7711	303		128 King Henry's Road NW3 3ST
NW4	Hendon Hall	MtCT	63%	£106	081-203 3341	52	yes	Ashley Lane NW4 1HE
NW8	Hilton International Regent	Hilton	73%	£148	071-722 7722	377		18 Lodge Road St John's Wood NW8 7JT
SW1	Forte Crest St James's	Forte	68%	£119	071-930 2111	256		81 Jermyn Street SW1Y 6JF
SW1	Grosvenor Thistle Hotel	MtCT	64%	£138	071-834 9494	366		101 Buckingham Palace Road SW1W 0SJ
SW1	Hyde Park Hotel	Forte	82%	£244	071-235 2000	185		66 Knightsbridge SW1Y 7LA
SW1	Royal Horseguards Thistle	MtCT	71%	£110	071-839 3400	376		2 Whitehall Court SW1A 2EJ
SW1	Royal Court Hotel	QMH	68%	£145	071-730 9191	102		Sloane Square SW1W 8EG
SW1	Royal Westminster Thistle	MtCT	71%	£146	071-834 1821	134		Buckingham Palace Road SW1W 0QT
SW1	Scandic Crown Victoria	Scandic	66%	£154	071-834 8123	210	yes	2 Bridge Place SW1V 1QA
SW1	Sheraton Park Tower	Sheraton	79%	£270	071-235 8050	295		101 Knightsbridge SW1X 7RN
SW1	Sheraton Belgravia	Sheraton	75%	£250	071-235 6040	89		20 Chesham Place SW1X 8HQ
SW1	Stakis St Ermin's	Stakis	71%	£159	071-222 7888	290		Caxton Street SW1H 0QW
SW5	Swallow International Hotel	Swallow	64%	£130	071-370 4200	417	yes	Cromwell Road SW5 0TH
SW7	Embassy House Hotel	Jarvis	59%	£106	071-584 7222	69		31 Queen's Gate SW7 5JA
SW7	Forum Hotel	Inter-Continental	62%	£144	071-370 5757	910		97 Cromwell Road SW7 4DN

Location	Establishment	Group	Grade	Price	Tel	Rooms	Pool	Address
SW7	Holiday Inn Kensington	Holiday Inns	68%	£185	071-373 2222	162		94-106 Cromwell Road SW7 4ER
SW7	Norfolk Hotel	QMH	69%	£125	071-589 8191	96		2 Harrington Road SW7 3ER
SW7	Vanderbilt Hotel	Edwardian	62%	£139	071-589 2424	223		68 Cromwell Road SW7 5BT
SW19	Cannizaro House	MtCT	76%	£138	081-879 1464	46		West Side Wimbledon Common SW19 4UF
W1	Berkshire Hotel	Edwardian	72%	£185	071-629 7474	147		350 Oxford Street W1N 0BY
W1	Britannia Inter-Continental	Inter-Continental	77%	£210	071-629 9400	317		Grosvenor Square W1A 3AN
W1	Brown's Hotel	Forte	74%	£239	071-493 6020	120		Albemarle Street W1A 4SW
W1	Churchill Inter-Continental	Inter-Continental	80%	£242	071-486 5800	414		30 Seymour Street Portman Square W1A 4ZX
W1	The Clifton-Ford	Doyle	72%	£196	071-486 6600	212		47 Welbeck Street W1M 8DN
W1	Cumberland Hotel	Forte	69%	£140	071-262 1234	390		Marble Arch W1A 4RF
W1	Forte Crest Regent's Park	Forte	64%	£121	071-388 2300	320		Carburton Street W1P 8EE
W1	Grafton Hotel	Edwardian	63%	£160	071-388 4131	324		130 Tottenham Court Road W1P 9HP
W1	Grosvenor House	Forte	83%	£256	071-499 6363	454	yes	90 Park Lane W1A 3AA
W1	Holiday Inn Mayfair	Holiday Inns	72%	£199	071-493 8282	185		3 Berkeley Street W1X 6NE
W1	Hospitality Inn Piccadilly	MtCT	64%	£149	071-930 4033	92		39 Coventry Street W1M 8EL
W1	Inter-Continental Hotel	Inter-Continental	84%	£307	071-409 3131	467		1 Hamilton Place Hyde Park Corner W1V 1QY
W1	The Langham	Hilton	75%	£222	071-636 1000	411		Portland Place W1N 3AA
W1	London Marriott Hotel	Marriott	77%	£279	071-493 1232	223		Grosvenor Square W1A 4AW
W1	London Mews Hilton on Park	Hilton	67%	£139	071-493 7222	72		2 Stanhope Row Park Lane W1Y 7HE
W1	London Hilton on Park Lane	Hilton	75%	£212	071-493 8000	448		22 Park Lane W1A 2HH
W1	Marble Arch Marriott	Marriott	68%	£177	071-723 1277	239	yes	134 George Street W1H 6DN
W1	May Fair Inter-Continental	Inter-Continental	79%	£271	071-629 7777	293	yes	Stratton Street W1A 2AN
W1	St George's Hotel	Forte	65%	£147	071-580 0111	86		Langham Place W1N 8QS
W1	The Selfridge	MtCT	75%	£181	071-408 2080	296		Orchard Street W1H 0JS
W1	Sherlock Holmes Hotel	Hilton	61%	£132	071-486 6161	125		108 Baker Street W1M 1LB
W1	The Westbury	Forte	75%	£203	071-629 7755	244		Conduit Street W1A 4UH
W2	Coburg Resort Hotel	Resort	64%	£102	071-221 2217	132		129 Bayswater Road W2 4RJ
W2	Hospitality Inn Bayswater	MtCT	60%	£102	071-262 4461	175		104 Bayswater Road W2 3HL
W2	London Embassy	Jarvis	68%	£132	071-229 1212	193		150 Bayswater Road W2 4RT
W2	Royal Lancaster Hotel	Rank	75%	£179	071-262 6737	418		Lancaster Terrace W2 2TY
W2	Whites Hotel	MtCT	77%	£198	071-262 2711	54		90 Lancaster Gate W2 3NR
W6	Novotel	Novotel	65%	£97	081-741 1555	640		1 Shortlands W6 8DR
		Copthorne	69%	£114	071-937 7211	829		Scarsdale Place Wrights Lane W8 5SR

	Hotel	Group		Price	Phone	No.		Address
W8	Kensington Palace Thistle	MtCT	67%	£131	071-937 8121	298		De Vere Gardens W8 5AF
W8	Kensington Close Hotel	Forte	59%	£99	071-937 8170	530		Wrights Lane W8 5JP
W8	Kensington Park Thistle Hotel	MtCT	67%	£166	071-937 8080	332		16-32 De Vere Gardens W8 5AG
W8	Royal Garden Hotel	Rank	82%	£191	071-937 8000	398		Kensington High Street W8 4PT
W11	Hilton International Kensington	Hilton	67%	£150	071-603 3355	603		179 Holland Park Avenue W11 4UL
W14	London Olympia Hilton	Hilton	66%	£149	071-603 3333	406		380 Kensington High Street W14 8NL
WC1	Forte Crest Bloomsbury	Forte	65%	£120	071-837 1200	284		Coram Street WC1N 1HT
WC1	Holiday Inn Kings Cross/Bloomsbury	Holiday Inns	69%	£135	071-833 3900	405	yes	1 Kings Cross Road WC1X 9HX
WC1	Kenilworth Hotel	Edwardian	63%	£172	071-637 3477	192		97 Great Russell Street WC1B 3LB
WC1	The Marlborough	Edwardian	69%	£190	071-636 5601	169		9-14 Bloomsbury Street WC1B 3QD
WC1	Hotel Russell	Forte	68%	£141	071-837 6470	328		Russell Square WC1B 5BE
WC2	Hampshire Hotel	Edwardian	77%	£220	071-839 9399	124		31 Leicester Square WC2H 7LH
WC2	Moat House	QMH	65%	£148	071-836 6666	153		10 Drury Lane WC2B 5RE
WC2	Mountbatten Hotel	Edwardian	70%	£193	071-836 4300	127		20 Monmouth Street Covent Garden WC2H 9HD
WC2	Royal Trafalgar Thistle	MtCT	65%	£135	071-930 4477	108		Whitcomb Street WC2 7HG
WC2	The Waldorf	Forte	83%	£206	071-836 2400	292		Aldwych WC2B 4DD

London Airport Heathrow

Hotel	Group		Price	Phone	No.		Address
Berkeley Arms Hotel	Jarvis	67%	£111	081-897 2121	56		Bath Road Cranford TW5 9QF
Excelsior Hotel	Forte	71%	£128	081-759 6611	839	yes	Bath Road West Drayton UB7 0DU
Forte Crest	Forte	68%	£99	081-759 2323	572		Sipson Road West Drayton UB7 0JU
Forte Posthouse (Ariel)	Forte	65%	£68	081-759 2552	180		Bath Road Hayes UB3 5AJ
Granada Lodge	Granada		£55	081-574 5875	46		M4 Junction 2/3 Heston TW5 9NA
Heathrow Hilton Hotel	Hilton	76%	£162	081-759 7755	400	yes	Terminal 4 Heathrow Airport Hounslow TW6 3AF
Holiday Inn Crowne Plaza	Holiday Inns	74%	£164	0895 445555	375	yes	Stockley Road West Drayton UB7 9NA
Park Hotel	MtCT	61%	£111	081-759 2400	306		Bath Road Longford West Drayton UB7 0EQ
Radisson Edwardian	Edwardian	76%	£206	081-759 6311	459		Bath Road Hayes UB3 5AW
Ramada Hotel Heathrow	Ramada	66%	£115	081-897 6363	636	yes	Bath Road Hounslow TW6 2AQ
Sheraton Heathrow Hotel	Sheraton	70%	£103	081-759 2424	415	yes	Bath Road West Drayton UB7 0HJ
Sheraton Skyline	Sheraton	73%	£164	081-759 2535	353	yes	Bath Road Hayes UB3 5BP

see also entries under Berkshire, Slough.

London Airport Gatwick

Location	Establishment	Group	Grade	Price	Tel	Rooms	Pool	Address
	Chequers Thistle	MtCT	63%	£106	0293 786992	78	yes	Brighton Road Horley RH6 8PH
	Copthorne Effingham Park	Copthorne	72%	£126	0342 714994	122	yes	West Park Road Copthorne RH10 3EU
	Copthorne London Gatwick	Copthorne	69%	£128	0342 714971	227		Copthorne nr Crawley RH10 3PG
	Europa Gatwick		68%	£117	0293 886666	211	yes	Balcombe Road Maidenbower nr Crawley RH10 4ZR
	Forte Crest Gatwick	Forte	74%	£99	0293 567070	474	yes	North Terminal Gatwick Airport RH6 0PH
	Forte Posthouse Gatwick	Forte	63%	£68	0293 771621	210		Povey Cross Road Horley RH6 0BA
	Gatwick Concorde Hotel	QMH	61%	£104	0293 53441	116		Church Road Lowfield Heath Crawley RH11 0PQ
	Gatwick Hilton International	Hilton	72%	£159	0293 518080	550	yes	Gatwick RH11 0PD
	Holiday Inn Gatwick	Holiday Inns	68%	£118	0293 529991	223	yes	Langley Drive Crawley RH11 7SX
	Moat House	QMH	62%	£74	0293 785599	121		Longbridge Roundabout Horley RH6 0AB
	Ramada Hotel Gatwick	Ramada	70%	£134	0293 820169	255	yes	Povey Cross Road Horley RH6 0BE

ENGLAND GROUP HOTELS

Key: QMH (Queens Moat Houses), MtCT (Mount Charlotte Thistle).
Note: This information comes from *Egon Ronay's Cellnet Guide 1994 Hotels & Restaurants*. Lodges (Forte Travelodge, Travel Inn, Granada, Campanile) and Inns are ungraded.
The price quoted is for a double room for two occupants with private bath and cooked breakfast in high season.
*Pool refers to an indoor swimming pool only; prices may be considerably cheaper at weekends and for stays of more than one night.
We recommend that you call to confirm family facilities before staying at the hotels listed.

Avon

Location	Establishment	Group	Grade	Price	Tel	Rooms	Pool	Address
Alveston	Forte Posthouse	Forte		62%	£68	0454 412521	74		Thornbury Road Alveston nr Bristol BS12 2LL
Bath	Bath Spa Hotel	Forte		87%	£183	0225 444424	100	yes	Sydney Road Bath BA2 6JF
Bath	Francis Hotel	Forte		67%	£125	0225 424257	93		Queen Square Bath BA1 2HH
Bath	Hilton National	Hilton		67%	£120	0225 463411	150	yes	Walcot Street Bath BA1 5BJ
Bath	Priory Hotel	Select		79%	£164	0225 331922	21		Weston Road Bath BA1 2XT
Bath	Royal Crescent Hotel	QMH		84%	£170	0225 319090	42		16 Royal Crescent Bath BA1 2LS
Bristol	Aztec Hotel	Shire Inns		74%	£102	0454 301090	88	yes	Aztec West Business Park Almondsbury Bristol BS12 4TS
Bristol	Bristol Marriott Hotel	Marriott		73%	£136	0272 294281	289	yes	Lower Castle Street Bristol BS1 3AD
Bristol	Forte Crest	Forte		67%	£107	0272 564242	197	yes	Filton Road Hambrook Bristol BS16 1QX
Bristol	Grand Hotel	MtCT		62%	£96	0272 291645	170		Broad Street Bristol BS1 2EL
Bristol	Hilton Hotel	Hilton		69%	£110	0272 260041	201	yes	Redcliffe Way Bristol BS1 6NJ
Bristol	Holiday Inn Crowne Plaza	QMH		72%	£105	0272 255010	132	yes	Victoria Street Bristol BS1 6HY
Bristol	Redwood Lodge	Country Club		64%	£85	0275 393901	108	yes	Beggar Bush Lane Failand Bristol BS8 3TG
Bristol	Stakis Bristol Hotel	Stakis		61%	£109	0454 201144	111	yes	Woodlands Lane Patchway Bristol BS12 4JF
Bristol	Swallow Royal Hotel	Swallow		77%	£118	0272 255100	242	yes	College Green Bristol BS1 5TE
Bristol	Unicorn Hotel	Rank		63%	£70	0272 230333	245		Prince Street Bristol BS1 4QF
Gordano	Forte Travelodge	Forte			£42	0275 373709	40		M5 Gordano Service Area nr Portbury BS20 9XG
Hunstrete	Hunstrete House	Clipper		72%	£150	0761 490490	24		Hunstrete Chelwood nr Bath BA18 4NS
Sedgemoor	Forte Travelodge	Forte			£42	0934 750831	40		M5 N'bound Welcome Break Sedgemoor Weston-super-Mare
Weston-super-Mare	Grand Atlantic	Forte		64%	£95	0934 626543	76		Beach Road Weston-super-Mare BS23 1BA
Winterbourne	Grange Resort Hotel	Resort		68%	£100	0454 777333	52	yes	Northwoods nr Winterbourne BS17 1RP

Bedfordshire

Location	Establishment	Group	Grade	Price	Tel	Rooms	Pool	Address
Bedford	Moat House	QMH	65%	£70	0234 355131	100		2 St Mary's Street Bedford MK42 0AR
Dunstable	Forte Travelodge	Forte		£42	0525 211177	28		A5 Watling Street Hockliffe Dunstable LU7 9LZ
Leighton Buzzard	The Swan	Resort	64%	£80	0525 372148	38		High Street Leighton Buzzard LU7 7EA
Luton	Forte Crest	Forte	60%	£90	0582 575911	93		Waller Avenue Luton LU4 9RU
Luton	Forte Posthouse	Forte	57%	£68	0582 575955	117		641 Dunstable Road Luton LU4 8RQ
Luton	Strathmore Thistle	MtCT	63%	£106	0582 34199	150		Arndale Centre Luton LU1 2TR
Marston	Forte Travelodge	Forte		£42	0234 766755	32		Jnct 13 M1/A421 Beancroft Rd Marston Moretaine MK43 0PZ
Toddington	Granada Lodge	Granada		£45	0525 873881	43		Toddington Service Area M1 Sbnd nr Dunstable LU5 6HR
Woburn	Bedford Arms	MtCT	63%	£104	0525 290441	55		George Street Woburn nr Milton Keynes MK17 9PX

Berkshire

Location	Establishment	Group	Grade	Price	Tel	Rooms	Pool	Address
Ascot	Berystede Hotel	Forte	67%	£129	0344 23311	91		Bagshot Road Sunninghill Ascot SL5 9JH
Ascot	Royal Berkshire	Hilton	76%	£126	0344 23322	63	yes	London Road Sunninghill Ascot SL5 0PP
Bracknell	Hilton National	Hilton	69%	£126	0344 424801	167		Bagshot Road Bracknell RG12 3QJ
Elcot	Elcot Park Resort Hotel	Resort	67%	£100	0488 58100	75	yes	Elcot nr Newbury RG16 8NJ
Hungerford	Bear Hotel	Resort	63%	£72	0488 682512	41		Charnham Street Hungerford RG17 0EL
Hurley	Ye Olde Bell	Resort	65%	£100	0628 825881	36		High Street Hurley nr Maidenhead SL6 5LX
Maidenhead/Windsor	Holiday Inn	Holiday Inns	66%	£147	0628 23444	189	yes	Manor Lane Maidenhead SL6 2RA
Newbury	Chequers Hotel	Forte	66%	£113	0635 38000	56		Oxford Street Newbury RG13 1JB
Newbury	Hilton National	Hilton	69%	£85	0635 529000	104	yes	Pinchington Lane Newbury RG14 7HL
Newbury	Stakis Newbury Hotel	Stakis	67%	£108	0635 247010	112	yes	Oxford Road Newbury RG16 8XY
Pingewood	Kirtons Farm Country Club	Resort	60%	£100	0734 500885	81	yes	Pingewood Reading RG3 3UN
Reading	Forte Posthouse	Forte	64%	£68	0734 875485	138	yes	500 Basingstoke Road Reading RG2 0SL
Reading	Forte Travelodge	Forte		£42	0734 750618	36		Basingstoke Road Reading RG2 0JE
Reading	Holiday Inn	QMH	71%	£119	0734 391818	112	yes	Richfield Avenue Caversham Bridge Reading RG1 8BD
Reading	Ramada Hotel	Ramada	68%	£109	0734 586222	194	yes	Oxford Road Reading RG1 7RH
Sindlesham	Reading Moat House	QMH	70%	£132	0734 351035	96		Mill Lane Sindlesham nr Wokingham RG11 5DF
Slough	Copthorne Hotel	Copthorne	71%	£135	0753 516222	219		Cippenham Lane Slough SL1 2YE
Slough	Courtyard by Marriott	Marriott	60%	£70	0753 551551	148	yes	Church Street Chalvey nr Slough SL1 2NH

Slough	Heathrow/Slough Marriott	Marriott	73%	£135	0753 544244	352	yes	Ditton Road Langley Slough SL3 8PT
Windsor	Castle Hotel	Forte	67%	£146	0753 851011	104		High Street Windsor SL4 1LJ
Windsor	Oakley Court	QMH	78%	£168	0628 74141	92		Windsor Road Water Oakley nr Windsor SL4 5UR
Wokingham	Stakis St Anne's Manor	Stakis	69%	£130	0734 772550	130	yes	London Road Wokingham RG11 1ST

Buckinghamshire

Aylesbury	Forte Posthouse	Forte	69%	£68	0296 393388	94	yes	Aston Clinton Road Aylesbury HP22 5AA
Beaconsfield	Bellhouse Hotel	De Vere	67%	£115	0753 887211	136	yes	Oxford Road Beaconsfield HP9 2XE
Burnham	Burnham Beeches Moat House	QMH	68%	£110	0628 603333	75	yes	Grove Road Burnham SL1 8DP
Chenies	Bedford Arms Thistle	MtCT	64%	£108	0923 283301	10		Chenies nr Rickmansworth WD3 6EQ
Gerrards Cross	Bull Hotel	De Vere	63%	£125	0753 885995	95		Gerrards Cross SL9 7PA
High Wycombe	Forte Posthouse	Forte	65%	£68	0494 442100	106		Crest Road High Wycombe HP11 1TL
Marlow	Compleat Angler Hotel	Forte	73%	£164	0628 484444	64		Marlow Bridge Marlow SL7 1RG
Milton Keynes	Forte Crest	Forte	68%	£107	0908 667722	151	yes	500 Saxon Gate Milton Keynes MK9 2HQ

Cambridgeshire

Cambridge	Cambridgeshire Moat House	QMH	63%	£78	0954 780555	100	yes	Bar Hill Cambridge CB3 8EU
Cambridge	Forte Posthouse	Forte	67%	£68	0223 237000	118	yes	Lakeview Bridge Road Impington Cambridge CB4 4PH
Cambridge	Garden House	QMH	69%	£135	0223 63421	118		Granta Place Mill Lane Cambridge CB2 1RT
Cambridge	Holiday Inn	Holiday Inns	68%	£115	0223 464466	199	yes	Downing Street Cambridge CB2 3DT
Cambridge	University Arms	De Vere	65%	£110	0223 351241	117		Regent Street Cambridge CB2 1AD
Ely	Forte Travelodge	Forte		£42	0353 668499	39		A10/A142 Roundabout Ely
Ely	Lamb Hotel	QMH	62%	£75	0353 663574	32		2 Lynn Road Ely CB7 4EJ
Fenstanton	Forte Travelodge	Forte		£42	0954 30919	40		A604 Eastbound Fenstanton nr Cambridge
Huntingdon	Old Bridge Hotel	Poste Hotels	68%	£90	0480 52681	26		1 High Street Huntingdon PE18 6TQ
Lolworth	Forte Travelodge	Forte		£42	0954 781335	20		A604 Huntingdon Road Lolworth Bar Hill CB3 8DR
Peterborough	Butterfly Hotel	Butterfly	63%	£70	0733 64240	70		Thorpe Meadows Longthorpe Parkway Pborough PE3 6GA
Peterborough	Forte Posthouse	Forte	60%	£68	0733 240209	90	yes	Gt North Rd Norman Cross Peterborough PE7 3TB
Peterborough	Forte Travelodge	Forte		£42	0733 231109	32		A1 Gt North Rd Alwalton Village nr Peterborough PE7 3UR
Peterborough	Moat House	QMH	64%	£92	0733 289000	125	yes	Thorpe Wood Peterborough PE3 6SG
Peterborough	Swallow Hotel	Swallow	69%	£99	0733 371111	163	yes	Lynch Road Peterborough PE2 0GB
Swavesey	Forte Travelodge	Forte		£42	0954 789113	36		A604 Cambridge Road Swavesey nr Cambridge
Wansford-in-England	Haycock Hotel	Poste Hotels	70%	£90	0780 782223	51		Wansford-in-England Peterborough PE8 6JA

Location	Establishment	Group	Grade	Price	Tel	Rooms	Pool	Address
Cheshire								
Alsager	Manor House	Compass	65%	£70	0270 884000	57	yes	Audley Road Alsager ST7 2QQ
Bramhall	Moat House	QMH	63%	£85	061-439 8116	65		Bramhall Lane South Bramhall SK7 2EB
Bunbury	Wild Boar	Rank	67%	£78	0829 260309	37		Whitchurch Road Bunbury nr Tarporley CW6 9NW
Burtonwood	Forte Travelodge	Forte		£42	0925 710376	40		M62 Welcome Break Burtonwood Warrington WA5 3AX
Chester	Abbots Well	Jarvis	62%	£85	0244 332121	127	yes	Whitchurch Road Christleton Chester CH3 5QL
Chester	Blossoms Hotel	Forte	63%	£107	0244 323186	64		St John Street Chester CH1 1HL
Chester	Chester International	QMH	69%	£145	0244 322330	152		Trinity Street Chester CH1 2BD
Chester	Chester Resort Hotel	Resort	62%	£60	0244 851551	113		Backford Cross Chester CH1 6PE
Chester	Forte Posthouse	Forte	62%	£68	0244 680111	105	yes	Wrexham Road Chester CH4 9DL
Crewe	Forte Travelodge	Forte		£42	0270 883157	42		Jnct 16 M6/A500 Alsager Rd Barthomley nr Crewe CW2 5PT
Knutsford	Cottons Hotel	Shire Inns	65%	£112	0565 650333	82	yes	Manchester Road Knutsford WA16 0SU
Knutsford	Forte Travelodge	Forte		£42	0565 652187	32		A556 Chester Road Tabley Knutsford WA16 0PP
Mottram St Andrew	Mottram Hall	De Vere	70%	£140	0625 828135	133	yes	Mottram St Andrew Prestbury SK10 4QT
Nantwich	Rookery Hall	Select	79%	£118	0270 610016	45		Worleston nr Nantwich CW5 6DQ
Parkgate	Ship Hotel	Forte	58%	£60	051-336 3931	26		The Parade Parkgate The Wirral L64 6SA
Runcorn	Campanile Hotel	Campanile		£44	0928 581771	53		Lowlands Road Runcorn WA7 5TP
Runcorn	Forte Posthouse	Forte	62%	£70	0928 714000	136	yes	Wood Lane Beechwood Runcorn WA7 3HA
Sandbach	Chimney House	Lansbury	62%	£81	0270 764141	48		Congleton Road Sandbach CW11 0ST
Stockport	Forte Travelodge	Forte		£42	0625 875292	32		A253 London Road South Adlington Stockport SK12 4NA
Stockport	Travel Inn	Travel Inns		£43	061-499 1944	41		Finney Lane Heald Green Stockport SK8 2QH
Warrington	Holiday Inn Garden Court	Holiday Inns	65%	£77	0925 838779	100		Woolston Grange Avenue Woolston Warrington WA1
Warrington	Lord Daresbury Hotel	De Vere	67%	£115	0925 267331	141	yes	Chester Road Daresbury Warrington WA4 4BB
Warrington	Travel Inn	Travel Inns		£43	0582 482224	40		Winwick Road Warrington WA1
Wilmslow	Moat House	QMH	58%	£96	0625 529201	125	yes	Altrincham Road Wilmslow SK9 4LR
Cleveland								
Crathorne	Crathorne Hall	Voyager	72%	£110	0642 700398	37		Crathorne nr Yarm Cleveland TS15 0AR
Middlesbrough	Hospitality Inn	MtCT	59%	£92	0642 232000	180		Fry Street Middlesbrough TS1 1JH
Stockton-on-Tees	Swallow Hotel	Swallow	67%	£92	0642 679721	124	yes	10 John Walker Square Stockton-on-Tees TS18 1AQ
Thornaby-on-Tees	Forte Posthouse	Forte	60%	£68	0642 591213	135		Low Lane By Stainton Village nr Thornaby-on-Tees TS17 9LW

Cornwall

Saltash	Granada Lodge	Granada		£45	0752 848408	31		A38 By-Pass Saltash PL12 6LF

Cumbria

Borrowdale	Stakis Lodore Swiss Hotel	Stakis	71%	£120	076 87 77285	70	yes	Borrowdale Keswick CA12 5UX
Bowness-on-Windermere	Belsfield Hotel	Forte	62%	£112	053 94 42448	64	yes	Kendal Road Bowness-on-Windermere LA23 3EL
Bowness-on-Windermere	Old England Hotel	Forte	65%	£136	053 94 42444	79		Church Street Bowness-on-Windermere LA23 3DF
Carlisle	Granada Lodge	Granada	59%	£45	069 74 73131	39		M6 Junction 41/42 Southwaite Carlisle CA4 0NT
Carlisle	Swallow Hilltop	Swallow	65%	£70	0228 29255	92	yes	London Road Carlisle CA1 2PQ
Grasmere	The Swan	Forte	65%	£148	053 94 35551	36		Grasmere nr Ambleside LA22 9RF
Keswick	Keswick Hotel	Principal	60%	£70	076 87 72020	66		Station Road Keswick CA12 4NQ
Penrith	Forte Travelodge	Forte		£42	0768 66958	32		A66 Redhills Penrith CA11 0DT
Penrith	North Lakes Hotel	Shire Inns	71%	£108	0768 68111	85	yes	Ullswater Road Penrith CA11 8QT
Ullswater	Leeming House	Forte	75%	£164	076 84 86622	40		Watermillock Ullswater CA11 0JJ
Wetheral	The Crown	Shire Inns	70%	£106	0228 561888	51	yes	Wetheral nr Carlisle CA4 8ES

Derbyshire

Castle Donington	Donington Thistle	MtCT	70%	£118	0332 850700	110	yes	East Midlands Airport Castle Donington DE74 2SH
Chesterfield	Forte Travelodge	Forte		£42	0246 455441	20		A61 Brimington Road North Wittington Moor Chesterfield
Derby	Forte Posthouse	Forte	61%	£68	0332 514933	62		Pastures Hill Littleover Derby DE3 7BA
Dovedale	Peveril of the Peak	Forte	60%	£102	033 529 333	47		Thorpe Dovedale nr Ashbourne DE6 2AW
Matlock Bath	New Bath Hotel	Forte	63%	£118	0629 583275	55	yes	New Bath Road Matlock Bath DE4 3PX
Morley	Breadsall Priory	Country Club	69%	£108	0332 832235	91		Moor Road Morley nr Derby DE7 6DL
Newton Solney	Newton Park	Jarvis	67%	£111	0283 703568	51	yes	Newton Solney Burton-on-Trent DE15 0SS
Rowsley	Peacock Hotel	Jarvis	64%	£116	0629 733518	14		Rowsley Matlock DE4 2EB
South Normanton	Swallow Hotel	Swallow	69%	£96	0773 812000	161	yes	Carter Lane East South Normanton DE55 2EH

Location	Establishment	Group	Grade Price	Tel	Rooms	Pool	Address
Devon							
Barnstaple	Imperial Hotel	Forte	60% £87	0271 45861	56		Taw Vale Parade Barnstaple EX32 8NB
Exeter	Forte Crest	Forte	69% £100	0392 412812	110	yes	Southernhay East Exeter EX1 1QF
Exeter	Rougemont Hotel	MtCT	63% £79	0392 54982	90		Queen Street Exeter EX4 3SP
Exeter	Royal Clarence	QMH	71% £98	0392 58464	56		Cathedral Yard Exeter EX1 1HD
Exmouth	Imperial Hotel	Forte	60% £116	0395 274761	57		The Esplanade Exmouth EX8 2SW
Okehampton	Forte Travelodge	Forte	£42	0837 52124	32		A30 Sourton Cross nr Okehampton EX20 4LY
Paignton	Palace Hotel	Forte	60% £100	0803 555121	52		Esplanade Road Paignton TQ4 6BJ
Plymouth	Campanile Hotel	Campanile	£44	0752 601087	50		Marsh Mills Longbridge Road Plymouth PL6 8LD
Plymouth	Copthorne Hotel	Copthorne	70% £118	0752 224161	135	yes	Armada Way Plymouth PL1 1AR
Plymouth	Forte Posthouse	Forte	65% £68	0752 662828	106		Cliff Road The Hoe Plymouth PL1 3DL
Plymouth	Moat House	QMH	70% £118	0752 662866	217	yes	Armada Way Plymouth PL1 2HJ
Plymouth	Novotel	Novotel	62% £70	0752 221422	100		Marsh Mills Roundabout Plymouth PL6 8NH
Tiverton	Forte Travelodge	Forte	£42	0884 821087	40		Sampford Peverell Service Area M5 J27 nr Tiverton EX16 4LY
Torquay	Imperial Hotel	Forte	81% £160	0803 294301	167	yes	Parkhill Road Torquay TQ1 2DG
Dorset							
Bournemouth	Forte Posthouse	Forte	59% £68	0202 553262	98		The Landsowne Bournemouth BH1 2PR
Bournemouth	Royal Bath Hotel	De Vere	73% £140	0202 555555	131	yes	Bath Road Bournemouth BH1 2EW
Bournemouth	Swallow Highcliff Hotel	Swallow	70% £120	0202 557702	157		St Michael's Road West Cliff Bournemouth BH2 5DU
Christchurch	Travel Inn	Travel Inns	£43	0202 485376	38		Somerford Road Christchurch Bournemouth BH23 3QG
Ferndown	Dormy Hotel	De Vere	71% £105	0202 872121	128	yes	New Road Ferndown BH22 8ES
Mudeford	Avonmouth Hotel	Forte	59% £99	0202 483434	41		95 Mudeford Christchurch BH23 3NT
Poole	Hospitality Inn	MtCT	63% £78	0202 666800	68		The Quay Poole BH15 1HD
Poole	Travel Inn	Travel Inns	NEW £43	0202 874210	35		Ringwood Road Tricketts Cross Ferndown BH22 9BB
Shaftesbury	Grosvenor Hotel	Forte	62% £87	0747 52282	35		The Commons Shaftesbury SP7 8JA
Sherborne	Eastbury Hotel	Clipper	67% £98	0935 813131	15		Long Street Sherborne DT9 3BY
Sherborne	Forte Posthouse	Forte	59% £68	0935 813191	59		Horsecastles Lane Sherborne DT9 6BB
Durham							
Darlington	Blackwell Grange Moat House	QMH	62% £98	0325 380888	99		Blackwell Grange Darlington DL3 8QH

Town	Hotel	Group	Discount	Price	Phone	Rooms	Address	
Darlington	St George Thistle	MtCT	56%	£79	0325 332631	59	Teesside Airport nr Darlington DL2 1RH	
Darlington	Swallow King's Head	Swallow	57%	£86	0325 380222	85	Priestgate Darlington DL1 1LW	
Durham	Royal County Hotel	Swallow	67%	£110	091-386 6821	150	Old Elvet Durham DH1 3JN	yes

Essex

Town	Hotel	Group	Discount	Price	Phone	Rooms	Address	
Basildon	Campanile Hotel	Campanile		£44	0268 530810	98	Southend Arterial Road Pipps Hill Basildon SS14 3AE	
Basildon	Forte Posthouse	Forte	59%	£68	0268 533955	110	Cranes Farm Road Basildon SS14 3DG	
Basildon	Travel Inn	Travel Inns		£43	0268 522227	42	Felmores East Mayne Basildon SS13 1BW	
Brentwood	Forte Posthouse	Forte		£42	0277 810819	22	A127 East Horndon nr Brentwood CM13 3LL	
Brentwood	Moat House	Forte	61%	£68	0277 260260	111	Brook Street Brentwood CM14 5NF	yes
Brentwood	Forte Posthouse	QMH	67%	£118	0277 225252	33	London Road Brentwood CM14 4NR	
Colchester	Forte Posthouse	Forte	61%	£68	0206 767740	110	A604 Abbots Lane Eight Ash Green CO6 3QL	
Epping	Saracen's Head	Forte	63%	£68	0992 573137	79	High Road Bell Common Epping CM16 4DG	yes
Great Dunmow	Green Man	Forte	58%	£97	0371 873901	24	High Street Great Dunmow CM6 1AG	
Harlow	Moat House	Forte	60%	£102	0279 442521	55	Mulberry Green Old Town Harlow CM17 0ET	
Harlow	Heybridge Moat House	QMH	68%	£72	0279 422441	120	Southern Way Harlow CM18 7BA	
Ingatestone	Blue Boar	QMH	68%	£85	0277 355355	22	Roman Road Ingatestone CM4 9AB	
Maldon	Moat House	QMH	59%	£97	0621 852681	28	3 Silver Street Maldon CM9 7QE	
North Stifford	Travel Inn	Forte	61%	£103	0375 390909	126	High Street North Stifford nr Grays RM16 1UE	
Old Harlow	Granada Lodge	Travel Inns		£43	0279 442545	38	Cambridge Road Old Harlow CM20 2EP	
Thurrock	Swallow Hotel	Granada		£55	0708 891111	35	M25 J 30/31 Dartford Crossing Thurrock RM16 3BG	
Waltham Abbey	Swallow Hotel	Swallow	66%	£110	0992 717170	163	Old Shire Lane Waltham Abbey EN9 3LX	

Gloucestershire

Town	Hotel	Group	Discount	Price	Phone	Rooms	Address	
Cheltenham	Golden Valley Thistle	MtCT	69%	£90	0242 232691	124	Gloucester Road Cheltenham GL51 0TS	yes
Cheltenham	Hotel de la Bere	Forte	64%	£98	0242 237771	57	Southam Cheltenham GL52 3NH	
Cheltenham	Queen's Hotel	Forte	69%	£119	0242 514724	74	The Promenade Cheltenham GL50 1NN	
Cheltenham	Travel Inn	Travel Inns		£43	0242 233447	40	Tewkesbury Road Uckington Cheltenham GL51 9SL	
Cirencester	Fleece Hotel	Resort	64%	£80	0285 658507	30	Market Square Cirencester GL7 4NZ	
Gloucester	Travel Inn	Travel Inns		£43	0452 862521	40	Witcombe nr Gloucester GL3 4SS	
Gloucester	Travel Inn	Travel Inns		£43	0452 532519	40	Tewkesbury Road Longford Gloucester GL2 9BE	
Stonehouse	Stonehouse Court	Clipper	68%	£98	0453 825155	37	Bristol Road Stonehouse GL10 3RA	
Stow-on-the-Wold	Unicorn Hotel	Forte	59%	£100	0451 830257	20	Sheep Street Stow-on-the-Wold GL54 1HQ	

Location	Establishment	Group	Grade	Price	Tel	Rooms	Pool	Address
Tewkesbury	Royal Hop Pole	Forte	66%	£105	0684 293236	29		Church Street Tewkesbury GL20 5RT
Tewkesbury	Tewkesbury Park	Country Club	62%	£98	0684 295405	78	yes	Lincoln Green Lane Tewkesbury GL20 7DN

Greater Manchester

Location	Establishment	Group	Grade	Price	Tel	Rooms	Pool	Address
Bolton	Forte Posthouse	Forte	58%	£68	0204 651511	96		Beaumont Road Bolton BL3 4TA
Bolton	Pack Horse Hotel	De Vere	62%	£60	0204 27261	73		Nelson Square Bradshawgate Bolton BL1 1DP
Manchester	Charterhouse Hotel	Hidden	72%	£121	061-236 9999	58		Oxford Street Manchester M60 7HA
Manchester	Copthorne Hotel	Copthorne	70%	£121	061-873 7321	166	yes	Clippers Quay Salford Quays Manchester M5 3DL
Manchester	Forte Posthouse	Forte	60%	£68	061-998 7090	190		Palatine Road Northenden Manchester M22 4EH
Manchester	Granada Lodge	Granada		£45	061-410 0076	37		M62 Junction 18/19 Birch Manchester OL10 2QH
Manchester	Holiday Inn Crowne Plaza	Holiday Inns	73%	£124	061-236 3333	503	yes	Peter Street Manchester M60 2DS
Manchester	Novotel	Novotel	62%	£80	061-799 3535	119		Worsley Brow Worsley Manchester M28 4YA
Manchester	Hotel Piccadilly	Jarvis	73%	£138	061-236 8414	271	yes	Piccadilly Plaza Manchester M60 1QR
Manchester	Portland Thistle	MtCT	69%	£120	061-228 3400	205	yes	Portland Street Manchester M1 6DP
Manchester	Ramada Hotel	Ramada	73%	£115	061-835 2555	200	yes	Blackfriars Street Manchester M3 2EQ
Manchester	Victoria & Albert Hotel	Granada	73%	£136	061-832 1188	132		Water Street Manchester M60 9EA
Manchester Airport	Forte Crest	Forte	65%	£107	061-437 5811	292	yes	Ringway Road Wythenshawe M22 5NS
Manchester Airport	Hilton International	Hilton	71%	£159	061-436 4404	223	yes	Outwood Lane Ringway Manchester Airport M22 5WP
Standish	Almond Brook Moat House	QMH	63%	£95	0257 425588	126	yes	Almond Brook Road Standish nr Wigan WN6 0SR
Stockport	Alma Lodge	Jarvis	61%	£94	061-483 4431	56		149 Buxton Road Stockport SK2 6EL

Hampshire

Location	Establishment	Group	Grade	Price	Tel	Rooms	Pool	Address
Alton	Forte Travelodge	Forte		£42	0420 62659	31		A31 Four Marks Winchester Road Alton GU34 5HZ
Alton	The Swan	Forte	58%	£80	0420 83777	36		High Street Alton GU34 1AT
Ampfield	Potters Heron Hotel	Lansbury	60%	£87	0703 266611	54		Ampfield nr Romsey SO51 9ZF
Andover	White Hart Inn	Forte		£82	0264 352266	20		Bridge Street Andover SP10 1BH
Barton Stacey	Forte Travelodge	Forte		£42	0264 72260	20		A303 Barton Stacey nr Andover SO21 3NP
Basingstoke	Audleys Wood	MtCT	75%	£123	0256 817555	71		Alton Road Basingstoke RG25 2JT
Basingstoke	Forte Travelodge	Forte		£42	0256 843566	32		Winchester Road Basingstoke RG22 6HN

Location	Hotel	Group	%	£	Phone	Rooms		Address
Basingstoke	Hilton National	Hilton	66%	£87	0256 460460	144	yes	Old Common Road Black Dam Basingstoke RG21 3PR
Basingstoke	The Ringway	Hilton	65%	£64	0256 20212	134	yes	Aldermaston Roundabout Ringway North Basingstoke RG24 9NV
Basingstoke	Travel Inn	Travel Inns		£43	0256 811477	49		Worting Road Basingstoke RG22 6PG
Brockenhurst	Balmer Lawn Hotel	Hilton	65%	£90	0590 23116	58	yes	Lyndhurst Road Brockenhurst SO42 7ZB
Brockenhurst	Rhinefield House	Voyager	68%	£95	0590 22922	34		Rhinefield Road Brockenhurst SO42 7QB
Eastleigh	Forte Travelodge	Forte		£42	0703 616813	32		Twyford Road Eastleigh nr Southampton
Eastleigh	Forte Crest Southampton	Forte	66%	£95	0703 619700	120	yes	Leigh Road Eastleigh SO5 5PG
Fareham	Forte Posthouse	Forte	61%	£68	0329 844644	126	yes	Cartwright Drive Titchfield Fareham
Farnham	Solent Hotel	Shire Inns	75%	£101	0489 880000	90	yes	Solent Business Park Whiteley Fareham PO15 7AJ
Farnborough	Forte Crest	Forte	66%	£119	0252 545051	110		Lynchford Road Farnborough GU14 6AZ
Fleet	Forte Travelodge	Forte		£42	0252 815578	40	yes	M3 Fleet Service Area Hartley Wintney Basingstoke RG27 8BN
Havant	Forte Posthouse	Forte	62%	£68	0705 465011	92		Northney Road Hayling Island Havant PO11 0NQ
Lymington	Stanwell House	Clipper	65%	£98	0590 677123	35		High Street Lymington SO41 9AA
Portsmouth	Forte Posthouse	Forte	66%	£68	0705 827651	163	yes	Pembroke Road Southsea Portsmouth PO1 2TA
Portsmouth	Hilton National	Hilton	61%	£93	0705 219111	122		Eastern Road Farlington Portsmouth PO6 1UN
Portsmouth	Hospitality Inn	MtCT	59%	£79	0705 731281	115		South Parade Southsea Portsmouth PO4 0RN
Portsmouth	Pendragon Hotel	Forte	73%	£87	0705 823201	49		Clarence Parade Southsea Portsmouth PO5 2HY
Portsmouth	Portsmouth Marriott Hotel	Marriott		£127	0705 383151	170	yes	North Harbour Cosham Portsmouth PO6 4SH
Romsey	White Horse Hotel	Forte	63%	£101	0794 512341	33		Market Place Romsey SO51 8ZJ
Southampton	Dolphin Hotel	Forte	60%	£82	0703 339955	73		High Street Southampton SO9 2DS
Southampton	Forte Posthouse	Forte	58%	£68	0703 330777	128	yes	Herbert Walker Avenue Southampton SO1 0HJ
Southampton	Hilton National	Hilton	68%	£94	0703 702700	135		Bracken Place Chilworth Southampton SO2 4HB
Southampton	Novotel	Novotel	62%	£85	0703 330550	121		1 West Quay Road Southampton SO1 0RA
Southampton	Polygon Hotel	Forte	65%	£77	0703 330055	119		Cumberland Place Southampton SO9 4GD
Southampton	Travel Inn	Travel Inns	NEW	£43	0703 732262	32		Romsey Road Nursling Southampton SO1 9XJ
Sutton Scotney North	Forte Travelodge	Forte		£42	0962 761016	31		A34 Northside Service Area nr Winchester SO21 3JY
Sutton Scotney South	Forte Travelodge	Forte		£42	0962 760779	40		A34 Southside Service Area nr Winchester SO21 3JY
Winchester	Forte Crest	Forte	69%	£68	0962 861611	94	yes	Paternoster Row Winchester SO23 9LQ

Hereford & Worcester

Location	Hotel	Group	%	£	Phone	Rooms		Address
Abberley	Elms Hotel	QMH	71%	£97	0299 896666	25		Stockton Road Abberley nr Worcester WR6 6AT
Broadway	Lygon Arms	Savoy Group	78%	£171	0386 852255	65	yes	High Street Broadway WR12 7DU
Bromsgrove	Perry Hall	Jarvis	56%	£93	0527 579976	58		Kidderminster Road Bromsgrove B61 7JN
Bromsgrove	Stakis Country Court	Stakis	69%	£116	021-447 7888	141	yes	Birmingham Road Bromsgrove B61 0JB

Location	Establishment	Group	Grade	Price	Tel	Rooms	Pool	Address
Droitwich	Forte Travelodge	Forte		£42	0527 86545	32		A38 Rashwood Hill Droitwich WR9 8DA
Hartlebury	Forte Travelodge	Forte		£42	0299 250553	32		A449 S'bound Shorthill Nurseries nr Kidderminster DY11 6DR
Hereford	Moat House	QMH	63%	£70	0432 354301	60		Belmont Road Hereford HR2 7BF
Hereford	Travel Inn	Travel Inns		£43	0432 274853	40		Holmer Road Holmer nr Hereford HR4 9RS
Malvern	Abbey Hotel	De Vere	62%	£70	0684 892332	107		Abbey Road Malvern WR14 3ET
Redditch	Campanile Hotel	Campanile		£44	0527 510710	50		Far Moor Lane Winyates Green Redditch B98 0SD
Stourport-on-Severn	Moat House	QMH	62%	£49	0299 827733	68		Hartlebury Road Stourport-on-Severn DY13 9LT
Worcester	Fownes Resort Hotel	Resort	70%	£100	0905 613151	61		City Walls Road Worcester WR1 2AP
Worcester	Giffard Hotel	Forte	61%	£62	0905 726262	103		High Street Worcester WR1 2QR

Hertfordshire

Location	Establishment	Group	Grade	Price	Tel	Rooms	Pool	Address
Baldock	Forte Travelodge	Forte		£42	0462 835329	40		A1 Great North Road Hinxworth nr Baldock SG7 5EX
Broxbourne	Cheshunt Marriott Hotel	Marriott	66%	£93	0992 451245	150	yes	Halfhide Lane Turnford Broxbourne Cheshunt EN10 6NP
Harpenden	Moat House	QMH	68%	£95	0582 764111	53		Southdown Road Harpenden AL5 1PE
Hemel Hempstead	Forte Posthouse	Forte	62%	£68	0442 251122	146	yes	A414 Breakspear Way Hemel Hempstead Hemp2 4UA
Hertingfordbury	White Horse Hotel	Forte	63%	£90	0992 586791	42		Hertingfordbury Road Hertingfordbury SG14 2LB
Markyate	Hertfordshire Moat House	QMH	57%	£94	0582 840840	89		London Road Markyate AL3 8HH
Rushden	Forte Travelodge	Forte		£42	0933 57008	40		A45 Saunders Lodge Rushden
South Mimms	Forte Posthouse	Forte	60%	£68	0707 643311	120	yes	Bignells Corner South Mimms nr Potters Bar EN6 3NH
South Mimms	Forte Travelodge	Forte		£42	0707 665440	52		M25 Service Area Bignells Corner nr Potters Bar EN6 3QQ
St Albans	Noke Thistle	MtCT	68%	£107	0727 854252	111		Watford Road St Albans AL2 3DS
Stansted Abbots	Briggens House	QMH	70%	£106	0279 792416	54		Stanstead Road Stanstead Abbots nr Ware SG12 8LD
Stevenage	Forte Posthouse	Forte	58%	£68	0438 365444	54		B197 Old London Road Broadwater Stevenage SG2 8DS
Stevenage	Novotel	Novotel	60%	£80	0438 742299	100		Knebworth Park Stevenage SG1 2AX
Tring	Travel Inn	Travel Inns		£43	0442 824819	30		Tring Hill Tring HP23 4LD
Watford	Hilton National	Hilton	64%	£109	0923 235881	198	yes	Elton Way Watford WD2 8HA

Humberside

Location	Establishment	Group	Grade	Price	Tel	Rooms	Pool	Address
Beverley	Beverley Arms	Forte	62%	£90	0482 869241	57		North Bar Within Beverley HU17 8DD

Location	Hotel	Group	%		Price	Phone	Rooms	Address
Hull	Campanile Hotel	Campanile	62%		£44	0482 25530	50	Beverley Road Freetown Way Hull HU2 9AN
Hull	Forte Posthouse	Forte	69%		£68	0482 645212	97	Ferriby High Road North Ferriby Hull HU14 3LG
Hull	Forte Crest	Forte	NEW		£89	0482 225221	99	Castle Street Hull HU1 2BX
Hull	Travel Inn	Travel Inn			£43	0482 645285	40	Ferriby Road Hessle Hull
South Cave	Forte Travelodge	Forte		yes	£42	0430 424455	40	A63 Eastbound Beacon Service Area South Cave Hull

Isle of Wight

Location	Hotel	Group	%		Price	Phone	Rooms	Address
Ventnor	Royal Hotel	Forte	60%		£66	0983 852186	54	Belgrave Road Ventnor PO38 1JJ

Kent

Location	Hotel	Group	%		Price	Phone	Rooms	Address
Ashford	Ashford International	QMH	71%	yes	£107	0233 611444	200	Simone Weil Avenue Ashford TN24 8UX
Ashford	Eastwell Manor	QMH	82%		£110	0233 635751	23	Eastwell Park Boughton Aluph Ashford TN25 4HR
Ashford	Forte Posthouse	Forte	66%		£68	0233 625790	60	Canterbury Road Ashford TN24 8QQ
Ashford	Holiday Inn Garden Court	Holiday Inns	65%		£70	0233 712333	104	Maidstone Road Hothfield Ashford TN26 1AR
Ashford	Travel Inn	Travel Inns			£43	0233 712571	40	Maidstone Road A20 Hothfield Common Ashford TN26 1AP
Bearsted	Tudor Park	Country Club	67%	yes	£109	3622 34334	120	Ashford Road Bearsted nr Maidstone ME14 4NQ
Bexley	Forte Crest	Forte	56%		£68	3322 526900	102	Black Prince Roundabout Southwold Road Bexley DA5 1ND
Bexleyheath	Swallow Hotel	Swallow	71%	yes	£94	081-298 1000	142	1 Broadway Bexleyheath DA6 7JZ
Brands Hatch	Brands Hatch Thistle	MtCT	70%		£97	0474 854900	137	Brands Hatch nr Dartford DA3 8PE
Canterbury	Chaucer Hotel	Forte	61%		£98	0227 464427	42	63 Ivy Lane Canterbury CT1 1TT
Canterbury	Slatters Hotel	QMH	57%		£75	0227 463271	31	St Margarets Street Canterbury CT1 2Dy
Dover	Forte Posthouse	Forte	63%		£67	0304 821222	67	Singledge Lane Whitfield Dover CT16 3LF
Dover	Moat House	QMH	66%		£75	0304 203270	79	Townwall Street Dover CT16 1SZ
Dover	Travel Inn	Travel Inns		yes	£43	0304 213339	30	Folkestone Road Dover CT15 7AB
Hollingbourne	Great Danes	Jarvis	64%		£65	0622 30022	126	Ashford Road Hollingbourne ME17 1RE
Maidstone	Larkfield Priory	Forte	62%		£71	0732 846858	52	812 London Road Maidstone ME20 6HJ
Maidstone	Stakis Country Court Hotel	Stakis	67%		£93	0622 34322	138	Bearsted Weavering Maidstone ME14 5AA
Rochester	Forte Posthouse	Forte	62%	yes	£68	0634 687111	105	Maidstone Road Rochester Airport Rochester ME5 9SF
Tonbridge	Rose & Crown	Forte	59%		£97	0732 357966	50	125 High Street Tonbridge TN9 1DD
Wrotham Heath	Forte Posthouse Maidstone	Forte	67%		£68	0732 883311	106	London Road Wrotham Heath nr Sevenoaks TN15 7RS
Wrotham Heath	Travel Inn	Travel Inns		yes	£43	0732 884214	40	London Road Wrotham Heath nr Sevenoaks TN15 7RX

Lancashire

Location	Establishment	Group	Grade Price	Tel	Rooms	Pool	Address
Blackburn	Moat House	QMH	58% £69	0254 264441	98		Preston New Road Blackburn BB2 7BE
Blackpool	Imperial Hotel	Forte	64% £114	0253 23971	183	yes	North Promenade Blackpool FY1 2HB
Broughton	Broughton Park	Country Club	65% £94	0772 864087	98	yes	418 Garstang Road Broughton nr Preston PR3 5JB
Burnley	Forte Travelodge	Forte	£42	0282 416039	32		Cavalry Barracks Barracks Road Burnley BB11 4AS
Burnley	Oaks Hotel	Shire Inns	63% £88	0282 414141	56	yes	Colne Road Reedley Burnley BB10 2LF
Lancaster	Forte Posthouse	Forte	69% £68	0524 65999	110	yes	Waterside Park Caton Road Lancaster LA1 3RA
Mellor	Millstone Hotel	Shire Inns	£84	0254 813333	21		Church Lane Mellor nr Blackburn BB2 7JR
Preston	Forte Posthouse	Forte	63% £68	0772 259411	126		The Ringway Preston PR1 3AU
Preston	Novotel	Novotel	62% £69	0772 313331	100		Redfield Place Walton Summit Preston PR5 6AB
Preston	Travel Inn	Travel Inns	£43	0772 720476	40		Blackpool Road Lea Preston PR4 0XL
Samlesbury	Swallow Trafalgar	Swallow	64% £72	0772 877351	78	yes	Preston New Road Samlesbury PR5 0UL
Worthington	Kilhey Court	Principal	65% £90	0257 472100	55	yes	Chorley Road Worthington Wigan WN1 2XN

Leicestershire

Location	Establishment	Group	Grade Price	Tel	Rooms	Pool	Address
Leicester	Forte Posthouse	Forte	64% £68	0533 630500	172		Braunston Lane East Leicester LE3 2FW
Leicester	Granada Lodge	Granada	£45	0530 244237	39		M1/A50 Junction 22 Markfield Leicester LE6 0PP
Leicester	Grand Hotel	Jarvis	66% £102	0533 555599	92		Granby Street Leicester LE1 6ES
Leicester	Holiday Inn	Holiday Inns	72% £114	0533 531161	188	yes	129 St Nicholas Circle Leicester LE1 5LX
Leicester	Leicester Forest Moat House	QMH	58% £73	0533 394661	34		Hinckley Road Leicester LE3 3GH
Leicester	Stakis Country Court	Stakis	69% £104	0533 630066	141	yes	Braunstone Leicester LE3 2WQ
Lockington	Hilton National E Midlands	Hilton	69% £113	0509 674000	151	yes	Derby Road Lockington DE7 2RH
Loughborough	King's Head	Jarvis	58% £96	0509 233222	78		High Street Loughborough LE11 2QL
Lutterworth	Denbigh Arms	Resort	66% £65	0455 553537	34		High Street Lutterworth LE17 5AD
Rothley	Rothley Court	Forte	67% £100	0533 374141	36		Westfield Lane Rothley LE7 7LG
Thrussington	Forte Travelodge	Forte	£42	0664 424525	32		A46 Thrussington Green Acres Filling Stations LE7 8TF
Uppingham	Forte Travelodge	Forte	£42	0572 87719	40		A47 Glaston Road Morcott nr Uppingham LE15 8SA

Lincolnshire

Location	Hotel	Group	%		Rooms	Price	Phone	Address
Boston	New England Hotel	Forte	56%		25	£78	0205 365255	49 Wide Bargate Boston PE21 6SH
Colsterworth	Forte Travelodge	Forte			32	£42	0476 861181	A1 Southbound Colsterworth nr Grantham NG33 5JJ
Grantham	Forte Travelodge	Forte			40	£42	0476 77500	A1 Grantham Service Area Gonerby Moor Grantham NG32 2AB
Grantham	Granada Lodge	Granada			38	£45	0476 860686	A1/A151 Colsterworth Grantham NG33 5JR
Lincoln	Forte Posthouse	Forte	63%		70	£68	0522 520341	Eastgate Lincoln LN2 1PN
Lincoln	White Hart	Forte	69%		50	£90	0522 526222	Bailgate Lincoln LN1 3AR
Sleaford	Forte Travelodge	Forte			40	£42	0529 414752	A17/A15 Holdingham Sleaford NG34 8PN
South Witham	Forte Travelodge	Forte			32	£42	0572 767586	A1 New Fox South Witham Colsterworth LE15 8AU
Stamford	The George of Stamford	Poste Hotels	72%		47	£100	0780 55171	71 St Martins Stamford PE9 2LB

Merseyside

Location	Hotel	Group	%		Rooms	Price	Phone	Address
Bebington	Forte Travelodge	Forte			31	£42	051-327 2489	A41 N'bound New Chester Rd Eastham Wirral L62 9AQ
Bromborough	Travel Inn	Travel Inns	NEW		32	£43	051-334 2917	High Street Bromborough Wirral L62 7HZ
Gayton	Travel Inn	Travel Inns	65%		37	£43	051-342 1982	Chester Road Gayton Wirral L60 3FD
Haydock	Forte Posthouse	Forte	65%	yes	136	£68	0942 717878	Lodge Lane Newton-le-Willows Haydock WA12 0JG
Haydock	Forte Travelodge	Forte			40	£42	0942 272055	A580 Piele Road Haydock St Helens WA11 9TL
Haydock	Haydock Thistle	MtCT	67%	yes	139	£107	0942 272000	Penny Lane Haydock St Helens WA11 9SG
Liverpool	Atlantic Tower	MtCT	65%		226	£103	051-227 4444	Chapel Street Liverpool L3 9RE
Liverpool	Campanile Hotel	Campanile			82	£44	051-709 8104	Chaloner Street Queen's Dock Liverpool L3 4AJ
Liverpool	Gladstone Hotel	Forte	58%		154	£90	051-709 7050	Lord Nelson Street Liverpool L3 5QB
Liverpool	Moat House	QMH	67%		251	£116	051-709 0181	Paradise Street Liverpool L1 8JD
Liverpool	St George's Hotel	Forte	60%		155	£70	051-709 7090	St John's Precinct Lime Street Liverpool L1 1NQ
Liverpool	Travel Inn	Travel Inns	NEW		40	£43	051-228 4724	Queens Drive West Derby Liverpool L13 0DL
Southport	Prince of Wales Hotel	Forte	65%		104	£74	0704 536688	Lord Street Southport PR8 1JS

Middlesex

Location	Hotel	Group	%		Rooms	Price	Phone	Address
Hayes	Travel Inn	Travel Inns			40	£43	081-573 7479	362 Uxbridge Road Hayes UB4 0HE
Heathrow Airport - see under London Airport Heathrow								
Kenton	Travel Inn	Travel Inns			43	£43	081-907 1671	Kenton Road Kenton HA3 8AT
Shepperton	Moat House	QMH	61%		180	£103	0932 241404	Felix Lane Shepperton TW17 8NP
Wembley	Hilton National	Hilton	65%		300	£129	081-902 8839	Empire Way Wembley HA9 8DS

Location	Establishment	Group	Grade	Price	Tel	Rooms	Pool	Address
Norfolk								
Acle	Forte Travelodge	Forte	59%	£42	0493 751970	40		A47 Acle Bypass Acle nr Norwich NR13 3BE
East Dereham	Phoenix Hotel	Forte	67%	£77	0362 692276	23		Church Street East Dereham NR19 1DL
Great Yarmouth	Carlton Hotel	Waveney	62%	£79	0493 855234	90		Marine Parade Great Yarmouth NR30 3JE
King's Lynn	Butterfly Hotel	Butterfly	60%	£67	0553 771707	50		Beveridge Way Hardwick Narrows King's Lynn PE30 4NB
King's Lynn	Duke's Head	Forte		£93	0553 774996	71		Tuesday Market Place King's Lynn PE30 1JS
King's Lynn	Forte Travelodge	Forte	63%	£42	0406 362230	40		A17 Wisbech Road Long Sutton King's Lynn PE12 9AG
Norwich	Forte Posthouse	Forte	68%	£68	0603 56431	113	yes	Ipswich Road Norwich NR4 6EP
Norwich	Friendly Hotel	Friendly	60%	£94	0603 741161	80	yes	2 Barnard Road Bowthorpe Norwich NR5 9JB
Thetford	The Bell	Forte	62%	£97	0842 754455	47		King Street Thetford IP24 2AZ
Northamptonshire								
Corby	Forte Posthouse	Forte	60%	£68	0536 401348	69		A6116 Rockingham Road Corby NN17 1AE
Crick	Forte Posthouse Northampton	Forte	64%	£68	0788 822101	88	yes	Crick NN6 7XR
Daventry	Daventry Resort Hotel	Resort	70%	£100	0327 301777	138		Ashby Road Daventry NN11 5SG
Desborough	Forte Travelodge	Forte		£42	0536 762034	32		A6 Southbound Harborough Road Desborough
Kettering	Kettering Park Hotel	Shire Inns	71%	£105	0536 416666	90		Kettering Parkway Kettering NN15 6XT
Milton Keynes	Friendly Hotel	Friendly	57%	£79	0908 561666	88	yes	Monks Way Two Mile Ash nr Milton Keynes MK8 8LY
Northampton	Courtyard by Marriott	Marriott	65%	£77	0604 22777	104		Bedford Road Northampton NN4 0YF
Northampton	Forte Travelodge	Forte		£42	0604 758395	40		A45 Upton Way Northampton NN5 6EG
Northampton	Moat House	QMH	63%	£93	0604 22441	138		Silver Street Northampton NN1 2TA
Northampton	Stakis Country Court	Stakis	68%	£107	0604 700666	139	yes	100 Watering Lane Collingtree Northampton NN4 0XW
Northampton	Swallow Hotel	Swallow	72%	£99	0604 768700	122	yes	Eagle Drive Northampton NN4 0HN
Northampton	Travel Inn	Travel Inns		£43	0604 832340	51		Harpole Turn Weedon Road Northampton NN7 4DD
Northampton	Westone Moat House	QMH	59%	£79	0604 406262	66		Ashley Way Weston Favell Northampton NN3 3EA
Oundle	Talbot Hotel	Forte	62%	£96	0832 273621	40		New Street Oundle PE8 4EA
Thrapston	Forte Travelodge	Forte		£42	0832 735199	40		A14 Link Road Thrapston By-Pass Thrapston
Towcester	Forte Travelodge	Forte		£42	0327 359105	33		A43 East Towcester By-Pass Towcester NN12 0DD
Weedon	Crossroads Hotel		63%	£52	0327 40354	48		High Street Weedon NN7 4PX

Northumberland

Location	Hotel	Group	%	Price	Phone	Rooms		Address
Chollerford	George Hotel	Swallow	59%	£95	0434 681611	50	yes	Chollerford nr Hexham NE46 4EW

Nottinghamshire

Location	Hotel	Group	%	Price	Phone	Rooms		Address
Barnby Moor	Ye Olde Bell	Principal	60%	£80	0777 705121	55		Barnby Moor nr Retford DN22 8QS
Blyth	Forte Travelodge	Forte		£42	0909 591775	32		A1 Blyth Worksop
Blyth	Granada Lodge	Granada		£45	0909 591836	39		A1M/A614 Blyth S82 8HG
Newark	Forte Travelodge	Forte	70%	£42	0636 703635	30		A1 North Muskham Newark NG23 6HT
Nottingham	Forte Crest	Forte		£92	0602 470131	130		St James's Street Nottingham NG1 6BN
Nottingham	Forte Posthouse	Forte	61%	£68	0602 397800	91		Bostocks Lane Sandiacre Nottingham NG10 5NJ
Nottingham	Holiday Inn Garden Court	Holiday Inns	65%	£70	0602 500600	100		Castle Marina Park Nottingham NG7 1GX
Nottingham	Moat House	QMH	59%	£88	0602 602621	172		Mansfield Road Nottingham NG5 2BT
Nottingham	Novotel	Novotel	62%	£70	0602 720106	108		Bostock Lane Long Eaton Nottingham NG10 4EP
Nottingham	Royal Moat House	QMH	70%	£101	0602 41444	201		Wollaton Street Nottingham NG1 5RH
Nottingham	Stakis Victoria Hotel	Stakis	62%	£72	0602 419561	166		Milton Street Nottingham NG1 3PZ
Nottingham	Strathdon Thistle	MtCT	66%	£106	0602 418501	69		44 Derby Road Nottingham NG1 5FT
Retford	Forte Travelodge	Forte		£42	0777 838091	40		A1 Northbound Markham Moor nr Retford DN22 0QU
Southwell	Saracen's Head	Forte	62%	£80	0636 812701	27		Market Place Southwell NG25 0HE
Worksop	Forte Travelodge	Forte		£42	0909 501528	40		A47 St. Anne's Drive Dunkeries Mill Worksop S80 3QD

Oxfordshire

Location	Hotel	Group	%	Price	Phone	Rooms		Address
Abingdon	Upper Reaches	Forte	62%	£106	0235 522311	25		Thames Street Abingdon OX14 3TA
Banbury	Moat House	QMH	62%	£79	0295 259361	48		27-29 Oxford Road Banbury OX16 9AH
Banbury	Whately Hall	Forte	65%	£105	0295 263451	74		Banbury Cross Banbury OX16 0AN
Burford	Bay Tree	Select	67%	£105	0993 822791	22		Sheep Street Burford OX8 4LW
Oxford	Eastgate Hotel	Forte	61%	£123	0865 248244	43		Merton Street The High Oxford OX1 4BE
Oxford	Forte Travelodge	Forte		£42	0865 75705	24		London Road Wheatley nr Oxford OX9 1JH
Oxford	Moat House	QMH	62%	£105	0865 59933	155		Wolvercote Roundabout Oxford OX2 8AL
Oxford	Randolph Hotel	Forte	68%	£161	0865 247481	109	yes	Beaumont Street Oxford OX1 2LN
Steeple Aston	Hopcrofts Holt Hotel	MtCT	63%	£80	0869 40259	88		Steeple Aston OX6 3QQ
Wallingford	George Hotel	MtCT	62%	£106	0491 836665	39		High Street Wallingford OX10 0BS
Weston-on-the-Green	Weston Manor	Hidden	61%	£100	0869 50621	37		Weston-on-the-Green OX6 8QL
Woodstock	Bear Hotel	Forte	66%	£120	0993 811511	45		Park Street Woodstock OX7 1SZ

Location	Establishment	Group	Grade	Price	Tel	Rooms	Pool	Address
Shropshire								
Ludlow	Forte Travelodge	Forte		£42	0584 711695	32		A49 Woofferton Ludlow SY8 4AL
Oswestry	Forte Travelodge	Forte		£42	0691 658178	40		A5/A483 Mile End Service Area Oswestry SY11 4JA
Shrewsbury	Lion Hotel	Forte	62%	£92	0743 353107	59		Wyle Cop Shrewsbury SY1 1UY
Shrewsbury	Prince Rupert Hotel	QMH	64%	£85	0743 236000	65		Butcher Row Shrewsbury SY1 1UQ
Telford	Forte Travelodge	Forte		£42	0952 251244	40		Admaston Road Shawbirch Telford TF1 3QA
Telford	Holiday Inn	Holiday Inns	68%	£108	0952 292500	100	yes	St Quentin Gate Telford TF3 4EH
Telford	Moat House	QMH	67%	£95	0952 291291	148	yes	Forgegate Telford TF3 4NA
Somerset								
Dunster	Luttrell Arms	Forte	64%	£107	0643 821555	27		High Street Dunster nr Minehead TA24 6SG
Ilminster	Forte Travelodge	Forte		£42	0460 53748	32		A303 Southfield Roundabout Horton Cross Ilminster PA19 9PT
Podimore	Forte Travelodge	Forte		£42	0935 840074	31		A303 Podimore nr Yeovil BA22 8JG
Taunton	County Hotel	Forte	61%	£97	0823 337651	66		East Street Taunton TA1 3LT
Taunton	Forte Posthouse	Forte	66%	£68	0823 332222	97		Deane Gate Avenue Taunton TA1 2UA
Taunton	Travel Inn	Travel Inns		£43	0823 321112	40		81 Bridgwater Road Taunton TA1 2DU
Yeovil	The Manor	Forte	63%	£97	0935 231161	41		Hendford Yeovil BA20 1TG
Staffordshire								
Barton-under-Needwood	Forte Travelodge North	Forte		£42	0283 716343	20		A38 Northbound nr Burton-on-Trent DE13 8EG
Barton-under-Needwood	Forte Travelodge South	Forte		£42	0283 716784	40		A38 Southbound nr Burton-on-Trent DE13 3EH
Cannock	Travel Inn	Travel Inns		£43	0543 572721	38		Watling Street Cannock WS11 1SJ
Lichfield	George Hotel	Jarvis	59%	£90	0543 414822	38		Bird Street Lichfield WS13 6PR
Newcastle-under-Lyme	Clayton Lodge	Jarvis	60%	£84	0782 613093	50		Clayton Road Newcastle-under-Lyme ST5 4AF
Newcastle-under-Lyme	Forte Posthouse	Forte	60%	£68	0782 717171	119	yes	Clayton Road Newcastle-under-Lyme ST5 4DL
Rugeley	Forte Travelodge	Forte		£42	0889 570096	32		A51/B5013 Western Springs Road Rugeley WS15 2AS
Stafford	Tillington Hall	De Vere	63%	£80	0785 53531	90	yes	Eccleshall Road Stafford ST16 1JJ
Stoke-on-Trent	North Stafford Hotel	Principal	61%	£90	0782 744477	69		Station Road Stoke-on-Trent ST4 2AE
Stoke-on-Trent	Stakis Grand Hotel	Stakis	68%	£96	0782 202361	128	yes	Trinity Street Hanley Stoke-on-Trent ST1 5NB
Stoke-on-Trent	Stoke-on-Trent Moat House	QMH	70%	£99	0782 219000	147	yes	Etruria Hall Festival Way Etruria Stoke-on-Trent ST1 5BQ

Town	Hotel	Group	%	Price	Phone	Rooms		Address
Tamworth	Granada Lodge	Granada		£45	0827 260123	63		M42/A5 Junction 10 Tamworth B77 5PH
Uttoxeter	Forte Travelodge	Forte		£42	0889 562043	32		A50/A5030 Ashbourne Road Uttoxeter ST14 5AA

Suffolk

Town	Hotel	Group	%	Price	Phone	Rooms		Address
Aldeburgh	Brudenell Hotel	Forte	60%	£107	0728 452071	47		The Parade Aldeburgh IP15 5BU
Barton Mills	Forte Travelodge	Forte		£42	0638 717675	32		A11 Barton Mills Mildenhall IP28 6AE
Bury St Edmunds	Butterfly Hotel	Butterfly	62%	£61	0284 760884	66		Symonds Road Bury St Edmunds IP32 7BW
Bury St Edmunds	Suffolk Hotel	Forte	59%	£93	0284 753995	33		38 Buttermarket Bury St Edmunds IP33 1DL
Copdock	Ipswich Moat House	QMH	64%	£68	0473 730444	74	yes	London Road Copdock nr Ipswich IP8 3JD
Felixstowe	Orwell Moat House	QMH	69%	£85	0394 285511	58		Hamilton Road Felixstowe IP11 7DX
Framlingham	The Crown	Forte	62%	£103	0728 723521	14		Market Hill Framlingham IP13 9AN
Ipswich	Forte Posthouse	Forte	63%	£68	0473 690313	112		London Road Ipswich IP2 0UA
Ipswich	Novotel	Novotel	61%	£78	0473 232400	101		Greyfriars Road Ipswich IP1 1UP
Lavenham	The Swan	Forte	71%	£120	0787 247477	47		High Street Lavenham nr Sudbury CO10 9QA
Long Melford	Bull Hotel	Forte	65%	£102	0787 378494	25		Hall Street Long Melford CO10 9JG
Newmarket	Moat House	QMH	62%	£78	0638 667171	47		Moulton Road Newmarket CB8 8DY
Stowmarket	Forte Travelodge	Forte		£42	0449 615347	40		A45 Stowmarket IP14 3PY

Surrey

Town	Hotel	Group	%	Price	Phone	Rooms		Address
Camberley	Frimley Hall	Forte	68%	£122	0276 28321	66		Portsmouth Road Camberley GU15 2BG
Chessington	Travel Inn	Travel Inns		£43	0372 744060	42		Leatherhead Road Chessington KT9 2NE
Cobham	Hilton National	Hilton	65%	£110	0932 864471	152	yes	Seven Hills Road South Cobham KT11 1EW
Cobham	Woodlands Park	Select	69%	£147	0372 843933	58		Woodlands Lane Stoke d'Abernon Cobham KT11 3QB
Croydon	Forte Posthouse	Forte	61%	£68	081-688 5185	83		Purley Way Croydon CR0 4LT
Croydon	Hilton National	Hilton	69%	£105	081-680 3000	168		Waddon Way Purley Way Croydon CR9 4HH
Croydon	Travel Inn	Travel Inns		£43	081-686 2030	40		Coombe Road Croydon CR0 5RB
Dorking	Forte Travelodge	Forte		£42	0306 740361	29		A25 Reigate Road Dorking RH4 1QB
Dorking	White Horse	Forte	62%	£80	0306 881138	68		High Street Dorking RH14 1BE
East Horsley	Thatchers Resort Hotel	Resort	63%	£100	0483 284291	59		Epsom Road East Horsley KT24 6TB
Farnham	Bush Hotel	Forte	62%	£103	0252 715237	66		The Borough Farnham GU9 7NN

Horley, Gatwick Airport *see under* **London Airport Gatwick**

Location	Establishment	Group	Grade	Price	Tel	Rooms	Pool	Address
Guildford	Forte Crest	Forte		68%	£108	0483 574444	111	yes	Egerton Road Guildford GU2 5XZ
Morden	Forte Travelodge	Forte			£42	081-640 8227	32		A24 Epsom Road Morden SM4 5PH
Nutfield	Nutfield Priory	Hidden		70%	£110	0737 822066	52	yes	Nutfield Redhill RH1 4EN
Seale	Hog's Back Hotel	Jarvis		64%	£108	0252 782345	89	yes	Seale nr Farnham GU10 1EX
Sutton	Holiday Inn	Holiday Inns		70%	£129	081-770 1311	116	yes	Gibson Road Sutton Surrey SM1 2RF
Weybridge	Ship Thistle	MtCT		63%	£116	0932 848364	39	yes	5 Monument Green Weybridge KT13 8BQ

East Sussex

Location	Establishment	Group	Grade	Price	Tel	Rooms	Pool	Address
Brighton	Grand Hotel	De Vere		74%	£160	0273 321188	200	yes	King's Road Brighton BN1 2FW
Brighton	Hospitality Inn	MtCT		77%	£155	0273 206700	204	yes	King's Road Brighton BN1 2GS
Cooden	Cooden Resort Hotel	Resort		60%	£75	0424 842281	41	yes	Cooden Sea Road Bexhill-on-Sea TN39 4TT
Eastbourne	Cavendish Hotel	De Vere		68%	£70	0323 410222	112		Grand Parade Eastbourne BN21 4DH
Eastbourne	Grand Hotel	De Vere		75%	£150	0323 412345	164	yes	King Edward's Parade Eastbourne BN21 4EQ
Eastbourne	Queen's Hotel	De Vere		67%	£80	0323 22822	108		Marine Parade Eastbourne BN21 3DY
Eastbourne	Wish Tower Hotel	Principal		66%	£80	0323 722676	65		King Edward's Parade Eastbourne BN21 4EB
Hailsham	Forte Travelodge	Forte			£42	0323 844556	40		A22 Boship Roundabout Hellingly Hailsham BN27 4DT
Hastings	Royal Victoria Hotel	Resort		70%	£75	0424 445544	52		The Marina St Leonards-on-Sea nr Hastings TN38 0BD
Lewes	Shelleys Hotel	MtCT		60%	£118	0273 472361	21		High Street Lewes BN7 1XS
Rye	George Hotel	Forte		62%	£97	0797 222114	22		High Street Rye TN31 7JP

West Sussex

Location	Establishment	Group	Grade	Price	Tel	Rooms	Pool	Address
Billingshurst	Forte Travelodge	Forte			£42	0403 782711	26		A29 Five Oaks Billingshurst RH14 9AE
Bognor Regis	Royal Norfolk	Forte		60%	£70	0243 826222	51		The Esplanade Bognor Regis PO21 2LH
Chichester	Dolphin & Anchor	Forte		63%	£102	0243 785121	49		West Street Chichester PO19 1QE
Crawley	George Hotel	Forte		64%	£76	0293 524215	86		High Street Crawley RH10 1BS
Fontwell	Forte Travelodge	Forte			£42	0243 543972	32		A27/A29 Fontwell BN18 0SB
Gatwick Airport - see under **London Airport Gatwick**								
Goodwood	Goodwood Park	Country Club	67%	£94	0243 775537	89	yes	Goodwood Nr Chichester PO18 0QB
Horsham	Travel Inn	Travel Inns			£43	0403 250141	40		57 North Street Horsham RH12 1RB

Tyne & Wear

Location	Hotel	Group	%	Price	Tel	Rooms		Address
Gateshead	Forte Travelodge	Forte	70%	£42	091-438 3333	41		A194 Leam Lane Wardley Whitemare Pool nr Gateshead
Gateshead	Newcastle Marriott Hotel	Marriott		£129	091-493 2233	150		MetroCentre Gateshead NE11 9XF
Gateshead	Springfield Hotel	Jarvis	63%	£88	091-477 4121	60		Durham Road Low Fell Gateshead NE9 5BT
Gateshead	Swallow Hotel	Swallow	60%	£88	091-477 1105	103	yes	High West Street Gateshead NE8 1PE
Newcastle-upon-Tyne	Copthorne Hotel	Copthorne	73%	£116	091-222 0333	156	yes	Quayside Newcastle-upon-Tyne NE1 3RT
Newcastle-upon-Tyne	County Thistle	MtCT	68%	£105	091-232 2471	115		Neville Street Newcastle-upon-Tyne NE99 1AH
Newcastle-upon-Tyne	Forte Crest	Forte	61%	£93	091-232 6191	166		New Bridge Street Newcastle-upon-Tyne NE1 8BS
Newcastle-upon-Tyne	Holiday Inn	Holiday Inns	70%	£121	091-236 5432	150	yes	Great North Road Seaton Burn Newcastle-upon-Tyne NE13 6BP
Newcastle-upon-Tyne	Moat House	QMH	59%	£68	091-262 8989	147		Coast Road Wallsend Newcastle-upon-Tyne NE28 1HP
Newcastle-upon-Tyne	Novotel	Novotel	63%	£81	091-214 0303	126		Ponteland Road Kenton Newcastle-upon-Tyne NE3 3HZ
Newcastle-upon-Tyne	Swallow Gosforth Park	Swallow	73%	£120	091-236 4111	178	yes	High Gosforth Park Newcastle-upon-Tyne NE3 5HN
Newcastle-upon-Tyne	Swallow Hotel	Swallow	63%	£88	091-232 5025	93	yes	2 Newgate Arcade Newcastle-upon-Tyne NE1 5SX
Newcastle-upon-Tyne	Airport Moat House	QMH	62%	£79	0661 824911	100		Woolsington Newcastle-upon-Tyne NE13 8DJ
Sunderland	Swallow Hotel	Swallow	70%	£95	091-529 2041	65	yes	Queen's Parade Seaburn Sunderland SR6 8DB
Sunderland	Travel Inn	Travel Inns	NEW	£43	091-548 9384	40		A1231/A19 Wessington Way Sunderland
Washington	Campanile Hotel	Campanile		£44	091-416 5010	77		Emerson Road Washington nr Newcastle-upon-Tyne NE37 1LE
Washington	Forte Posthouse	Forte	59%	£68	091-416 2264	138		Emerson District 5 Washington NE37 1LB
Washington	Granada Lodge	Granada		£45	091-410 0076	35		A1M Washington DH3 2SJ
Washington	Moat House	QMH	66%	£93	091-417 2626	106	yes	Stone Cellar Rd High Usworth District 12 Washington

Warwickshire

Location	Hotel	Group	%	Price	Tel	Rooms		Address
Ansty	Ansty Hall	Hidden	71%	£108	0203 612222	31		Ansty nr Coventry CV7 9HZ
Brandon	Brandon Hall	Forte	65%	£107	0203 542571	60		Brandon nr Coventry CV8 3FW
Charlecote	Charlecote Pheasant	QMH	62%	£85	0789 470333	67		Charlecote nr Warwick CV35 9EN
Kenilworth	De Montfort Hotel	De Vere	63%	£100	0926 55944	96		Kenilworth CV8 1ED
Leamington Spa	Courtyard by Marriott	Marriott	65%	£70	0926 425522	97		Olympus Avenue Europa Way Leamington Spa CV34 6RJ
Nuneaton	Forte Travelodge	Forte		£42	0203 382541	40		A444 Bedworth Nuneaton Coventry CV12 0BN
Nuneaton	Travel Inn	Travel Inns		£43	0203 343584	30		Coventry Road Nuneaton CV10 7PJ
Stratford-upon-Avon	Alveston Manor	Forte	65%	£115	0789 204581	108		Clopton Bridge Stratford-upon-Avon CV37 7HP
Stratford-upon-Avon	Billesley Manor	QMH	76%	£135	0789 400888	41	yes	Billesley Alcester nr Stratford-upon-Avon B49 6NF
Stratford-upon-Avon	Falcon Hotel	QMH	63%	£94	0789 205777	73		Chapel Street Stratford-upon-Avon CV37 6HA
Stratford-upon-Avon	Forte Posthouse	Forte	59%	£68	0789 266761	60		Bridgefoot Stratford-upon-Avon CV37 7LT

Location	Establishment	Group	Grade	Price	Tel	Rooms	Pool	Address
Stratford-upon-Avon	Moat House International	QMH	71%	£125	0789 414411	247	yes	Bridgefoot Stratford-upon-Avon CV37 6YR
Stratford-upon-Avon	Shakespeare Hotel	Forte	69%	£127	0789 294771	63		Chapel Street Stratford-upon-Avon CV37 6ER
Stratford-upon-Avon	White Swan	Forte	62%	£112	0789 297022	37		Rother Street Stratford-upon-Avon CV37 6NH
Warwick	Hilton National	Hilton	66%	£140	0926 499555	181	yes	Stratford Road Warwick CV34 6RE
Wishaw	The Belfry	De Vere	73%	£110	0675 470301	219	yes	Lichfield Road Wishaw B76 9PR

West Midlands

Location	Establishment	Group	Grade	Price	Tel	Rooms	Pool	Address
Birmingham	Campanile Hotel	Campanile		£44	021-622 4925	50		Irving Street Lee Bank, Birmingham B1 1DH
Birmingham	Copthorne Hotel	Copthorne	70%	£127	021-200 2727	212	yes	Paradise Circus Birmingham B3 3HJ
Birmingham	Forte Crest	Forte	68%	£97	021-643 8171	253	yes	Smallbrook Queensway Birmingham B5 4EW
Birmingham	Forte Posthouse	Forte	60%	£68	021-357 7444	192	yes	Chapel Lane Great Barr Birmingham B43 7BG
Birmingham	Granada Lodge	Granada		£45	021-550 3261	60		M5 Junction 3/4 Frankley Birmingham B32 4AR
Birmingham	Holiday Inn	Holiday Inns	70%	£124	021-631 2000	288	yes	Holliday Street Birmingham B1 1HH
Birmingham	Hyatt Regency	Hyatt	77%	£162	021-643 1234	319	yes	2 Bridge Street Birmingham B1 2JZ
Birmingham	Novotel	Novotel	61%	£100	021-643 2000	148		70 Broad Street Birmingham B1 2HT
Birmingham	Plough & Harrow	Forte	59%	£107	021-454 4111	44		135 Hagley Road Edgbaston Birmingham B16 8LS
Birmingham	Royal Angus Thistle	MtCT	65%	£102	021-236 4211	133		St Chads Queensway Birmingham B4 6HY
Birmingham	Strathallan Thistle	MtCT	63%	£103	021-455 9777	167		225 Hagley Road Edgbaston Birmingham B16 9RY
Birmingham	Swallow Hotel	Swallow	77%	£120	021-452 1144	98		12 Hagley Road Five Ways Birmingham B16 8SJ
Birmingham Airport	Forte Posthouse	Forte	61%	£68	021-782 8141	136	yes	Coventry Road Birmingham Airport Birmingham B26 3QW
Birmingham Airport	Novotel	Novotel	65%	£92	021-782 7000	195		Birmingham International Airport Birmingham B26 3QL
Brierley Hill	Copthorne Hotel	Copthorne	71%	£118	0384 482882	138		The Waterfront Level Street Brierley Hill DY5 1UR
Coventry	De Vere Hotel	De Vere	69%	£85	0203 633733	190	yes	Cathedral Square Coventry CV1 5RP
Coventry	Forte Crest	Forte	66%	£98	0203 613261	147		Hinckley Road Coventry CV2 2HP
Coventry	Forte Posthouse	Forte	60%	£68	0203 402151	184		Rye Hill Allesley Coventry CV5 9PH
Coventry	Novotel	Novotel	62%	£78	0203 365000	100		Wilsons Lane Longford Coventry CV6 6HL
Coventry (North)	Campanile Hotel	Campanile		£44	0203 622311	50		Wigston Road Walsgrave Coventry CV2 2SD
Coventry (South)	Campanile Hotel	Campanile		£44	0203 639922	50		Abbey Road Whitley Coventry CV3 4BJ
Dudley	Forte Travelodge	Forte		£42	0384 481579	32		A461 Dudley Road Dudley DY5 1LQ
Dunchurch	Forte Travelodge	Forte		£42	0788 521528	40		A45 London Road Thurlaston Dunchurch nr Rugby CV23 9LG
Hagley	Travel Inn	Travel Inns		£43	0562 883120	40		Birmingham Road Hagley nr Stourbridge DY9 9JS

Town	Hotel	Group	%	£	Phone	Rooms		Address
Meriden	Forest of Arden Hotel	Country Club	70%	£110	0676 22335	152	yes	Maxstoke Lane Meriden CV7 7HR
Meriden	Manor Hotel	De Vere	64%	£85	0676 22735	74		Main Road Meriden CV7 7NH
Oldbury	Forte Travelodge	Forte		£42	021-552 2967	33		A4123 Wolverhampton Road Oldbury Warly B69 2BH
Solihull	George Hotel	Jarvis	66%	£116	021-711 2121	130		The Square Solihull B91 3RF
Solihull	Moat House	QMH	69%	£108	021-711 4700	115	yes	Homer Road Solihull B91 3QD
Solihull	St John's Swallow Hotel	Swallow	63%	£97	021-711 3000	177	yes	651 Warwick Road Solihull B91 1AT
Solihull	Travel Inn	Travel Inns		£43	021-744 2942	40		Stratford Road Shirley Solihull B90 4PT
Sutton Coldfield	Forte Travelodge	Forte		£42	021-355 0017	32		Boldmere Road Sutton Coldfield B72 5UP
Sutton Coldfield	New Hall	MtCT	78%	£129	021-378 2442	60		Walmley Road Sutton Coldfield B76 8QX
Sutton Coldfield	Penns Hall	Jarvis	66%	£132	021-351 3111	114		Penns Lane Walmley Sutton Coldfield B76 8LH
Walsall	Forte Posthouse	Forte	61%	£68	0922 33555	98		Birmingham Road Walsall WS5 3AB
West Bromwich	Moat House	QMH	59%	£89	021-553 6111	172		Birmingham Road Bromwich B70 6RS
Wolverhampton	Mount Hotel	Jarvis	60%	£102	0902 752055	56	yes	Mount Road Tettenhall Wood Wolverhampton WV6 8HL

Wiltshire

Town	Hotel	Group	%	£	Phone	Rooms		Address
Amesbury	Forte Travelodge	Forte		£42	0980 624966	32		A303 Amesbury SP4 7AS
Beanacre	Beechfield House	Hidden	70%	£80	0225 703700	24		Beanacre nr Melksham SN12 7PU
Chippenham	Granada Lodge	Granada		£45	0666 837097	35		M4 Junction 17/18 Leigh Delamere Chippenham SN4 6LB
Malmesbury	Old Bell Hotel	Clipper	64%	£98	0666 822344	37		Abbey Row Malmesbury SN16 0BW
Salisbury	Rose & Crown	QMH	56%	£98	0722 327908	28		Harnham Road Harnham Salisbury SP2 8QJ
Salisbury	White Hart	Forte	63%	£106	0722 327476	68		1 St John Street Salisbury SP1 2SD
Swindon	De Vere Hotel	De Vere	69%	£100	0793 878785	154	yes	Shaw Ridge Leisure Park Whitehill Way Swindon SN5 7DW
Swindon	Forte Posthouse	Forte	63%	£68	0793 524601	100	yes	Marlborough Road Swindon SN3 6AQ
Swindon	Forte Crest	Forte	62%	£100	0793 831333	91		Oxford Road Stratton St Margaret Swindon SN3 4TL
Swindon	Swindon Marriott Hotel	Marriott	71%	£123	0793 512121	153	yes	Pipers Way Swindon SN3 1SH
Swindon	Wiltshire Hotel	MtCT	62%	£100	0793 528282	95		Fleming Way Swindon SN1 1TN
Warminster	Granada Lodge	Granada		£45	0985 219639	31		A36/A350 Warminster BA12 7RU

North Yorkshire

Town	Hotel	Group	%	£	Phone	Rooms		Address
Harrogate	The Crown	Forte	67%	£98	0423 567755	121		Crown Place Harrogate HG1 2RZ
Harrogate	Hospitality Inn	MtCT	61%	£98	0423 564601	71		West Park Prospect Place Harrogate HG1 1LB
Harrogate	Imperial Hotel	Principal	65%	£95	0423 565071	85		Prospect Place Harrogate HG1 1LA
Harrogate	Majestic Hotel	Forte	64%	£114	0423 568972	156	yes	Ripon Road Harrogate HG1 2HU

Location	Establishment	Group	Grade	Price	Tel	Rooms	Pool	Address
Harrogate	Moat House	QMH	64%	£125	0423 500000	214		King's Road Harrogate HG1 1XX
Harrogate	Hotel St George	Swallow	63%	£105	0423 561431	93	yes	Ripon Road Harrogate HG1 2SY
Helmsley	Black Swan	Forte	69%	£111	0439 70466	44		Market Place Helmsley YO6 5BJ
Scarborough	The Crown	Forte	63%	£97	0723 373491	78		Esplanade Scarborough YO11 2AG
Scotch Corner	Forte Travelodge	Forte		£42	0748 823768	40		A1 Scotch Corner Skeeby nr Richmond DL10 5EQ
Skipton	Forte Travelodge	Forte		£42	0756 798091	32		A65/A59 Roundabout Gargrave Road Skipton BD23 1UD
South Milford	Forte Posthouse Leeds/Selby	Forte	65%	£68	0977 682711	105	yes	South Milford nr Leeds LS25 5LF
York	Abbey Park Resort Hotel	Resort	57%	£75	0904 658301	85		The Mount York YO2 2BN
York	Forte Posthouse	Forte	65%	£68	0904 707921	139		Tadcaster Road York YO2 2QF
York	Forte Travelodge	Forte		£42	0973 531823	40		A64 Eastbound Bilbrough nr York
York	Novotel	Novotel	62%	£85	0904 611660	124	yes	Fishergate York YO1 4AD
York	Royal York Hotel	Principal	65%	£100	0904 653681	145		Station Road York YO2 2AA
York	Stakis York	Stakis	68%	£130	0904 648111	128		Tower Street York YO1 1SB
York	Swallow Hotel	Swallow	64%	£105	0904 701000	113	yes	Tadcaster Road York YO2 2QQ
York	Viking Hotel	QMH	69%	£113	0904 659822	188		North Street York YO1 1JF

South Yorkshire

Location	Establishment	Group	Grade	Price	Tel	Rooms	Pool	Address
Barnsley	Ardsley Moat House	QMH	65%	£60	0226 289401	73		Doncaster Road Ardley Barnsley S71 5EH
Barnsley	Forte Travelodge	Forte		£42	0226 298799	32		A633/635 Stairfoot Roundabout Barnsley
Bawtry	The Crown	Forte	64%	£88	0302 710341	57		High Street Bawtry DN10 6JW
Carcroft	Forte Travelodge	Forte		£42	0302 330841	40		A1 Great North Road Carcroft nr Doncaster
Doncaster	Campanile Hotel	Campanile		£44	0302 370770	50		Doncaster Leisure Park Bawtry Doncaster DN4 7PD
Doncaster	Danum Swallow Hotel	Swallow	64%	£86	0302 342261	66		High Street Doncaster DN1 1DN
Doncaster	Moat House	QMH	68%	£88	0302 310331	100		Warmsworth Doncaster DN4 9UX
Rotherham	Campanile Hotel	Campanile		£44	0709 700255	50		Lowton Way off Denby Way Hellaby Ind Estate S66 8RY
Rotherham	Moat House	QMH	69%	£68	0709 364902	83		Moorgate Road Rotherham S60 2BG
Rotherham	Travel Inn	Travel Inns		£43	0709 543216	37		Bawtry Road Rotherham S65 3JB
Sheffield	Forte Crest	Forte	65%	£93	0742 670067	136	yes	Manchester Road Sheffield S10 5DX
Sheffield	Grosvenor House	Forte	67%	£77	0742 720041	103		Charter Square Sheffield S1 3EH
Sheffield	Holiday Inn Royal Victoria	Holiday Inns	67%	£107	0742 768822	200		Station Approach Sheffield S4 7XE
Sheffield	Moat House	QMH	71%	£100	0742 375376	95	yes	Chesterfield Road South Sheffield S8 8BW
Sheffield	St George Swallow Hotel	Swallow	64%	£96	0742 583811	141	yes	Kenwood Road Sheffield S7 1NQ

West Yorkshire

Location	Hotel	Group	%	Price	Tel	Rooms		Address
Bingley	Bankfield Hotel	Jarvis	61%	£105	0274 567123	103		Bradford Road Bingley BD16 1TU
Bradford	Novotel	Novotel	60%	£70	0274 683683	132		Merrydale Road Bradford BD4 6SA
Bradford	Stakis Norfolk Gardens	Stakis	65%	£106	0274 734734	120		Hall Ings Bradford BD1 5SH
Bradford	Victoria Hotel	Forte	61%	£77	0274 728706	59		Bridge Street Bradford BD1 1JX
Bramhope	Forte Crest	Forte	66%	£98	0532 842911	126	yes	Bramhope nr Leeds LS16 9JJ
Bramhope	Parkway Hotel	Jarvis	63%	£122	0532 672551	103	yes	Otley Road Bramhope nr Leeds LS16 8AG
Brighouse	Forte Crest	Forte	68%	£98	0484 400400	94	yes	Coalpit Lane Clifton Village Brighouse HD6 4HW
Ferrybridge	Granada Lodge	Granada		£45	0977 670488	35		M62/A1 Junction 33 Ferrybridge WF11 0AF
Garforth	Hilton National	Hilton	61%	£94	0532 866556	144		Wakefield Road Garforth nr Leeds LS25 1LH
Hartshead Moor	Forte Travelodge	Forte		£42	0274 851706	40	yes	Hartshead Moor Service Area Clifton Brighouse HD6 4RJ
Huddersfield	George Hotel	Principal	62%	£85	0484 515444	60		St George's Square Huddersfield HD1 1JA
Huddersfield	Pennine Hilton National	Hilton	66%	£95	0422 375431	118		Ainley Top Huddersfield HD3 3RH
Leeds	Hilton International	Hilton	69%	£105	0532 442000	206	yes	Neville Street Leeds LS1 4BX
Leeds	Holiday Inn Crowne Plaza	Holiday Inns	71%	£150	0532 442200	125		Wellington Street Leeds LS1 4DL
Leeds	Merrion Thistle Hotel	MtCT	65%	£101	0532 439191	109		Merrion Centre Wade Lane Leeds LS2 8NH
Leeds	Queen's Hotel	Forte	70%	£119	0532 431323	190	yes	City Square Leeds LS1 1PL
Wakefield	Campanile Hotel	Campanile		£44	0924 201054	77		Monckton Road Wakefield WF2 7AL
Wakefield	Forte Posthouse	Forte	64%	£68	0924 276388	99		Queen's Drive Ossett Wakefield WF5 9BE
Wakefield	Granada Lodge	Granada		£45	0924 830569	31		M1 Junction 38/39 Woolley Edge Wakefield WF4 4LQ
Wakefield	Swallow Hotel	Swallow	58%	£86	0924 372111	63		Queen Street Wakefield WF1 1JU
Wentbridge	Forte Travelodge	Forte		£42	0977 620711	56		A1 Barnsdale Bar Wentbridge nr Pontefract WS8 3JB
Wentbridge	Wentbridge House	Select	63%	£75	0977 620444	12		Wentbridge nr Pontefract WF8 3JJ

SCOTLAND GROUP HOTELS

Location	Establishment	Group	Grade	Price	Tel	Rooms	Pool	Address

Key: QMH (Queens Moat Houses), MtCT (Mount Charlotte Thistle).
Note: This information comes from *Egon Ronay's Cellnet Guide 1994 Hotels & Restaurants.* Lodges (Forte Travelodge, Travel Inn, Granada, Campanile and Inns are ungraded.
The price quoted is for a double room for two occupants with private bath and cooked breakfast in high season.
'Pool' refers to an indoor swimming pool only; prices may be considerably cheaper at weekends and for stays of more than one night.
We recommend that you call to confirm family facilities before staying at the hotels listed.

Borders

Location	Establishment	Group	Grade	Price	Tel	Rooms	Pool	Address
Peebles	Tontine Hotel	Forte	57%	£80	0721 720892	37		High Street Peebles EH45 8AJ

Central

Location	Establishment	Group	Grade	Price	Tel	Rooms	Pool	Address
Dunblane	Stakis Dunblane Hydro	Stakis	61%	£131	0786 822551	214	yes	Perth Road Dunblane FK15 0HG
Stirling	Granada Lodge	Granada		£45	0786 815033	37		M90/M80 Junction 9 Stirling FK7 8EU

Dumfries & Galloway

Location	Establishment	Group	Grade	Price	Tel	Rooms	Pool	Address
Gretna Green	Forte Travelodge	Forte		£42	0461 37566	41		A74 Trunk Road Gretna Green CA6 5HQ

Fife

Location	Establishment	Group	Grade	Price	Tel	Rooms	Pool	Address
Dunfermline	King Malcolm Thistle	MtCT	65%	£93	0383 722611	48		Queensferry Road Dunfermline KY11 5DS
St Andrews	Rusacks Hotel	Forte	74%	£150	0334 74321	50		Pilmour Links St Andrews KY16 9JQ

Grampian

Aberdeen	Caledonian Thistle	MtCT	68%	£125 0224 640233	80		Union Terrace Aberdeen AB9 1HE
Aberdeen	Copthorne Hotel	Copthorne	68%	£129 0224 630404	89		122 Huntly Street Aberdeen AB1 1SU
Aberdeen	Holiday Inn Crowne Plaza	Holiday Inns	69%	£112 0224 713911	144	yes	Oldmeldrum Road Bucksburn Aberdeen AB2 9LN
Aberdeen	Stakis Tree Tops	Stakis	63%	£127 0224 313377	110	yes	161 Springfield Road Aberdeen AB9 2QH
Aberdeen	Travel Inn	Travel Inns		£43 0224 821217	40		Murcar Bridge of Don Aberdeen AB2 8BP
Aberdeen Airport	Aberdeen Marriott Hotel	Marriott	70%	£141 0224 770011	154	yes	Riverview Drive Farburn Dyce Aberdeen AB2 0AZ
Aberdeen Airport	Airport Skean Dhu Hotel	MtCT	65%	£110 0224 725252	148		Argyll Road Dyce Aberdeen AB2 0DU

Highland

Aviemore	Aviemore Highlands Hotel	Principal	61%	£70 0479 810771	103		Aviemore Centre Aviemore PH22 1PJ
Aviemore	Stakis Aviemore Four Seasons	Stakis	70%	£100 0479 810681	89	yes	Aviemore PH22 1PF
Aviemore	Stakis Coylumbridge Resort	Stakis	62%	£96 0479 810661	175	yes	Aviemore PH22 1QN
Fort William	Mercury Hotel	MtCT	58%	£79 0397 703117	86		Achintore Road Fort William PH33 6RW
Inverness	Caledonian Hotel	Jarvis	69%	£99 0463 235181	106	yes	33 Church Street Inverness IV1 1DX
Inverness	Kingsmills Hotel	Swallow	67%	£110 0463 237166	84	yes	Culcabock Road Inverness IV2 3LP
Inverness	Mercury Hotel	MtCT	62%	£85 0463 239666	118		Millburn Road North Kessoch Bridge Inverness IV2 3TR

Lothian

Edinburgh	The Balmoral	Forte	83%	£190 031-556 2414	189	yes	Princes Street Edinburgh EH2 2EQ
Edinburgh	Barnton Thistle	MtCT	63%	£85 031-339 1144	50		Queensferry Road Edinburgh EH4 6AS
Edinburgh	Caledonian Hotel	QMH	79%	£192 031-225 2433	240		Princes Street Edinburgh EH1 2AB
Edinburgh	Forte Travelodge	Forte		£42 031-441 4296	40		A720 Dreghorn Link City By-Pass Edinburgh EH13 9QR
Edinburgh	Forte Posthouse	Forte	62%	£68 031-334 0390	200		Corstorphine Road Edinburgh EH12 6UA
Edinburgh	George Inter-Continental	Inter-Continental	74%	£186 031-225 1251	195		19 George Street Edinburgh EH2 2PB
Edinburgh	Granada Lodge	Granada		£45 031-653 2427	44		A1 Musselburgh By-Pass Musselburgh Edinburgh EH21 8RE
Edinburgh	Hilton National	Hilton	68%	£152 031-332 2545	144		69 Belford Road Edinburgh EH4 3DG
Edinburgh	Holiday Inn Garden Court	Holiday Inns	65%	£93 031-332 2442	119		107 Queensferry Road Edinburgh EH4 3HL
Edinburgh	Howard Hotel	Select	75%	£180 031-557 3500	16		36 Great King Street Edinburgh EH3 6QH
Edinburgh	King James Thistle	MtCT	70%	£126 031-556 0111	147		St James Centre 107 Leith Street Edinburgh EH1 3SW

Location	Establishment	Group	Grade	Price	Tel	Rooms	Pool	Address
Edinburgh	Scandic Crown Hotel	Scandic	68%	£155	031-557 9797	238	yes	80 High Street The Royal Mile Edinburgh EH1 1TH
Edinburgh	Sheraton Grand Hotel	Sheraton	79%	£199	031-229 9131	263	yes	1 Festival Square Edinburgh EH3 9SR
Edinburgh	Stakis Grosvenor Hotel	Stakis	64%	£115	031-226 6001	136		Grosvenor Street Edinburgh EH12 5EF
Edinburgh	Swallow Royal Scot	Swallow	65%	£120	031-334 9191	259	yes	111 Glasgow Road Edinburgh EH12 8NF
Edinburgh	Travel Inn	Travel Inns	NEW	£43	031-661 3396	39		228 Willowbrae Road Edinburgh EH8 7NG
Ingliston	Norton House	Voyager	66%	£115	031-333 1275	47		Ingliston nr Edinburgh EH28 8LX
Kirknewton	Dalmahoy Hotel	Country Club	78%	£125	031-333 1845	115	yes	Kirknewton EH27 8EB
North Berwick	Marine Hotel	Forte	62%	£100	0620 2406	84		Cromwell Road North Berwick EH39 4LZ
South Queensferry	Forth Bridges Moat House	QMH	61%	£114	031-331 1199	108	yes	South Queensferry EH30 9SF

Strathclyde

Location	Establishment	Group	Grade	Price	Tel	Rooms	Pool	Address
Abington	Forte Travelodge	Forte		£42	08642 782	54		A74/M74 Welcome Break Services Abington Biggar ML12 6RG
Ayr	Caledonian Hotel	Jarvis	64%	£99	0292 269331	114	yes	Dalblair Road Ayr KA7 1UG
Cumbernauld	Travel Inn	Travel Inns		£43	0236 725339	37		4 South Muirhead Road Cumbernauld nr Glasgow G67 1AX
Dumbarton	Forte Travelodge	Forte		£42	0389 65202	32		A82 Milton Dumbarton G82 2TY
East Kilbride	Bruce Swallow Hotel	Swallow	59%	£75	0355 229771	79		Cornwall Street East Kilbride G74 1AF
East Kilbride	Travel Inn	Travel Inns	NEW	£43	0355 222809	40		Brunel Way The Murray East Kilbride G75 0JY
Erskine	Forte Posthouse	Forte	62%	£68	041-812 0123	166	yes	by Erskine Bridge PA8 6AN
Giffnock	Macdonald Thistle	MtCT	64%	£102	041-638 2225	56		Eastwood Toll Giffnock nr Glasgow G46 6RA
Glasgow	Copthorne Hotel	Copthorne	64%	£122	041-332 6711	140		George Square Glasgow G2 1DS
Glasgow	Forte Crest	Forte	74%	£117	041-248 2656	254		Bothwell Street Glasgow G2 7EN
Glasgow	Glasgow Hilton	Hilton	78%	£140	041-204 5555	321	yes	1 William Street Glasgow G3 8HT
Glasgow	Glasgow Marriott Hotel	Marriott	73%	£136	041-226 5577	298	yes	Argyle Street Anderston Glasgow G3 8RR
Glasgow	Hospitality Inn	MtCT	67%	£130	041-332 3311	307		36 Cambridge Street Glasgow G2 3HN
Glasgow	Jurys Pond Hotel	Jurys	59%	£78	041-334 8161	137		2 Shelly Road Great Western Road Glasgow G12 0XP
Glasgow	Kelvin Park Lorne Hotel	QMH	63%	£81	041-334 4891	99		923 Sauchiehall Street Glasgow G3 7TE
Glasgow	Moat House International	QMH	69%	£126	041-204 0733	282	yes	Congress Road Glasgow G3 8QT
Glasgow	Stakis Grosvenor	Stakis	66%	£99	041-339 8811	95		Grosvenor Terrace Glasgow G12 0TA
Glasgow	Swallow Hotel	Swallow	61%	£92	041-427 3146	119	yes	517 Paisley Road West Glasgow G51 1RW
Glasgow	Tinto Firs Hotel	MtCT	62%	£85	041-637 2353	30		470 Kilmarnock Road Glasgow G43 2BB
Glasgow	Town House	Hidden	70%	£110	041-332 3320	34		54 West George Street Glasgow G2 1NG

Location	Establishment	Group	Grade	Price	Tel	Rooms	Pool	Address
Glasgow Airport	Forte Crest	Forte		68%	£95	041-887 1212	300		Abbotsinch nr Paisley PA3 2TR
Glasgow Airport	Stakis Normandy	Stakis		61%	£102	041-886 4100	141		Inchman Road Renfrew Glasgow Airport PA4 5EJ
Gourock	Stakis Gantock Hotel	Stakis		64%	£95	0475 634671	99	yes	Cloch Road Gourock PA15 1AR
Irvine	Hospitality Inn	MtCT		68%	£86	0294 74272	128	yes	46 Annick Road Irvine KA11 4LD
Milngavie	Black Bull Thistle	MtCT		59%	£70	041-956 2291	27		Main Street Milngavie G62 6BH
Newhouse	Travel Inn	Travel Inns			£43	0698 860277	40		Glasgow Road Newhouse nr.Motherwell ML1 5SY

Tayside

Location	Establishment	Group	Grade	Price	Tel	Rooms	Pool	Address
Dundee	Angus Thistle	MtCT		69%	£108	0382 26874	58		Marketgait Dundee DD1 1QU
Dundee	Travel Inn	Travel Inns			£43	0382 561115	40		Kingsway West Invergowrie Dundee DD2 5JU
Kinross	Granada Lodge	Granada			£45	0577 64646	35		M90 Junction 6 Kinross KY13 7NQ
Perth	Royal George Hotel	Forte		62%	£95	0738 24455	42		Tay Street Perth PH1 5LD
Perth	Stakis City Mills Hotel	Stakis		59%	£90	0738 28281	76		West Mill Street Perth PH1 5QP

WALES GROUP HOTELS

Location	Establishment	Group	Grade	Price	Tel	Rooms	Pool	Address
Clwyd, Halkyn	Forte Travelodge	Forte			£42	0352 780952	31		A55 Halkyn CH8 8RF
Clwyd, Llangollen	Hand Hotel	MtCT		55%	£66	0978 860303	57		Bridge Street Llangollen LL20 8PL
Clwyd, Llangollen	Royal Hotel	Forte		59%	£82	0978 860202	33		Bridge Street Llangollen LL20 8PG
Clwyd, Northop Hall	Forte Travelodge	Forte			£42	0244 816473	40		A55 Northop Hall Mold CH7 6HB
Clwyd, Wrexham	Forte Travelodge	Forte			£42	0978 365705	32		A483/A5152 Wrexham By-Pass Rhostyllen LL14 4EJ

Key: QMH (Queens Moat Houses), MtCT (Mount Charlotte Thistle).

Note: This information comes from *Egon Ronay's Cellnet Guide 1994 Hotels & Restaurants*. Lodges (Forte Travelodge, Travel Inn, Granada, Campanile and Inns are ungraded.
The price quoted is for a double room for two occupants with private bath and cooked breakfast in high season.
'Pool refers to an indoor swimming pool only; prices may be considerably cheaper at weekends and for stays of more than one night.
We recommend that you call to confirm family facilities before staying at the hotels listed.

Location	Establishment	Group	Grade	Price	Tel	Rooms	Pool	Address
Dyfed, Carmarthen	Ivy Bush Royal	Forte	59%	£60	0267 235111	75		Spilman Street Carmarthen SA31 1LG
Dyfed, Cross Hands	Forte Travelodge	Forte		£42	0269 845700	32		A48 Cross Hands nr Llanelli SA14 6NW
Mid Glamorgan, Bridgend	Forte Travelodge	Forte		£42	0656 659218	40		M4 J36 Service Area Sarn Park nr Bridgend CF32 9RW
Mid Glamorgan, Miskin	Miskin Manor	Select	70%	£107	0443 224204	32	yes	Pendylan Road Pontyclun Miskin CF7 8ND
Mid Glamorgan, Pencoed	Forte Travelodge	Forte		£42	0656 864404	40		Old Mill Felindre Road Pencoed nr Bridgend CF3 5HU
South Glamorgan, Cardiff	Angel Hotel	QMH	66%	£114	0222 232633	91		Castle Street Cardiff CF1 2QZ
South Glamorgan, Cardiff	Campanile Hotel	Campanile		£44	0222 549044	50		Caxton Place Pentwyn Cardiff CF2 7HA
South Glamorgan, Cardiff	Cardiff Marriott Hotel	Marriott	69%	£131	0222 399944	182	yes	Mill Lane Cardiff CF1 1EZ
South Glamorgan, Cardiff	Copthorne Hotel	Copthorne	70%	£119	0293 599100	135	yes	Culver House Cross Cardiff CF5 6XJ
South Glamorgan, Cardiff	Forte Crest	Forte	69%	£93	0222 388681	155		155 Castle Street Cardiff CF1 2XB
South Glamorgan, Cardiff	Forte Posthouse	Forte	63%	£68	0222 73-212	139	yes	Pentwyn Road Cardiff CF2 7XA
South Glamorgan, Cardiff	Forte Travelodge	Forte		£42	0222 549564	32		Circle Way East off A48M Llanederyn Cardiff CF3 7ND
South Glamorgan, Cardiff	Moat House	QMH	70%	£103	0222 732520	135	yes	Circle Way East Llanederyn Cardiff CF3 7XF
South Glamorgan, Cardiff	Park Hotel	MtCT	70%	£108	0222 383471	119		Park Place Cardiff CF1 3UD
South Glamorgan, Cardiff	Travel Inn	Travel Inns		£43	0633 680070	49		Newport Road Castleton nr Cardiff CF3 8UQ
West Glamorgan, Port Talbot	Travel Inn	Travel Inns		£43	0639 813017	40		Baglan Road Port Talbot SA12 8ES
West Glamorgan, Swansea	Forte Crest	Forte	69%	£95	0792 651074	99	yes	39 The Kingsway Swansea SA1 5LS
West Glamorgan, Swansea	Hilton National	Hilton	65%	£88	0792 310330	120		Phoenix Way Enterprise Park Llansamlet SA7 9EG
West Glamorgan, Swansea	Swansea Marriott Hotel	Marriott	67%	£123	0792 642020	118	yes	Maritime Quarter Swansea SA1 3SS
Gwent, Tintern Abbey	Beaufort Hotel	Jarvis	60%	£92	0291 689777	24		Tintern Abbey nr Chepstow NP6 6SF
Gwent, Newport	Hilton National	Hilton	61%	£93	0633 412777	119		The Coldra Newport NP6 2YG
Gwent, Newport	Stakis Country Court Hotel	Stakis	69%	£112	0633 413733	141	yes	Chepstow Road Langstone Newport NP6 2LX
Gwynedd, Llandudno	Bodysgallen Hall	Historic House	77%	£155	0492 584466	28	yes	Llandudno LL30 1RS
Powys, Presteigne	Radnorshire Arms	Forte	61%	£124	0544 267406	16		High Street Presteigne LD8 2BE

Maps

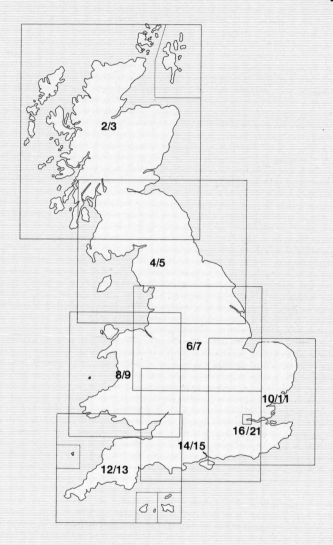

2/3

4/5

6/7

8/9

10/11

16/21

14/15

12/13

	Motorways	● Food
	Primary Routes	□ Accommodation
	Other Roads	▣ Accommodation and Food
	County Boundaries	○ Family Pub

Leading Guides Ltd.

Designed and Produced by
European Map Graphics Ltd. Berks.

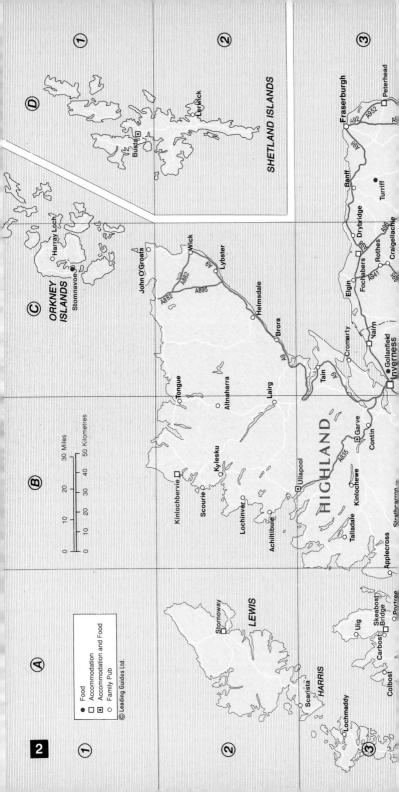

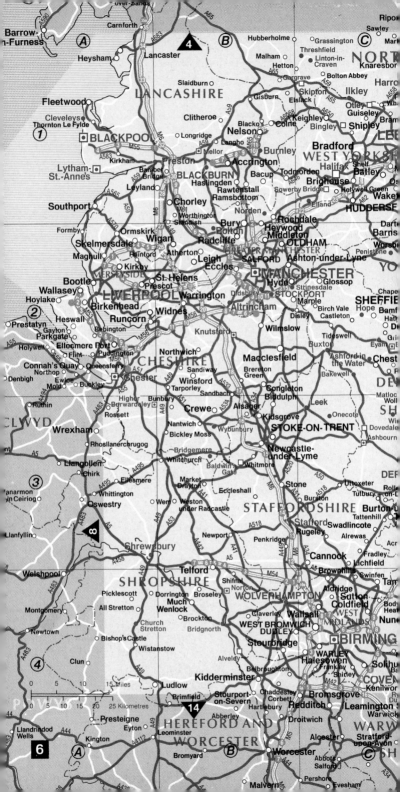

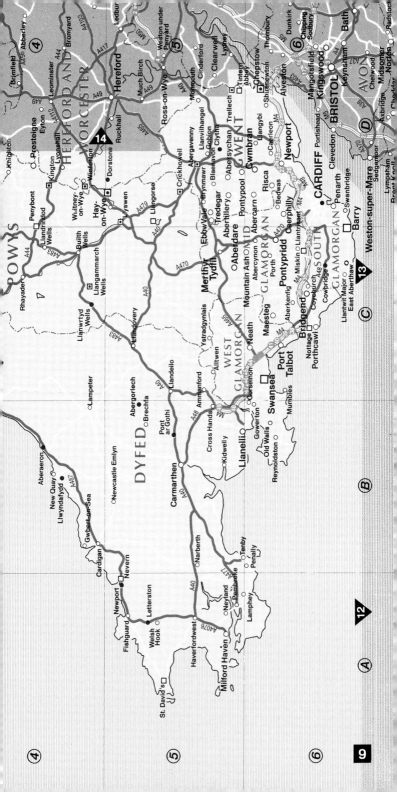

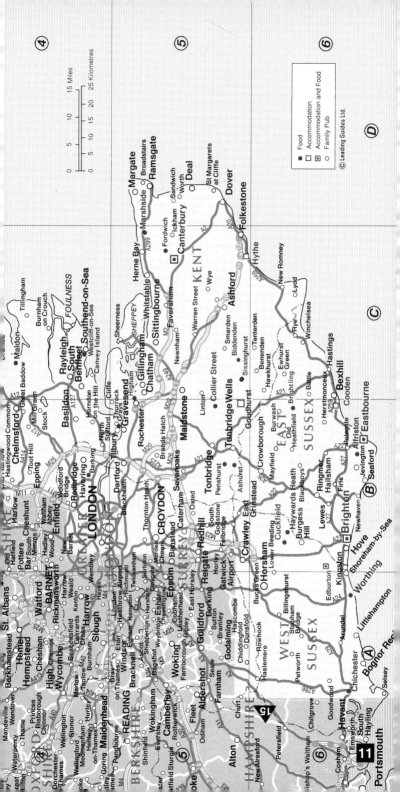

④

⑤

⑥

15 Miles

0   5   10   15   20   25 Kilometres
0   5   10   15 Miles

● Food
□ Accommodation
▣ Accommodation and Food
○ Family Pub

© Leading Guides Ltd.

Ⓓ

Ⓒ

KENT

Margate
Broadstairs
Ramsgate
Marshside
Sandwich
Worth
Deal
St Margarets
at Cliffe
Fordwich
Ickham
Canterbury
Dover
Herne Bay
Whitstable
Folkestone
Sittingbourne
Hythe
Faversham
Warren Street
Wye
Ashford
New Romney
Newnham
Lydd
Smarden
Tenterden
Bliddenden
Benenden
Sissinghurst
Winchelsea
Rye
Ewhurst
Green
Hawkhurst
Hastings

EAST SUSSEX

Sheerness
SHEPPEY
Gillingham
Chatham
Collier Street
Linton
Tunbridge
Wells
Goudhurst
Burwash
Brightling
Herstmonceux
Battle
Bexhill
Cooden
Eastbourne
Seaford

Tillingham
Burnham
on Crouch
Maldon
Great Baddow
Rayleigh
South
Benfleet
Southend-on-Sea
Westcliff-on-Sea
Canvey Island
Basildon
Hadleigh
Pitsea
Hornden
on the Hill
North
Stifford
Grays
Thurrock
Tilbury
Cliffe
Higham
Gravesend
Rochester
Brands Hatch
Maidstone
Crowborough
Mayfield
Heathfield
Blackboys
Firle
Alfriston
Jevington
Polegate

Chelmsford
Stock
Mill Green
Billericay
Dartford
Blackheath
Bexleyheath
Barking
Havering
Woodford
Redbridge
Waltham
Abbey
Cheshunt
Enfield
New
Barnet
Epping
Harlow
Hastingwood Common
Hatfield
Old
Hatfield
Potters
Bar
Hadley
Green
South
Mimms
Thornton Heath

SURREY

LONDON
Wembley
Kenton
Harrow
Harrow
Weald
Hayes
Ruislip
Pinner
London
(Heathrow) Airport
Richmond
Twickenham
Hampton
Morden
Cheam
Sutton
Banstead
Caterham
Croydon
Redhill
Reigate
Oxted
Godstone
South
Godstone
Felbridge
East
Grinstead
Crawley
Gatwick
Airport
Horley
Copthorne

St. Albans
Barnet
Watford
Rickmansworth
Chorleywood
Croxley
Green
Bushey

HERTFORDSHIRE

Berkhamsted
Hemel
Hempstead
Chesham
High
Wycombe
Beaconsfield
Burnham
Marlow
Bourne End
Taplow
Maidenhead
Windsor
Eton
Slough

Wendover
Mandeville
Princes
Risborough
Chinnor

OXFORDSHIRE
Thame
Dorchester
on Thames
Wallingford
Goring
Pangbourne
Henley
on-Thames
Medmenham
Hurley

BERKSHIRE
READING
Bracknell
Wokingham
Eversley
Shinfield
Sturgis
Hartfield

HAMPSHIRE
Basingstoke
Odiham
Hook
Rotherwick
Fleet
Church
Crookham
Aldershot
Farnham
Alton
New Alresford
Petersfield
Bishop's Waltham
Waltham
Cosham
Havant
Emsworth
South
Hayling
Hayling
Portsmouth

Camberley
Bagshot
Sandhurst
Bisley
Woking
Weybridge
Byfleet
Cobham
Esher
Ripley
Guildford
Shere
Dorking
Godalming
Chiddingfold
Dunsfold
Bramley
Hascombe
Rowhook
Haslemere
Petworth
Churt
Chilgrove
Goodwood
Chichester
Selsey
Bognor Regis
Littlehampton

WEST SUSSEX
Billingshurst
Stopham
Bridge
Buck's Green
Horsham
Lower Beeding
Cuckfield
Haywards Heath
Burgess
Hill
Lindfield
Ardingly
Edburton
Shoreham-by-Sea
Worthing
Kingston
Hove
Brighton
Newhaven
Lewes
Ringmer
Hailsham
Arundel

Ⓐ

Ⓑ

15

11

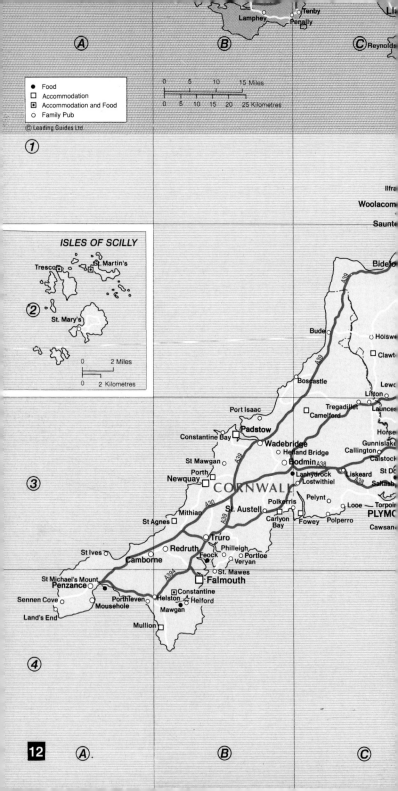

Food
Accommodation
Accommodation and Food
Family Pub

© Leading Guides Ltd.

0   5   10   15 Miles
0   5   10   15   20   25 Kilometres

Ⓐ

Ⓑ

Ⓒ Reynolds

①

Lamphey   Tenby
           Penally

Lla

Ilfra
Woolacom
Saunte

Bide

ISLES OF SCILLY

Tresco   St.Martin's

② St. Mary's

0   2 Miles
0   2 Kilometres

CORNWALL

Bude   ○ Holswe
            □ Clawt

Boscastle   Lewa
            Litton ○
Port Isaac   Tregadillet   Launces
              □ Camelford
Padstow   Horse
Constantine Bay   Gunnislake
         Wadebridge   Callington
         ○ Helland Bridge   Calstoc
St Mawgan ○ Bodmin   St Do
Porth   ● Lanhydrock   Liskeard
Newquay   Lostwithiel   Saltash
Mithian   Polkerris   Pelynt   Looe   Torpoin
St Agnes □ St. Austell   PLYMO
           Carlyon   Fowey Polperro
           Bay   Cawsan
St Ives ○   Truro
         Redruth   Philleigh
Camborne   Feock ● Portloe
St Michael's Mount   Veryan
Penzance   ● St. Mawes
Sennen Cove ○ Porthleven ● Falmouth
Mousehole   Helston Constantine
Land's End   Helford
              Mawgan
         Mullion

③

④

12   Ⓐ   Ⓑ   Ⓒ

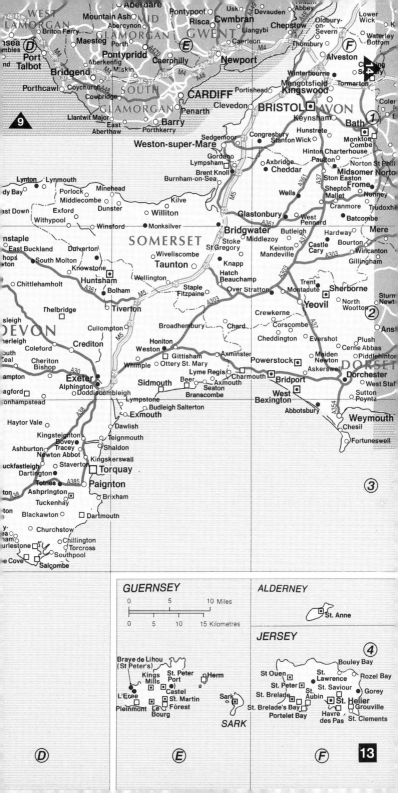

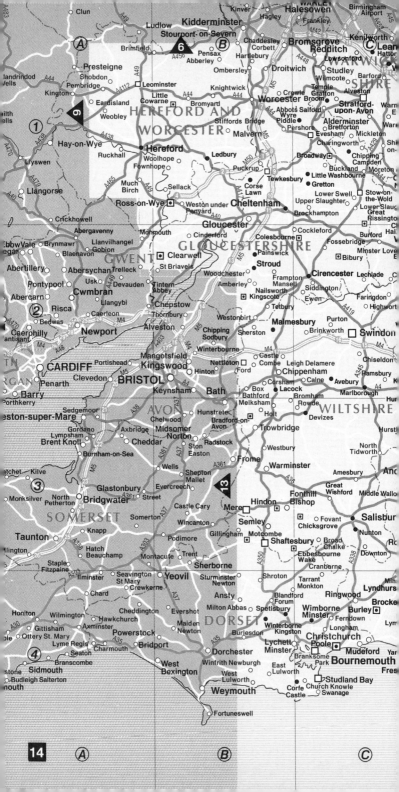

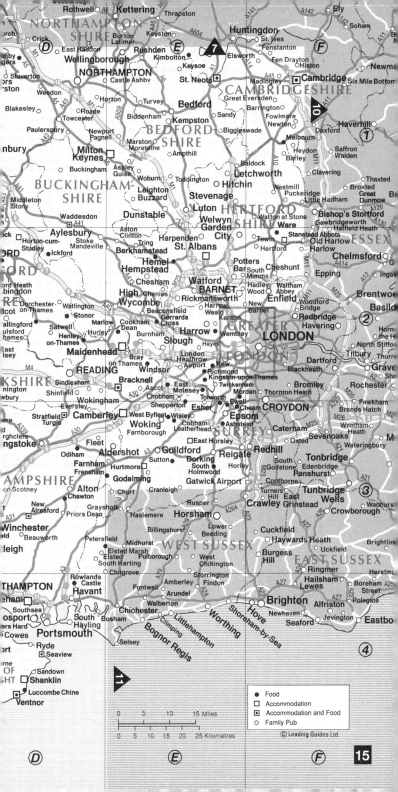

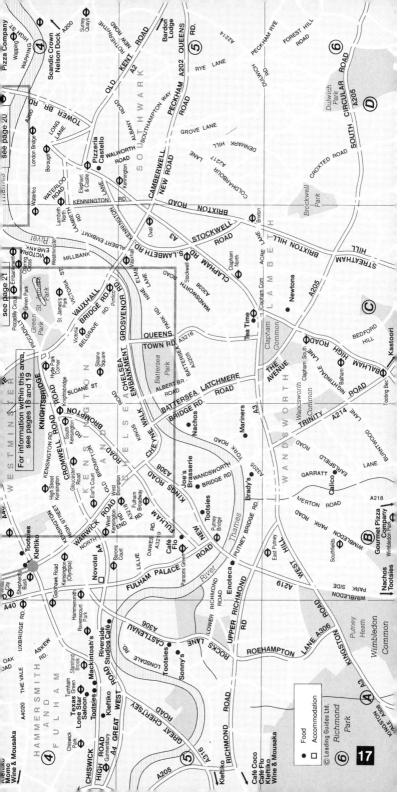

Food ●
Accommodation □

17

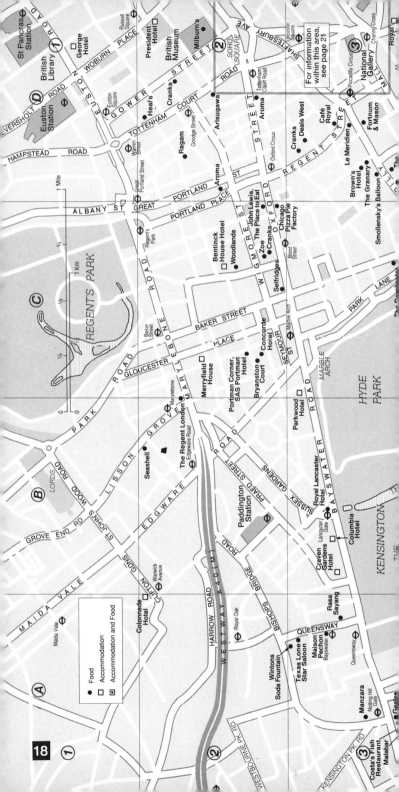

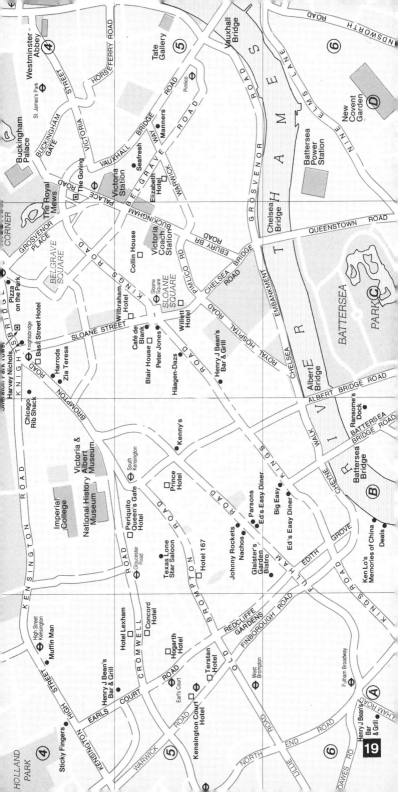

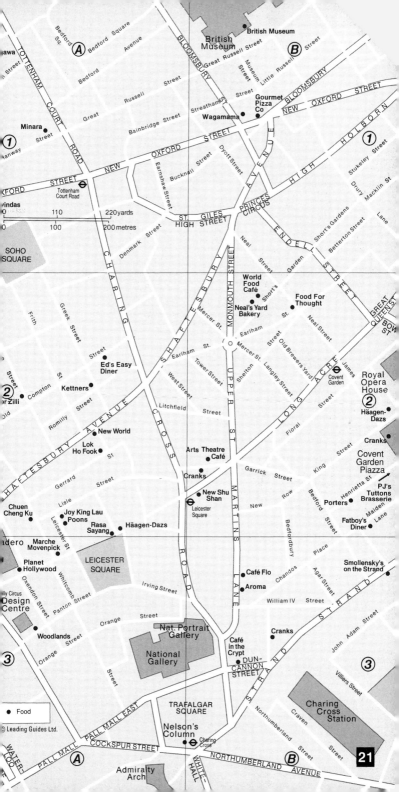

Recommended by
EGON RONAY'S GUIDES
1994

YOUR GUARANTEE
OF
QUALITY AND INDEPENDENCE

- Establishment inspections are anonymous

- Inspections are undertaken by qualified
  Egon Ronay's Guides' inspectors

- The Guides are completely independent
  in their editorial selection

- The Guides do not accept advertising,
  hospitality or payment from listed
  establishments

Hotels & Restaurants   Pubs & Inns
Just A Bite   Oriental Restaurants
.... And Baby Comes Too   Ireland
Paris Restaurants & Bistros   Europe

Index

Index

Recommended by

EGON RONAY'S GUIDES

1994

*YOUR GUARANTEE
OF
QUALITY AND INDEPENDENCE*

- Establishment inspections are anonymous

- Inspections are undertaken by qualified
Egon Ronay's Guides' inspectors

- The Guides are completely independent
in their editorial selection

- The Guides do not accept advertising,
hospitality or payment from listed
establishments

Hotels & Restaurants	Pubs & Inns
Just A Bite	Oriental Restaurants
. . . . And Baby Comes Too	Ireland
Paris Restaurants & Bistros	Europe

Egon Ronay's Guides are available from all good bookshops or can be
ordered from Leading Guides, 73 Uverdale Road, London SW10 0SW
Tel: 071-352 2485/352 0019 Fax: 071-376 5071

READERS' COMMENTS

Please use this sheet, and the continuation overleaf, to recommend restaurants of **really outstanding quality.**

  Complaints about any of the Guide's entries will be treated seriously and passed on to our inspectorate, but we would like to remind you always to take up your complaint with the management at the time.

  We regret that owing to the volume of readers' communications received each year we will be unable to acknowledge these forms, but your comments will certainly be seriously considered.

Please post to: **Egon Ronay's Guides, 73 Uverdale Road, London SW10 0SW**

Please use an up-to-date Guide. We publish annually. (... and Baby Comes Too 1994)

Name and address of establishment	Your recommendation or complaint

442

Readers' Comments continued

Name and address of establishment   **Your recommendation or complaint**

_____ _____

_____ _____

_____ _____

_____ _____

_____ _____

_____ _____

_____ _____

_____ _____

_____ _____

_____ _____

_____ _____

_____ _____

_____ _____

Your Name (BLOCK LETTERS PLEASE)

_____

Address

_____

_____

_____

_____

READERS' COMMENTS

Please use this sheet, and the continuation overleaf, to recommend
restaurants of **really outstanding quality.**

    Complaints about any of the Guide's entries will be treated seriously and
passed on to our inspectorate, but we would like to remind you always to
take up your complaint with the management at the time.

    We regret that owing to the volume of readers' communications received
each year we will be unable to acknowledge these forms, but your
comments will certainly be seriously considered.

Please post to: **Egon Ronay's Guides, 73 Uverdale Road, London SW10 0SW**

Please use an up-to-date Guide. We publish annually. (... and Baby Comes Too 1994)

Name and address of establishment   **Your recommendation or complaint**

444

Readers' Comments continued

Name and address of establishment   **Your recommendation or complaint**

Your Name (BLOCK LETTERS PLEASE)

Address

READERS' COMMENTS

Please use this sheet, and the continuation overleaf, to recommend restaurants of **really outstanding quality.**

   Complaints about any of the Guide's entries will be treated seriously and passed on to our inspectorate, but we would like to remind you always to take up your complaint with the management at the time.

   We regret that owing to the volume of readers' communications received each year we will be unable to acknowledge these forms, but your comments will certainly be seriously considered.

Please post to: **Egon Ronay's Guides, 73 Uverdale Road, London SW10 0SW**

Please use an up-to-date Guide. We publish annually. (... and Baby Comes Too 1994)

Name and address of establishment   **Your recommendation or complaint**

Readers' Comments continued

Name and address of establishment   **Your recommendation or complaint**

Your Name (BLOCK LETTERS PLEASE)

Address

READERS' COMMENTS

Please use this sheet, and the continuation overleaf, to recommend restaurants of **really outstanding quality.**

Complaints about any of the Guide's entries will be treated seriously and passed on to our inspectorate, but we would like to remind you always to take up your complaint with the management at the time.

We regret that owing to the volume of readers' communications received each year we will be unable to acknowledge these forms, but your comments will certainly be seriously considered.

Please post to: **Egon Ronay's Guides, 73 Uverdale Road, London SW10 0SW**

Please use an up-to-date Guide. We publish annually. (... and Baby Comes Too 1994)

Name and address of establishment	Your recommendation or complaint

Readers' Comments continued

Name and address of establishment	Your recommendation or complaint

Your Name (BLOCK LETTERS PLEASE)

Address